# The Faber Book of Gay Short Fiction

Edmund White is acknowledged to be one of the leading inter-preters of gay culture. In *The Faber Book of Gay Short Fiction* he has created a rich anthology that explores the literary expression of male homosexuality in the American and English tradition, from the oblique beginnings of Forster and Firbank, through the mid-century fiction of Isherwood and Welch, to the bolder recent work of Vidal, William, Burroughs and Baldwin, and contemporary works through the age of AIDS.

White's thoughtful introductory essay describes his personal experience of gay literature and provides an insightful historical and psychological context for the stories. As he points out, gay writers are "not just reporting the past but also shaping the future, forging an identity as much as revealing it."

'An excellent read.' – *San Francisco Review of Books*

'A distinguished anthology. . . . Offers a revealing and re-warding excursion into a subculture's language and mores.' – *Publishers Weekly*

'Don't get this for the gay lit collection. . . . Get it for the lit col-lection, period.' – *Booklist*

Edmund White is the author of *A Boy's Own Story* and *The Beautiful Room is Empty*. He is a professor of English at Brown University and is completing a biography of Jean Genet.

*The Faber Book of*

# GAY SHORT FICTION

**EDITED BY**
**EDMUND WHITE**

*faber and faber*
BOSTON • LONDON

First published in 1991 in the United States by Faber and Faber, Inc.,
50 Cross Street, Winchester, MA 01890 and in the United Kingdom by
Faber and Faber Ltd., 3 Queen Square, London WC1N 3AU

This paperback edition first published in 1992

Library of Congress Cataloging-in-Publication Data
The Faber book of gay short fiction / edited by Edmund White.
    p.   cm.
  ISBN 0-571-12908-0 (paper) : $15.95
  1. Gay men—Fiction.  2. Gays' writings, English.  3. Gays'
writings, American  4. Short stories, American.  5. Short stories,
English.  I. White, Edmund, 1940–    .
PR1309.H57F33    1992
823'.0108920642—dc20                                    92-19700
                                                            CIP

Jacket shows "Cilindrone" by Clemente/Warhol/Basquiat, courtesy
Galerie Bruno Bischofberger, Zurich

Jacket design by Mary Maurer

Printed in the United States of America

# Contents

# Acknowledgements

The editor would like to express his gratitude to Alex Jeffers.

We are indebted to the following copyright holders for permission to print the stories in this volume.

PAUL BAILEY: from *Trespasses*, published in 1989 by Penguin Books Ltd, first published in 1970 by Jonathan Cape, copyright © 1969, 1970 by Paul Bailey, by permission of the author; JAMES BALDWIN: from *Just Above My Head*, published by The Dial Press, New York, copyright © 1978, 1979 by James Baldwin; NEIL BARTLETT: 'Three Wedding Ceremonies' from *Ready to Catch Him Should He Fall*, published in 1990 by Serpent's Tail, copyright © Neil Bartlett, by permission of the author; PAUL BOWLES: 'Pages from Cold Point' from *The Delicate Prey*, copyright © 1950 by Paul Bowles; WILLIAM S. BURROUGHS: 'The Wild Boys' from *The Wild Boys*, published in 1982 in a collection by Pan Books Ltd, first published in 1972 by Calder & Boyars Ltd, copyright © 1969, 1970, 1971, 1972, 1982 William S. Burroughs, by permission of Aitken & Stone Ltd; SIMON BURT: 'Good Fortune', copyright © Simon Burt, by permission of the author; ALFRED CHESTER: 'In Praise of Vespasian' from *Behold Goliath*, first published in 1965 by André Deutsch Ltd, copyright © 1955, 1957, 1960, 1961, 1962, 1964 by Alfred Chester, by permission of André Deutsch Ltd and A. M. Heath & Co Ltd; DENNIS COOPER: 'My Mark' from *Safe*, published in 1984 by The Sea Horse Press Ltd, New York, copyright © 1984 by Dennis Cooper, by permission of Ira Silverberg Communications, New York; JAMES M. ESTEP: 'BM', copyright © James M. Estep, by permission of the author; RONALD FIRBANK: 'Concerning the Eccentricities of Cardinal Pirelli' from *The Complete Ronald Firbank*, published in 1988 by Picador Classics (Pan Books Ltd), first published in 1961 by Gerald Duckworth and Co Ltd, copyright © 1961 by Thomas Firbank; E. M. FORSTER: 'Dr Woolacott', published in 1975, 1979, 1983, 1984, 1987, 1988 by Penguin Books Ltd, first published in 1972 by Edward Arnold, copyright © 1972 by The Provost and Scholars of King's College, Cambridge, by permission of King's College, Cambridge and The Society of Authors as the literary representatives of the E. M. Forster Estate; PATRICK GALE: 'The List', copyright © Patrick Gale, by permission of the author; ROBERT GLÜCK: 'Denny Smith', copyright © Robert Glück, by permission of the author; ALLAN GURGAnus: 'Forced Use', copyright © Allan Gurganus, by permission of the author; WILLIAM HAYWOOD HENDERSON: from *Native*, copyright © William Haywood Henderson, by permission of the author; ANDREW HOLLERAN: 'Sunday Morning: Key West', copyright © Andrew Holleran, by permission of the author; ALAN HOLLINGHURST: from *The Swimming-Pool Library*, published in 1988 by Chatto & Windus Ltd, copyright © 1988 by Alan Hollinghurst, by permission of the author; TIMOTHY IRELAND: from *The Novice*, published in 1988 by GMP Publishers Ltd, copyright © 1988 by Timothy Ireland, by permission of the author; CHRISTOPHER ISHERWOOD: 'Mr Lancaster' from *Down There on a Visit*, first published in 1962 by Methuen & Co Ltd, copyright © 1962 by Christopher Isherwood, by permission of the Estate of Christopher Isherwood; HENRY JAMES: 'The Pupil' from *Fourteen Stories by Henry James* selected by David Garnett, published in 1946; DAVID LEAVITT: 'When You Grow to Adultery', copyright © David Leavitt, by permission of Wylie, Aitken & Stone, Inc., New York; DAVID MALOUF: 'Southern Skies' from *Antipodes*, published in 1986 by Penguin Books Ltd, first published in 1985 by Chatto & Windus, the Hogarth Press, copyright © 1985 by David Malouf, by permission of the author; ADAM MARS-JONES: 'The Changes of Those Terrible Years', copyright © Adam Mars-Jones, by permission of the author; ARMISTEAD MAUPIN: 'Suddenly Home', copyright © Armistead Maupin, by permission of the author; DAVID PLANTE: 'The Secret of the Gentiles', copyright © David Plante, by permission of the author; JAMES PURDY: 'Dawn' from *The Candles of Your Eyes*, published by Peter Owen Ltd, London, originally published by Weidenfeld and Nicolson, New York, copyright © 1967, 1970, 1974, 1975, 1976, 1978, 1979, 1984, 1987 by James Purdy; LEV RAPHAEL: 'Another Life', copyright © Lev Raphael, by permission of the author; GORE VIDAL: 'Pages from an Abandoned Journal' from *A Thirsty Evil*, copyright © 1956 by Gore Vidal; TOM WAKEFIELD: 'Darts' from *Forties' Child*, published by Serpent's Tail, first published in 1980 by Routledge & Kegan Paul Ltd, copyright © 1980 by Tom Wakefield, by permission of Richard Scott Simon Ltd; DENTON WELCH: 'When I was Thirteen' from *The Stories of Denton Welch*, published in 1985 by E. P. Dutton, New York, copyright © 1966, 1985 by the University of Texas, by permission of David Higham Associates; EDMUND WHITE: 'Skinned Alive', published in 1989 in *Granta* 27, copyright © 1989 by Edmund White, by permission of the author; TENNESSEE WILLIAMS: 'Two on a Party' from *Hard Candy*, copyright © 1954 by Tennessee Williams, by permission of the Estate of Tennessee Williams.

Faber and Faber Limited apologizes for any errors or omissions in the above list and would be grateful to be notified of any corrections that should be incorporated in the next edition or reprint of this volume.

# Foreword

Since no one is brought up to be gay, the moment he recognizes the difference he must account for it. Such accounts are a kind of primitive gay fiction, the oral narrations told and retold as pillow talk or in pubs or on the psychoanalytic couch. Every gay man has polished his story through repetition, and much gay fiction is a version of this first tale. 'Coming out' is the rite that marks the passage from homosexual desire to gay identity, and this transition begins and ends in avowal. Philosophers may object that the urge to avow is itself a trap, based as it is on Christian confession and assuming as it does that sexual identity is profound, hidden, constitutive, more a matter of being than doing.

Despite such objections, gays continue to believe their gayness is in fact something they are rather than something they do (notice, for instance, the number of celibate priests who have felt the need to bear witness to their gayness, even though their sexuality is held firmly in abeyance).

If gays tell each other – or the hostile world around them – the stories of their lives, they're not just reporting the past but also shaping the future, forging an identity as much as revealing it. Most gay men believe they did not choose to be homosexual, that this orientation was imposed on them, although whether by nature or nurture they have no way of knowing. Many men recollect homosexual desires amongst their earliest childhood memories, although they often attempt to keep those longings separate, in quarantine or between parentheses. Acknowledging

homosexual desires and integrating them into a larger notion of
the self is the first bold act of gay fiction, whether written or
whispered. Sometimes these revisions of the self approach nullity
– or universality. As a character remarks in Christopher Isherwood's 'Mr Lancaster': 'What I am has refashioned itself throughout the days and years, and until now almost all that remains
constant is the mere awareness of being conscious. And that
consciousness belongs to everybody; it isn't a particular person.'

Sometimes, naturally, gay men, such as Paul Bailey's narrator,
feel that they were born too early, before the redefinitions effected
by gay liberation changed everyone's life. These men tell stories,
but their stories are tales of loss, regret and bitterness: 'I'm very
out of date, aren't I? I scarcely fit into this modern society. I can't
get used to freedom; I suppose I crave the martyr's crown. The
dirty back-streets and the stinking lavatories are my hunting-
grounds; they're fit settings for humiliation; the clubs and bars,
with everyone so open and happy, they only oppress me. They
tear at my heart because I remember what I had and anyway, I
always did hate my kind en masse.'

I suppose I'm suggesting that being gay is a bit like being a
writer, just as exalting or annihilating and always as perilous. Like
most writers, most gays are urban, at least in the years necessary
for consolidating their identity. Almost all the men in this
anthology once lived or still live in London, New York or San
Francisco. The city is the big human market-place that allows even
quite strange people to seek out those of fellow feeling; it offers the
economic independence, the anonymity and the randomness
needed to sponsor original styles of life. Writers drift to the big city
and learn how a writer lives from observing others of his kind, just
as homosexuals perfect their values and manners by imitating
older exemplars.

Many writers – creatures with working-class salaries, middle-
class origins and upper-class pretensions – have taken a bitter
refuge in dandyism; homosexuals, even in the recent past, have
found consolation for their low status in comparable fantasies of
aristocratic camp – not for nothing do they call themselves

'queens'. A novelist, even if he is a swaggering he-man such as Hemingway or Tolstoy or a misogynist such as Flaubert, must not only interest himself in 'female things' such as dress, manners and romantic adventure, he must also at certain moments of writing even *become* a woman. The male homosexual often has a more direct access to women's secrets than the average man; more importantly, the homosexual man has *lived* from the inside the problem of dealing with male arrogance and even brutality, since gay men not only are men but must also live with them.

I could go on inventing ways that gays are like writers, but I don't want to exaggerate the resemblance. I just want to point out that if everyone acknowledges that the writer's greatest gift is to look at familiar things from an odd angle, then the gay man inevitably enjoys what is both an advantage and a curse – a permanent sense of alienation from the tribe. This is the famous 'defamiliarization' that the Russian Formalists first discussed: it is built into the social identity of being gay. Just as a Russian aristocrat, Vladimir Nabokov, wrote best about American motels and nymphets, just as the unmarried Jane Austen wrote best about courtship, just as today the most discerning writers about Britain are of Indian or Pakistani or Chinese or Japanese extraction, so the novelists who have best described power and how it couples with sex – even heterosexual sex – are Henry James and Marcel Proust, and the fantasists who found silvery comedy in the tragic seriousness of marriage are Oscar Wilde and Ronald Firbank.

The recognition of the link between gays and other minorities is pondered in very different ways in Lev Raphael's 'Another Life' and David Plante's 'The Secret of the Gentiles', in which a separate but parallel world is Jewish, while in William Haywood Henderson's 'Native' that reflecting surface can be seen in the black stare of an American Indian's dancing eyes. In two other stories (Patrick Gale's 'The List' and Tom Wakefield's 'Darts') gay men (implied or potential) look at lesbians. In a working-class pub a young boy in Wakefield's story learns that lesbians are called 'willdews' ('When they are at home it must be "will yer do this or will yer do that". Got it? So, they are willdews.'), a bit of folk anthropology by a friendly heterosexual not unlike the explanations gays themselves derive from science, astrology, Freud, religion, folklore, Foucault or the ancient Greeks. Homosexuality demands an explanation, and gay fiction is often an attempt to provide it.

Sometimes homosexuality seeks itself out in travel, as though acceptance and adventure will be found only *elsewhere*. For E. M. Forster, who'd travelled enough to be disillusioned, 'elsewhere' turns out to be supernatural. But in many of the other stories in this anthology, I was struck by how often they take place 'abroad'. Another country promises compassion or at least promiscuity, the land of marvels, where the traveller's inner contradictions will be resolved or where the tyranny of reproductive society will suddenly, unaccountably be set aside. Gore Vidal's innocent abroad all too quickly becomes an initiate completely at home in a sophisticated Paris. Alfred Chester explores the *pissotières* of Paris as thoroughly as Vidal examines men who used to be called 'pissy queens'. In Denton Welch's 'When I Was Thirteen' an English cast of characters goes to Switzerland to discover that desire itself is always pure, no matter what lewd constructions may be put on it by corrupt observers. Similarly Paul Bowles's characters travel far to unearth (or conjure up) forbidden longings. Tennessee Williams sets his odd couple in perpetual motion; the speed of their travels belies the timid slowness with which they acknowledge their mutual love.

If one of the main impulses behind gay fiction is avowal and self discovery, another is surely sexual affirmation. James Baldwin's young men look at each other with a real hunger, a simple wonder before the flesh of another man, so similar and yet so radically different: '. . . a miracle of spinal column, neck to buttocks, shoulders and shoulderblades, elbows, wrists, thighs, ankles, a miracle of bone and blood and muscle and flesh and music.' This simple catechism is one the gay lover never tires of telling, a language that has been suppressed as often as it was invented and that must be created again and again.

Of course if some gay fiction was an apology addressed to the straight world, other books, badly printed and sold under the counter, were pornography aimed at the gay reader. Even today gay fiction retains the identifying marks of this double heritage – the obligation to explain and the ambition to excite.

Some new writers, of course, are trying to get beyond these twin urges. Allan Gurganus in 'Forced Use' bans the vocabulary, the folkways and the conventional confessions of gay life in order to find once again the inherent strangeness of sexual desires that are inassimilable. Timothy Ireland goes daringly in the opposite direction; his characters announce with dazzling simplicity, 'We are married.' If Lev Raphael's characters, Nat and Mark, also hope to introduce their new wine into old skins, Henderson's men, Blue and Sam, don't want to acknowledge their desires at all, and this very denial lends an edgy, indeterminate sexuality to everything they do and think, even to the landscape that dwarfs them. In Dennis Cooper's fiction sex is reinvented through the dislocations in the language that describes it and in the constant, chilling pairing of love and death. Robert Glück is a writer who startles us with his odd conjunctions, passionate emphases and sophisticated ellipses. He's capable of dilating scenes that are ordinarily elided and gliding over passages that would be obligatory in any other writer's work. His treatment of love in 'Denny Smith' is at once fanciful and literal, since he combines literary parody and wild digressions with the use of the names of real people, products and contemporary political figures.

Of course, the dominant fact of gay life today is AIDS, and this anthology includes several stories on that theme, including my own. Adam Mars-Jones touches on the question of our responsibility to the ill, and Andrew Holleran shows how people attempt to domesticate what can only be a scandal. The enormous body of fiction that has sprung up in the United States and the rest of the English-speaking world about AIDS in the last few years reveals that literature is still the gay community's strongest response to crisis.

For me the evolution of the gay novel has seemed breathlessly rapid and strangely personal. As a boy I looked desperately for things to read that might confirm an identity I was piecing together and accommodate a sexuality that fate seemed to have thrust on me without my ever having chosen it. In the early 1950s one of the few books I could find in the Evanston Public Library was the biography of Nijinsky by his wife in which she obliquely deplored the demonic influence of the impresario Diaghilev on her saintly husband, the great dancer. I alternated between grim psychiatric case studies and the outrageous Anthony Blanche scenes in Evelyn Waugh's *Brideshead Revisited*. I caught dim echoes of the scandalous Oscar Wilde trial – all bits of half-information to convey the then prevailing notions of homosexuality as sin, madness or crime.

In the 1960s I was lucky enough to discover Christopher Isherwood's *A Single Man*, a sane, unapologetic picture of an English professor living in Los Angeles. He muddles through a long, eventful day and confides his feelings to his straight friends, which proves a breakthrough in several different ways, since the protagonist suffers as everyone does, from the death of loved ones, the numbing of routine, the fear of loneliness, but not in the specially damned or debilitated sense supposedly peculiar to homosexuals. André Gide's journals and his memoir *If It Die* showed a civilized adult mind given over to far-ranging interests (classical piano music, Greek theatre, Russian politics, travel in Africa), as well as to a frank attraction to boys. William S. Burroughs' *Naked Lunch*, John Rechy's *City of Night* and Jean Genet's *Our Lady of the Flowers* moved in the opposite direction, towards rendering gay life as exotic, marginal, even monstrous, as possible. Not incidentally, these books were all original and genuine works of art. Burrough's collage techniques, Rechy's ear for gay speech and sympathy for the gay underdog, Genet's way of turning all ordinary values upside down – these were shock tactics for transforming our received notions of reality.

The beginning of gay liberation in 1969 did not produce straight off a new crop of fiction, but by 1978 the new gay novel was beginning to emerge. That was the year Larry Kramer's controversial *Faggots* and Andrew Holleran's romantic *Dancer from the Dance* were published; among other things both books documented the new gay culture that had been spawned by liberation, prosperity and a society-wide tolerance.

In 1980, seven New York gay writers formed a casual club named The Violet Quill. We'd meet once a month in one another's apartments. Four of us each time would read our latest pages, then settle down to high tea. We were more competitive about the richness of our desserts than the quality of our prose. The mood was certainly friendly and collaborative; we thought of calling our organization The All-Praise Club. Nevertheless the atmosphere was sufficiently challenging to prompt us to our best efforts.

The members were Felice Picano, who was working on a gay psychological thriller, *The Lure*, and later on an elegaic love story, *Late in the Season*, Andrew Holleran, at work on stories and his second novel *Nights in Aruba*, Robert Ferro (*The Family of Max Desir*), George Whitmore (*The Confessions of Danny Slocum* and *Nebraska*), Chris Cox (*Key West: A Traveler's Companion*), Michael Grumley (then at work on *Life Studies*, remarkable for its lyrical language) and I (*A Boy's Own Story*). Our occasional visitor was Vito Russo, who was writing the authoritative book about gays in Hollywood, *The Celluloid Closet*.

All of us, however, were linked to other book people. Felice was the publisher of The Sea Horse Press, Chris Cox became an editor at Dutton and later Ballantine. Many of us were published by *Christopher Street* magazine, which was for a long while virtually the only serious gay literary review in America. Michael Grumley was later a regular contributor to the New York *Native*. Whitmore, Cox and I were all professional journalists and we all frequently wrote on gay topics. We were in touch with such gay editors as Bill Whitehead and Michael Denneny and the gay writer and psychotherapist Charles Silverstein. Most of us knew the playwright Harvey Fierstein (*The Torchsong Trilogy*), the historian Jonathan

Katz (*Gay American History*) and the literary critic David Kalstone, who at that time was finishing his book *Five Temperaments*, a study of Adrienne Rich, Elizabeth Bishop, James Merrill, John Ashbery and – as the sole heterosexual – Robert Lowell.

In 1983 I moved to Paris. When I came back to the States in 1990 this literary map had been erased. George Whitmore, Michael Grumley, Robert Ferro and Chris Cox were dying and Vito Russo was dead. Of our original group only Felice Picano, Andrew Holleran and I were still alive. Better than anyone else, Holleran has captured our sense of living posthumously in his personal essays, *Ground Zero*. Many younger writers had also died; of those I knew I could count Tim Dlugos, Richard Youmans, Gregory Kolovakis, the translator Matt Ward and the novelist John Fox (who'd been my student at Columbia). My two closest friends, David Kalstone and my editor, Bill Whitehead, had died.

For me these losses were definitive. The witnesses to my life, the people who had shared the same references and sense of humour, were gone. More important, the 'novels' these friends were living, were creating daily out of their very existence, stories I had wanted to unfold at a leisurely pace and with a wealth of detail, had been rudely summarized or slammed shut in mid-tale. I speak only of personal losses. The loss of all the books these young people might have written was incalculable.

Curiously enough, AIDS, which had destroyed so many of these distinguished writers, had also, as a phenomenon, made homosexuality a much more familar part of the American landscape. It had also divided the gay community along ideological lines which have been reflected in gay literature. A lesbian writer, Sarah Schulman, has written eloquently about AIDS activism in her novel *People Like Us*, as has Larry Kramer in his plays and essays; both writers are openly polemical, in contrast with less angry, more elegaic writers like Holleran and me. Similarly, a new puritansim is setting in. Felice Picano is especially vocal in his denunciation of novelists who exclude sex scenes from their books, accusing them of hypocrisy and cynicism. 'A gay man who writes without including sex in his work is a traitor,' he thunders. 'Such neutering is just internalized homophobia – after all, sex is the only thing that defines homosexuality.' Many younger gays, however, feel that unbridled sex scenes in fiction are irresponsible and even criminally dangerous.

My own belief is that censorship of any sort is to be feared. Cultural and affectional ties are as defining of homosexuality as sexual practices, and those writers (such as David Leavitt) who reflect in their work the erotic conservatism of their generation are well within their rights, but so are frankly sexual writers such as Dennis Cooper and Alan Hollinghurst. What is being played out in gay fiction reflects the more general conflict between gay assimilationists and gay militants.

Despite such controversies, gay and lesbian studies are on the way to being institutionalized in the United States. Hundreds of lesbian and gay scholars have just met at Harvard. Several universities are offering courses in lesbian and gay history and culture. Yale's Beinecke Library hopes to collect the papers of the Violet Quill – a development that would a decade ago have surprised those of us who read to one another in our Manhattan apartments. Not long ago I wrote that gay culture seemed to be following a rapid trajectory – oppressed in the 1950s, liberated in the 1960s, exalted in the 1970s and wiped out in the 1980s. Perhaps I was too hasty. The 1990s may be the decade when gay fiction will be institutionalized.

For that to happen, however, several questions will have to be answered or at least framed. Do gays really constitute something like an ethnic minority? Does an author's sexuality represent a more crucial part of his identity than his social class, generation, race or regional origins? Is gay literature of more than passing interest to people outside the gay community, or is it like sci-fi or murder mysteries – essential to adepts but dispensable to everyone else?

These questions have already prompted considerable debate and will long continue to be discussed. What seems indisputable, however, is that, now more than ever before, if gay books of universal appeal do happen to be written, they will have a real chance of being published, read and recognized.

Edmund White, March 1991

# The Pupil

**HENRY JAMES**

## I

The poor young man hesitated and procrastinated: it cost him such an effort to broach the subject of terms, to speak of money to a person who spoke only of feelings and, as it were, of the aristocracy. Yet he was unwilling to take leave, treating his engagement as settled, without some more conventional glance in that direction than he could find an opening for in the manner of the large, affable lady who sat there drawing a pair of soiled *gants de Suède* through a fat, jewelled hand and, at once pressing and gliding, repeated over and over everything but the thing he would have liked to hear. He would have liked to hear the figure of his salary; but just as he was nervously about to sound that note the little boy came back – the little boy Mrs Moreen had sent out of the room to fetch her fan. He came back without the fan, only with the casual observation that he couldn't find it. As he dropped this cynical confession he looked straight and hard at the candidate for the honour of taking his education in hand. This personage reflected, somewhat grimly, that the first thing he should have to teach his little charge would be to appear to address himself to his mother when he spoke to her – especially not to make her such an improper answer as that.

When Mrs Moreen bethought herself of this pretext for getting rid of their companion, Pemberton supposed it was precisely to approach the delicate subject of his remuneration. But it had been only to say some things about her son which it was better that a boy of eleven shouldn't catch. They were extravagantly to his advantage, save when she lowered her voice to sigh, tapping her left side familiarly: 'And all over clouded by *this*, you know – all at the mercy of a weakness – !'. Pemberton gathered that the weakness was in the region of the heart. He had known the poor child was not robust: this was the basis on which he had been invited to treat, through an English lady, an Oxford acquaintance, then at Nice, who happened to know both his needs and those of the amiable American family looking out for something really superior in the way of a resident tutor.

The young man's impression of his prospective pupil, who had first come into the room, as if to see for himself, as soon as Pemberton was admitted, was not quite the soft solicitation the visitor had taken for granted. Morgan Moreen was, somehow, sickly without being delicate, and that he looked intelligent (it is true Pemberton wouldn't have enjoyed his being stupid) only added to the suggestion that, as with his big mouth and big ears he really couldn't be called pretty, he might be unpleasant. Pemberton was modest – he was even timid; and the chance that his small scholar might prove cleverer than himself had quite figured, to his nervousness, among the dangers of an untried experiment. He reflected, however, that these were risks one had to run when one accepted a position, as it was called, in a private family; when as yet one's University honours had, pecuniarily speaking, remained barren. At any rate, when Mrs Moreen got up as if to intimate that, since it was understood he would enter upon his duties within the week she would let him off now, he succeeded, in spite of the presence of the child, in squeezing out a phrase about the rate of payment. It was not the fault of the conscious smile which seemed a reference to the lady's expensive identity, if the allusion did not sound rather vulgar. This was exactly because she became still more gracious to reply: 'Oh! I can assure you that all that will be quite regular.'

Pemberton only wondered, while he took up his hat, what 'all that' was to amount to – people had such different ideas. Mrs Moreen's words, however, seemed to commit the family to a pledge definite enough to elicit from the child a strange little comment, in the shape of the mocking, foreign ejaculation '*Oh, là-là!*'

Pemberton, in some confusion, glanced at him as he walked slowly to the window with his back turned, his hands in his pockets and the air in his elderly shoulders of a boy who didn't play. The young man wondered if he could teach him to play, though his mother had said it would never do and that this was why school was impossible. Mrs Moreen exhibited no discomfiture; she only continued blandly: 'Mr Moreen will be delighted to meet your wishes. As I told you, he has been called to London for a week. A soon as he comes back you shall have it out with him.'

This was so frank and friendly that the young man could only reply, laughing as his hostess laughed: 'Oh! I don't imagine we shall have much of a battle.'

'They'll give you anything you like,' the boy remarked unexpectedly, returning from the window. 'We don't mind what anything costs – we live awfully well.'

'My darling, you're too quaint!' his mother exclaimed, putting out to caress him a practised but ineffectual hand. He slipped out of it, but looked with intelligent, innocent eyes at Pemberton, who had already had time to notice that from one moment to the other his small satiric face seemed to change its time of life. At this moment it was infantine; yet it appeared also to be under the influence of curious intuitions and knowledges. Pemberton rather disliked precocity, and he was disappointed to find gleams of it in a disciple not yet in his teens. Nevertheless he divined on the spot that Morgan wouldn't prove a bore. He would prove on the contrary a kind of excitement. This idea held the young man, in spite of a certain repulsion.

'You pompous little person! We're not extravagant!' Mrs Moreen gaily protested, making another unsuccessful attempt to draw the boy to her side. 'You must know what to expect,' she went on to Pemberton.

'The less you expect the better!' her companion interposed. 'But we *are* people of fashion.'

'Only so far as *you* make us so!' Mrs Moreen mocked, tenderly.

'Well, then, on Friday – don't tell me you're superstitious – and mind you don't fail us. Then you'll see us all. I'm so sorry the girls are out. I guess you'll like the girls. And, you know, I've another son, quite different from this one.'

'He tries to imitate me,' said Morgan to Pemberton.

'He tries? Why, he's twenty years old!' cried Mrs Moreen.

'You're very witty,' Pemberton remarked to the child – a proposition that his mother echoed with enthusiasm, declaring that Morgan's sallies were the delight of the house. The boy paid no heed to this; he only inquired abruptly of the visitor, who was surprised afterwards that he hadn't struck him as offensively forward: 'Do you *want* very much to come?'

'Can you doubt it, after such a description of what I shall hear?' Pemberton replied. Yet he didn't want to come at all; he was coming because he had to go somewhere, thanks to the collapse of his fortune at the end of a year abroad, spent on the system of putting his tiny patrimony into a single full wave of experience. He had had his full wave, but he couldn't pay his hotel bill. Moreover, he had caught in the boy's eyes the glimpse of a far-off appeal.

'Well, I'll do the best I can for you,' said Morgan; with which he turned away again. He passed out of one of the long windows; Pemberton saw him go and lean on the parapet of the terrace. He remained there while the young man took leave of his mother, who, on Pemberton's looking as if he expected a farewell from him, interposed with: 'Leave him, leave him; he's so strange!' Pemberton suspected she was afraid of something he might say. 'He's a genius – you'll love him,' she added. 'He's much the most interesting person in the family.' And before he could invent some civility to oppose to this, she wound up with: 'But we're all good, you know!'

'He's a genius – you'll love him!' were words that recurred to Pemberton before the Friday, suggesting, among other things, that geniuses were not invariably lovable. However, it was all the better if there was an element that would make tutorship absorbing: he had perhaps taken too much for granted that it would be dreary. As he left the villa after his interview, he looked up at the balcony and saw the child leaning over it. 'We shall have great larks!' he called up.

Morgan hesitated a moment; then he answered, laughing: 'By the time you come back I shall have thought of something witty!'

This made Pemberton say to himself: 'After all he's rather nice.'

II

On the Friday he saw them all, as Mrs Moreen had promised, for her husband had come back and the girls and the other son were at home. Mr Moreen had a white moustache, a confiding manner and, in his buttonhole, the ribbon of a foreign order – bestowed, as Pemberton eventually learned, for services. For what services he never clearly ascertained: this was a point – one of a large number – that Mr Moreen's manner never confided. What it emphatically did confide was that he was a man of the world. Ulick, the firstborn, was in visible training for the same profession – under the disadvantage as yet, however, of a buttonhole only feebly floral and a moustache with no pretensions to type. The girls had hair and figures and manners and small fat feet, but had never been out alone. As for Mrs Moreen, Pemberton saw on a nearer view that her elegance was intermittent and her parts didn't always match. Her husband, as she had promised, met with enthusiasm Pemberton's ideas in regard to a salary. The young man had endeavoured to make them modest, and Mr Moreen confided to him that *he* found them positively meagre. He further assured him that he aspired to be intimate with his children, to be their best friend, and that he was always looking out for them. That was what he went off for, to London and other places – to look out; and this vigilance was the theory of life, as well as the real occupation, of the whole family. They all looked out, for they were very frank on the subject of its being necessary. They desired it to be understood that they were earnest people, and also that their fortune, though quite adequate for earnest people, required the most careful administration. Mr Moreen, as the parent bird,

sought sustenance for the nest. Ulick found sustenance mainly at
the club, where Pemberton guessed that it was usually served on
green cloth. The girls used to do up their hair and their frocks
themselves, and our young man felt appealed to be glad, in regard
to Morgan's education, that, though it must naturally be of the
best, it didn't cost too much. After a little he *was* glad, forgetting at
times his own needs in the interest inspired by the child's nature
and education and the pleasure of making easy terms for him.

During the first weeks of their acquaintance Morgan had been
as puzzling as a page in an unknown language – altogether
different from the obvious little Anglo-Saxons who had misrepre-
sented childhood to Pemberton. Indeed the whole mystic volume
in which the boy had been bound demanded some practice in
translation. Today, after a considerable interval, there is something phantasmagoric, like a prismatic reflection or a serial novel,
in Pemberton's memory of the queerness of the Moreens. If it
were not for a few tangible tokens – a lock of Morgan's hair, cut by
his own hand, and the half-dozen letters he got from him when
they were separated – the whole episode and the figures peopling
it would seem too inconsequent for anything but dreamland. The
queerest thing about them was their success (as it appeared to him
for a while at the time), for he had never seen a family so brilliantly
equipped for failure. Wasn't it success to have kept him so
hatefully long? Wasn't it success to have drawn him in that first
morning at *déjeuner*, the Friday he came – it was enough to *make*
one superstitious – so that he utterly committed himself, and this
not by calculation or a *mot d'ordre*, but by a happy instinct which
made them, like a band of gypsies, work so neatly together? They
amused him as much as if they had really been a band of gypsies.
He was still young and had not seen much of the world – his
English years had been intensely usual; therefore the reversed
conventions of the Moreens (for they had their standards) struck
him as topsyturvy. He had encountered nothing like them at
Oxford; still less had any such note been struck to his younger
American ear during the four years at Yale in which he had richly
supposed himself to be reacting against Puritanism. The reaction

of the Moreens, at any rate, went ever so much further. He had thought himself very clever that first day in hitting them all off in his mind with the term 'cosmopolite'. Later, it seemed feeble and colourless enough – confessedly, helplessly provisional.

However, when he first applied it to them he had a degree of joy – for an instructor he was still empirical – as if from the apprehension that to live with them would really be to see life. Their sociable strangeness was an intimation of that – their chatter of tongues, their gaiety and good humour, their infinite dawdling (they were always getting themselves up, but it took for ever, and Pemberton had once found Mr Moreen shaving in the drawing-room), their French, their Italian and, in the spiced fluency, their cold, tough slices of American. They lived on macaroni and coffee (they had these articles prepared in perfection), but they knew recipes for a hundred other dishes. They overflowed with music and song, were always humming and catching each other up, and had a kind of professional acquaintance with continental cities. They talked of 'good places' as if they had been strolling players. They had at Nice a villa, a carriage, a piano and a banjo, and they went to official parties. They were a perfect calendar of the 'days' of their friends, which Pemberton knew them, when they were indisposed, to get out of bed to go to, and which made the week larger than life when Mrs Moreen talked of them with Paula and Amy. Their romantic initiations gave their new inmate at first an almost dazzling sense of culture. Mrs Moreen had translated something, at some former period – an author whom it made Pemberton feel *borné* never to have heard of. They could imitate Venetian and sing Neapolitan, and when they wanted to say something very particular they communicated with each other in an ingenious dialect of their own – a sort of spoken cipher, which Pemberton at first took for Volapuk, but which he learned to understand as he would not have understood Volapuk.

'It's the family language – Ultramoreen,' Morgan explained to him drolly enough; but the boy rarely condescended to use it himself, though he attempted colloquial Latin as if he had been a little prelate.

Among all the 'days' with which Mrs Moreen's memory was
taxed she managed to squeeze in one of her own, which her
friends sometimes forgot. But the house derived a frequented air
from the number of fine people who were freely named there and
from several mysterious men with foreign titles and English
clothes whom Morgan called the princes and who, on sofas with
the girls, talked French very loud, as if to show they were saying
nothing improper. Pemberton wondered how the princes could
ever propose in that tone and so publicly: he took for granted
cynically that this was what was desired of them. Then he
acknowledged that even for the chance of such an advantage Mrs
Moreen would never allow Paula and Amy to receive alone. These
young ladies were not at all timid, but it was just the safeguards
that made them so graceful. It was a houseful of Bohemians who
wanted tremendously to be Philistines.

In one respect, however, certainly, they achieved no rigour –
they were wonderfully amiable and ecstatic about Morgan. It was
a genuine tenderness, an artless admiration, equally strong in
each. They even praised his beauty, which was small, and were
rather afraid of him, as if they recognized that he was of a finer
clay. They called him a little angel and a little prodigy and pitied
his want of health effusively. Pemberton feared at first that their
extravagance would make him hate the boy, but before this
happened he had become extravagant himself. Later, when he
had grown rather to hate the others, it was a bribe to patience for
him that they were at any rate nice about Morgan, going on tiptoe
if they fancied he was showing symptoms, and even giving up
somebody's 'day' to procure him a pleasure. But mixed with this
was the oddest wish to make him independent, as if they felt that
they were not good enough for him. They passed him over to
Pemberton very much as if they wished to force a constructive
adoption on the obliging bachelor and shirk altogether a responsibility. They were delighted when they perceived that Morgan
liked his preceptor, and could think of no higher praise for the
young man. It was strange how they contrived to reconcile the
appearance, and indeed the essential fact, of adoring the child

with their eagerness to wash their hands of him. Did they want to
get rid of him before he should find them out? Pemberton was
finding them out month by month. At any rate, the boy's relations
turned their backs with exaggerated delicacy, as if to escape the
charge of interfering. Seeing in time how little he had in common
with them (it was by *them* he first observed it – they proclaimed it
with complete humility), his preceptor was moved to speculate on
the mysteries of transmission, the far jumps of heredity. Where
his detachment from most of the things they represented had
come from was more than an observer could say – it certainly had
burrowed under two or three generations.

As for Pemberton's own estimate of his pupil, it was a good
while before he got the point of view, so little had he been
prepared for it by the smug young barbarians to whom the
tradition of tutorship, as hitherto revealed to him, had been
adjusted. Morgan was scrappy and suprising, deficient in many
properties supposed common to the *genus* and abounding in
others that were the portion only of the supernaturally clever.
One day Pemberton made a great stride: it cleared up the question
to perceive that Morgan *was* supernaturally clever and that,
though the formula was temporarily meagre, this would be the
only assumption on which one could successfully deal with him.
He had the general quality of a child for whom life had not been
simplified by school, a kind of homebred sensibility which might
have been bad for himself but was charming for others, and a
whole range of refinement and perception – little musical vib-
rations as taking as picked-up airs – begotten by wandering about
Europe at the tail of his migratory tribe. This might not have been
an education to recommend in advance, but its results with
Morgan were as palpable as a fine texture. At the same time he
had in his composition a sharp spice of stoicism, doubtless the
fruit of having had to begin early to bear pain, which produced the
impression of pluck and made it of less consequence that he might
have been thought at school rather a polyglot little beast. Pemberton indeed quickly found himself rejoicing that school was out of
the question: in any million of boys it was probably good for all but

one, and Morgan was that millionth. It would have made him
comparative and superior – it might have made him priggish.
Pemberton would try to be school himself – a bigger seminary
than five hundred grazing donkeys; so that, winning no prizes,
the boy would remain unconscious and irresponsible and amusing – amusing, because, though life was already intense in his
childish nature, freshness still made there a strong draught for
jokes. It turned out that even in the still air of Morgan's various
disabilities jokes flourished greatly. He was a pale, lean, acute,
undeveloped little cosmopolite, who liked intellectual gymnastics
and who, also, as regards the behaviour of mankind, had noticed
more things than you might suppose, but who nevertheless had
his proper playroom of superstitions, where he smashed a dozen
toys a day.

III

At Nice once, towards evening, as the pair sat resting in the open
air after a walk, looking over the sea at the pink western lights,
Morgan said suddenly to his companion: 'Do you like it – you
know, being with us all in this intimate way?'

'My dear fellow, why should I stay if I didn't?'

'How do I know you will stay? I'm almost sure you won't, very
long.'

'I hope you don't mean to dismiss me,' said Pemberton.

Morgan considered a moment, looking at the sunset. 'I think if I
did right I ought to.'

'Well, I know I'm supposed to instruct you in virtue; but in that
case don't do right.'

'You're very young – fortunately,' Morgan went on, turning to
him again.

'Oh yes, compared with you!'

'Therefore, it won't matter so much if you do lose a lot of time.'

'That's the way to look at it,' said Pemberton accommodatingly.

They were silent a minute; after which the boy asked: 'Do you
like my father and mother very much?'

'Dear me, yes. They're charming people.'

Morgan received this with another silence; then, unexpectedly, familiarly, but at the same time affectionately, he remarked: 'You're a jolly old humbug!'

For a particular reason the words made Pemberton change colour. The boy noticed in an instant that he had turned red, whereupon he turned red himself and the pupil and the master exchanged a longish glance in which there was a consciousness of many more things than are usually touched upon, even tacitly, in such a relation. It produced for Pemberton an embarrassment; it raised, in a shadowy form, a question (this was the first glimpse of it), which was destined to play as singular and, as he imagined, owing to the altogether peculiar conditions, an unprecedented part in his intercourse with his little companion. Later, when he found himself talking with this small boy in a way in which few small boys could ever have been talked with, he thought of that clumsy moment on the bench at Nice as the dawn of an understanding that had broadened. What had added to the clumsiness then was that he thought it his duty to declare to Morgan that he might abuse him (Pemberton) as much as he liked, but must never abuse his parents. To this Morgan had the easy reply that he hadn't dreamed of abusing them; which appeared to be true: it put Pemberton in the wrong.

'Then why am I a humbug for saying *I* think them charming?' the young man asked, conscious of a certain rashness.

'Well – they're not *your* parents.'

'They love you better than anything in the world – never forget that,' said Pemberton.

'Is that why you like them so much?'

'They're very kind to me,' Pemberton replied, evasively.

'You *are* a humbug!' laughed Morgan, passing an arm into his tutor's. He leaned against him, looking off at the sea again and swinging his long, thin legs.

'Don't kick my shins,' said Pemberton, while he reflected: 'Hang it, I can't complain of them to the child!'

'There's another reason, too,' Morgan went on, keeping his legs still.

'Another reason for what?'

'Besides their not being your parents.'

'I don't understand you,' said Pemberton.

'Well, you will before long. All right!'

Pemberton did understand, fully, before long; but he made a fight even with himself before he confessed it. He thought it the oddest thing to have a struggle with the child about. He wondered he didn't detest the child for launching him in such a struggle. But by the time it began the resource of detesting the child was closed to him. Morgan was a special case, but to know him was to accept him on his own odd terms. Pemberton had spent his aversion to special cases before arriving at knowledge. When at last he did arrive he felt that he was in an extreme predicament. Against every interest he had attached himself. They would have to meet things together. Before they went home that evening, at Nice, the boy had said, clinging to his arm:

'Well, at any rate you'll hang on to the last.'

'To the last?'

'Till you're fairly beaten.'

'*You* ought to be fairly beaten!' cried the young man, drawing him closer.

## IV

A year after Pemberton had come to live with them Mr and Mrs Moreen suddenly gave up the villa at Nice. Pemberton had got used to suddenness, having seen it practised on a considerable scale during two jerky little tours – one in Switzerland the first summer, and the other late in the winter, when they all ran down to Florence and then, at the end of ten days, liking it much less than they had intended, straggled back in mysterious depression. They had returned to Nice 'for ever', as they said; but this didn't prevent them from squeezing, one rainy, muggy May night, into a second-class railway-carriage – you could never tell by which class they would travel – where Pemberton helped them to stow away a wonderful collection of bundles and bags. The explanation of this manœuvre was that they had determined to spend the summer 'in some bracing place'; but in Paris they dropped into a small furnished apartment – a fourth floor in a third-rate avenue, where there was a smell on the staircase and the *portier* was hateful – and passed the next four months in blank indigence.

The better part of this baffled sojourn was for the preceptor and his pupil, who, visiting the Invalides and Notre Dame, the Conciergerie and all the museums, took a hundred remunerative rambles. They learned to know their Paris, which was useful, for they came back another year for a longer stay, the general character of which in Pemberton's memory today mixes pitiably and confusedly with that of the first. He sees Morgan's shabby knickerbockers – the everlasting pair that didn't match his blouse and that as he grew longer could only grow faded. He remembers the particular holes in his three or four pairs of coloured stockings.

Morgan was dear to his mother, but he never was better dressed than was absolutely necessary – partly, no doubt, by his own fault, for he was as indifferent to his appearance as a German philosopher. 'My dear fellow, you *are* coming to pieces,' Pemberton would say to him in sceptical remonstrance; to which the child would reply, looking at him serenely up and down: 'My dear fellow, so are you! I don't want to cast you in the shade.' Pemberton could have no rejoinder for this – the assertion so closely represented the fact. If however the deficiencies of his own wardrobe were a chapter by themselves he didn't like his little charge to look too poor. Later he used to say: 'Well, if we are poor, why, after all, shouldn't we look it?' and he consoled himself with thinking there was something rather elderly and gentlemanly in Morgan's seediness – it differed from the untidiness of the urchin who plays and spoils his things. He could trace perfectly the degrees by which, in proportion as her little son confined himself to his tutor for society, Mrs Moreen shrewdly forbore to renew his garments. She did nothing that didn't show, neglected him because he escaped notice, and then, as he illustrated this clever

policy, discouraged at home his public appearances. Her position
was logical enough – those members of her family who did show
had to be showy.

During this period and several others Pemberton was quite
aware of how he and his comrade might strike people; wandering
languidly through the Jardin des Plantes as if they had nowhere to
go, sitting, on the winter days, in the galleries of the Louvre, so
splendidly ironical to the homeless, as if for the advantage of the
*calorifère*. They joked about it sometimes: it was the sort of joke
that was perfectly within the boy's compass. They figured themselves as part of the vast, vague, hand-to-mouth multitude of the
enormous city and pretended they were proud of their position in
it – it showed them such a lot of life and made them conscious of a
sort of democratic brotherhood. If Pemberton could not feel a
sympathy in destitution with his small companion (for after all
Morgan's fond parents would never have let him really suffer),
the boy would at least feel it with him, so it came to the same
thing. He used sometimes to wonder what people would think
they were – fancy they were looked askance at, as if it might be a
suspected case of kidnapping. Morgan wouldn't be taken for a
young patrician with a preceptor – he wasn't smart enough;
though he might pass for his companion's sickly little brother.
Now and then he had a five-franc piece, and except once, when
they bought a couple of lovely neckties, one of which he made
Pemberton accept, they laid it out scientifically in old books. It was
a great day, always spent on the quays, rummaging among the
dusty boxes that garnish the parapets. These were occasions that
helped them to live, for their books ran low very soon after the
beginning of their aquaintance. Pemberton had a good many in
England, but he was obliged to write to a friend and ask him
kindly to get some fellow to give him something for them.

If the bracing climate was untasted that summer the young man
had an idea that at the moment they were about to make a push
the cup had been dashed from their lips by a movement of his
own. It had been his first blow-out, as he called it, with his
patrons; his first successful attempt (though there was little other

success about it), to bring them to a consideration of his impossible position. As the ostensible eve of a costly journey the moment
struck him as a good one to put in a signal protest – to present an
ultimatum. Ridiculous as it sounded he had never yet been able to
compass an uninterrupted private interview with the elder pair or
with either of them singly. They were always flanked by their
elder children, and poor Pemberton usually had his own little
charge at his side. He was conscious of its being a house in which
the surface of one's delicacy got rather smudged; nevertheless he
had kept the bloom of his scruple against announcing to Mr and
Mrs Moreen with publicity that he couldn't go on longer without a
little money. He was still simple enough to suppose Ulick and
Paula and Amy might not know that since his arrival he had only
had a hundred and forty francs; and he was magnanimous
enough to wish not to compromise their parents in their eyes. Mr
Moreen now listened to him, as he listened to every one and to
everything, like a man of the world, and seemed to appeal to him –
though not of course too grossly – to try and be a little more of one
himself. Pemberton recognized the importance of the character
from the advantage it gave Mr Moreen. He was not even
confused, whereas poor Pemberton was more so than there was
any reason for. Neither was he surprised – at least any more than a
gentleman had to be who freely confessed himself a little shocked,
though not, strictly, at Pemberton.

'We must go into this, mustn't we, dear?' he said to his wife. He
assured his young friend that the matter should have his very best
attention; and he melted into space as elusively as if, at the door,
he were taking an inevitable but deprecatory precedence. When,
the next moment, Pemberton found himself alone with Mrs
Moreen it was to hear her say: 'I see, I see,' stroking the roundness
of her chin and looking as if she were only hesitating between a
dozen easy remedies. If they didn't make their push Mr Moreen
could at least disappear for several days. During his absence his
wife took up the subject again spontaneously, but her contribution to it was merely that she had thought all the while
they were getting on so beautifully. Pemberton's reply to this

revelation was that unless they immediately handed him a substantial sum he would leave them for ever. He knew she would wonder how he would get away, and for a moment expected her to inquire. She didn't, for which he was almost grateful to her, so little was he in a position to tell.

'You won't, you know you won't – you're too interested,' she said. 'You *are* interested, you know you are, you dear, kind man!' She laughed, with almost condemnatory archness, as if it were a reproach (but she wouldn't insist), while she flirted a soiled pocket-handkerchief at him.

Pemberton's mind was fully made up to quit the house the following week. This would give him time to get an answer to a letter he had despatched to England. If he did nothing of the sort – that is, if he stayed another year and then went away only for three months – it was not merely because before the answer to his letter came (most unsatisfactory when it did arrive), Mr Moreen generously presented him – again with all the precautions of a man of the world – three hundred francs. He was exasperated to find that Mrs Moreen was right, that he couldn't bear to leave the child. This stood out clearer for the very reason that, the night of his desperate appeal to his patrons, he had seen fully for the first time where he was. Wasn't it another proof of the success with which those patrons practised their arts that they had managed to avert for so long the illuminating flash? It descended upon Pemberton with a luridness which perhaps would have struck a spectator as comically excessive, after he had returned to his little servile room, which looked into a close court where a bare, dirty opposite wall took, with the sound of shrill clatter, the reflection of lighted back-windows. He had simply given himself away to a band of adventurers. The idea, the word itself, had a sort of romantic horror for him – he had always lived on such safe lines. Later it assumed a more interesting, almost a soothing, sense: it pointed a moral, and Pemberton could enjoy a moral. The Moreens were adventurers not merely because they didn't pay their debts, because they lived on society, but because their whole view of life, dim and confused and instinctive, like that of clever colour-blind animals, was speculative and rapacious and mean. Oh! they were 'respectable', and that only made them more *immondes*. The young man's analysis of them put it at last very simply – they were adventurers because they were abject snobs. That was the completest account of them – it was the law of their being. Even when this truth became vivid to their ingenious inmate he remained unconscious of how much his mind had been prepared for it by the extraordinary little boy who had now become such a complication in his life. Much less could he then calculate on the information he was still to owe to the extraordinary little boy.

v

But it was during the ensuing time that the real problem came up – the problem of how far it was excusable to discuss the turpitude of parents with a child of twelve, of thirteen, of fourteen. Absolutely inexcusable and quite impossible it of course at first appeared; and indeed the question didn't press for a while after Pemberton had received his three hundred francs. They produced a sort of lull, a relief from the sharpest pressure. Pemberton frugally amended his wardrobe and even had a few francs in his pocket. He thought the Moreens looked at him as if he were almost too smart, as if they ought to take care not to spoil him. If Mr Moreen hadn't been such a man of the world he would perhaps have said something to him about his neckties. But Mr Moreen was always enough a man of the world to let things pass – he had certainly shown that. It was singular how Pemberton guessed that Morgan, though saying nothing about it, knew something had happened. But three hundred francs, especially when one owed money, couldn't last for ever; and when they were gone – the boy knew when they were gone – Morgan did say something. The party had returned to Nice at the beginning of the winter, but not to the charming villa. They went to an hotel, where they stayed three months, and then they went to another hotel, explaining that they had left the first because they had waited and waited and couldn't get the rooms they wanted. These apartments, the rooms they wanted, were generally very splendid; but fortunately they never *could* get them – fortunately, I mean, for Pemberton, who reflected always that if they had got them there would have been still less for educational expenses. What Morgan said at last was said suddenly, irrelevantly, when the moment came, in the middle of a lesson, and consisted of the apparently unfeeling words: 'You ought to *filer*, you know – you really ought.'

Pemberton stared. He had learnt enough French slang from Morgan to know that to *filer* meant to go away. 'Ah, my dear fellow, don't turn me off!'

Morgan pulled a Greek lexicon towards him (he used a Greek–German), to look out a word, instead of asking it of Pemberton. 'You can't go on like this, you know.'

'Like what, my boy?'

'You know they don't pay you up,' said Morgan, blushing and turning his leaves.

'Don't pay me?' Pemberton stared again and then feigned amazement. 'What on earth put that into your head?'

'It has been there a long time,' the boy replied, continuing his search.

Pemberton was silent, then he went on: 'I say, what are you hunting for? They pay me beautifully.'

'I'm hunting for the Greek for transparent fiction,' Morgan dropped.

'Find that rather for gross impertinence, and disabuse your mind. What do I want of money?'

'Oh, that's another question!'

Pemberton hesitated – he was drawn in different ways. The severely correct thing would have been to tell the boy that such a matter was none of his business and bid him go on with his lines. But they were really too intimate for that; it was not the way he was in the habit of treating him; there had been no reason it should be. On the other hand Morgan had quite lighted on the truth – he really shouldn't be able to keep it up much longer; therefore why not let him know one's real motive for forsaking him? At the same time it wasn't decent to abuse to one's pupil the family of one's pupil; it was better to misrepresent than to do that. So in reply to Morgan's last exclamation he just declared, to dismiss the subject, that he had received several payments.

'I say – I say!' the boy ejaculated, laughing.

'That's all right,' Pemberton insisted. 'Give me your written rendering.'

Morgan pushed a copybook across the table, and his companion began to read the page, but with something running in his head that made it no sense. Looking up after a minute or two he found the child's eyes fixed on him, and he saw something strange in them. Then Morgan said: 'I'm not afraid of the reality.'

'I haven't yet seen the thing that you *are* afraid of – I'll do you that justice!'

This came out with a jump (it was perfectly true), and evidently gave Morgan pleasure. 'I've thought of it a long time,' he presently resumed.

'Well, don't think of it any more.'

The child appeared to comply, and they had a comfortable and even an amusing hour. They had a theory that they were very thorough, and yet they seemed always to be in the amusing part of lessons, the intervals between the tunnels, where there were waysides and views. Yet the morning was brought to a violent end by Morgan's suddenly leaning his arms on the table, burying his head in them and bursting into tears. Pemberton would have been startled at any rate; but he was doubly startled because, as it then occurred to him, it was the first time he had ever seen the boy cry. It was rather awful.

The next day, after much thought, he took a decision and, believing it to be just, immediately acted upon it. He cornered Mr and Mrs Moreen again and informed them that if, on the spot, they didn't pay him all they owed him, he would not only leave their house, but would tell Morgan exactly what had brought him to it.

'Oh, you *haven't* told him? cried Mrs Moreen, with a pacifying hand on her well-dressed bosom.

'Without warning you? For what do you take me?'

Mr and Mrs Moreen looked at each other, and Pemberton could see both that they were relieved and that there was a certain alarm in their relief. 'My dear fellow,' Mr Moreen demanded, 'what use *can* you have, leading the quiet life we all do, for such a lot of money?' – an inquiry to which Pemberton made no answer, occupied as he was in perceiving that what passed in the mind of his patrons was something like: 'Oh, then, if we've felt that the child, dear little angel, has judged us and how he regards us, and we haven't been betrayed, he must have guessed – and, in short, it's *general*!' an idea that rather stirred up Mr and Mr Moreen, as Pemberton had desired that it should. At the same time, if he had thought that his threat would do something towards bringing them around, he was disappointed to find they had taken for granted (how little they appreciated his delicacy!) that he had already given them away to his pupil. There was a mystic uneasiness in their parental breasts, and that was the way they had accounted for it. None the less his threat did touch them; for if they had escaped it was only to meet a new danger. Mr Moreen appealed to Pemberton, as usual, as a man of the world; but his wife had recourse, for the first time since the arrival of their inmate, to a fine *hauteur*, reminding him that a devoted mother, with her child, had arts that protected her against gross misrepresentation.

'I should misrepresent you grossly if I accused you of common honesty!' the young man replied; but as he closed the door behind him sharply, thinking he had not done himself much good, while Mr Moreen lighted another cigarette, he heard Mrs Moreen shout after him, more touchingly:

'Oh, you do, you *do*, put the knife to one's throat!'

The next morning, very early, she came to his room. He recognized her knock, but he had no hope that she brought him money; as to which he was wrong, for she had fifty francs in her hand. She squeezed forward in her dressing-gown, and he received her in his own, between his bath-tub and his bed. He had been tolerably schooled by this time to the 'foreign ways' of his hosts. Mrs Moreen was zealous, and when she was zealous she didn't care what she did; so she now sat down on his bed, his clothes being on the chairs, and, in her preoccupation, forgot, as she glanced round, to be ashamed of giving him such a nasty room. What Mrs Moreen was zealous about on this occasion was to persuade him that in the first place she was very good-natured to bring him fifty francs, and, in the second, if he would only see it, he was really too absurd to expect to be *paid*. Wasn't he paid enough, without perpetual money – wasn't he paid by the comfortable, luxurious home that he enjoyed with them all, without a care, an anxiety, a solitary want? Wasn't he sure of his position, and wasn't that everything to a young man like him, quite unknown, with singularly little to show, the ground of whose exorbitant pretensions it was not easy to discover? Wasn't he paid, above all, by the delightful relation he had established with Morgan – quite ideal, as from master to pupil – and by the simple privilege of knowing and living with so amazingly gifted a child, than whom really – she meant literally what she said – there was no better company in Europe? Mrs Moreen herself took to appealing to him as a man of the world; she said 'Voyons, mon cher', and 'My dear sir, look here now'; and urged him to be reasonable, putting it before him that it was really a chance for him. She spoke as if, according as he *should* be reasonable, he would prove himself worthy to be her son's tutor and of the extraordinary confidence they had placed in him.

After all, Pemberton reflected, it was only a difference of theory, and the theory didn't matter much. They had hitherto gone on that of remunerated, as now they would go on that of gratuitous, service; but why should they have so many words about it? Mrs Moreen, however, continued to be convincing; sitting there with her fifty francs she talked and repeated, as women repeat, and bored and irritated him, while he leaned against the wall with his hands in the pockets of his wrapper, drawing it together round his legs and looking over the head of his visitor at the grey negations of his window. She wound up with saying: 'You see I bring you a definite proposal.'

'A definite proposal?'

'To make our relations regular, as it were – to put them on a comfortable footing.'

'I see – it's a system,' said Pemberton. 'A kind of blackmail.'

Mrs Moreen bounded up, which was what the young man wanted.

'What do you mean by that?'

'You practise on one's fears – one's fears about the child if one should go away.'

'And, pray, what would happen to him in that event?' demanded Mrs Moreen, with majesty.

'Why, he'd be alone with *you*.'

'And pray, with whom *should* a child be but with those whom he loves most?'

'If you think that, why don't you dimiss me?'

'Do you pretend that he loves you more than he loves *us*?' cried Mrs Moreen.

'I think he ought to. I make sacrifices for him. Though I've heard of those *you* make, I don't see them.'

Mrs Moreen stared a moment; then, with emotion, she grasped Pemberton's hand. '*Will* you make it – the sacrifice?'

Pemberton burst out laughing. 'I'll see – I'll do what I can – I'll stay a little longer. Your calculation is just – I *do* hate intensely to give him up; I'm fond of him and he interests me deeply, in spite of the inconvenience I suffer. You know my situation perfectly; I haven't a penny in the world, and occupied as I am with Morgan, I'm unable to earn money.'

Mrs Moreen tapped her undressed arm with her folded bank-note. 'Can't you write articles? Can't you translate, as *I* do?'

'I don't know about translating; it's wretchedly paid.'

'I am glad to earn what I can,' said Mrs Moreen virtuously, with her head high.

'You ought to tell me who you do it for.' Pemberton paused a moment, and she said nothing; so he added: 'I've tried to turn off some little sketches, but the magazines won't have them – they're declined with thanks.'

'You see then you're not such a phoenix – to have such pretensions,' smiled his interlocutress.

'I haven't time to do things properly,' Pemberton went on. Then as it came over him that he was almost abjectly good-natured to give these explanations he added: 'If I stay on longer it must be on one condition – that Morgan shall know distinctly on what footing I am.'

'Mrs Moreen hesitated. 'Surely you don't want to show off to a child?'

'To show *you* off, do you mean?'

Again Mrs Moreen hesitated, but this time it was to produce a still finer flower. 'And *you* talk of blackmail!'

'You can easily prevent it,' said Pemberton.

'And *you* talk of practising on fears,' Mrs Moreen continued.

'Yes, there's no doubt I'm a great scoundrel.'

His visitor looked at him a moment – it was evident that she was sorely bothered. Then she thrust out her money at him. 'Mr Moreen desired me to give you this on account.'

'I'm much obliged to Mr Moreen; but we have no account.'

'You won't take it?'

'That leaves me more free,' said Pemberton.

'To poison my darling's mind?' groaned Mrs Moreen.

'Oh, your darling's mind!' laughed the young man.

She fixed him a moment, and he thought she was going to break out tormentedly, pleadingly: 'For God's sake, tell me what *is* in it!' But she checked this impulse – another was stronger. She pocketed the money – the crudity of the alternative was comical – and swept out of the room with the desperate concession: 'You may tell him any horror you like!'

VI

A couple of days after this, during which Pemberton had delayed to profit by Mrs Moreen's permission to tell her son any horror, the two had been for a quarter of an hour walking together in silence when the boy became sociable again with the remark: 'I'll tell you how I know it; I know it through Zénobie.'

'Zénobie? Who in the world is *she*?'

'A nurse I used to have – ever so many years ago. A charming woman. I liked her awfully, and she liked me.'

'There's no accounting for tastes. What is it you know through her?'

'Why, what their idea is. She went away because they didn't pay her. She did like me awfully, and she stayed two years. She told me all about it – that at last she could never get her wages. As soon as they saw how much she liked me they stopped giving her anything. They thought she'd stay for nothing, out of devotion. And she did stay ever so long – as long as she could. She was only a poor girl. She used to send money to her mother. At last she couldn't afford it any longer, and she went away in a fearful rage one night – I mean of course in a rage against *them*. She cried over me tremendously, she hugged me nearly to death. She told me all about it,' Morgan repeated. 'She told me it was their idea. So I guessed, ever so long ago, that they have had the same idea with you.'

'Zénobie was very shrewd,' said Pemberton. 'And she made you so.'

'Oh, that wasn't Zénobie; that was nature. And experience!' Morgan laughed.

'Well, Zénobie was a part of your experience.'

'Certainly I was a part of hers, poor dear!' the boy exclaimed. 'And I'm a part of yours.'

'A very important part. But I don't see how you know that I've been treated like Zénobie.'

'Do you take me for an idiot?' Morgan asked. 'Haven't I been conscious of what we've been through together?'

'What we've been through?'

'Our privations – our dark days.'

'Oh, our days have been bright enough.'

Morgan went on in silence for a moment. Then he said: 'My dear fellow, you're a hero!'

'Well, you're another!' Pemberton retorted.

'No, I'm not; but I'm not a baby. I won't stand it any longer. You must get some occupation that pays. I'm ashamed, I'm ashamed!' quavered the boy in a little passionate voice that was very touching to Pemberton.

'We ought to go off and live somewhere together,' said the young man.

'I'll go like a shot if you'll take me.'

'I'd get some work that would keep us both afloat,' Pemberton continued.

'So would I. Why shouldn't *I* work? I ain't such a *crétin*!'

'The difficulty is that your parents wouldn't hear of it,' said Pemberton. 'They would never part with you; they worship the ground you tread on. Don't you see the proof of it? They don't dislike me; they wish me no harm; they're very amiable people; but they're perfectly ready to treat me badly for your sake.'

The silence in which Morgan received this graceful sophistry struck Pemberton somehow as expressive. After a moment Morgan repeated: 'You *are* a hero!' Then he added: 'They leave me with you altogether. You've all the responsibility. They put me off on you from morning till night. Why, then, should they object to my taking up with you completely? I'd help you.'

'They're not particularly keen about my being helped, and they delight in thinking of you as *theirs*. They're tremendously proud of you.'

'I'm not proud of them. But you know *that*,' Morgan returned.

'Except for the little matter we speak of they're charming people,' said Pemberton, not taking up the imputation of lucidity, but wondering greatly at the child's own, and especially at this fresh reminder of something he had been conscious of from the first – the strangest thing in the boy's large little composition, a temper, a sensibility, even a sort of ideal, which made him privately resent the general quality of his kinsfolk. Morgan had in secret a small loftiness which begot an element of reflection, a domestic scorn not imperceptible to his companion (though they never had any talk about it), and absolutely anomalous in a

juvenile nature, especially when one noted that it had not made
this nature 'old-fashioned', as the word is of children – quaint or
wizened or offensive. It was as if he had been a little gentleman
and had paid the penalty by discovering that he was the only such
person in the family. This comparison didn't make him vain; but it
could make him melancholy and a trifle austere. When Pemberton
guessed at these young dimnesses he saw him serious and
gallant, and was partly drawn on and partly checked, as if with a
scruple, by the charm of attempting to sound the little cool
shallows which were quickly growing deeper. When he tried to
figure to himself the morning twilight of childhood, so as to deal
with it safely, he perceived that it was never fixed, never arrested,
that ignorance, at the instant one touched it, was already flushing
faintly into knowledge, that there was nothing that at a given
moment you could say a clever child didn't know. It seemed to
him that *he* both knew too much to imagine Morgan's simplicity
and too little to disembroil his tangle.

The boy paid no heed to his last remark; he only went on: 'I
should have spoken to them about their idea, as I call it, long ago,
if I hadn't been sure what they would say.'

'And what would they say?'

'Just what they said about what poor Zénobie told me – that it
was a horrid, dreadful story, that they had paid her every penny
they owed her.'

'Well, perhaps they had,' said Pemberton.

'Perhaps they've paid you!'

'Let us pretend they have, and *n'en parlons plus*.'

'They accused her of lying and cheating,' Morgan insisted
perversely. 'That's why I don't want to speak to them.'

'Lest they should accuse me, too?'

To this Morgan made no answer, and his companion, looking
down at him (the boy turned his eyes, which had filled, away),
saw that he couldn't have trusted himself to utter.

'You're right. Don't squeeze them,' Pemberton pursued.
'Except for that, they *are* charming people.'

'Except for *their* lying and *their* cheating?'

'I say – I say!' cried Pemberton, imitating a little tone of the lad's which was itself an imitation.

'We must be frank, at the last; we *must* come to an understanding,' said Morgan, with the importance of the small boy who lets himself think he is arranging great affairs – almost playing at shipwreck or at Indians. 'I know all about everything,' he added.

'I daresay your father has his reasons,' Pemberton observed, too vaguely, as he was aware.

'For lying and cheating?'

'For saying and managing and turning his means to the best account. He has plenty to do with his money. You're an expensive family.'

'Yes, I'm very expensive,' Morgan rejoined, in a manner which made his preceptor burst out laughing.

'He's saving for *you*,' said Pemberton. 'They think of you in everything they do.'

'He might save a little – ' The boy paused. Pemberton waited to hear what. Then Morgan brought out oddly: 'A little reputation.'

'Oh, there's plenty of that. That's all right!'

'Enough of it for the people they know, no doubt. The people they know are awful.'

'Do you mean the princes? We mustn't abuse the princes.'

'Why not? They haven't married Paula – they haven't married Amy. They only clean out Ulick.'

'You *do* know everything!' Pemberton exclaimed.

'No, I don't, after all. I don't know what they live on, or how they live, or *why* they live! What have they got and how did they get it? Are they rich, are they poor, or have they a *modeste aisance*? Why are they always chiveying about – living one year like ambassadors and the next like paupers? Who are they, anyway, and what are they? I've thought of all that – I've thought of a lot of things. They're so beastly worldly. That's what I hate most – oh, I've *seen* it! All they care about is to make an appearance and to pass for something or other. What do they want to pass for? What *do* they, Mr Pemberton?'

'You pause for a reply,' said Pemberton, treating the inquiry as a joke, yet wondering too, and greatly struck with the boy's intense, if imperfect, vision. 'I haven't the least idea.'

'And what good does it do? Haven't I seen the way people treat them – the "nice" people, the ones they want to know? They'll take anything from them – they'll lie down and be trampled on. The nice ones hate that – they just sicken them. You're the only really nice person we know.'

'Are you sure? They don't lie down for me!'

'Well, you shan't lie down for them. You've got to go – that's what you've got to do,' said Morgan.

'And what will become of you?'

'Oh, I'm growing up. I shall get off before long. I'll see you later.'

'You had better let me finish you,' Pemberton urged, lending himself to the child's extraordinarily competent attitude.

Morgan stopped in their walk, looking up at him. He had to look up much less than a couple of years before – he had grown, in his loose leanness, so long and high. 'Finish me?' he echoed.

'There are such a lot of jolly things we can do together yet. I want to turn you out – I want you to do me credit.'

Morgan continued to look at him. 'To give you credit – do you mean?'

'My dear fellow, you're too clever to live.'

'That's just what I'm afraid you think. No, no; it isn't fair – I can't endure it. We'll part next week. The sooner it's over the sooner to sleep.'

'If I hear of anything – any other chance, I promise to go,' said Pemberton.

Morgan consented to consider this. 'But you'll be honest,' he demanded; 'you won't pretend you haven't heard?'

'I'm much more likely to pretend I have.'

'But what can you hear of, this way, stuck in a hole with us? You ought to be on the spot, to go to England – you ought to go to America.'

'One would think you were *my* tutor!' said Pemberton.

Morgan walked on, and after a moment he began again: 'Well,

now that you know that I know and that we look at the facts and keep nothing back – it's much more comfortable, isn't it?'

'My dear boy, it's so amusing, so interesting, that it surely will be quite impossible for me to forgo such hours as these.'

This made Morgan stop once more. 'You *do* keep something back. Oh, you're not straight – *I* am!'

'Why am I not straight?'

'Oh, you've got your idea!'

'My idea?'

'Why, that I probably shan't live, and that you can stick it out till I'm removed.'

'You *are* too clever to live!' Pemberton repeated.

'I call it a mean idea,' Morgan pursued. 'But I shall punish you by the way I hang on.'

'Look out or I'll poison you!' Pemberton laughed.

'I'm stronger and better every year. Haven't you noticed that there hasn't been a doctor near me since you came?'

'*I'm* your doctor,' said the young man, taking his arm and drawing him on again.

Morgan proceeded, and after a few steps he gave a sigh of mingled weariness and relief. 'Ah, now that we look at the facts, it's all right!'

## VII

They looked at the facts a good deal after this; and one of the first consequences of their doing so was that Pemberton stuck it out, as it were, for the purpose. Morgan made the facts so vivid and so droll, and at the same time so bald and so ugly, that there was fascination in talking them over with him, just as there would have been heartlessness in leaving him alone with them. Now that they had such a number of perceptions in common it was useless for the pair to pretend that they didn't judge such people; but the very judgement, and the exchange of perceptions, created another tie. Morgan had never been so interesting as now that he himself was made plainer by the sidelight of these confidences.

What came out in it most was the soreness of his characteristic pride. He had plenty of that, Pemberton felt – so much that it was perhaps well it should have had to take some early bruises. He would have liked his people to be gallant, and he had waked up too soon to the sense that they were perpetually swallowing humble-pie. His mother would consume any amount, and his father would consume even more than his mother. He had a theory that Ulick had wriggled out of an 'affair' at Nice: there had once been a flurry at home, a regular panic, after which they all went to bed and took medicine, not to be accounted for on any other supposition. Morgan had a romantic imagination, fed by poetry and history, and he would have liked those who 'bore his name' (as he used to say to Pemberton with the humour that made his sensitiveness manly) to have a proper spirit. But their one idea was to get in with people who didn't want them and to take snubs as if they were honourable scars. Why people didn't want them more he didn't know – that was people's own affair; after all they were not superficially repulsive – they were a hundred times cleverer than most of the dreary grandees, the 'poor swells' they rushed about Europe to catch up with. 'After all, they *are* amusing – they are!' Morgan used to say, with the wisdom of the ages. To which Pemberton always replied: 'Amusing – the great Moreen troupe? Why, they're altogether delightful; and if it were not for the hitch that you and I (feeble performers!) make in the *ensemble*, they would carry everything before them.'

What the boy couldn't get over was that this particular blight seemed, in a tradition of self-respect, so undeserved and so arbitrary. No doubt people had a right to take the line they liked; but why should *his* people have liked the line of pushing and toadying and lying and cheating? What had their forefathers – all decent folk, so far as he knew – done to them, or what had *he* done to them? Who had poisoned their blood with the fifth-rate social ideal, the fixed idea of making smart acquaintances and getting into the *monde chic*, especially when it was foredoomed to failure and exposure? They showed so what they were after; that was what made the people they wanted not want *them*. And never a movement of dignity, never a throb of shame at looking each other in the face, never any independence or resentment or disgust. If his father or his brother would only knock some one down once or twice a year! Clever as they were they never guessed how they appeared. They were good-natured, yes – as good-natured as Jews at the doors of clothing-shops! But was that the model one wanted one's family to follow? Morgan had dim memories of an old grandfather, the maternal, in New York, whom he had been taken across the ocean to see, at the age of five: a gentleman with a high neckcloth and a good deal of pronunciation, who wore a dress-coat in the morning, which made one wonder what he wore in the evening, and had, or was supposed to have, 'property' and something to do with the Bible Society. It couldn't have been but that *he* was a good type. Pemberton himself remembered Mrs Clancy, a widowed sister of Mr Moreen's, who was as irritating as a moral tale and had paid a fortnight's visit to the family at Nice shortly after he came to live with them. She was 'pure and refined', as Amy said, over the banjo, and had the air of not knowing what they meant and of keeping something back. Pemberton judged that what she kept back was an approval of many of their ways; therefore it was to be supposed that she too was of a good type, and that Mr and Mrs Moreen and Ulick and Paula and Amy might easily have been better if they would.

But that they wouldn't was more and more perceptible from day to day. They continued to 'chivey', as Morgan called it, and in due time became aware of a variety of reasons for proceeding to Venice. They mentioned a great many of them – they were always strikingly frank, and had the brightest friendly chatter, at the late foreign breakfast in especial, before the ladies had made up their faces, when they leaned their arms on the table, had something to follow the *demi-tasse*, and, in the heat of familiar discussion as to what they 'really ought' to do, fell inevitably into the languages in which they could *tutoyer*. Even Pemberton liked them, then; he could endure even Ulick when he heard him give his little flat voice for the 'sweet sea-city'. That was what made him have a sneaking kindness for them – that they were so out of the workaday world and kept him so out of it. The summer had waned when, with cries of ecstasy, they all passed out on the balcony that overhung the Grand Canal; the sunsets were splendid – the Dorringtons had arrived. The Dorringtons were the only reason they had not talked of at breakfast; but the reasons that they didn't talk of at breakfast always came out in the end. The Dorringtons, on the other hand, came out very little; or else, when they did, they stayed – as was natural – for hours, during which periods Mrs Moreen and the girls sometimes called at their hotel (to see if they had returned) as many as three times running. The gondola was for the ladies; for in Venice too there were 'days', which Mrs Moreen knew in their order an hour after she arrived. She immediately took one herself, to which the Dorringtons never came, though on a certain occasion when Pemberton and his pupil were together at St Mark's – where, taking the best walks they had ever had and haunting a hundred churches, they spent a great deal of time – they saw the old lord turn up with Mr Moreen and Ulick, who showed him the dim basilica as if it belonged to them. Pemberton noted how much less, among its curiosities, Lord Dorrington carried himself as a man of the world; wondering too whether, for such services, his companions took a fee from him. The autumn, at any rate, waned, the Dorringtons departed, and Lord Verschoyle, the eldest son, had proposed neither for Amy nor for Paula.

One sad November day, while the wind roared round the old palace and the rain lashed the lagoon, Pemberton, for exercise and even somewhat for warmth (the Moreens were horribly frugal about fires – it was a cause of suffering to their inmate), walked up and down the big bare *sala* with his pupil. The scagliola floor was cold, the high battered casements shook in the storm, and the stately decay of the place was unrelieved by a particle of furniture. Pemberton's spirits were low, and it came over him that the fortune of the Moreens was now even lower. A blast of desolation, a prophecy of disaster and disgrace, seemed to draw through the comfortless hall. Mr Moreen and Ulick were in the Piazza, looking out for something, strolling drearily, in mackintoshes, under the arcades; but still, in spite of mackintoshes, unmistakable men of the world. Paula and Amy were in bed – it might have been thought they were staying there to keep warm. Pemberton looked askance at the boy at his side, to see to what extent he was conscious of these portents. But Morgan, luckily for him, was now mainly conscious of growing taller and stronger and indeed of being in his fifteenth year. This fact was intensely interesting to him – it was the basis of a private theory (which, however, he had imparted to his tutor) that in a little while he should stand on his own feet. He considered that the situation would change – that, in short, he should be 'finished', grown up, producible in the world of affairs and ready to prove himself of sterling ability. Sharply as he was capable, at times, of questioning his circumstances, there were happy hours when he was as superficial as a child; the proof of which was his fundamental assumption that he should presently go to Oxford, to Pemberton's college, and, aided and abetted by Pemberton, do the most wonderful things. It vexed Pemberton to see how little, in such a project, he took account of ways and means: on other matters he was so sceptical about them. Pemberton tried to imagine the Moreens at Oxford, and fortunately failed; yet unless they were to remove there as a family there would be no *modus vivendi* for Morgan. How could he live without an allowance, and where was the allowance to come from? He (Pemberton) might live on Morgan; but how could Morgan live on him? What was to become of him anyhow? Somehow, the fact that he was a big boy now, with better prospects of health, made the question of his future more difficult. So long as he was frail the consideration that he inspired seemed enough of an answer to it. But at the bottom of Pemberton's heart was the recognition of his probably being strong enough to live and not strong enough to thrive. He himself, at any rate, was in a period of natural, boyish rosiness about all this, so that the beating of the tempest seemed to him only the voice of life and the challenge of fate. He had on his shabby little overcoat, with the collar up, but he was enjoying his walk.

It was interrupted at last by the appearance of his mother at the end of the *sala*. She beckoned to Morgan to come to her, and while Pemberton saw him, complacent, pass down the long vista, over the damp false marble, he wondered what was in the air. Mrs Moreen said a word to the boy and made him go into the room she had quitted. Then, having closed the door after him, she directed her steps swiftly to Pemberton. There *was* something in the air, but his wildest flight of fancy wouldn't have suggested what it proved to be. She signified that she had made a pretext to get Morgan out of the way, and then she inquired – without hesitation – if the young man could lend her sixty francs. While, before bursting into a laugh, he stared at her with surprise, she declared that she was awfully pressed for the money; she was desperate for it – it would save her life.

'Dear lady, *c'est trop fort!*' Pemberton laughed. 'Where in the world do you suppose I should get sixty francs, *du train dont vous allez?*'

'I thought you worked – wrote things; don't they pay you?'

'Not a penny.'

'Are you such a fool as to work for nothing?'

'You ought surely to know that.'

Mrs Moreen stared an instant, then she coloured a little. Pemberton saw she had quite forgotten the terms – if 'terms' they could be called – that he had ended by accepting from herself; they had burdened her memory as little as her conscience. 'Oh, yes, I see what you mean – you have been very nice about that; but why go back to it so often?' She had been perfectly urbane with him ever since the rough scene of explanation in his room, the morning he made her accept *his* 'terms' – the necessity of his making his case known to Morgan. She had felt no resentment, after seeing that there was no danger of Morgan's taking the matter up with her. Indeed, attributing this immunity to the good taste of his influence with the boy, she had once said to Pemberton: 'My dear fellow; it's an immense comfort you're a gentleman.' She repeated this, in substance, now. 'Of course you're a gentleman – that's a bother the less!' Pemberton reminded her that he had not 'gone back' to anything; and she also repeated her prayer that, somewhere and somehow, he would find her sixty francs. He took the liberty of declaring that if he could find them it wouldn't be to lend them to *her* – as to which he consciously did himself injustice, knowing that if he had them he would certainly place them in her hand. He accused himself, at bottom and with some truth, of a fantastic, demoralized sympathy with her. If misery made strange bedfellows it also made strange sentiments. It was moreover a part of the demoralization and of the general bad effect of living with such people that one had to make rough retorts, quite out of the tradition of good manners. 'Morgan, Morgan, to what pass have I come for you?' he privately exclaimed, while Mrs Moreen floated voluminously down the *sala* again, to liberate the boy; groaning, as she went, that everything was too odious.

Before the boy was liberated there came a thump at the door communicating with the staircase, followed by the apparition of a dripping youth who poked in his head. Pemberton recognized him as the bearer of a telegram and recognized the telegram as addressed to himself. Morgan came back as, after glancing at the signature (that of a friend in London), he was reading the words: 'Found jolly job for you – engagement to coach opulent youth on own terms. Come immediately.' The answer, happily, was paid, and the messenger waited. Morgan, who had drawn near, waited too, and looked hard at Pemberton; and Pemberton, after a moment, having met his look, handed him the telegram. It was really by wise looks (they knew each other so well) that, while the telegraph-boy, in his waterproof cape, made a great puddle on the floor, the thing was settled between them. Pemberton wrote the answer with a pencil against the frescoed wall, and the messenger departed. When he had gone Pemberton said to Morgan:

'I'll make a tremendous charge; I'll earn a lot of money in a short time, and we'll live on it.'

'Well, I hope the opulent youth will be stupid – he probably will –' Morgan parenthesized, 'and keep you a long time.'

'Of course, the longer he keeps me the more we shall have for our old age.'

'But suppose *they* don't pay you!' Morgan awfully suggested.

'Oh, there are not two such – !' Pemberton paused, he was on the point of using an invidious term. Instead of this he said 'two such chances!'

Morgan flushed – the tears came to his eyes. *'Dites toujours*, two such rascally crews!' Then, in a different tone, he added: 'Happy opulent youth!'

'Not if he's stupid!'

'Oh, they're happier then. But you can't have everything, can you?' the boy smiled.

Pemberton held him, his hands on his shoulders. 'What will become of *you*, what will you do?' He thought of Mrs Moreen, desperate for sixty francs.

'I shall turn into a man.' And then, as if he recognized all the bearings of Pemberton's allusion: 'I shall get on with them better when you're not here.'

'Ah, don't say that – it sounds as if I set you against them!'

'You do – the sight of you. It's all right; you know what I mean. I shall be beautiful. I'll take their affairs in hand; I'll marry my sisters.'

'You'll marry yourself!' joked Pemberton; as high, rather tense pleasantry would evidently be the right, or the safest, tone for their separation.

It was, however, not purely in this strain that Morgan suddenly asked: 'But I say – how will you get to your jolly job? You'll have to telegraph to the opulent youth for money to come on.'

Pemberton bethought himself. 'They won't like that, will they?'

'Oh, look out for them!'

Then Pemberton brought out his remedy. 'I'll go to the American Consul; I'll borrow some money off him – just for the few days, on the strength of the telegram.'

Morgan was hilarious. 'Show him the telegram – then stay and keep the money!'

Pemberton entered into the joke enough to reply that, for Morgan, he was really capable of that; but the boy, growing more serious, and to prove he hadn't meant what he said, not only hurried him off to the Consulate (since he was to start that evening, as he had wired to his friend), but insisted on going with him. They splashed through the tortuous perforations and over the humpbacked bridges, and they passed through the Piazza, where they saw Mr Moreen and Ulick go into a jeweller's shop. The Consul proved accommodating (Pemberton said it wasn't the letter, but Morgan's grand air), and on their way back they went into St Mark's for a hushed ten minutes. Later they took up and kept up the fun of it to the very end; and it seemed to Pemberton a part of that fun that Mrs Moreen, who was very angry when he had announced to her his intention, should charge him, grotesquely and vulgarly, and in reference to the loan she had vainly endeavoured to effect, with bolting lest they should 'get something out' of him. On the other hand he had to do Mr Moreen and Ulick the justice to recognize that when, on coming in, *they* heard the cruel news, they took it like perfect men of the world.

VIII

When Pemberton got at work with the opulent youth, who was to be taken in hand for Balliol, he found himself unable to say whether he was really an idiot or it was only, on his own part, the long associations with an intensely living little mind that made him seem so. From Morgan he heard half-a-dozen times: the boy wrote charming young letters, a patchwork of tongues, with indulgent postscripts in the family Volapuk and, in little squares and rounds and crannies of the text, the drollest illustrations – letters that he was divided between the impulse to show his present disciple, as a kind of wasted incentive, and the sense of something in them that was profanable by publicity. The opulent youth went up, in due course, and failed to pass; but it seemed to add to the presumption that brilliancy was not expected of him all at once that his parents, condoning the lapse, which they good-naturedly treated as little as possible as if it were Pemberton's, should have sounded the rally again, begged the young coach to keep his pupil in hand another year.

The young coach was now in a position to lend Mrs Moreen sixty francs, and he sent her a post-office order for the amount. In return for this favour he received a frantic, scribbled line from her: 'Implore you to come back instantly – Morgan dreadfully ill.' They were on the rebound, once more in Paris – often as Pemberton had seen them depressed he had never seen them crushed – and communication was therefore rapid. He wrote to the boy to ascertain the state of his health, but he received no answer to his letter. Accordingly he took an abrupt leave of the opulent youth and, crossing the Channel, alighted at the small hotel, in the quarter of the Champs Elysées, of which Mrs Moreen had given him the address. A deep if dumb dissatisfaction with this lady and her companions bore him company: they couldn't be vulgarly honest, but they could live at hotels, in velvety *entresols*, amid a smell of burnt pastilles, in the most expensive city in Europe. When he had left them, in Venice, it was with an irrepressible suspicion that something was going to happen; but the only thing that had happened was that they succeeded in getting away. 'How is he? where is he?' he asked of Mrs Moreen; but before she could speak, these questions were answered by the pressure round his neck of a pair of arms, in shrunken sleeves, which were perfectly capable of an effusive young foreign squeeze.

'Dreadfully ill – I don't see it!' the young man cried. And then, to Morgan: 'Why on earth didn't you relieve me? Why didn't you answer my letter?'

Mrs Moreen declared that when she wrote he was very bad, and Pemberton learned at the same time from the boy that he had answered, every letter he had received. This led to the demonstration that Pemberton's note had been intercepted. Mrs Moreen was prepared to see the fact exposed, as Pemberton perceived, the moment he faced her, that she was prepared for a good many other things. She was prepared above all to maintain that she had acted from a sense of duty, that she was enchanted she had got him over, whatever they might say; and that it was useless of him to pretend that he didn't *know*, in all his bones, that his place at such a time was with Morgan. He had taken the boy away from

them, and now he had no right to abandon him. He had created
for himself the gravest responsibilities; he must at least abide by
what he had done.

'Taken him away from you?' Pemberton exclaimed indignantly.

'Do it – do it, for pity's sake; that's just what I want. I can't stand
*this* – and such scenes. They're treacherous!' These words broke
from Morgan, who had intermitted his embrace, in a key which
made Pemberton turn quickly to him, to see that he had suddenly
seated himself, was breathing with evident difficulty and was very
pale.

'*Now* do you say he's not ill – my precious pet?' shouted his
mother, dropping on her knees before him with clasped hands,
but touching him no more than if he had been a gilded idol. 'It will
pass – it's only for an instant; but don't say such dreadful things!'

'I'm all right – all right,' Morgan panted to Pemberton, whom he
sat looking up at with a strange smile, his hands resting on either
side on the sofa.

'Now do you pretend I've been treacherous – that I've
deceived?' Mrs Moreen flashed at Pemberton as she got up.

'It isn't *he* says it, it's I!' the boy returned, apparently easier, but
sinking back against the wall; while Pemberton, who had sat
down beside him, taking his hand, bent over him.

'Darling child, one does what one can; there are so many things
to consider,' urged Mrs Moreen. 'It's his *place* – his only place. You
see *you* think it is now.'

'Take me away – take me away,' Morgan went on, smiling to
Pemberton from his white face.

'Where shall I take you, and how – oh, *how*, my boy?' the young
man stammered, thinking of the rude way in which his friends in
London held that, for his convenience, and without a pledge of
instantaneous return, he had thrown them over; of the just resentment with which they would already have called in a successor, and
of the little help as regarded finding fresh employment that resided
for him in the flatness of his having failed to pass his pupil.

'Oh, we'll settle that. You used to talk about it,' said Morgan. 'If
we can only go, all the rest's a detail.'

'Talk about it as much as you like, but don't think you can attempt it. Mr Moreen would never consent – it would be so precarious,' Pemberton's hostess explained to him. Then to Morgan she explained: 'It would destroy our peace, it would break our hearts. Now that he's back it will be all the same again. You'll have your life, your work and your freedom, and we'll all be happy as we used to be. You'll bloom and grow perfectly well, and we won't have any more silly experiments, will we? They're too absurd. It's Mr Pemberton's place – every one in his place. You in yours, your papa in his, me in mine – *n'est-ce pas, chéri*? We'll all forget how foolish we've been, and we'll have lovely times.'

She continued to talk and to surge vaguely about the little draped, stuffy *salon*, while Pemberton sat with the boy, whose colour gradually came back; and she mixed up her reasons, dropping that there were going to be changes, that the other children might scatter (who knew? – Paula had her ideas), and that then it might be fancied how much the poor old parent-birds would want the little nestling. Morgan looked at Pemberton, who wouldn't let him move; and Pemberton knew exactly how he felt at hearing himself called a little nestling. He admitted that he had had one or two bad days, but he protested afresh against the iniquity of his mother's having made them the ground of an appeal to poor Pemberton. Poor Pemberton could laugh now, apart from the comicality of Mrs Moreen's producing so much philosophy for her defence (she seemed to shake it out of her agitated petticoats, which knocked over the light gilt chairs), so little did the sick boy strike him as qualified to repudiate any advantage.

He himself was in for it, at any rate. He should have Morgan on his hands again indefinitely; though indeed he saw the lad had a private theory to produce which would be intended to smooth this down. He was obliged to him for it in advance; but the suggested amendment didn't keep his heart from sinking a little, any more than it prevented him from accepting the prospect on the spot, with some confidence moreover that he would do so even better if he could have a little supper. Mrs Moreen threw out more hints about the changes that were to be looked for, but she was such a mixture of smiles and shudders (she confessed she was very nervous), that he couldn't tell whether she were in high feather or only in hysterics. If the family were really at last going to pieces why shouldn't she recognize the necessity of pitching Morgan into some sort of lifeboat? This presumption was fostered by the fact that they were established in luxurious quarters in the capital of pleasure; that was exactly where they naturally *would* be established in view of going to pieces. Moreover didn't she mention that Mr Moreen and the others were enjoying themselves at the opera with Mr Granger, and wasn't *that* also precisely where one would look for them on the eve of a smash? Pemberton gathered that Mr Granger was a rich, vacant American – a big bill with a flourishy heading and no items; so that one of Paula's 'ideas' was probably that this time she had really done it, which was indeed an unprecedented blow to the general cohesion. And if the cohesion was to terminate what was to become of poor Pemberton? He felt quite enough bound up with them to figure, to his alarm, as a floating spar in case of a wreck.

It was Morgan who eventually asked if no supper had been ordered for him; sitting with him below, later, at the dim, delayed meal, in the presence of a great deal of corded green plush, a plate of ornamental biscuit and a languor marked on the part of the waiter. Mrs Moreen had explained that they had been obliged to secure a room for the visitor out of the house; and Morgan's consolation (he offered it while Pemberton reflected on the nastiness of lukewarm sauces) proved to be, largely, that this circumstance would facilitate their escape. He talked of their escape (recurring to it often afterwards), as if they were making up a 'boy's book' together. But he likewise expressed his sense that there was something in the air, that the Moreens couldn't keep it up much longer. In point of fact, as Pemberton was to see, they kept it up for five or six months. All the while, however, Morgan's contention was designed to cheer him. Mr Moreen and Ulick, whom he had met the day after his return, accepted that return like perfect men of the world. If Paula and Amy treated it even with less formality an allowance was to be made for them, inasmuch as Mr Granger had not come to the opera after all. He had only placed his box at their service, with a bouquet for each of the party; there was even one apiece, embittering the thought of his profusion, for Mr Moreen and Ulick. 'They're all like that,' was Morgan's comment; 'at the very last, just when we think we've got them fast, we're chucked!'

Morgan's comments, in these days, were more and more free; they even included a large recognition of the extraordinary tenderness with which he had been treated while Pemberton was away. Oh, yes, they couldn't do enough to be nice to him, to show him they had him on their mind and make up for his loss. That was just what made the whole thing so sad, and him so glad, after all, of Pemberton's return – he had to keep thinking of their affection less, and less sense of obligation. Pemberton laughed out at this last reason, and Morgan blushed and said: 'You know what I mean.' Pemberton knew perfectly what he meant; but there were a good many things it didn't make any clearer. This episode of his second sojourn in Paris stretched itself out wearily, with their resumed readings and wanderings and maunderings, their pot-terings on the quays, their hauntings of the museums, their occasional lingerings in the Palais Royal, when the first sharp weather came on and there was a comfort in warm emanations, before Chevet's wonderful succulent window. Morgan wanted to hear a great deal about the opulent youth – he took an immense interest in him. Some of the details of his opulence – Pemberton could spare him none of them – evidently intensified the boy's appreciation of all his friend had given up to come back to him; but in addition to the greater reciprocity established by such a renunciation he had always his little brooding theory, in which there was a frivolous gaiety too, that their long probation was drawing to a close. Morgan's conviction that the Moreens couldn't go on much longer kept pace with the unexpended impetus with which, from month to month, they did go on. Three weeks after Pemberton had rejoined them they went on to another hotel, a dingier one than the first; but Morgan rejoiced that his tutor had at

least still not sacrified the advantage of a room outside. He clung
to the romantic utility of this when the day, or rather the night,
should arrive for their escape.

For the first time, in this complicated connection, Pemberton
felt sore and exasperated. It was, as he had said to Mrs Moreen in
Venice, *trop fort* – everything was *trop fort*. He could neither really
throw off his blighting burden nor find in it the benefit of a
pacified conscience or of a rewarded affection. He had spent all
the money that he had earned in England, and he felt that his
youth was going and that he was getting nothing back for it. It was
all very well for Morgan to seem to consider that he would make
up to him for all inconveniences by settling himself upon him
permanently – there was an irritating flaw in such a view. He saw
what the boy had in his mind; the conception that as his friend had
had the generosity to come back to him he must show his
gratitude by giving him his life. But the poor friend didn't desire
the gift – what could he do with Morgan's life? Of course at the
same time that Pemberton was irritated he remembered the
reason, which was very honourable to Morgan and which consisted simply of the fact that he was perpetually making one forget
that he was after all only a child. If one dealt with him on a
different basis one's misadventures were one's own fault. So
Pemberton waited in a queer confusion of yearning and alarm for
the catastrophe which was held to hang over the house of Moreen,
of which he certainly at moments felt the symptoms brush his
cheek and as to which he wondered much in what form it would
come.

Perhaps it would take the form of dispersal – a frightened *sauve
qui peut*, a scuttling into selfish corners. Certainly they were less
elastic than of yore; they were evidently looking for something
they didn't find. The Dorringtons hadn't reappeared, the princes
had scattered; wasn't that the beginning of the end? Mrs Moreen
had lost her reckoning of the famous 'days'; her social calendar
was blurred – it had turned its face to the wall. Pemberton
suspected that the great, the cruel, discomfiture had been the
extraordinary behaviour of Mr Granger, who seemed not to know

what he wanted, or, what was much worse, what *they* wanted. He kept sending flowers, as if to bestrew the path of his retreat, which was never the path of return. Flowers were all very well, but – Pemberton could complete the proposition. It was now positively conspicuous that in the long run the Moreens were a failure; so that the young man was almost grateful the run had not been short. Mr Moreen, indeed, was still occasionally able to get away on business, and, what was more surprising, he was also able to get back. Ulick had no club, but you could not have discovered it from his appearance, which was as much as ever that of a person looking at life from the window of such an institution; therefore Pemberton was doubly astonished at an answer he once heard him make to his mother, in the desperate tone of a man familiar with the worst privations. Her question Pemberton had not quite caught; it appeared to be an appeal for a suggestion as to whom they could get to take Amy. 'Let the devil take her!' Ulick snapped; so that Pemberton could see that not only they had lost their amiability, but had ceased to believe in themselves. He could also see that if Mrs Moreen was trying to get people to take her children she might be regarded as closing the hatches for the storm. But Morgan would be the last she would part with.

One winter afternoon – it was a Sunday – he and the boy walked far together in the Bois de Boulogne. The evening was so splendid, the cold lemon-coloured sunset so clear, the stream of carriages and pedestrians so amusing and the fascination of Paris so great, that they stayed out later than usual and became aware that they would have to hurry home to arrive in time for dinner. They hurried accordingly, arm-in-arm, good-humoured and hungry, agreeing that there was nothing like Paris after all and that after all, too, that had come and gone they were not yet sated with innocent pleasures. When they reached the hotel they found that, though scandalously late, they were in time for all the dinner they were likely to sit down to. Confusion reigned in the apartments of the Moreens (very shabby ones this time, but the best in the house), and before the interrupted service of the table (with objects displaced almost as if there had been a scuffle, and a great wine stain from an overturned bottle), Pemberton could not blink the fact that there had been a scene of proprietary mutiny. The storm had come – they were all seeking refuge. The hatches were down – Paula and Amy were invisible (they had never tried the most casual art upon Pemberton, but he felt that they had enough of an eye to him not to wish to meet him as young ladies whose frocks had been confiscated), and Ulick appeared to have jumped overboard. In a word, the host and his staff had ceased to 'go on' at the pace of their guests, and the air of embarrassed detention, thanks to a pile of gaping trunks in the passage, was strangely commingled with the air of indignant withdrawal.

When Morgan took in all this – and he took it in very quickly – he blushed to the roots of his hair. He had walked, from his infancy, among difficulties and dangers, but he had never seen a public exposure. Pemberton noticed, in a second glance at him, that the tears had rushed into his eyes and that they were tears of bitter shame. He wondered for an instant, for the boy's sake, whether he might successfully pretend not to understand. Not successfully, he felt, as Mr and Mrs Moreen, dinnerless by their extinguished hearth, rose before him in their little dishonoured *salon*, considering apparently with much intensity what lively capital would be next on their list. They were not prostrate, but they were very pale, and Mrs Moreen had evidently been crying. Pemberton quickly learned however that her grief was not for the loss of her dinner, much as she usually enjoyed it, but on account of a necessity much more tragic. She lost no time in laying this necessity bare, in telling him how the change had come, the bolt had fallen, and how they would all have to turn themselves about. Therefore cruel as it was to them to part with their darling she must look to him to carry a little further the influence he had so fortunately acquired with the boy – to induce his young charge to follow him into some modest retreat. They depended upon him, in a word, to take their delightful child temporarily under his protection – it would leave Mr Moreen and herself so much more free to give the proper attention (too little, alas! had been given) to the readjustment of their affairs.

'We trust you – we feel that we can,' said Mrs Moreen, slowly rubbing her plump white hands and looking, with compunction, hard at Morgan, whose chin, not to take liberties, her husband stroked with a tentative paternal forefinger.

'Oh, yes; we feel that we can. We trust Mr Pemberton fully, Morgan,' Mr Moreen conceded.

Pemberton wondered again if he might pretend not to understand; but the idea was painfully complicated by the immediate perception that Morgan had understood.

'Do you mean that he may take me to live with him – for ever and ever?' cried the boy. 'Away, away, anywhere he likes?'

'For ever and ever? *Comme vous-y-allez!*' Mr Moreen laughed indulgently. 'For as long as Mr Pemberton may be so good.'

'We've struggled, we've suffered,' his wife went on; 'but you've made him so your own that we've already been through the worst of the sacrifice.'

Morgan had turned away from his father – he stood looking at Pemberton with a light in his face. His blush had died out, but something had come that was brighter and more vivid. He had a moment of boyish joy, scarcely mitigated by the reflection that, with his unexpected consecration of his hope – too sudden and too violent; the thing was a good deal less like a boy's book – the 'escape' was left on their hands. The boyish joy was there for an instant, and Pemberton was almost frightened at the revelation of gratitude and affection that shone through his humiliation. When Morgan stammered 'My dear fellow, what do you say to *that*?' he felt that he should say something enthusiastic. But he was still more frightened as something else that immediately followed and that made the lad sit down quickly on the nearest chair. He had turned very white and had raised his hand to his left side. They were all three looking at him, but Mrs Moreen was the first to bound forward. 'Ah, his darling little heart!' she broke out; and this time, on her knees before him and without respect for the idol, she caught him ardently in her arms. 'You walked him too far, you hurried him too fast!' she tossed over her shoulder at Pemberton. The boy made no protest, and the next instant his mother, still holding him, sprang up with her face convulsed and with the terrified cry 'Help, help! he's going, he's gone!' Pemberton saw, with equal horror, by Morgan's own stricken face, that he *was* gone. He pulled him half out of his mother's hands, and for a moment, while they held him together, they looked, in their dismay, into each other's eyes. 'He couldn't stand it, with his infirmity,' said Pemberton – 'the shock, the whole scene, the violent emotion.'

'But I thought he *wanted* to go to you!' wailed Mrs Moreen.

'I *told* you he didn't, my dear,' argued Mr Moreen. He was trembling all over, and he was, in his way, as deeply affected as his wife. But, after the first, he took his bereavement like a man of the world.

# Concerning the Eccentricities of Cardinal Pirelli

### RONALD FIRBANK

Midnight had ceased chiming from the Belfry tower, and the last seguidilla had died away. Looking fresh as a rose, and incredibly juvenile in his pyjamas of silver-grey and scarlet (the racing colours of Vittoria, Duchess of Vizeu), the Cardinal seemed disinclined for bed.

Surveying in detachment the preparatives for his journey (set out beneath an El Greco Christ, with outspread, delicate hands), he was in the mood to dawdle.

'These for the Frontier. Those for the train,' he exclaimed aloud, addressing a phantom porter.

Among the personalia was a passport, the likeness of identity showing him in a mitre, cute to tears, though, essentially, orthodox; a flask of Napoleon brandy, to be 'declared' if not consumed before leaving the Peninsula; and a novel, *Self-Essence*, on the Index, or about to be.

'A coin, child, and put them for me on the rack,' he enjoined the wraith, regarding through the window the large and radiant stars.

The rhythmic murmur of a weeping fountain filled momentously the night.

Its lament evoked the Chicklet's sobs.

'Did I so wrong, my God, to punish him? Was I too hasty?' the Primate asked, repairing towards an ivory crucifix by Cano; 'yet, Thou knowest, I adore the boy!'

He paused a moment astonished by the revelation of his heart.

'It must have been love that made me do it,' he smiled,

considering the incident in his mind. Assuredly the rebuff was unpremeditated springing directly from the boy's behaviour, spoiling what might have been a ceremony of something more than ordinary poignance.

It had come about so.

There had been held previously during the evening, after the Basilica's scheduled closing hour, a service of 'Departure', fastidiously private, in the presence only of the little Ostensoir-swinger 'Chicklet', who, missing all the responses, had rushed about the cathedral after mice; for which the Cardinal, his sensitiveness hurt by the lad's disdain and frivolity, had afterwards confined him alone with them in the dark.

'Had it been Miguilito or Joaquin, I should not have cared a straw for their interest in the mice! But somehow this one –' the Cardinal sighed.

Adjusting in capricious abstraction his cincture, he turned towards the window.

It was a night like most.

Uranus, Venus, Saturn showed overhead their wonted lights, while in the sun-weary cloisters, brightly blue-drenched by the moon, the oleanders in all their wonder – (how swiftly fleeting is terrestrial life) – were over, and the bougainvillaeas reigned instead.

'It must have been that,' he murmured, smiling up at the cathedral towers.

Poor little Don Wilful. The chapter-mice, were they something so amusing to pursue? 'I've a mind, do you know, to join you, boy; I declare I feel quite rompish!' he told himself, gathering up, with a jocund pounce, a heavy mantle of violet cloth-of-gold.

'Tu-whit, tu-whoo.'

Two ominous owls answered one another across the troubled garden.

'I declare I feel –' his hand sought vaguely his heart: it went pit-a-pat for almost nothing now! 'The strain of the diocese,' he breathed, consulting a pier-glass of the period of Queen Isabella 'the Ironical'.

'The Court may favour Paul Orna, but in my opinion no one can rival Joey Paquin's "line"; I should like to see him "tailor" our Madonna; one of the worst and most expensively dressed little saints in the world,' his Eminence commented, folding toga-wise the obedient tissues about his slender form.

An aspect so correctly classic evoked the golden Rome of the Imperial Caesars rather than the so tedious Popes.

Repeating a sonorous line from Macrobius, the Cardinal measured himself a liqueur-glass of bandy.

Poor little Don Bright-eyes, alone in the obscurity. It was said a black dervish 'walked' the Coro – one of the old habitués of the Mosque.

'Jewel-boy. Yum-yum,' he murmured, setting a mitre like a wondrous mustard-pot upon his head. *Omnia vanitas*; it was intended for St Peter's.

'Tu-whit, tu-whoo!'

Grasping a Bishop's stave, remotely shepherdessy, his Eminence opened softly the door.

Olé, the Styx!

Lit by Uranus, Venus and Saturn only, the consummate tapestries on the stairs recording the Annunciation, Conception, Nativity, Presentation, Visitation, Purification and Ascension of the Virgin made welcome milestones.

' . . . Visitation, Purification.' The Primate paused on the penultimate step.

On a turn of the stair by the 'Conception', a sensitive panel, chiefly white, he had the impression of a wavering shadow, as of someone following close behind.

Continuing, preoccupied, his descent, he gained a postern door. A few deal cases, stoutly corded for departure, were heaped about it. 'His Holiness, I venture to predict, will appreciate the excellence of our home-grown oranges, not to be surpassed by those of any land,' the Primate purred, sailing forth into the garden.

Oh, the lovely night! Oh, the lovely night! He stood, leaning on his wand, lost in contemplation of the miracle of it.

'Kek, kek, kex.'

In the old lead aqua-but, by the Chapter-house, the gossiping bull-frogs were discussing their great horned and hoofed relations . . .

'There was never yet one that didn't bellow!'

'Kek, kek, kex.'

'*Los toros*, forsooth!'

'A blessed climate . . .' The Primate pursued his way.

It was in the face of a little door like the door of a tomb in the cathedral's bare façade (troubled only by the fanciful shadows of the trees) that he presently slipped his key.

Olé, the Styx!

He could distinguish nothing clearly at first beyond the pale forked fugitive lightning through the triple titanic windows of the chancel.

'Sunny-locks, Don Sunny-locks?' the Cardinal cooed, advancing diffidently, as though mistrustful of meeting some charwoman's pail.

Life had prepared him for these surprises.

Traversing on his crozier a spectral aisle, he emerged upon the nave.

Flanked by the chapels of the Crucifix, of the Virgin, of the Eldest Son of God, and of divers others, it was here as bright as day.

Presumably Don April-showers was too self-abashed to answer, perhaps too much afraid. '. . . If I recollect, the last time I preached was on the theme of Flagellation,' the Primate mused, considering where it caught the moon the face of a fakir in ecstasy carved amid the corbels.

'A sermon I propose to publish,' he resolved, peering into the chapel of Santa Lucia. It was prepared, it seemed, in anticipation of a wedding, for stately palms and branches of waxen peach-bloom stood all about. 'Making circulation perilous,' the Primate mused, arrested by the determined sound of a tenacious mouse gnawing at a taper-box.

'An admirable example in perseverance!' he mentally told himself, blinking at the flickering mauve flowers of light in the sanctuary lamps.

Philosophizing, he penetrated the engrailed silver doors connecting the chapel of the Magdalen.

The chapel was but seldom without a coffin, and it was not without one now.

Since the obsequies of the brilliant Princess Eboli it had enjoyed an unbroken vogue.

Besides the triumphal monument of the beloved of Philip II, the happy (though, perhaps, not the happiest) achievement of Jacinto Bisquert, there were also mural tablets to the Duchesses of Pampeluna (*née* Mattosinhos), Polonio (*née* Charona), and Sarmento (*née* Tizzi-Azza), while the urn and ashes of the Marchioness of Orcasitas (*née* Ivy Harris) were to be found here too, far from the race and turmoil of her native New York.

'Misericordia! Are you there, boy?' the Cardinal asked, eyeing abstractedly the twin hooded caryatides that bore the fragile casket white as frozen snow containing the remains of the all-amiable princess.

Folded in dainty sleep below, he perceived the lad.

Witching as Eros, in his loose-flowing alb, it seemed profane to wake him!

'. . . And lead us not into temptation,' the Primate murmured, stooping to gaze on him.

Age of bloom and fleeting folly: Don Apple-cheeks!

Hovering in benison he had almost a mind to adopt the boy, enter him for Salamanca, or, remoter, Oxford, and perhaps (by some bombshell codicil) even make him his heir.

'How would you like my Velasquez, boy? . . .' His Eminence's hand framed an airy caress. 'Eh, child? Or my Cano Crucifix? . . . I know of more than one bottle-nosed dowager who thinks she'll get it! . . . You know my Venetian glass, Don Endymion, is among the choicest in Spain . . .'

There was a spell of singing silence, while the dove-grey mystic lightning waxed and waned.

Aroused as much by it as the Primate's hand, the boy started up with a scream of terror.

'Ouch, sir!'

'Olé, boy?'

The panic appeared to be mutual.

'Oufarella! . . .' With the bound of a young faun the lad was enskied amid the urns and friezes.

The heart in painful riot, the Primate dropped to a chair.

Ouching, Oléing and Oufarellaing it, would they never have done? Paternostering Phoebe Poco (shadowing her master) believed they never would. 'Old ogre: why can't he be brisk about it and let a woman back to bed?' she wondered.

Thus will egotism, upon occasion, eclipse morality outright.

'And always be obedient, dear child,' the Cardinal was saying; 'it is one of the five things in Life that matter most.'

'Which are the others, sir?'

'What others, boy?'

'Why, the other four!'

'Never mind now. Come here.'

'Oh, tral-a-la, sir.' Laughing like some wild spirit, the lad leapt (Don Venturesome, Don Venturesome, his Eminence trembled) from the ledge of A Virtuous Wife and Mother (Sarmento, *née* Tizzi-Azza) to the urn of Ivy, the American marchioness.

'You'd not do that if you were fond of me, boy!' The Cardinal's cheek had paled.

'But I *am* fond of you, sir! Very. Caring without caring: don't you know?'

'So you do care something, child?'

'I care a lot! . . .'

Astride the urn of Ivy – poised in air – the Chicklet pellucidly laughed.

'Tell me so again,' the Cardinal begged, as some convent-bell near by commenced sounding for office before aurora.

For behind the big windows the stars were fading.

'It's today they draw the Lottery, sir.'

'Ah; well, I had nothing in it . . .'

'00050 – that's me!'

The Cardinal fetched a breath.

'Whose is it, boy?' He pointed towards the bier.

'A Poet, sir.'

'A Poet?'

'The name, though, he had escapes me . . .'

'No matter then.'

'Where would his soul be now, sir?'

'Never mind, boy; come here.'

'In the next world I should like to meet the Cid, and Christopher Columbus!'

'Break your neck, lad, and so you will.'

'Pablo Pedraza too . . .'

'Who's that, boy?'

'He was once the flower of the ring, sir; superior even to Tancos; you may recollect he was tossed and ruptured at Ronda; the press at the time was full of it.'

'Our press, dear youth, our press! ! ! . . .' the Primate was about to lament, but an apologetic sneeze from a chapel somewhere in the neighbourhood of the Eldest Son of God arrested him.

It seemed almost to confirm the legend of old, Mosque-sick 'Suliman', said to stalk the temple aisles.

The Cardinal twirled challengingly his stave – Bible v. Koran; a family case; cousins; Eastern, equally, each; hardy old perennials, no less equivocal and extravagant, often, than the ever-adorable Arabian Nights! 'If only Oriental literature sprawled less, was more concise! It should concentrate its roses,' he told himself, glancing out, enquiringly, into the nave.

Proffoudly soft and effaced, it was a place full of strange suggestion. Intersecting avenues of pillared arches, upbearing waving banners, seemed to beckon towards the Infinite.

'Will you be obliged to change, sir; or shall you go straight through?'

'Straight through, boy.'

'I suppose, as you cross the border, they'll want to know what you have to declare.'

'I have nothing, child, but myself.'

'If 00050 is fortunate, sir, I hope to travel, too – India, Persia, Peru! . . . Ah, it's El Dorado, then.'

'El Dorado, boy?' The Cardinal risked an incautious gesture.

'Oh, tral-a-la, sir.' Quick as Cupid the lad eluded him on the evasive wings of a laugh; an unsparing little laugh, sharp and mocking, that aroused the Primate like the thong of a lash.

Of a long warrior line, he had always regarded disobedience (in others) as an inexcusable offence. What would have happened before the ramparts of Zargoza, Valladolid, Leon, Burgos, had the men commanded by Ipolito Pirelli in the Peninsular War refused to obey? To be set at defiance by a youngster, a mere cock-robin, kindled elementary ancestral instincts in the Primate's veins.

'Don't provoke me, child, again.'

From pillared ambush Don Prudent saw well, however, to effect a bargain.

'You'd do the handsome by me, sir; you'd not be mean?'

'Eh? . . .'

'The Fathers only give us texts; you'd be surprised, your Greatness, at the stinginess of some!'

'. . . ?'

'You'd run to something better, sir; you'd give me something more substantial?'.

'I'll give you my slipper, child, if you don't come here!' his Eminence warned him.

'Oufarella . . .'

Sarabandish and semi-mythic was the dance that ensued. Leading by a dozen derisive steps Don Light-of-Limb took the nave. In the dusk of the dawn it seemed to await the quickening blush of day like a white-veiled negress.

'Olé, your Purpleship!'

Men (eternal hunters, novelty seekers, insatiable beings), men in their natural lives, pursue the concrete no less than the ideal – qualities not seldom found combined in fairy childhood.

'Olé.'

Oblivious of sliding mantle the Primate swooped.

Up and down, in and out, round and round 'the Virgin', over the worn tombed paving, through Saint Joseph, beneath the cobweb banners from Barocco to purest Moorish, by early Philip, back to Turân-Shâh – 'Don't exasperate me, boy' – along the raised tribunes of the choristers and the echoing coro – the great fane (after all) was nothing but a cage; God's cage; the cage of God! . . .

Through the chancel windows the day was newly breaking as the oleanders will in spring.

Dispossessed of everything but his fabulous mitre, the Primate was nude and elementary now as Adam himself.

'As you can perfectly see, I have nothing but myself to declare,' he addressed some phantom image in the air.

With advancing day Don Skylark *alias* Bright-eyes *alias* Don Temptation it seemed had contrived an exit, for the cathedral was become a place of tranquillity and stillness.

'Only myself.' He had dropped before a painting of old Dominic Theotocópuli, the Greek, showing the splendour of Christ's martyrdom.

Peering expectantly from the silken parted curtains of a confessional, paternostering Phoebe Poco caught her breath.

Confused not a little at the sight before her, her equilibrium was only maintained by the recollection of her status: 'I'm an honest widow; so I know what men are, bless them!' And stirred to romantic memories she added: 'Poor soul, he had the prettiest teeth . . .'

Fired by fundamental curiosity, the dame, by degrees, was emboldened to advance. All over was it, with him, then? It looked as though his Eminence was far beyond Rome already.

'May God show His pity on you, Don Alvaro of my heart.'

She remained a short while lost in mingled conjecture. It was certain no morning bell would wake him.

'So.' She stopped to coil her brier-wood chaplet about him in order that he might be less uncovered. 'It's wonderful what us bits of women do with a string of beads, but they don't go far with a gentleman.'

Now that the ache of life, with its fevers, passions, doubts, its routine, vulgarity, and boredom, was over, his serene, unclouded face was a marvelment to behold. Very great distinction and sweetness was visible there, together with much nobility, and love, all magnified and commingled.

'*Adios*, Don Alvaro of my heart,' she sighed, turning away towards the little garden door ajar.

Through the triple windows of the chancel the sky was clear and blue – a blue like the blue of lupins. Above him stirred the wind-blown banners in the Nave.

# Dr Woolacott

## E. M. FORSTER

*For this, from stiller seats we came*
*Cymbeline V.iv*

I

People, several of them, crossing the park . . .

Clesant said to himself, 'There is no reason I should not live for years now that I have given up the violin,' and leant back with the knowledge that he had faced a fact. From where he lay, he could see a little of the garden and a little of the park, a little of the fields and the river, and hear a little of the tennis; a little of everything was what was good for him, and what Dr Woolacott had prescribed. Every few weeks he must expect a relapse, and he would never be able to travel or marry or manage the estates, still there, he didn't want to much, he didn't much want to do anything. An electric bell connected him with the house, the strong beautiful slightly alarming house where his father had died, still there, not so very alarming, not so bad lying out in the tepid sun and watching the colourless shapeless country people . . .

No, there was no reason he should not live for years.

'In 1990, why even 2000 is possible, I am young,' he thought. Then he frowned, for Dr Woolacott was bound to be dead by 2000, and the treatment might not be continued intelligently. The anxiety made his head ache, the trees and grass turned black or crimson, and he nearly rang his bell. Soothed by the advancing figures, he desisted. Looking for mushrooms apparently, they soothed him because of their inadequacy. No mushrooms grew in the park. He felt friendly and called out in his gentle voice, 'Come here.'

'Oh aye,' came the answer.

'I'm the squire, I want you a moment, it's all right.'

Set in motion, the answerer climbed over the park fence. Clesant had not intended him to do this, and fearful of being bored said: 'You'll find no mushrooms here, but they'll give you a drink or anything else you fancy up at the house.'

'Sir, the squire, did you stay?'

'Yes; I pass for the squire.'

'The one who's sick?'

'Yes, that one.'

'I'm sorry.'

'Thank you, thanks,' said the boy, pleased by the unexpected scrap of sympathy.

'Sir . . .'

'All right, what is it?' he smiled encouragingly.

'Sick of what illness?'

Clesant hesitated. As a rule he resented that question, but this morning it pleased him, it was as if he too had been detected by friendly eyes zigzagging in search of a treasure which did not exist. He replied: 'Of being myself perhaps! Well, what they call functional. Nothing organic. I can't possibly die, but my heart makes my nerves go wrong, my nerves my digestion, then my head aches, so I can't sleep, which affects my heart, and round we go again. However, I'm better this morning.'

'When shall you be well?'

He gave the contemptuous laugh of the chronic invalid. 'Well? That's a very different question. It depends. It depends on a good many things. On how carefully I live. I must avoid all excitement, I must never get tired, I mustn't be –' He was going to say 'mustn't be intimate with people', but it was no use employing expressions which would be meaningless to a farm-worker, and such the man appeared to be, so he changed it to 'I must do as Dr Woolacott tells me.'

'Oh, Woolacott . . .'

'Of course you know him, everyone round here does, marvellous doctor.'

'Yes, I know Woolacott.'

Clesant looked up, intrigued by something positive in the tone of the voice.

'Woolacott, Woolacott, so I must be getting on.' Not quite as he had come, he vaulted over the parked palings, paused, repeated 'Woolacott' and walked rapidly after his companions, who had almost disappeared.

A servant now answered the bell. It had failed to ring the first time, which would have been annoying had the visitor proved tedious. The little incident was over now, and nothing else disturbed the peace of the morning. The park, the garden, the sounds from the tennis, all reassumed their due proportions, but it seemed to Clesant that they were pleasanter and more significant than they had been, that the colours of the grass and the shapes of the trees had beauty, that the sun wandered with a purpose through the sky, that the little clouds, wafted by westerly airs, were moving against the course of doom and fate, and were inviting him to follow them.

II

Continuance of convalescence . . . tea in the gun-room. The gun-room, a grand place in the old squire's time, much energy had flowed through it, intellectual and bodily. Now the bookcases were locked, the trophies between them desolate, the tall shallow cupboard designed for fishing-rods and concealed in the wainscoting contained only medicine-bottles and air cushions. Still, it was Clesant's nearest approach to normality, for the rest of his household had tea in the gun-room too. There was innocuous talk as they flitted out and in, pursuing their affairs like birds, and troubling him only with the external glint of their plumage. He knew nothing about them, although they were his guardians and familiars; even their sex left no impression on his mind. Throned on the pedestal of a sofa, he heard them speak of their wishes and plans, and give one another to understand that they had passionate impulses, while he barricaded himself in the circle of his thoughts.

He was thinking about music.

Was it quite out of the question that he should take up the violin again? He felt better, the morning in the garden had started him upon a good road, a refreshing sleep had followed. Now a languorous yearning filled him, which might not the violin satisfy? The effect might be the contrary, the yearning might turn to pain, yet even pain seemed unlikely in this kindly house, this house which had not always been kindly, yet surely this afternoon it was accepting him.

A stranger entered his consciousness – a young man in good if somewhat provincial clothes, with a pleasant and resolute expression upon his face. People always were coming into the house on some business or other; and then going out of it. He stopped in the middle of the room, evidently a little shy. No one spoke to him for the reason that no one remained: they had all gone away while Clesant followed his meditations. Obliged to exert himself for a moment, Clesant said: 'I'm sorry – I expect you're wanting one of the others.'

He smiled and twiddled his cap.

'I'm afraid I mustn't entertain you myself. I'm something of an invalid, and this is my first day up. I suffer from one of those wretched functional troubles – fortunately nothing organic.'

Smiling more broadly, he remarked: 'Oh aye.'

Clesant clutched at his heart, jumped up, sat down, burst out laughing. It was that farm-worker who had been crossing the park.

'Thought I'd surprise you, thought I'd give you a turn,' he cried gaily. 'I've come for that drink you promised.'

Clesant couldn't speak for laughing, the whole room seemed to join in, it was a tremendous joke.

'I was around in my working-kit when you invited me this morning, so I thought after I'd washed myself up a bit and had a shave my proper course was to call and explain,' he continued more seriously. There was something fresh and rough in his voice which caught at the boy's heart.

'But who on earth are you, who are you working for?'

'For you.'

'Oh nonsense, don't be silly.'

"Tisn't nonsense, I'm not silly, I'm one of your farm-hands. Rather an unusual one, if you like. Still, I've been working here for the last three months, ask your bailiff if I haven't. But I say – I've kept thinking about you – how are you?'

'Better – because I saw you this morning!'

'That's fine. Now you've seen me this afternoon you'll be well.'

But this last remark was flippant, and the visitor through making it lost more than the ground he had gained. It reminded Clesant that he had been guilty of laughter and of rapid movements, and he replied in reproving tones: 'To be well and to be better are very different. I'm afraid one can't get well from one's self. Excuse me if we don't talk any more. It's so bad for my heart.' He closed his eyes. He opened them again immediately. He had had, during that instant of twilight, a curious and pleasurable sensation. However, there was the young man still over at the farther side of the room. He was smiling. He was attractive – fresh as a daisy, strong as a horse. His shyness had gone.

'Thanks for that tea, a treat,' he said, lighting a cigarette. 'Now for who I am. I'm a farmer – or rather, going to be a farmer. I'm only an agricultural labourer now – exactly what you took me for this morning. I wasn't dressing up or posing with that broad talk. It's come natural to say "Oh aye", especially when startled.'

'Did I startle you?'

'Yes, you weren't in my mind.'

'I thought you were looking for mushrooms.'

'So I was. We all do when we're shifting across, and when there's a market we sell them. I've been living with that sort all the summer, your regular hands, temporaries like myself, tramps, sharing their work, thinking their thoughts when they have any.' He paused. 'I like them.'

'Do they like you?'

'Oh well . . .' He laughed, drew a ring off his finger, laid it on the palm of his hand, looked at it for a moment, put it on again. All his gestures were definite and a trifle unusual. 'I've no pride anyway, nor any reason to have. I only have my health, and I didn't always have that. I've known what it is to be an invalid, though no one guesses it now.' He looked across gently at Clesant. He seemed to say: 'Come to me, and you shall be as happy as I am and as strong.' He gave a short account of his life. He dealt in facts, very much so when they arrived – and the tale he unfolded was high-spirited and a trifle romantic here and there, but in no way remarkable. Aged twenty-two, he was the son of an engineer at Wolverhampton, his two brothers were also engineers, but he himself had always taken after his mother's family, and preferred country life. All his holidays on a farm. The war. After which he took up agriculture seriously, and went through a course of Cirencester. The course terminated last spring, he had done well, his people were about to invest money in him, but he himself felt 'too scientific' after it all. He was determined to 'get down into the manure' and feel people instead of thinking about them. 'Later on it's too late.' So off he went and roughed it, with a few decent clothes in a suitcase, and now and then, just for the fun of the thing, he took them out and dressed up. He described the estate, how decent the bailiff was, how sorry people seemed to be about the squire's illness, how he himself got a certain amount of time off, practically any evening. Extinguishing his cigarette, he put back what was left of it into his case for future use, laid a hand upon either knee, smiled.

There was a silence. Clesant could not think of anything to say, and began to tremble.

'Oh, my name –'

'Oh yes, of course, what's your name?'

'Let me write it down, my address too. Both my Wolver-hampton address I'll give you, also where I'm lodging here so if ever – got a pencil?'

'Yes.'

'Don't get up.'

He came over and sat on the sofa; his weight sent a tremor, the warmth and sweetness of his body began casting nets.

'And now we've no paper.'

'Never mind,' said Clesant, his heart beating violently.

'Talking's better, isn't it?'

'Yes.'

'Or even not talking.' His hand came nearer, his eyes danced round the room, which began to fill with golden haze. He beckoned, and Clesant moved into his arms. Clesant had often been proud of his disease but never, never of his body, it had never occurred to him that he could provoke desire. The sudden revelation shattered him, he fell from his pedestal, but not alone, there was someone to cling to, broad shoulders, a sunburnt throat, lips that parted as they touched him to murmur – 'And to hell with Woolacott.'

Woolacott! He had completely forgotten the doctor's existence. Woolacott! The word crashed between them and exploded with a sober light, and he saw in the light of the years that had passed and would come how ridiculously he was behaving. To hell with Woolacott, indeed! What an idea! His charming new friend must be mad. He started, recoiling, and exclaimed: 'Whatever made you say that?'

The other did not reply. He looked rather foolish, and he too recoiled, and leant back in the opposite corner of the sofa, wiping his forehead. At last he said: 'He's not a good doctor.'

'Why, he's our family doctor, he's everyone's doctor round here!'

'I didn't mean to be rude – it slipped out. I just had to say it, it must have sounded curious.'

'Oh, all right then,' said the boy, willing enough to be mollified. But the radiance had passed and no effort of theirs could recall it.

The young man took out his unfinished cigarette, and raised it towards his lips. He was evidently a good deal worried. 'Perhaps I'd better explain what I meant,' he said.

'As you like, it doesn't matter.'

'Got a match?'

'I'm afraid I haven't.'

He went for one to the farther side of the room, and sat down there again. Then he began: 'I'm perfectly straight – I'm not trying to work in some friend of my own as your doctor. I only can't bear to think of this particular one coming to your house – this grand house – you so rich and important at the first sight and yet so awfully undefended and deceived.' His voice faltered. 'No, we won't talk it over. You're right. We've found each other, nothing else matters, it's a chance in a million we've found each other. I'd do anything for you, I'd die if I could for you, and there's this one thing you must do straight away for me: sack Woolacott.'

'Tell me what you've got against him instead of talking sentimentally.'

He hardened at once. 'Sentimental, was I? All right, what I've got against Woolacott is that he never makes anyone well, which seems a defect in a doctor. I may be wrong.'

'Yes, you're wrong,' said Clesant; the mere repetition of the doctor's name was steadying him. 'I've been under him for years.'

'So I should think.'

'Of course, I'm different, I'm not well, it's not natural for me to be well, I'm not a fair test, but other people –'

'Which other people?'

The names of Dr Woolacott's successful cases escaped him for the moment. They filled the centre of his mind, yet the moment he looked at them they disappeared.

'Quite so,' said the other. 'Woolacott,' he kept on saying. 'Woolacott! I've my eye on him. What's life after twenty-five? Impotent, blind, paralytic. What's life before it unless you're fit? Woolacott! Even the poor can't escape. The crying, the limping, the nagging, the medicine-bottles, the running sores – in the cottages too; kind Dr Woolacott won't let them stop . . . You think I'm mad, but it's not your own thought you're thinking: Woolacott stuck it ready diseased into your mind.'

Clesant sighed. He looked at the arms now folded hard against each other, and longed to feel them around him. He had only to say, 'Very well, I'll change doctors,' and immediately . . . But he

never hesitated. Life until 1990 or 2000 retained the prior claim.
'He keeps people alive,' he persisted.

'Alive for what?'

'And there's always the marvellously unselfish work he did
during the war.'

'Did he not. I saw him doing it.'

'Oh – it was in France you knew him?'

'Was it not. He was at his marvellously unselfish work night
and day, and not a single man he touched ever got well. Woolacott
dosed, Woolacott inoculated, Woolacott operated, Woolacott
spoke a kind word even, and there they were and here they are.'

'Were you in hospital yourself?'

'Oh aye, a shell. This hand – ring and all mashed and twisted,
the head – hair's thick enough on it now, but brain stuck out then,
so did my guts, I was a butcher's shop. A perfect case for
Woolacott. Up he came with his "Let me patch you up, do let me
just patch you up", oh, patience itself and all that, but I took his
measure, I was only a boy then, but I refused.'

'Can one refuse in a military hospital?'

'You can refuse anywhere.'

'I hadn't realized you'd been wounded. Are you all right now?'

'Yes, thanks,' and he resumed his grievances. The pleasant
purple-grey suit, the big well-made shoes and soft white collar, all
suggested a sensible country lad on his holiday, perhaps on
courtship – farm-hand or farmer, countrified anyway. Yet with
them went this wretched war-obsession, this desire to be
revenged on a man who had never wronged him and must have
forgotten his existence. 'He is stronger than I am,' he said angrily.
'He can fight alone, I can't. My great disadvantage – never could
fight alone. I counted on you to help, but you prefer to let me
down, you pretended at first you'd join up with me – you're no
good.'

'Look here, you'll have to be going. So much talk is fatal for me,
I simply mustn't get overtired. I've already far exceeded my
allowance, and anyhow I can't enter into this sort of thing. Can

you find your own way out, or shall I ring this bell?' For inserted into the fabric of the sofa was an electric bell.

'I'll go. I know where I'm not wanted. Don't you worry, you'll never see me again.' And he slapped his cap on to his head and swung to the door. The normal life of the house entered the gun-room as he opened it – servants, inmates, talking in the passages, in the hall outside. It disconcerted him, he came back with a complete change of manner, and before ever he spoke Clesant had the sense of an incredible catastrophe moving up towards them both.

'Is there another way out?' he inquired anxiously.

'No, of course not. Go out the way you came in.'

'I didn't tell you, but the fact is I'm in trouble.'

'How dare you, I mustn't be upset, this is the kind of thing that makes me ill,' he wailed.

'I can't meet those people – they've heard of something I did out in France.'

'What was it?'

'I can't tell you.'

In the sinister silence, Clesant's heart resumed its violent beating, and though the door was now closed voices could be heard through it. They were coming. The stranger rushed at the windows and tried to climb out. He plunged about, soiling his freshness, and whimpering, 'Hide me.'

'There's nowhere.'

'There must be . . .'

'Only that cupboard,' said Clesant in a voice not his own.

'I can't find it,' he gasped, thumping stupidly on the panelling. 'Do it for me. Open it. They're coming.'

Clesant dragged himself up and across the floor, he opened the cupboard, and the man bundled in and hid, and that was how it ended.

Yes, that's how it ends, that's what comes of being kind to handsome strangers and wanting to touch them. Aware of all his weaknesses, Dr Woolacott had warned him against this one. He crawled back to the sofa, where a pain stabbed him through the heart and another struck between the eyes. He was going to be ill.

The voices came nearer, and with the cunning of a sufferer he decided what he must do. He must betray his late friend and pretend to have trapped him on purpose in the cupboard, cry 'Open it . . .'

The voices entered. They spoke of the sounds of a violin. A violin had apparently been heard playing in the great house for the last half-hour, and no one could find out where it was. Playing all sorts of music, gay, grave and passionate. But never completing a theme. Always breaking off. A beautiful instrument. Yet so unsatisfying . . . leaving the hearers much sadder than if it had never performed. What was the use (someone asked) of music like that? Better silence absolute than this aimless disturbance of our peace. The discussion broke off, his distress had been observed, and like a familiar refrain rose up 'Telephone, nurse, doctor . . .' Yes, it was coming again – the illness, merely functional, the heart had affected the nerves, the muscles, the brain. He groaned, shrieked, but love died last; as he writhed in convulsions he cried: 'Don't go to the cupboard, no one's there.'

So they went to it. And no one was there. It was as it had always been since his father's death – shallow, tidy, a few medicine-bottles on the upper shelf, a few cushions stored on the lower.

### III

Collapse . . . He fell back into the apparatus of decay without further disaster, and in a few hours any other machinery for life became unreal. It always was like this, increasingly like this, when he was ill. Discomfort and pain brought their compensation, because they were so superbly organized. His bedroom, the anteroom where the night-nurse sat, the bathroom and tiny kitchen, throbbed like a nerve in the corner of the great house, and elsewhere normal life proceeded, people pursued their avocations in channels which did not disturb him.

Delirium . . . The nurse kept coming in, she performed medical incantations and took notes against the doctor's arrival. She did not make him better, he grew worse, but disease knows its harmonies as well as health, and through its soft advances now rang the promise, 'You shall live to grow old.'

'I did something wrong, tell me, what was it?' It made him happy to abase himself before his disease, nor was this colloquy their first.

'Intimacy,' the disease replied.

'I remember . . . Do not punish me this once, let me live and I will be careful. Oh, save me from him.'

'No – from yourself. Not from him. He does not exist. He is an illusion, whom you created in the garden because you wanted to feel you were attractive.'

'I know I am not attractive, I will never excite myself again, but he does exist, I think.'

'No.'

'He may be death, but he does exist.'

'No. He never came into the gun-room. You only wished that he would. He never sat down on the sofa by your side and made love. You handed a pencil, but he never took it, you fell into his arms, but they were not there, it has all been a daydream of the kind forbidden. And when the others came in and opened the cupboard: your muscular and intelligent farm-hand, your saviour from Wolverhampton in his Sunday suit – was he there?'

'No, he was not,' the boy sobbed.

'No, he was not,' came an echo, 'but perhaps I am here.'

The disease began to crouch and gurgle. There was the sound of a struggle, a spewing sound, a fall. Clesant, not greatly frightened, sat up and peered into the chaos. The nightmare passed, he felt better. Something survived from it, an echo that said 'Here, here'. And, he not dissenting, bare feet seemed to walk to the little table by his side, and hollow, filled with the dark, a shell of nakedness bent towards him and sighed 'Here'.

Clesant declined to reply.

'Here is the end, unless you . . .' Then silence. Then, as if emitted by a machine, the syllables 'Oh aye'.

Clesant, after thought, put out his hand and touched the bell.

'I put her to sleep as I passed her, this is my hour, I can do that much . . .' He seemed to gather strength from any recognition of his presence, and to say, 'Tell my story for me, explain how I got here, pour life into me and I shall live as before when our bodies touched.' He sighed. 'Come home with me now, perhaps it is a farm. I have just enough power. Come away with me for an evening to my earthly lodging, easily managed by a . . . the . . . such a visit would be love. Ah, that was the word – love – why they pursued me and still know I am in the house; love was the word they cannot endure, I have remembered it at last.'

Then Clesant spoke, sighing in his turn. 'I don't even know what is real, so how can I know what is love? Unless it is excitement, and of that I am afraid. Do not love me, whatever you are; at all events this is my life and no one shall disturb it; a little sleep followed by a little pain.'

And his speech evoked strength. More powerfully the other answered now, giving instances and arguments, throwing into sentences the glow they had borne during daylight. Clesant was drawn into a struggle, but whether to reach or elude the hovering presence he did not know. There was always a barrier either way, always his own nature. He began calling for people to come, and the adversary, waxing lovely and powerful, struck them dead before they could waken and help. His household perished, the whole earth was thinning, one instant more, and he would be alone with his ghost – and then through the walls of the house he saw the lights of a car rushing across the park.

It was Dr Woolacott at last.

Instantly the spell broke, the dead revived, and went downstairs to receive life's universal lord; and he – he was left with a human being who had somehow trespassed and been caught, and blundered over the furniture in the dark, bruising his defenceless body, and whispering, 'Hide me.'

And Clesant took pity on him again, and lifted the clothes of the bed, and they hid.

Voices approached, a great company, Dr Woolacott leading his army. They touched, their limbs intertwined, they gripped and grew mad with delight, yet through it all sounded the tramp of that army.

'They are coming.'

'They will part us.'

'Clesant, shall I take you away from all this?'

'Have you still the power?'

'Yes, until Woolacott sees me.'

'Oh, what is your name?'

'I have none.'

'Where is your home?'

'Woolacott calls it the grave.'

'Shall I be with you in it?'

'I can promise you that. We shall be together for ever and ever, we shall never be ill, and never grow old.'

'Take me.'

They entwined more closely, their lips touched never to part, and then something gashed him where life had concentrated, and Dr Woolacott, arriving too late, found him dead on the floor.

The doctor examined the room carefully. It presented its usual appearance, yet it reminded him of another place. Dimly, from France, came the vision of a hospital ward, dimly the sound of his own voice saying to a mutilated recruit, 'Do let me patch you up, oh but you must just let me patch you up . . .'

# When I Was Thirteen

### DENTON WELCH

When I was thirteen, I went to Switzerland for the Christmas holidays in the charge of an elder brother, who was at that time still up at Oxford.

In the hotel we found another undergraduate whom my brother knew. His name was Archer. They were not at the same college, but they had met and evidently had not agreed with each other. At first my brother would say nothing about Archer; then one day, in answer to a question of mine, he said: 'He's not very much liked, although he's a very good swimmer.' As he spoke, my brother held his lips in a very firm, almost pursed, line which was most damaging to Archer.

After this I began to look at Archer with more interest. He had broad shoulders but was not tall. He had a look of strength and solidity which I admired and envied. He had rather a nice pug face with insignificant nose and broad cheeks. Sometimes, when he was animated, a tassel of fair, almost colourless, hair would fall across his forehead, half covering one eye. He had a thick beautiful neck, rather meaty barbarian hands, and a skin as smooth and evenly coloured as a pink fondant.

His whole body appeared to be suffused with this gentle pink colour. He never wore proper skiing clothes of waterproof material like the rest of us. Usually he came out in nothing but a pair of grey flannels and a white cotton shirt with all the buttons left undone. When the sun grew very hot, he would even discard this thin shirt, and ski up and down the slopes behind the hotel in nothing but his trousers. I had often seen him fall down in this half-naked state and get buried in snow. The next moment he would jerk himself to his feet again, laughing and swearing.

After my brother's curt nod to him on our first evening at the hotel, we had hardly exchanged any remarks. We sometimes passed on the way to the basement to get our skis in the morning, and often we found ourselves sitting near one another on the glassed-in terrace; but some Oxford snobbery I knew nothing of, or some more profound reason, always made my brother throw off waves of hostility. Archer never showed any signs of wishing to approach. He was content to look at me sometimes with a mild inoffensive curiosity, but he seemed to ignore my brother completely. This pleased me more than I would have admitted at that time. I was so used to being passed over myself by all my brother's friends that it was pleasant when someone who knew him seemed to take a sort of interest, however slight and amused, in me.

My brother was often away from the hotel for days and nights together, going for expeditions with guides and other friends. He would never take me because he said I was too young and had not enough stamina. He said that I would fall down a crevasse or get my nose frostbitten, or hang up the party by lagging behind.

In consequence I was often alone at the hotel; but I did not mind this; I enjoyed it. I was slightly afraid of my brother and found life very much easier and less exacting when he was not there. I think other people in the hotel thought that I looked lonely. Strangers would often come up and talk to me and smile, and once a nice, absurd Belgian woman, dressed from head to foot in a babyish suit of fluffy orange knitted wool, held out a bright five-franc piece to me and told me to go and buy chocolate caramels with it. I think she must have taken me for a much younger child.

On one of these afternoons when I had come in from the Nursery Slopes and was sitting alone over my tea on the sun terrace, I noticed that Archer was sitting in the corner huddled over a book, munching greedily and absentmindedly.

I, too, was reading a book, while I ate delicious rum-babas and little tarts filled with worm-castles of chestnut purée topped with caps of whipped cream. I have called the meal tea, but what I was drinking was not tea but chocolate. When I poured out, I held the pot high in the air, so that my cup, when filled, should be covered in a rich froth of bubbles.

The book I was reading was Tolstoy's *Resurrection*. Although I did not quite understand some parts of it, it gave me intense pleasure to read it while I ate the rich cakes and drank the frothy chocolate. I thought it a noble and terrible story, but I was worried and mystified by the words 'illegitimate child' which had occurred several times lately. What sort of child could this be? Clearly a child that brought trouble and difficulty. Could it have some terrible disease, or was it a special sort of imbecile? I looked up from my book, still wondering about this phrase 'illegitimate child', and saw that Archer had turned in his creaking wicker chair and was gazing blankly in my direction. The orchestra was playing 'The Birth of the Blues' in a rather remarkable Swiss arrangement, and it was clear that Archer had been distracted from his book by the music, only to be lulled into a daydream, as he gazed into space.

Suddenly his eyes lost their blank look and focused on my face. 'Your brother off up to the Jungfrau Joch again, or somewhere?' he called out.

I nodded my head, saying nothing, becoming slightly confused.

Archer grinned. He seemed to find me amusing.

'What are you reading?' he asked.

'This,' I said, taking my book over to him. I did not want to call out either the word 'Resurrection' or 'Tolstoy'. But Archer did not make fun of me for reading a 'classic', as most of my brother's friends would have done. He only said: 'I should think it's rather good. Mine's frightful; it's called *The Story of my Life*, by Queen Marie of Romania.' He held the book up and I saw an extraordinary photograph of a lady who looked like a snake-charmer in full regalia. The headdress seemed to be made of white satin, embroidered with beads, stretched over cardboard. There were tassels and trailing things hanging down everywhere.

I laughed at the amusing picture and Archer went on: 'I always

read books like this when I can get them. Last week I had Lady
Oxford's autobiography, and before that I found a perfectly
wonderful book called *Flaming Sex*. It was by a French woman who
married an English knight and then went back to France to shoot a
French doctor. She didn't kill him, of course, but she was sent to
prison, where she had a very interesting time with the nuns who
looked after her in the hospital. I also lately found an old book by a
Crown Princess of Saxony who ended up picnicking on a haystack
with a simple Italian gentleman in a straw hat. I love these "real
life" stories, don't you?'

I again nodded my head, not altogether daring to venture on a
spoken answer. I wondered whether to go back to my own table or
whether to pluck up courage and ask Archer what an 'illegitimate
child' was. He solved the problem by saying 'Sit down' rather
abruptly.

I subsided next to him with 'Tolstoy' on my knee. I waited for a
moment and then plunged.

'What exactly does "illegitimate child" mean?' I asked rather
breathlessly.

'Outside the law – when two people have a child although
they're not married.'

'Oh.' I went bright pink. I thought Archer must be wrong. I still
believed that it was quite impossible to have a child unless one
was married. The very fact of being married produced the child. I
had a vague idea that some particularly reckless people
attempted, without being married, to have children in places
called 'night-clubs', but they were always unsuccessful, and this
made them drink, and plunge into the most hectic gaiety.

I did not tell Archer that I thought he had made a mistake, for I
did not want to hurt his feelings. I went on sitting at his table and,
although he turned his eyes back to his book and went on reading,
I knew that he was friendly.

After some time he looked up again and said: 'Would you like to
come out with me tomorrow? We could take our lunch, go up the
mountain and then ski down in the afternoon.'

I was delighted at the suggestion, but also a little alarmed at my own shortcomings. I thought it my duty to explain that I was not a very good skier, only a moderate one, and that I could only do stem turns. I hated the thought of being a drag on Archer.

'I expect you're much better than I am. I'm always falling down or crashing into something,' he answered.

It was all arranged. We were to meet early, soon after six, as Archer wanted to go to the highest station on the mountain railway and then climb on skis to a nearby peak which had a small rest-house of logs.

I went to bed very excited, thankful that my brother was away on a long expedition. I lay under my enormous feather-bed eiderdown, felt the freezing mountain air on my face, and saw the stars sparkling through the open window.

I got up very early in the morning and put on my most sober ski socks and woollen shirt, for I felt that Archer disliked any suspicion of bright colours or dressing-up. I made my appearance as workmanlike as possible, and then went down to breakfast.

I ate several crackly rolls, which I spread thickly with dewy slivers of butter and gobbets of rich black cherry jam; then I drank my last cup of coffee and went to wax my skis. As I passed through the hall I picked up my picnic lunch in its neat grease-proof paper packet.

The nails in my boots slid and then caught on the snow, trodden hard down to the basement door. I found my skis in their rack, took them down and then heated the iron and the wax. I loved spreading the hot black wax smoothly on the white wood. Soon they were both done beautifully.

I will go like a bird, I thought.

I looked up and saw Archer standing in the doorway.

'I hope you haven't put too much on, else you'll be sitting on your arse all day,' he said gaily.

How fresh and pink he looked! I was excited.

He started to wax his own skis. When they were finished, we went outside and strapped them on. Archer carried a rucksack and he told me to put my lunch and my spare sweater into it.

We started off down the gentle slopes to the station. The sun was shining prickingly. The lovely snow had rainbow colours in it. I was so happy I swung my sticks with their steel points and basket ends. I even tried to show off, and jumped a little terrace which I knew well. Nevertheless it nearly brought me down. I just regained my balance in time. I would have hated at that moment to have fallen down in front of Archer.

When we got to the station we found a compartment to ourselves. It was still early. Gently we were pulled up the mountain, past the water station stop and the other three halts.

We got out at the very top where the railway ended. A huge unused snowplough stood by the side of the track, with its vicious shark's nose pointed at me. We ran to the van to get out our skis. Archer found mine as well as his own and slung both pairs across his shoulders. He looked like a very tough Jesus carrying two crosses, I thought.

We stood by the old snowplough and clipped on our skis; then we began to climb laboriously up the ridge to the wooden rest-house. We hardly talked at all, for we needed all our breath, and also I was still shy of Archer. Sometimes he helped me, telling me where to place my skis, and, if I slipped backwards, hauling on the rope which he had half-playfully tied round my waist.

In spite of growing tired, I enjoyed the grim plodding. It gave me a sense of work and purpose. When Archer looked round to smile at me, his pink face was slippery with sweat. His white shirt above the small rucksack was plastered to his shoulder blades. On my own face I could feel the drops of sweat just being held back by my eyebrows. I would wipe my hand across my upper lip and break all the tiny beads that had formed there.

Every now and then Archer would stop. We would put our skis sideways on the track and rest, leaning forward on our sticks. The sun struck down on our necks with a steady seeping heat and the light striking up from the snow was as bright as the fiery dazzle of a mirror. From the ridge we could see down into two valleys; and standing all round us were the other peaks, black rock and white snow, tangling and mixing until the mountains looked like vast teeth which had begun to decay.

I was so tired when we reached the long gentle incline to the rest-house that I was afraid of falling down. The rope was still round my waist, and so the slightest lagging would have been perceptible to Archer. I think he must have slackened his pace for my benefit, for I somehow managed to reach the iron seats in front of the hut. I sank down, still with my skis on. I half-shut my eyes. From walking so long with my feet turned out, my ankles felt almost broken.

The next thing I knew was that Archer had disappeared into the rest-house. He came out carrying a steaming cup.

'You must drink this,' he said, holding out black coffee which I hated. He unwrapped four lumps of sugar and dropped them in the cup.

'I don't like it black,' I said.

'Never mind,' he answered sharply, 'drink it.'

Rather surprised, I began to drink the syrupy coffee. 'The sugar and the strong coffee will be good for you,' said Archer. He went back into the rest-house and brought out a glass of what looked like hot water with a piece of lemon floating in it. The mountain of sugar at the bottom was melting into thin Arabian Nights wreaths and spirals, smoke-rings of syrup.

'What else has it got in it?' I asked, with an attempt at worldliness.

'Rum!' said Archer.

We sat there on the terrace and unwrapped our picnic lunches. We both had two rolls, one with tongue in it, and one with ham, a hard-boiled egg, sweet biscuits, and a bar of delicious bitter chocolate. Tangerine oranges were our dessert.

We began to take huge bites out of our rolls. We could not talk for some time. The food brought out a thousand times more clearly the beauty of the mountain peaks and sun. My tiredness made me thrillingly conscious of delight and satisfaction. I wanted to sit there with Archer for a long time.

At the end of the meal Archer gave me a piece of his own bar of chocolate, and then began to skin pigs of tangerine very skilfully and hand them to me on his outstretched palm, as one offers a lump of sugar to a horse. I thought for one moment of bending down my head and licking the pigs up in imitation of a horse; then I saw how mad it would look.

We threw the brilliant tangerine peel into the snow, which immediately seemed to dim and darken its colour.

Archer felt in his hip pocket and brought out black, cheap Swiss cigarettes, wrapped in leaf. They were out of a slot machine. He put one between my lips and lighted it. I felt extremely conscious of the thing jutting out from my lips. I wondered if I would betray my ignorance by not breathing the smoke in and out correctly. I turned my head a little away from Archer and experimented. It seemed easy if one did not breathe too deeply. It was wonderful to be really smoking with Archer. He treated me just like a man.

'Come on, let's get cracking,' he said, 'or, if anything happens, we'll be all night.'

I scrambled to my feet at once and snapped the clips of the skis round my boot heels. Archer was in high spirits from the rum. He ran on his skis along the flat ridge in front of the rest-house and then fell down.

'Serves me right,' he said. He shook the snow off and we started properly. In five minutes we had swooped down the ridge we had climbed so painfully all morning. The snow was perfect; new and dry with no crust. We followed a new way which Archer had discovered. The ground was uneven with dips and curves. Often we were out of sight of each other. When we came to the icy path through a wood, my courage failed me.

'Stem like hell and don't get out of control,' Archer yelled back at me. I pointed my skis together, praying that they would not cross. I leant on my sticks, digging their metal points into the compressed snow. Twice I fell, though not badly.

'Well done, well done!' shouted Archer, as I shot past him and out of the wood into a thick snowdrift. He hauled me out of the snow and stood me on my feet, beating me all over to get off the snow, then we began the descent of a field called the 'Bumps'. Little hillocks, if manoeuvred successfully, gave one that thrilling sinking and rising feeling experienced on a scenic railway at a fun fair.

Archer went before me, dipping and rising, shouting and yelling in his exuberance. I followed more sedately. We both fell several times, but in that not unpleasant, bouncing way which brings you to your feet again almost at once.

Archer was roaring now and trying to yodel in an absurd, rich contralto.

I had never enjoyed myself quite so much before. I thought him the most wonderful companion, not a bit intimidating, in spite of being rather a hero.

When at last we swooped down to the village street, it was nearly evening. Early orange lights where shining in the shop windows. We planked our skis down on the hard, iced road, trying not to slip.

I looked in at the *pâtisserie, confiserie* window, where all the electric bulbs had fluffy pink shades like powder-puffs. Archer saw my look.

'Let's go in,' he said. He ordered me hot chocolate with whipped cream, and *croissant* rolls. Afterwards we both went up to the little counter and chose cakes. I had one shaped like a little log. It was made of soft chocolate, and had green moss trimmings made in pistachio nut. When Archer went to pay the bill he bought me some chocolate caramels, in a little bird's eye maple box, and a bar labelled '*Chocolat Polychrome*'. Each finger was a different-coloured cream: mauve, pink, green, yellow, orange, brown, white, even blue.

We went out into the village street and began to climb up the path to the hotel. About halfway up Archer stopped outside a little wooden chalet and said: 'This is where I hang out.'

'But you're staying at the hotel,' I said incredulously.

'Oh yes, I have all my meals there, but I sleep here. It's a sort of little annexe when there aren't any rooms left in the hotel. It's only got two rooms; I've paid just a bit more and got it all to myself. Someone comes every morning and makes the bed and stokes the boiler and the stove. Come in and see it.'

I followed Archer up the outside wooden staircase and stood
with him on the little landing outside the two rooms. The place
seemed wonderfully warm and dry. The walls were unpainted
wood; there were double windows. There was a gentle creaking in
all the joint of the wood when one moved. Archer pushed open
one of the doors and ushered me in. I saw in one corner a huge
white porcelain stove, the sort I had only before seen in pictures.
Some of Archer's skiing gloves and socks were drying round it on
a ledge. Against another wall were two beds, like wooden troughs
built into the wall. The balloon-like quilts bulged up above the
wood.

'I hardly use the other room,' said Archer. 'I just throw my
muck into it and leave my trunks there.' He opened the connecting door and I saw a smaller room with dirty clothes strewn on the
floor; white shirts, hard evening collars, some very short pants,
and many pairs of thick grey socks. The room smelled mildly of
Archer's old sweat. I didn't mind at all.

Archer shut the door and said: 'I'm going to run the bath.'

'Have you a bathroom too – all your own?' I exclaimed
enviously. 'Every time anyone has a bath at the hotel, he has to
pay two francs fifty to the fraulein before she unlocks the door.
I've only had two proper baths since I've been here. I don't think it
matters though. It seems almost impossible to get really dirty in
Switzerland, and you can always wash all over in your bedroom
basin.'

'Why don't you have a bath here after me? The water's lovely
and hot, although there's not much of it. If you went back first and
got your evening clothes, you could change straight into them.'

I looked at Archer a little uncertainly. I longed to soak in hot
water after my wonderful but gruelling day.

'Could I really bathe here?' I asked.

'If you don't mind using my water. I'll promise not to pee in it.
I'm not really filthy, you know.'

Archer laughed and chuckled, because he saw me turning red at
his coarseness. He lit another of his peasant cigarettes and began

to unlace his boots. He got me to pull them off. I knelt down, bowed my head and pulled. When the ski boot suddenly flew off, my nose dipped forward and I smelled Archer's foot in its woolly, hairy, humid casing of sock.

'Would you just rub my foot and leg?' Archer said urgently, a look of pain suddenly shooting across his face. 'I've got cramp. It often comes on at the end of the day.'

He shot his leg out rigidly and told me where to rub and message. I felt each of his curled toes separately and the hard tendons in his leg. His calf was like a firm sponge ball. His thigh, swelling out, amazed me. I likened it in my mind to the trumpet of some musical instrument. I went on rubbing methodically. I was able to feel his pain melting away.

When the tense look had quite left his face, he said, 'Thanks,' and stood up. He unbuttoned his trousers, let them fall to the ground, and pulled his shirt up. Speaking to me with his head imprisoned in it, he said: 'You go and get your clothes and I'll begin bathing.'

I left him and hurried up to the hotel, carrying my skis on my shoulder. I ran up to my room and pulled my evening clothes out of the wardrobe. The dinner jacket and trousers had belonged to my brother six years before, when he was my age. I was secretly ashamed of this fact, and had taken my brother's name from the inside of the breast pocket and had written my own in elaborate lettering.

I took my comb, face flannel and soap, and getting out my toboggan slid back to Archer's chalet in a few minutes. I let myself in and heard Archer splashing. The little hall was full of steam and I saw Archer's shoulders and arms like a pink smudge through the open bathroom door.

'Come and scrub my back,' he yelled; 'it gives me a lovely feeling.' He thrust a large stiff nailbrush into my hands and told me to scrub as hard as I could.

I ran it up and down his back until I'd made harsh red tramlines. Delicious tremors seemed to be passing through Archer.

'Ah! go on!' said Archer in a dream, like a purring cat. 'When

I'm rich I'll have a special back-scratcher slave.' I went on industriously scrubbing his back till I was afraid that I would rub the skin off. I liked to give him pleasure.

At last he stood up all dripping and said: 'Now it's your turn.'

I undressed and got into Archer's opaque, soapy water. I lay back and wallowed. Archer poured some very smelly salts on to my stomach. One crystal stuck in my navel and tickled and grated against me.

'This whiff ought to cover up all remaining traces of me!' Archer laughed.

'What's the smell supposed to be?' I asked, brushing the crystals off my stomach into the water, and playing with the one that lodged so snugly in my navel.

'Russian pine,' said Archer, shutting his eyes ecstatically and making inbreathing dreamy noises. He rubbed himself roughly with the towel and made his hair stand up on end.

I wanted to soak in the bath for hours, but it was already getting late, and so I had to hurry.

Archer saw what difficulty I had in tying my tie. He came up to me and said: 'Let me do it.' I turned round relieved, but slightly ashamed of being incompetent.

I kept very still, and he tied it tightly and rapidly with his ham-like hands. He gave the bows a little expert jerk and pat. His eyes had a very concentrated, almost crossed look and I felt him breathing down on my face. All down the front our bodies touched featherily; little points of warmth came together. The hard-boiled shirts were like slightly warmed dinner plates.

When I had brushed my hair, we left the chalet and began to walk up the path to the hotel. The beaten snow was so slippery, now that we were shod only in patent-leather slippers, that we kept sliding backwards. I threw out my arms, laughing, and shouting to Archer to rescue me; then, when he grabbed me and started to haul me to him, he too would begin to slip. It was a still, Prussian-blue night with rather weak stars. Our laughter seemed to ring across the valley, to hit the mountains and then to travel on and on and on.

We reached the hotel a little the worse for wear. The soles of my patent-leather shoes had become soaked, and there was snow on my trousers. Through bending forward, the studs in Archer's shirt had burst undone, and the slab of hair hung over one of his eyes. We went into the cloak-room to readjust ourselves before entering the dining-room.

'Come and sit at my table,' Archer said; then he added: 'No, we'll sit at yours; there are two places there already.'

We sat down and began to eat Roman *gnocchi*. (The proprietor of the hotel was Italian-Swiss.) I did not like mine very much and was glad when I could go on to *oeufs au beurre noir*. Now that my brother was away I could pick and choose in this way, leaving out the meat course, if I chose to, without causing any comment.

Archer drank Pilsner and suggested that I should too. Not wanting to disagree with him, I nodded my head, although I hated the pale, yellow, bitter water.

After the meal Archer ordered me *crème de menthe* with my coffee; I had seen a nearby lady drinking this pretty liquid and asked him about it. To be ordered a liqueur in all seriousness was a thrilling moment for me. I sipped the fumy peppermint, which left such an artificial heat in my throat and chest, and thought that apart from my mother who was dead, I had never liked anyone so much as I liked Archer. He didn't try to interfere with me at all. He just took me as I was and yet seemed to like me.

Archer was now smoking a proper cigar, not the leaf-rolled cigarettes we had had at lunchtime. He offered me one too, but I had the sense to realize that he did not mean me to take one and smoke it there before the eyes of all the hotel. I knew also that it would have made me sick, for my father had given me a cigar when I was eleven, in an attempt to put me off smoking for ever.

I always associated cigars with middle-aged men, and I watched Archer interested, thinking how funny the stiff fat thing looked sticking out of his young mouth.

We were sitting on the uncurtained sun-terrace, looking out on to the snow in the night; the moon was just beginning to rise. It

made the snow glitter suddenly, like fish-scales. Behind us people
were dancing in the salon and adjoining rooms. The music came
to us in angry snatches, some notes distorted, others quite
obliterated. Archer did not seem to want to dance. He seemed
content to sit with me in silence.

Near me on a what-not stand stood a high-heeled slipper made
of china. I took it down and slipped my hand into it. How
hideously ugly the china pom-poms were down the front! The
painted centipede climbing up the red heel wore a knowing,
human expression. I moved my fingers in the china shoe,
pretending they were toes.

'I love monstrosities too,' said Archer, as I put the shoe back
inside the fern in its crinkly paper-covered pot.

Later we wandered to the buffet bar and stood there drinking
many glasses of the *limonade* which was made with white wine. I
took the tinkly pieces of ice into my mouth and sucked them,
trying to cool myself a little. Blood seemed to rise in my face; my
head buzzed.

Suddenly I felt full of *limonade* and lager. I left Archer to go to the
cloak-room, but he followed and stood beside me in the next china
niche, while the water flushed and gushed importantly in the
polished copper tubes, and an interesting, curious smell came
from the wire basket which held some strange disinfectant
crystals. Archer stood so quietly and guardingly beside me there
that I had to say: 'Do I look queer?'

'No, you don't look queer; you look nice,' he said simply.

A rush of surprise and pleasure made me hotter still. We
clanked over the tiles and left the cloak-room.

In the hall, I remembered that I had left all my skiing clothes at
the chalet.

'I shall need them in the morning,' I said to Archer.

'Let's go down there, then I can make cocoa on my spirit-lamp,
and you can bring the clothes back with you.'

We set out in the moonlight; Archer soon took my arm, for he
saw that I was drunk, and the path was more slippery than ever.
Archer sang 'Silent Night' in German, and I began to cry. I could

not stop myself. It was such a delight to cry in the moonlight with Archer singing my favourite song; and my brother far away up the mountain.

Suddenly we both sat down on our behinds with a thump. There was a jarring pain at the bottom of my spine but I began to laugh wildly; so did Archer. We lay there laughing, the snow melting under us and soaking through the seats of our trousers and the shoulders of our jackets.

Archer pulled me to my feet and dusted me down with hard slaps. My teeth grated together each time he slapped me. He saw that I was becoming more and more drunk in the freezing air. He propelled me along to the chalet, more or less frog-marching me in an expert fashion. I was quite content to leave myself in his hands.

When he got me upstairs, he put me into one of the bunks and told me to rest. The feathers ballooned out round me. I sank down deliciously. I felt as if I were floating down some magic staircase for ever.

Archer got his little meta-stove out and made coffee – not cocoa as he had said. He brought me over a strong cup and held it to my lips. I drank it unthinkingly and not tasting it, doing it only because he told me to.

When he took the cup away, my head fell back on the pillow, and I felt myself sinking and floating away again. I was on skis this time, but they were liquid skis, made of melted glass, and the snow was glass too, but a sort of glass that was springy, like gelatine, and flowing like water.

I felt a change in the light, and knew that Archer was bending over me. Very quietly he took off my shoes, undid my tie, loosened the collar and unbuttoned my braces in front. I remember thinking, before I finally fell asleep, how clever he was to know about undoing the braces; they had begun to feel so tight pulling down on my shoulders and dragging the trousers up between my legs. Archer covered me with several blankets and another quilt.

When I woke in the morning, Archer was already up. He had made me some tea and had put it on the stove to keep warm. He brought it over to me and I sat up. I felt ill, rather sick. I remembered what a glorious day yesterday had been, and thought how extraordinarily it was that I had not slept in my own bed at the hotel, but in Archer's room, in my clothes.

I looked at him shamefacedly. 'What happened last night? I felt peculiar,' I said.

'The lager and the lemonade, and the *crème de menthe* made you a bit tight, I'm afraid,' Archer said, laughing. 'Do you feel better now? We'll go up to the hotel and have breakfast soon.'

I got up and washed and changed into my skiing clothes. I still felt rather sick. I made my evening clothes into a neat bundle and tied them on to my toboggan. I had the sweets Archer had given me in my pocket.

We went up to the hotel, dragging the toboggan behind us.

And there on the doorstep we met my brother with one of the guides. They had had to return early, because someone in the party had broken a ski.

He was in a temper. He looked at us and then said to me: 'What have you been doing?'

I was at a loss to know what to answer. The very sight of him had so troubled me that this added difficulty of explaining my actions was too much for me.

I looked at him miserably and mouthed something about going in to have breakfast.

My brother turned to Archer fiercely, but said nothing.

Archer explained: 'Your brother's just been down to my place. We went skiing together yesterday and he left some clothes at the chalet.'

'It's very early,' was all my brother said; then he swept me on into the hotel before him, without another word to the guide or to Archer.

He went with me up to my room and saw that the bed had not been slept in.

I said clumsily: 'The maid must have been in and done my room early.' I could not bear to explain to him about my wonderful day, or why I had slept at the chalet.

My brother was so furious that he took no more notice of my weak explanations and lies.

When I suddenly said in desperation, 'I feel sick,' he seized me, took me to the basin, forced his fingers down my throat and struck me on the back till a yellow cascade of vomit gushed out of my mouth. My eyes were filled with stinging water; I was trembling. I ran the water in the basin madly, to wash away this sign of shame.

Gradually I grew a little more composed. I felt better, after being sick, and my brother had stopped swearing at me. I filled the basin with freezing water and dipped my face into it. The icy feel seemed to bite round my eye-sockets and make the flesh round my nose firm again. I waited, holding my breath for as long as possible.

Suddenly my head was pushed down and held. I felt my brother's hard fingers digging into my neck. He was hitting me now with a slipper, beating my buttocks and my back with slashing strokes, hitting a different place each time, as he had been taught when a prefect at school, so that the flesh should not be numbed from a previous blow.

I felt that I was going to choke. I could not breathe under the water, and realized that I would die. I was seized with such a panic that I wrenched myself free and darted round the room, with him after me. Water dripped on the bed, the carpet, the chest of drawers. Splashes of it spat against the mirror in the wardrobe door. My brother aimed vicious blows at me until he had driven me into a corner. There he beat against my uplifted arms, yelling in a hoarse, mad, religious voice: 'Bastard, Devil, Harlot, Bugger!'

As I cowered under his blows, I remember thinking that my brother had suddenly become a lunatic and was talking gibberish in his madness, for, of the words he was using, I had not heard any before, except 'Devil'.

# Mr Lancaster

## CHRISTOPHER ISHERWOOD

Now, at last, I'm ready to write about Mr Lancaster. For years I have been meaning to, but only rather halfheartedly; I never felt I could quite do him justice. Now I see what my mistake was; I always used to think of him as an isolated character. Taken alone, he is less than himself. To present him entirely, I realize I must show how our meeting was the start of a new chapter in my life, indeed a whole series of chapters. And I must go on to describe some of the characters in those chapters. They are all, with one exception, strangers to Mr Lancaster. (If he could have known what was to become of Waldemar, he would have cast him forth from the office in horror.) If he could ever have met Ambrose, or Geoffrey, or Maria, or Paul – but no, my imagination fails! And yet, through me, all these people are involved with each other, however much they might have hated to think so. And so they are all going to have to share the insult of each other's presence in this book.

In the spring of 1928, when I was twenty-three years old, Mr Lancaster came to London on a business trip and wrote my mother a note suggesting he should call on us. We had neither of us ever met him. All I knew about him was that he managed the office of a British shipping company in a North German harbour city. And that he was the stepson of my maternal grandmother's brother-in-law; there is perhaps a simpler way of saying this. Even my mother, who delighted in kinship, had to admit that he wasn't, strictly speaking, related to us. But she decided it would be nice if we called him 'Cousin Alexander', just to make him feel more at home.

I agreed, although I didn't care a damn what we called him or how he felt about it. As far as I was concerned, everyone over forty belonged, with a mere handful of honourable exceptions, to an alien tribe, hostile by definition but in practice ridiculous rather than formidable. The majority of them I saw as utter grotesques, sententious and gaga, to be regarded with indifference. It was only people of my own age who seemed to me better than half-alive. I was accustomed to say that when we started getting old – a situation which I could theoretically foresee but never quite believe in – I just hoped we would die quickly and without pain.

Mr Lancaster proved to be every bit as grotesque as I had expected. Nevertheless, hard as I tried, I couldn't be indifferent to him; for, from the moment he arrived, he managed to enrage and humiliate me. (It's obvious to me now that this was quite unintentional; he must have been desperately shy.) He treated me as though I were still a schoolboy, with a jocular, patronizing air. His worst offence was to address me as 'Christophilos' – giving the name an affected classical pronunciation which made it sound even more mockingly insulting.

'I'm willing to wager, most excellent Christophilos, that you've never seen the inside of a tramp steamer. No? Then let me counsel you, for the salvation of your immortal soul, let go of your Lady Mother's apron strings for once, and come over to visit us on one of the company's boats. Show us you can rough it. Let's see you eat bacon fat in the middle of a nor'easter, and have to run for the rail while the old salts laugh. It might just possibly make a man of you.'

'I'll be delighted to come,' I said, just as nonchalantly as I knew how.

I said it because, at that moment, I loathed Mr Lancaster and therefore couldn't possibly refuse his challenge. I said it because, at that time, I would have gone anywhere with anyone; I was wild with longing for the whole unvisited world. I said it also because I suspected Mr Lancaster of bluffing.

I was wrong. About three weeks later, a letter came for me from the London office of his company. It informed me, as a matter already settled, that I should be sailing on such and such a day, on board the company's freighter *Coriolanus*. An employee would be sent to guide me to the ship, if I would meet him at noon outside the dock gates in the West India Dock Road.

Just for a moment, I was disconcerted. But then my fantasy took the situation over. I started to play the lead in an epic drama, adapted freely from Conrad, Kipling, and Browning's 'What's become of Waring?' When a girl phoned and asked me if I could come to a cocktail party a week from Wednesday, I replied tersely, with a hint of grimness, 'Afraid not. Shan't be here.'

'Oh, really? Where *will* you be?'

'Don't know exactly. Somewhere in the middle of the North Sea. On a tramp steamer.'

The girl gasped.

Mr Lancaster and this shipping company didn't fit into my epic. It was humiliating to have to admit that I was only going as far as the north coast of Germany. When speaking to people who didn't know me well, I contrived to suggest that this would be merely the first port of call on an immense and mysterious voyage.

And now before I slip back into the convention of calling this young man 'I', let me consider him as a separate being, a stranger almost, setting out on this adventure in a taxi to the docks. For, of course, he *is* almost a stranger to me. I have revised his opinions, changed his accent and his mannerisms, unlearned or exaggerated his prejudices and his habits. We still share the same skeleton, but its outer covering has altered so much that I doubt if he would recognize me on the street. We have in common the label of our name, and a continuity of consciousness; there has been no break in the sequence of daily statements that I am I. But *what* I am has refashioned itself throughout the days and years, until now almost all that remains constant is the mere awareness of being conscious. And that awareness belongs to everybody; it isn't a particular person.

The Christopher who sat in that taxi is, practically speaking, dead; he only remains reflected in the fading memories of us who knew him. I can't revitalize him now. I can only reconstruct him from his remembered acts and words and from the writings he has left us. He embarrasses me often, and so I'm tempted to sneer at him; but I will try not to. I'll try not to apologize for him, either. After all, I owe him some respect. In a sense he is my father, and in another sense my son.

How alone he seems! Not lonely, for he has many friends and he can be lively with them and make them laugh. He is even a sort of leader amongst them. They are apt to look to him to know what they shall think next, what they are to admire and what hate. They regard him as enterprising and aggressive. And yet, in the midst of their company, he is isolated by his self-mistrust, anxiety and dread of the future. His life has been lived, so far, within narrow limits and he is quite naïve about most kinds of experience; he fears it and yet he is wildly eager for it. To reassure himself, he converts it into epic myth as fast as it happens. He is forever play-acting.

Even more than the future, he dreads the past – its prestige, its traditions and their implied challenge and reproach. Perhaps his strongest negative motivation is ancestor-hatred. He has vowed to disappoint, disgrace and disown his ancestors. If I were sneering at him, I should suggest that this is because he fears he will never be able to live up to them; but that would be less than half true. His fury is sincere. He is genuinely a rebel. He knows instinctively that it is only through rebellion that he will ever learn and grow.

He is taking with him on this journey a secret which is like a talisman; it will give him strength as long as he keeps it to himself. Yesterday, his first novel was published – and, of all the people he is about to meet, not one of them knows this! Certainly, the captain and the crew of the *Coriolanus* don't know it; probably no one in the whole of Germany knows. As for Mr Lancaster, he has already proved himself utterly unworthy of being told; he doesn't know and he never will. Unless, of course, the novel has such a success that he eventually reads about it in a newspaper . . . But this thought is censored with superstitious haste. No – no – it is bound to fail. All literary critics are corrupt and in the pay of the enemy . . . And why, anyhow, put your trust in treacherous hopes of this kind, when the world of the epic myth offers unfailing comfort and safety?

*That spring, totally disregarded by the crass and conceited* littérateurs *of the time, an event took place which, as we can all agree, looking backward on this, its tenth anniversary, marked the beginning of the modern novel as we know it:* All the Conspirators *was published. Next day, it was found that Isherwood was no longer in London. He had vanished without a trace or a word. His closest friends were bewildered and dismayed. There were even fears of his suicide. But then – months later – strange rumours were whispered around the salons – of how, on that same morning, a muffled figure had been glimpsed, boarding a tramp steamer from a dock on the Isle of Dogs –*

No, I will never sneer at him. I will never apologize for him. I am proud to be his father and his son. I think about him and I marvel, but I must beware of romanticizing him. I must remember that much of what looks like courage is nothing but brute ignorance. I keep forgetting that he is as blind to his own future as the dullest of the animals. As blind as I am to mine. His is an extraordinary future in many ways – far happier, luckier, more interesting than most. And yet, if I were he and could see it ahead of me, I'm sure I should exclaim in dismay that it was more than I could possibly cope with.

As it is, he can barely foresee the next five minutes. Everything that is about to happen is strange to him and therefore unpredictable. Now, as the taxi ride comes to an end, I shut down my own foresight and try to look out through his eyes.

The company's employee, a clerk scarcely older than I, named Hicks, met me at the dock gates as arranged. He was not a

character I would have chosen for my epic, being spotty-skinned
and wan from the sooty glooms and fogs of Fenchurch Street.
Also, he was in a fussy hurry, which epic characters never are.
'Whew,' he exclaimed, glancing at his watch, 'we'd better look
smart!' He seized hold of the handle of my suitcase and broke into
a trot. Since I wouldn't let go and leave him to carry it alone, I had
to trot, too. My entrance upon Act One of the drama was lacking
in style.

'There she is,' said Hicks. 'That's her.'

The *Coriolanus* was even smaller and dirtier looking than I had
expected. The parts of her that weren't black were of a yellowish
brown; the same colour, I thought – though this may have been
merely association of ideas – as vomit. Two cranes were still
dangling crates over her deck, which was swarming with dock
hands. They were shouting at the top of their voices, to make
themselves heard above the rattle of winches and the squawking
of the sea gulls that circled overhead.

'But we needn't have hurried!' I said reproachfully to Hicks. He
answered indifferently that Captain Dobson liked passengers to
be on board in plenty of time. He had lost interest in me already.
With a mumbled goodbye, he left me at the gangplank, like a
parcel he had delivered and for which he felt no further responsibility.

I elbowed my way aboard, nearly getting myself pushed into
the open hold. Captain Dobson saw me from the bridge and came
down to greet me. He was a small, fattish man with a weather-
scarlet face and the pouched, bulging eyes of a comedian.

'You're going to be sick, you know,' he said. 'We've had some
good men here, but they all failed.' I tried to look suitably anxious.

Below decks, I found a Chinese cook, a Welsh cabin boy and a
steward who looked like a jockey. He had been on the Cunard
Line for twelve years, he told me, but liked this better. 'You're on
your own here.' He showed me my cabin. It was tiny as a
cupboard and quite airless; the porthole wouldn't unscrew. I went
into the saloon, but its long table was occupied by half a dozen
clerks, scribbling frantically at cargo lists. I climbed back up on

deck again and found a place in the bows where, by making myself very small, I stayed out of everybody's way.

An hour later, we sailed. It took a long time getting out of the dock into the river, for we had to pass through lock gates. Lively slum children hung on them, watching us. One of the cargo clerks came and stood beside me at the rail.

'You'll have it choppy,' he said. 'She's a regular dancing master.' And, without another word, he vaulted athletically over the rail onto the already receding wharf, waved briefly to me, and was gone.

Then we had high tea in the saloon. I made the acquaintance of the mate and the two engineers. We ate soused mackerel and drank the tea out of mugs; it was brassily strong. I went back on deck, to find that a quiet, cloudy evening had set in. We were leaving the city behind us. The docks and the warehouses gave way to cold grey fields and marshes. We passed several light-ships. The last of them was called Barrow Deep. Captain Dobson passed me and said, 'This is the first stage of our daring voyage.' In his own way, he was trying to create an epic atmosphere. All right – I awarded him marks for effort.

Back to my cabin, for it was now too dark to see anything. The steward looked in. He had come to propose that I should pay him a pound for my food during the voyage, and eat as much as I liked. I could see he thought this was a stiff bargain, because he was sure I'd be seasick. 'There was another gentleman with us a couple of months ago,' he told me with relish. 'He was taken very bad. You'll knock on the wall if you want anything in the night, won't you, sir?'

I smiled to myself after he had left. For I had a second secret, which I intended to guard as closely as my other. These seafolk were really quite endearingly simple, I thought. They appeared to be absolutely ignorant of the advances of medical science. Natur-ally, I had taken my precautions. In my pocket was a small cardboard box with capsules in it, wrapped in silver paper. The capsules contained either pink powders or grey powders. You had to take one of each; once before sailing, and thereafter twice a day.

When I woke next morning, the ship was rolling powerfully. Between rolls, she thrust her bows steeply into the air, staggered slightly, fell forward with a crash that shook everything in the cabin. I had just finished swallowing my capsules when the door opened and the steward looked in. I knew from the disappointment in his face what it was he'd been hoping to see.

'I thought you wasn't feeling well, sir,' he said reproachfully. 'I looked in half an hour ago, and you lay there and didn't say a word.'

'I was asleep,' I said. 'I slept like a log.' And I gave this vulture a beaming smile.

At breakfast, the second engineer had his arm in a sling. A pipe had burst in the engines during the night, and he had scalded his hand. Teddy, the Welsh cabin boy, cut up his bacon for him. Teddy was clumsy in doing this, and the second engineer told him sharply to hurry. For this the second engineer was reproved by the first engineer: 'You won't half be a bloody old bugger when you're older – my God you will!'

Despite the second engineer's semi-heroic injury, I was beginning to lose my sense of the epic quality of this voyage. I had expected to find that the crew of this ship belonged to a race of beings apart – men who lived only for the sea. But, as a matter of fact, none of them quite corresponded to my idea of a seaman. The mate was too handsome, rather like an actor. The engineers might just as well have been working in a factory; they were simply engineers. The steward was like any other kind of professional servant. Captain Dobson wouldn't have looked out of place as the owner of a pub. I had to face the prosaic truth: all kinds of people go to sea.

Actually, their thoughts seemed entirely ashore. They talked about films they had seen. They discussed a recent scandalous divorce case: 'She's what you might call a respectable whore.' They entertained me by asking riddles: 'What is it that a girl of fourteen hasn't got, a girl of sixteen is expecting, and Princess Mary never will get?' Answer: 'An insurance card.' I told the story about the clergyman, the drunk and the waifs and strays. When I got to the payoff line: 'If you wore your trousers the same way round as your collar . . .' I faltered, not sure that it would be good taste to mimic a Cockney accent, since both engineers had one. However, the story went over quite well. They were all very friendly. But the answer to that constantly repeated young man's question, 'What do they really think of me?' seemed to be, as usual, 'They don't.' They weren't even sufficiently interested in me to be surprised when I took a second helping of bacon, although the ship was going up and down like a seesaw.

All day long we lurched and slithered through the rugged sea. On deck the sea glitter was so brilliant that I felt half stupefied by it. Now that everything was battened down and squared away, the ship seemed to have grown to twice its original size. I walked the empty deck like a prize turkey. Now and then Captain Dobson, who stood benevolently on the bridge smoking a brier pipe and wearing an old felt hat, pointed out passing ships to me. Whenever he did this I felt bound to hurry to the rail and scrutinize them with professional intentness. Later he embarrassed me by bringing me a deck chair and setting it up with his own hands. 'Now you'll be as happy as the boy who killed his father,' he said. And he added: 'I'd like your opinion of this,' as he gave me a paperbound book with a sexy picture on the cover. It was called *The Bride of the Brute* and contained a lot of scenes like: 'He cupped her ripe breasts in his burning hands, then savagely crushed them together till she cried out in pain and desire.' If I had been in London among my friends, we should all have felt bound to make sophisticated fun of this book. It was the sort of book you were supposed to dismiss as ridiculous. But here I could admit to myself that, absurd as it was, it excited me hotly. Captain Dobson took it as a compliment that I read right through the book in an hour. Meanwhile, Teddy served me mugs of tea with large jam puffs.

In the middle of the night I woke, just as if somebody had roused me. Kneeling on my bunk, I peered out through the porthole. And there were the first lights of Germany shining across the black water, blue and green and red.

Next morning we steamed up the river. Captain Dobson drank with the German pilot in the chartroom and became very cheerful. He had exchanged his old felt hat for a smart white cap, which made him look more than ever like a comic music-hall sea dog. We passed barges which were as snug as homes, with gay curtained windows and pots of flowers. Captain Dobson showed me various places of interest along the shore. Pointing to one factory building, he said, 'They've got hundreds of girls in there, cleaning the wool. It's so hot, they strip to the waist.' He winked. I leered politely.

In the harbour, the *Coriolanus* became tiny again, as she made her way humbly to her berth amidst all the great ships. Captain Dobson shouted greetings to them as we passed, and was greeted in return. He appeared to be universally popular.

When we tied up, our deck was so far below the level of the dock that the gangplank had to be nearly vertical. A police officer, who had come to inspect my passport, hesitated to descend it. Captain Dobson mocked him: 'Go 'vay, Tirpitz! Go 'vay!' He had called the pilot 'Tirpitz', too, and all the captains of the ships he had hailed. The police officer climbed down cautiously backward, laughing but holding on very tight.

After the stamping of my passport, there were no other formalities. I shook hands with the steward (who was sulking a little; a bad loser), tipped Teddy and waved goodbye to Captain Dobson. 'Give my love to the girls!' he shouted from the bridge. The police officer obligingly came with me to the dock gates and put me on a tram which stopped outside Mr Lancaster's office.

It was an impressive place, even larger than I'd expected, on the ground floor, with revolving glass doors. Half a dozen girls and about twice that many men were at work there. A youth of sixteen ushered me into Mr Lancaster's private room.

I had remembered Mr Lancaster as tall, but I had forgotten how very, very tall he was. How tall and how thin. Obeying the strong subconscious physical reaction which is part of every meeting, I defensively became a fraction of a millimetre shorter, broader, more compact, as I shook his bony hand.

'Well, Cousin Alexander, here I am!'

'Christopher,' he said, in his deep, languid voice. It was a statement, not an exclamation. I expanded it to mean: Here you are, and it doesn't astonish me in the least.

His head was so small that it seemed feminine. He had very large ears, a broad, wet moustache, and a peevish mouth. He looked sulky, frigid, dyspeptic. His nose was long and red, with a suggestion of moisture at the end of it. And he wore a high, hard collar and awkward black boots. No – I could find no beauty in him. All my earlier impressions were confirmed. I reminded myself with approval of one of my friend Hugh Weston's dicta: 'All ugly people are wicked.'

'I shall be ready in exactly –' Mr Lancaster looked at his watch and seemed to make some rapid but complicated calculation – 'eighteen minutes.' He walked back to his desk.

I sat down on a hard chair in the corner and felt an indignant gloom fill me from my toes to my head. I was violently disappointed. Why? What had I expected? A warm welcome, questions about the voyage, admiration for my freedom from seasickness? Well – yes. I *had* expected that. And I had been a fool, I told myself. I should have known better. Now, here I was, trapped for a week with this frigid old ass.

Mr Lancaster had begun to write something. Without looking up, he took a newspaper from the desk and tossed it over to me. It was a London *Times*, three days old.

'Thank you – sir,' I said, as spitefully as I dared. It was my declaration of war. Mr Lancaster didn't react in any way.

Then he began to telephone. He telephoned in English, French, German and Spanish. All these languages he spoke in exactly the same tone and with the same inflections. Every now and then he boomed, and I realized that he was listening to his own voice and liking the way it sounded. It was noticeably ecclesiastical and it also had something of the government minister in it; nothing of the businessman. Several times he became commanding. Once he was almost gracious. He couldn't keep his hands still for a moment, and the least problem made him irritable and excited.

He wasn't ready for more than half an hour.

Then, without warning, he rose, said, 'That's all,' and walked out, leaving me to follow. All of the adult employees had left the outer office, presumably to get their lunch. The youth was on duty. Mr Lancaster said something to him in German, from which I learned only that his name was Waldemar. As we went out, I grinned at him, trying instinctively to draw him into a conspiracy against Mr Lancaster. But he remained expressionless and merely made me a small, stiff German bow. It really shocked me to see an adolescent boy bow like that. Mr Lancaster certainly broke them in young. Or did he – horrible thought! – class me with Mr Lancaster and therefore treat me with the same mocking-contemptuous respect? I thought not. Waldemar was probably every bit as stuffy as his employer, and tried to imitate his behaviour as a model of gentlemanly deportment.

We took a tram back to Mr Lancaster's home. It was a warm, humid day of spring. Carrying my suitcase and wearing – in order to transport it – my overcoat, made me sweat; but I enjoyed the weather. It disturbed and excited me. I was glad that the tram was crowded – not only because I thus became separated from Mr Lancaster and didn't have to make conversation with him, but also because I was pressed up close against the bodies of young Germans of my own age, boys and girls; and the nationality barrier between them and me seemed to rub off as the swaying car swung us into a tight-packed huddle. Outside there were more young people, on bicycles. The schoolboys wore caps with shiny peaks and bright-coloured shirts with laces instead of buttons, open at the neck. The gaily painted tram sped clanking and tolling its bell down long streets of white houses, where broad creeper leaves shadowed fronts of embossed stucco, in gardens dense with lilac. We passed a fountain – a sculptured group of Laocoön and his sons writhing in the grip of the snakes. In this sunshine you could almost envy them. For the snakes were vomiting cool water over the hot, naked bodies of the men, and their deadly wrestling match appeared lazy and sensual.

Mr Lancaster lived in the ground-floor flat of a large house that faced north. Its rooms were high, ugly and airy. They had big white sliding doors which shot open at a touch, with uncanny momentum, making a bang which resounded through the building. The place was furnished in Germanic *art nouveau* style. The chairs, tables, closets and bookcases were grim, angular shapes which seemed to express a hatred of comfort and an inflexible puritanism. An equally grim stencilled frieze of leafless branches ran around the walls of the living-room, and the hanging centre lamp was an austere sour-green glass lotus bud. The place must have been dreary beyond words in winter; now at least it had the merit of being cool. Mr Lancaster's only obvious contribution to the décor were a few school and regimental group photographs.

The most arresting of Mr Lancaster's photographs was a large one showing a vigorous, bearded old man of perhaps seventy-five. What a beard! It was the real article, no longer obtainable, made of sterling silver; the beard of the genuine Victorian paterfamilias. It roared in torrents from his finely arched nostrils and his big-lobed ears, foamed over his cheeks in two tidal waves that collided below his chin to form boiling rapids in which no boat could have lived. What a beard-conscious old beauty – tilting his head up to be admired, with an air of self-indulged caprice!

'My dear old father,' said Mr Lancaster, making it clear, by his memorial tone of voice, that The Beard was now with God. 'Before he was sixteen he had rounded the Horn and been north of the Aleutians, right up to the edge of the ice. By the time he was *your* age, Christopher –' this was a faint reproach – 'he was second mate, sailing out of Singapore on the China Seas run. He used to translate Xenophon during the typhoons. Taught me everything I know.'

Lunch was cold. It consisted of black bread, hard yellow Dutch cheese and various kinds of sausage – the indecently pink kind, the kind that smells gamy, the kind full of lumps of gristle, the kind that looks in cross-section like a very old stained-glass window in a church.

Before we had eaten anything, Mr Lancaster informed me that he didn't approve of after-dinner naps. 'When I was managing the company's office at Valparaiso, my second in command was always telling me I ought to take a siesta, like the rest of them did. So I said to him, "That's the time when the white man steals a march on the dagoes." '

This, I was to discover, was a characteristic specimen of Mr Lancaster's line of bold reactionary talk. No doubt, in my case, he was using it for educational reasons, taking it for granted that I must have romantic, liberal views which needed a counter-balance. There he was both right and wrong. I did have liberal views, in a vague, unthoughtout way; but he was quite wrong in thinking that by expressing opposite opinions he could startle me. I should have been startled only if he had agreed with me; as it was, I accepted his prejudices as a matter of course, without curiosity, finding them entirely in character.

Actually, I think, Mr Lancaster felt himself to be beyond left or right. He took his stand on the infallibility of his experience and his weary knowledge that he had seen everything worth seeing. He was also beyond literature. He told me that he spent his evenings carpentering in a small workshop at the back of the flat – 'to keep myself from reading.'

'I've got no use for books as books,' he announced. 'When I've taken what I need out of them, I throw them away . . . Whenever anyone comes and tells me about some philosophy that's just been discovered, some new idea that's going to change the world, I turn to the classics and see which of the great Greeks expressed it best . . . Scribbling, in these latter days, is nothing but a nervous disease. And it's spreading everywhere. I don't doubt, my poor Christophilos, that before long you'll have sunk so low as to commit a novel yourself!'

'I've just published one.'

The moment I had spoken, I was horrified and ashamed. Not until the words were in my mouth had I known what I was going to say. Mr Lancaster couldn't have provoked me more artfully into a confession if he'd been a prosecuting lawyer.

The most humiliating aspect of my confession was that it didn't even seem to surprise or interest him in the least. 'Send me a copy sometime,' he told me blandly. 'I'll let you have it back by return post, with all the split infinitives underlined in red pencil and all the non sequiturs in blue.' He patted my shoulder; I winced with dislike. 'Oh, by the way,' he added, 'we have a trifling foolish banquet towards –' he spoke this line in a special, whimsical tone, as if to draw my respectful attention to the fact that here was a quotation from the Divine Swan in playful mood – 'All the local worthies from the shipping companies, the consulates and so forth will be there. I've arranged for you to come.'

'No,' I said. And I meant it. I had had enough. There was a limit to the amount of my valuable life I could afford to waste on this ignorant, offensive, self-satisfied fool. I would simply walk out on him, at once, this very afternoon. I had some money. I'd go to a travel bureau and find out how much it would cost to get back to England third class by the ordinary, civilized means. If I hadn't enough, I would take a room in a hotel and telegraph my mother for more. It was perfectly easy. Mr Lancaster wasn't dictator of the world, and there was nothing he could do to stop me. He knew this as well as I did. I wasn't a child. And yet –

And yet – for some absurd, irrational, infuriating, humiliating reason – I was afraid of him! Incredible, but true. So afraid that my defiance made me tremble and my voice turned weak. Mr Lancaster didn't appear to have heard me.

'It'll be an experience for you,' he said, munching his hard old cheese.

'I can't.' This time, I spoke much too loudly, because of overcompensation.

'Can't what?'

'Can't come.'

'Why not?' His manner was quite indulgent; an adult listening to the excuses of a schoolboy.

'I – I haven't got a dinner jacket.' Again, I horrified myself. This betrayal was as involuntary as the other; and, up to the moment of speaking, I'd supposed I was going to tell him I was leaving.

'I didn't expect you would have one,' said Mr Lancaster, imperturbably. 'I've already asked my second in command to lend you his. He's about your size, and he has to stay at home tonight. His wife's expecting another baby. Her fifth. They breed like vermin. That's the real menace of the future, Christopher. Not war. Not disease. Starvation. They'll spawn themselves to death. I warned them, back in '21. Wrote a long letter to *The Times*, forecasting the curve of the birth rate. I've been proved right already. But they were afraid. The facts were too terrible. They only printed my first paragraph –' He rose abruptly to his feet. 'You can go out and look around town. Be back here at six, sharp. No – better say five fifty-five. I have to work now.' And with that, he left me alone.

The banquet was held in some private rooms above a big restaurant in the middle of the city.

As soon as we arrived, Mr Lancaster's manner became preoccupied. He glanced rapidly away from me in all directions and kept leaving me to go over and speak to groups of guests as they arrived. He wore a greenish-black dinner jacket of pre-1914 cut and carried a white silk handkerchief inside his starched cuff. My own borrowed dinner jacket was definitely too large for me; I felt like an amateur conjurer – but one without any rabbits to produce out of his big pockets.

Mr Lancaster was nervous! He evidently felt a need to explain to me what was worrying him, but he couldn't. He couldn't say anything coherent. He muttered broken sentences, while his eyes wandered around the room.

'You see – this annual meeting. A formality, usually. But this year – certain influences – absolute firmness – make them see clearly what's at stake. Because the alternative is. Same thing everywhere today. Got to be fought. Uncompromisingly. State my position – once and for all. We shall see. I don't quite think they'll dare to –'

Evidently this meeting, whatever it was, would take place at once. For already the guests were moving towards a door at the other end of the room. Without even telling me to wait for him, Mr Lancaster followed them. I had no alternative but to stay where I was, sitting at the extreme end of one of the settees, facing a large mirror on the wall.

Very very occasionally in the course of your life – goodness knows how or why – a mirror will seem to catch your image and hold it like a camera. Years later, you have only to think of that mirror in order to see yourself just as you appeared in it then. You can even recall the feelings you had as you were looking into it. For example, at the age of nine, I shot a wildly lucky goal in a school football game. When I got back from the field, I looked into a mirror in the changing room, feeling that this improbable athletic success must somehow have altered my appearance. It hadn't; but I still know exactly how I looked and felt. And I know how I looked and felt as I stared into that restaurant mirror.

I see my twenty-three-year-old face regarding me with large, reproachful eyes, from beneath a cowlick of streaky blond hair. A thin, strained face, so touchingly pretty that it might have been photographed and blown up big for a poster appealing on behalf of the world's young: 'The old hate us because we're so cute. Won't *you* help?'

And now I experience what that face is experiencing – the sense which the young so constantly have of being deserted. Their god forsakes them many times a day; they are continually crying out in despair from their crosses. It isn't that I feel angry with Mr Lancaster for having deserted me; I hardly blame him at all. For he seems to me to be an almost impersonal expression, at this moment, of the world's betrayal of the young.

I am in mortal dread of being challenged by the manager of the restaurant or by any one of the various waiters who are hanging around the room, waiting for the banquet to begin. Suppose they ask me what I'm doing here – why, if I'm a bona fide dinner guest, I'm not with the others attending the meeting?

Therefore I concentrate all my will upon the desired condition of not being accosted. Fixing my eyes upon my reflection in the mirror, I try to exclude these men utterly from my consciousness, to eradicate every vestige of a possible telepathic bond between us. It is a tremendous strain. I tremble all over and feel sick to my stomach. Sweat runs down my temples.

The meeting lasted nearly an hour and a half.

The guests returned from it mostly by twos and threes, but Mr Lancaster was alone. He came straight over to me.

'We've got to eat now,' he told me with an air of nervous impatience, just as though I had raised some objection. 'I've had them put you next to old Machado. He'll tell you all about Peru. He's their vice-consul here. You speak French, I suppose?'

'Not one word.' This was quite untrue. But I wanted to disconcert Mr Lancaster, and so punish him a little for leaving me alone by making him feel guilty.

But he wasn't even listening. 'Good. It'll be an experience for you.' And he was off again. I joined the crowd that was now moving into the dining room.

It was a very big place, a real banqueting hall. There were four long tables in it. What was evidently the table of honour was placed along the far wall, under an arrangement of many national flags. At this table I saw Mr Lancaster already in the act of sitting down. It was equally easy to identify the least important table, right by the door. And, sure enough, one of its place cards had my name on it. On my right I read the name of Emilio Machado; and, a moment later, Sr Machado himself took his seat at my side. He was a tiny man in his seventies. He had a benevolent mahogany-brown face netted with wrinkles – these were a slightly paler shade of brown – and hung with a drooping white moustache. His lips moved in a rather pathetic, silly smile as he watched the expressions on the faces of some loudly chattering guests across the table, but I didn't have the impression that he wanted to be spoken to.

The dinner, to my surprise, was excellent. (I associated everything in this city so completely with Mr Lancaster that I was apt to forget he couldn't possibly have had anything to do with the catering.) As soon as the soup course was over, the guests began to toast each other, pair by pair. To do this, a guest would half rise to his feet, glass in hand, and wait until he had succeeded in catching the desired eye. The other guest, when caught, would also rise; glasses would be raised, bows exchanged. It was obvious that this was a serious matter. I felt sure that no toast went unremembered, and that to omit any of them would have led to grave consequences in your subsequent business dealings.

Watching all his toasting made me aware that I myself had nothing to drink. It appeared that the drinks didn't come with the dinner; they had to be ordered separately. In the fuss of changing my clothes, I had forgotten my money; I would have to send the bill over to Mr Lancaster to be paid. But this didn't bother me. Serve him right, I thought, for his neglect. I made up my mind to speak to Sr Machado, and ask him to share a bottle of wine with me. He didn't have any, either. I drew a deep breath: '*Si vous voulez, Monsieur, j'aimerais bien boire quelque chose –*'

He didn't hear me. I felt my face getting hot with shame. But now I heard a voice in my other ear: 'You are the nephew of Mr Lancaster, yes?'

I started guiltily. For I had been so absorbed in the problem of communicating with Machado that I'd scarcely noticed my other neighbour. He was a smiling, greedy-faced man, with a gleam in his eye and no chin. His sleek, thin grey hair was brushed immaculately back from his forehead. An unused monocle hung down on a broad silk ribbon against his shirtfront. His mouth pulled down at the corners, giving him a slight resemblance to a shark – but not a very dangerous one; not a man-eater, certainly. Squinting at his place card, I read a Hungarian name which no one but a Hungarian could possibly pronounce.

'I'm not his nephew,' I said. 'I'm not related to him at all, as a matter of fact.'

'You are not?' This delighted the Shark. 'You are just friends?'

'I suppose so.'

'A frriend?' He rolled the *r* lusciously: 'Mr Lancaster has a young friend!'

I grinned. Already I felt that I knew the Shark very well indeed.

'But he leaves you alone, no? That is not very friendly.'

'Well, now I've got you to look after me.'

My reply sent the Shark off into peals of screaming laughter. (On second thoughts, he was also partly a parrot.)

'I look after you, yes?' said Parrot-Shark: 'Oh, very good! I shall look after you. Do not be afraid of that, please. I shall do it.' He beckoned to a waiter. 'You will help me drink one great big bottle of wine, yes? Very bad for me, if I must every time drink up all alone.'

'Very bad.'

'And now tell me, please – you are the friend of Mr Lancaster, since how long?'

'Since this morning.'

'This morning, only!' This didn't really shock Parrot-Shark, as he pretended; but it did puzzle him sincerely. 'And he leaves you alone already?'

'Oh, I'm used to that!'

He was looking at me much more inquisitively now, aware, perhaps, that here was something not quite usual, just a bit uncanny, even. Maybe if he could have seen what a very odd young fish he had at the end of his line, he would have fled screaming from the room. However, at this moment the wine arrived, and soon his curiosity was forgotten.

From then on, dinner became quite painless. It was easy enough to keep Parrot-Shark amused, especially after we had finished the first bottle and he had ordered another. At the end of the meal, the lights were turned out and the waiters brought in ice puddings with coloured lamps inside them. Then the speeches began. A fat, bald man rose to his feet with the assurance of a celebrity. Parrot-Shark whispered to me that this was the mayor. The mayor told stories. Someone had once explained to me the technique of storytelling in German; you reserve, if possible, the whole point of the story and pack it into the final verb at the end of the last sentence. When you reach this sentence, you pause dramatically, then you cast forth the heavy, clumsy, polysyllabic verb, like a dice thrower, upon the table.

At the end of each story the audience roared and wiped perspired faces with their handkerchiefs. But, by the time it was Mr Lancaster's turn to speak, they were getting tired and not so easy to please. His speech was followed by applause that was no more than barely polite.

'Mr Lancaster is in bad humour tonight.' Parrot-Shark told me, with evident sly satisfaction.

'Why is he in a bad humour?'

'Here we have a club for the foreign people who have work in this city. Mr Lancaster is the president of our club for three years now. Always before, he is elected with no opposition – because he represents so powerful a shipping firm –'

'And this year you elected someone else?'

'Oh no. We elect him. But only after much discussion. We elect him because we are afraid of him.'

'Ha, ha! That's very funny!'

'It is true! We are all afraid of Mr Lancaster. He is our schoolmaster. No – do not tell him that, please! I joke only.'

'I'm not afraid of him,' I boasted.

'Ah, for you it is different! You also are English. I think when you are Mr Lancaster's age, people will be afraid of *you*.' But Parrot-Shark did not mean this; he didn't believe it for one instant. He patted my hand. 'I like every time to tease you a little bit, no?' On this understanding we drank each other's healths and finished a third bottle.

The rest of the evening I remember only rather vaguely. After the speeches, the whole company rose. Some, I suppose, went home. The majority got possession of chairs in the outer room, where they ordered more drinks. Little tables appeared from somewhere to put the drinks on. Those who had nowhere to sit wandered about, on the alert to capture an empty place. The lights seemed very bright. The tremendous clatter of conversation tuned itself down in my ears into a deep, drowsy hum. I was sitting at a table in an alcove. Parrot-Shark was still looking after me, and several of his friends had joined him. I don't think they were all

Hungarians – indeed one of them seemed obviously French and another Scandinavian – but they had the air of belonging together. It was as if they were all members of a secret society, and their talk was full of passwords and smilingly acknowledged countersigns. I felt intuitively that they had all been involved in the opposition to Mr Lancaster's re-election. They didn't seem very formidable; it was no wonder that he had defeated them. But they were more dangerous and more determined than they looked. They were smiling enemies, snipers, heel-biters, quick to scurry away, but sure to return.

Machado had long since disappeared. But I kept getting glimpses of Mr Lancaster. I was surprised to realize that he was every bit as drunk as I was. I had supposed he would be extremely abstinent, either from conviction or caution, or else that he would have a very strong head. We were drinking liqueur brandy, now; I had begun to loll on the table. 'Feeling sleepy?' Parrot-Shark asked. 'I fix you up, eh?' He called the waiter and gave a detailed order in German, winking at his friends as he did so. They all laughed. I laughed too. Really and truly, I didn't care what they did with me.

The waiter brought the drink. I sniffed at it. 'What is it?' I asked.

'Just a small special medicine, yes?' The faces of Parrot-Shark and his fellow-conspirators had moved in very close, now. They formed a circle within which I felt myself hypnotically enclosed. Their eyes followed my every movement with an intentness which pleased and flattered me. It was certainly a change, being at the burning-point of such focused attention. I sniffed the drink again. It was some kind of a cocktail; I could distinguish only a musky odour which perhaps contained cloves.

But now something made me turn my head. And there was Mr Lancaster. My sense of distance had become a bit tricky; he appeared to be about twenty-five yards away and at least twelve feet tall. Actually, he must have been standing right behind my chair. He said sharply, 'Don't drink that stuff, Christopher. It's a plot –' (or perhaps, 'It's a lot'; I can't be sure).

There was a long pause during which, I suppose, I grinned

idiotically. Parrot-Shark said, smiling, 'You hear what Herr Lancaster says? You are not to drink it.'

'No.' I said, 'I certainly won't. I won't disoblige my dearest Coz.' With these words, I raised the glass to my lips and drained the entire drink. It was like swallowing a skyrocket. The shock made me quite sober for a moment. 'That's very interesting,' I heard myself saying; 'pure reflex action. I mean – you see – if he'd told me *not* to drink it – I mean, I shouldn't –'

My voice trailed off and I just could not be bothered to say any more. Looking up, I was surprised to find that Mr Lancaster was no longer there. Probably several minutes had gone by.

'He doesn't like you,' I abruptly told Parrot-Shark.

Parrot-Shark grinned. 'It is because he is afraid that I steal you from him, no?'

'Well, what are you waiting for?' I asked aggressively. 'Don't you *want* to steal me?'

'We shall steal you,' said Parrot-Shark, but he kept glancing apprehensively toward Mr Lancaster, who had reappeared in the middle distance. 'There is a bar,' he whispered to me, 'down by the harbour. It is very amusing.'

'What do you mean – amusing?'

'You will see.'

He words broke the spell. I was suddenly, catastrophically bored. Oh yes, in my own sadistic way, I had been flirting with Parrot-Shark; daring him to overpower my will, to amaze me, to master me, to abduct me. Poor timid creature, he couldn't have abducted a mouse! He had no faith in his own desires. He was fatally lacking in shamelessness. I suppose he thought of himself as a seducer. But his method of seduction had gone out with the nineties. It was like an interminable and very badly written book which I now knew I had never meant to read.

'Amusing?' I said. '*Amusing?*'

With that I rose, in all the dignity of my drunkenness, and walked slowly across to where Mr Lancaster was sitting. 'Take me home,' I told him, in a commanding voice. It must have been commanding, because he instantly obeyed!

*

The next morning, at breakfast, Mr Lancaster seemed very much under the weather. His poor nose was redder than ever and his face was grey. He sat listlessly at the table and let me get the food from the kitchen. I hummed to myself as I did so. I felt unusually cheerful. I was aware that Mr Lancaster was watching me.

'I hope you take cold baths, Christopher.'

'I took one this morning.'

'Good boy! It's one of the habits you can judge a man by.'

I wanted to laugh out loud. Because I never took a cold bath unless I had been drunk, and would indeed have thought it shameful and reactionary to take one for any other reason. I agreed with Mr Lancaster, for once: cold bath taking was a habit you could judge a man by – it marked him as one of the enemy. Nevertheless – I had to confess that part of myself, a spaniel side of me that I deplored, eagerly licked up Mr Lancaster's misplaced praise!

Altogether, I felt a distinct improvement in our relations; at any rate, on my side. I felt that I had definitely scored over him and could therefore afford to be generous. I had defied him last night about drinking that drink, and had got away with it. I had had a glimpse behind the scenes of his business life and realized that he wasn't quite invulnerable; he was at least subject to petty ambition. Best of all, he had a hang-over this morning and I hadn't – well, not much of one.

'I'm afraid I was a little preoccupied, yesterday evening,' he said. 'I should have taken you aside and explained things to you quietly. It was a very delicate situation. I had to act quickly –' I became aware that Mr Lancaster didn't really want to tell me about the club and his fight for re-election; it wouldn't have sounded important enough. So he took refuge in grandiose generalizations: 'There are evil things abroad in the world. I've been in Russia, and I know. I know Satanists when I see them. And they're getting bolder every year. They no longer crawl the gutters. They sit in the seats of power. I'm going to make a prophecy – listen, I want you to remember this – ten years from now, this city will be a place you couldn't bring your mother, or your wife, or any pure woman to visit. It will be – I don't say worse, because that would be impossible – but as bad – as bad as Berlin!'

'Is Berlin so bad?' I asked, trying not to sound too interested.

'Christopher – in the whole of *The Thousand and One Nights*, in the most shameless rituals of the Tantras, in the carvings on the Black Pagoda, in the Japanese brothel pictures, in the vilest perversions of the Oriental mind, you couldn't find anything more nauseating than what goes on there, quite openly, every day. That city is doomed, more surely than Sodom ever was. Those people don't even realize how low they have sunk. Evil doesn't know itself there. The most terrible of all devils rules – the devil without a face. You've led a sheltered life, Christopher. Thank God for it. You could never imagine such things.'

'No – I'm sure I couldn't.' I said meekly. And then and there I made a decision – one that was to have a very important effect on the rest of my life. I decided that, no matter how, I would get to Berlin just as soon as ever I could and that I would stay there a long, long time.

That afternoon Mr Lancaster arranged that Waldemar should take me to see the sights. We looked at the paintings in the Rathaus and visited the cathedral. Captain Dobson had made me curious to see the Bleikeller, the lead cellar, under it, in which corpses of human beings and animals are preserved. Captain Dobson had described how he had been to see these corpses with his brother: 'One of them's a woman, you know. She's wearing a pair of black drawers. So I thought to myself, I'd like to see how things had panned out down there. There was a caretaker on guard, but he'd got his back turned to us. So I said to my brother, just keep an eye on old Tirpitz. And then I lifted them up. And, do you know, there was nothing – nothing at all! The rats must have been at her.'

The flesh of the corpses had shrivelled on their bones so that they were hardly more than skeletons; it looked like black rubber. There was a caretaker on this occasion, too; but he didn't turn his back and I had no chance of testing Captain Dobson's story. The thought of it made me smile; I wished I could tell it to Waldemar.

An American lady who was down in the cellar with us asked me how the corpses had been preserved. When I told her I didn't know, she suggested I should ask Waldemar. I had to explain that I couldn't. Whereupon, she cried to her companion: 'Say – isn't this cute? This young man can't speak any Germany and his friend doesn't speak any English!'

I didn't think it was cute at all. Being with Waldemar embarrassed me. He was probably a nice boy. He was certainly nice looking; in fact he was quite beautiful, in a high-cheekboned, Gothic style. He looked like one of the carved stone angels in the cathedral. No doubt the twelfth-century sculptor had used just such a boy – maybe a direct ancestor of Waldemar – for his model. But an angel isn't a very thrilling companion, especially if he doesn't speak your language; and Waldemar seemed so passive. He just followed me around without showing any initiative. My guess was that he found me as tiresome as the sights and only consoled himself by reflecting that it would be even more boring back in the office.

The four days which I now spent with Mr Lancaster seemed like a whole life together. I doubt if I should have gotten to known him any better in four months or four years.

I was bored, of course; but that didn't bother me particularly. (Most of the young are bored most of the time – if they have any spirit at all. That is to say, they are outraged – and quite rightly so – because life isn't as wonderful as they feel it ought to be.)

But I had decided to make the best of Mr Lancaster. I was ashamed of my adolescent reactions to him that first day. Wasn't I a novelist? At college, my friend Allen Chalmers and I had been fond of exchanging the watchword 'All pains!' This was short for Matthew Arnold's line in his sonnet on Shakespeare: 'All pains the immortal spirit must endure.' We used it to remind each other that, to a writer, everything is potential material and that he has no business quarrelling with his bread and butter. Mr Lancaster, I now reminded myself, was part of 'all pains', and I resolved to accept him and study him scientifically.

So the first time I found myself alone in his flat, I searched it carefully for clues. I felt ridiculously guilty doing this. There were no rugs on the floors, and the noise of my footsteps was so loud that I was tempted to take off my shoes. In a corner of the living-room stood a pair of skis. They looked somehow so like Mr Lancaster that they might have been his familiars watching me. I used to make faces at them. I was being watched, anyway, by the photograph of The Beard. How dearly he would have liked to have me aboard his ship, to be ordered aloft in a blizzard off the Horn! When you looked at him and then considered his victim and pupil, Mr Lancaster, you realized how much the old monster had to answer for.

On the whole, my search was disappointing. I found almost nothing. There was a locked writing desk which might possibly contain secrets; I would watch for a chance to see inside it. Otherwise, all the drawers and cupboards were open. My only discovery of any interest was that Mr Lancaster kept a British Army captain's uniform in the wardrobe with his other clothes. So he was one of those dreary creatures who made a cult of their war experiences! Well, I might have known it. At least it was some-thing to begin on.

At supper that night – our only eatable meal, since it was cooked by a woman who came in – I got him on to the subject. It certainly wasn't difficult. I barely had to mention the word 'war' to start him intoning:

'Loos – Armentières – Ypres – St Quentin – Compiègne – Abbeville – Épernay – Amiens – Bethune – St Omer – Arras –' His voice had gone into its ecclesiastical singsong, and I had begun to wonder if he would ever stop. But he did, abruptly. Then, in a much lower voice, he said 'Le Cateau', and was silent for several moments. He had pronounced the name in his most specially sacred tone. And now he explained: 'It was there that I wrote what I regret to say is one of the very few great lines of poetry on the war.' Again, his voice rose into a chant: 'Only the monstrous anger of the guns.'

'But surely,' I voluntarily exclaimed, 'that's by – ?' Then I quickly checked myself, as I realized the full beauty of this discovery. Mr Lancaster had genuine delusions of grandeur!

'I could have been a writer,' he continued. 'I had that power which only the greatest writers have – the power of looking down on all human experience with absolute objectivity.' He said this with such conviction that there was something almost spooky about it. I was reminded of the way the dead talk about themselves in Dante.

'Tolstoy had it,' Mr Lancaster mused, 'but Tolstoy was dirty. I know, because I've lived in six countries. He couldn't look at a peasant girl without thinking of her breasts under her dress.' He paused, to let me recover from the shock of this powerful language. He was in the role of the great novelist now, talking simply and brutally of life as he sees it without fear or desire. 'Some day, Christopher, you must go there and see it for yourself. Those steppes stretching thousands of miles beyond the horizon, and all the squalor and the hopelessness. All the terrible rot of sloth. The utter lack of backbone. Then you'll know why Russia is being run today by a pack of atheist Jews . . . We in England never produced anyone greater than Keats. Keats was a clean-hearted lad, but he couldn't see clearly. He was too sick. You have to have a healthy mind in a healthy body. Oh, I know you young Freudians sneer at such things, but history will prove you wrong. Your generation will pay and pay and pay. The sun's touching the horizon already. It's almost too late. The night of the barbarian is coming on. I could have written all that. I could have warned them. But I'm a man of action, really –

'I'll tell you what, most excellent Christophilos – I'm going to make you a present. I'll give you the idea for a book of short stories that will make your reputation as a writer. It's something that's never been done. No one has dared to do it. Their heads were full of this so-called expressionism. They thought they were being subjective. Pooh! They hadn't the stamina. Their minds were costive. All that they could produce was as dry as sheep droppings –

'You see, these fools imagine that realism is writing *about* emotions. They think they're being very daring because they name things by the catchwords these Freudians have invented. But that's only puritanism turned inside out. The puritans forbid the use of the names; so now the Freudians order the use of the names. That's all. That's the only difference. There's nothing to choose between them. In their dirty little hearts, the Freudians fear the names just as much as the puritans do – because they're still obsessed by this miserable medieval Jewish necromancy – the Rabbi Loew and all that . . . But the true realism – the kind nobody dares to attempt – has no use for names. The true realism goes behind the names –

'So what I would do is this –'

Here Mr Lancaster paused impressively, rose, crossed the room, opened a drawer, took out a pipe, filled it, lighted it, shut the drawer, came back to his chair. The process took nearly five minutes. His face remained dead-pan throughout it. But I could sense that he was simply delighted to keep me in suspense – and, in spite of myself, I really was.

'What I would do,' he at last continued, 'is to write a series of stories which do not describe an emotion, but create it. Think of it, Christopher – a story in which the word "fear" is never mentioned and the emotion of fear is never described, but which *induces* fear in the reader. Can you imagine how terrible that fear would be?

'There'd be a story inducing hunger and thirst. And a story arousing anger. And then there'd be another story – the most terrible of all. Perhaps almost too terrible to write –'

(The story inducing sleep? I didn't say this, but I thought it – very loud.)

'The story,' said Mr Lancaster, speaking very slowly now to get the maximum effect, 'which arouses the instinct of – repro-duction.'

My efforts to view Mr Lancaster scientifically were not merely for art's sake. I realized by now that he was capable of having a truly shocking effect on my character. It was very dangerous for me to stop regarding him as a grotesque and start thinking of him

humanly, because then I should hate him for bullying me. And if I
went on hating him and letting myself be bullied by him, I should
sink into a vicious, degenerate bitchery; the impotent bitchery of
the slave. If there was such a thing as reincarnation – and why
not? – I might well have been Mr Lancaster's slave secretary in the
days of classical Rome. We had probably lived out in a tumble-
down villa on the wrong side of the Appian Way. I would have
been the sort of slave who fancies himself as a poet and philosopher, but is condemned to waste his time transcribing the
maunderings of his master and endure his earth-shakingly trivial
thoughts about the mysteries of nature. My master would have
been poor, of course, and stingy, too. I would have had to double
my duties, fetching wood and water, and maybe cooking as well.
But I would have put on airs with the slaves from the other villas
and pretended that I never had to do anything menial. At night I
would lie awake planning his murder. But I should never dare go
through with it, for fear of being caught and crucified.

No – Mr Lancaster had to be taken scientifically or not at all.
You had to study him like lessons. I actually made notes of his
table talk:

'The worst of this work I'm doing now is, it doesn't really use
more than a hundredth part of my brain. I get mentally constipated. In the war, my battery major used to set me gunnery
problems. I'd solve them in the day. Gave three alternative
solutions to each – without mathematics –

'There's one thing, Christopher, that you *must* realize. It is
necessary in this world to believe in a positive force of evil. And
the joy of life – the *whole* joy of life – is to fight that evil. If we lose
sight of that, we lose the meaning of life. We fall into the ghastly
despair of Glycon:

> *Panta gelōs, kī panta konis, kī panta to māden,*
> *panta gar ex alogōn esti ta ginomena . . .*

> *All is but laughter, dust and nothingness,*
> *All of unreason born . . .*

That's where the Pagans came to an end, the edge of the shoreless sea. That was all they knew. But we have no excuse to follow them. For against their negation we can now put Gareth's tremendous affirmation, his reply to his mother when she urged him to stay at home and amuse himself with the distractions of a purposeless life:

> Man am I grown, a man's work must I do.
> Follow the deer? follow the Christ, the King,
> Live pure, speak true, right wrong, follow the King –
> Else, wherefore born?

Never forget that, Christopher. Repeat it to yourself every morning, as you wake up. Else, wherefore born? Never ask, Can we win? Fight, fight!

> Charge once more, then, and be dumb!
> Let the victors, when they come,
> When the forts of folly fall,
> Find thy body by the wall.

None of your clever modern men has Arnold's voice. Meredith had it. William Watson had it – he was the last. Then the clever-clever moderns swarmed on to the stage, and we lost the message.

'I could have given it back to them. I could have revived it. But I heard another call. It was one morning in early summer – at the edge of the Mer de Glace, just below Mont Blanc. I stood looking out over that vast dazzling sea of ice, and a voice asked me: Which will you be? Choose. And I said: Help me to choose. And the voice asked: Do you want love? And I said: Not at the price of service. And the voice asked: Do you want wealth? And I said: Not at the price of love. And the voice asked: Do you want fame? And I said: Not at the price of truth. And then there was a long silence. And I waited, knowing that it would speak again. And at last the voice said: Good, my son. Now I know what to give you –

'You have everything before you. Christopher. Love hasn't come to you, yet. But it will. It comes to all of us. And it only comes once. Make no mistake about that. It comes and it goes. A man must make himself ready for it; and he must know when it comes. Some are unworthy. They degrade themselves and are unfit to receive it. Some hold back from receiving it – call it pride, call it fear – fear of one's own good fortune – who shall judge? Be ready for the moment. Christopher. Be ready –'

One morning, when Mr Lancaster had started out for the office, I saw that the writing desk he usually kept locked was standing open. As he had left the key, with his key bunch attached to it, sticking in the keyhole, I guessed he would soon discover his mistake and come back. So my investigations had to be quick.

The first thing I found was an army service revolver, evidently another of Mr Lancaster's sentimental war souvenirs. This couldn't have interested me less; I felt certain the desk must contain some worthier secrets. I leafed through old paid bills and obsolete railway timetables; handled bits of wire, blackened light bulbs, broken picture frames, rusty parts of some small engine, perished rubber bands. It was as if Mr Lancaster had sternly bundled up all that was untidy in his character and stowed it away here out of sight.

However, in the top drawer – the most prominent and there-fore, least likely place, I had thought, which was why I looked there last – I found a thick notebook with a shiny black cover. I was thrilled to see that it was full of poetry in Mr Lancaster's handwriting; a long, narrative poem, apparently. I could do no more than hastily skim through it – lots of nature, of course – mountains, seas, stars, boyhood rambles and ruminations in the manner of Wordsworth – and God – lots and lots of God – and travel – and the war – oh dear, yes, the war – and more travel – hm – hm – hm – aha, what was this? Now we were getting somewhere at last!

> *And there was One –*
> *Long, long, ago – dear God, how very long –*
> *Who, when the lilac breathed in breathless bloom*
> *And later buds their secrets still withheld*

*Yet promised to reveal, as soon they must,*
*Since it was so ordained – as evening came*
*She too was there, her presence felt ere seen*
*By him who watched for it. She never knew*
*What meaning filled the twilight with her step,*
*What emptiness, for him, the twilight brought*
*When, soon, she came no more – the ways of Life*
*Leading her elsewhere. And she never knew,*
*Going her ways about the world, what deed,*
*Unknowing, she had done; into what heart*
*She had brought beauty and left bitter pain.*

I can't remember how the lines struck me then, because I regarded them simply and solely as a find. My treasure hunt was successful. I was triumphant. Seizing pencil and paper, I scribbled them down, thinking only of how I would read them aloud to my friends when I got back to London.

I had barely finished my copying when I realized that Mr Lancaster had re-entered the flat. He had made far less noise than usual. There was no time to cover up the traces of my search. All I could do – and I think it showed great presence of mind – was to drop the notebook into the drawer and take out the revolver. It was at least less embarrassing, I thought, to be caught examining a revolver than an autobiographical poem.

'Put that down!' Mr Lancaster barked hoarsely.

He had never used that tone to me before; it startled and enraged me. 'It isn't loaded,' I said. 'And, anyhow, I'm not a child.' I put the revolver back in the drawer and walked straight out of the room.

(Looking back, I now reinterpret Mr Lancaster's behaviour. I see how his conversation was full of attempts to arouse my interest in him. Didn't he expect, for example, that I'd ask him what it was that that voice on the Mont Blanc glacier had finally given him? Hadn't he even hoped that I'd beg him to tell me about his love life? And wasn't the leaving of the key in his desk a deliberate, if subconscious, attempt to make me read his poem? If I'm right –

and I think I am – then my cruelty to Mr Lancaster was in my lack of curiosity. My would-be scientific study of him was altogether unscientific, because I was sure in advance of what I was going to find – which no scientist should be. I was sure he was a bore.

So, when Mr Lancaster came in and found me looking at the revolver instead of the notebook, he must have been bitterly disappointed; even if he couldn't have explained to himself why. Hence his outburst of temper.

As for the revolver, maybe he had almost forgotten its existence. And maybe it was actually I who reminded him that it was lying there, all the time, in the bottom drawer, a gross metallic fact in the midst of his world of fantasy.)

Two days before I was due to return to England, Mr Lancaster took me sailing. He didn't ask me if I wanted to do this; he simply announced his plan and I accepted it. I didn't really care what happened, now. Since the incident of the revolver, our relations were chilly. I was merely counting the hours till I could leave.

We left after the office closed that evening, in his car, to drive out to the village on the river where he kept his boat. On the way, we picked up Sr Machado. I was glad to have him with us, for I didn't want to spend any more time alone with Mr Lancaster. Much later, it occurred to me that Machado was probably the only one of Mr Lancaster's acquaintances left who would agree to come with him on a trip of this kind. No doubt many of them had tried it – once.

The three of us were squeezed into the front seat of Mr Lancaster's little car, with the outboard engine, under its tarpaulin cover, sitting up in the back. Quite soon we lost our way. Mr Lancaster, who had forgotten to bring the map, became increasingly jittery as we bumped along a narrow sand road in the twilight, skirting a marsh. Old farmhouses stood half awash amidst water meadows. A crane walked stiffly along the wall of the dike and went flapping away over the lush, wet landscape. I felt a dreamy, romantic contentment steal over me. What did it matter where we were? Why be anywhere in particular? But Mr Lancaster was frantic.

Just as it began to get really dark, two figures appeared out on the marsh in a punt. Mr Lancaster stopped the car, ran up on to the dike and hailed them. They were very small and towheaded, a boy and a girl. It was almost incredible that they could manage the punt at all, and this made them seem more like very intelligent animals than terribly stupid children. They stood hand in hand in the punt, staring up at Mr Lancaster with their big, vacant blue eyes, their mouths open, as if they expected he was going to feed them. Mr Lancaster addressed them – as he told me later – in High and Low German. He spoke as one speaks to idiots, so slowly and with such elaborate pantomime that even I could understand what he said. But not those children. They just stared and stared. Mr Lancaster began to shout and wave his arms but they didn't flinch. They were too stupid to be afraid of him. At last he gave it up in despair, turned the car around and drove back the way we had come.

Very late at night we finally arrived at our destination. The place was crowded with holiday-makers, and only one room was vacant at the inn. It must have been one of the best rooms, however, for it had an imposing bed on a dais, as well as a studio couch. The chief decoration was a photogravure of an almost nude woman in an 'artistic' pose; this stood on an easel with a piece of figured material like tapestry draped around it. Mr Lancaster decided that he would sleep on the couch and Sr Machado on the bed. I was to go back to the cabin of Mr Lancaster's boat. 'It'll be an experience for me,' I said sarcastically, before he could say it. But Mr Lancaster was deaf to sarcasm.

I woke in the early but already brilliant morning, and found myself undecided whether to romanticize my situation or sulk. My situation was romantic, I had to admit. Here I was, all alone in this foreign land, in sole occupancy of a sailing boat! No doubt these people were watching me and wondering about me. Although it was barely six o'clock, most of the holiday-makers seemed to be up.

The village was built along the riverbank, with beer gardens running down to the water's edge. The boats were decorated with sprays of poplar at their mastheads; and schoolboys had fastened them to the handle bars of their bikes. On board the boats there were gramophones, and people were playing concertinas and singing. Beer was being drunk and sausages munched, and you could smell the delicious smell of out-of-door coffee. The girls were plump and pretty; the men were cropped blond and piggy-pink. As they sang they shaved or combed their hair, and were temporarily silenced as they brushed their teeth in the river.

All this filled me with joy. But on the debit side of the day there was my stiffness from sleeping curled up on the tiny bunk in the cabin, plus a headache. And there was Mr Lancaster, who now appeared and was cross because I hadn't tidied the cabin or finished dressing; I was, in fact, sprawling on the deck in the sun. By the time we had had breakfast at the inn and I had become constipated – my usual reaction to having to use strange lavatories and being told to hurry – the sulks were on.

And then the engine was mounted on the boat, but it wouldn't start. A mechanic had to be fetched from the garage; while he was working, quite a large crowd gathered. All that Mr Lancaster could contribute was his fussing and nagging. Nevertheless, he made the occasion a text for one of his reminiscent sermons: 'This reminds me of the war. I remember getting out of a village near Loos just before dawn, because we knew the Hun would start shelling as soon as it got light. I was curious to see how I would stand the strain, because our colonel obviously had the wind up. So I took my pulse. It was *absolutely* normal. I found my brain was functioning so well that, as I was giving orders to my sergeant-major, I visualized a chess problem I'd read in *The Times* a few days before. It was black to play and mate in three moves, and I *saw* the solution, Christopher. I didn't have to think about it at all. I simply looked at it, as you look at the map of a town and say to yourself: "Well, quite obviously, *that's* the quickest way to the market square." There couldn't be any question. And I have no doubt whatsoever that I could have played at least half a dozen games simultaneously at that moment, and won all of them. What is it Sophocles says about the greatness of man when his mind rises to its highest in the face of fate –?' And he was off again into a long, straggling string of Greek. How right Hugh Weston was in saying that it is the most hideous of all languages!

At last we were off, heading towards the sea. Mr Lancaster snapped at me because I dropped some of his fishing gear. I scowled back at him. To snub me and show me my place he then concentrated on Machado, talking to him in Spanish. This was nothing but a relief, as far as I was concerned; but it worried Machado, whose courtly Latin manners demanded that he should communicate with me, now that he was aware of my existence. (I'm sure he simply did not remember we had sat next to each other at that dinner.) So he spoke to me from time to time In French, which I had great difficulty in understanding because of his fearful accent. The worst of Machado's remarks was that they were not only hard to understand but harder still to develop into any kind of conversation. For example, he said: '*Je suppose que le sujet le plus intéressant pour un écrivain, c'est la prostitution.*' To which I could only reply enthusiastically: '*Monsieur, vous avez parfaitement raison.*' And there we stuck.

We were in the estuary now; the river was already very wide. Mr Lancaster ordered me to steer the boat while he got the fishing rods ready for action. 'You've got to be on the alert from the first moment,' he told me. 'This river's full of sand bars. Careful. Careful! CAREFUL! Look at the colour of the water ahead! Dead slow through here! Steady, now! Steady. Steady. Steady. Steady. *Now* – open her up! OPEN! Quick, man! Port! HARD to port! Do you want to swamp us?' (There was a very mild swell as we left the river mouth; you could hardly even feel the change of motion.) 'Away, now. Dead ahead! Hold her two degrees sou'west of the point. Hold her in her course. HOLD HER! Careful, man! Good. *Good*! Oh, good man! *Very* pretty! Well steered, sir! I'm greatly afraid, Christopher, that we're going to make a sailor out of you yet!'

I had done nothing to be praised for, except that I hadn't run us into a buoy as big as a haystack. Mr Lancaster's enthusiasm was as crazy as his anxiety. Yet once again – as in the case of the cold bath – I was idiotically flattered. Ah, if he had realized how easily manageable I was; how instantly I responded to the crudest compliment! No – even if he had realized it, this would have made no difference in his treatment of me. Flattery was something Mr Lancaster would never have bestowed upon me; he would have regarded it as bad for my soul.

I suppose he felt no responsibility for Machado's soul. For he began to butter him up in a manner that was absolutely shameless, speaking French, now, for my benefit. He called Machado a 'good sport', using the English words and then explaining them in French, until Machado understood and clapped his hands with delight: 'Good spot! I – good spot? Oh, yes!'

'Isn't he a dear old man?' said Mr Lancaster to me, benevolently. 'He's three quarters Peruvian Indian, you know. His father probably chewed coca and never wore shoes. That's your real unspoiled dago for you. Doesn't matter what age he is – he always stays a child.'

We were now quite far out on the flat shallow sea; the low shore of dunes was already only a pale line between the sparkle of the water and the shine of the sky. White sails were curving all over the seascape. Mr Lancaster, evidently feeling very pleased with himself, stood in the bows intoning:

> Pervixi: neque enim fortuna malignior unquam
> erepiet nobis quod prior hora dedit.

I knew, with sudden intense force, just how awful the Odyssey and the voyage of the *Pequod* must have been, and that I would have sooner or later jumped overboard rather than listen to either of those ghastly sea bores, Ulysses and Ahab.

Presently Mr Lancaster announced that it was time for us to fish. Machado and I were given the rods. We trailed our lines inexpertly in the water. This might have been quite restful, if heaven hadn't rebuked my laziness by performing a most tire-

some miracle – nothing less than a miraculous draught. We ran
into a school of mackerel!

Mr Lancaster was absolutely beside himself. 'Careful! CARE-
FUL, MAN! Easy – easy – easy! Don't let the line slack! You'll lose
him! Play him, man! Keep playing him! Fight him! He's a wily
devil! He'll trick you yet! Don't look at *me*, man! Watch him!
WATCH HIM! keep your head! Keep calm! NOW –'

All of this was more superfluous than words can tell, for, in fact,
there was nothing – absolutely nothing – we could have done to
avoid catching those miserable fish – short of throwing the rods
away and lying down in the bottom of the boat. Machado wasn't
speaking French now, or even Spanish. He emitted what sounded
like tribal hunting sounds, maybe in some Indian dialect of the
Andes. At first I caught some of their excitement and yanked the
fish in as fast as I could. Then I began to get tired. Then rather
disgusted. It was so indecently easy. By the time we were
through, I think we had at least thirty fish in the boat.

After the catch Mr Lancaster set himself to clean some of the fish
we were to eat, so he didn't pay much attention to Machado. I was
steering. Happening to glance over in the old man's direction, I
saw that he was leaning right over the side. His back was tense
and his legs were stiffly straddled. My first thought was that he
was having a stroke. But no – he was pulling desperately at
something in the water. He looked as if he were trying to haul up
the bottom of the sea. He turned his head toward me, half
strangling with the exertion. '*Poisson!*' he gurgled, only it sounded
more like 'possum!'

Naturally, I jumped to my feet to help him. What was my
amazement – and subsequent fury – when I received a violent
backhander in the chest from Mr Lancaster! He knocked me right
over backwards, and I sat down very hard. I think if I'd had a knife
I'd have whipped it out right then and there, and finished him. As
it was, I merely mentally shouted: 'Touch me again, you old goat,
and I'll throttle you!' Mr Lancaster, meanwhile, was yelling in my
face: 'Leave him alone, you silly little fool!' I suppose he saw the
blazing hate in my eyes, for he added, somewhat less hysterically,

'*Never* help a man when he's landing a fish! NEVER! Don't you even know *that*?'

He turned from me to attend to Machado, who was heaving in his line. Mr Lancaster knelt beside him, speaking to him in French, soothing him, urging him, entreating him, imploring him to breathe deeply, to relax, to keep up the pressure, gentle and slow. '*Ça va mieux, n'est-ce pas? Ça marche? Mais naturellement* –' He was absurdly like a midwife encouraging a woman in labour. And sure enough, slowly, slowly, with infinite pain, Machado was delivered of an enormous fish – a tuna, Mr Lancaster said. When he had gaffed it we let it trail in the water behind the boat, to keep it fresh.

Then Mr Lancaster cooked the mackerel on a spirit stove. I would have liked to be strong-minded and refuse to eat. But I was ragingly hungry. And although Mr Lancaster, with his usual incompetence, had burned the fish badly, it smelled and tasted delicious. Besides, I was in an awkward position because I couldn't possibly be nasty to Machado, who was in a state of utter triumph and had to be congratulated repeatedly. Quite probably, this would be the last really happy day of his life. I compromised by ignoring Mr Lancaster. He didn't appear to notice this.

In this mood, we started for home. Mr Lancaster kept remarking complacently on his own foresight; he had calculated our timetable so that we were going with the tide both ways. But the long, chugging voyage seemed tedious enough, even so. As we got into the river mouth, I was steering again and Mr Lancaster was nagging at me. We must have been off course, but how was I to know? It was no use trying to follow his pseudonautical directions. I just went ahead by sight.

Suddenly he screamed: 'SAND! SAND AHEAD! PUT HER ABOUT! HARD! HARD OVER!'

What happened next was quite unplanned. At least, I had no conscious knowledge of what I was going to do. Nevertheless, I did it. I had the feel of the tiller by this time; I could sense pretty well how much it would stand. All I did was to obey Mr Lancaster's order just the merest shade too energetically. I swung the tiller hard over – very hard. And with the most exquisitely satisfactory, rending crack, the crosspiece to which the outboard engine was clamped broke off, and the engine fell into the water.

I looked up at Mr Lancaster and I nearly grinned.

For a moment I thought he would swallow his Adam's apple. 'You fool!' he screamed. 'You fool! You confounded little idiot!' He stepped over to me, making the boat rock. But I wasn't in the least scared now. I knew he wouldn't – couldn't – hit me. And he didn't.

As a matter of fact, the water was so shallow that we didn't have much trouble in dragging up the engine. But of course there was no question of getting it started again; it needed to be thoroughly cleaned first. So there was nothing for it but to sail back to the village.

The sail lasted all the rest of the day. There was very little wind, and Mr Lancaster seemed to be making the worst possible use of it, for nearly every boat on the river passed us. He steered, glumly. Machado was peacefully asleep after his exertions. Finally we were taken in tow by a pleasure steamer. Mr Lancaster had to accept this courtesy because it was beginning to get dark, but I could see how it humiliated him. A man and a woman, neither of them slender or young, were sitting in the stern of the steamer, invisible to the other passengers but right in front of us. Throughout the trip they made love with abandon. And this, too, was a sort of humiliation for Mr Lancaster, because the lovers evidently felt that his reactions weren't worth bothering about. I felt that I was on the side of the lovers, and smiled at them approvingly; but they weren't bothering about my reactions, either.

As for myself, I was in a wonderful mood. The semi-deliberate ditching of the outboard engine had discharged all my aggression, like a great orgasm. Now I no longer felt the least resentment against Mr Lancaster. Indeed, I had stopped thinking about him. My thoughts had gone racing on ahead of my life, of me on this sailing boat; they had left Mr Lancaster and Germany far behind. They were back in London, in my room, at my desk. But I wasn't even unduly impatient to return there physically, for, meanwhile,

I had plenty to think about. After all – despite Mr Lancaster – this silly day would be memorable to me throughout my life. For, right in the midst of it – maybe at the very instant when that engine had splashed into the water – I had had a visitation. A voice had said: 'The two women – the ghosts of the living and the ghosts of the dead – the Memorial.' And, in a flash, I had seen it all – the pieces had moved into place – the composition was instantaneously *there*. Dimly, but with intense excitement, I recognized the outline of a new novel.

The day came for my return to England. The *Coriolanus* was sailing in the evening.

That morning Mr Lancaster informed me, with his usual nonchalance, that Waldemar was to take me to the art gallery. Waldemar and I were to have lunch together – since Mr Lancaster had a business appointment – and I was to be back at the flat at four fifteen precisely. I made no comment.

But, as soon as Waldemar and I were alone on the gallery steps and Mr Lancaster had disappeared around the corner, I turned to him and firmly shook my head. '*Nein*,' I said.

Waldemar looked puzzled. Pointing to the gallery entrance, he asked: '*Nein?*'

'*Nein*,' I repeated, smiling. Then I pantomimed a breast stroke.

Waldemar's face brightened instantly. '*Ach – schwimmen! Sie wollen, dass wir schwimmen gehen?*'

'*Ja*,' I nodded. '*Swimmen.*'

Waldemar beamed at me. I had never seen him smile like that before. It changed his whole face. He no longer looked at all angelic.

He took me to a big municipal open-air pool. I had passed this place several times, but with my almost utter lack of German, had never had the nerve to go in there alone. Waldemar didn't seem passive now. He bought our tickets, got me my towel and soap, greeted numerous friends, steered me into the locker room, made me take a shower and showed me how to tie on one of the triangular red bathing slips he had rented. When he undressed, it was as if he took off his entire office personality. It was astonishing how he had managed to disguise his physically mature, animally relaxed brown body in that prim office suit. He no longer behaved to me as if I were forty years old and in league with Mr Lancaster. We smiled at each other tentatively, then started to wrestle, splashed and ducked each other, swam races. But though we were playing like kids, I was chiefly aware of the fact that he was already a young man.

Presently we were joined by a friend, a boy of his own age named Oskar. Oskar was monkey-faced, impudent, dark and grinning. He spoke fairly fluent English. He was a page, he told me, in one of the large hotels. And I was aware of the page mentality in him; he had been around, he knew the score, and he looked at me speculatively, like one of his hotel guests who might have special requirements he could satisfy in exchange for a tip. He had giggly asides with Waldemar and I knew they were discussing me; but I didn't mind, because Oskar took great trouble to make me feel one of the party.

After swimming, we went to a restaurant for lunch. Both the boys smoked and drank beer. I had the impression that Waldemar was anxious to appear as sophisticated as his friend. By this time, we were calling each other Oskar and Christoph.

Waldemar said something to Oskar and they both roared with laughter.

'What's the joke?' I asked.

'Walli says he thinks his bride will like you,' Oskar told me.

'Well – good. Is she coming here?'

'We go to see her. Soon. All right?'

'All right.'

'All right!' Waldemar laughed very heartily. He was slightly drunk. He reached across the table and shook my hand hard. Oskar explained: 'Walli's bride likes also older gentlemen. Not too old. You – very good! Pretty boy!'

I blushed. A most delicious gradual apprehension began to creep over me.

'You have five marks?'

'Yes.' I produced them.

This amused the boys. 'No, no – for later.'

'But, Oskar –' I felt we were somehow at cross-purposes – 'if she's Walli's bride – and, anyhow, isn't he much too young to have a bride?'

'Already at twelve I have a bride. Walli also.'

'But – won't he be jealous if I –?'

More laughter. Oskar told me: 'We shall not leave you alone with her.' I must have looked more and more bewildered, for he patted my hand reassuringly. 'You need not be shy, Christoph. First, you watch us. Then you see how easy it is.' He translated his joke to Waldemar and they laughed till the tears ran down their faces.

*Braut* in dictionary German means a bride or fiancée. But boys like Oskar and Waldemar used it to refer to any girl they happened to be going with. This, my first lesson in the language, I learned during the unforgettable, happy, shameless afternoon – an afternoon of closed Venetian blinds, of gramophone music and the slippery sounds of nakedness, of Turkish cigarettes, cushion dust, crude perfume and healthy sweat, of abruptly exploding laughter and wheezing sofa springs.

I didn't return to Mr Lancaster's flat until nearly six o'clock. I was too dazed with pleasure to have cared if he had scolded me; but he didn't. In fact, he appeared to be back in the mood in which he had received me on the day of my arrival. He just didn't seem particularly interested in my existence. 'Give my regards to your mother' was all he said when we parted. I felt hurt by his coldness. However little *I* might care, I was still sincerely surprised when my indifference was returned.

When I got back to London, I found that my novel was indeed a flop. The reviews were even worse than I had expected. My friends loyally closed ranks against the world in its defence, declaring that a masterpiece had been assassinated by the thugs of mediocrity. But I didn't really care. My head was full of my new novel and a crazy new scheme I had of becoming a medical student. And always, in the background, was Berlin. It was calling me every night, and its voice was the harsh sexy voice of the gramophone records I had heard in the bed-sitting room of Waldemar's 'bride'. Sooner or later, I should get there. I was sure of that. Already I had begun to teach myself German, by one of those learn-it-in-three-months methods. While riding on buses, I recited irregular verbs. To me they were like those incantations in *The Arabian Nights* which will make you master of a paradise of pleasures.

\*

I never sent a copy of *All the Conspirators* to Mr Lancaster, of course. But I wrote him a thank-you letter – one of those thankless, heartless documents I had been trained since my childhood to compose. He didn't answer it.

When I tried to describe him to my friends, I found I could make very little of him as a significant or even a farcical character. I just did not have the key to him, it seemed. And when I read my copy of his poem to Allen Chalmers, we were both rather embarrassed. It simply wasn't bad enough in the right way. Chalmers had to be polite and pretend that it was much more ridiculous than it actually was.

I also touched on the subject of Mr Lancaster's love life in talking to my mother. She smiled vaguely and murmured, 'Oh, I hardly think *that* was the trouble.' I then learned from her what she hadn't thought even worth telling me before – that Mr Lancaster had actually been married for a few months, after the war, but that his wife left him and they had separated legally. 'Because,' said my mother dryly, 'Cousin Alexander wasn't – so one was given to understand – at all adequate as a husband.' This revelation of Mr Lancaster's impotence quite shocked me. Not on his account – it was pretty much what I would have expected – but on my mother's. I never fail to be shocked by the ability of even the most ladylike ladies to live in cozy matter-of-fact intimacy with the facts of nature. My mother was surprised and rather pleased by my reaction. She was aware that she had managed for once to say something 'modern', though she couldn't altogether understand how she had done it.

I suppose I should have forgotten all about Mr Lancaster if he hadn't regained my interest in the most dramatic way possible. Toward the end of November that same year he shot himself.

The news came in a letter from Mr Lancaster's assistant manager, the 'second in command' who had lent me his dinner jacket for the banquet. I had met him briefly after that at the office and thanked him. I remembered him only as a florid little Yorkshireman with a broad accent and a capable, good-natured manner.

The letter informed us of the bare facts in a tidy, businesslike style. Mr Lancaster had shot himself one evening at his flat, but the body had not been discovered until next day. No suicide note had been found, nor any papers 'of a personal nature'. (He must have burned the notebook with his poem, I supposed.) He had not been unwell at the time. He was in no financial difficulties, and the affairs of the company were giving him no cause for anxiety. The assistant manager concluded with a line of formal condolence with us on our 'great loss'. No doubt he mistook us for blood relatives, or felt that we had anyhow to represent the family, since there was nobody else to do it.

Mr Lancaster's act impressed me a great deal. I strongly approved of suicide on principle, because I thought of it as an act of protest against society. I wanted to make a saga around Mr Lancaster's protest. I wanted to turn him into a romantic figure. But I couldn't. I didn't know how.

The next year I did at last go to Berlin, having thrown up my medical career before it was properly started. And there, some while later, I ran into Waldemar. He had grown bored with his native city and had come to Berlin to seek his fortune.

Waldemar, naturally, knew very little about Mr Lancaster's death. But he told me something which amazed me. He told me that Mr Lancaster had often spoken of me, after I had left, to people in the office. Waldemar had heard him say that I had written a book, that it had been a failure in England because the critics were all fools, but that I should certainly be recognized one day as one of the greatest writers of my time. Also, he had always referred to me as his nephew.

'I believe he was really fond of you,' said Waldemar, sentimentally. 'He never had any sons of his own, did he? Who knows, Christoph, if you'd been there to look after him, he might have been alive today!'

If only things were as uncomplicated as that!

I think I see now that Mr Lancaster's invitation to me was his last attempt to re-establish relations with the outside world. But of course it was already much too late. If my visit had any decisive effect on him, it can only have been to show him what it was that prevented him from having any close contact with anybody. He had lived too long inside his sounding box, listening to his own reverberations, his epic song of himself. He didn't need me. He didn't need any kind of human being; only an imaginary nephew-disciple to play a supporting part in his epic. After my visit he created one.

Then suddenly, I suppose, he ceased to believe in the epic any more. Despair is something horribly simple. And though Mr Lancaster had been so fond of talking about it, he probably found it absolutely unlike anything he had ever imagined. But, in his case, I hope and believe, it was short-lived. Few of us can bear much pain of this kind and remain conscious. Most of the time, thank goodness, we suffer quite stupidly and unreflectingly, like the animals.

# In Praise of Vespasian

**ALFRED CHESTER**

When the telephone rang this morning and a friend said: 'There's very bad news from Barcelona,' I knew at once what it must be, and through the rest of our conversation, and even now as I write, I contain a fixed image of Joaquin. It is a 'still' from him in motion. He is caught, somewhat blurred, in the midst of walking rapidly past a plane tree on the Boulevard St Germain. A summer night, very hot, starless and moist. The green-black leaves of the plane tree are carved in detail by streetlights. Joaquin's short-sleeved white shirt is unbuttoned to the waist and on the ribbed chest a crucifix hangs. His trousers are cut American-style: long in the crotch, baggy, wide at the cuff. His eyes are nervous and alert, the eyes of the hunter and the hunted in one, for he is looking for love. He is viewing the men around him and also those down the street, queuing up at the *pissotière*. In a moment, if my still releases him, he will join the queue. And my heart sinks now just as it did when the image appeared to me during the telephone conversation. I refuse to free him, refuse to unfreeze the picture of him. Why? Because he is dead, and because if the still turns to motion, death will wall Joaquin's young life into its myriad urinals.

Though I liked Joaquin, I was never really easy in his presence; the fibre of him seemed somehow always to be quaking; he was too intense, too fragilely built. Also his way of talking irritated me; whatever language he used, he used it with a clattering, tooth-rattling accent, as if he had castanets in place of molars. But he was good-looking, nearly beautiful, and today, thinking of his face, I remember the proud well-shaped bone under it, the pronounced mortality, over which the glowing skin was pulled taut. And those black restless eyes again, so black and so brilliant, for all their fierceness they often made me think of rabbits – not of their eyes but of that quivery-shivery business at their noses. He was already past thirty when I left Paris three years ago, but he looked much younger, as faggots often will, so young in fact that when I asked him how it happened he wasn't afraid of the brutal-looking labourers or the Algerian *voyous* he was constantly picking up – Paris being his sky of love, the *pissoirs* were its stars, and the men he found there its angels: *'Je les arrache des astres, mes anges desastreux'* – he told me that as soon as they reached his hotel room he warned them they must be very cautious, very quiet, as he was a minor, the implication being that he had nothing, they everything, to lose should he scream for the police. (Twice he was put to the test by Arabs who hadn't understood, believed or cared. He was beaten and robbed both times and, if anger and humiliation are interchangeable with unwillingness, raped.)

Joaquin had two passions, and he lived with the hope that through these he would find fulfilment. From men he sought love – not theirs but his own. The male body presented itself to him like a sealed envelope, a grain not yet unhusked; within was that magic word, that nourishment that would call out my friend's love. At least he believed it would. In city upon city, night after night, sometimes man after man, Joaquin ravaged his heart and his body for the sought-after emotion: the envelope was always empty, the grain seemed to have suffered a pestilence. But if one can laugh at and be charmed by the void and the rot – and the stories Joaquin told were often very funny – it means that hope or, more important, energy is springing eternal. So on he went. Love would be found; it *could* be found. And this was not hearsay, for he himself had found it once, when he was seventeen and studying for the priesthood:

'He was a labourer of course – *au moins je reste fidèle à mes gouts* – and he would come downhill past the seminary and over to the road on the right that led down into the city. Every morning.

Six a.m. I used to watch him from the window on the landing
outside my dormitory. He was part or all gypsy, that was easy to
see. But he had such *fine* features and tiny round ears like the
Kikuyu. And gigantically hung to judge by the basket in those
blue denims. All those months that I watched him I thought it was
envy I felt – even with it sticking out in front of me. It's true I
thought so. Envy, but a beautiful warm envy that wasn't corrupt-
ing and was no sin. I envied him his freedom, his dark skin, his
beauty, his ears, that enormous basket. I wanted to *be* him.
Imagine me, *mon lapin*, in blue denims coming down a hill, butch
as can be, and going off to work in a factory or at the harbour! Four
or five months I watched him, and of course we never spoke. I
don't think he ever even noticed me at the window. And then –
Oh, a terrible thing happened. One morning, to my astonishment, I saw one of the younger boys from the seminary run out on
the road when my lover was passing. They talked a minute and
then disappeared laughing into the orange grove across from the
church. *Là, oh là là, quelle déception, imagines-toi!* It's possible it was
altogether innocent – maybe they were cousins or something.
Though we were all rich boys at the seminary, a lot of us had poor
relatives – why not a gypsy cousin? But I didn't speculate then. I
knew they were strangers, and I was cut to pieces with jealousy,
absolutely shredded. And this wasn't the worst. The worst was
that, without understanding or imagining what could be passing
between them in the orchard, I felt that something truly odd was
happening, and I was revolted. I was too sickened ever to go near
the window again, and for weeks afterwards when I'd pass that
boy in the halls I'd have to turn my face away. He nauseated me.'

It took Joaquin a year before he could understand and imagine.
Comprehension came only when he himself went into the orange
grove with a travelling salesman, a Belgian who sold vestments
and church supplies. The hour in the orchard was followed by a
month in the infirmary where he lay dizzy with the fright and awe
of remembered ecstasy and bent double with the first attack of that
mysterious ailment which nailed pain more-or-less permanently
to his innards and finally killed him last week. Also he prayed,

fasted, wept and longed for death – not to end his sin nor punish his guilt, but that he might have good reason to call a priest to his bedside for confession. It seemed to Joaquin, as he lay there, that his whole past had been one of passionate, orgiastic desire operating behind his blindness. It suddenly seemed to him that every man he had ever known – father, brother, uncles, friends, shopkeepers, soldiers, priests – all had struck an unrecognizable but violent flame in his blood. He had wanted every single man he had ever laid eyes on, never mind how old or fat or ugly. It seemed to him he had desired without pause, had run his eighteen years ragged in a bedevilled foray, in wildest pursuit, and he'd never even been aware of it. So he lay, appalled by the invisible salaciousness of the distant past and giddy with delight of the recent past, and in addition heartsick that he had not known enough to run out on the road to meet the gypsy the year before. Simultaneously, his sense of sin – like a caryatid propping up the future – drove not only anguish and agony into his soul and his intestines, but made him wonder more practically what, under the circumstances, he was to do. Could a priest vow away lust for men as he vowed away lust for women? This was something else altogether, like vowing away not merely sight or hearing, but also a blind eye, a deaf ear. Finally, while still in the infirmary, he had a dream which pointed the way:

'I was in a sacristy with the Belgian and I think he was trying to make me buy one of those vestments he sold. Anyway, he kept pulling them out of a little suitcase on the floor. I was simply dying to try one on, but I knew that for some reason I mustn't show any interest. Then, unexpectedly, out came a robe so exquisite, I couldn't resist. I was all golden, shot through with red and silver, marvellous for my colouring. I reached for it, *mais ce vilain garçon*, pushed me away and put the robe on himself. Of course I became furious, and we both started shouting, and it seemed very natural that we should fall to our knees opposite each other, each of us with a great sword growing out from between his legs, and that these swords should begin duelling of themselves. While this battle was going on, I happened to look at his face and, to my

horror, it wasn't the Belgian at all, but the gypsy. Oh, what a
mistake! *Comme il était adorable, ma cocotte*, and I knew he was naked
underneath the robe. I began trembling with excitement, and my
lips hurt so much I thought they would fall off. My arms rose and
opened to him, but he didn't notice; he was that busy watching the
swords. How could I get past those blades and take the gypsy in my
arms? What a problem! I jerked my hips, twitched my thighs,
wiggled my ass, moved this way and that, but the swords were
always in my way. And all the time my arms, my poor open arms
were waiting. At last, I knew there was only one thing to do – to
fling myself forward, though this must surely mean we'd die. I
hesitated, and before I had the courage I woke up.'

He woke from the dream to a nostalgia and a sorrow for himself
or rather for the figure with open arms who, blind and witless,
had blindly and witlessly longed to hold so many men. So when
the pain in his intestines receded, his loyalty to the open-armed
figure was greater than his loyalty to himself, and knowing
confession would be hypocritical, he withdrew from the seminary
and returned to his home in Barcelona. But from here too he was
soon forced to withdraw, for his factory-owning family could not
have been expecting to be told the truth when they asked Joaquin
why he had returned. They made plans to send him to a
monastery, to get him a post with the army, to put him in school in
Madrid, to ship him hither or send him thither. But Joaquin did
not wait. He sold his jewellery – watches, rings, cuff-links (a taste
his mother had always indulged) – and took a bus north to
Figueras and from there went by foot to the French frontier which
he crossed without difficulty at night. His original goal was
Holland, for the Belgian salesman had told him that in Amsterdam all the men were beautiful and queer. Joaquin did not want all
the men or even many of them; but among them perhaps would
be one like the gypsy – and this one he wanted. It took him nearly
six years to reach Amsterdam, and by that time he was a French
citizen, for the Dutch route led through Paris, and by Paris was he
overcome.

He arrived there within a week of quitting Barcelona, and within a month he had a number of acquaintances who advised him to ask the government for political asylum – something he would not have thought of by himself, since his family and schools had never indicated that Franco was someone to run away from. As this was soon after the Second World War, Joaquin had little trouble acquiring refugee status and, in 1951, he was granted citizenship. It was during his first year in Paris that Joaquin's two passions developed. The second one was –

No! I will not lie! I will not tell you of his ambitions nor how he earned his living, for there was no second passion in Joaquin, and if I seek to fabricate one, to accent (more than he did) certain other aspects of his character and life, it is because I wish you not to see him as a faggot. Joaquin was no lisping, gesturing, eye-flashing, tail-wagging queen of the gay bars or the salons. He was no fraud. He was the real thing. And he was never offended if one mistook him for a heterosexual. I would prefer to deal with Joaquin as he dealt with himself, in his diaries for example. Ah, his diaries, that record of his life from the age of fifteen – what has become of them? Probably he took them back to Barcelona and, after his funeral, the factory-owners found them filling up most of one suitcase and, without daring to peer into the books, burnt them. I will quote only from one entry; it concerns the day he went into the orange grove with the Belgian, and Joaquin writes in ecstatic detail of falling to the ground with the man, of the acute perfume of the orange leaf, of the astonishment and shock of his first kisses – and then there is a sudden break in the writing. The boy hesitates to put down the truth and is humiliated by this hesit-ation. Then, to punish himself – not for the truth, mind you, but for the hesitation – he writes as penance across each line, down the whole length of three pages: 'He buggered me. He buggered me. He buggered me.'

So I am writing this because for me there is nothing left of Joaquin but the image of him on the Boulevard St Germain, and I want to honour and fulfil him. I have kept him frozen in the still since, as I said, should I allow him to move, he will move down the street and into the *pissotière* which is all right with a full life ahead of him. But now that he is dead, I forbid him his urinals, for I imagine there are better, worthier, nobler, holier things to do. Like what, for instance? Oh, like anything, I suppose. After all, democracy dignifies almost everything. There are monuments, murals, songs, books, poems, great statues of marble and bronze to ennoble the roles we play and give meaning to the triviality, the absurdity of our democratic lives. The factory worker, the movie star, the housewife, the cancer victim, the bum, the whore, the postman, even the queen pederast and the paralysed child can render up his last breath with a sigh of fulfilment; *what* he was has already been set on a pedestal. But Joaquin? For Joaquin these words must be his pedestal. And make no mistake, I am not begging love off you. First of all, another's love was never something he really hungered for – only his own, much more hardly obtained. And secondly, fulfilment as we know it comes to a man through an Idea of Man, and as I seek to fulfil Joaquin I must make an abstraction of him. And who can love an Idea of Man? In spite of all the eternal flames, nobody loves the Unknown Soldier. We can only love known soldiers. We may honour that anonymously he caught a bullet at the Marne and perhaps saved us from doing likewise at the Mississippi; we honour the Idea, and a man may therein be fulfilled. It has nothing to do with love, not even when Eros himself is the Unknown Soldier.

Then, move, Joaquin! Break from the shadow of the plane tree and whirl your eyes across the masses of love everywhere along the boulevard – on the street, on café terraces, on the line outside the circular triptych where hope and water run.

Joaquin moves with the long reckless stride of his skinny legs, and he goes up the street hastily, joins the queue at the *pissotière*. A half-dozen men are ahead of him, awaiting their turn; they are uninteresting even in the soft of the summer Paris night – a couple of businessmen, an Algerian peanut vendor, a rather dapper young Parisian, a long American very elegant in Levis but with too much movement at the pelvis and a face lovely though composed of merely recollected lust and dead eyes, like a Hollywood leading lady *en chasse*. Joaquin is disheartened, for these obviously will be the men he must meet inside. A moment of indecision and reflection. He is about to leave when unexpected magnificence is disgorged from the mouth of the *pissoir*. The rumour of a military band starts up in Joaquin's heart, and the music of anticipated love knocks through his veins. Behold a massive young Arab of delicate, arrogant beauty, with the ears of the Kikuyu and curly black oil-soaked hair. Joaquin's tongue trembles remembering the taste of the new olive, and his cheeks grow hot for knowing they will be pressed against that moist Mohammedan head. The relaxed young Arab strolls past Joaquin, catches his gaze, smiles but hardly smiles, strolls on.

Overcome by this recognition, it is several seconds before Joaquin recovers himself enough to dash from the line and make off in pursuit. He walks rapidly north on the Boulevard St Germain, pushing through the lazy evening crowds, and in a moment nears the Algerian who, sensing Joaquin, turns, smiles, *really* smiles and breaks wide the night with unbelievably good teeth and the soft movement of soft thick lips – and then he turns away and hurries along the boulevard. Joaquin follows more swiftly; the Arab smiles back and walks on more quickly still. Since this is a reversal of the usual procedure – for in general when an Algerian is engaged it is he who pursues, inexorably, and coyness is unthinkable – our hero pauses in his chase, wondering if he is being discouraged rather than teased. But when Joaquin stops, so too does the young Arab and gives a quick upward shake to his head. With a burst of speed Joaquin rushes forward, almost reaches his goal when the other rushes away, shoving pedestrians aside and laughing aloud. Puzzled by this game, Joaquin tries a new tempo: he slows to a stroll. So too does the Algerian. Thus, separated by ten yards, they begin a walk that takes them clear across Paris to the Place Blanche.

And the Arab has not chosen the shortest route, for once across the Seine he decides to amble (Joaquin's pace permitting) up the Champs-Elysées to the Etoile. He likes to look in shop windows, and to examine café terraces, and to study the passing automobiles, and to admire the elegant ladies, and to make sure that Joaquin is not too close, nor too quick, nor too discouraged. But Joaquin is not at all discouraged; he does not understand the game but he loves it, and he now knows the rules. When the Algerian stops to look at the world, Joaquin stops and looks at the Algerian; they both look and examine and admire. And in our hero's heart there is no mere rumour of a military band but all the brass and drums of it. *This*, this surely is love, and off the lovers go, north from the Etoile, up the Avenue Kléber, out of the Place de Ternes with its brilliant cafés into the hush and stillness of the Boulevard de Courcelles. And then the rules of the game seem about to change.

The Algerian slips into an empty *pissoir* outside the Parc Monceau. Aflush with joy Joaquin hastens after and in the glow from the moon-shaped light overhead he sees his beloved urinating calmly and tranquilly smiling. Our hero stands beside him, longs but hesitates to speak: this love affair is so embedded in silence that the exchange of a word threatens to alter the depth of it. So instead, Joaquin's hand gropes out uncertainly, reaches – but to nothing. For, still leaking, the Algerian bursts into happy laughter and flies past Joaquin out to the street, buttoning himself on the run. Because his hand is forward and still upon nothing, our hero suffers a moment of weariness and woe. But only a moment.

The lovers continue their promenade – up the Courcelles and up the Batignolles, to the first exciting glow of Montmartre night life. Joaquin's legs have grown tired, for he is not as strong as the Algerian who, it appears, is still so full of energy he might easily do another turn around Paris. But no: Eros is kind, even if long-winded. They have reached their final avenue, the Boulevard de Clichy, and it is mobbed and raucous and aflame with colour and carnival. Joaquin, however, notices nothing except his lover who, as they approach the Place Pigalle, is entering yet another *pissotière*. Our hero's patience is tested further, for the *tasse* is filled and the queue lengthy. Joaquin submits to the waiting, and the line moves slowly because only two places are free: the Algerian refuses to relinquish the third. At last it is Joaquin's turn. He enters, moves in deeply to greet his lover, and as he does so, the Algerian sways forward, opens, unfolds his lips. Our hero does not merely kiss them – but with a sigh, a groan, the whole of him falls against them. When the Algerian steps back his lips are shut tight, for he knows he holds Joaquin's soul in his mouth, and he has no intention of releasing it. Immediately, he raises his hand and rubs thumb against forefinger to indicate that he will accept money in exchange for love.

Joaquin, without a soul and with the smell of oil in his nostrils and the taste of the Arab on his tongue, is in despair. Not because his lover is a whore but because he has perhaps fifty francs in his pocket. Frenzied and miserable, he reaches down and tears his pockets out wide; two or three coins fall through the grating at his feet and into the sink of the urinal.

The noise attracts attention from the queue outside, but Joaquin doesn't care. He cries out to his lover with exasperation: 'I have nothing, nothing, but I love you! I love you!'

'Be quiet, little fool!' the Algerian whispers nervously.

'No, I won't be. I'll – '

'All right, let's go.' He is evidently annoyed but he follows the elated Joaquin out of the *pissotière*. On the street he grumbles a bit about money but his irritation vanishes when our hero rubs against him and reminds him of the goodness of love. Soon they are hurrying once more, but this time side by side to seek out goodness in the Arab's room in a hotel near the Place Blanche. We leave them now, that they may make much ecstasy and many joys, and later fall asleep in one another's arms.

But before dawn, Joaquin wakes. The air is grey and smells of cold lamb; his feet ache; the oil is rancid on his tongue; the delicate face next to him is gross with sleep; the military band has long since gone home; his cheek is frozen where it was pressed against the Mohammedan head. And his soul is out of the loving mouth and back in a loveless bosom. Quietly, oh so stealthily and quietly, he slips from the bed, throws on his clothes, runs from the room and down the stairs to the chill, abandoned streets. Alone, and with no distractions, he sets off across Paris, on foot once again, having left his bus money in the sink of the urinal.

It is not always Joaquin's heart that drives him into what the English sensibly call *Conveniences*. Sometimes, quite as acute if not so inspired, a lesser organ insists. (I say lesser, yet perhaps I should say greater, for it was the bowel that killed him and not the heart, though the murderer bowel was born of the heart, as death is inevitably born of life, as love must always create its slayer.) So we find our hero on his first trip to London at the beck of the assassin bowel, going down a dingy flight of steps, putting a penny into a coin-lock, and entering a little badly-lighted wooden booth whose decorated walls strike from the dimness, glorious as the Sistine Chapel, pious as Pompeii, breathless as Lascaux, ideal as Eden. *Honi soit qui mal y pense*, though who could think evil here where it seems a thousand generations of Britons have come to pencil and carve out their dreams. Joaquin feels that through some error or some magic he has found his way into the British Unconscious, and it is one unexpectedly tumultuous with joy, a teeming womb in which all men – drawn to scale – take on the proportions of royal kings. As his reverent eyes follow the graffiti, he notices suddenly that the walls of the Unconscious begin about twenty inches above the ground, and on the floor to his right, in what must evidently be another Unconscious, a black shoe is making a rapid, soundless tapping motion. The ever-alert heart of Joaquin suspects at once that this must be the telepathy of love, and without hesitation he mimics his neighbour, setting up a soundless tap of his own. The English boot, overjoyed or over-come, pauses an instant, then with a certain diffidence, a shy formality moves ever so slowly towards the space under the partition. Joaquin responds to this, and consequently the solid English boot and the frail Parisian sandal begin a series of dances. On either side of the wall, they cautiously minuet, then timidly waltz, then tentatively fox-trot, then anxiously tango, then briefly and frenetically rumba – and the manly boot comes abruptly but gently to rest upon the quivering sandal.

Joaquin hears his toes cry out: 'Tell me, O thou whom my soul loveth, where thou feedest thy flock, where thou makest it to rest at noon: for why should I be as one that is veiled . . .' But, as in all courtships, there exists the problem of how two Unconsciouses are going to become one when a partition separates them, has in fact created them.

A sudden scratching on the wall – and Joaquin's blood rises. He puts his ear against the sculptured crotch of James I, listening, waiting. The scratching ceases. He listens and waits. Silence. But then the boot prods the sandal, and looking down Joaquin sees that a hand has come under the partition – a too white, too fine, too hairy, too naked English hand, and that it wears no glove in his world of walls and shoes outrages our hero's sense of propriety. All love and desire recoil at the sight of the unclothed hand, but curiosity remains, for there is a piece of folded toilet-paper lying on the palm. A love letter? The map of a trysting place? Avoiding contact with the flesh, Joaquin lifts the paper and unfolds it. The message is written in red ink: 'Would you like to blow me? How old are you?'

Joaquin strangles his laughter and throws the paper into the bowl. The English boot has its toe lifted anxiously, the suitor at the mercy of his lady-love, awaiting a reply. The Parisian sandal does not deign to budge. A moment goes by, and another. The anxious boot now seems pensive, and suddenly there is some more, more frantic scratching on the wall. Once again the naked hand slithers under the partition, and this time there is not only a note but also a fountain pen. Joaquin takes the offerings and unfolds the second message: 'Would you like to blow me? How old are you?'

But now Joaquin's laughter cannot be controlled; it bursts spluttering across the Unconscious. He tears a bit of paper from the roll behind him and leaning it on the wall, below a drawing of Edward and Gaveston, he unscrews the fountain pen and writes his reply in red ink: 'I am only four years old and would not like to blow you.' Pen and paper are once more about to be passed under the partition when Joaquin becomes conscious of his own hand. He is repelled by its nudity, its slenderness, its swarthiness, and suggestive swell of its knuckles. To avoid exposure, he slips the square of toilet-paper under the clip of the fountain pen and then passes the pen under the partition, his hand concealed. The offering is snapped away greedily. The note is apparently read. The boot withdraws from the sandal. There is a rustle of clothing. Flush! goes the toilet. The coin-lock clicks and the door bangs open. And away, away, flies Joaquin's first English romance, up the stairs into the crowded city.

From where our hero still sits, he can hear the rumbling tonnage of London street-life; the buses, the pedestrians, the wagons and automobiles. And among it all he believes he can hear the black boots crying down to the sandals with a despair that pierces and grieves him, makes him regret: 'A garden shut up is my sister, my bride; a spring shut up, a fountain sealed.'

Our hero also went to Sodom for a time. I shall not tell you how he came to go there, for this would involve details that distract from his memorial and would be tantamount to carving out beside the Unknown Soldier his marching orders or the Articles of War. Joaquin merely went, as the Soldier went to battle.

Sodom – for those of you who haven't been there – is an island about ten miles in length by about two miles in width. There is no depth to it at all. It was built by men as a memorial to God, for much the same reasons that I am writing this: to praise and fulfil Him because they had heard He was dead and because His work had apparently come to nothing. The great buildings of Sodom are shaped like tombstones, and the island is populated almost entirely by robots. Man created the robots in his own image, and he created the island in the image of a cemetery. Like Man and God, the robots are omnipotent and omniscient – except in four ways: they cannot be anything but robots, they cannot love, they cannot know they are robots, and they cannot know they cannot love. (They can, however, have suspicions, and therefore are they frequently uneasy. To alleviate this, they have invented robot Mechanics who are in six ways inferior to Man and God, and in two ways inferior to other robots: the Mechanics cannot have suspicions and they cannot know they cannot have suspicions. So all the other robots go to them for adjustment, hoping that *their* suspicions will be removed.) Where the robots can eat food, they eat chemicals instead, as one would expect. Where they can live and act, they sit in dark rooms and watch others do it for them. Where they can have faith, they mistrust the honest. Where they can have suspicions, they believe the treacherous. Where they can suffer, they prefer to be tranquil. Where they can laugh, they snicker. Where they can praise, they scorn. Where they can scorn, they worship. Where they can do almost anything but love, they do nearly nothing but hate. And where they can hate, they imagine that they love.

To this unhappy island, then, comes Joaquin. And almost from the moment of disembarkation he senses that all who enter Sodom must abandon love and, worse still, the hope of it. For here only lust is to be found, and Sodom offers it as generously as in other places Nature offers her own green womb: the grasses of lust smother all the treeless streets and avenues, the mosses of lust suffocate the great buildings, the vines of lust overhang the bars, bouquets of lust – or solitary fruits and flowers of it – perfume the hotels, the cinemas, the subways, the restaurants, the shops, the doorways, the windows. But for our hero, love is the only soil from which lust may grow, and with revulsion he disdains the gifts of Sodom.

He disdains them, but he cannot ignore them.

At night, Joaquin cannot sleep, so heavy are his glands, so turbulent his blood. Up in a room on the fifteenth storey, his hand anchored to the crucifix upon his breast, he stares out the window across a length of the dark island toward where the sky flames and fumes above the fiery heart of Sodom. And he stares towards that whorl of crimson sky into which extends the monster building of the island, the tallest tombstone in the world. To Joaquin the building is Satan with his head in the holocaust and his three red mouths that break and chew and his two white eyes spinning slowly round and round in eternal soul-gathering. Despite the mouths and his own revulsion, Joaquin relinquishes his anchor, is hooked by the wheeling white eyes, sails round with them. He

wheels and spins until regardless of the time of night or morning
he can no longer resist: the weight of his glands must yield to the
pull of lust from below.

A tall, thin, tight-lipped, grey-faced robot in a grey business suit
becomes Joaquin's guide. The robot has large faded-blue eyes
whose fixed hypnotic quality is intensified by the lashes: short and
thick and stiff and extremely black as if mascara'd. When the robot
walks by, Joaquin's eyes meet his and there is no alternative to
obedience. Our hero feels neither will nor compulsion to follow,
as the guide seems to feel neither will nor compulsion to lead.
There is no apparent connection between them. They are like
objects floating down a belt conveyor. The island floats them
along. And presently, one behind the other, they enter the
subway, go through a turnstile, walk across a deserted stone
landing and drop before a door marked, in spite of the nature of
Sodom, MEN. The robot enters. Our hero follows.

It is a fairly small white-tiled chamber with a concrete floor and a
nipping smell of disinfectant. Joaquin finds that, including himself and his guide, eight male persons are present, but there is
nothing in their behaviour to indicate that they are in any way
aware of one another. At the adjacent urinals against the left wall,
two robots stand motionless. Along the right wall, in each of the
pair of cabinets that either never had doors or from which the
doors have been removed, a seated and motionless robot is
visible. At the far wall stand the three remaining motionless
robots, of whom one is Joaquin's guide, staring into space from
between his black rigid lashes. Our hero, just across the threshold
of the chamber, stands frozen. There is no sound, no breath. The
Spanish heart in Joaquin's paralysed chest seems unwilling to
beat, throbs only at long intervals but with a compensating
violence that stabs the blood into his fingertips and scalp. At first,
Joaquin is expectant, but as he waits, and as the silence and
stillness continue, the thrust of his heart gentles, for he begins to
suppose that nothing is going to happen, that whatever is
supposed to happen is now happening: that perhaps the most
pure and powerful expression of lust is utter indifference. Though

Joaquin wishes now to withdraw from the chamber, he finds he cannot. He is frozen into place by the transfixed robots, by his guide's rigid stare, by the very tile and odour of the room. Therefore, he remains, petrified, minute after minute.

Then, as if a button had been pushed, the place is stormed by motion. The robots spring from the wall, dash from the urinals, jump from the cabinets. Joaquin is whipped into the midst of them, astonished at their frenzy, unable to partake but aware that he is being partaken of. Legs and arms and faces and bodies flail as the robots like cowboys go leaping to saddle, or the robots like stallions go bucking their riders. Stampeding madness must be pursuing them for they gallop with fury, and they rave, they shout, they cry, they shriek and babble nonsensically. No, no! It isn't nonsense! Joaquin abruptly understands that their cries are *not* wordless, that they are in fact all bellowing in the same thing, that through the froth and foam of their mouths pulled askew by the wind they gallop through, they are all wailing: 'I love you' and again 'I love you' and again and continually, wailing their love as they hump across the wild and limitless prairies, a little ahead, so hardly ahead, of the stampeding madness.

Until someone in this vast wilderness screams, 'I'm coming!' Joaquin sees who has screamed: his guide's stallion. The stallion has called out his death but the guide's eyes are still as fixed as glass, focused on space, passionless though he rides and bellows, 'I love you. I love you.' Thunder bursts open the wilderness, a spasm crashes across the chamber, a shudder rolls from wall to wall and, suddenly, as if a button had been pressed, the crowd of robots explodes and each of the eight is flung back to the place he had come from.

No one now speaks. Once more there is silence and motionlessness, except for sighing chests and laboured breathing. But soon these grow quiet. The robots stand transfixed. Nothing remains.

Paris again: a chill autumn evening and the city is strangling on fog. Yet despite the thick bluish valley vapour that clutches at stone and bone, there is gaiety at the Place Denfert where the cafés and streets are filled with those who have been freed by their offices, shops and factories. Like everyone else, Joaquin has worked all day and is having a drink before going home to *pot-au-feu*, boiled potatoes, salad, camembert, and another painful evening of happy-family-life. Medical expenses – he has recently done another month in the hospital having his bowels reinvestigated – have obliged him to give up his hotel room and move in with friends. So he is at the Place Denfert to catch a bus for the southern suburbs, but his soul aches with discontent and he longs for love. Perhaps tonight, in spite of the family that awaits him and the doctor's instructions that he must rest in the evenings, he will not go home at all; perhaps he will tonight make the urinary stations of the cross, cruise the whole of the city from *pissotière* to *pissotière*. Pulling up the collar of his raincoat, he leaves his drink and the café.

In the *pissoir* down the avenue, no legs show; nonetheless Joaquin pauses at the corner an instant, attendant upon Destiny. And Destiny of course arrives, but is so modest in appearance that our hero almost overlooks it: a labourer in raincoat and blue beret, a middle-aged man, square-faced and squarely built, greying temples, flushed winey complexion, gentle-seeming, fatherly. Joaquin is not really drawn to him, but he watches him enter the *tasse* and sees his legs go round to the centre urinal. *Eh bien, pourquoi pas – enfin, rien à perdre.* Besides this is only the first, and need not be the last, of all the stations of the cross. So our hero follows the man inside where, presently, they shift eyes, shake shoulders, sneak looks, smile, bow, and at last exchange visiting cards.

After a long silence, Destiny leans forward and his breath riots red wine: '*T'es joli, mon petit, bien?*'

Joaquin is grateful for the compliment: 'You're not bad yourself.'

'Do you have a place we can go to?'

'No – and you?'

The labourer shakes his head. '*Ah, je veux bien te baiser.*'

'I'd like it too.'

'It would give you pleasure?'

Joaquin realizes that the intent of the question is to sharpen his excitement, and it does. Now, passionately, he begins to want the man, to love him, is eager to have him, longs to suggest going to a hotel – but he cannot afford the price of a room, and he hesitates to ask Destiny to pay, for he probably hasn't the money either. Besides, Joaquin knows that among Frenchmen the most over-whelming of passions is thrift, and he is already too fond of the labourer to risk a test of the man's feelings, except indirectly.

'If only there were *somewhere* . . .' our hero ventures, eyes shyly, slyly lowered.

'Ah, if only . . .' agrees Destiny, reaching up to pet Joaquin's cheeks and hair with a gesture that is, though drunkenly broken, so tender that our hero's lids grow heavy, are closed by languor and love. 'Ah, *petit*, if we had somewhere to go I would screw your little ass off.'

Joaquin knows that this is no idle boast, no vain promise, but since under the circumstances all boasts will prove idle and all promises vain, our hero says: 'I must leave now.'

'What a pity.'

They button up and exit together, shaking hands on the street. 'Maybe we'll meet again,' says Destiny sadly as they draw apart and lose each other in the fog.

Even more discontented than he had been earlier, Joaquin now pushes listlessly through the streets for a while, then resolving to cruise northward he is obliged to cross the Place Denfert again. And as he crosses, he sees the bus he should be taking home – and there at a window towards the front sits Destiny talking to someone opposite him. Well, thinks Joaquin, why not go home? He can at least spend the journey with his beloved labourer and – who knows? – there may in the fog of the countryside be an empty lot, an abandoned barn; they may yet have their moment. So Joaquin springs up into the bus. All the seats are taken and the aisle is packed, but still he shoves his way through until his eyes meet Destiny's. And though Joaquin smiles, almost laughs, with delight, there is no sign of recognition in the labourer's face – or wait! yes! a flicker in the cheekbones that seems to be, impossibly, fear. Confused, Joaquin lets the crowd drive him down the aisle to the back of the bus where, though his heart and mind are on Destiny, his hand, thinking of Accident, reaches up to hold a strap against the moment of departure. The car is overheated, it stinks, and bodies are crushed together. Joaquin sickens from the smell of ammonia, exhaust fumes, sweat, undigested garlic, French-women. He shuts his eyes fiercely, drops back upon the moment of tenderness in the *pissotière*, and is so ravished by the dream, by the promise, by a dream of the imagined fulfilment of the promise and the boast, that when at last he opens his eyes the bus is already out beyond the Porte d'Orléans. Although he cannot see him because of the packed aisle, Joaquin is grateful that only a few yards away Destiny sits chatting with a companion or perhaps dozing from his wine and the swinging of the bus.

Joaquin becomes aware of raised voices and of general move-ment along the aisle: thrusts, jostlings, then complaints about it all. He looks towards the front of the bus and there sees Destiny with flushed furious face, flailing his way through the crowd.

'That queer! I'll get that dirty fag!' he is shouting, and Joaquin's intestines leap at the words. Ferocious Destiny is making straight for our hero, bawling: 'You pansy, you lousy little bugger, I'll fix you.'

Joaquin groans as pain begins to flash through his belly. The labourer is there beside him now, shaking with rage, his fists out before him threateningly; but he doesn't actually touch our hero, he merely roars: 'I recognize you. I know who you are. You're the one. You're the lousy little fag who made a pass at me in the shithouse.' He looks sweepingly at the people roundabout: 'Stinking fairies everywhere these days. A man isn't even safe pissing any more.'

All the faces in the bus, all expressionless, all interested but utterly detached, all are turned upon Joaquin who stands astonished, humiliated, the love in him wounded and dazed. Yet he stands upright for the intestinal ache has gathered his spirit into a spear upon which he and his heart are impaled, held rigid. As Destiny – this labourer, this lover, this tender promising father –

flings slop at him, he longs to say something, to pretend outrage, to plead innocence, to beg mercy, to threaten. But he can say nothing, for he has forgotten the French language – and also the Spanish language, and the English language, and all the incomprehensible, pointless, useless tongues of humanity. He can speak only with the divine tongue of pain. If he opens his mouth the tongue will burst forth howling and shrieking the agony that enflames and scorches his bowel, that slashes and shreds him and cleaves him and rives him and that will ultimately bring him to a hospital in Barcelona where a further slit will be cut in his belly and where his anus will be sewn tight, more like judgement than treatment. And there in Barcelona will he lie for a week under an oxygen tent, surrounded by faces curious but indifferent, while he rattles his miserable way towards a destination he doesn't want to reach, stuffed at last with hopeless heart and returned at last to his family, all in one piece and still bearing his old Catalan name, yet like the glorious soldier – Mutilated and Unknown.

Joaquin, Joaquin, if I had a voice I would sing to you who have no ears, and I would not sing a dirge but a cradle-song: to the child so freshly lain within the Spanish ground. I would sing, Joaquin, how your drying corpse became Earth's newborn heart making her hunger to love, and how your healing wounds became Earth's restless eyes making her hunt for love, and how your slowly dissolving agony became Earth's fury, Earth's inexorable courage, so that when failure stoked the fire in her gut, when futility cancered and fouled her, when desperation festered her, tumoured her, gangrened her, poisoned her and made the whole of her rot, she still went on cruising, the raging insane beast of the cosmos, making all the planetary stations of the cross, until she herself was cut to pieces and was laid herself like a newborn heart into the ground of this loveless universe.

Once more, and finally, Joaquin will move.

At the Porte d'Auteuil, the most westerly gate of Paris, where the city abruptly strips and flings itself out upon the weeds and forests of Boulogne, there is a great boulevard named for Exel-

mans, a known soldier. Running along the middle of this boulevard is a tremendous stone bridge which, though now unused,
was once part of a railway that circled Paris. Buses have made it
obsolete. It stands graceful and monstrous, its underside full of
vaultings and gloomy arcades that shelter bums, lovers, open
markets. At one turning of the bridge, embedded in the wall, is
the city's empress *pissotière*. This is not a round but a long one and
can accommodate perhaps a score of men. On mild nights, or even
on cold ones, the place is usually jammed. Seldom will you find a
foreigner here; this is the great melting-pot of French society –
French *male* society that is to say, for the only women present are
Aphrodite and Undine, both foreigners – and all levels are
represented: students, industrialists, functionaries, ambassadors,
ordinary faggots, labourers, husbands and fathers, all. Towards
one o'clock in the morning, the *tasse* becomes quite daring in its
activity. The men pair off; some leave and some, as in Sodom,
stay.

A bitter winter night, the pavement sparkling with frost.
Auteuil, this quarter of the upper-upper middle class, sleeps.
Joaquin comes down Exelmans and slips into the *pissotière*, taking
the one available urinal, almost in the centre next to a sailor. He
looks up and down the long row speculatively. At first it is too
dark to see clearly, but soon his eyes adjust, and faces,
expressions, desires begin to emerge. Hands move, feet shift,
there are whispers and rustlings, moans and the sounds of moist
flesh. Then suddenly a hush, a held breath – something unusual is
happening.

An extraordinary figure has swaggered in, his hands plunged
into the pockets of a heavy woollen windbreaker. He is a
monument of a man, much too tall to be French. Asia or Africa
must at one time have raped his ancestry and his complexion,
since even in the dimness Joaquin can tell that the colour of his
skin is not altogether European. His head is large and crowned
with generous waves of red-blond hair, probably dyed. His eyes
are dark. The ears are round and small like the Kikuyu. His neck is
powerful. His shoulders wing worldward without cowardice. Up

and back he swaggers behind the line of men, offering himself to their eyes and promising perfect love. And twenty men are each of them alone with him. But whom will he choose? Up and back he goes, up and back.

At last, decisively, he pauses behind the centre urinal and, without removing his hands from his pockets, jabs his elbow against the sailor's ribs and indicates by an upward thrust of the head that he wants not him but his place. Deferentially the sailor vacates; one has no alternative with heroes.

Hands now on hips, the swaggerer stands at the urinal revealing himself to all and accepting reverence. From both ends, like the lines of a cathedral, attention focuses towards the centre, towards the swaggering giant with gleaming hair who, as in Joaquin's dream, seems now invested in a robe of gold, shot through with red and silver. Twenty pairs of devout eyes genuflect and twenty hearts bring tribute. The eyes chant. The hearts carol. Undine sings. Aphrodite hums. Now, in this frozen night of joy, there are no swords between men. There are no secret jealousies, no envies, no rivalries, no rancour against the hero's choice, against him who will know the ultimate accomplishment of love. And Joaquin, beside the swaggerer, closes his eyes, drops to his knees violently as if suffering a conversion or revelation and, throwing wide his arms to grasp him who comes to them, opens his lips upon Life Everlasting.

# The Wild Boys

## WILLIAM S. BURROUGHS

'They have incredible stamina. A pack of wild boys can cover fifty miles a day. A handful of dates and a lump of brown sugar washed down with a cup of water keep them moving like that. The noise they make just before they charge . . . well I've seen it shatter a greenhouse fifty yards away. Let me show you what a wild-boy charge is like.' He led the way into the projection room. 'These are actual films of course but I have arranged them in narrative sequence. As you know I was with one of the first expeditionary forces sent out against the wild boys. Later I joined them. Seen the charges from both sides. Well here's one of my first films.'

The Colonel reins in his horse. It is a bad spot. Steep hills slope down to a narrow dry river bed. He scans the hillsides carefully through his field glasses. The hills slope up to black mesas streaked with iron ore.

'Since our arrival in the territory the regiment had been fêted by the local population who told us how glad they were the brave English soldiers had come to free them from the wild boys. The women and children pelted us with flowers in the street. It reeked of treachery but we were blinded by the terrible Bor Bor they were putting in our food and drink. Bor Bor is the drug of female illusion and it is said that he who takes Bor Bor cannot see a wild boy until it is too late.

'The regiment is well into the valley. It is a still hot afternoon with sullen electricity in the air. And suddenly there they are on both sides of us against the black mesas. The valley echoes to their terrible charge cry a hissing outblast of breath like a vast WHOOO? . . . Their eyes light up inside like a cat's and their hair stands on end. And they charge down the slope with incredible speed leaping from side to side. We open up with everything we have and they still keep coming. They aren't human at all more like vicious little ghosts. They carry eighteen-inch bowie knives with knuckle-duster handles pouring into the river bed above and below us leaping down swinging their knives in the air. When one is killed a body is dragged aside and another takes his place. The regiment formed a square and it lasted about thirty seconds.

'I had prudently stashed my assets in a dry well where peering out through thistles I observed the carnage. I saw the Colonel empty his revolver and go down under ten wild boys. A moment later they tossed his bleeding head into the air and started a ball game. Just at dusk the wild boys got up and padded away. They left the bodies stripped to the skin many with the genitals cut off. The wild boys make little pouches from human testicles in which they carry their hashish and *khat*. The setting sun bathed the torn bodies in a pink glow. I walked happily about munching a chicken sandwich stopping now and again to observe an interesting cadaver.

'There are many groups scattered over a wide area from the outskirts of Tangier to the Blue Desert of Silence . . . glider boys with bows and laser guns, rollerskate boys – blue jockstraps and steel helmets, eighteen-inch bowie knives – naked blowgun boys long hair down their backs a kris at the thigh, slingshot boys, knife throwers, bowmen, bare-hand fighters, shaman boys who ride the wind and those who have control over snakes and dogs, boys skilled in bone-pointing and Juju magic who can stab the enemy reflected in a gourd of water, boys who call the locusts and the fleas, desert boys shy as little sand foxes, dream boys who see each other's dreams and the silent boys of the Blue Desert. Each group developed special skills and knowledge until it evolved into humanoid subspecies. One of the more spectacular units is the dreaded Warrior Ants made up of boys who have lost both hands in battle. They wear aluminium bikinis and sandals and tight steel helmets. They are attended by musicians and dancing boys, medical and electronic attendants who carry the weapons that are screwed into their stumps, buckle them into their bikinis, lace their sandals wash and anoint their bodies with a musk of genitals, roses, carbolic soap, gardenias, jasmine, oil of cloves, ambergris and rectal mucus. This overpowering odour is the first warning of their presence. The smaller boys are equipped with razor-sharp pincers that can snip off a finger or sever a leg tendon. And they click their claws as they charge. The taller boys have long double-edged knives that can cut a scarf in the air screwed into both stumps.'

On the screen the old regiment same canyon same Colonel. The Colonel sniffs uneasily. His horse rears and neighs. Suddenly there is a blast of silver light reflected from helmets knives and sandals. They hit the regiment like a whirlwind the ground ants cutting tendons, the shock troops slashing with both arms wade through the regiment heads floating in the air behind them. It is all over in a few seconds. Of the regiment there are no survivors. The wild boys take no prisoners. The first to receive attention were those so seriously wounded they could not live.

The Colonel paused and filled his kif pipe. He seemed to be looking at something far away and long ago and I flinched for I was a snippy Fulbright queen at the time dreading some distastefully intimate *experience* involving the amorous ghost of an Arab boy. What a bore he is with his tacky old Lawrence sets faithful native youths dying in his arms.

'As I have told you the first wild-boy tribes were fugitive survivors from the terror of Colonel Arachnid ben Driss. These boys in their early- and mid-teens had been swept into a whirlwind of riots, burning screams, machine guns and lifted out of time. Migrants of ape in gasoline crack of history. Officials denied that any repressive measures had followed nonexistent riots.

'"There is no Colonel Arachnid in the Moroccan Army" said a spokesman for the Ministry of the Interior.

'No witnesses could be found who had noticed anything out of
the ordinary other than the hottest August in many years. The
gasoline boys and Colonel Arachnid were hallucinated by a
drunken Reuters man who became temporarily deranged when
his houseboy deserted him for an English pastry cook. I was
myself the Reuters man as you may have gathered.'

Here are the boys cooking over campfires . . . quiet valley by a
stream calm young faces washed in the dawn before creation. The
old phallic Gods of Greece and the assassins of Alamout still linger
in the Moroccan hills like sad pilots waiting to pick up survivors.
The piper's tune drifts down a St Louis street with the autumn
leaves.

On screen an old book with gilt edges. Written in golden script
*The Wild Boys*. A cold spring wind ruffles the pages.

Weather boys with clouds and rainbows and Northern lights in
their eyes study the sky.

Glider boys ride a blue flash sunset on wings of pink and rose
and gold laser guns shooting arrows of light. Roller-skate boys
turn slow circles in ruined suburbs China-blue half-moon in the
morning sky.

Blue evening shadows in the old skating rink, smell of empty
locker rooms and mouldy jockstraps. A circle of boys sit on a gym
mat hands clasped around the knees. The boys are naked except
for blue steel helmets. Eyes move in a slow circle from crotch to
crotch, silent, intent, they converge on one boy a thin dark youth
his face spattered with adolescent pimples. He is getting stiff. He
steps to the centre of the circle and turns around three times. He
sits down knees up facing the empty space in the circle where he
sat. He pivots slowly looking at each boy in turn. His eyes lock
with one boy. A fluid click a drop of lubricant squeezes out the tip
of his phallus. He lies back his head on a leather cushion. The boy
selected kneels in front of the other studying his genitals. He
presses the tip open and looks at it through a lens of lubricant. He
twists the tight nuts gently runs a slow precise finger up and down
the shaft drawing lubricant along the divide line feeling for
sensitive spots in the tip. The boy who is being masturbated rocks

back hugging knees against his chest. The circle of boys sits silent lips parted watching faces calmed to razor sharpness. The boy quivers transparent suffused with blue light the pearly glands and delicate coral tracings of his backbone exposed.

A naked boy on perilous wings soars over a blue chasm. The air is full of wings . . . gliders launched from skis and sleds and skates, flying bicycles, sky-blue gliders with painted birds, an air schooner billowing white sails stabilized by autogiros. Boys climb in the rigging and wave from fragile decks.

Boy on a bicycle with autogiro wings sails off a precipice and floats slowly down into a valley of cobblestone streets and deep-blue canals. In a golf course sand pit hissing snake boys twist in slow copulations guarded by a ring of cobras.

The legend of the wild boys spread and boys from all over the world ran away to join them. Wild boys appeared in the mountains of Mexico, the jungles of South American and Southeastern Asia. Bandit country, guerrilla country, is wild-boy country. The wild boys exchange drugs, weapons, skills on a world-wide network. Some wild-boy tribes travel constantly taking the best cannabis seeds to the Amazon and bringing back cuttings of the Yage vine for the jungles of Southern Asia and Central Africa. Exchange of spells and potions. A common language based on variable transliteration of a simplified hieroglyphic script is spoken and written by the wild boys. In remote dream rest areas the boys fashion these glyphs from wood, metal, stone and pottery. Each boy makes his own picture set. Sea chest in an attic room, blue wallpaper ship scenes, copies of *Adventure* and *Amazing Stories*, a .22 pump-action rifle on the wall. A boy opens the chest and takes out the words one by one . . . The erect phallus which means in wild-boy script as it does in Egyptian to stand before or in the presence of, to confront to regard attentively . . . a phallic statue of ebony with star sapphire eyes a tiny opal set in the tip of the phallus . . . two wooden statues face each other in a yellow oak rocking chair. The boy statues are covered with human skin tanned in ambergris, carbolic soap, rose petals, rectal mucus, smoked in hashish and burning leaves . . . a yellow-haired boy straddles a copper-skinned Mexican, feet braced muscles carved in orgasm . . . an alabaster boy lights up blue inside, piper boy with a music box, roller-skate boy of blue slate with a bowie knife in his hand, a post card world of streams, freckled boy, blue outhouses covered with morning glory and rose vines where the boys jack off on July afternoons shimmers in a Gysin painting . . . little peep shows . . . flickering silver titles . . . others with colours and odours and raw naked flesh . . . tight nuts crinkle to autumn leaves . . . blue chasms . . . a flight of birds. These word objects travel on the trade routes from hand to hand. The wild boys see, touch, taste, smell the words. Shrunken head of a CIA man . . . a little twisted sentry his face cyanide blue . . .

(A highly placed narcotics official tells a grim President: 'The wild-boy thing is a cult based on drugs, depravity and violence more dangerous than the hydrogen bomb.')

At a long work bench in the skating rink boys tinker with tiny jet engines for their skates. They forge and grind eighteen-inch bowie knives bolting on handles of ebony and the ironwoods of South America that must be worked with metal tools . . .

The roller-skate boys swerve down a wide palm-lined avenue into a screaming blizzard of machine-gun bullets, sun glinting on their knives and helmets, lips parted eyes blazing. They slice through a patrol snatching guns in the air.

Jungle work bench under a thatched roof . . . a ten-foot blowgun with telescopic sights operated by compressed air . . . tiny blowguns with darts no bigger than a mosquito sting tipped with serum jaundice and strange fevers . . .

In houseboats, basements, tents, tree houses, caves, and lofts the wild boys fashion their weapons . . . a short double-edged knife bolted to a strong spring whipped back and forth slices to the bone . . . kris with a battery vibrator in the handle . . . karate sticks . . . a knob of ironwood protrudes between the first and second fingers and from each end of the fist . . . loaded gloves and knuckle-dusters . . . crossbows and guns powered by thick rubber sliced from an inner tube. These guns shoot a lead slug fed in from a magazine above the launching carriage. Quite accurate up to twenty yards . . . a cyanide injector shaped like a pistol. The needle is unscrewed from the end of the barrel, the pistol cocked by drawing back a spring attached to the plunger. A sponge soaked in cyanide solution is inserted, the needle screwed back in place. When the trigger releases the spring a massive dose of cyanide is squeezed into the flesh causing instant death. When not in use the needle is capped by a Buck Rogers Death Ray . . . cyanide darts and knives with hollow perforated blades . . . a flintlock pistol loaded with crushed glass and cyanide crystals . . .

Cat boys fashion claws sewn into heavy leather gloves that are strapped around the wrist and forearm, the incurving hollow claws packed with cyanide paste. The boys in green jockstraps wait in a tree for the jungle patrol. They leap down on the soldiers, deadly claws slashing, digging in. Boys collect the weapons from twisted blue hands. They wash off blood and poison in a stream and pass around a kif pipe.

Snake boys in fish-skin jockstraps wade out of the bay. Each boy has a venomous speckled sea snake coiled around his arm. They move through scrub and palm to an electric fence that surrounds the officer's club. Through flowering shrubs Americans can be seen in the swimming pool blowing and puffing. The boys extend their arms through the fence index finger extended. The snakes drop off and glide towards the swimming pool. A jungle patrol in Angola . . . suddenly black mambas streak down from trees on both sides of their path mouths open fangs striking necks and arms lashing up from the ground. Mamba boys black as obsidian with mamba-skin jockstraps and kris glide forward.

Five naked boys release cobras above a police post. As the snakes glide down the boys move their heads from side to side. Phalluses sway and stiffen. The boys snap their heads forward mouths open and ejaculate. Strangled cries from the police box. Faces impassive the boys wait until their erections subside.

Boys sweep a cloud of bubonic fleas like a net with tiny black knots into an enemy camp.

A baby and semen black market flourished in the corrupt border cities, and we recruited male infants from birth. You could

take your boy friend's sperm to market, contact a broker who
would arrange to inseminate medically inspected females. Nine
months later the male crop was taken to one of the remote
peaceful communes behind the front lines. A whole generation
arose that had never seen a woman's face nor heard a woman's
voice. In clandestine clinics fugitive technicians experimented
with test-tube babies and cuttings. Brad and Greg got out just
under a 'terminate with extreme prejudice' order . . . And here is
their clinic in the Marshan Tangier. Laughing, comparing a line of
boys jack off into test tubes . . .

Here is a boy on his way to the cutting room. Brad and Greg
explain they are going to take a cutting from the rectum very small
and quite painless and the more excited he is when they take the
cutting better chance there is that the cutting will *make* . . . They
arrange him on a table with his knees up rubber slings behind the
knees to keep him spread and turn an orgone funnel on his ass
and genitals. Then Brad slips a vibrating cutting tube up him.
These are in hard rubber and plastic perforated with pinpoint
holes. Inside is a rotary knife operated from the handle. When the
ring expands it forces bits of the lining through the holes which are
then clipped off by the knife.

Brad switches on the vibrator. The boy's pubic hairs crackle
with blue sparks, tight nuts pop egg-blue worlds in air . . . Some
boys red out rose-red delicate sea-shell pinks come rainbows and
Northern lights . . . Here are fifty boys in one ward room, bent
over hands on knees, on all fours, legs up. Greg throws the master
switch. The boys writhe and squirm, leap about like lemurs, eyes
blazing blue chasms, semen pulsing sparks of light. Little phantom figures dance on their bodies, slide up and down their pulsing
cocks, and ride the cutting tubes . . .

Little boy without a navel in a 1920 classroom. He places an
apple on the teacher's desk.

'I am giving you back your apple teacher.'

He walks over to the blackboard and rubs out the word
MOTHER.

Flanked by Brad and Greg he steps to the front of the stage and takes a bow to an audience of cheering boys eating peanuts and jacking off.

Now the cuttings are no longer needed. The boys create offspring known as Zimbus. Brad and Greg have retired to a remote YMCA. Zimbus are created after a battle when the forces of evil are in retreat . . .

The first to receive attention were those so seriously wounded that they could not live . . . A red-haired boy who had been shot through the liver was quickly stripped of bikini and sandals and propped up in a sitting position. Since they believe that the spirit leaves through the back of the head a recumbent position is considered unfavourable. The pack stood around the dying boy in a circle and a technician deftly removed the helmet. I saw then that the helmet was an intricate piece of electronic equipment. The technician took an eighteen-inch cylinder from a leather carrying case. The cylinder is made up of alternate layers of thin iron and human skin taken from the genitals of slain enemies. In the centre of the cylinder is an iron tube which protrudes slightly from one end. The tube was brought within a few inches of the boy's wound. This has the effect of reducing pain or expediting the healing of a curable wound. Pain-killing drugs are never used since the cell-blanketing effect impedes departure of the spirit. Now a yoke was fitted over the boy's shoulders and what looked like a diving helmet was placed over his head. This helmet covered with leather on the outside is in two pieces one piece covering the front of the head the other the back. The technician made an adjustment and suddenly the back section shot back to the end of the yoke where it was caught and held by metal catches. Two sections are of magnetized iron inside the technician adjusting the direction of magnetic flow so that by a repelling action the two sections spring apart pushing the spirit out the back of the head. The flow is then reversed so that the two sections are pulling towards each other but held apart. This pulls the spirit out. A luminous haze like heat waves was quite visibly draining out the boy's head. The dancing boys who had gathered in a circle around the dying boy began playing their flutes a haunting melody of Pan pipes train whistles and lonely sidings as the haze shot up into the afternoon sky. The body went limp and the boy was dead. I saw this process repeated a number of times. When the dying had been separated from their bodies by this device those with curable wounds were treated. The cylinder was brought within an inch of the wound and moved up and down. I witnessed the miracle of almost immediate healing. A boy with a great gash in his thigh was soon hobbling about the wound looking as if it had been received some weeks before. The firearms were divided among the dancing boys and attendants. The boys busied themselves skinning the genitals of the slain soldiers pegging the skins out and rubbing in pastes and unguents for curing. They butchered the young soldiers removing the heart and liver and bones for food and carted the cadavers some distance from the camp. These chores accomplished the boys spread out rugs and lit hashish pipes. The warriors were stripped by their attendants massaged and rubbed with musk. The setting sun bathed their lean bodies in a red glow as the boys gave way to an orgy of lust. Two boys would take their place in the centre of a rug and copulate to drums surrounded by a circle of silent naked onlookers. I observed fifteen or twenty of these circles, copulating couples standing, kneeling, on all fours, faces rapt and empty. The odour of semen and rectal mucus filled the air. When one couple finished another would take its place. No words were spoken only the shuddering gasps and the pounding drums. A yellow haze hovered over the quivering bodies as the frenzied flesh dissolved in light. I noticed that a large blue tent had been set up and that certain boys designated by the attendants retired to this tent and took no part in the orgy. As the sun sank the exhausted boys slept in naked heaps. The moon rose and boys began to stir and light fires. Here and there hashish pipes glowed. The smell of cooking meat drifted through the air as the boys roasted the livers and hearts of the slain soldiers and made broth from the bones. Desert thistles shone silver in the moonlight. The boys formed a circle in a natural amphitheatre that sloped down to a platform of sand. On this platform they spread a round blue rug about eight feet in diameter. The four directions were indicated on this rug by arrows and its position was checked against a compass. The rug looked like a map crisscrossed with white lines and shaded in striations of blue from the lightest egg blue to blue black. The musicians formed an inner circle around the rug playing on their flutes the haunting tune that had sped the dying on their way. Now one of the boys who had taken no part in the recent orgy stepped forward onto the rug. He stood there naked sniffing quivering head thrown back scanning the night sky. He stepped to the North and beckoned with both hands. He repeated the same gesture to the South East and West. I noticed that he had a tiny blue copy of the rug tattooed on each buttock. He knelt in the centre of the rug studying the lines and patterns looking from the rug to his genitals. His phallus began to stir and stiffen. He leaned back until his face was turned to the sky. Slowly he raised both hands palms up and his hands drew a blue mist from the rug. He turned his hands over palms down and slowly lowered them pulling blue down from the sky. A pool of colour swirled about his thighs. The mist ran into a vague shape as the colour shifted from blue to pearly grey pink and finally red. A red being was now visible in front of the boy's body lying on his back knees up transparent thighs on either side of his flanks. The boy knelt there studying the red shape of his eyes moulding the body of a red-haired boy. Slowly he placed his hands behind knees that gave at his touch and moved them up to trembling ears of red smoke. A red boy was lying there buttocks spread the rectum a quivering rose that seemed to breathe, the body clearly outlined but still transparent. Slowly the boy penetrated the phantom body I could see his penis inside the other and as he moved in and out the soft red gelatin clung to his penis thighs and buttocks young skin taking shape legs in the air kicking spasmodically a red face on the rug lips parted the body always more solid. The boy leaned forward and fastened his lips to the other mouth spurting sperm inside and suddenly the red boy was solid buttocks quivering against the boy's groin as they breathed in and out of each other's lungs locked together the red body solid from the buttocks and penis to the twitching feet. They remained there quivering for thirty seconds. A red mist steamed off the red boy's body. I could see freckles and leg hairs. Slowly the boy withdrew his mouth. A red-haired boy lay there breathing deeply eyes closed. The boy withdrew his penis, straightened the red knees and lay the newborn Zimbu on his back. Now two attendants stepped forward with a litter of soft leather. Carefully they lifted the Zimbu onto the litter and carried him to the blue tent.

Another boy stepped on to the rug. He stood in the centre of the rug and leaned forward hands on knees his eyes following the lines and patterns. His penis stiffened. He stood upright and walked to the four directions lifting his hands each time and saying one word I did not catch. A little wind sprang up that stirred the boy's pubic hairs and played over his body. He began to dance to the flutes and drums and as he danced a blue will-o'-the-wisp took shape in front of him shifting from one side of the rug to the other. The boy spread out his hands. The will-o'-the-wisp tried to dodge past but he caught it and brought his arms together pulling the blue shape against him. The colour shifted from blue to pearly grey streaked with brown. His hands were stroking a naked flank and caressing a penis out of the air buttocks flattened against his body as he moved in fluid gyrations lips parted teeth bared. A brown body solid now ejaculated in shuddering gasps sperm hitting the rug left white streaks and spots that soaked into the crisscross of white lines. The boy held the Zimbu up pressing his chest in and out with his own breathing quivering to the blue tattoo. The Zimbu shuddered and ejaculated again. He hung limp in the other's arms. The attendants stepped forward with another litter. The Zimbu was carried away to the blue tent.

A boy with Mongoloid features steps on to the rug playing a flute to the four directions. As he plays phantom figures swirl around him taking shape out of moonlight, campfires and shadows. He kneels in the centre of the rug playing his flute faster and faster. The shape of a boy on hands and knees is forming in front of him. He puts down his flute. His hands mould and knead the body in front of him pulling it against him with stroking movements that penetrate the pearly grey shape caressing it inside. The body shudders and quivers against him as he forms the buttocks around his penis stroking silver genitals out of the moonlight grey then pink and finally red the mouth parted in a gasp shuddering genitals out of the moon's haze a pale blond boy spurting thighs and buttocks and young skin. The flute player kneels there arms wrapped tightly around the Zimbu's chest breathing deeply until the Zimbu breathes with his own breathing quivering to the blue tattoo. The attendants step forward and carry the pale blond Zimbu to the blue tent.

A tall boy black as ebony steps on to the rug. He scans the sky. He walks around the rug three times. He walks back to the centre of the rug. He brings both hands down and shakes his head. The music stops. The boys drift away.

It was explained to me that the ceremony I had just witnessed was performed after a battle in case any of the boys who had just been killed wished to return and that those who had lost their hands might wish to do since the body is born whole. However most of the spirits would have gone to the Blue Desert of Silence. They might want to return later and the wild boys made periodic expeditions to the Blue Desert. The Zimbus sleep in the blue tent. Picture in an old book with gilt edges. The picture is framed with roses intertwined . . . two bodies stuck together pale wraith of a blond boy lips parted full moon a circle of boys in silver helmets naked knees up. Under the picture in gold letters. Birth of a Zimbu. Boy with a flute charming a body out of the air. I turn the page. Boy with Mongoloid features is standing on a circular rug. He looks down at his stiffening phallus. A little wind stirs his pubic hairs. Buttocks tight curving inward at the bottom of the two craters a round blue tattoo miniature of the rug on which he stands. I turn the page. A boy is dancing will-o'-the-wisp dodges in front of him. I turn the page. Will-o'-the-wisp in his arms gathering outline luminous blue eyes trembling buttocks flattened against his body holding the Zimbu tight against his chest. His breathing serves as the Zimbu's lungs until his breathing is his own quivering to the blue tattoo children of lonely sidings, roses, afternoon sky. I turn the pages. Dawn shirt framed in roses dawn wind between his legs distant lips.

# Pages from an Abandoned Journal

GORE VIDAL

I

April 30, 1948

After last night, I was sure they wouldn't want to see me again but evidently I was wrong because this morning I had a call from Steven . . . he spells it with a 'v' . . . asking me if I would like to come to a party at Elliott Magren's apartment in the Rue du Bac. I should have said no but I didn't. It's funny: when I make up my mind *not* to do something I always end up by doing it, like meeting Magren, like seeing any of these people again, especially after last night. Well, I guess it's experience. What was it Pascal wrote? I don't remember what Pascal wrote . . . another sign of weakness. I should look it up when I don't remember . . . the book is right here on the table but the thought of leafing through all those pages is discouraging so I pass on.

Anyway, now that I'm in Paris I've got to learn to be more adaptable and I do think, all in all, I've handled myself pretty well . . . until last night in the bar when I told everybody off. I certainly never thought I'd see Steven again . . . that's why I was so surprised to get his call this morning. Is he still hopeful after what I said? I can't see how. I was *ruthlessly* honest. I said I wasn't interested, that I didn't mind what other people did, etc., just as long as they left me alone, that I was getting married in the fall when I got back to the States (WRITE HELEN) and that I don't go in for any of that, never did and never will. I also told him in no uncertain terms that it's very embarrassing for a grown man to be treated like some idiot girl surrounded by a bunch of seedy, middle-aged Don Juans trying to get their hooks into her . . . him. Anyway, I really let him have it before I left. Later, I felt silly but I was glad to go on record like that once and for all: now we know where we stand and if they're willing to accept me on *my* terms, the way I am, then there's no reason why I can't see them sometimes. That's really why I agreed to meet Magren who sounds very interesting from what everybody says, and everybody talks a lot about him, at least in those circles which must be the largest and busiest circles in Paris this spring. Well, I shouldn't complain: this is the Bohemian life I wanted to see. It's just that there aren't many girls around, for fairly obvious reasons. In fact, except for running into Hilda Devendorf at American Express yesterday, I haven't seen an American girl to talk to in the three weeks I've been here.

My day: after the phone call from Steven, I worked for two and a half hours on Nero and the Civil Wars . . . I wish sometimes I'd picked a smaller subject for a doctorate, not that I don't like the period but having to learn German to read a lot of books all based on sources available to anybody is depressing: I could do the whole thing from Tacitus but that would be cheating, no bibliography, no footnotes, no scholastic quarrels to record and judge between. Then, though the day was cloudy, I took a long walk across the river to the Tuileries where the gardens looked fine. Just as I was turning home into the rue de l'Université it started to rain and I got wet. At the desk Madame Revenel told me Hilda had called. I called her back and she said she was going to Deauville on Friday to visit some people who own a hotel and why didn't I go too? I said I might and wrote down her address. She's a nice girl. We were in high school together back in Toledo; I lost track of her when I went to Columbia.

Had dinner here in the dining room (veal, french fried potatoes, salad and something like a pie but very good . . . I like the way Madame Revenel cooks). She talked to me all through dinner, very fast, which is good because the faster she goes the less chance you have to translate in your head. The only other people in the dining room were the Harvard professor and his wife. They both read while they ate. He's supposed to be somebody important in the English Department but I've never heard of him . . . Paris is like that: everyone's supposed to be somebody important only you've never heard of them. The Harvard professor was reading a mystery story and his wife was reading a life of Alexander Pope . . .

I got to the Rue du Bac around ten-thirty. Steven opened the door, yelling: 'The beautiful Peter!' This was about what I expected. Anyway, I got into the room quickly . . . if they're drunk they're apt to try to kiss you and there was no point in getting off on the wrong foot again . . . but luckily he didn't try. He showed me through the apartment, four big rooms one opening off another . . . here and there an old chair was propped against a wall and that was all the furniture there was till we got to the last room where, on a big bed with a torn canopy, Elliott Magren lay, fully dressed, propped up by pillows. All the lamps had red shades. Over the bed was a painting of a nude man, the work of a famous painter I'd never heard of (read Berenson!).

There were about a dozen men in the room, most of them middle-aged and wearing expensive narrow suits. I recognized one or two of them from last night. They nodded to me but made no fuss. Steven introduced me to Elliott who didn't move from the bed when he shook hands; instead, he pulled me down beside him. He had a surprisingly powerful grip, considering how pale and slender he is. He told Steven to make me a drink. Then he gave me a long serious look and asked me if I wanted a pipe of opium. I said I didn't take drugs and he said nothing which was unusual: as a rule they give you a speech about how good it is for you or else they start defending themselves against what they feel is moral censure. Personally, I don't mind what other people do. As a matter of fact, I think all this is very interesting and I sometimes wonder what the gang back in Toledo would think if they could've seen me in a Left-Bank Paris apartment with a male prostitute who takes drugs. I thought of those college boys who sent T. S. Eliot the record 'You've Come a Long Way From St Louis'.

Before I describe what happened, I'd better write down what I've heard about Magren since he is already a legend in Europe, at least in these circles. First of all, he is not very handsome. I don't know what I'd expected but something glamorous, like a movie star. He is about five foot ten and weighs about 160 pounds. He has dark straight hair that falls over his forehead; his eyes are black. The two sides of his face don't match, like Oscar Wilde's, though the effect is not as disagreeable as Wilde's face must've been from the photographs. Because of drugs, he is unnaturally pale. His voice is deep and his accent is still Southern; he hasn't picked up that phoney English accent so many Americans do after five minutes over here. He was born in Galveston, Texas about thirty-six years ago. When he was sixteen he was picked up on the beach by a German baron who took him to Berlin with him. (I always wonder about details in a story like this: what did his parents say about a stranger walking off with their son? was there a scene? did they know what was going on?) Elliott then spent several years in Berlin during the twenties which were the great days, or what these people recall now as the great days . . . I gather the German boys were affectionate: it all sounds pretty disgusting. Then Elliott had a fight with the Baron and he walked, with no money, nothing but the clothes he was wearing, from Berlin to Munich. On the outskirts of Munich, a big car stopped and the chauffeur said that the owner of the car would like to give him a lift. The owner turned out to be a millionaire-ship-owner from Egypt, very fat and old. He was intrigued with Elliott and he took him on a yachting tour of the Mediterranean. But Elliott couldn't stand him and when the ship got to Naples, Elliott and a Greek sailor skipped ship together after first stealing two thousand dollars from the Egyptian's state-room. They went to Capri where they moved into the most expensive hotel and had a wonderful time until the money ran out and the sailor deserted Elliott for a rich American woman. Elliott was about to be taken off to jail for not paying his bill when Lord Glenellen, who was just checking in the hotel, saw him and told the police to let him go, that *he* would pay his bill . . . here again: how would Glenellen know that it would be worth his while to help this stranger? I mean you can't tell by looking at him that Elliott is queer. Suppose he hadn't been? Well, maybe that soldier I met on Okinawa the night of the hurricane was right: they can always tell about each other, like Masons. Glenellen kept Elliott for a number of years. They went to England together and Elliott rose higher and higher in aristocratic circles until he met the late King Basil who was then a Prince. Basil fell in love with him and Elliott went to live with him until Basil became King. They didn't see much of each other after that because the war started and Elliott went to California to live. Basil died during the war, leaving Elliott a small trust fund which is what he lives on now. In California, Elliott got interested in Vedanta and tried to stop taking drugs and lead a quiet . . . if not a normal . . . life. People say he was all right for several years but when the war ended he couldn't resist going back to Europe. Now he does nothing but smoke opium, his courtesan life pretty much over. This has been a long account but I'm glad I got it all down because the story is an interesting one and I've heard so many bits and pieces of it since I got here that it helps clarify many things just writing this down in my journal . . . It is now past four o'clock and I've got a hangover already from the party but I'm going to finish, just as discipline. I never seem to finish anything which is a bad sign, God knows.

While I was sitting with Elliott on the bed, Steven brought him his opium pipe, a long painted wooden affair with a metal chimney. Elliott inhaled deeply, holding the smoke in his lungs as long as he could; then he exhaled the pale medicinal-scented smoke, and started to talk. I can't remember a word he said. I was aware, though, that this was probably the most brilliant conversation I'd ever heard. It might have been the setting which was certainly provocative or maybe I'd inhaled some of the opium which put me in a receptive mood but, no matter the cause, I sat listening to him, fascinated, not wanting him to stop. As he talked, he kept his eyes shut and I suddenly realized why the lampshades were red: the eyes of drug addicts are hypersensitive to light; whenever he opened his eyes he would blink painfully and the tears would streak his face, glistening like small watery rubies in the red light. He told me about himself, pretending to be a modern Candide, simple and bewildered but actually he must have been quite different, more calculating, more resourceful. Then he asked me about myself and I couldn't tell if he was really interested or not because his eyes were shut and it's odd talking to someone who won't look at you. I told him about Ohio and high school and the University and now Columbia and the doctorate I'm trying to get in History and the fact I want to teach, to marry Helen . . . but as I talked I couldn't help but think how dull my life must sound to Elliott. I cut it short. I couldn't compete with him . . . and didn't want to. Then he asked me if I'd see him some evening, alone, and I said I would like to but . . . and this was completely spur of the moment . . . I said I was going down to Deauville the next day, with a girl. I wasn't sure he'd heard any of this because at that moment Steven pulled me off the bed and tried to make me dance with him which I wouldn't do, to the amusement of the others. Then Elliott went to sleep so I sat and talked for a while with an interior decorator from New York and, as usual, I was floored by the amount these people know: painting, music, literature, architecture . . . where do they learn it all? I sit like a complete idiot, supposedly educated, almost a PhD, while they talk circles around me: Fragonard, Boucher, Leonore Fini, Gropius, Sacheverell Sitwell, Ronald Firbank, Jean Genet, Jean Giono, Jean Cocteau, Jean Brown's body lies a'mouldering in Robert Graves. God damn them all. I have the worst headache and outside it's dawn. Remember to write Helen, call Hilda about Deauville, study German two hours tomorrow instead of one, start boning up on Latin again, read Berenson, get a book on modern art (what book?), read Firbank . . .

II

May 21, 1948
Another fight with Hilda, this time about religion. She's a

Christian Scientist. It all started when she saw me taking two aspirins this morning because of last night's hangover. She gave me a lecture on Christ-Scientist and we had a long fight about God on the beach (which was wonderful today, not too many people, not too hot). Hilda looked more than ever like a great golden seal. She is a nice girl but like so many who go to Bennington feels she must continually be alert to the life about her. I think tonight we'll go to bed together. Remember to get suntan oil, change money at hotel, finish Berenson, study German grammar! See if there's a Firbank in a paper edition.

May 22, 1948

It wasn't very successful last night. Hilda kept talking all the time which slows me down, also she is a good deal softer than she looks and it was like sinking into a feather mattress. I don't think she has bones, only elastic webbing. Well, maybe it'll be better tonight. She seemed pleased but then I think she likes the idea better than the actual thing. She told me she had her first affair at fourteen. We had another argument about God. I told her the evidence was slight, etc. but she said evidence had nothing to do with faith. She told me a long story about how her mother had cancer last year but wouldn't see a doctor and the cancer went away. I didn't have the heart to tell her that Mother's days are unpleasantly numbered. We had a wonderful dinner at that place on the sea, lobster, *moules*. Write Helen.

May 24, 1948

A fight with Hilda, this time about Helen whom she hardly knows. She felt that Helen was pretentious. I said who isn't? She said many people weren't. I said name me one. She said *she* wasn't pretentious. I then told her all the pretentious things she'd said in the past week starting with that discussion about the importance of an aristocracy and ending with atonalism. She then told me all the pretentious things I'd said, things I either didn't remember saying or she had twisted around. I got so angry I stalked out of her room and didn't go back: just as well. Having sex with her is

about the dullest pastime I can think of. I went to my room and
read Tacitus in Latin, for practice.

My sunburn is better but I think I've picked up some kind of
liver trouble. Hope it's not jaundice: a burning feeling right where
the liver is.

May 25, 1948

Hilda very cool this morning when we met on the beach. Beautiful
day. We sat on the sand a good yard between us, and I kept
thinking how fat she's going to be in a few years, only fit for child-
bearing. I also thought happily of those agonizing 'painless'
childbirths she'd have to endure because of Christian Science. We
were just beginning to quarrel about the pronunciation of a French
word when Elliott Magren appeared . . . the last person in the
world I expected to see at bright noon on that beach. He was
walking slowly, wearing sunglasses and a pair of crimson trunks.
I noticed with surprise how smooth and youthful his body was,
like a boy. I don't know what I'd expected: something gaunt and
hollowed out I suppose, wasted by drugs. He came up to me as
though he'd expected to meet me right where I was. We shook
hands and I introduced him to Hilda who fortunately missed the
point to him from the very beginning. He was as charming as ever.
It seems he had to come to Deauville alone . . . he hated the sun
but liked the beach . . . and, in answer to the golden Hilda's
inevitable question, no, he was not married. I wanted to tell her
everything, just to see what would happen, to break for a moment
that beaming complacency, but I didn't . . .

May 27, 1948

Well, this afternoon, Hilda decided it was time to go back to Paris.
I carried her bag to the station and we didn't quarrel once. She was
pensive but I didn't offer the usual small change for her thoughts.
She didn't mention Elliott and I have no idea how much she
suspects; in any case, it's none of her business, none of mine
either. I think, though, I was nearly as shocked as she was when

he came back to the hotel this morning with that fourteen-year-old boy. We were sitting on the terrace having coffee when Elliott, who must've got up very early, appeared with this boy. Elliott even introduced him to us and the little devil wasn't faintly embarrassed, assuming, I guess, that we were interested in him, too. Then Elliott whisked him off to his room and, as Hilda and I sat in complete silence, we could hear from Elliott's room on the first floor the hoarse sound of the boy's laughter. Not long after, Hilda decided to go back to Paris.

Wrote a long letter to Helen, studied Latin grammar . . . I'm more afraid of my Latin than of anything else in either the written or the orals: can't seem to concentrate, can't retain all those irregular verbs. Well, I've come this far. I'll probably get through all right.

May 28, 1948

This morning I knocked on Elliott's door around eleven o'clock. He'd asked me to pick him up on my way to the beach. When he shouted come in! I did and found both Elliott and the boy on the floor together, stark naked, putting together a Meccano set. Both were intent on building an intricate affair with wheels and pulleys, a blueprint between them. I excused myself hurriedly but Elliott told me to stay . . . they'd be finished in a moment. The boy who was the colour of a terracotta pot gave me a wicked grin. Then Elliott, completely unselfconscious, jumped to his feet and pulled on a pair of trunks and a shirt. The boy dressed, too, and we went out on the beach where the kid left us. I was blunt. I asked Elliott if this sort of thing wasn't very dangerous and he said yes it probably was but life was short and he was afraid of nothing, except drugs. He told me then that he had had an electrical shock treatment at a clinic shortly before I'd first met him. Now, at last, he was off opium and he hoped it was a permanent cure. He described the shock treatment, which sounded terrible. Part of his memory was gone: he could recall almost nothing of his childhood . . . yet he was blithe even about this: after all, he believed only in the present . . . Then when I asked him if he always went in for young boys he said yes and he made a joke about how, having lost all memory of his own childhood, he would have to live out a new one with some boy.

May 29, 1948

I had a strange conversation with Elliott last night. André went home to his family at six and Elliott and I had an early dinner on the terrace. A beautiful evening: the sea green in the last light . . . a new moon. Eating fresh sole from the Channel, I told Elliott all about Jimmy, told him things I myself had nearly forgotten, had wanted to forget. I told him how it had started at twelve and gone on, without plan or thought or even acknowledgement until, at seventeen, I went to the army and he to the Marines and a quick death. After the army, I met Helen and forgot him completely; his death, like Elliott's shock treatment, took with it all memory, a thousand summer days abandoned on a coral island. I can't think now why on earth I told Elliott about Jimmy, not that I'm ashamed but it was, after all, something intimate, something nearly forgotten . . . anyway, when I finished, I sat there in the dark, not daring to look at Elliott, shivering as all in a rush the warmth left the sand about us and I had that terrible feeling I always have when I realize too late I've said too much. Finally, Elliott spoke. He gave me a strange disjointed speech about life and duty to oneself and how the moment is all one has and how it is dishonourable to cheat oneself of that . . . I'm not sure that he said anything very useful or very original but sitting there in the dark, listening, his words had a peculiar urgency for me and I felt, in a way, that I was listening to an oracle . . .

June 1, 1948

Shortly before lunch, the police came and arrested Elliott. Luckily, I was down on the beach and missed the whole thing . . . The hotel's in an uproar and the manager's behaving like a madman. It seems André stole Elliott's camera. His parents found it and asked him where he got it. He wouldn't tell. When they threatened him, he said Elliott gave him the camera and then, to make this story credible, he told them that Elliott had tried to seduce him . . . The whole sordid business then proceeded logically: parents to police . . . police to Elliott . . . arrest. I sat down shakily on the terrace and wondered what to do. I was . . . I am frightened. While I was sitting there, a gendarme came out on the terrace and told me Elliott wanted to see me, in prison. Meanwhile, the gendarme wanted to know what I knew about Mr Magren. It was only too apparent what his opinion of *me* was: another *pédérast américain*. My voice shook and my throat dried up as I told him I hardly knew Elliott . . . I'd only just met him . . . I knew nothing about his private life. The gendarme sighed and closed his notebook: the charges against Elliott were *très grave, très grave,* but I would be allowed to see him tomorrow morning. Then, realizing I was both nervous and uncooperative, the gendarme gave me the address of the jail and left. I went straight to my room and packed. I didn't think twice. All I wanted was to get away from Deauville, from Elliott, from the crime . . . and it *was* a crime, I'm sure of that. I was back in Paris in time for supper at the hotel.

June 4, 1948

Ran into Steven at the Café Flore and I asked him if there'd been any news of Elliott. Steven took the whole thing as a joke: yes, Elliott had called a mutual friend who was a lawyer and everything was all right. Money was spent; the charges were dropped and Elliott was staying on in Deauville for another week . . . doubtless to be near André. I was shocked but relieved to hear this. I'm not proud of my cowardice but I didn't want to be drawn into something I hardly understood.

Caught a glimpse of Hilda with some college boy, laughing and chattering as they left the brasserie across the street. I stepped behind a kiosk, not wanting Hilda to see me. Write Helen. See the doctor about wax in ears, also liver. Get tickets for Roland Petit ballet.

III

December 26, 1953

The most hideous hangover! How I hate Christmas, especially this one. Started out last night at the *Caprice* where the management gave a party, absolutely packed. The new room is quite stunning, to my surprise: black walls, white driftwood but not artsy-craftsy, a starlight effect for the ceiling . . . only the upholstery is really *mauvais goût* tufted velveteen in SAFFRON! . . . but then Piggy has no sense of colour and why somebody didn't stop him I'll never know. All the tired old faces were there. Everyone was going to the ballet except me and there was all the usual talk about who was sleeping with whom, such a bore . . . I mean who cares who . . . whom dancers sleep with? Though somebody did say that Niellsen was having an affair with Dr Bruckner which is something of a surprise considering what a mess there was at Fire Island last summer over just that. Anyway, I drank too many vodka martinis and, incidentally, met Robert Gammadge the English playwright who isn't at all attractive though he made the biggest play for me. He's supposed to be quite dreary but makes tons of money. He was with that awful Dickie Mallory whose whole life is devoted to meeting celebrities, even the wrong ones. Needless to say, he was in seventh heaven with his playwright in tow. I can't understand people like Dickie: what fun do they get out of always being second fiddle? After the *Caprice* I went over to Steven's new apartment on the river; it's in a remodelled tenement house and and I must say it's fun and the Queen Anne desk I sold him looks perfect heaven in his living room. I'll say one thing for him: Steven is one of the few people who has the good sense simply to let a fine piece go in a room. There were quite a few people there and we had New York champagne which is drinkable when you're already full of vodka. Needless to say, Steven pulled me off to one corner to ask about Bob. I wish people wouldn't be so sympathetic not that they really are of course but they feel they must *pretend* to be: actually, they're only curious. I said Bob *seemed* all right when I saw him last month. I didn't go into any details though Steven did his best to worm the whole story out of me. Fortunately, I have a good grip on myself nowadays and I am able to talk about the break-up quite calmly. I always tell everybody I hope Bob will do well in his new business and that I like Sydney very much . . . actually, I hear things are going badly, that the shop is doing *no* business and that Bob is drinking again which means he's busy cruising the streets and getting into trouble. Well, I'm out of it and any day now I'll meet somebody . . . though it's funny how seldom you see anyone who's really attractive. There was a nice young Swede at Steven's but I never did get his name and anyway he is being kept by that ribbon clerk from the Madison Avenue Store. After Steven's I went to a real brawl in the Village: a studio apartment, packed with people, dozens of new faces, too. I wish now I hadn't got so drunk because there were some really attractive people there. I was all set, I thought, to go home with one but the friend intervened at the last moment and it looked for a moment like there was going to be real trouble before our host separated us . . . I never did get the host's name, I think he's in advertising. So I ended up alone. Must call doctor about hepatitis pills, write Leonore Fini, check last month's invoices (re, missing Sheraton receipt), call Mrs Blaine-Smith about sofa.

December 27, 1953

I finally had tea with Mrs Blaine-Smith today . . . one of the most beautiful women I've ever met, so truly chic and well-dressed . . . I'm hopelessly indebted to Steven for bringing us together: she practically keeps the shop going. She had only six or seven people for tea, very much *en famille*, and I couldn't've been more surprised and pleased when she asked me to stay on. (I expect she knows what a discount I gave her on that Heppelwhite sofa.) Anyway, one of her guests was an Italian Count who was terribly nice though unattractive. We sat next to each other on that delicious ottoman in the library and chatted about Europe after the war: what a time that was! I told him I hadn't been back since 1948 but even so we knew quite a few people in common. Then, as always, the name Elliott Magren was mentioned. He's practically a codeword . . . if you know Elliott, well, you're on the inside and of course the Count (as I'd expected all along) knew Elliott and we exchanged bits of information about him, skirting carefully drugs and small boys because Mrs Blaine-Smith though she knows everyone (and everything) *never* alludes to that sort of thing in any way, such a relief after so many of the queen bees you run into. Hilda, for instance, who married the maddest designer in Los Angeles and gives, I am told, the crudest parties with everyone drunk from morning till night. (Must stop drinking so much: nothing *after* dinner, that's the secret . . . especially with my liver.) We were discussing Elliott's apartment in the Rue du Bac and that marvellous Tchelichew that hangs over his bed when a little Englishman whose name I never did get, turned and said: did you know that Elliott Magren died last week? I must say it was stunning news, sitting in Mrs Blaine-Smith's library so far, far away . . . The Count was even more upset than I (could he have been one of Elliott's numerous admirers?). I couldn't help recalling then that terrible time at Deauville when Elliott was arrested and I had had to put up bail for him and hire a lawyer, all in French! Suddenly everything came back to me in a flood: that summer, the affair with Hilda . . . and Helen (incidentally, just this morning got a Christmas card from Helen, the first word in years: a photograph of her husband and three ghastly children, all living in Toledo: well, I suppose she's happy). But what an important summer that was, the chrysalis burst at last which, I think, prepared me for all the bad luck later when I failed my doctorate and had to go to work in Steven's office . . . And now Elliott's dead. Hard to believe someone you once knew is actually dead, not like the war where sudden absences in the roster were taken for granted. The Englishman told us the whole story. It seems Elliott was rounded up in a police raid on dope addicts in which a number of very famous people were caught, too. He was told to leave the country; so he piled everything into two taxicabs and drove to the Gare St Lazare where he took a train for Rome. He settled down in a small apartment off the Via Veneto. Last fall he underwent another series of shock treatment, administered by a quack doctor who cured him of drugs but lost his memory for him in the process. Aside from this, he was in good health and looked as young as ever except that for some reason he dyed his hair red . . . too mad! Then, last week, he made a date to go to the opera with a friend. The friend arrived . . . the door was open but, inside, there was no Elliott. The friend was particularly annoyed because Elliott often would not show up at all if, en route to an appointment, he happened to see someone desirable in the street. I remember Elliott telling me once that his greatest pleasure was to follow a handsome stranger for hours on end through the streets of a city. It was not so much the chase which interested him as the identification he had with the boy he followed: he would become the other, imitating his gestures, his gait, becoming himself young, absorbed in a boy's life. But Elliott had followed no one that day. The friend finally found him face down in the bathroom, dead. When the autopsy was performed, it was discovered that Elliott had had a malformed heart, an extremely rare case, and he might have died as suddenly at any moment in his life . . . the drugs, the shock treatments and so on had contributed nothing to his death. He was buried Christmas day in the Protestant cemetery close to Shelley, in good company to the end. I must say I can't imagine him with red hair . . . The Count asked me to have dinner with him tomorrow at the Colony (!) and I said I'd be delighted. Then Mrs Blaine-Smith told the most devastating story about the Duchess of Windsor in Palm Beach.

Find out about Helen Gleason's sphinxes. Call Bob about the keys to the back closet. Return Steven's copy of 'Valmouth'. *Find out the Count's name before dinner tomorrow.*

# Two on a Party

## TENNESSEE WILLIAMS

He couldn't really guess the age of the woman, Cora, but she was certainly not any younger than he, and he was almost thirty-five. There were some mornings when he thought she looked, if he wasn't flattering himself, almost old enough to be his mother, but there were evenings when the liquor was hitting her right, when her eyes were lustrous and her face becomingly flushed, and then she looked younger than he. As you get to know people, if you grow to like them, they begin to seem younger to you. The cruelty or damaging candour of the first impression is washed away like the lines in a doctored photograph, and Billy no longer remembered that the first night he met her he had thought of her as 'an old bag'. Of course, that night when he first met her she was not looking her best. It was in a Broadway bar; she was occupying the stool next to Billy and she had lost a diamond ear-clip and was complaining excitedly about it to the barman. She kept ducking down like a diving seal to look for it among the disgusting refuse under the brass rail, bobbing up and down and grunting and complaining, her face inflamed and swollen by the exertion, her rather heavy figure doubled into ludicrous positions. Billy had the uncomfortable feeling that she suspected him of stealing the diamond ear-clip. Each time she glanced at him his face turned hot. He always had that guilty feeling when anything valuable was lost, and it made him angry; he thought of her as an irritating old bag. Actually she wasn't accusing anybody of stealing the diamond ear-clip; in fact she kept assuring the barman that the clasp on the ear-clip was loose and she was a goddamn fool to put it on.

Then Billy found the thing for her, just as he was about to leave the bar, embarrassed and annoyed beyond endurance; he noticed the sparkle of it almost under his shoe, the one on the opposite side from the ducking and puffing 'old bag'. With the sort of school-teacherish austerity that he assumed when annoyed, when righteously indignant over something, an air that he had picked up during his short, much earlier, career as an English instructor at a midwestern university, he picked up the clip and slammed it wordlessly down on the bar in front of her and started to walk away. Two things happened to detain him. Three sailors off a Norwegian vessel came one, two, three through the revolving door of the bar and headed straight for the vacant stools just beyond where he had been sitting, and at the same instant, the woman, Cora, grabbed hold of his arm, shouting, Oh, don't go, the least you can do is let me buy you a drink! And so he had turned right around, as quickly and precisley as the revolving door through which the glittering trio of Norsemen had entered. OK, why not? He resumed his seat beside her, she bought him a drink, he bought her a drink, inside of five minutes they were buying beer for the sailors and it was just as if the place was suddenly lit up by a dozen big chandeliers.

Quickly she looked different to him, not an old bag at all but really sort of attractive and obviously more to the taste of the dazzling Norsemen than Billy could be. Observing the two of them in the long bar mirror, himself and Cora, he saw that they looked good together, they made a good pair, they were mutually advantageous as a team for cruising the Broadway bars. She was a good deal darker than he and more heavily built. Billy was slight and he had very blond skin that the sun turned pink. Unfortunately for Billy, the pink also showed through the silky, thin yellow hair on the crown of his head where the baldness, so fiercely but impotently resisted, was now becoming a fact that he couldn't disown. Of course, the crown of the head doesn't show in the mirror unless you bow to your image in the glass, but there is no denying that the top of a queen's head is a conspicuous area on certain occasions which are not unimportant. That was how he put it, laughing about it to Cora. She said, Honey, I swear to Jesus I think you're more self-conscious about your looks and your age than I am! She said it kindly, in fact, she said everything kindly. Cora was a kind person. She was the kindest person that Billy had ever met. She said and meant everything kindly, literally everything; she hadn't a single malicious bone in her body, not a particle of jealousy or suspicion or evil in her nature, and that was what made it so sad that Cora was a lush. Yes, after he stopped thinking of her as 'an old bag', which was almost immediately after they got acquainted, he started thinking of Cora as a lush, yes, but not as kindly as Cora thought about him, for Billy was not, by nature, as kind as Cora. Nobody else could be. Her kindness was monumental, the sort that simply doesn't exist any more, at least not in the queen world.

Fortunately for Billy, Billy was fairly tall. He had formed the defensive habit of holding his head rather high so that the crown of it wouldn't be so noticeable in bars, but unfortunately for Billy, he had what doctors had told him was a calcium deposit in the ears which made him hard of hearing and which could only be corrected by a delicate and expensive operation – boring a hole in the bone. He didn't have much money; he had just saved enough to live, not frugally but carefully, for two or three more years before he would have to go back to work at something. If he had the ear operation, he would have to go back to work right away and so abandon his sybaritic existence which suited him better than the dubious glory of being a somewhat better than hack writer of Hollywood film scenarios and so forth. Yes, and so forth!

Being hard of hearing, in fact, progressively so, he would have to crouch over and bend sidewise a little to hold a conversation in a bar, that is, if he wanted to understand what the other party was saying. In a bar it's dangerous not to listen to the other party, because the way of speaking is just as important as the look of the face in distinguishing between good trade and dirt, and Billy did not at all enjoy being beaten as some queens do. So he would have

to bend sidewise and expose the almost baldness on the crown of
his blond head, and he would cringe and turn red instead of pink
with embarrassment as he did so. He knew that it was ridiculous
of him to be that sensitive about it. But as he said to Cora, age does
worse things to a queen than it does to a woman.

She disagreed about that and they had great arguments about it.
But it was a subject on which Billy could hold forth as eloquently
as a southern Senator making a filibuster against the repeal of the
poll tax, and Cora would lose the argument by default, simply not
able to continue it any longer, for Cora did not like gloomy topics
of conversation so much as Billy liked them.

About her own defects of appearance, however, Cora was
equally distressed and humble.

You see, she would tell him, I'm really a queen myself. I mean
it's the same difference, honey, I like and do the same things,
sometimes I think in bed if they're drunk enough they don't know
I'm a woman, at least they don't act like they do, and I don't blame
them. Look at me, I'm a mess I'm getting so heavy in the hips and
I've got these big udders on me!

Nonsense, Billy would protest, you have a healthy and beautiful female body, and you mustn't low-rate yourself all the time
that way, I won't allow it!

And he would place his arm about her warm and Florida-sun-
browned shoulders, exposed by her backless white gown (the
little woolly-looking canary yellow jacket being deposited on a
vacant bar stool beside her), for it was usually quite late, almost
time for the bars to close, when they began to discuss what the
years had done to them, the attritions of time. Beside Billy, too,
there would be a vacant bar stool on which he had placed the hat
that concealed this thinning hair from the streets. It would be one
of those evenings that gradually wear out the exhilaration you
start with. It would be one of those evenings when lady luck
showed the bitchy streak in her nature. They would have had one
or two promising encounters which had fizzled out, coming to a
big fat zero at three a.m. In the game they played, the true
refinement of torture is to almost pull in a catch and then the line

breaks, and when that happens, each not pitying himself as much as he did the other, they would sit out the final hour before closing, talking about the wicked things time had done to them, the gradual loss of his hearing and his hair, the fatty expansion of her breasts and buttocks, forgetting that they were still fairly attractive people and still not old.

Actually, in the long run their luck broke about fifty-fifty. Just about every other night one or the other of them would be successful in the pursuit of what Billy called 'the lyric quarry'. One or the other or both might be successful on the good nights, and if it was a really good night, then both would be. Good nights, that is, really good nights, were by no means as rare as hen's teeth nor were they as frequent as streetcars, but they knew very well, both of them, that they did better together than they had done separately in the past. They set off something warm and good in each other that strangers responded to with something warm and good in themselves. Loneliness dissolved any reserve and suspicion, the night was a great warm comfortable meeting of people, it shone, it radiated, it had the effect of a dozen big chandeliers, oh, it was great, it was grand, you simply couldn't describe it, you got the coloured lights going, and there it all was, the final pattern of it and the original pattern, all put together, made to fit exactly, no, there were simply no words good enough to describe it. And if the worst happened, if someone who looked like a Botticelli angel drew a knife, or if the law descended suddenly on you, and those were eventualities the possibility of which a queen must always consider, you still could say you'd had a good run for your money.

Like everyone whose life is conditioned by luck, they had some brilliant streaks of it and some that were dismal. For instance, that first week they operated together in Manhattan. That was really a freak; you couldn't expect a thing like that to happen twice in a lifetime. The trade was running as thick as spawning salmon up those narrow cataracts in the Rockies. Head to tail, tail to head, crowding, swarming together, seemingly driven along by some immoderate instinct. It was not a question of catching; it was simply a question of deciding which ones to keep and which to throw back in the stream, all glittering, all swift, all flowing one way which was towards you!

That week was in Manhattan, where they teamed up. It was, to be exact, in Emerald Joe's at the corner of Forty-second and Broadway that they had met each other the night of the lost diamond clip that Billy had found. It was the week of the big blizzard and the big Chinese Red offensive in North Korea. The combination seemed to make for a wildness in the air, and trade is always best when the atmosphere of a city is excited whether it be over a national election or New Year's or a championship prize-fight or the World Series baseball games; anything that stirs up the whole population makes it better for cruising.

Yes, it was a lucky combination of circumstances, and that first week together had been brilliant. It was before they started actually living together. At that time, she had a room at the Hotel Pennsylvania and he had one at the Astor. But at the end of that week, the one of their first acquaintance, they gave up separate establishments and took a place together at a small East Side Hotel in the Fifties, because of the fact that Cora had an old friend from her hometown in Louisiana employed there as the night clerk. This one was a gay one that she had known long ago and innocently expected to be still the same. Cora did not understand how some people turn bitter. She had never turned bitchy and it was not understandable to her that others might. She said this friend on the desk was a perfect set up; he'd be delighted to see them bringing in trade. But that was the way in which it failed to work out . . .

That second week in New York was not a good one. Cora had been exceeding her usual quota of double ryes on the rocks and it began all at once to tell on her appearance. Her system couldn't absorb any more; she had reached the saturation point, and it was no longer possible for her to pick herself up in the evening. Her face had a bloated look and her eyes remained bloodshot all the time. They looked, as she said, like a couple of poached eggs in a sea of blood, and Billy had to agree with her that they did. She started looking her oldest and she had the shakes.

Then about Friday of that week the gay one at the desk turned bitchy on them. Billy had expected him to turn, but Cora hadn't. Sooner or later, Billy knew, that frustrated queen was bound to get a severe attack of jaundice over the fairly continual coming and going of so much close-fitting blue wool, and Billy was not mistaken. When they brought their trade in, he would slam down the key without looking at them or speaking a word of greeting. Then one night they brought in a perfectly divine-looking pharmacist's mate of Italian extraction and his almost equally attractive buddy. The old friend of Cora's exploded, went off like a spit-devil.

I'm sorry, he hissed, but this is *not* a flea-bag! You should have stayed on Times Square where you started.

There was a scene. He refused to give them their room-key unless the two sailors withdrew from the lobby. Cora said, Fuck you, Mary, and reached across the desk and grabbed the key from the hook. The old friend seized her wrist and tried to make her let go.

Put that key down, he shrieked, or you'll be sorry!

He started twisting her wrist; then Billy hit him; he vaulted right over the desk and knocked the son-of-a-bitch into the switchboard.

Call the police, call the police, the clerk screamed to the porter.

Drunk as she was, Cora suddenly pulled herself together. She took as much command of the situation as could be taken.

You boys wait outside, she said to the sailors, there's no use in you all getting into S.P. trouble.

One of them, the Italian, wanted to stay and join in the roughhouse, but his buddy, who was the bigger one, forcibly removed him to the sidewalk. (Cora and Billy never saw them again.) By the time, Billy had the night clerk by the collar and was giving him slaps that bobbed his head right and left like something rubber, as if that night clerk was everything that he loathed in a hostile world. Cora stopped him. She had that wonderful, that really invaluable faculty of sobering up in a crisis. She pulled Billy off her old friend and tipped the coloured porter ten dollars not to call in the law. She turned on all her southern charm and sweetness, trying to straighten things out. You darling, she said, you poor darling, to the bruised night clerk. The law was not called, but the outcome of the situation was far from pleasant. They had to check out, of course, and the hysterical old friend said he was going to write Cora's family in Alexandria, Louisiana, and give them a factual report on how she was living here in New York and how he supposed she was living anywhere else since she'd left home and he knew her.

At that time Billy knew almost nothing about Cara's background and former life, and he was surprised at her being so upset over this hysterical threat, which seemed unimportant to him. But all the next day Cora kept alluding to it, speculating whether or not the bitch would really do it, and it was probably on account of this threat that Cora made up her mind to leave New York. It was the only time, while they were living together, that Cora ever made a decision, at least about places to go and when to go to them. She had none of that desire to manage and dominate which is a typically American perversion of the female nature. As Billy said to himself, with that curious harshness of his towards things he loved, she was like a big piece of seaweed. Sometimes he said it irritably to himself, just like a big piece of seaweed washing this way and that way. It isn't healthy or normal to be so passive, Billy thought.

Where do you want to eat?

I don't care.

No, tell me, Cora, what place would you prefer?

I really don't care, she'd insist, it makes no difference to me.

Sometimes out of exasperation he would say, All right, let's eat at the Automat.

Only then would Cara demur.

Of course, if you want to, honey, but couldn't we eat some place with a liquor licence?

She was agreeable to anything and everything; she seemed to be grateful for any decision made for her, but this one time, when they left New York, when they made their first trip together, it was Cora's decision to go. This was before Billy began to be

terribly fond of Cora, and at first, when Cora said, Honey, I've got
to leave this town or Hugo (the hotel queen) will bring up Bobo
(her brother who was a lawyer in Alexandria and who had played
some very unbrotherly legal trick on her when a certain inheritance was settled) and there will be hell to pay, he will freeze up
my income – then, at this point, Billy assumed that they would go
separate ways. But at the last moment Billy discovered that he
didn't want to go back to a stag existence. He discovered that
solitary cruising had been lonely, that there were spirtual comforts
as well as material advantages in their double arrangements. No
matter how bad luck was, there was no longer such a thing as
going home by himself to the horrors of a second or third-class
hotel bedroom. Then there *were* the material advantages, the fact
they actually did better operating together, and the fact that it was
more economical. Billy had to be somewhat mean about money
since he was living on savings that he wanted to stretch as far as he
could, and Cora more than carried her own weight in the expense
department, She was only too eager to pick up a check and Billy
was all too willing to let her do it. She spoke of her income but she
was vague about what it was or came from. Sometimes looking
into her handbag she had a fleeting expression of worry that made
Billy wonder uncomfortably if her finances, like his, might not be
continually dwindling toward an eventual point of eclipse. But
neither of them had a provident nature or dared to stop and
consider much of the future.

Billy was a light traveller, all he carried with him was a three-
suiter, a single piece of hand luggage and his portable typewriter.
When difficulties developed at a hotel, he could clear out in five
minutes or less. He rubbed his chin for a minute, then he said,
Cora, how about me going with you?

They shared a compartment in the Sunshine Special to Florida.
Why to Florida? One of Cora's very few pretensions was a little
command of French; she was fond of using little French phrases
which she pronounced badly. Honey, she said, I have a little *pied-
à-terre* in Florida.

*Pied-à-terre* was one of those little French phrases that she was proud of using, and she kept talking about it, her little *pied-à-terre* in the Sunshine State.

Whereabouts is it, Billy asked her.

No place fashionable, she told him, but just wait and see and you might be surprised and like it.

That night in the shared compartment of the Pullman was the first time they had sex together. It happened casually, it was not important and it was not very satisfactory, perhaps because they were each too anxious to please the other, each too afraid the other would be disappointed. Sex has to be slightly selfish to have real excitement. Start worrying about the other party's reactions and the big charge just isn't there, and you've got to do it a number of times together before it becomes natural enough to be a completely satisfactory thing. The first time between strangers can be like a blaze of light, but when it happens between people who know each other well and have an established affection, it's likely to be self-conscious and even a little embarrassing, most of all afterwards.

Afterwards they talked about it with a slight sense of strain. They felt they had gotten that sort of thing squared away and would not have to think about it between them again. But perhaps, in a way, it did add a little something to the intimacy of their living together; at least it had, as they put it, squared things away a bit. And they talked about it shyly, each one trying too hard to flatter the other.

Gee, honey, said Cora, you're a wonderful lay, you've got wonderful skin, smooth as a baby's, gee, it sure was wonderful, honey, I enjoyed it so much, I wish you had. But I know you didn't like it and it was selfish of me to start it with you.

*You* didn't like it, he said.

I swear I *loved* it, she said, but I knew that *you* didn't like it, so we won't do it again.

He told Cora that she was a wonderful lay and that he had loved it every bit as much as she did and maybe more, but he agreed they'd better not do it again.

Friends can't be lovers, he said.

No, they can't, she agreed with a note of sadness.

Then jealousy enters in.

Yes, they get jealous and bitchy . . .

They never did it again, at least not that completely, not any time during the year and two months since they started living together. Of course, there were some very drunk, *blind* drunk nights when they weren't quite sure what happened between them after they fell into bed, but you could be pretty certain it wasn't a sixty-six in that condition. Sixty-six was Cora's own slightly inexact term for a normal lay, that is, a lay that occurred in the ordinary position.

What happened? Billy would ask when she'd had a party.

Oh, it was wonderful, she would exclaim, a sixty-six!

Good Jesus, drunk as he was?

Oh, I sobered him up, she'd laugh.

And what did you do, Billy? Take the sheets? Ha ha, you'll have to leave this town with a board nailed over your ass!

Sometimes they had a serious conversation, though most of the time they tried to keep the talk on a frivolous plane. It troubled Cora to talk about serious matters, probably because matters were too serious to be talked about with comfort. And for the first month or so neither of them knew that the other one actually had a mind that you could talk to. Gradually they discovered about each other the other things, and although it was always their mutual pursuit, endless and indefatigable, of 'the lyric quarry' that was the mainstay of their relationship, at least upon its surface, the other things, the timid and tender values that can exist between people, began to come shyly out and they had a respect for each other, not merely to like and enjoy, as neither had ever respected another person.

It was a rare sort of moral anarchy, doubtless, that held them together, a really fearful shared hatred of everything that was restrictive and which they felt to be false in the society they lived in and against the grain of which they continually operated. They did not dislike what they called 'squares'. They loathed and despised them, and for the best of reasons. Their existence was a

never-ending contest with the squares of the world, the squares
who have such a virulent rage at everything not in their book.
Getting around the squares, evading, defying the phony rules of
convention, that was maybe responsible for half their pleasure in
their outlaw existence. They were a pair of kids playing cops and
robbers: except for that element, the thrill of something lawless,
they probably would have gotten bored with cruising. Maybe not,
maybe so. Who can tell? But hotel clerks and house dicks and
people in adjoining hotel bedrooms, the spectre of Cora's family
in Alexandria, Louisiana, the spectre of Billy's family in Montgo-
mery, Alabama, the various people involved in the niggardly
control of funds, almost everybody that you passed when you
were drunk and hilariously gay on the street, especially all those
bull-like middle-aged couples that stood off sharply and glared at
you as you swept through a hotel lobby with your blushing trade –
all, all, of those were natural enemies to them, as well as the one
great terrible, worst of all enemies, which is the fork-tailed,
cloven-hoofed, pitchfork-bearing devil of time!

Time, of course, was the greatest enemy of all, and they knew
that each day and each night was cutting down a little on the
distance between the two of them running together and that
demon pursuer. And knowing it, knowing that nightmarish fact,
gave a wild sort of sweetness of despair to their two-ring circus.

And then, of course, there was also the fact that Billy was, or
had been at one time, a sort of artist *manqué* and still had a touch of
homesickness for what that was.

Sometime, said Cora, you're going to get off the party.

Why should I get off the party?

Because you're a serious person. You are fundamentally a
serious sort of a person.

I'm not a serious person any more than you are. I'm a goddamn
remittance man and you know it.

No, I don't know it, said Cora. Remittance men get letters
enclosing cheques, but you don't even get letters.

Billy rubbed his chin.

Then how do you think I live?

Ha ha, she said.

What does 'Ha Ha' mean?

It means I know what I know!

Balls, said Billy, you know no more about me than I do about you.

I know, said Cora, that you used to write for a living, and that for two years you haven't been writing but you're still living on the money you made as a writer, and sooner or later, you're going to get off the party and go back to working again and being a serious person. What do you imagine I think of that portable typewriter you drag around with you everywhere we go, and that big fat portfolio full of papers you tote underneath your shirts in your three-suiter? I wasn't born yesterday or the day before yesterday, baby, and I know that you're going to get off the party some day and leave me on it.

If I get off the party, we'll get off it together, said Billy.

And me do *what*? she'd ask him, realistically.

And he would not be able to answer that question. For she knew and he knew, both of them knew it together, that they would remain together only so long as they stayed on the party, and not any longer than that. And in his heart he knew, much as he might deny it, that it would be pretty much as Cora predicted in her Cassandra moods. One of those days or nights it was bound to happen. He would get off the party, yes, he would certainly be the one of them to get off it, because there was really nothing for Cora to do but stay on it. Of course, if she broke down, that would take her off it. Usually or almost always it's only a breakdown that takes you off a party. A party is like a fast-moving train – you can't jump off it, it thunders past the stations you might get off at, very few people have the courage to leap from a thing that is moving that fast, they have to stay with it no matter where it takes them. It only stops when it crashes, the ticker wears out, a blood vessel bursts, the liver or kidneys quit working. But Cora was tough. Her system had absorbed a lot of punishment, but from present appearances it was going to absorb a lot more. She was too tough to crack up any time soon, but she was not tough enough to make the clean break, the daring jump off, that Billy knew, or felt that he knew, that he was still able to make when he was ready to make it. Cora was five or maybe even ten years older than Billy. She rarely looked it, but she was that much older and time is one of the biggest differences between two people.

I've got news for you, baby, and you had better believe it.

What news?

This news, Cora would say. You're going to get off the party and leave me on it!

Well, it was probably true, as true as anything is, and what a pity it was that Cora was such a grand person. If she had not been such a nice person, so nice that at first you thought it must be phony and only gradually came to see it was real, it wouldn't matter so much. For usually queens fall out like a couple of thieves quarrelling over the split of the loot. Billy remembered the one in Baton Rouge who was so annoyed when he confiscated a piece she had a lech for that she made of Billy an effigy of candle wax and stuck pins in it with dreadful imprecations, kept the candle-wax effigy on her mantel and performed black rites before it. But Cora was not like that. She didn't have a jealous bone in her body. She took as much pleasure in Billy's luck as her own. Sometimes he suspected she was more interested in Billy having good luck than having it herself.

Sometimes Billy would wonder. Why do we do it?

We're lonely people, she said, I guess it's as simple as that . . .

But nothing is ever quite so simple as it appears when you are comfortably loaded.

Take this occasion, for instance.

Billy and Cora are travelling by motor. The automobile is a joint possession which they acquired from a used-car dealer in Galveston. It is a '47 Buick convertible with a brilliant new scarlet paint-job. Cora and Billy are outfitted with corresponding brilliance; she has on a pair of black and white checked slacks, a cowboy shirt with a bucking broncho over one large breast and a roped steer over the other, and she has on harlequin sun-glasses with false diamonds encrusting the rims. Her freshly peroxided hair is bound girlishly on top of her head with a diaphanous scarf of magenta chiffon; she has on her diamond ear-clips and her multiple slave-bracelets, three of them real gold and two of them only gold-plated, and hundreds of little tinkling gold attachments, such as tiny footballs, liberty bells, hearts, mandolins, choo-choos, sleds, tennis rackets, and so forth. Billy thinks she has overdone it a little. It must be admitted, however that she is a noticeable person, especially at the wheel of this glittering scarlet Roadmaster. They have swept down the Camino Real, the Old Spanish Trail, from El Paso eastward instead of westward, having decided at the last moment to resist the allure of Southern California on the other side of the Rockies and the desert, since it appears that the Buick has a little tendency to overheat and Cora notices that the oil pressure is not what it should be. So they have turned eastward instead of westward, with a little side trip to Corpus Christi to investigate the fact or fancy of those legendary seven connecting glory-holes in a certain tearoom there. It turned out to be fancy or could not be located. Says Cora: You queens know places but never know where places are!

A blowout going into New Orleans. That's to be expected, said Cora, they never give you good rubber. The spare is no good either. Two new tyres had to be bought in New Orleans and Cora paid for them by hocking some of her baubles. There was some money left over and she buys Billy a pair of cowboy boots. They are still on the Wild West kick. Billy also presents a colourful appearance in a pair of blue jeans that fit as if they had been painted on him, the fancily embossed cowboy boots and a sport shirt that is covered with leaping dolphins, Ha ha! They have never had so much fun in their life together, the coloured lights are going like pinwheels on the Fourth of July, everything is big and very bright celebration. The Buick appears to be a fairly solid investment, once it has good rubber on it and they get those automatic devices to working again . . .

It is a mechanical age that we live in, they keep saying.

They did Mobile, Pensacola, West Palm Beach and Miami in one continual happy breeze! The scoreboard is brilliant! Fifteen lays, all hitching on the highway, since they got the convertible. It's all we ever needed to hit the jackpot, Billy exults . . .

Then comes the badman into the picture!

They are on the Florida keys, just about midway between the objective, Key West, and on the tip of the peninsula. Nothing is visible about them but sky and mangrove swamp. Then all of a sudden that used-car dealer in Galveston pulls the grinning joker out of his sleeve. Under the hood of the car comes a loud metallic noise as if steel blades are scraping. The fancy heap will not take the gas. It staggers gradually to a stop, and trying to start it again succeeds only in running the battery down. Moreover, the automatic top has ceased to function; it is the meridian of a day in early spring which is as hot as midsummer on the Florida Keys . . .

Cora would prefer to make light of the situation, if Billy would let her do so. The compartment of the dashboard is filled with roadmaps, a flashlight and a thermos of dry martinis. The car has barely uttered its expiring rattle and gasp when Cora's intensely ornamented arm reaches out for this unfailing simplification of the human dilemma. For the first time in their life together, Billy interferes with her drinking, and out of pure meanness. He grabs her wrist and restrains her. He is suddenly conscious of how disgusted he is with what he calls her Oriental attitude toward life. The purchase of this hoax was her idea. Two thirds of the investment was also her money. Moreover she had professed to be a pretty good judge of motors. Billy himself had frankly confessed that he couldn't tell a spark plug from a carburetor. So it was Cora who had examined and appraised the possible buys on the used-car lots of Galveston and come upon this 'bargain'! She had looked under the hoods and shimmied fatly under the chassis of dozens of cars before she arrived at this remarkably misguided choice. The car had been suspiciously cheap for a '47 Roadmaster with such a brilliantly smart appearance, but Cora said it was just as sound as the American dollar! She put a thousand dollars into the deal and Billy put in five hundred which had come in from the resale to pocket editions of a lurid potboiler he had written under a pseudonym a number of years ago when he was still an active member of the literary profession.

Now Cora was reaching into the dashboard compartment for a thermos of martinis because the car whose purchase was her responsibility had collasped in the middle of nowhere . . .

Billy seizes her wrist and twists it.

Let go of that godamn thermos, you're not gonna get drunk!

She struggles with him a little, but soon she gives up and suddenly goes feminine and starts to cry.

After that a good while passes in which they sit side by side in silence in the leather-lined crematorium of the convertible.

A humming sound begins to be heard in the distance. Perhaps it's a motorboat on the other side of the mangroves, perhaps something on the highway . . .

Cora begins to jingle and jangle as she twists her ornamented person this way and that way with nervous henlike motions of the head and shoulder and torso, peering about on both sides and half rising and flopping awkwardly back down again, and finally grunting eagerly and piling out of the car, losing her balance, sprawling into a ditch, ha ha, scrambling up again, taking the middle of the road and making great frantic circles with her arms as a motorcycle approaches. If the cyclist had desired to pass them it would have been possible. Later Billy will remind her that it was *she* who stopped it. But right now Billy is enchanted, not merely at the prospect of a rescue but much more by the looks of the potential instrument of rescue. The motorcyclist is surely something dispatched from a sympathetic region back of the sun. He has one of those blond and block-shaped heads set upon a throat which is as broad as the head itself and has the smooth and supple muscularity of the male organ in its early stage of tumescence. This bare throat and blond head above it have never been in a country where the sun is distant. The hands are enormous square knobs to the golden doors of Paradise. And the legs that straddle the quiescent fury of the cycle (called Indian) could not have been better designed by the appreciative eyes and fingers of Michelangelo or Phidias or Rodin. It is in the direct and pure line of those who have witnessed and testified in stone what they have seen of a simple physical glory in mankind! The eyes are behind sunglasses. Cora is a judge of eyes but she has to see them to judge them. Sometimes she will say to a young man wearing sunglasses, will you kindly uncover the windows of your soul? She considers herself to be a better judge of good and bad trade than is Billy whose record contains a number of memorable errors. Later Cora will remember that from the moment she saw this youth on the motorcycle something whispered *Watch Out* in her ear. Honey, she will say, later, he had more Stop signs on him than you meet when you've got five minutes to get to the station! Perhaps this will be an exaggerated statement, but it is true that Cora had misgivings in exact proportion to Billy's undisguised enchantment.

As for right now, the kid seems fairly obliging. He swings his great legs off the cycle which he rests upon a metal support. He hardly says anything. He throws back the hood of the car and crouches into it for a couple of minutes, hardly more than that, then the expressionless blond cube comes back into view and announces without inflection, Bearings gone out.

What does that mean, asks Cora.

That means you been screwed, he says.

What can we do about it?

Not a goddamn thing. You better junk it.

What did he say, inquires Billy.

He said, Cora tells him, that the bearings have gone out.

What are bearings?

The cyclist utters a short barking laugh. He is back astraddle the frankly shaped leather seat of his Indian, but Cora has once more descended from the Buick and she has resorted to the type of flirtation that even most queens would think common. She has fastened her bejewelled right hand over the elevated and narrow front section of the saddle which the boy sits astride. There is not only proximity but contact between their two parties, and all at once the boy's blond look is both contemptuous and attentive, and his attitude towards their situation has undergone a drastic alteration. He is now engaged in it again.

There's a garage on Boca Raton, he tells them. I'll see if they got a tow truck. I think they got one.

Off he roars down the Keys!

One hour and forty-five minutes later the abdicated Roadmaster is towed into a garage on Boca Raton, and Cora and Billy plus their new-found acquaintance are checking, all three, into a tourist cabin at a camp called The Idle-wild, which is across the highway from the garage.

Cora has thought to remove her thermos of martinis from the dashboard compartment, and this time Billy has not offered any objection. Billy is restored to good spirits. Cora still feels guilty, profoundly and abjectly guilty, about the purchase of the glittering fraud, but she is putting up a good front. She knows, however, that Billy will never quite forgive and forget and she does not understand why she made that silly profession of knowing so much about motors. It was, of course, to impress her beloved companion. He knows so much more than she about so many things, she has to pretend, now and then, to know *something* about *something*, even when she knows in her heart that she is a comprehensive and unabridged dictionary of human ignorance on nearly all things of importance. She sighs in her heart because she's become a pretender, and once you have pretended, is it ever possible to stop pretending?

Pretending to be a competent judge of a motor has placed her in the sad and embarrassing position of having cheated Billy out of five hundred dollars. How can she make it up to him?

A whisper in the heart of Cora: *I love him!*

Whom does she love?

There are three persons in the cabin, herself, and Billy and the young man from the highway.

Cora despises herself and she has never been much attracted to men of an altogether physical type.

So there is the dreadful answer! She is in love with Billy!

I am in love with Billy, she whispers to herself.

That acknowledgement seems to call for a drink.

She gets up and pours herself another martini. Unfortunately someone, probably Cora herself, has forgotten to screw the cap back on the thermos bottle and the drinks are now tepid. No drink is better than an ice-cold martini, but no drink is worse than a martini getting warm. However, be that as it may, the discovery just made, the one about loving Billy, well, after *that* one the temperature of a drink is not so important so long as the stuff is still liquor!

She says to herself: I have admitted a fact! Well, the only thing to do with a fact is admit it, but once admitted, you don't have to keep harping on it.

Never again, so long as she stays on the party with her companion, will she put into words her feelings for him, not even in the privacy of her heart . . .

*Le coeur a ses raisons que la raison ne connait pas!*

That is one of those little French sayings that Cora is proud of knowing and often repeats to herself as well as to others.

Sometimes she will translate it, to those who don't know French language, as follows.

The heart knows the scoop when the brain is ignorant of it!

Ha ha!

Well, now she is back in the cabin after a mental excursion that must have lasted at least a half an hour.

Things have progressed thus far.

Billy has stripped down to his shorts and he has persuaded the square-headed blond to do likewise.

Cora herself discovers that she has made concessions to the unseasonable warmth of the little frame building.

All she is wearing is her panties and bra.

She looks across without real interest at the square-headed stranger. Yes. A magnificent torso, as meaningless, now, to Cora as a jigsaw puzzle which put together exhibits a cow munching grass in a typical one-tree pasture.

Excuse me, people, she remarks to Billy. I just remembered I promised to make a long-distance call to Atlanta.

A long-distance call to Atlanta is a code message between herself and Billy.

What it means is this: The field is yours to conquer!

Cora goes out, having thrown on a jacket and pulled on her checkerboard slacks.

Where does Cora go? Not far, not far at all.

She is leaning against a palm tree not more than five yards distant from the cabin. She is smoking a cigarette in a shadow.

Inside the cabin the field is Billy's to conquer.

Billy says to the cyclist: How do you like me?

Huh . . .

(That is the dubious answer to his question!)

Billy gives him a drink, another one, thinking that this may evoke a less equivocal type of response.

How do you like me, now?

You want to know how I like you?

Yes!

I like you the way that a cattleman loves a sheepherder!

I am not acquainted, says Billy, with the likes and dislikes of men who deal in cattle.

Well, says the square-headed blond, if you keep messing around I'm going to give you a demonstration of it!

A minute is a microscope view of eternity.

It is less than a minute before Cora hears a loud sound.

She knew what it was before she even heard it, and almost before she heard it, that thud of a body not falling but thrown to a floor, she is back at the door of the cabin and pushing it open and returning inside.

*Hello*! is what she says with apparent good humour.

She does not seem to notice Billy's position and bloody mouth on the floor . . .

Well, she says, I got my call through to Atlanta!

While she is saying this, she is getting out of her jacket and checkerboard slacks, and she is not stopping there.

Instant diversion is the doctor's order.

She is stripped bare in ten seconds, and on the bed.

Billy has gotten outside and she is enduring the most undesired embrace that she can remember in all her long history of desired and undesired and sometimes only patiently borne embraces . . .

Why do we do it?

We're lonely people. I guess it's simple as that . . .

But nothing is ever that simple! Don't you know it?

And so the story continues where it didn't leave off . . .

Trade ceased to have much distinction. One piece was fundamentally the same as another, and the nights were like waves rolling in and breaking and retreating again and leaving you washed up on the wet sands of morning.

Something continual and something changeless.

The sweetness of their living together persisted.

We're friends! said Cora.

She meant a lot more than that, but Billy is satisfied with this spoken definition, and there's no other that can safely be framed in language.

Sometimes they look about them, privately and together, and what they see is something like what you see through a powerful telescope trained upon the moon, flatly illuminated craters and treeless plains and a vacancy of light – much light, but an emptiness in it.

Calium is the element of this world.

Each has held some private notion of death. Billy thinks his death is going to be violent. Cora thinks hers will be ungraciously slow. Something will surrender by painful inches . . .

Meanwhile they are together.

To Cora that's the one important thing left.

Cities!

You queens know places, but never know where places are!

No Mayor has ever handed them a gold key, nor have they entered under a silken banner of welcome, but they have gone to them all in the northern half of the western hemisphere, this side of the Arctic Circle! Ha ha, just about all . . .

*Many cities!*

Sometimes they wake up early to hear the awakening tumult of a city and to reflect upon it.

They're two on a party which has made a departure and a rather wide one.

Into brutality? No. It's not that simple.

Into vice? No. It isn't nearly that simple.

Into what, then?

Into something unlawful? Yes, of course!

But in the night, hands clasping and no questions asked.

In the moring, a sense of being together no matter what comes, and the knowledge of not having struck nor lied nor stolen.

A female lush and a fairy who travel together, who are two on a party, and the rush continues.

They wake up early, sometimes, and hear the city coming awake, the increase of traffic, the murmurous shuffle of crowds on their way to their work, the ordinary resumption of daytime life in a city, and they reflect upon it a little from their, shall we say, bird's-eye situation.

There's the radio and the newspaper and there is TV, which Billy says means 'Tired Vaudeville,' and everything that is known is known very fully and very fully stated.

But after all, when you reflect upon it at the only time that is suitable for reflection, what can you do but turn your other cheek to the pillow?

Two queens sleeping together with sometimes a stranger between them . . .

One morning a phone will ring.

Cora will answer, being the lighter sleeper and the quicker to rise.

*Bad news!*

Clapping a hand over the shrill mouthpiece, instinctive gesture of secrecy, she will cry to Billy.

Billy, Billy, wake up! They've raided the Flamingo! The heat is on! Get packed!

Almost gainly this message is delivered and the packing performed, for it's fun to fly away from a threat of danger.

(Most dreams are about it, one form of it or another, in which man remembers the distant mother with wings . . .)

Off they go, from Miami to Jacksonville, from Jacksonville to Savannah or Norfolk, all winter shuttling about the Dixie circuit, in spring going back to Manhattan, two birds flying together against the wind, nothing real but the party, and even that sort of dreamy.

In the morning, always Cora's voice addressing room service, huskily, softly, not to disturb his sleep before the coffee arrives, and then saying gently, Billy, Billy, your coffee . . .

Cup and teaspoon rattling like castanets as she hands it to him. often spilling a little on the bedclothes and saying, Oh, Honey, excuse me, ha ha!

# Pages from Cold Point

**PAUL BOWLES**

Our civilization is doomed to a short life: its component parts are too heterogeneous. I personally am content to see everything in the process of decay. The bigger the bombs, the quicker it will be done. Life is visually too hideous for one to make the attempt to preserve it. Let it go. Perhaps some day another form of life will come along. Either way, it is of no consequence. At the same time, I am still a part of life, and I am bound by this to protect myself to whatever extent I am able. And so I am here. Here in the Islands vegetation still has the upper hand, and man has to fight even to make his presence seen at all. It is beautiful here, the trade winds blow all year, and I suspect that bombs are extremely unlikely to be wasted on this unfrequented side of the island, if indeed on any part of it.

I was loath to give up the house after Hope's death. But it was the obvious move to make. My university career always having been an utter farce (since I believe no reason inducing a man to 'teach' can possibly be a valid one), I was elated by the idea of resigning, and as soon as her affairs had been settled and the money properly invested, I lost no time in doing so.

I think that week was the first time since childhood that I had managed to recapture the feeling of there being a content in existence. I went from one pleasant house to the next, making my adieux to the English quacks, the Philosophy fakirs, and so on – even to those colleagues with whom I was merely on speaking terms. I watched the envy in their faces when I announced my departure by Pan American on Saturday morning; and the greatest pleasure I felt in all this was in being able to answer, 'Nothing,' when I was asked, as invariably I was, what I intended to do.

When I was a boy people used to refer to Charles as 'Big Brother C.', although he is only a scant year older than I. To me now he is merely 'Fat Brother C.', a successful lawyer. His thick, red face and hands, his back-slapping joviality, and his fathomless hypocritical prudery, these are the qualities which make him truly repulsive to me. There is also the fact that he once looked not unlike the way Racky does now. And after all, he still is my big brother, and disapproves openly of everything I do. The loathing I feel for him is so strong that for years I have not been able to swallow a morsel of food or a drop of liquid in his presence without making a prodigious effort. No one knows this but me – certainly not Charles, who would be the last one I should tell about it. He came up on the late train two nights before I left. He got quickly to the point – as soon as he was settled with a highball.

'So you're off for the wilds,' he said, sitting forward in his chair like a salesman.

'If you can call it the wilds,' I replied. 'Certainly it's not wild like Mitichi.' (He has a lodge in northern Quebec.) 'I consider it really civilized.'

He drank and smacked his lips together stiffly, bringing the glass down hard on his knee.

'And Racky. You're taking him along?'

'Of course.'

'Out of school. Away. So he'll see nobody but you. You think that's good.'

I looked at him. 'I do,' I said.

'By God, if I could stop you legally, I would!' he cried, jumping up and putting his glass on the mantel. I was trembling inwardly with excitement, but I merely sat and watched him. He went on. 'You're not fit to have custody of the kid!' he shouted. He shot a stern glance at me over his spectacles.

'You think not?' I said gently.

Again he looked at me sharply. 'D'ye think I've forgotten?'

I was understandably eager to get him out of the house as soon as I could. As I piled and sorted letters and magazines on the desk, I said: 'Is that all you came to tell me? I have a good deal to do tomorrow and I must get some sleep. I probably shan't see you at breakfast. Agnes'll see that you eat in time to make the early train.'

All he said was: 'God! Wake up! Get wise to yourself! You're not fooling anybody, you know.'

That kind of talk is typical of Charles. His mind is slow and obtuse; he constantly imagines that everyone he meets is playing some private game of deception with him. He is so utterly incapable of following the functioning of even a moderately evolved intellect that he finds the will to secretiveness and duplicity everywhere.

'I haven't time to listen to that sort of nonsense,' I said, preparing to leave the room.

But he shouted, 'You don't want to listen! No! Of course not! You just want to do what you want to do. You just want to go on off down there and live as you've a mind to, and to hell with the consequences!' At this point I heard Racky coming downstairs. C. obviously heard nothing, and he raved on. 'But just remember, I've got your number all right, and if there's any trouble with the boy I'll know who's to blame.'

I hurried across the room and opened the door so he could see that Racky was there in the hallway. That stopped his tirade. It was hard to know whether Racky had heard any of it or not. Although he is not a quiet young person, he is the soul of discretion, and it is almost never possible to know any more about what goes on inside his head than he intends one to know.

I was annoyed that C. should have been bellowing at me in my own house. To be sure, he is the only one from whom I would accept such behaviour, but then, no father likes to have his son see him take criticism meekly. Racky simply stood there in his bathrobe, his angelic face quite devoid of expression, saying: 'Tell Uncle Charley good night for me, will you? I forgot.'

I said I would, and quickly shut the door. When I thought Racky was back upstairs in his room, I bade Charles good night. I have never been able to get out of his presence fast enough. The effect he has on me dates from an early period of our lives, from days I dislike to recall.

Racky is a wonderful boy. After we arrived, when we found it impossible to secure a proper house near any town where he might have the company of English boys and girls his own age, he showed no sign of chagrin, although he must have been disappointed. Instead, as we went out of the renting office into the glare of the street, he grinned and said: 'Well, I guess we'll have to get bikes, that's all.'

The few available houses near what Charles would have called 'civilization' turned out to be so ugly and so impossibly confined in atmosphere that we decided immediately on Cold Point, even though it was across the island and quite isolated on its seaside cliff. It was beyond a doubt one of the most desirable properties on the island, and Racky was as enthusiastic about its splendours as I.

'You'll get tired of being alone out there, just with me,' I said to him as we walked back to the hotel.

'Aw, I'll get along all right. When do we look for the bikes?'

At his insistence we bought two the next morning. I was sure I should not make much use of mine, but I reflected that an extra bicycle might be convenient to have around the house. It turned out that the servants all had their own bicycles, without which they would not have been able to get to and from the village of Orange Walk, eight miles down the shore. So for a while I was forced to get astride mine each morning before breakfast and pedal madly along beside Racky for a half hour. We would ride through the cool early air, under the towering silk-cotton trees near the house, and out to the great curve in the shoreline where the waving palms bend landward in the stiff breeze that always blows there. Then we would make a wide turn and race back to the house, loudly discussing the degrees of our desires for the various items of breakfast we knew were awaiting us there on the terrace. Back home we would eat in the wind, looking out over the Caribbean, and talk about the news in yesterday's local paper, brought to us by Isiah each morning from Orange Walk. Then Racky would disappear for the whole morning on his bicycle, riding furiously along the road in one direction or the other until he had discovered an unfamiliar strip of sand along the shore that he could consider a new beach. At lunch he would describe it in detail to me, along with a recounting of all the physical hazards involved in hiding the bicycle in among the trees, so that natives passing along the road on foot would not spot it, or in climbing down unscalable cliffs that turned out to be much higher than they had appeared at first sight, or in measuring the depth of the water preparatory to diving from the rocks, or in judging the efficacy of the reef in barring sharks and barracuda. There is never any element of bragadoccio in Racky's relating of his exploits – only the joyous excitement he derives from telling how he satisfies his inexhaustible curiosity. And his mind shows its alertness in all directions at once. I do not mean to say that I expect him to be an 'intellectual'. That is no affair of mine, nor do I have any particular interest in whether he turns out to be a thinking man or not. I know he will always have a certain boldness of manner and a great purity of spirit in judging values. The former will prevent his becoming what I call a 'victim': he never will be brutalized by realities. And his unerring sense of balance in ethical considerations will shield him from the paralysing effects of present-day materialism.

For a boy of sixteen Racky has an extraordinary innocence of vision. I do not say this as a doting father, although God knows I can never even think of the boy without the familiar overwhelming sensation of delight and gratitude for being vouchsafed the privilege of sharing my life with him. What he takes so completely as a matter of course, our daily life here together, is a source of never-ending wonder to me; and I reflect upon it a good part of each day, just sitting here being conscious of my great good fortune in having him all to myself, beyond the reach of prying eyes and malicious tongues. (I suppose I am really thinking of C.

when I write that.) And I believe that a part of the charm of sharing Racky's life with him consists precisely in his taking it all so utterly for granted. I have never asked him whether he likes being here – it is so patent that he does, very much. I think if he were to turn to me one day and tell me how happy he is here, that somehow, perhaps, the spell might be broken. Yet if he were to be thoughtless and inconsiderate, or even unkind to me, I feel that I should be able only to love him the more for it.

I have reread that last sentence. What does it mean? And why should I even imagine it could mean anything more than it says?

Still, much as I may try, I can never believe in the gratuitous, isolated fact. What I must mean is that I feel that Racky already has been in some way inconsiderate. But in what way? Surely I cannot resent his bicycle treks; I cannot expect him to want to stay and sit talking with me all day. And I never worry about his being in danger; I know he is more capable than most adults of taking care of himself, and that he is no more likely than any native to come to harm crawling over the cliffs or swimming in the bays. At the same time there is no doubt in my mind that something about our existence annoys me. I must resent some detail in the pattern, whatever that pattern may be. Perhaps it is just his youth, and I am envious of the lithe body, the smooth skin, the animal energy and grace.

For a long time this morning I sat looking out to sea, trying to solve that small puzzle. Two white herons came and perched on a dead stump east of the garden. They stayed a long time there without stirring. I would turn my head away and accustom my eyes to the bright sea-horizon, then I would look suddenly at them to see if they had shifted position, but they would always be in the same attitude. I tried to imagine the black stump without them – a purely vegetable landscape – but it was impossible. All the while I was slowly forcing myself to accept a ridiculous explanation of my annoyance with Racky. It had made itself manifest to me only yesterday, when instead of appearing for lunch, he sent a young coloured boy from Orange Walk to say that he would be lunching in the village. I could not help noticing that the boy was riding Racky's bicycle. I had been waiting lunch a good half hour for him, and I had Gloria serve immediately as the boy rode off, back to the village. I was curious to know in what sort of place and with whom Racky could be eating, since Orange Walk, as far as I know, is inhabited exclusively by Negroes, and I was sure Gloria would be able to shed some light on the matter, but I could scarcely ask her. However, as she brought on the dessert, I said: 'Who was that boy that brought the message from Mister Racky?'

She shrugged her shoulders. 'A young lad of Orange Walk. He's named Wilmot.'

When Racky returned at dusk, flushed from his exertion (for he never rides casually), I watched him closely. His behaviour struck my already suspicious eye as being one of false heartiness and a rather forced good humour. He went to his room early and read for quite a while before turning off his light. I took a long walk in the almost day-bright moonlight, listening to the songs of the night insects in the trees. And I sat for a while in the dark on the stone railing of the bridge across Black River. (It is really only a brook that rushes down over the rocks from the mountain a few miles inland, to the beach near the house.) In the night it always sounds louder and more important than it does in the daytime. The music of the water over the stones relaxed my nerves, although why I had need of such a thing I find it difficult to understand, unless I was really upset by Racky's not having come home for lunch. But if that were true it would be absurd, and moreover, dangerous – just the sort of the thing the parent of an adolescent has to beware of the fight against, unless he is indifferent to the prospect of losing the trust and affection of his offspring permanently. Racky must stay out whenever he likes, with whom he likes, and for as long as he likes, and I must not think twice about it, much less mention it to him, or in any way give the impression of prying. Lack of confidence on the part of a parent is the one unforgivable sin.

Although we still take our morning dip together on arising, it is three weeks since we have been for the early spin. One morning I found that Racky had jumped on to his bicycle in his wet trunks while I was still swimming, and gone by himself, and since then there has been an unspoken agreement between us that such is to be the procedure; he will go alone. Perhaps I held him back; he likes to ride so fast.

Young Peter, the smiling gardener from Saint Ives Cove, is Racky's special friend. It is amusing to see them together among the bushes, crouched over an ant-hill or rushing about trying to catch a lizard, almost of an age the two, yet so disparate – Racky with his tan skin looking almost white in contrast to the glistening black of the other. Today I know I shall be alone for lunch, since it is Peter's day off. On such days they usually go together on their bicycles into Saint Ives Cove, where Peter keeps a small rowboat. They fish along the coast there, but they have never returned with anything so far.

Meanwhile I am here alone, sitting on the rocks in the sun, from time to time climbing down to cool myself in the water, always conscious of the house behind me under the high palms, like a large glass boat filled with orchids and lilies. The servants are clean and quiet, and the work seems to be accomplished almost automatically. The good, black servants are another blessing of the islands; the British, born here in this paradise, have no conception of how fortunate they are. In fact, they do nothing but complain. One must have lived in the United States to appreciate the wonder of this place. Still, even here ideas are changing each day. Soon the people will decide that they want their land to be a part of today's monstrous world, and once that happens, it will be all over. As soon as you have that desire, you are infected with the deadly virus, and you begin to show the symptoms of the disease. You live in terms of time and money, and you think in terms of society and progress. Then all that is left for you is to kill the other people who think the same way, along with a good many of those who do not, since that is the final manifestation of the malady. Here for the moment at any rate, one has a feeling of staticity – existence ceases to be like those last few seconds in the hour-glass when what is left of the sand suddenly begins to rush through to the bottom all at once. For the moment, it seems suspended. And if it seems, it is. Each wave at my feet, each bird-call in the forest at my back, does *not* carry me one step nearer the final disaster. The disaster is certain, but it will suddenly have happened, that is all. Until then, time stays still.

I am upset by a letter in this morning's mail: the Royal Bank of Canada requests that I call in person at its central office to sign the deposit slips and other papers for a sum that was cabled from the bank in Boston. Since the central office is on the other side of the island, fifty miles away, I shall have to spend the night over there and return the following day. There is no point in taking Racky along. The sight of 'civilization' might awaken a longing for it in him; one never knows. I am sure it would have in me when I was his age. And if that should once start, he would merely be unhappy, since there is nothing for him but to stay here with me, at least for the next two years, when I hope to renew the lease, or, if things in New York pick up, buy the place. I am sending word by Isiah when he goes home into Orange Walk this evening, to have the McCoigh car call for me at seven-thirty tomorrow morning. It is an enormous old open Packard, and Isiah can save the ride out to work here by piling his bicycle into the back and riding with McCoigh.

The trip across the island was beautiful, and would have been highly enjoyable if my imagination had not played me a strange trick at the very outset. We stopped in Orange Walk for gasoline, and while that was being seen to, I got out and went to the corner store for some cigarettes. Since it was not yet eight o'clock, the store was still closed, and I hurried up the side street to the other little shop which I thought might be open. It was, and I bought my cigarettes. On the way back to the corner I noticed a large black woman leaning with her arms on the gate in front of her tiny house, staring into the street. As I passed by her, she looked straight into my face and said something with the strange accent of the island. It was said in what seemed an unfriendly tone, and ostensibly was directed at me, but I had no notion what it was. I got back into the car and the driver started it. The sound of the words had stayed in my head, however, as a bright shape outlined by darkness is likely to stay in the mind's eye, in such a way that when one shuts one's eyes one can see the exact contour of the shape. The car was already roaring up the hill toward the overland road when I suddenly reheard the very words. And they were: 'Keep your boy at home, mahn.' I sat perfectly rigid for a moment as the open countryside rushed past. Why should I think she had said that? Immediately I decided that I was giving an arbitrary sense to a phrase I could not have understood even if I had been paying strict attention. And then I wondered why my subconscious should have chosen that sense, since now that I whispered the words over to myself they failed to connect with any anxiety to which my mind might have been disposed. Actually I have never given a thought to Racky's wanderings about Orange Walk. I can find no such preoccupation no matter how I put the question to myself. Then, could she really have said those words? All the way through the mountains I pondered the question, even though it was obviously a waste of energy. And soon I could no longer hear the sound of her voice in my memory: I had played the record over too many times, and worn it out.

Here in the hotel a gala dance is in progress. The abominable orchestra, comprising two saxophones and one sour violin, is playing directly under my window in the garden, and the serious-looking couples slide about on the waxed concrete floor of the terrace in the light of strings of paper lanterns. I suppose it is meant to look Japanese.

At this moment I wonder what Racky is doing there in the house with only Peter and Ernest the watchman to keep him company. I wonder if he is asleep. The house, which I am accustomed to think of as smiling and benevolent in its airiness, could just as well be in the most sinister and remote regions of the globe, now that I am here. Sitting here with the absurd orchestra bleating downstairs, I picture it to myself, and it strikes me as terribly vulnerable in its isolation. In my mind's eye I see the moonlit point with its tall palms waving restlessly in the wind, its dark cliffs licked by the waves below. Suddenly, although I struggle against the sensation, I am inexpressibly glad to be away from the house, helpless there, far on its point of land, in the silence of the night. Then I remember that the night is seldom silent. There is the loud sea at the base of the rocks, the droning of the thousands of insects, the occasional cries of the night birds – all the familiar noises that make sleep so sound. And Racky is there surrounded by them as usual, not even hearing them. But I feel profoundly guilty for having left him, unutterably tender and sad at the thought of him, lying there alone in the house with the two Negroes the only human beings within miles. If I keep thinking of Cold Point I shall be more and more nervous.

I am not going to bed yet. They are all screaming with laughter down there, the idiots; I could never sleep anyway. The bar is still open. Fortunately it is on the street side of the hotel. For once I need a few drinks.

Much later, but I feel no better; I may be a little drunk. The dance is over and it is quiet in the garden, but the room is too hot.

As I was falling asleep last night, all dressed, and with the overhead light shining sordidly in my face, I heard the black woman's voice again, more clearly even than I did in the car yesterday. For some reason this morning there is no doubt in my mind that the words I heard are the words she said. I accept that and go on from there. Suppose she did tell me to keep Racky home. It could only mean that she, or someone else in Orange Walk, has had a childish altercation with him; although I must say it is hard to conceive of Racky's entering into any sort of argument or feud with those people. To set my mind at rest (for I do seem to be taking the whole thing with great seriousness), I am going to stop in the village this afternoon before going home, and try to see the woman. I am extremely curious to know what she could have meant.

I had not been conscious until this evening when I came back to Cold Point how powerful they are, all those physical elements that go to make up its atmosphere: the sea and wind-sounds that isolate the house from the road, the brilliancy of the water, sky and sun, the bright colours and strong odours of the flowers, the feeling of space both outside and within the house. One naturally accepts these things when one is living here. This afternoon when I returned I was conscious of them all over again, of their existence and their strength. All of them together are like a powerful drug; coming back made me feel as though I had been disintoxicated and were returning to the scene of my former indulgences. Now at eleven it is as if I had never been absent an hour. Everything is the same as always, even to the dry palm branch that scrapes against the window screen by my night table. And indeed, it is only thirty-six hours since I was here; but I always expect my absence from a place to bring about irremediable changes.

Strangely enough, now that I think of it, I feel that something *has* changed since I left yesterday morning, and that is the general attitude of the servants – their collective aura, so to speak. I noticed that difference immediately upon arriving back, but was unable to define it. Now I see it clearly. The network of common understanding which slowly spreads itself through a well-run household has been destroyed. Each person is by himself now. No unfriendliness, however, that I can see. They all behave with the utmost courtesy, excepting possibly Peter, who struck me as looking unaccustomedly glum when I encountered him in the kitchen after dinner. I meant to ask Racky if he had noticed it, but I forgot and he went to bed early.

In Orange Walk I made a brief stop on the pretext to McCoigh that I wanted to see the seamstress in the side street. I walked up and back in front of the house where I had seen the woman, but there was no sign of anyone.

As for my absence, Racky seems to have been perfectly content, having spent most of the day swimming off the rocks below the terrace. The insect sounds are at their height now, the breeze is cooler than usual, and I shall take advantage of these favourable conditions to get a good long night's rest.

Today has been one of the most difficult days of my life. I arose early, we had breakfast at the regular time, and Racky went off in the direction of Saint Ives Cove. I lay in the sun on the terrace for a while, listening to the noises of the household's regime. Peter was all over the property, collecting dead leaves and fallen blossoms in a huge basket and carrying them off to the compost heap. He appeared to be in an even fouler humour than last night. When he came near to me at one point on his way to another part of the garden I called to him. He set the basket down and stood looking at me; then he walked across the grass towards me slowly – reluctantly, it seemed to me.

'Peter, is everything all right with you?'

'Yes, sir.'

'No trouble at home?'

'Oh, no, sir.'

'Good.'

'Yes, sir.'

He went back to his work. But his face belied his words. Not only did he seem to be in a decidedly unpleasant temper; out here in the sunlight he looked positively ill. However, it was not my concern, if he refused to admit it.

When the heavy heat of the sun reached the unbearable point for me, I got out of my chair and went down the side of the cliff along the series of steps cut there into the rock. A level platform is below, and a diving board, for the water is deep. At each side, the rocks spread out and the waves break over them, but by the platform the wall of rock is vertical and the water merely hits against it below the springboard. The place is a tiny amphitheatre, quite cut off in sound and sight from the house. There too I like to lie in the sun; when I climb out of the water I often remove my trunks and lie stark naked on the springboard. I regularly make fun of Racky because he is embarrassed to do the same. Occasionally he will do it, but never without being coaxed. I was spread out there without a stitch on, being lulled by the slapping of the water, when an unfamiliar voice very close to me said: 'Mister Norton?'

I jumped with nervousness, nearly fell off the springboard, and sat up, reaching at the same time, but in vain, for my trunks, which were lying on the rock practically at the feet of a middle-aged mulatto gentleman. He was in a white duck suit, and wore a high collar with a black tie, and it seemed to me that he was eyeing me with a certain degree of horror.

My next reaction was one of anger at being trespassed upon in this way. I rose and got the trunks, however, donning them calmly and saying nothing more meaningful than: 'I didn't hear you come down the steps.'

'Shall we go up?' said my caller. As he led the way, I had a definite premonition that he was here on an unpleasant errand. On the terrace we sat down, and he offered me an American cigarette which I did not accept.

'This is a delightful spot,' he said, glancing out to sea and then at the end of his cigarette, which was only partially aglow. He puffed at it.

I said, 'Yes,' waiting for him to go on; presently he did.

'I am from the constabulary of this parish. The police, you see.' And seeing my face, 'This is a friendly call. But still it must be taken as a warning, Mister Norton. It is very serious. If anyone else comes to you about this it will mean trouble for you, heavy trouble. That's why I want to see you privately this way and warn you personally. You see.'

I could not believe I was hearing his words. At length I said faintly: 'But what about?'

'This is not an official call. You must not be upset. I have taken it upon myself to speak to you because I want to save you deep trouble.'

'But I *am* upset!' I cried, finding my voice at last. 'How can I help being upset, when I don't know what you're talking about?'

He removed his chair close to mine, and spoke in a very low voice.

'I have waited until the young man was away from the house so we could talk in private. You see, it is about him.'

Somehow that did not surprise me. I nodded.

'I will tell you very briefly. The people here are simple country folk. They make trouble easily. Right now they are all talking about the young man you have living here with you. He is your son, I hear.' His inflection here was sceptical.

'Certainly he's my son.'

His expression did not change, but his voice grew indignant. 'Whoever he is, that is a bad young man.'

'What do you mean?' I cried, but he cut in hotly: 'He may be your son; he may not be. I don't care who he is. That is not my affair. But he is bad through and through. We don't have such things going on here, sir. The people in Orange Walk and Saint Ives Cove are very cross now. You don't know what these folk do when they are aroused.'

I thought it my turn to interrupt. 'Please tell me why you say my son is bad. What has he done?' Perhaps the earnestness in my voice reached him, for his face assumed a gentler aspect. He leaned still closer to me and almost whispered.

'He has no shame. He does what he pleases with all the young boys, and the men too, and gives them a shilling so they won't tell about it. But they talk. Of course they talk. Every man for twenty miles up and down the coast knows about it. And the women too, they know about it.' There was a silence.

I had felt myself preparing to get to my feet for the last few seconds because I wanted to go into my room and be alone, to get away from that scandalized stage whisper. I think I mumbled 'Good morning' or 'Thank you,' as I turned away and began walking toward the house. But he was still beside me, still whispering like an eager conspirator into my ear: 'Keep him home, Mister Norton. Or send him away to school, if he is your son. But make him stay out of these towns. For his own sake.'

I shook hands with him and went to lie on my bed. From there I heard his car door slam, heard him drive off. I was painfully trying to formulate an opening sentence to use in speaking to Racky about this, feeling that the opening sentence would define my stand. The attempt was merely a sort of therapeutic action, to avoid thinking about the thing itself. Every attitude seemed impossible. There was no way to broach the subject. I suddenly realized that I should never be able to speak to him directly about it. With the advent of this news he had become another person – an adult, mysterious and formidable. To be sure, it did occur to me that the mulatto's story might not be true, but automatically I rejected the doubt. It was as if I wanted to believe it, almost as if I had already known it, and he had merely confirmed it.

Racky returned at midday, panting and grinning. The inevitable comb appeared and was used on the sweaty, unruly locks. Sitting down to lunch, he exclaimed: 'Gosh! Did I find a swell beach this morning! But what a job to get to it!' I tried to look unconcerned as I met his gaze; it was as if our positions had been reversed, and I were hoping to stem his rebuke. He prattled on about thorns and vines and his machete. Throughout the meal I kept telling myself: 'Now is the moment. You must say something.' But all I said was: 'More salad? Or do you want dessert now?' So the lunch passed and nothing happened. After I had finished my coffee I went into my bedroom and looked at myself in the large mirror. I saw my eyes trying to give their reflected brothers a little courage. As I stood there I heard a commotion in the other wing of the house: voices, bumpings, the sound of a scuffle. Above the noise came Gloria's sharp voice, imperious and excited: 'No, mahn! Don't strike him!' And louder: 'Peter, mahn, no!'

I went quickly towards the kitchen, where the trouble seemed to be, but on the way I was run into by Racky, who staggered into the hallway with his hands in front of his face.

'What is it, Racky?' I cried.

He pushed past me into the living room without moving his hands away from his face; I turned and followed him. From there he went into his own room, leaving the door open behind him. I heard him in his bathroom running the water. I was undecided what to do. Suddenly Peter appeared in the hall doorway, his hat in his hand. When he raised his head, I was surprised to see that his cheek was bleeding. In his eyes was a strange, confused expression of transient fear and deep hostility. He looked down again.

'May I please talk with you, sir?'

'What was all the racket? What's been happening?'

'May I talk with you outside, sir?' He said it doggedly, still not looking up.

In view of the circumstances, I humoured him. We walked slowly up the cinder road to the main highway, across the bridge, and through the forest while he told me his story. I said nothing.

At the end he said: 'I never wanted to, sir, even the first time, but after the first time I was afraid, and Mister Racky was after me every day.'

I stood still, and finally said: 'If you had only told me this the first time it happened, it would have been much better for everyone.'

He turned his hat in his hands, studying it intently. 'Yes, sir. But I didn't know what everyone was saying about him in Orange Walk until today. You know I always go to the beach at Saint Ives Cove with Mister Racky on my free days. If I had known what they were all saying I wouldn't have been afraid, sir. And I wanted to keep on working here. I needed the money.' Then he repeated what he had already said three times. 'Mister Racky said you'd see about it that I was put in the jail. I'm a year older than Mister Racky, sir.'

'I know, I know,' I said impatiently; and deciding that severity was what Peter expected of me at this point I added: 'You had better get your things together and go home. You can't work here any longer, you know.'

The hostility in his face assumed terrifying proportions as he said: 'If you killed me I would not work any more at Cold Point, sir.'

I turned and walked briskly back to the house, leaving him standing there in the road. It seems he returned at dusk, a little while ago, and got his belongings.

In his room Racky was reading. He had stuck some adhesive tape on his chin and over his cheekbone.

'I've dismissed Peter,' I announced. 'He hit you, didn't he?'

He glanced up. His left eye was swollen, but not yet black.

'He sure did. But I landed him one, too. And I guess I deserved it anyway.'

'I rested against the table. 'Why?' I asked nonchalantly.

'Oh, I had something on him from a long time back that he was afraid I'd tell you.'

'And just now you threatened to tell me?'

'Oh, no! He said he was going to quit the job here, and I kidded him about being yellow.'

'Why did he want to quit? I thought he liked the job.'

'Well, he did, I guess, but he didn't like me.' Racky's candid gaze betrayed a shade of pique. I still leaned against the table. I persisted. 'But I thought you two got on fine together. You seemed to.'

'Nah. He was just scared of losing his job. I had something on him. He was a good guy, though; I liked him all right.' He paused. 'Has he gone yet?' A strange quaver crept into his voice as he said the last words, and I understood that for the first time Racky's heretofore impeccable histrionics were not quite equal to the occasion. He was very much upset at losing Peter.

'Yes, he's gone,' I said shortly. 'He's not coming back, either.' And as Racky, hearing the unaccustomed inflection in my voice, looked up at me suddenly with faint astonishment in his young eyes, I realized that this was the moment to press on, to say: 'What did you have on him?' But as if he had arrived at the same spot in my mind a fraction of a second earlier, he proceeded to snatch away my advantage by jumping up, bursting into loud song, and pulling off all his clothes simultaneously. As he stood before me naked, singing at the top of his lungs, and stepped into his swimming trunks, I was conscious that again I should be incapable of saying to him what I must say.

He was in and out of the house all afternoon: some of the time he read in his room, and most of the time he was down on the diving board. It is strange behaviour for him; if I could only know what is in his mind. As evening approached, my problem took on a purely obsessive character. I walked to and fro in my room, always pausing at one end to look out the window over the sea, and at the other end to glance at my face in the mirror. As if that could help me! Then I took a drink. And another. I thought I might be able to do it at dinner, when I felt fortified by the whisky. But no. Soon he will have gone to bed. It is not that I expect to confront him with any accusations. That I know I never can do. But I must find a way to keep him from his wanderings, and I must offer a reason to give him, so that he will never suspect that I know.

We fear for the future of our offspring. It is ludicrous, but only a little more palpably so than anything else in life. A length of time has passed; days which I am content to have known, even if now they are over. I think that this period was what I had always been waiting for life to offer, the recompense I had unconsciously but firmly expected, in return for having been held so closely in the grip of existence all these years.

That evening seems long ago only because I have recalled its details so many times that they have taken on the colour of legend. Actually my problem already had been solved for me then, but I did not know it. Because I could not perceive the pattern, I foolishly imagined that I must cudgel my brains to find the right words with which to approach Racky. But it was he who came to me. That same evening, as I was about to go out for a solitary stroll which I thought might help me hit upon a formula, he appeared at my door.

'Going for a walk?' he asked, seeing the stick in my hand.

The prospect of making an exit immediately after speaking with him made things seem simpler. 'Yes,' I said, 'but I'd like to have a word with you first.'

'Sure. What?' I did not look at him because I did not want to see the watchful light I was sure was playing in his eyes at this moment. As I spoke I tapped with my stick along the designs made by the tiles in the floor. 'Racky, would you like to go back to school?'

'Are you kidding? You know I hate school.'

I glanced up at him. 'No, I'm not kidding. Don't look so horrified. You'd probably enjoy being with a bunch of fellows your own age.' (That was not one of the arguments I had meant to use.)

'I might like to be with guys my own age, but I don't want to have to be in school to do it. I've had school enough.'

I went to the door and said lamely: 'I thought I'd get your reactions.'

He laughed. 'No, thanks.'

'That doesn't mean you're not going,' I said over my shoulder as I went out.

On my walk I pounded the highway's asphalt with my stick, stood on the bridge having dramatic visions which involved such eventualities as our moving back to the States, Racky's having a bad spill on his bicycle and being paralysed for some months, and even the possibility of my letting events take their course, which would doubtless mean my having to visit him now and then in the governmental prison with gifts of food, if it meant nothing more tragic and violent. 'But none of these things will happen,' I said to myself, and I knew I was wasting precious time; he must not return to Orange Walk tomorrow.

I went back towards the point at a snail's pace. There was no moon and very little breeze. As I approached the house, trying to tread lightly on the cinders so as not to awaken the watchful Ernest and have to explain to him that it was only I, I saw that there were no lights in Racky's room. The house was dark save for the dim lamp on my night table. Instead of going in, I skirted the entire building, colliding with bushes and getting my face sticky with spider webs, and went to sit a while on the terrace where there seemed to be a breath of air. The sound of the sea was far out on the reef, where the breakers sighed. Here below, there were only slight watery chugs and gurgles now and then. It was unusually low tide. I smoked three cigarettes mechanically, having ceased even to think, and then, my mouth tasting bitter from the smoke, I went inside.

My room was airless. I flung my clothes on to a chair and looked at the night table to see if the carafe of water was there. Then my mouth opened. The top sheet of my bed had been stripped back to the foot. There on the far side of the bed, dark against the whiteness of the lower sheet, lay Racky asleep on his side, and naked.

I stood looking at him for a long time, probably holding my breath, for I remember feeling a little dizzy at one point. I was whispering to myself, as my eyes followed the curve of his arm, shoulder, back, thigh, leg: 'A child. A child.' Destiny, when one perceives it clearly from very near, has no qualities at all. The recognition of it and the consciousness of the vision's clarity leave no room on the mind's horizon. Finally I turned off the light and softly lay down. The night was absolutely black.

He lay perfectly quiet until dawn. I shall never know whether or not he was really asleep all that time. Of course he couldn't have been, and yet he lay so still. Warm and firm, but still as death. The darkness and silence were heavy around us. As the birds began to sing, I sank into a soft, enveloping slumber; when I awoke in the sunlight later, he was gone.

I found him down by the water, cavorting alone on the springboard; for the first time he had discarded his trunks without my suggesting it. All day we stayed together around the terrace and on the rocks, talking, swimming, reading, and just lying flat in the hot sun. Nor did he return to his room when night came. Instead after the servants were asleep, we brought three bottles of champagne in and set the pail on the night table.

Thus it came about that I was able to touch on the delicate subject that still preoccupied me, and profiting by the new understanding between us, I made my request in the easiest, most natural fashion.

'Racky, would you do me a tremendous favour if I asked you?'

He lay on his back, his hands beneath his head. It seemed to me his regard was circumspect, wanting in candour.

'I guess so,' he said. 'What is it?'

'Will you stay around the house for a few days – a week, say? Just to please me? We can take some rides together, as far as you like. Would you do that for me?'

'Sure thing,' he said, smiling.

I was temporizing, but I was desperate.

Perhaps a week later – (it is only when one is not fully happy that one is meticulous about time, so that it may have been more or less) – we were having breakfast. Isiah stood by, in the shade, waiting to pour us more coffee.

'I noticed you had a letter from Uncle Charley the other day,' said Racky. 'Don't you think we ought to invite him down?'

My heart began to beat with great force.

'Here? He'd hate it here,' I said casually. 'Besides, there's no room. Where would he sleep?' Even as I heard myself saying the words, I knew that they were the wrong ones, that I was not really participating in the conversation. Again I felt the fascination of complete helplessness that comes when one is suddenly a conscious on-looker at the shaping of one's fate.

'In my room,' said Racky. 'It's empty.'

I could see more of the pattern at that moment than I had ever suspected existed. 'Nonsense,' I said. 'This is not the sort of place for Uncle Charley.'

Racky appeared to be hitting in an excellent idea. 'Maybe if I wrote and invited him,' he suggested, motioning to Isiah for more coffee.

'Nonsense,' I said again, watching still more of the pattern reveal itself, like a photographic print becoming constantly clearer in a tray of developing solution.

Isiah filled Racky's cup and returned to the shade. Racky drank slowly, pretending to be savouring the coffee.

'Well, it won't do any harm to try. He'd appreciate the invitation,' he said speculatively.

For some reason, at this juncture I knew what to say, and as I said it, I knew what I was going to do.

'I thought we might fly over to Havana for a few days next week.'

He looked guardedly interested, and then he broke into a wide grin. 'Swell!' he cried. 'Why wait till next week?'

The next morning the servants called 'goodbye' to us as we drove up the cinder road to the McCoigh car. We took off from the airport at six that evening. Racky was in high spirits; he kept the stewardess engaged in conversation all the way to Camagüey.

He was delighted also with Havana. Sitting in the bar at the Nacional, we continued to discuss the possibility of having C. pay us a visit at the island. It was not without difficulty that I eventually managed to persuade Racky that writing him would be inadvisable.

We decided to look for an apartment right there in Vedado for Racky. He did not seem to want to come back here to Cold Point. We also decided that living in Havana he would need a larger income than I. I am already having the greater part of Hope's estate transferred to his name in the form of a trust fund which I shall administer until he is of age. It was his mother's money, after all.

We bought a new convertible, and he drove me out to Rancho Boyeros in it when I took my plane. A Cuban named Claudio with very white teeth, whom Racky had met in the pool that morning, sat between us.

We were waiting in front of the landing field. An official finally unhooked the chain to let the passengers through. 'If you get fed up, come to Havana,' said Racky, pinching my arm.

The two of them stood together behind the rope, waving to me, their shirts flapping in the wind as the plane started to move.

The wind blows by my head; between each wave there are thousands of tiny licking and chopping sounds as the water hurries out of the crevices and holes; and a part-floating, part-submerged feeling of being in the water haunts my mind even as the hot sun burns my face. I sit here and I read, and I wait for the pleasant feeling of repletion that follows a good meal, to turn slowly, as the hours pass along, into the even more delightful, slightly stirring sensation deep within, which accompanies the awakening of the appetite.

I am perfectly happy here in reality, because I still believe that nothing very drastic is likely to befall this part of the island in the near future.

# Dawn

JAMES PURDY

It wasn't as if Timmy had made his living posing nude and having his picture in the flesh magazines. Tim modelled clothes mostly and was making good money. But he did do one underwear modelling job and that was the one his dad saw in North Carolina. Wouldn't you know it would be! So his dad thought there must be more and worse ones. Nude ones, you know. His dad was a pill.

His dad came in to New York from the place he had lived in all his life. Population about four hundred people, probably counting the dead.

Well, his dad was something. He arrived in the dead of night or rather when the first streaks of morning were reaching the Empire State.

'Where is Timmy?' he said without even saying hello or telling me who he was (I recognized him from one of Tim's snapshots). He pushed right past me into the front room like a house detective with the passkey.

'Well, where is he?' He roared his question this time.

'Mr Jaqua,' I replied. 'He just stepped out for a moment.'

'I bet,' the old man quipped. 'Where does he sleep when he is at home?' he went on while looking around the apartment as if for clues.

I showed him the little room down the hall. He took a quick look inside and clicked his tongue in disapproval, and rushed right on back to the front room and helped himself to the big easy chair.

He brought out a raggedy clipping from his breast pocket.

'Have you laid eyes on this?' He beckoned for me to come over and see what he was holding.

It was the magazine ad of Tim all right, posing in very scanty red shorts.

I coloured by way of reply and Mr Jaqua studied me.

'I suppose there are more of these in other places,' he accused me.

'Well!' He raised his voice when I did not reply.

'I don't poke my nose into his business,' I said lamely. I coloured again.

'I can't blame you if you don't.' He was a bit conciliatory.

'See here, Freddy . . . You are Freddy, I suppose, unless he's changed room-mates. Pay me mind. I wanted Tim to be a lawyer and make good money and settle down, but he was stagestruck from a boy of ten.' Mr Jaqua seemed to be talking to a large assembly of people, and he looked out through my small apartment window into the street. 'I've sent him enough money to educate four boys,' he went on. 'I could even have stood it, I think, if he had made good on the stage. But where are the parts he should have found? You tell me!' His eyes moved away from outdoors, and his gaze rested on me.

'He failed,' the old man finished and looked at the underwear ad fiercely.

'But Tim had some good parts, Mr Jaqua. Even on Broadway.' I began my defence, but I was so stricken by this man's rudeness and insensitivity that I found myself finally just studying him as a spectacle.

'There's a screw loose somewhere.' He ignored my bits of information about Tim's acting career. 'I've come to take him home, Freddy.'

He looked at me now very sadly as if by studying me, the underwear ad, the acting career, and the loose screw would all at last be explained.

'See here. Everybody saw this ad back home.' He tapped the clipping with his finger. 'The damned thing was in the barbershop, then it turned up in the pool parlour, I'm told, and the dentist's office, and God knows maybe finally in Sunday school and church.'

'It paid good money, though, Mr Jaqua.'

'Good money,' he repeated and I remembered then he was a trial lawyer.

'I should think it would, Freddy,' he sneered as if finally dismissing me as a witness.

'It's very tough being an actor, Mr Jaqua.' I interrupted his silence. 'I know because I am one. There's almost no serious theatre today, you see.'

'Do you have any coffee in the house, Freddy?' he said after another prolonged silence.

'I have fresh breakfast coffee, sir. Would you like a cup?'

'Yes, that would be nice.' He folded the advertisement of the red shorts and put it back in his pocket until it would be produced again later on.

'What I'd like better, though,' he said after sipping a little of my strong brew, 'would you let me lie down on his bed and get some rest pending his arrival?'

Mr Jaqua never waited for my nod of approval, for he went immediately to the bedroom and closed the door energetically.

'Your dad is here,' I told Timmy as he came through the door.

'No,' he moaned. He turned deathly pale, almost green. 'Jesus,' he whimpered.

'He's lying down on your bed,' I explained.

'Oh, Freddy,' he said. 'I was afraid this would happen one day . . . What does he want?'

'Seems he saw you in that underwear ad.'

Tim made a grimace with his lips that looked like the smile on a man I once saw lying dead of gunshot wounds on the street. I looked away.

'He expects you to go home with him, Timmy,' I warned him.

'Oh, Christ in heaven!' He sat down in the big chair, and picked up the coffee cup his dad had left and sipped some of it. It was my turn to show a queer smile.

Tim just sat on there then for an hour or more while I pretended
to do some cleaning up of our apartment, all the while watching
him every so often and being scared at what I saw.

Then all at once, as if he had heard his cue, he stood up, squared
his shoulders, muttered something, and without a look or word to
me, he went to the bedroom door, opened it, and went in.

At first the voices were low, almost whispers, then they rose in a
high, dizzy crescendo, and there was cursing and banging and so
on as in all domestic quarrels. Then came a silence, and after that
silence I could hear Tim weeping hard. I had never heard him or
seen him cry in all our three years of living together. I felt terribly
disappointed somehow. He was crying like a little boy.

I sat down stunned as if my own father had come back from the
dead and pointed out all my shortcomings and my poor record as
an actor and a man.

Finally they came out together, and Tim had his two big
suitcases in hand.

'I'm going home for a while, Freddy,' he told me, and this time
he smiled his old familiar smile. 'Take this.' He extended a big
handful of bills.

'I don't want it, Timmy.'

His father took the bills from him then – there were several
hundred-dollar ones – and pressed them hard into my hand.
Somehow I could accept them from Mr Jaqua.

'Tim will write you when he gets settled back home. Won't you,
Tim?' the old man inquired as they went out the door.

After their footsteps died away, I broke down and cried, not like
a young boy, but like a baby. I cried for over an hour. And strange
to say I felt almost refreshed at shedding so many bitter tears. I
realized how badly I had suffered in New York, and how much I
loved Timmy, though I knew he did not love me very much in
return. And I knew then as I do now I would never see him again.

# *From* Just Above My Head

## JAMES BALDWIN

It was a heavy, slow Saturday afternoon in Atlanta, and they were free until Sunday morning. Webster had disappeared early, with many a vivid warning, and they were glad to be on their own; but his warnings remained with them, and the heat was as heavy as the region's molasses. They would have liked to discover the town, and they walked awhile, but they did not dare walk very far. If they got lost, they would have to ask someone for directions, and so they panicked whenever they saw more white faces than black faces. They had been made to know that they were from the North, and that their accents betrayed them and might land them on the chain gang. It happened every day down here, and, the Lord knew, Webster wouldn't be able to help them.

And the city was like a checkerboard. They would walk a block which was all black, then suddenly turn a corner and find themselves surrounded by nothing but white faces. They wanted to run, but, of course, to run meant that the white mob would run after them and they would, then, be lynched. At such moments, they smiled aimlessly, looked in a store window, if there was one, or else elaborately admired the view, slowing their walk to a shuffle. Then, as though the same idea had hit them at the same moment – which it had – they slowly turned and slowly walked back the way they had come. Sometimes they nearly exploded with the terrified laughter they had not dared release until they were again surrounded by black people, or back in the rooming house.

So this Saturday afternoon, they returned to the café next to the rooming house. Webster had prepaid their Saturday lunch and dinner. They had a little money in their pockets – not very much, for they had not been paid yet. Webster had all their money. This frightened them, too, but they did not know what to do about it. They had to trust Webster. Wordlessly, though, they trusted Crunch, who was the only one of them who might be able to intimidate Webster.

They sat down in the café, which was nearly empty – they had not yet realized that Southerners move about as little as possible on hot summer afternoons: in general, that is, due to imponderables to which they were reacting, but did not understand – and Peanut and Crunch went to the counter, and brought back four Pepsi-Colas.

'Tell you,' said Red. 'This trip is starting to fuck with my nerves. Can't wait to get back to Seventh Avenue.'

'When you was there,' said Arthur, smiling, 'you couldn't wait to get away.' He lit a cigarette and put the pack on the table. 'But I know how you feel.'

'We just ain't used to it,' Peanut said. 'And we don't know nobody. Be different, next time.'

'How?' asked Red. 'How we going to get to know somebody *next* time? You going to write a letter to the governor?'

Crunch laughed, and picked up the pack of cigarettes, and lit one.

'Well,' said Peanut, 'if we keep coming back, we *bound* to get to know – *somebody* –'

They all laughed, and, after a moment, Peanut laughed. Crunch said, 'Well, *you* know somebody – at least, you *knew* somebody – them cousins of yours in Charlotte –'

Peanut sighed and looked down at the table. 'Yeah. I'm sorry about that.'

Crunch leaned across the table and clapped Peanut on the shoulder. 'What *you* sorry about? *You* can't help it if your cousins are fools.'

Peanut is the lightest of us, and Crunch is the darkest, and Peanut's cousins *proved* that they did not like dark meat. They hurt Crunch's feelings, and they reminded Peanut of his bewildering grandmother.

'Oh, little by little, we'll figure out how to move,' Red said cheerfully. 'I'll find me a swinging chick at one of these church socials and make her be our guide.'

'These chicks all looking to get married, man,' Crunch said. 'And they don't want to marry none of us. What do a bank president's daughter want with – a wandering *troubador?*'

'Oh, hell, Crunch,' said Peanut. 'Love will find a way.'

'Not down here, in the land of cotton,' Arthur said, and they laughed.

'Anyway,' Crunch said after a moment, 'little Arthur's the only one liable to come down here next time.'

They all looked at Crunch. 'Why?' asked Arthur.

Crunch looked at Arthur. 'Where's your brother?'

Arthur said, 'My brother?' and stared at Crunch. His heart thundered like an express train, stopped.

'Oh, shit,' said Red. 'You right.'

'Right about what?' Arthur asked. But he knew. He had never thought of it.

'Uncle Sam is saving some people over yonder,' Crunch said. 'He's making the world safe for democracy again, and he needs some niggers for the latrine detail.'

The table became very silent.

'Shit,' Red said again.

Arthur said nothing. He did not know what to say. He did not dare look up. He looked at the white marble table, and the brown rings made by the Pepsi-Cola bottles. Then he looked very carefully at the flypaper suspended from the ceiling, with flies sticking, stuck, on the yellow paper. He wondered how many flies there were, and thought of counting them. He was suddenly aware that there was an electric fan whirring nearby – if you put your fingers in the fan, the blades would chop your fingers off. He did not think of me at all – he was not thinking.

'Well, let's not sit here like this,' Peanut said shakily. 'Let's do something.'

Yes, but what? A movie would have been ideal, but then, there was the question of whether black people sat in the balcony, or came in through the back door. None of them knew how it worked down here – they had forgotten to ask, or couldn't remember the answers.

'Hell,' Red said, suddenly, 'there's a black pool hall on the corner, let's go shoot some pool.'

'Okay,' Crunch said, and everybody rose except Arthur. They all looked at him.

'Ain't you coming?'

'Look,' Arthur said calmly, with a smile, 'you all go ahead. I might pick you up later. I got a little headache, I just want to lie down.'

Crunch raised that eyebrow at him. 'You sure?'

'Yeah, I'm all right. You cats go on, I'll dig you later.'

'OK.'

The three of them pranced out into the sun, paused for a moment, laughing, before the great glass window. Arthur waited until they had disappeared. Then he rose slowly, leaning lightly on the table, and walked outside. The sun was like a blow. He looked in the direction the boys had taken – saw them, on the still, far corner, ambling across the street.

Then he turned in the opposite direction. The rooming house was next door, really more like a hotel, a narrow, three-storey building. Peanut and Red and Webster were on the ground floor. He and Crunch were on the top floor. He walked into the long, dark, narrow hall, which was absolutely silent, and slowly, shaking, climbed the stairs.

He was covered with cold sweat by the time he reached the top floor, and his hands were shaking so hard he could hardly get the key in the lock, but, at last, the door swung open. Sunlight hammered on the room, and he crossed to the window and pulled down the shade. He ran cold water in the sink, and plunged his face and head under, blindly found the towel, and dried himself.

He kicked off his shoes, unpeeled his socks, took off his shirt and trousers, and lay down on Crunch's bed. *Korea*.

He lay there for a long time, numb, as empty as the listening silence, stunned. He lay on his back. The air did not move. He did not move. The sun would not move, the earth, the stars, the moon, the planets, whatever held it all together, the big wheel and the little wheel, and the boulder of his sorrow, which had dropped on him and pinned him to his bed, nothing would move, until he saw Crunch. *Korea*. He fell asleep.

Crunch shook him gently. The room was half dark, not dark yet. Crunch sat on the edge of the bed, looking at him carefully, with that eyebrow raised, half smiling, half frowning.

'You feel better?'

Arthur stared, saying nothing, then he smiled.

'You're back.'

'Of course I'm back. You feel better?'

Arthur moved and put his head in Crunch's lap, holding on to him and staring up at him.

The room grew darker. They were alone. Crunch leaned down, and kissed him. Arthur held on to Crunch with all his strength, with all his tears, tears he had not yet begun to shed. Crunch leaned up.

'Let me lock the door,' he whispered.

Arthur sat up, and watched Crunch lock the door.

He did it very elaborately, and then turned, grinning, with one finger to his lips.

'We all alone, now, little fellow. Ain't nobody on this floor but us. And it's Saturday night, anyway, *everybody's* out.' He grinned, and then his face changed, he stood at the door, looking at Arthur.

'Where's Peanut and Red?'

Arthur was whispering, and Crunch whispered, 'I left them in the pool hall. They found some friends.'

'They coming back?'

'I told them I was taking you someplace.'

He sat down on the bed again, and started taking off his shoes. He looked over at Arthur. 'Did I do right?'

'Sure.'

'Get under the covers.'

Arthur watched as Crunch stripped – Crunch was whistling, low in his throat: and it came to Arthur, with great astonishment, that Crunch was whistling because he was happy – was happy to be here, with Arthur. Arthur watched as Crunch unbuttoned his shirt, watched the long, dark fingers against the buttons and the cloth, watched the cloth fly across the room to land on the other bed, watched as he unbuckled his belt, dropped his trousers, raising one knee then the other, sitting on the bed again to pull the trousers past the big feet, then folding the trousers, and rising to place them on the other bed, pulling off his undershirt, kicking off his shorts, his whole, long, black self padding to the small sink, where he looked, briefly, into the mirror, ran cold water, gargled, his dark body glowing in the darkening room, a miracle of spinal column, neck to buttocks, shoulders and shoulder blades, elbows, wrists, thighs, ankles, a miracle of bone and blood and muscle and flesh and music. Arthur was still wearing his undershirt and his shorts. He hated being naked in front of anyone, even me – perhaps, especially me; I had sometimes given him his bath: but that had been under another condition, for which he had not been responsible, and which he was not compelled to remember. Nakedness had not, then, been a confession, or a vow. Arthur was frightened; then, he wasn't frightened; but he found that he could not move. He could not take off his undershirt. He could not take off his shorts. Crunch turned, and Arthur, in a kind of peaceful terror, watched as the face, and the eyes in that face, and the neck and the chest, and the nipples on the chest, and the ribs and the long flat belly and the belly button and the jungle of hair spinning upward from the long, dark, heavy, swinging sex approached, and Crunch got under the covers, and took Arthur in his arms.

Crunch sighed, a weary, trusting sigh, and put his hands under Arthur's undershirt and pulled it over Arthur's head, and, suddenly, they both laughed, a whispering laugh. Crunch dropped the undershirt on the floor.

'That's called progress,' Crunch whispered. 'And now,' he said, 'let's see what we can do down yonder.'

He put his hands at Arthur's waist, pulled the shorts down, got them past one foot. Arthur's prick rose.

Crunch stroked it, and grinned. 'That's enough progress, for now,' he said, but he put his rigid sex against Arthur's, and then they simply lay there, holding on to each other, unable to make another move. They really did not know where another move might carry them. Arthur was afraid in one way, and Crunch in another. It was also as though they had expended so much energy to arrive at this moment that they had to fall out and catch their breath, this moment was almost enough. But it was only a moment: the train was boarded, the engine ready to roll. They held on to each other. This might be the beginning; it might be the beginning of the end. The train was boarded, the engine pulsing, great doors were slamming shut behind them, the train would soon be moving, a journey had begun. They might lose each other on this journey; nothing could be hidden on this journey. They might look at each other, miles from now, when the train stopped at some unimaginable place, and wish never to see each other again. They might be ashamed – they might be debased: they might be for ever lost.

Arthur was less frightened than Crunch. He simply held on to Crunch and stroked him and kissed him, for in the centre of his mind's eye, there was Crunch in uniform, Crunch gone, Crunch forever gone, and, now that he had found him, his mind became as still and empty as the winter sky, at the thought of losing him. He held this blankness as far inside him as he held his tears – for, something told him that Crunch could not bear his tears, could not bear anybody's tears. Tears were a weapon you could use against Crunch.

And Crunch – ah, Crunch. He held my brother, falling in love – falling in love with the little fellow. Crunch was older than Arthur, lonelier than Arthur, knew more about himself than Arthur knew. He had never been on this train, true; but he had been landed in some desolate places. He held him closer, falling in love, his prick stiffening, his need rising, his hope rising; the train began to move, Arthur held him closer, and Crunch moved closer, becoming more naked, praying that Arthur would receive his nakedness.

His long self covered Arthur, his tongue licked Arthur's nipples, his armpits, his belly button. He did not dare go further, yet; shaking, he raised himself to Arthur's lips. He took Arthur's sex in his fist.

'Do me like I do you,' he whispered. 'Little fellow, come on, this is just the beginning,' and Arthur, with a kind of miraculous understanding, kissed Crunch's nipples, slid down to kiss his sex, moved up to his lips again. As he felt Crunch pulsing, he pulsed with Crunch, coaxed the pulsing vein at the underside of the organ as Crunch coaxed his, scarcely breathing. Crunch groaned, *little fellow*, groaned again, they seemed to hang for a second in a splintered, blinding air, then Crunch's sperm shot out against Arthur's belly, Arthur's shot against his, it was as though each were coming through the other's sex.

They lay in each other's arms.

Crunch looked into his Arthur's eyes.

'Hi.'

'Hi, yourself.'

Their breathing slowed. Neither wanted to move.

'You think we making progress?'

'I'm with you.'

They laughed, holding on to each other, wet with each other.

Crunch asked shyly, 'Do you still love me?'

'Maybe we should make some more progress.'

Crunch shook with laughter, silently, and Arthur shook with joy, watching him. 'Right now?'

'Whenever you ready.'

'Oh – come on – !' said Crunch.

'That's what I said.'

'You – you something –'

'I love you. I'd do anything for you,' said Arthur.

Crunch watched him. 'For true?'

'For true.'

Crunch held him tighter.

'I want to make love with you – every way possible – I don't care what happens – as long as I can hold you.' He watched Arthur's eyes; but he was beginning to feel at peace.

'You want to make progress, *I'll* make progress. We'll make progress together.'

Crunch asked, 'You and me, then?'

'You and me.'

The room was dark. They heard the night outside. They did not want to leave each other's arms.

Crunch asked, 'You hungry?'

'No – not now.'

'You want to wash up?'

'No. Not yet.'

'What you want to do then?'

'Maybe sleep a little – next to you.'

'OK.'

They curled into each other, spoon fashion, Arthur cradled by Crunch.

They did not sleep long. Arthur woke up, and peed in the sink, as quietly as possible. He ran the water as quietly as possible. He lifted the shade, and looked out of the window. It was night, he guessed it to be around nine or ten o'clock; there were not as many people in the street as there would have been on a Saturday night in Harlem. Most of the people were already inside some place, or they were on their way, and their voices, and their music, muffled, filled the air, filled the room. He dropped the shade.

Crunch lay as he had left him. One arm was at his side, one arm lay stretched where Arthur had been. His breathing was deep and slow – yet Arthur sensed that Crunch was not entirely lost in sleep. Arthur crawled back into bed, pulling the covers back up. The moment he crawled into bed, Crunch, still sleeping, pulled Arthur into his arms.

And yet, Crunch lay as one helpless. Arthur was incited by this helplessness, the willing helplessness of the body in his arms. He kissed Crunch, who moaned, but did not stir. He ran his hands up and down the long body. He seemed to discover the mystery of geography, of space and time, the lightning flash of tension between one – moment? – one breath and the next breath. The breathing in – the breathing out. The miracle of air, entering, and the chest rose: the miracle of air transformed into the miracle of breath, coming out, into your face, mixed with Pepsi-Cola, hamburgers, mustard, whatever was in the bowels: and the chest fell. He lay in this urgency for a while, terrified, and happy.

He held Crunch closer, running his fingers up and down the barely tactile complex telegraph system of the spine. His hands dared to discover Crunch's beautiful buttocks, his ass, his behind. He stroked the gift between his legs whch held the present and the future. Their sex became rigid. Crunch growled, turned on his back, still holding Arthur.

Arthur moved, in Crunch's arms, belly to belly. Pepsi-Cola, mustard, and onions and hamburgers and Crunch's rising prick: Crunch moaned. Arthur knew something that he did not know he knew – he did not know that he knew that Crunch waited for Arthur's lips at his neck, Arthur's tongue at the nipples of his chest. Pepsi-Cola, mustard, hamburgers, ice cream, surrendered to funkier, unknown odours; Crunch moaned again, surrendering, surrendering, as Arthur's tongue descended Crunch's long black self, down to the raging penis. He licked the underside of the penis, feeling it leap, and he licked the balls. He was setting Crunch free – he was giving Crunch what he, somehow, knew that Crunch longed and feared to give him. He took the penis into his mouth, it moved, with the ease of satin, past his lips, into his throat. For a moment, he was terrified: what now? For the organ was hard and huge and throbbing, Crunch's hands came down, but lightly, on Arthur's head, he began to thrust upward, but carefully, into Arthur's mouth.

Arthur understood Crunch's terror – the terror of someone in the water, being carried away from the shore – and this terror, which was his own terror, soon caused him to gasp, to attempt to pull away, at the same time that he held on. His awareness of

Crunch's terror helped him to overcome his own. He had never done this before. In the same way that he knew how Crunch feared to be despised – by him – he knew, too, that he, now, feared to be despised by Crunch. *Cocksucker*.

Well. It was Crunch's cock, and so he sucked it; with all the love that was in him, and a moment came when he felt that love being trusted, and returned. A moment came when he felt Crunch pass from a kind of terrified bewilderment into joy. A friendly, a joyful movement, began. *So high, you can't get over him.*

Sweat from Arthur's forehead fell onto Crunch's belly.

*So low* – and Crunch gasped as Arthur's mouth left his prick standing in the cold, cold air, as Arthur's tongue licked his sacred balls – *you can't get under him.* Arthur rose, again, to Crunch's lips. *So wide. You can't get around him.* It was as though, with this kiss, they were forever bound together. Crunch moaned, in an absolute agony, and Arthur went down again.

'Little fellow. Baby. Love.'

*You must come in at the door.*

He held the prick in his mouth again, sensing, awaiting, the eruption. He, and he alone, had dragged it up from the depths of his lover.

'Oh. Little fellow.'

Then, shaking like an earthquake, 'Oh, my love. Oh, love.'

Atlanta was still. The world was still. Nothing moved in the heavens.

'Oh. Love.'

Curious, the taste, as it came, leaping, to the surface: of Crunch's prick, of Arthur's tongue, into Arthur's mouth and throat. He was frightened, but triumphant. He wanted to sing. The taste was volcanic. This taste, the aftertaste, this anguish, and this boy had changed all tastes for ever. The bottom of his throat was sore, his lips were weary. Every time he swallowed, from here on, he would think of Crunch, and this thought made him smile as, slowly, now, and in a peculiar joy and panic, he allowed Crunch to pull him up, upward, into his arms.

He dared to look into Crunch's eyes. Crunch's eyes were wet

and deep *deep like a river*, and Arthur found that he was smiling *peace like a river*.

Arthur asked Crunch, 'All right? do you feel all right?'

Crunch put Arthur's head on his chest, ran one long hand up and down Arthur.

'You're the most beautiful thing ever happened to me, baby,' he said. 'That's how I feel.' Then, 'Thank you, Arthur.'

'For what?' Arthur asked – teasing, bewildered, triumphant – and safe in Crunch's arms.

'For loving me,' Crunch said.

After a moment, he pulled up the covers. They went to sleep, spoon fashion, Arthur cradling Crunch.

# Darts

## TOM WAKEFIELD

The Utic's Nest is a funny name for a pub. If a Utic had a nest then it must have been a bird. I'd never heard of a bird called a Utic and nobody else had, but that was the name of the public house just down the road from where we lived. If you asked anyone what a Utic was, they just shrugged their shoulders or shook their heads as though you were asking a daft or silly question. A pub was a pub and its name obviously was of little account or interest to its customers. I would never have gone there in the first place if my mother's working shifts had not been changed. She worked 'nights' in a factory in Darlaston. For some reason, she was required to work on a Saturday night. This gave her Wednesday and Thursday night free. It changed the lean social arrangements that my parents were limited to – the Saturday night at the Working Men's Club was now in abeyance.

It was substituted by a Thursday night visit to The Utic's Nest. I suppose that in accordance with licensing laws children should have been barred entrance. They never were; the licensee did not seem at all uncomfortable when the local bobby came in for a pint. There were other children there besides me, either the policeman didn't mind or he chose not to see us. In any event, we were always limited to one bottle of Vimto and a bag of crisps. If you took little sips the bottle lasted all night. I never shared my crisps, nor did I join the other children who sat and talked quietly around a large table set apart in the end of the pub, well away from the bar. The pub only possessed one very long, oblong-shaped room and everything that went on happened in it. I usually sat to the right of my father, he on a chair, me on a stool. My mother always faced us, her back resting on the wall. The three or four couples that joined them at their table never varied much. Sometimes one of my aunties or uncles would join us, but they never stayed long. I would listen to the grown-up talk, the men talked to men and the women talked to women.

Neither paid much heed to me, I didn't expect them to. Occasionally one of the men would say, 'Alright then Tom lad?' and nod his head. The women might say, 'You've got a Wakefield look but your mam's eyes.' There really wasn't much that I could say to these acknowledgements so I kept quiet. I was never bored. Other things happened at The Utic's Nest.

Each night a man would play the piano for a short time and at the end of his repertoire there would be a call for a song. It was always the same lady. And she always sang the same song. She was fat, older than my parents, and her name was Mrs Welch. She was a widow. She wore a black dress with sequins decorating its bosom. The song was called 'Love's Last Word is Spoken, Cherie'. She sang it beautifully and at the end she never failed to wipe her eyes as she had moved herself to tears by the quality of her own performance. Some of the women in the pub cried a little too – but not my mother. She did clap though and would say 'lovely voice, Elsie has a lovely voice.'

A darts match was also played. The Utic's Nest was part of a kind of league. If other teams lost at The Utic's Nest there was always an undercurrent of dissent or grumbling. Not that the game had been played unfairly but on account of the four members who made up the darts team. All of them wore trousers, all of them wore shirts. But two of the players had trousers which buttoned down the side, no fly-hole in the front. These two also had breasts, but their hair was short. They were known as Billy and Mac. They were well liked at The Utic. They would always greet my parents and often buy me an extra bag of crisps or supply me with another bottle of Vimto. Sometimes, they would ruffle my hair but they never said much. In fact, I hardly ever saw them a yard apart from one another. They puzzled me.

If I wanted to know something, mostly I would ask my father. He knew everything about everybody in the pub. I don't know what prompted me to interrogate my mother. I half expected a curt reply. I was surprised.

'Mam, those two, Billy and Mac, are they men or women?' she paused and sipped at her milk stout, licked the froth from the top of her lip and looked at me directly.

'They're good people,' she said.

'Are they men or women?' Other women around the table had heard me repeat the question. I think they were as interested in her response as I was.

'They're willdews,' she said.

'Willdews, willdews, what's a willdew?' She threw back her head and chortled, this was rare for her and I thought that she had dismissed my question with her mirth.

'Well, it's like this. They are ladies, they'll never be anything else. But they won't marry because they live together in a bungalow. And when they are at home it must be "will yer do this or will yer do that". Got it? So, they are willdews.' At this the other women laughed. I still did not understand but accepted the explanation. However, she did not let it end there. She addressed the other women.

'That's why the other teams get upset, well some of them do if they lose. Behave like bloody little kids, grown men, yes they do. I don't know why. Their lives are their own, as I say, they're good women.'

'Oh, I know that Esther, we'd never get ambulance drivers like those two ever again. They were ever so good when they took my mother to Stafford hospital. Do you know, they even took her in some flowers on the Sunday. Off duty they were, it was their day off. My mother said they were golden, yes, she said that to me about them before she died. And Esther, I think you're right, people often sling a bit of squitch in their direction – but they've no grounds for it. No, they wouldn't do anybody any harm. They are good, they mind their own business and lead their own lives. They'd help anybody yer know.' The other women nodded respectfully.

It was later that I noticed that when an opposing team lost, one or two of the losing men would say something nasty to Billy or Mac. Billy and Mac ignored the insult but the men did not get away free. One of the married women sitting drinking would hurl abuse at them, others would join in and Billy and Mac basked in their defence. After a time, no man dared say bad things to them. But my dad told me that Billy and Mac were only allowed to play in home games, not away games, not in other pubs. Darts was a man's game. It seemed that Billy and Mac could only fit in at The Utic's Nest. They were always there – every Thursday.

# Good Fortune

## SIMON BURT

ONE

Missing the train didn't help.

His German, needless to say, was not up to much. So he listened very carefully to the man at the ticket office – *Der beamte; ein Beamter*; a verbal noun – when he told him when and from what platform the connection to Mannheim left. He made him repeat it, in German and in English, because he still had trouble with the twenty-four-hour clock, to make doubly sure.

He hated stations. He felt even lonelier than usual on stations. Stations and launderettes. He went out of his way to avoid them. What room in his two large and very heavy suitcases was not taken up by books was filled with dirty clothes.

The train left from platform four, at 9.32. When he got to the platform there was a train already there. A cross, by the looks of it, between a goods train and a cattle truck. He sat and read – *The Unquiet Grave* by Palinurus – and waited for it to leave.

He should have known.

He waited and waited, but the goods train showed no sign of leaving. Eventually he got up and went back to the ticket office and said, Look. Are you sure you've got it right? There's this goods train on my platform. I've got to get to Mannheim in time for the express.

Yes, they said. That's right. That's the 9.32 to Mannheim.

The goods train, he said.

That's right, they said. There's a passenger compartment at the front. Hadn't he seen?

So he went, as fast as his heavy luggage would allow him – That was one of the things he hated about stations. He was terrified all the time that someone was going to steal his luggage. He had to cart it about with him. – back to the platform, but the train had gone.

He panicked, of course.

He just stood there. He didn't know how long for.

Then he went back to the ticket office and told them what had happened.

Not to worry, they said. There was a tram stop round the corner. The tram would get him there in plenty of time.

So he went to the tram stop.

The tram, when it arrived, was full. There was just enough room for him to stand in the aisle with his luggage between his legs.

The journey was maddeningly slow. Most of it he spent muttering, Come on, Come *on*, between his teeth, and jerking his body forwards as if to add its impetus to the tram's.

Not sensible, but by this time he was barely in control.

On the outskirts of Mannheim he got a seat. He hooked his legs over his cases and chewed the skin round his fingernails. The tram seemed to stop every hundred yards. Eventually they stopped at the station and he ran to the inquiry counter.

It wasn't easy to run with half a hundredweight in either hand.

The express, they said, was at platform seven. But hurry. It's about to leave.

Hurry!

They could not, he supposed, have looked too closely at him. He was dripping with sweat. His face must have been scarlet.

He hurried.

But it didn't do any good. He arrived at platform seven in time to see the express leave. He watched the tail lights disappear up the track. He felt pretty bloody awful.

He sat on his cases and damn near cried. It was half-past twelve at night, and all he had in his pocket was his ticket home, five pounds in English money, and about forty Marks.

And *The Unquiet Grave*. Not ideal reading for desperate circumstances, which is what he felt his circumstances were.

Maybe he did cry a bit.

The next time he looked at his watch it was one o'clock. The station was nearly empty. He went back to the inquiry desk, but it was closed. He found a timetable and worked out that the next train for Ostend was at eleven o'clock the next morning. It had been hard enough to reserve a seat on the train he'd missed. He'd probably have to stand half way across Europe.

The left-luggage office was closed, and there was a sign on the lockers that said that facilities were suspended until further notice owing to terrorist activity. Which meant that he would have to stay awake all night to guard his cases. He had slept little the night before and was tired. Not that he could see himself getting much sleep stretched out on a bench, which seemed to be the only recourse left open to him, but it would have been nice to have had the option.

The cafeteria was closed.

The waiting room was dark, and he couldn't find the light, and it smelt of beer and vomit anyway.

There didn't seem to be anything else to do. He picked up his cases, which got heavier by the minute, and walked out into the town.

About a hundred yards down the street – he had switched his suitcases from hand to hand twice already – he found a café that was still open.

It did not look the cleanest place in the world, but he couldn't think of anything else to do but go in and blow some of his Marks on a coffee.

There were four or five people sitting here and there about the room, and they seemed no cleaner than the café. He bought a coffee and sat in a corner.

No one looked at him.

No one said anything.

He took out *The Unquiet Grave* and began to read, but he couldn't concentrate, so he sat and stirred his coffee. He drew lines and

circles on the froth with his spoon. He felt very sleepy. Every now
and then he took a sip. He had all night, and could not afford
many coffees.

He was nodding over the dregs of his second cup when the door
opened and a woman came in. He looked up as she passed, but
their eyes met, and she smiled, so he looked quickly down again.
He reopened *The Unquiet Grave*. The next thing he knew she was
standing at his table holding two cups of coffee.

Entropy, she said. Coffee gets cold. You look as if you need
another one.

She put one cup down in front of him, and pulled out the chair
opposite his.

May I? she said.

He nodded, and closed *The Unquiet Grave*.

She put her coffee on the table and moved his two empty cups
to the edge. She sat down and offered him a cigarette. He didn't
smoke, but he took it. It seemed easier.

So, she said.

So. What brings you to this place?

He could, he felt, have asked the same of her. She looked more
out of place than he did. He was wearing his old duffle-coat. He
was dirty and unkempt. She looked as if she had just stepped out
of Harrods – or whatever the Mannheim equivalent was. Head-
scarf. Burberry mackintosh. Tweeds, pearls. About forty to forty-
five, he guessed. Slightly horsy about the hip and jaw. Carefully
waved greying hair.

She smiled.

What is your name? she said.

McHale, he said. J. J. McHale. I've come from Heidelberg. I've
missed the train.

J. J., she said. What do they stand for?

I call myself J. J., he said. They stand for Julian and Justin.

I can see why you wouldn't use them, she said.

He stirred his coffee. She held her cup to her lips, but didn't
drink.

So, J. J., she said. Why Heidelberg?

## TWO

That was not an easy question.

Mainly because he himself was none too clear about the reason.

Like almost everything else he did it was more or less an accident. The result of someone else's decision.

He was not good at deciding what to do. He had left school because he was the right age to leave school. He had got all the necessary A levels because he had been unable to think of anything else to do but work for them. He had been accepted by Trinity College, Dublin, for the following September – again someone else's choice: his housemaster had said, Why not Trinity? and he agreed, and sent off the forms, and they took him – and he would have been quite happy to stay at home until September came round. But everyone said, No, you must travel. What a waste of opportunity if you don't travel. So he said he would travel, and that left only the question of where he was to go.

Which is where his father came in. One of his father's friends, it appeared, had a school in Heidelberg. Why didn't he go there? Heidelberg was a beautiful city, and he could enrol in the school, and learn German.

So he had gone.

He had enrolled at the Lyceum Palatinum, Heidelberg, a gracious, balconied building, overlooking the Neckar and the Old Bridge, opposite the castle.

But then the plan had broken down.

He started to learn German. He sat in a class with about thirty other people. Greeks, French, Danes. Most of whom, it had transpired, were Freemasons. And for a while he had worked quite hard at it. But he couldn't keep it up somehow.

He hadn't really warmed to any of his fellow students. Most of them spent most of their time drinking, as far as he could see, and singing songs. One of them, a spectacularly handsome Dane called Björn, used to get thrown out of bars for declaiming in enormous tones some of Mussolini's less restrained speeches. *Popolo abissinio. Popolo barbaro, incivile.*

He had taken to his bed. He lay there listening to everyone else getting up and going jollily down to breakfast and the morning lesson.

Then he read one or other of his books. Wherever he went he bought books. He had arrived in Heidelberg with two, and was leaving with nearly two cases. He bought them at the second-hand stalls round the Heiliggeistkirche.

Then Herr Koechlin, his father's friend, would come in and start saying *Warum? warum?* and *Dies' ist kein Hotel.* And he would get up. He would take his book up on to the Philosophenweg, where Goethe and Schiller used to commune with nature and each other, and spend the afternoon there, looking down over the town, and thinking, I am in Germany.

In the evening, when the rest went off to get drunk, and play the Stiefel game, which involved passing round a huge beer-filled glass boot, and guzzling as much as possible, the person who didn't finish – that is to say the person before the one who did – having to pay for the boot, he walked round the town, until it was time to go back to his room and sleep.

He had to share his room. In all the time he was there he had not exchanged a single word with his room-mate, and not many with anyone else.

Only one person had called him J. J. since he had left England. Everyone at the Lyceum, when they called him anything, called him Yustin.

I don't really know, he said. I suppose it just happened.

How nice to be so footloose, the woman said. I envy you. Now I am here for a reason.

She drank, and put down her cup. He drank, too, and coughed over his cigarette.

I cannot sleep, she said. You are lucky to be young, and not know the sorrow of insomnia. So I walk. And drop into places like this. My name is Magda.

Hello, Magda, he said. I was at school in Heidelberg. Learning

German. I didn't learn much. I'm on my way back to England. I missed the train.

And what, she said, have you learned from that?

Learned? he said.

What was there to learn?

Let us see, she said. We could start with your telling me why you are going home so obviously in the middle of term.

It was a well-known fact, his books told him, that one can say to a stranger what one cannot say to anyone closer. Not that he had anyone particularly close.

Of course and as usual, he didn't really know why, exactly why, he was leaving, why he had had enough, except that he was not the sort of person who could cope with that sort of thing. In fact, he was still waiting to discover something he could cope with, but there you are. But he could give a pretty clear outline of the last straw.

So he did.

She had asked him after all, and didn't he always do what he was asked?

He told her. He told her about the sort of person he was, and about how he spent his time at the Lyceum.

And he told her about Konradin.

Konradin was the name of a boy who had arrived about a month after he had, during the time when he still went to lessons, when he was only not enjoying it a little.

He was not – in case she had any trouble working it out – the sort of person who made friends easily. All his way through school, for instance, he had had only two. He preferred it that way. Not that he didn't envy people who found it easy to make friends. He just wasn't that sort of person.

His first two terms at school he had known no one. Then, at the beginning of his third term, there was a boy in the dormitory who asked him the way to the lavatory, and they were friends for two years.

He couldn't remember now why they had quarrelled. It had something to do with a box of After Eights, his or his friend's, which either he or his friend had eaten, without reference to the other. They never spoke to each other again.

It took his next friend a year to break through to him. After a while, he found, you got used to being alone. You liked it. But he did break through. At the end of term they had gone on a long walk together, and he had gone back the next term thinking, I must not expect him to speak to me. I must not trade on one walk's worth of acquaintance.

But he did talk. And they were friends for the two years till they left. They spent every available minute together. They never parted without naming the time and place of their next meeting. I have to pee. See you back here in five minutes.

His friend was in Barcelona now, learning Spanish.

He badly missed him.

Actually, to be honest, he badly missed the life they had led together. Which was not quite the same thing.

And Konradin?

Konradin was to be his next special friend.

It was Konradin whom he wanted for his next special friend.

They had sat at the same table in the dining room, the day of Konradin's arrival. He had been very quiet. He had spent the evening playing the piano rather than out drinking.

And that was it.

That was all.

He had decided. Then, on that first evening.

Over the next few weeks, Konradin settled in to the school. He became lively at table. He did not play the piano again. He went out in the evenings and came home only slightly less drunk than the rest. But by then it was too late.

He had not said a word. He had not known how to start. He watched Konradin. At class. At meals. Whenever he could. It was good to know that he was around.

But then he stopped going to class, and didn't go to many meals, so he saw much less of him.

He did not make friends easily.

### THREE

In the end, Konradin spoke to him.

It had been a tiresome day. After lunch, Herr Koechlin had obviously decided that it was time he did something for the son of his old friend, and instead of *waruming*, and *Dies'-ist-kein-Hotel-ing*, he invited him to his room for a glass of sherry.

Sherry.

After lunch.

They had a long talk. At least, Herr Koechlin spoke for a long time. There had been much hand-clasping, and What's-the-mattering, and Really, my dear Yustin, you must let me help you.

He stonewalled. He sat and stared at his feet.

Eventually Herr Koechlin gave up, and he had promised that he would try and do better. In pursuit of that promise he had gone to the afternoon lesson, on the Perfect Tense of Separable Verbs and how to express Absence of Obligation. And he went to the evening meal, where, for the first time, Konradin sat next to him, and he stared hard at his plate.

He stopped talking, and drank some coffee.

He asked Magda for a cigarette.

What would life be, she said, without coffee and cigarettes? People would never speak to each other. Neither strangers nor old friends. I'll get some more.

While she was at the counter he wiped his hands on his trousers.

More people had come into the café. Shabby people mostly. Magda looked even more out of place than ever. She came back with two more coffees and two glasses of brandy.

Like your fellow students, she said, we are going to drink. They have no Stiefel here, I'm afraid.

Oh well, he said. I couldn't afford to pay for it anyway.

You imply, she said, that I would drink the more. That is impolite. So it is, too, to emphasize that I am paying.

I'm sorry, he said.

You must learn, she said. Other people exist independently of you. They need and they feel. They have life.

I am sorry, he said.

You are sorry, she said. Where does that get us?

He stared at his hands in his lap.

We must not quarrel, she said. The night is only half over.

She lifted her glass.

Drink, she said.

They drank.

You stared at your plate, she said.

He often did. He could write a book. Plates I have known.

He said nothing throughout the meal. Konradin was quiet too. When the plates had been taken away, and they were waiting for Herr Koechlin to ring the bell and dismiss them, he spoke.

Are you bored? Konradin said.

He thought, What? Yes. Um. Oh God, what am I going to say?

Yes, he said.

I too, Konradin said. I am very bored. The people here, they are children.

Yes, he said.

I am Konradin, Konradin said.

I know, he said.

You are Yustin, Konradin said.

J. J., he said.

J. J., Konradin said. He got the Js right.

Herr Koechlin rang his bell, and he was about to stand up, like everybody else. But Konradin put his hand on his arm.

Wait, he said. We were talking.

Herr Koechlin nodded at him on his way out.

I'm not really bored, he said. I just said that. I don't know what's wrong with me. I'm lonely, I think.

I'm not surprised, Konradin said. Who would not be lonely in a place like this?

The dining-room was empty now, apart from them. Konradin looked out of the window at the Neckar and the illuminated Castle opposite.

A beautiful view, he said. But man does not live by views alone. What are we going to do tonight? While the children drink.

I don't know, he said.

Positive thought, Konradin said. And positive action. Don't tell me you've been in Heidelberg all this time, and can't think of anything to do. No concerts? No poetry readings? My dear J.J., you have been wasting your time.

Yes, he said. I expect I have. I'm not very good on my own.

Well, Konradin said. Now you have me. And I have not been wasting my time. Tonight we will go out, and I will show you Heidelberg. We may even get a little drunk. Like the children. But we will do it properly. I will show you how.

So they went out.

And they got drunk.

They went to a jazz bar in the new city, which was full of American soldiers who bought them beer. They moved on to a wine bar in the Hauptstrasse which was full of university students who bought them wine. They ended up playing the Stiefel game in a dirty bar in a back street by the river, with a group of motor mechanics.

At eleven o'clock the landlord threw everyone out except for them, and a few favoured customers, whom he gathered round a central table. He served them all with a glass of schnapps, and lifted his hand for silence. Then he went to a box on the wall, which had the words *Spezialität Gulaschsuppe* written on it in Gothic script, and, with an elaborate gesture, opened it.

Inside was a picture of Hitler in the robes and armour of a Ritter. Everyone stood up and shouted *Sieg Heil!*

He wasn't drunk enough not to be embarrassed.

But Konradin's arm was up, and he was shouting *Sieg Heil* like all the rest, and soon so was he.

Then they all shouted *Hoch!* and downed their schnapps, and Konradin took him out.

They sat on a bench by the river after that, and he was sick. Konradin put his arm round his shoulder while he puked, and gave him his handkerchief to wipe his mouth.

Now, he said, to the real business of the evening. You have had too much fresh air. What you need is a smoky room and a coffee. I know just the place.

I ought to go to bed, he said.

That too, Konradin said.

I'm not used to this, he said.

You are doing very well, Konradin said. It all comes with practice. Soon it will be second nature.

He put Konradin's handkerchief in his pocket.

He could not walk straight for very far, so Konradin put his arm round his waist.

The wind was cold.

They sang.

After a long while they wobbled up to a neon-lit doorway, and Konradin rang the bell.

Inside was a dim room with alcoves, into one of which they fell, and a crooning jukebox.

He heard Konradin say, Coffee for my friend and brandy for me, and he fell asleep.

He was still drunk when he woke up.

His tie was loose.

His belt was undone.

His head was in a girl's lap.

He sat up.

His coffee was cold.

The girl was not very pretty.

Konradin was dancing with a woman who did not look very young.

He waved at Konradin, who brought his partner back to the table.

How do you like the girls? he said. I'm afraid they can't speak English. Shall you mind?

The song on the jukebox stopped. His girl leapt to her feet and yelled, *Musik! Musik!* Konradin's girl jumped up and down.

They want another record, Konradin said. I don't have any money. Do you?

He scooped a handful of change on to the table, and Konradin's girl disappeared with it. The music started again.

His girl put her hand on his thigh.

A waiter appeared with a tray of drinks. Konradin said, Bring the bottle.

He handed a note to the waiter, who took it, and returned with a half-empty bottle of brandy.

They danced.

And drank.

And danced.

And drank again.

He paid.

When the bar closed, the girls took them back to their place.


### FOUR

To be honest, the thought that, whatever he was going to do, Konradin was going to be doing it in the room next door, added rather a lot to his excitement.

The only trouble was, when they got to the girls' apartment it immediately became apparent that there was no room next door.

It was a big room, but there was only one of them.

And there was only one bed in it.

Konradin's girl started to undress him as soon as they arrived, and he stood very still as his girl started on him. When they were both naked he looked across at Konradin.

Konradin's body was slim and pale, and his girl clucked appreciatively at it as she took off her own clothes. She went to the bed and drew Konradin down on top of her, where he lay, kissing her, and pumping her belly with his hips.

His girl took off her clothes and led him to her side of the bed. She sat on the bed and took his cock in her mouth.

It didn't do any good.

He was staring at Konradin, at Konradin's luminous body.

His girl released his cock and lay down. She must have noticed where he was looking, because she leaned across and stroked Konradin's buttocks, and smiled.

He stood by the bed.

His girl opened her arms, and her legs, and he clambered between them. They kissed for a while. She sucked his tongue down her throat, and ground her hips against his.

It didn't do any good.

It hurt his tongue. That was all he felt. An ache at the root of his tongue.

Konradin and his girl had changed position. She was concentrating now on his lower half, and he was lying back against the pillow with his eyes closed.

Again his girl must have seen where he was looking, because she said something in German, and Konradin opened his eyes and looked at him. He pulled himself up the bed a little. His girl must have taken this for a signal of some sort, because she lifted her head, but Konradin pushed it back again, and said something that he couldn't hear.

His girl pushed him towards Konradin. He thought, he really did, that Konradin was going to say something. He had no idea what. Encouragement maybe. Advice maybe. But he kissed him.

His girl turned round and burrowed between his legs. Again she took his cock in her mouth.

Out of the corner of his eye, as Konradin kissed him, he could see her legs wedged up against the wall.

He pulled his mouth from Konradin's mouth, and his cock from her mouth, and climbed off the bed.

It took him for ever to find his clothes. He dressed with his back to the bed. When he turned round his girl was straddling Konradin's face.

Konradin's girl was sitting on the edge of the bed. As he looked she lifted and separated Konradin's legs, licked her finger, and slid it into his anus.

She was looking at him. Her face was perfectly matter of fact.

She took her finger out of Konradin's anus and beckoned him with it.

He simply could not help himself. He followed her finger. He knelt full clothed on the bed. She took his head in her hands, and pushed his face between Konradin's legs. It must, he thought, be tiring to keep your legs in the air for so long.

Then she took Konradin's cock and pushed it into his mouth. Konradin swung his legs over his back and crossed them, so that he was trapped.

He fought, but between them they held him there.

He couldn't breathe. He was the only one who couldn't. The others were snorting like horses. He didn't know whether they were panting with laughter or pleasure. He was in no position to find out. But in one case at least he suspected laughter.

He stopped fighting and relaxed, which may have taken the fun out of things, because Konradin's girl pulled him off Konradin, and pushed him off the bed.

Like an angry schoolteacher she took him by the ear and led him to the door.

Stark naked she led him down the stairs and into the street.

She patted his cheek, kissed him, and closed the door on him.

He got hopelessly lost on the way home. He wandered for what felt like hours. He hid whenever he chanced on some fellow wanderer.

He thought that he might never stop blushing.

It was that final kiss that did it. All the rest he could handle. More or less.

Most of his walk he spent with a raging erection.

But that pat on the face, that kiss on the forehead, they were too much.

He'd read books. He knew, at second-hand admittedly, but he knew about numerous situations none too different from the one he had just found himself in. He had, in fact, imagined things not too dissimilar, although his own performance had been more professional in imagination than in fact.

He knew, too, that desire often outstrips performance, or comes too late to be of any use.

And he admitted the desire. His erection bespoke it.

He could, he swore, handle all that.

It was the kiss that did it.

To be dismissed in that kindly, almost motherly, way. That was more than he could take. That was what made his face blaze, and sent him scuttling into corners every time he heard a step on the street.

It would take him some time to stop remembering that.

He sat down in one of the corners he had scuttled into, and hugged his knees.

FIVE

He woke to grey dawn.

Six thirty by his watch.

He was lost, but after a shortish walk he came across a tramline which he followed to a stop.

He had an enormous headache.

When the tram arrived he discovered that he had lost his wallet, so he couldn't get on. His travellers cheques were in his wallet. All of them. Silly, of course, to carry them about like that, but it was one of his neuroses. Like with his suitcases. He like to have important things to hand. To know where they were.

He walked along the tramlines till he got his bearings.

He crossed the Old Bridge at a quarter past eight, and arrived at the Lyceum when everyone was clattering jollily down to breakfast. He met his room-mate at the door of his room, but said nothing.

He spent the morning lying on his bed, trying to sleep. It came to him suddenly as he lay there that he was going home.

Today.

Tonight.

He went through his drawers looking for money. But all he could find was a five pound note and a couple of half-crowns.

That stumped him for a while.

From downstairs came the sound of lessons ending, and students trooping jollily into lunch.

He waited till everything was quiet, and went down the corridor to Konradin's room. The room was empty, the sheets on both beds tumbled, so Konradin must have got back sometime.

He found a hundred and fifty marks in a drawer and took it. He figured Konradin owed him. He left his two half-crowns in their place.

It didn't take him long to pack. There was not enough room for all his books and dirty clothes in his suitcase, so he went back to Konradin's room and took one of his.

When he had finished he hid the cases under his bed, and went to the bathroom to wash and shave.

Then he lay down again.

He saw Konradin again at dinner. He sat at the other end of the table and was too busy chatting and laughing to do more than wave.

He felt pretty spry considering.

He ate quickly, and did not wait for Herr Koechlin to ring his dismissal bell. People looked surprised when he got up to leave, but he had a train to catch.

He nodded to Konradin on his way out.

He felt good on the way to the station. His bags were heavy but his heart was light. But it didn't last.

There was a queue at the ticket office.

He managed to book almost the last seat on the Ostend express.

The ticket cost ninety-eight marks, which left little enough to get home on.

And he missed the train.

Magda fetched more coffee and brandy.

Of course, you know your problem, she said when she got back. You realize that you haven't even once described your friend to me. All I know of him is that he is slim and pale when naked, and that could be said of many people.

Yes, he said. I know. I'm self-absorbed. It's my fault.

Other people exist, she said. You do not like it, but it is so.

She banged her coffee spoon on the table. People looked across at them. He looked at his lap.

It is so, she said.

I shall try to remember, he said.

Remember! she said. You remember too much. You have altogether too good a memory. Which is why you only had your erection looking backwards.

He could think of nothing to say.

Of course, you know, she said, what follows from everything you've been saying.

What? he said.

That all fortune is good fortune, she said.

That was too much.

He gulped.

As if it weren't all bad enough without that.

There he was, all in all, he felt justified in thinking, in a fairly lousy state, and all she could come up with was that. Some tinpot apophthegm that solved nothing. That left everything exactly as it was.

He couldn't think why he had told her anything if she was going to miss the point like that.

He groped in his pocket for his handkerchief, because he was going to cry. When he pulled it out he saw that it was Konradin's handkerchief, still stained with his vomit.

That did it.

He cried.

Magda waited for him to stop.

While he was stopping she said something he didn't catch.

Oh well, he said. I suppose it will come out in the end.

He put the handkerchief away. Magda looked at him. She was obviously waiting for him to say something.

I shall try to see things, he said, in this new light.

She got up and went to the counter again. While she was away he realized what it was she had said.

He squirmed in his chair. He spilled his coffee. He grabbed his brandy and downed it in one, which made him choke.

The trouble was, he wasn't sure.

She had either offered him a bed for the night, or offered to share her bed with him.

That, he felt, was a point it would be as well to be clear on.

Magda came back to the table.

You'll need this, she said. They close soon. I must be going.

All she was carrying was one glass of brandy.

He looked at the brandy.

He looked at the cases.

He looked at his watch.

Yes, Magda said. You have a problem. Don't you.


### SIX

They cleaned him out.

That last brandy had been a mistake.

He had gone, after Magda left, back to the station – *zum Bahnhof zurück*; or was it *zur*; he still had trouble with gender – and sat, suitcases gripped firmly in either hand, on a bench, where his eyes unfocused, his head lolled forward on his breast, and he surrendered, reluctantly but the brandy was too much for him, to unconsciousness.

While he slept they cleaned him out.

Gently they unclasped his hands from his cases. Gently they laid him flat on the bench, and rifled his pockets.

He woke to the sight of the station roof.

He did not know where he was.

He looked at his wrist and wondered why he wasn't wearing his watch.

His neck was stiff. His mouth was dry.

Christ!

Jesus!

Jesus Christ!

He jumped to his feet. His head swam but he didn't have time to care.

Oh God! Oh God! Oh God!

His cases, his watch, his passport, his ticket, his five-pound note, his Marks, even *The Unquiet Grave*, all were gone. Even Konradin's handkerchief.

He turned and ran. He turned and ran back.

He sat on the bench.

He closed his eyes, but this made him feel sick, so he opened them again.

He clasped his head in his hands, but this made it swim worse than ever, so he stopped.

He felt a sudden blow to his shoulder, but when he turned round there was no one there.

He retreated into his duffle-coat. He turned up the hood and pulled it down over his eyes. He hunched his elbows in at his waist and thrust his hands into his pockets.

He waited.

There was something in his pocket.

This, he thought, is happening to me.

In his pocket were a ten-pfennig coin and a penny.

He rubbed them together.

The station was cold. In default of anything else to do, he might as well go for a walk.

He walked off the concourse and out along a platform to where the light ended and the night hung like a curtain.

He walked up the line.

Taking care to keep his feet on the sleepers he walked and walked up the line.

The sleepers were narrowly spaced and made him take shorter strides than usual, which occupied his mind so that it was some time before he looked up to see where he was going, and was immediately arrested by the beauty of the rails.

They swept.

They curved.

They shone in the blue night.

He looked back along them to the station.

He looked forward along them into the air.

He took the two coins out of his pocket and rubbed them together again. Then he threw them as far as he could along the rails, so far that, although he listened very hard, he couldn't hear them land.

He filled his lungs with air and slowly expelled it.

He turned and started to walk back to the station.

Which is when it happened.

A line of ice ran up his spine and punched him in the neck. A line of fire ran through his limbs and a great light slapped him behind the eyes.

He ran.

He whooped.

He leaped.

He punched the air.

He ran back along the lines to the station. He ran across the concourse and out on to the street. He ran past Magda's café. Laughing and shouting he ran until he couldn't run any more. Giggling he leaned against a wall. His legs buckled and he curled up into his duffle-coat and, smiling, slept.

It was full day when he woke.

The pavement under his cheek was orange.

Feet walked past his face.

A coin fell by his nose.

Rubbing his eyes he pulled himself up on to his elbow.

Around him on the pavement were chalked a parquet of lively coloured scenes: landscapes, Rhinescapes, portraits, a copy of Dürer's *Praying Hands*.

And on the pictures lay a scatter of coins.

And past him as he lay on the pictures walked Mannheim on its way to work, dropping coins and more coins around him.

He stood up, shook himself, stretched, and set about collecting the coins.

## *from* Trespasses

### PAUL BAILEY

Welcome to Auntie Bernard's palatial parlour and mind your head on the chandelier – it hangs low, like all the best things.

Nothing gives me greater pleasure than to talk about myself. I once said to Mums – after she'd gone over to Rome, that is – that if I ever went too, the priest would never get away, I'd have him fixed with my glittering eye, he'd be in that box all day and night while I had a good old wallow. *You have been warned.*

I could never compete with Mums in the personality stakes. I say that in all humility. She was an extraordinary creature, she really was. Had there been more like her, I feel sure that England would have had a revolution. Blood would have flowed in the streets and heads would have tumbled. There must have been dozens of shop assistants – from Harrods and Fortnum's and many points between – who would have been willing to man the barricades, if only for the chance of taking a pot-shot at her. She was not the world's most lovable lady.

She never arrived at places, she descended on them. Swooped down, rather. She swooped down on to my school a few times – yes, it *was* public and yes, the masters *did* fondle our bums while they were correcting our Latin – and every time she came she appeared to be a bit less real. You could smell her scent for days after. All the other boys were terribly envious – 'I say, Proctor, your mother is a *riot*' – and some of them even told me, it was intended as a compliment, that they kept her in mind when they were exercising their wrists. I told her so years later and she smiled sweetly and said she was deeply touched. She omitted to tell me that she had seduced our house-captain on one of her visits. He told me himself.

Mums's father – she called him Dads – owned a salon in Mayfair and left her a good deal of money. He died – and so did his wife, Mums's Mums – before I was born. They were killed in a car accident near Monte Carlo. I remember once standing with her in silence – her silences were so rare that I can't help but remember them – at the crossing where it had happened.

That was our only holiday together and a pretty fatal one it was, too. As I have no doubt mentioned before, I caught my first dose of clap – in the place where men are supposed to catch it – from a chorus boy with liquid eyes, and I had to give up champagne and devote long hours of every day to fun with my water-pistol. A French farce, that one was, to end them all.

However, back to Mums. My father, who lived off her for years, left her for an actress when I was ten. 'Is she a famous actress, Mums?' I asked. 'Goodness no, dear,' she replied. 'She sounds distinctly tuppenny-ha'penny. They're living in a boarding-house. She's a strolling player by the sound of it.' So, after that, Father's lady-love – and I think he *must* have loved her because we heard from our cook, who had heard it from someone else, that he had actually taken a job somewhere – after that, Father's girl friend was always referred to as The Strolling Player (Mums adored giving people names) with one or two variations like The Pocket Bernhardt or The Thespian. Father became – and there were no variations for him – The Bastard, although this was abbreviated to The B. in letters.

Mums's letters! I have most of them to this day. When I'm really in the dumps, when my pecker is in need of lifting up, I undo the blue ribbon and read some of the more hilarious passages. Her letters may not be in the Lady Mary Wortley Montagu class (Confession Number One: I've never read Her Ladyship) but, by God, they *are* funny. One sentence and there she is, as vividly and monstrously alive as ever. I once wrote to tell her that I'd seen my first opera – *Figaro*. Her reply – from the Royal Picardy, Le Touquet – said she was so pleased I had developed a taste for opera, which was such a very civilized pastime, but would I give her my assurance that I'd never, on any account, become an admirer of the monstrous Wagner. She was not objecting to the velvet-jacketed gentleman's charming political leanings, because – I'm ashamed to say – she was a bit of a fascist herself. No, her objections were purely aesthetic. 'It's all so long and everyone looks so disgustingly robust. There are no clothes to speak of in Wagner. An evening spent in contemplation of a well-filled shift is not my idea of delight.'

Another time I wrote saying that I wanted to be a poet when I grew up. I even sent her some of my poems, which were all very homo in theme – wince-making words like 'lad' kept cropping up and there were references to 'lovely limbs' and 'dew-glistening thighs'. I'd describe the style now as Scoutmaster Tasteful Classical. Nasty repressed stuff it was *and* absolute nonsense – I mean, if your thighs were glistening with dew you'd be dead from pneumonia within the week, wouldn't you? Anyway, 'I want to be a poet,' I wrote. 'If you keep writing,' she answered, 'there is no reason why you shouldn't become another Keats or Shelley. Only don't die as they did. So young, the pair of them, starving in that appalling garret – their Mumses must have been shattered at losing them. You are not to die young – that is an order!'

But mostly the letters contained gossip – who was doing what to whom and where. They made wonderful bedtime reading in the dormitory. Mum's ears must have worked overtime under her blue rinse. And all the lovers she had – I was kept up to date on that score, too. She made my life seem very drab – there were no sun-tanned youths sending me red roses or smiling beguilingly at me from behind a glass of chilled white wine. Far from it. A burst of acne had hit my poor face, which only made my pathetic attempts to entice the heartiest and hairiest boy in the school into my maiden bed the more doomed to certain failure. The Proctor stomach turned over every time he appeared – clad or otherwise, but especially otherwise. Twenty years later we met in Bruton

Street: he was even heartier and hairier, sporting the most ridiculous handle-bar moustache. 'Let's have a pint of bitter together, old man,' he said. So I said I only drank gin, a bottle of which I had in my bijou abode some ten minutes' walk away: would *that* be acceptable? 'Just the job. We can have a good old chinwag in comfort.' He strode along beside me. No sooner had we entered the flat than his great hairy hand pounced on to my bottom and fixed itself there. 'May I, old man?' he asked. 'An't please your worship,' I said back, and I tried to drop a grateful curtsy, which perplexed him rather. That was the extent of our chinwag. When the doing was done, he shook my hand and slapped my back and marched off into obscurity again.

But, as usual, I digress. I was talking about Mums's letters, wasn't I? Well, for many, many years they were my only contact with her. If I had a mother it was by long distance. It was probably a blessing in disguise, as they say. I was monstrous enough without her; *with* her I'd have been totally unbearable. The mere thought of my years at Oxford – oh, them gleaming spires! – makes me shudder. It's not the outrageous clothes and the outrageous behaviour so much as our absolute and total ignorance of the way most people in England were living at the time. While we were all whooping it up and spending small fortunes on drag parties, hungry men were marching to London from the north and in some parts of this sceptr'd isle a tin shack was considered a desirable property. God rot us for not noticing and not caring.

However, I'm jumping the gun again. I came down to the great metropolis and I continued to live it up: my social conscience was still some months away. I worked, in the loosest possible sense, for a publisher – translating engineering manuals and such into readable English. I spent all my earnings – and some of my allowance from Mums – at theatres and restaurants and then, to round off a perfect day, on guardsmen. Those pre-war prices were most reasonable: two-and-six for handicrafts and as little some-times as five shillings for a full-scale operation, complete with trimmings. I must have had dozens of them – one of my friends swore he'd seen two account cards in my wallet, one for a department store and the other for Chelsea barracks. It was like a drug for me, except that the effects always wore off so quickly. I often trudged out in search of my injection in weather that would have deterred Nanook of the North.

It was on just such a search that I met Jim, the love of my life. Oh dear, it does sound so sordid, doesn't it? Still, the truth is the truth and this particular Miss Capulet met her Mr Montague in a dark and gloomy lavatory in the vicinity of Blackfriars Bridge. It was *so* dark and gloomy, in fact, that we had to walk out into the street to see what we both looked like. We saw and we fell and from that moment romance bloomed. How many couples can boast such an enchanted beginning?

He was barely literate but he taught me a good few values. So many people today assume that having an education is like having a passport to understanding and decency. It's a myth, I fear. Jim couldn't help being anything but decent and kind yet writing a letter was, for him, as daunting an ordeal as swimming the Channel. He put me in my place several times. 'Can't you ever behave naturally? Why do you have to speak in that stupid voice? You're talking to *me*, you know.'

We decided we'd share my flat and he insisted on paying half the rent from the meagre wages he earned as a carpenter's apprentice. He had great trouble getting away from his parents, particularly his mother, old Ada Burris, who was so ghastly that La Divina Goacher seems almost human by comparison. I was called into her presence one cheerless Sunday afternoon and I must say I felt distinctly uneasy as I climbed the stairs at Empress Dwellings. The squalor! Ada, Sid, Evie and Jim all lived together in two rooms at the very top. There was no electricity and one water tap in the forecourt served the entire house. The main reason for my uneasiness, though, was because I was convinced that I was about to play the role of the future bride being inspected by the groom's family. I certainly did get stared at that day, but only Ada – whose eyes were the kind that wool had never been pulled over – guessed what was going on between her son and the gentleman caller. We ate vinegar-soaked cucumber sandwiches and drank tea the colour of ox-blood as Ada prattled on about how pleased she was that her boy had made such a good friend and one, what's more, who had a shilling or two to spare; it was such an honour for them to have – beg pardon the expression – a toff come to call and sit down and take a bite with them. I tried to appear as relaxed as I could. Her choicest phrases were all repeated at full volume for the benefit of Sid, on whose deaf side she had cleverly seated herself. Evie, who was fat and plain and wore a surgical boot, looked at me as though I was a creature from another world – which, in a way, I was. I caught her eye once or twice and I could sense how insincere and forced my smile was. I felt so ashamed: she sat there, a lump, marked out by Mother Nature to be unloved, casting looks of adoration at her young brother. She obviously hadn't realized – and Jim afterwards bore this out – that she was doomed to a life of drudgery. Ada ran the family with words, Evie with deeds. Ages later, she wrote to tell me of her mother's death. I invited her to dinner. She came, and – at the age of forty-seven – drank her first glass of wine. She choked to begin with but after that, she said, it went down very nicely, although she couldn't see herself making a habit of it. We talked about Jim, she was proud of him being brave but she would have preferred him alive for all that. She would see her deaf old father to his last rest and then, who knew, she'd have to do more than taking in ironing and sewing to earn her daily bread, wouldn't she? I said she must go home by taxi. She complained of the extravagance. I insisted. In the street, I hailed a cab. Clump, clump, clump down the stairs she came. We stood for a moment on the doorstep, embarrassed. She cupped my face in her hands and kissed me. She waved as the taxi drew off. I somehow managed to close the front door. I bent over, I remember, and I wept. I have seldom in my life been so honoured.

I seem to have strayed again, as is my wont. I love that phrase, don't you – as is my wont? Well, the evening after my Sunday visit, Jim came round to the flat carrying a small suitcase which, he said, contained all his possessions. His farewell to the Dwellings, I

soon learned, had not been pleasant: decidedly *un*pleasant, in
fact, with Ada screaming loudly from a balcony. 'I don't want a
bleeding brown-hatter for a son' was the phrase that rang
melodiously in his ears all the way to Aldgate station. She had, it
seemed, goaded him – by way of scarcely veiled references – into
blurting out the truth about us. She had settled for 'brown-hatter'
only after exploring all the other possibilities: Nancy, pansy, arse-
hole prodder. (She obviously couldn't conceive of her son being
passive.) At one point in her recital she had even invoked the
Almighty. 'Do you think the Lord gave you a pair of ballocks', she
wanted to know, 'so as you could let them run to waste?'

And so began – as they say in memoirs – the happiest period of
my life. To start with, I treated him a bit like Eliza Doolittle – you
know, introducing him ever so gently to what we privileged
mortals call culture. Bedtime readings from the classics and so
forth. I once took him to the ballet – the stress is on the second
syllable – and I was so proud of him: he laughed loudly all the way
through some terrible piece, a positive feast of fish-net, called *The
Triumph of Death*. As soon as the serpent began to rape the heroine,
we had to leave: accompanied, I might add, by sibilant cries of
'Philistines!' Oh, I adored him that evening. The theatre was filled
with earnest queens all saying '*So* profound', 'Serge has never
offered us anything as meaningful as this' and there was Jim,
bright-eyed with disbelief, trusting his native intelligence and
coming to the right conclusion.

Re-enter Mums. She rang one afternoon and Jim answered the
phone – he was still unaccustomed to it, so he shouted into the
mouthpiece, holding the receiver a good foot away from him.
'*Who* was that?' asked Mums as soon as she realized that her
darling boy was on the other end of the line. 'Have you got a
workman in?' When I'd recovered from the fit of hysterics brought
on by her question I managed to reply 'Not at the moment' and
immediately collapsed again. We arranged to meet at the Ritz for
tea.

We met. Picture the scene. Me, in my most discreet apparel,
pretending to listen intently as Mums – little finger crooked above

the handle of her cup, her free hand soaring and dropping – describes the last few months on Capri. She finishes. I embark on a slab of walnut cake. It is time now for seriousness.

MUMS: You were quite extraordinary on the telephone today, dear. Your Mums wondered if you were really of sound mind.

ME: Yes, Mums, I'm sorry. It was a private joke, you see.

MUMS: With the man who nearly deafened me?

ME: Yes, Mums. Mums – (I concentrate on the crumbs on my plate, arranging them into patterns) – I have something to tell you.

MUMS: Tell me then.

ME: It might come as a shock to you.

MUMS: Does anything shock me, dear? I doubt it.

ME: This might. It's my private life –

MUMS: Yes, dear – what about it?

ME: It's my tendencies –

MUMS: What about them?

ME: (I cough away the phlegm that has gathered in my throat. A whisper escapes from me.) I'm a homosexual.

MUMS: I know you are, dear. What about it?

ME: How *could* you know, Mums?

MUMS: How *couldn't* I, you mean. It's as plain as a pikestaff, dear. You were always – what's the expression? – a sensitive plant. I'm glad you are: there are far too many brutes in this world. Those beautiful poems you sent me from school, they told me the whole story. Who wants to be normal anyway? The greatest artists were all homosexual –

ME: Now, Mums –

MUMS: Of course they were. Don't argue. This is one subject I *do* know about. Michelangelo, Leonardo, Shakespeare, Beethoven – all of them.

ME: The man who answered the phone, Mums, is my lover.

MUMS: But he sounded so common –

ME: He was born in the East End –

MUMS: You *must* be careful. Being different is perfectly all right, nothing wrong with it at all, but you *must* be careful in your choice of friends. You can't go scouring the gutters, dear. Working people are all very well, they perform a useful service, but it's absolutely necessary to keep one's distance from them. They take liberties, otherwise; they betray one. Follow my advice, dear, and find yourself someone from a good school. Or from Sandhurst – I'd like to think of you married to a handsome young officer.

ME: I love him, Mums.

MUMS: Now, dear, control yourself. You can't take him to the best parties – you know that, don't you? Let's change the subject. Have you heard from The Bastard?

ME: No. Should I have done?

MUMS: I simply wondered. I suppose he *is* still with The Strolling Player?

ME: I suppose so, Mums.

And the touching scene drew to its close.

Where Mums failed, Hitler succeeded. The war began and Jim went away. The army, to my amazement, declined the offer of my services. Blood pressure. I remained in London, working for the fire service.

I shan't inflict all the details of my Great Sorrow on you. I've nothing but contempt for people who do it to me. 'I do not wish to hear,' I say to them, ever so brusquely. What I *will* say, though, is that I was a different man when I was with Jim, I wasn't always a parody pansy. I lived quite simply; I even spoke simply, which took some doing.

Memory's a great one with her little tricks, isn't she? It all seems so idyllic from this distance. Would we have been able to continue in that happy, uneventful way? It's a chilling thought – granted more time together we might have become (like so many do) a couple of bickerers: 'queens' means 'scenes'. Or the kind who ask each other twenty-four hours every day: 'Do you still love me? You *do*, don't you?' Or the kind who can enjoy each other only when they're indulging in threesomes. Or the kind who just break up. To return to the actual plot. I received that card from Germany and went into a decline. 'Only disconnect' became my motto. I saw no one. Another period I look back on with a shudder: I floundered in self-pity, I realize now. I took to injection-hunting once more. There was plenty of scope, the war hadn't ended. I was obliged in several doorways. I lost interest when I was spoken to: I preferred a nod or a wink; I preferred it quick and brutal.

I hadn't seen Mums since the tête-à-tête over the Earl Grey. News had reached her in faraway Suffolk of Jim's death. Could she call on me with a gentleman friend? 'A lover, Mums?' 'No dear, quite the reverse. A priest.' She rang off before I could ask why she was bringing a priest to see me. I soon discovered the reason.

I don't think I can do justice to Father Flynn. He was seven feet tall, he had protruding teeth, hands like sides of beef and eyes out on stalks. Centuries of inbreeding are responsible for you, I thought as he sent the chandelier tinkling. Mums, you're a marvel, you've brought this clown to cheer me up. Alas no, she hadn't. Father Flynn was a deadly serious specimen, it quickly became clear. He held my hand in his – he covered it, rather – and patted it as gently as he could. 'Have you something in your eye?' I asked and then it dawned on me that he wasn't squinting but giving me the Clerical Look of Sympathy. (You know the one – you peer closely at your victim and you nod slowly, as if to say 'You don't have to speak. I understand.') 'Could I possibly have my hand back?' I asked eventually. 'I have to prepare something dainty for the trolley.' 'Of course, of course.' 'You're about to back into the fireplace,' I said, 'so would you kindly sit down?' And I added, wickedly, 'For Christ's sake.'

I heard, from the kitchen, the lilt of the Emerald Isle: 'He's obviously been under a great deal of stress.' 'And a great many Irish labourers, too,' I called out. What is known as a pregnant silence ensued.

'Tea up!' I chirped brightly as I entered with a plate of fish-paste sandwiches. 'I don't want to see any of these left.' Which was perfectly true: Jim had bought a jar of the disgusting stuff five

years before and it had remained in the Proctor pantry the entire
time. Waste not, want not – Father Flynn's visit was heaven-sent
in one respect at least. Nineteen of the twenty sandwiches
prepared found their way into the priestly intestines; Mums bit
into the remaining one and then, with horror etched large across
her features, returned it to the plate.

Pregnant silences seemed to be the order of the day. To relieve
the monotony I said, 'Mums, whatever is the matter? You're not
your usual old self at all.'

'I certainly am not, dear. I'm a new woman.'

'A new woman? Does that mean you have a good lover?'

'In a sense, dear, in a sense. I have Jesus Christ.'

'Mrs Proctor has been re-born in the spirit,' said Father Flynn.

Oh no, I thought, the silly cow *hasn't* become a Holy Roman.
Not *that*.

'My life has meaning at last,' she said. 'I have come out of the
wilderness.'

'Mrs Proctor is at peace with herself. Joy is in her heart.'

I looked at Father Flynn. 'Is it? She doesn't appear very joyful.
Tell me, Father, has she confessed to you?'

'She has, my son.'

'I bet it was entertaining, wasn't it?'

Those Irish eyes didn't smile. 'Your mother has taken a very
serious decision. She has cleansed herself.'

'Yes, Bernard, it's true. I am clean.' A meaningful pause.
Something's up, I said to myself, something *is* up. 'You could be
clean, too. Father Flynn is ready and willing to help you.'

'Are you, Father?'

'I am, my son. Shall I go on, Mrs Proctor?' Mums nodded. It was
all very strange. 'Your mother has told me about your problem.
Believe me, I *do* understand, I know what agonies you must go
through.'

'Do you, Father? I'm a trifle confused – which problem of mine
are you referring to?'

'Would you rather we discussed it man to man? If there's
another room – '

I brought him to heel. 'You have not answered my question, Father. Which problem?'

'*The* one.'

I was remorseless by now. '*The* one?'

'Yes. Your *physical* one.'

'But *which* physical one?' I asked sweetly.

I realized suddenly that my decline was over; my appetite for living was back. But then Mums brought my fun and games to a halt by saying, 'I told Father Flynn about your queer leanings, Bernard.'

'That's right. And I *do* understand, I know what agonies you must go through.'

'How do you know, Father?'

'I have been called to.' The blandness of it!

'Oh, I see. You spoke with such certainty I wondered if you too were in the club.'

'Which club?'

Mums to the rescue once more: 'My son is being offensive, Father. Take no notice. Do behave yourself, Bernard.'

'This *is* my flat, Mums,' I reminded her. 'Would you mind telling me the purpose of your visit?'

'What a silly question, dear. We haven't seen each other for years. I came to find out how you were – '

'Then why did you bring the clergy with you?'

'Because, dear, because I want you to experience the same happiness that I now have. Losing your friend – '

'The one you advised me to throw over? The one I couldn't take with me to the best parties?' I launched into an aria of obscenities; Ada Burris herself could not have surpassed me. I told Mums that I despised and hated her: her shallowness and stupidity, her vanity, her snobbishness, her cruelty. But most of all I loathed her for her hypocrisy, for the ease with which she assumed it was possible to wipe away fifty years of thoughtlessness by offering herself up to some senseless Deity.

I stood there snorting like a bull. Mums said nothing. I glared at Father Flynn.

'God is doing his work inside you,' he said. 'You have just shed a load of bitterness.'

I bawled at them to leave. They went out crossing themselves, like Mrs Goacher's mad lodger.

After that joyous outburst it seemed only right and proper that Bernard Proctor should prove to the world that he wasn't as thoughtless as he had accused his mother of being. He wanted to be of use to someone.

So – back we go into the first person – I applied for a post that I'd seen advertised in a weekly journal. I went before this forbidding board and explained to them why I considered myself the best person there was to take evening classes in English literature a stone's throw from the sound of Bow Bells. I rattled off the names of all the authors I'd read, from Beowulf onwards. I kept my legs apart and made absolutely sure that not a single hairpin was dropped.

I can honestly say that the job I have somehow managed to cling on to all these years has given me more satisfaction than anything else in life, except for those few months in You-know-who's company. My business and my pleasure have been kept strictly apart, although I've been sorely tempted many times – as you can well imagine, working where I do. I have never dallied with any of the golden youths who have passed through my metaphorical hands.

I haven't finished with Mums yet, I'm afraid. I heard from her – or rather, from the put-upon nurse who was looking after her – for the last time. The pain-killing drugs she was taking had made her temporarily deranged: the nurse had discovered her in the sitting-room one morning pissing (Nursie, of course, said 'passing water') into the Meissen tea-cups. Mrs Proctor was now in hospital.

Mums and her wayward son made their last contact.

'Have they told you what's wrong with me?'

'Yes,' I said.

'Frightful place to have it in, isn't it?' It was – she had cancer of the rectum. 'I laugh about it when it isn't hurting me.'

I simply couldn't believe it: a courageous Mums, a dignified Mums? And I performed an about-face, too: I asked her forgiveness for what I'd said. It was granted. She also apologized for trying to convert me. She knew now it was a personal matter, it had to rise up in you, it had to come from your heart. As far as she was concerned, sweet Jesus was the only man who had ever made any sense to her in this bloody world.

I stayed with her until she died, two days later. A priest gave her the last rites. Her face was serene.

Out in the street, I felt my old hatred seething up – what right had she to die so well? People whose lives had been decent and good and blessed with love went out screaming their heads off. Mums the selfish, Mums the cruel, Mums the every vice you could put a name to, had died as beautifully as any saint.

I came home to the gin bottle and then I went cruising. I prowl the streets and scatter the good seed on the hand. Many an old haunt was revisited that night. A Negro said he could give me twelve inches if I gave *him* five pounds. I had little in cash – would he accept a cheque? No, he said, he hadn't yet opened a bank account. *Ciao*.

After which, it was hard by the shore of silver-streaming Thames and into the most notorious lavatory in the south-west area. Was it empty? Almost, but not quite. One tall gentleman at the very end. Yes, just the job, tall and broad with it. A strong profile. A handsome, rugged face. And what a nice smile, so full and generous, such fine white teeth. And *what* a lovely appendage, not up to the promised five pounds' worth but enough – *more* than enough – for gin-soaked, motherless, Jim-less Bernard. Notes were compared – do you like mine? I like *yours* – and hands explored and then I found myself in a van, seated next to an old queen, the lines on whose face had been partly obscured with orange make-up and down whose cheeks enormous tears – of the kind one only ever seems to see in films – rolled and rolled and rolled. Before we drove away at midnight, we had been joined by four others.

In the dingy court-room the following morning I stood,
unwashed and unshaven, and listened as the magistrate described me as 'a shameful man' and Police-Constable Jenkins,
Ronald Percival, stated in a loud, clear voice that I had made a
grossly indecent proposal to him. (Marry me, Police-Constable
Jenkins, Ronald Percival, marry me do.) I said I was a clerk and
paid my fine (yes, they would accept a cheque) and I walked
slowly home, hoping against hope that the authorities wouldn't
find out and take my job away from me. They didn't. It's some
kind of a miracle that no one read the little item at the bottom of
page three in that Sunday newspaper, next to the advertisement
that promised relief from constipation. Or perhaps someone did
read it, but took pity on me and decided not to protest. That
person – it might even be persons – has my gratitude, I do assure
him. Or her. It was another miracle that I passed out on the
kitchen floor the night I heard about poor Ellie – I know the police
don't get up to those wicked tricks any more, but something
equally nasty might have happened with me in that condition.

I was the chief mourner at Mums's funeral. Oh, that hateful
ritual! When it's my turn, as they say, please Someone, just shove
me arse-upwards into a dustbin and set me alight. Then you can
scatter me to the winds. Thanks. Meanwhile, back at the grave-
yard: when it was all over, I was stopped by an elderly man. He
had receding sandy hair and there were gaps in his dentures – his
breath was so foul that I had to brush a hand against my nose
whenever he spoke. 'Hullo, old chap,' he said. 'I'm your father. I
don't suppose you wish to speak to me.' 'Hullo,' I said. We shook
hands. 'I came to pay my last respects. Ended up RC, did she?'
'Yes.' 'I saw when the funeral was from the back page of *The Times*.
I haven't much work on at the moment, business is always bad at
this time of the year, so I thought I'd come, pay my last respects,
see her off as it were.' 'Yes,' was still all I could say. 'Well then, I'd
better get back to Alice.' 'The – actress?' (I'd nearly said 'The
Strolling Player'.) 'Yes, she *was* on the boards. She gave it up. I've
been the breadwinner for many a long year.' You – a breadwinner? – in that shabby raincoat, in those cracked shoes . . . I

reached for my wallet, automatically. 'Christ no, old chap, I'm not on the scrounge. I must be off.' And off he fled.

And there you have me, if you'll pardon the expression. I'm very out of date, aren't I? I scarcely fit into this modern society. I can't get used to freedom; I suppose I crave the martyr's crown. The dirty back-streets and the stinking lavatories are my hunting-grounds; they're fit settings for humiliation: the clubs and bars, with everyone so open and happy, they only oppress me. They tear at my heart because I remember what I had. And anyway, I always did hate my kind *en masse*.

It's most unreasonable. But, if I'm honest, I have to confess that I enjoy putting on a show for all you normal specimens. It gives me pleasure. I'm one of that wretched number who thrive on pain. It keeps me going; it makes me tick. And, like a child, I expect you to applaud me.

So clap your hands now. My glittering eye is getting spots before it. I need my rest, I'm not as young as I was, and I *do* have a class tomorrow. England is still a terrible place, class is still warring against class; whatever they say, there is still some darkness shrouding this land of ours. I believe in what I do, and I hope and pray I do it well. I hope I lighten a few dark corners in my children's minds.

# The Secret of the Gentiles

## DAVID PLANTE

He went to live in Italy after he graduated from a Jesuit college in Boston, class of 1960. In Rome, he thought the only way to learn Italian was to go out into the street and shops and try to speak. He bought a bag of vegetables and salads wrapped in newspaper from a young woman at a stand in the cobbled street, and she, leaning over artichokes and carrots and fennel to hand him his change, smiled and asked his name. It made him feel a foreigner, which he liked, to give the Italian version, and, smiling back, he said, 'Davide.' She looked at him more closely, without smiling, then she tilted her head to the side, which was a gesture he recognized of Roman indifference, and said, 'E un nome antico.'

In Rome, *antico* meant to David ancient, and he went back to his apartment in the old part of the city feeling a little that he belonged there, his name being, like the stones, ancient.

David lived on Via del Gesù. In the courtyard of the *palazzo* was a fountain. His small apartment was just under the roof.

On his way to and from the English School, where he taught English to Italians, he walked along the narrow streets, paved from side to side with square stones so there was no sidewalk. David often found his arm rising to touch the walls he passed, the mottled walls of rough, sometimes cracked, pink, red. They had big white phalluses chalked on them. There was always the sound of running water.

A late autumn day, David was walking along a garden wall. Over it hung branches with small oranges. The garden wall was attached to a very big *palazzo*. In the basement was what looked like a junk shop with a low doorway to the street. Outside the doorway, on the cobbles, was an old trunk. When David stopped to look at it, a bald man wearing a grey, grease-stained overall came out of the shop and he and David looked at it together. The steamer trunk was covered in grey canvas that was torn, and the lock was rusty. David asked in Italian if it was for sale.

The man must have been in his middle seventies. Instead of answering, he asked David, 'Where are you from?'

David told him.

He smiled. 'What is your name?'

'Davide.'

The man's smile went and he stared at David for a moment before he said, 'The trunk is for sale, but I have to tell you, frankly, that it is not an antique.'

Again, they looked at the trunk.

'How much is it?' David asked.

'A thousand lire.'

'That's very little.'

'I don't think it's worth more.'

'I'd like to buy it,' David said.

'I'll give it to you for seven hundred and fifty.'

'No, no, I'll pay the thousand.'

'Don't you want to see inside first?'

The man lifted the lid. The inside was lined with pale blue paper. The smell of naphthalene rose up. Both men leaned to look deeper into the trunk.

'You'll take it for seven hundred and fifty?' the man said.

'I'll take it,' David said.

After he paid, with frayed lire notes, the man said, 'But how will you get it home?'

'I didn't think.'

The man said something David didn't understand, and David frowned. Raising his hands, the man told him to wait where he was, just for a minute, and he hurried along the street to two narrow wooden doors in the garden wall through which he went, leaving the doors open. A minute later he came out driving a three-wheel van, dented and rusty, with ropes dangling from the back. His expression was intent.

David helped him get the trunk on to the van. The man, moving quickly, locked his shop, then motioned to David to get into the little cab.

The van swayed from side to side as the man drove down the streets David pointed to.

David thought: Most Americans would suspect a Roman of trying to cheat them.

In the courtyard of the *palazzo* where he lived, David told the man he'd manage to get the trunk up the stairs himself, and if he couldn't he'd ask the *portiere* for help.

No, the old man said, he'd help, if they went slowly, slowly.

'Please,' David said, 'you've already – ' And here his Italian broke down. 'You're very generous,' he said, which may or may not have been the thing to say, but it was what came to him. 'You're too generous.'

The old man insisted. The corners of the trunk bumped against the walls of the narrow stairwell. The old man and David rested on the landings. They placed the trunk in the middle of the living room, where David saw it was too big for his apartment.

He asked the old man to sit, and he brought him a glass of wine. The man drank it straight down and handed the empty glass to David.

'*È molto carino qui,*' he said.

Standing before him, David thanked him.

'Sit down, sit down,' the man said, and extended his hand as if to push David down.

He sat on a chair across from the man. The idea flashed in his mind that the old man wanted to try to get him to do something with him that he wouldn't want to do, and David wondered how he could get rid of him, politely. He searched for something to say, but he couldn't find the Italian words.

The old man smiled at him and said something, and the only word David recognized was *ebreo*: Jew.

David thought, He believes I'm a Jew.

The man spread out his arms and said, 'The Jews – ,' and something incomprehensible.

Maybe, David thought, he was a little crazy.

His hands now on his chest, the old man said, 'They are the master race.'

This startled David, and it occurred to him that if the old man was not himself a Jew, he might have had Jewish friends who were killed by the Nazis. Or, worse for him, he might have revealed to the Germans where certain Jews had been in hiding, and ever since had been trying to make up for this to every Jew he met.

David said, 'I'm not a Jew.'

The man sat back. 'No? But with such a name – '

'Mine is a very common name in America among Christians.'

The old man said quietly, 'Here, recently, Christians call their sons David. They think the name is Anglo-Saxon. But those who were born during the war, as you must have been, who are called David – ' He raised his shoulders.

'I was born a Catholic,' David said.

He offered the man another glass of wine, but the man rose to go. Shaking David's hand in both of his, he said, 'It doesn't matter if you're not a Jew.' But some intensity had gone out of his brown, whisker-bristling face.

He eyed the steamer trunk as he left.

David wondered, Why didn't I let him think I was a Jew?

Shortly after, crossing the Piazza Navona, he heard a father call out to his little son, who was running away from him, 'Davide, Davide,' and David paused to look at the father rush to the little boy and grab him under his arms and lift him, laughing, into the air. Perhaps the father considered the name to be Anglo-Saxon.

Then David thought: What do I feel about Jews? What did he feel without telling himself what he should and shouldn't feel? What did he feel from some spot far back, as far back, say, as his

first seven years, when, according to the Church, he didn't have a
fully developed reason and couldn't be held culpable for what he
felt and thought? What feelings about Jews did he learn from
before he knew if the feelings were right or wrong?

Whenever he heard the Italian word for 'down', which was
'*giù*', he reacted with a little start.

He could not afford his apartment: kitchen, living-room, and two
bedrooms. One of the bedrooms he called his study, so small the
steamer trunk had to be put on the bed. There was no space for it
in the other rooms. The floors of the apartment were of red-
brown, waxed tiles, many cracked, and the walls were white. A
little terrace had a view over a rooftop where nuns hung out their
laundry, and beyond was Rome. There were orange trees in pots
on the terrace. David didn't want to move out, but he didn't know
how he would pay his rent.

An American friend said he should pin up a note on the notice
board in the entrance hall of the school asking for someone to
share.

'I'd have to give up my study.'

'Study?' she said. 'What do you need a study for?'

He was too embarrassed to say he wrote there. 'I guess, for
nothing.'

'And look,' she said, 'put in your notice that you'd like to have
an American man share with you. Sharing an apartment with
someone whose toilet and eating and sleeping habits, never mind
language, you understand, makes life much easier, I can tell you.'

'I don't know,' he said.

'I mean it. I shared for a month with a Somalian girl. It didn't
work out.'

'But what's the point of being in Rome if, in your apartment,
you're in America?' he asked.

He didn't indicate that he was looking for an American to share
his apartment, but he wrote the notice in American, using
expressions he had stopped using since he came abroad: Guy
looking for guy –

An Italian telephoned him. His name, he said, was Antonio. For a moment David hesitated.

Antonio came to see the apartment. He was a few years older than David, about twenty-five. He wore a white shirt with stiff collar and cuffs under a black pullover, and he was thin and good-looking. David made coffee, and they sat on the terrace among the orange trees and talked. Antonio was from Milan, where his parents lived. In Rome, he taught Italian to foreigners. His shoes were highly polished and the creases in his trousers were sharp.

David looked down at his corduroys and scuffed shoes and told himself he must dress better.

Antonio spoke very good English. He thrust out his tongue to make the difficult 'th' sound, and if he made a mistake, such as 'the people is' or 'the news are', he corrected himself.

On the flat rooftop across the way, two nuns, in black habits, were hanging white sheets on clothes-lines. They propped up the lines with poles. The sheets hid the view of Rome.

After the coffee, Antonio, rather than David, brought up the subject of the apartment.

'Oh yes,' David said, as if he'd forgotten.

While he showed Antonio around, ending with the study, David looked at him when Antonio looked the other way. He wondered if he wanted to live with him. Looking around the study, Antonio touched the smooth skin of his cheek with just the tips of his fingers, and David saw that hand as though it were another man's hand touching Antonio. A little frightened of what he might do, David imagined himself, on impulse, touching Antonio on his cheek.

Antonio was studying the steamer trunk on the bed. Then, as if Antonio knew he was being studied, he turned towards David. Antonio smiled. David didn't smile.

He thought he could use the trunk as an excuse not have Antonio stay.

Touching it, he said, 'This is a problem.'

'What about it?' Antonio asked.

'There's no room for it except on this bed.'

'That's no problem. We can ask the *portiere* to store it in the *fondo* of the *palazzo*.'

Now David had his excuse. He put his hands to his forehead. 'But I didn't first clear it with the *portiere* if I can rent out a room.'

'You did the right thing. You shouldn't tell anyone you're renting a room. Otherwise, the rent will go up. I'm only a visiting friend.'

Carrying one side of the trunk by a leather handle while Antonio took the other, David went first down the stone steps to the *fondo* where the *portiere* said the trunk could be stored. David thought: But there must be a way to stop him from moving in. They climbed the stairs in silence.

Antonio declined another coffee, which David felt he had to offer. 'I've got to go,' Antonio said, looking at his watch, 'I've got an appointment.' Italians always had appointments, even at the oddest hours. Shaking David's hand, Antonio said, '*Dunque, siamo d'accordo.*'

'*Sì.*'

David showed him to the door of what was going to be his apartment for only one night more. As he was leaving, Antonio stopped and turned round to face David again, and, smiling, he put his hands on his shoulders. David flinched, but Antonio didn't appear to notice.

'Look,' Antonio said, 'I have a girlfriend, and I want to ask you, with your permission, if I can, from time to time and with the greatest discretion, bring her up to my room.'

David said, 'You can do what you want.'

He sat on the small terrace. The convent roof was empty of laundry. The evening sky was grey, pink and blue, and swallows were swooping. David heard the swish of their wings when they passed close over his head.

Antonio moved in, then immediately went out and left David alone. Opening the door to Antonio's room slowly, he entered to look around: at Antonio's slim briefcase on the seat of the chair before the desk, his shirt over the back of the chair, and on his desk a pile of loose change and a smooth piece of red coral inserted in a silver cap to make a charm.

When Antonio wasn't seeing his girlfriend Anna in the evening, he and David ate out in a small trattoria called Suora Carolina near the Pantheon. Walking back together, David stopped at a window in a shop in which holy vestments were displayed on wooden frames, a satin green chasuble embroidered in gold thread standing at the centre, and Antonio stopped to look with him. Among the vestments were chalices. In one corner of the window was a brass seven-branched candelabra.

Pointing to it, David asked, 'What's that doing there?'

'What do you mean?' Antonio asked.

'Isn't it Jewish?'

Antonio looked at him and frowned. 'Aren't you a Jew?' he asked.

Looking at Antonio, David, too, frowned. 'No,' he said, and suddenly he understood that Antonio was, and that Antonio had taken the room because he thought he, David, was. For a moment displaced by this, David, to try to place himself, turned back to the candelabra in the window. In a voice meant to be deep with acceptance, and, more, with reverence, he said, 'I know it's called a minorah.'

They both studied the minorah for a while, then walked off.

In the Piazza Rotunda, Antonio said, 'I just remembered I have an appointment.'

'All right,' David said.

Antonio walked away from him over the black cobbles.


A pair of Antonio's shoes were on a sheet of newspaper under the kitchen table where he left them when he intended to polish them.

David got out the shoe polishing bag and, crouching over the newspaper, smeared black polish over Antonio's shoes.

He should try to remember what his parents, what his aunts and uncles, thought about Jews.

Come on, he said to himself, admit the worst of what they said.

He had never heard anyone in his family use the word 'kike'. Never.

Of course, there was Aunt Claire, who had lived in New York for a few years as a hospital nurse, and who sometimes told stories about her experiences with her Jewish landlady, such as: when Aunt Claire came home from the hospital on Friday afternoon, the landlady would be waiting on the landing, and she'd say, 'Don't you have something for me?' to which Aunt Claire always replied, 'You'll have to wait for the rent, Mrs Zimmerman, until I open my purse.' Jews existed in New York, and some In New Jersey. A very few lived in Boston, but none he knew of in Providence.

David put Antonio's polished shoes back under the table just as he heard Antonio come into the apartment with Anna. The three of them had coffee in the living-room, and while David, silent, listened to Antonio and Anna talk in Italian, a sudden shame came over him for having polished Antonio's shoes. David went into the kitchen and picked up the shoes to examine them. Maybe, he thought, he could scuff them up so they'd look like they did before he'd polished them. But that wouldn't work, and Antonio would wonder even more what had happened to them. David looked out the window.

Antonio came in with the coffee cups, which he rinsed and placed on a rack above the sink. Then he stood by David at the window.

'By the way,' David said, 'I had a few minutes to spare this evening, and I polished your shoes.'

Antonio frowned a little.

David simply asked, 'Where's Anna?'

'She's waiting in my room.'

'I see.'

Antonio seemed reluctant to leave, as if there was something he had to say, maybe about the shoes. He stepped away. 'Shall I shut off the light in the living-room?' he asked.

'Sure thing,' David said.

Antonio left, and David thought, I can't un-polish his shoes.

In his room, which was next to Antonio's, David lay on his bed and thought of the people he'd worked with when he'd gone to New York to work for a summer to save enough money to move to Rome. He remembered, possibly because he was in the mood to remember her, a girl named Sharon. She was not pretty. Her face was coarse and greasy, but she had beautiful hair. She took care of her hair. Perhaps her mother kept telling her, 'You've got nice hair.' She had a big Jewish nose.

She was the kind of girl David would become close to, as if, given her looks, there was no way she could suppose that David was after her for what girls with good looks always complained men were after them for. David was wrong to suppose this. Sometimes, walking back to the office from lunch with her, they didn't speak in the heavy heat, but David sensed her big body close, filled, it seemed to him, with heavy thinking. He told Sharon he was going to leave New York and go live in Rome, and he felt in all the thinking emanating from her a sudden, small convulsion.

'Are you a Catholic?' she asked.

'I was, but I'm nothing now.'

'Then why are you going to Rome?'

'To lead a life of sin,' David said.

At the office, she went into the ladies' room and emerged with her hair combed in smooth waves. She came to David's desk and stood before it. The time he most liked in the office was in the morning or before the lunch hour ended, when there were just a few people, all quietly thinking about what they wanted to think about. During these moments, he wrote short poems on office stationery. Sharon interrupted his writing. She smiled.

'You know,' she said, 'you are a David.'

She left it to him to figure out what that meant.

From time to time, if everyone else in the little office gang was off shopping or meeting others, David and Sharon would have lunch together, but there was no longer from Sharon the sense that her very body had wild, or at least uncontrollable, thoughts. She and David became quietly friendly.

Sharon wore a silver star of David on a chain around her throat. In the heat, it stuck to her skin.

One day, she told David that she was going to Israel.

'That's great,' he said.

In fact, he felt sad for her, as though there was no other place for her to go, as though she wasn't pretty enough, or imaginative enough, to go to any other place but Israel, where, because she was a Jew, she had to be accepted.

But he felt sadder, in a larger way, about Israel itself, and he didn't know why.

Could that have had to do, not with what the Jews felt, but with something he, a Christian, felt? Whenever, in church, he'd heard the priest almost intone from a psalm, 'O Israel,' a longing came over him.

On a sheet of office paper, he wrote:

> Israel, Israel,
> I am not a Jew
> But let me pray against your broken wall –
> I have no soul,
> But let me weep among your ruins –

Sharon came over to his desk to say a few words before she left in the evening. He usually had to stay later than anyone else to catch up on his work. Without considering it much, he said to her, 'I wrote this poem for you,' and gave it to her.

She touched her hair delicately as she read it. Her hand at her head went still and she frowned. Having stared at the poem as if all together, she handed it back to him without comment.

After she left, he read it and wondered how it could have offended her, if it had. Didn't she understand it? The meaning was so clear, he thought; he did not believe he had a soul, and yet he longed for something, which, because he did not have a soul, he could not have. The poem expressed the sadness he'd been trying to define. Maybe it was a Christian poem, however, and Sharon couldn't understand it.

Sharon went off to Israel before he went to Rome, and she sent him a postcard.

In Rome, lying on his bed, he asked himself, what did he feel about the Jews?

The shoes were gone, as were Antonio and Anna, when David went into the kitchen the next morning to make his coffee. It was Saturday. David watched young nuns, on the flat convent roof, play handball. Their long skirts and veils swung, and they laughed when they hit the ball. David did nothing with his day, and this, by sunset, made him anxious.

Antonio came in alone. He was wearing the shoes. David was sitting in a wicker chair in the living-room, and Antonio sat in the wicker double-seater. He put a package on the cushion beside him.

'How was your day?' David asked.

'I spent it with Anna.'

'Then it was a nice day.'

'We went to bookshops.'

'You bought some books?'

'I bought you one.'

David felt something rise in him that strained for more expression than just a smile.

Antonio held the package out to him, and David reached for it, then sat back and took the paper from the book. It was *Gli occhiali d'oro* by Giorgio Bassani, which David thumbed through so the pages fell softly on one another. He looked up at Antonio with the expectation that Antonio would be as moved as he was, though David didn't know why he was moved. Antonio sat still in his chair and watched David, who pretended to read the book, but incomprehensible words – *rifuterebbe* – appeared to magnify then shrink into the text.

David's impulse was to get up and go to Antonio and, leaning over him, put his arms around him, and this impulse came, David knew, from a longing to love Antonio for sadness greater than any sadness David had ever known. The recognition of this longing surprised David and almost removed him from it to wonder about it but while he was thinking, How strange, tears rose into his eyes.

Antonio said, 'I'm sorry you were alone today.' His eyes were large and so dark it was as if his dark irises filled them. Then he smiled.

He wasn't sad, David thought. Antonio wasn't sad, and David could see on his eyes the bemusement, which, though, was a little amused, of why David was.

'You could have come with Anna and me,' Antonio said.

'No.'

'With us, you would see parts of Rome you never saw.'

'I was all right.'

'Were you, really?'

'Sure,' David said.

Antonio said, 'You spend too much time alone, I think.'

'I have friends if I want to see people.'

'You should see them. You shouldn't be alone.'

For a moment, David did see sadness in Antonio's face, and he knew immediately that it was for him, for David. He didn't want to be the cause of anyone's sad concern, and he tried to think of a way of getting Antonio's attention off him. Turning over the pages of the book, he asked Antonio, 'Did you have a lovely day?'

Antonio's lips rose at the corners into not quite a smile. 'A very lovely day,' he said. 'I always have lovely days.'

David looked down at the book and read a line, which he understood.

Antonio got up and said, 'I'll leave you to read,' and as he passed David he touched him on the shoulder.

In his room, David started the novel. He had a dictionary by him. The book was difficult to read, and sometimes he didn't know what was happening. But if he didn't understand exactly, he had a sense of what was happening. A young Italian Jew identified himself with an ageing man who loved young men, and who, after exposing his love, killed himself.

He fell asleep at dawn. In the late morning when he got up, the

apartment was empty. He went out onto the terrace to look over
Rome as he drank his coffee. After he showered and shaved and
dressed, he went out.

When he returned to the apartment, he found Antonio, alone,
sitting in the sunlight that came through the glass doors to the
terrace. He had taken off his shoes and placed them on a
sheepskin rug before his wicker chair.

David didn't want to be alone with him.

'Where's Anna?' he asked.

Antonio shrugged.

'You didn't have a fight, I hope,' David said.

'No. I think it's good for her not to see me all the time or she
would start to take me for granted.'

David laughed. 'That sounds very Italian.'

'That's what I am.'

Antonio asked David what he'd been doing, and David told
him, then David asked Antonio what he'd been doing, and
Antonio told him, and then they went silent.

Antonio said, 'Let's not eat at Suora Carolina's this evening.
Let's treat ourselves to a better place. We'll go to Otello's.'

David knew that if he were any less enthusiastic than Antonio,
his room-mate would be disappointed, and he made his voice go
high. 'That'd be great.'

The restaurant had a glassed-in front, and through the glass
David saw, in the illuminated courtyard outside, a sleek man and
a sleek woman examining a basket of plums by the fountain.
Antonio was studying the couple. 'I know those people,' he said.
He and David kept looking around the restaurant at the people at
other tables, but they avoided looking at one another.

Then Antonio said to David, 'Next weekend, you and I will take
a little tour of Rome. I can borrow Anna's car.'

'She has a car?'

'Anna's rich. But that's beside the point. She'll let me borrow
her car.'

David wondered if Anna, too, was Jewish. He asked, 'What kind of family does Anna come from?'

'Let's not talk about her now.'

Antonio drove Anna's car, a convertible, with driving gloves. He took David to a park. The park was a botanical institute. Antonio walked quickly as though to get away from David, who stopped to look to his left through the sloping branches of a tree at a statue of a male nude, its pedestal and feet covered with moss. When David looked towards Antonio again, he was turning off the main drive, going down a footpath. David descended the path, bordered by ferns and waist-high fibrous plants, over which he saw green hills and small dales beneath dark cypress trees and palms. The earth was running with water, and the narrow path muddy. At points, the lawns on either side of the path opened up into springs, and the water flowed into small rocaille pools which David crossed on bridges, through the shadows of pine trees.

As if trying to escape, Antonio was swiftly climbing an incline, and passed a row of green wooden benches. David sat on a bench. Antonio had gone out of sight.

What do I want from him? David thought.

He waited for Antonio to come back. Antonio was frowning. He said, 'I got lost,' and then he laughed.

They went to Suora Carolina's for their Sunday lunch. David wished Anna was having lunch with them.

The *pancetta* in the *carbonara* was not crisp enough, Antonio said over and over as he ate, and he told Carolina's daughter this when she came to clear the pasta plates and serve the next course.

Antonio finished his cutlet and let his body fall against the chair so his head was thrown back a little, and, his chin raised, he looked at David eat as if from a long distance.

David said to Antonio, 'Tell me what you feel being a Jew.'

Antonio raised his eyebrows.

'Tell me what makes you a Jew. You're not like any of the Jews I knew in America.'

'I have no idea,' Antonio said.

'You mean, you don't want to say.'

Antonio raised his eyebrows higher than before.

'You're not interested, is that it?' David asked.

'What are you trying to make me say?'

'I want to know what you feel.'

'Why?'

'Because I want to know.'

'I feel very little,' Antonio said.

'I can't believe that.'

'Why are you trying to force feelings on me that I don't have?'

'But all your suffering has to mean something to you.'

Antonio shrugged. 'To me personally, no.'

'I don't believe it,' David said. 'I don't. Why can't you admit to me that you've suffered? Tell me. Go on, tell me you've suffered.'

'I haven't.'

'But I'm sure you have.'

Antonio said, 'I think you could only really love me if I said, Yes. And I'd like you to love me. For that, I'd like to tell you I have suffered. But I have not.' He raised his hands so his shirt cuffs fell down his wrists. 'I have not.'

David asked, 'And Israel? Doesn't Israel mean anything to you?'

'No,' Antonio said.

Antonio went off to see Anna after dinner, and David, looking down at his scuffed shoes from time to time, walked about Rome. As if following in the direction his body took him, he went down the wide Via dei Fori Imperiali, along the Forum. Among the floodlit ruins, the fragments of brick walls with bushes growing out of them, he saw the Arch of Titus. He hadn't come to see it, but when he did he stopped to stare at it. He continued along the Via dei Fori Imperiali. At the end of the avenue, having to wait a long time for a pause in the traffic, he crossed over to the Colosseum.

He walked around the big, broken amphitheatre. Blocks of stone, with ruined edges and holes and grooves, emerged into the electric light from the shadows under the arches. David walked close to but did not enter those dark arches. He kept glancing in. Here, a man in New York told him when he told the man he was going to Rome, things happened at night. David had never, at night, done anything but walk around the Colosseum. A man was standing still just where the electric illumination was cut off by a pillar. David walked past quickly.

The apartment was empty. He left the lights off and went into his room and shut the door. On his bed, he told himself that he should have gone deeper into the Colosseum.

As he was falling asleep, he thought he heard Antonio come into his room undress and get into his bed.

They were in an enormous bed and, neither able to sleep, they were talking.

'Tell me what you feel about the Jews,' Antonio said to him.

'Feel?'

'I want to know.'

'What do you think I feel?'

The room was empty except for the bed and grey metal loudspeakers in each corner, over which a voice shouted, 'You hate us. You hate our very bodies.'

'That's not true,' a voice, not quite David's, tried to answer. 'That's not true.'

'Tell me what you think!' Then the screaming voice went down to a whisper. 'Tell me something I've never heard before.'

'If I hated the Jews, I'd tell you. I don't hate the Jews.'

'You could hate the Jews until your heart was bursting with hatred, and I wouldn't be interested, because I know about hatred towards the Jews. Tell me something I don't know, something a Jew would never, ever suspect a Gentile ever thought about him. I'm sure, I'm absolutely sure, that the Gentiles feel something about the Jews that they, the Gentiles, keep a secret. What is it?'

'You want to know what a Gentile feels towards a Jew that goes deeper than hatred?'

'Yes.'

'Our secret?'

'Yes. Yes.'

The voices rose and fell over a low, dark, devastated field, in which was a bed.

'We long for Israel to be destroyed.'

Wind blew over the field.

'But how can we tell the Jews that? How can we let them know they've suffered to teach us that this world has meaning only when destroyed, because eternity alone matters, and eternity is commensurate with the suffering of the Jews? How can we tell them our secret is that we know they have suffered for us?'

David and Antonio were in the bed, in the windy field. Antonio, looking straight at David, said, 'I knew all that.'

Leaning towards him, David kissed him on his bare shoulder.

# Skinned Alive

## EDMUND WHITE

I first saw him at a reading in Paris. An American writer, whom everyone had supposed dead, had come to France to launch a new translation of his classic book, originally published twenty-five years earlier. The young man in the audience who caught my eye had short red-blond hair and broad shoulders (bodyguard broad, commando broad) and an unsmiling gravity. When he spoke English, he was very serious; when he spoke French, he looked amused.

He was seated on the other side of the semi-circle surrounding the author, who was slowly, sweetly, suicidally disappointing the young members of his audience. They had all come expecting to meet Satan, for hadn't he summed up in his pages a brutish vision of gang rape in burned-out lots, of drug betrayals and teenage murders? But what they faced now was a reformed drunk given to optimism, offering us brief recipes for recovery and serenity – not at all what the spiky-haired audience had had in mind. I was charmed by the writer's hearty laugh and pleased that he'd been able to trade in his large bacchanalian genius for a bit of happiness. But his new writings were painful to listen to and my eyes wandered restlessly over the book shelves. I was searching out interesting new titles, saluting familiar ones, reproaching a few.

And then I had the young man to look at. He had on black trousers full in the calf and narrow in the thighs, his compact waist cinched in by a thick black belt and a gold buckle. His torso was concealed by an extremely ample, long-sleeved black shirt, but despite its fullness I could still see the broad, powerful chest, the massive shoulders and biceps – the body of a professional killer. His neck was thick, like cambered marble.

My French friend Hélène nudged me and whispered. 'There's one for you.' Maybe she said that later, during the discussion period after the young man had asked a question that revealed his complete familiarity with the text. He had a tenor voice he'd worked to lower or perhaps he was just shy – one, in any event, that made me think of those low notes a cellist draws out of his instrument by slowly sawing the bow back and forth while fingering a tremolo with the other hand.

From his accent I couldn't be certain he was American; he might be German, a nationality that seemed to accommodate his contradictions better – young but dignified, athletic but intellectual. There was nothing about him of the brash American college kid, the joker who has been encouraged to express all his opinions, including those that have just popped into his head. The young man respected the author's classic novel so much that he made me want to take it more seriously. I liked the way he referred to specific scenes as though they were literary sites known to everyone. This grave young man was probably right, the scandalous books always turn out to be the good ones.

Yes, Hélène must have nudged me after his question, because she's attracted to men only if they're intelligent. If they're literary, all the better, since, when she's not reading, she's talking about books. I'll phone her towards noon and she'll say. 'I'm in China,' or, 'Today, it's the Palais Royal,' or, 'Another unhappy American childhood,' depending on whether the book is a guide, a memoir or a novel. She worries about me and wants me to find someone, preferably a Parisian, so I won't get any funny ideas about moving back to New York. She and I always speak in English. If I trick her into continuing in French after an evening with friends, she'll suddenly catch herself and say indignantly, 'But why on earth are we speaking French!' She claims to be bilingual, but she speaks

French to her cats. People dream in the language they use on their cats.

She is too discreet, even with me, her closest friend, to solicit any details about my intimate life. Once, when she could sense Jean-Loup was making me unhappy, I said to her, 'But you know I do have two other . . . people I see from time to time,' and she smiled, patted my hand and said, 'Good. Very good. I'm delighted.' Another time she shocked me. I asked her what I should say to a jealous lover, and she replied, 'The answer to the question, "Are you faithful, chéri?" is always "Yes".' She made vague efforts to meet and even charm the different men who passed through my life (her Japanese clothes, low voice and blue-tinted glasses impressed them all). But I could tell she disapproved of most of them. 'It's Saturday,' she would say. 'Jean-Loup must be rounding you up for your afternoon shopping spree.' If ever I said anything against him, she would dramatically bite her lip, look me in the eye and nod.

But I liked to please Jean-Loup. And if I bought him his clothes every Saturday, he would let me take them off again, piece by piece, to expose his boyish body, a body as lean-hipped and priapic as those Cretan youths painted on the walls of Minos's palace. On one hip, the colour of wedding-gown satin, he had a mole, which the French more accurately call a grain de beauté.

Since Jean-Loup came from a solid middle-class family but had climbed a social rung, he had the most rigid code of etiquette, and I owe him the slight improvements I've made in my impressionistic American table manners, learned thirty years ago among boarding-school savages. Whereas Americans are taught to keep their unused hand in their laps at table, the French are so filthy-minded they assume hidden hands are the devil's workshop. Whereas Americans clear each plate as soon as it's finished, the French wait for everyone to complete his or her meal. That's the sort of thing he taught me. To light a match after one has smelled up a toilet. To greet the most bizarre story with the comment: 'But that's perfectly normal.' To be careful to serve oneself from the cheese tray no more than once. ('Cheese is the only course a guest has the right to refuse,' he told me, 'and the only dish that should never be passed twice'.)

Also not to ask so many questions or volunteer so many answers. After a two-hour train ride he'd ask me if I had had enough time to confide to the stranger at my side all the details of my unhappy American childhood. Like most Frenchmen who have affairs with Americans, he was attracted by my 'niceness' and 'simplicity' (ambiguous compliments at best), but had set out to reform those very qualities, which became weaknesses once I was granted the high status of honorary Frenchman. 'Not Frenchman,' he would say. 'You'll never be French. But you are a Parisian. No one can deny that.' Then to flatter me he would add, '*Plus parisien tu meurs*,' though just then I felt I'd die if I were less, not more Parisian.

But if Jean-Loup was always 'correct' in the salon, he was 'vicious' and 'perverse' (high compliments in French) in the boudoir. The problem was that he didn't like to see me very often. He loved me but wasn't in love with me, that depressing (and all too translatable) distinction ('*Je t'aime mais je ne suis pas amoureux*'). He was always on the train to Bordeaux, where his parents lived and where he'd been admitted to several châteaux, including some familiar even to me because they were on wine labels. He'd come back with stories of weekend country parties at which the boys got drunk and tore off the girls' designer dresses and then everyone went riding bareback at dawn. He had a set of phrases for describing these routs ('*On s'éclatait*'; '*On se démarrait*'; *On était fou, mais vraiment fou et on a bien rigolé*'), which all meant they had behaved disreputably with the right people within decorous limits. After all they were all in their own 'milieu'. He slept with a few of the girls and was looking to marry one who would be intelligent, not ugly, distinguished, a good sport and a slut in bed. He was all those things, so he was only looking for his counterpart. He even asked me to help him. 'You go everywhere, you meet everyone,' he said, 'you've fixed up so many of your friends, find me someone like Brigitte but better groomed, a good slut who likes men. Of course, even if I married that would never affect our relationship.' Recently he'd decided that he would inform his bride-to-be that he was homosexual; he just knew she'd be worldly about it.

With friends Jean-Loup was jolly and impertinent, quick to trot out his 'horrors', as he called them, things that would make the girls scream and the boys blush. Twice he showed his penis at mixed dinner parties. Even so, his 'horrors' were, while shocking, kind-hearted and astute. He never asked about money or class, questions that might really embarrass a French man. He would sooner asked about blow-jobs than job prospects, cock-size than the size of a raise. In our funny makeshift circle – which I had cobbled together to amuse him and which fell apart when he left me – the girls were witty, uncomplicated and heterosexual, and the boys handsome and homo. We were resolutely silly and made enormous occasions out of each other's birthdays and saint's days. Our serious, intimate conversations took place only between two people, usually over the phone.

I neglected friends my own age. I never spoke English or talked about books except with Hélène. A friend from New York said, after staying with me for a week, that I was living in a fool's paradise, a gilded play-pen filled with enchanting, radiant nymphs and satyrs who offered me 'no challenge'. He disapproved of the way I was willing to take just crumbs from Jean-Loup.

Brioche crumbs, I thought.

I didn't know how to explain that now that so many of my old friends in New York had died – my best friend, and also my editor, a real friend as well – I preferred my play-pen, where I could be twenty-five again but French this time. When reminded of my real age and nationality, I then *played* at being older and American. Youth and age seemed equally theatrical. Maybe the unreality was the effect of living in another language, of worrying about how many slices of *chèvre* one could take and of buying pretty clothes for a bisexual Bordelais. At about this time a punk interviewed me on television and asked, 'You are known as a homosexual, a writer and an American. When did you first realize you were an American?'

'When I moved to France,' I said.

That Jean-Loup was elusive could not be held against him. He warned me from the first he was in full flight. What I didn't grasp was that he was running towards someone even he couldn't name yet. Despite his lucid way of making distinctions about other people ('She's not a liar but a mythomaniac; her lying serves no purpose') he was indecisive about everything in his own future: Would he marry or become completely gay? Would he stay in business or develop his talent, drawing adult comic strips? Would he remain in Paris or continue shuttling between it and Bordeaux? I teased him, calling him, 'Monsieur Charnière' ('Mister Hinge').

Where he could be decisive was in bed. He had precise and highly coloured fantasies, which I deduced from his paces and those he put me through. He never talked about his desires until the last few times we had sex, just before the end of our 'story' as the French call an affair; his new talkativeness I took as a sign that he'd lost interest in me or at least respect for me, and I was right. Earlier he had never talked about his desire, but hurled it against me: he needed me here not there, like this not that. I felt desired for the first time in years.

My friends, especially Hélène, but even the other children in the play-pen, assumed Jean-Loup was genteelly fleecing me with my worldly, cheerful complicity, but I knew I had too little money to warrant such a speculation. He'd even told me that if it was money he was after he could find a man far richer than me. In fact I knew I excited him. That's why I had to find him a distinguished slut for a wife. I had corrupted him, he told me, by habituating him to sex that was 'hard', which the French pronounce 'ard' as in *ardent* and, out of a certain deference, never elide with the preceding word.

He didn't mind if I talked during sex, telling him who he was, where we were and why I had to do all this to him. I was used to sex raps from the drug-taking 1970s. Now, of course, there were no drugs and I had to find French words for my obsessions, and when I sometimes made a mistake in gender or verb form Jean-Loup would wince. He wouldn't mention it later; he didn't want to talk anything over later. Only once, after he'd done something very strange to me, he asked, laughing as he emerged from the shower, 'Are you the crazy one or am I? I think we're both crazy.' He seemed very pleased.

For the first year we'd struggled to be 'lovers' officially, but he devoted more of his energy to warding me off than embracing me. He had a rule that he could never stay on after a dinner at my place; he would always leave with the other members of the play-pen. To stay behind would look too domestic, he thought, too queer, too *pédé*. After a year of such partial intimacy I got fed up. More likely I became frightened that Jean-Loup, who was growing increasingly remote, would suddenly drop me. I broke up with him over dinner in a restaurant. He seemed relieved and said, 'I would never have dared to take the first step.' He was shaken for two or three days, then recovered nicely. As he put it, he 'supported celibacy' quite effortlessly. It felt natural to him, it was his natural condition.

I went to New York for a week. By chance he went there after I returned. When we saw each other again in Paris we were as awkward as adolescents. His allergies were acting up; American food had made him put on two kilos; a New York barber had thrown his meaty ears into high relief. 'It's terrible,' Jean-Loup said, 'I wanted my independence, but now that I have it . . . Undress me.' I did so, triumphant while registering his admission that he was the one after all who had wanted to be free.

After that we saw each other seldom but when we did it was always passionate. The more people we told that we were no longer lovers, the more violent our desire for each other became. I found his heavy balls, which he liked me to hold in my mouth while I looked up at him. I found the mole on his smooth haunch. Because of his allergies he couldn't tolerate colognes or deodorants; I was left with his natural kid-brother smell. We had long passed through the stage of smoking marijuana together or using sex toys or dressing each other up in bits of finery. Other couples I knew became kinkier and kinkier over the years if they continued having sex or else resigned themselves to the most routine, suburban relief. We were devouring each other with a desire that was ever purer and sharper. Of course such a desire is seldom linked to love. It can be powerful when solicited but quickly forgotten when absent, since it may never have played a part in one's dreams of the future.

Perhaps the threat of ending things altogether, which we'd just averted, had made us keener. More likely, Jean-Loup, now that he thought he'd become less homosexual by shedding a male lover, me, felt freer to indulge drives that had become more urgent precisely because they were less well defined. Or perhaps I'm exaggerating my importance in his eyes; as he once said, he didn't like to wank his head over things like that ('Je ne me branle pas trop la tête').

I was in love with him and, during sex, thought of that love, but I tried to conceal it from him.

I tried to expect nothing, see him when I saw him, pursue other men, as though I were strictly alone in the world. For the first time when he asked me if I had other lovers I said I did and even discussed them with him. He said he was relieved, explaining that my adventures exonerated him from feeling responsible for me and my happiness. He was a lousy lover, he said, famous for being elusive; even his girlfriends complained about his slipperiness. That elusiveness, I would discover, was his protest against his own passivity, his longing to be owned.

Things changed day by day between us. He said he wasn't searching for other sexual partners; he preferred to wait until he fell in love, revealing that he didn't see us becoming lovers again. Nor was he in such a hurry to find a distinguished and sympathetic slut for a wife. When I asked him about his marital plans, he said that he was still looking forward to settling down with a wife and children some day but that now he recognized that when he thought of rough sex, of *la baise harde*, he thought of men. And again he flatteringly blamed me for having corrupted him even while he admitted he was looking for someone else, another man, to love.

Once in a very great while he referred to me playfully as his 'husband', despite his revulsion against camp. I think he was trying to come up with a way that would let our friendship continue while giving each of us permission to pursue other people. Once he sombrely spoke of me as his patron but I winced and he quickly withdrew the description. I wouldn't have minded playing his father, but that never occurred to him.

I'm afraid I'm making him sound too cold. He also had a sweet kid-brother charm, especially around women. All those former débutantes from Bordeaux living in Paris felt free to ask him to run an errand or install a bookcase, which he did with unreflecting devotion. He was careful (far more careful than any American would have been) to distinguish between a pal and a friend, but the true friends exercised an almost limitless power over him. Jean-Loup was quite proud of his capacity for friendship. When he would say that he was a rotten lover – elusive, unsure of his direction – he'd also assure me that he'd always remain my faithful friend, and I believed him. I knew that he was, in fact, waiting for our passion to wear itself out so that a more decent friendship could declare itself.

He wasn't a friend during sex or just afterwards, he'd always shower, dress and leave as quickly as possible. Once, when he glanced back at the rubble we had made of the bedroom, he said all that evidence of our bestiality disgusted him. Nor was he specially kind to me around our playmates. To them, paradoxically, he enjoyed demonstrating how thoroughly he was at home in my apartment. He was the little lord of the manor. Yet he'd compliment me on how well I 'received' people and assure me I could always open a restaurant in New York some day if my career as a writer petered out. He didn't take my writing too seriously. It had shocked him the few times he'd dipped into it. He preferred the lucidity and humanism of Milan Kundera, his favourite writer.

In fact none of our playmates read me, and their indifference pleased me. It left me alone with my wet sand.

He took a reserved interest in my health. He was relieved that my blood tests every six months suggested the virus was still dormant. He was pleased I no longer smoked or drank (though like most French people he didn't consider champagne alcoholic). During one of our sex games he poured half a bottle of red Sancerre down my throat; the etiquette of the situation forbade my refusal, but it was the only time I had tasted alcohol in nearly ten years. We were convinced that the sort of sex we practised might be demented but was surely safe; in fact we had made it demented since it had to stay safe.

He was negative. While he waited for his results, he said that if they turned out positive his greatest regret would be that he wouldn't be able to father children. A future without a family seemed unbearable. As long as his boy's body with its beautifully shaped man's penis remained unmarked, without a sign of its past or a curse over its future, he was happy to lend himself to our games.

Sometimes his laugh was like a shout – boyish, the sound, but the significance, knowing and Parisian. He laughed to show that he hadn't been taken in or that he had caught the wicked allusion. When I was in the kitchen preparing the next course, I'd smile if I heard his whoop. I liked it that he was my husband, so at home, so sociable, so light-hearted, but our marriage was just a poor invention of my own fancy.

It reassured me that his sexuality was profoundly, not modishly, violent. He told me that when he had been a child, just seven or eight, he had built a little town out of cardboard and plywood, painted every shutter and peopled every house, and then set the whole construction afire and watched the conflagration with a bone-hard, inch-long erection. Is that why just touching me made him hard now (bone-hard, foot-long)? Could he see I was ablaze with ardour for him (ardour with a silent *h*)?

The violence showed up again in the comic strips he was always drawing. He had invented a sort of Frankenstein monster in good French clothes, a creature disturbed by his own half-human sentiments in a world otherwise populated by robots. When I related his comics to the history of art, he'd smile a gay, humiliated smile, the premonitory form of his whooping, disabused Parisian laugh. He was ashamed I made so much of his talent, though his talent was real enough.

He didn't know what to do with his life. He was living as ambitious, healthy young men live who have long vistas of time before them: despairingly. I, who had already outlived my friends and had fulfilled some of my hopes but few of my desires (desire won't stay satisfied), lived each day with joy and anguish. Jean-Loup expected his life to be perfect: there was apparently going to be so much of it.

Have I mentioned that Jean-Loup had such high arches that walking hurt him? He had one of his feet broken, lowered and screwed shut in metal vices that were removed six months later. His main reason for the operation was to escape the bank for a few weeks. His clinic room was soon snowed under with comic strip adventures. After that he walked with a bit of a Chaplinesque limp when he was tired.

I often wondered what his life was like with the other young Bordelais counts and countesses at Saint Jean-de-Luz every August. I was excluded from that world – the chance of my being introduced to his childhood friends had never even once entered his head – which made me feel like a *demi-mondaine* listening avidly to her titled young lover's accounts of his exploits in the great world. Although I presented Jean-Loup to my literary friends in London, he had few opinions about them beyond his admiration for the men's clothes and the women's beauty and apparent intelligence. 'It was all so fast and brilliant,' he said, 'I scarcely understood a word.' He blamed me for not helping him with his English, though he hated the sounds I made when I spoke my native language. 'You don't have an accent in French – oh, you have your little accent, but it's nothing, very charming. But in American you sound like a duck, it's frightful!'

I suppose my English friends thought it was a sentimental autumn-and-spring affair. One friend, who lent us her London house for a few days, said, 'Don't let the char see you and Jean-Loup nude.' I thought the warning seemed bizarre until I understood it as an acknowledgement of our potential for sensual mischief. Perhaps she was particularly alive to sensual possibilities, since she was so proud of her own handsome, young husband.

After I returned to Paris, I spent my days alone reading and writing, and in fair weather I'd eat a sandwich on the quay. That January the Seine overflowed and flooded the highway on the Right Bank. Seagulls flew upstream and wheeled above the turbulent river, crying, as though mistaking Notre Dame for Mont-St Michel. The floodlights trained on the church's façade projected ghostly shadows of the two square towers up into the foggy night sky, as though spirits were doing axonometric drawings of a cathedral I had always thought of as malign. The gargoyles were supposed to ward off evil, but to me they looked like dogs straining to leap away from the devil comfortably lodged within.

I went to Australia and New Zealand for five weeks. I wrote Jean-Loup many letters, in French, believing that the French language tolerated love better than English, but when I returned to Paris Jean-Loup complained of my style. He found it '*mièvre*', 'wimpy' or 'wet'.

He said I should write about his ass one day, but in a style that was neither pornographic nor wimpy. He wanted me to describe his ass as Francis Ponge describes soap: an objective, exhaustive, whimsical catalogue of its properties.

I wanted someone else, but I distrusted that impulse, because it seemed, if I looked back, I could see that I had never been happy in love and that with Jean-Loup I was happier than usual. As he pointed out, we were still having sex after two years, and he ascribed the intensity to the very infrequency that I deplored. Even so, I thought there was something all wrong, fundamentally wrong, with me: I set up a lover as a god, then burned with rage when he proved mortal. I lay awake, next to one lover after another, in a rage, dreaming of someone who'd appreciate me, give me the simple affection I imagined I wanted.

When I had broken off with Jean-Loup over dinner he had said, 'You deserve someone better, someone who will love you completely.' Yet the few times I had been loved 'completely' I felt suffocated. Nor could I imagine a less aristocratic lover, one who'd sit beside me on the couch, hand in hand, and discuss the loft bed, the 'mezzanine', we should buy with the cunning little chair and matching desk underneath.

But when I was alone night after night, I resented Jean-Loup's independence. He said I deserved something better, and I knew I merited less but needed more.

It was then I saw the redhead at the reading. Although I stared holes through him, he never looked at me once. It occurred to me that he might not be homosexual, except that his grave military bearing was something only homosexuals could (or would bother to) contrive if they weren't actually soldiers. His whole look and manner were studied. Let's say he was the sort of homosexual other homosexuals recognize but that heterosexuals never suspect.

The next day I asked the owner of the bookstore if she knew the redhead. 'He comes into the shop every so often,' she said, with a quick laugh to acknowledge the character of my curiosity, 'but I don't know his name. He bought one of your books. Perhaps he'll come to your reading next week.'

I told her to be sure to get his name if he returned. 'You were a diplomat once,' I reminded her. She promised but when I phoned a few days later she said he hadn't been in. Then on the night of my reading I saw him sitting in the same chair as before and I went up to him with absolute confidence and said, 'I'm so glad you came tonight. I saw you at the last reading, and my *copine* and I thought you looked so interesting we wished we knew you.' He looked so blank that I was afraid he hadn't understood and I almost started again in French. I introduced myself and shook his hand. He went white and said, 'I'm sorry for not standing up,' and then stood up and shook my hand, and I was afraid he'd address me as 'sir'.

Now that I could look at his hair closely I noticed that it was blond, if shavings of gold are blond, only on the closely cropped sides but that it was red on top – the reverse of the sun-bleached strawberry blond. He gave me his phone number, and I thought this was someone I could spend the rest of my life with, however brief that might be. His name was Paul.

I phoned him the next day to invite him to dinner, and he said that he had a rather strange schedule, since he worked four nights a week for a disco.

'What do you do?' I asked.

'I'm the physiognomist. The person who recognizes the regulars and the celebrities. I have to know what Brigitte Bardot looks like *now*. I decide who comes in, who stays out, who pays, who doesn't. We have a house rule to let all models in free.' He told me people called him Cerberus.

'But how do you recognize everyone?'

'I've been on the door since the club opened seven years ago. So I have ten thousand faces stored in my memory.' He laughed. 'That's why I could never move back to America. I'd never find a job that paid so well for just twenty hours' work a week. And in America I couldn't do the same job, since I don't know any faces there.'

We arranged an evening and he arrived dressed in clothes by one of the designers he knew from the club. Not even my reactionary father, however, would have considered him a popinjay. He did nothing that would risk his considerable dignity. He had white tulips in his surprisingly small, elegant hand.

All evening we talked literature, and, as two good Americans, we also exchanged confidences. Sometimes his shyness brought all the laughter and words to a queasy halt, and it made me think of that becalmed moment when a sailboat comes around and the mainsail luffs before it catches the wind again. I watched the silence play over his features.

He was from a small town in Georgia. His older brother and he had each achieved highest scores in the state-wide scholastic aptitude test. They had not pulled down good grades, however; they read Plato and *Naked Lunch*, staged *No Exit* and brawls with the boys in the next town, experimented with hallucinogens and conceptual art. Paul's brother made an 'art work' out of his plans to assassinate President Ford and was arrested by the FBI.

'I just received the invitation to my tenth high-school reunion,' Paul said.

'I'll go with you,' I said. 'I'll go as your spouse.'

He looked at me and breathed a laugh, save it was voiced just at the end, the moving bow finally touching the bass string and waking sound in it.

Paul's older brother had started a rock band, gone off to New York, where he died of AIDS – another musician punished. He had been one of the first heterosexual male victims – dead already in 1981. He contracted the disease from a shared needle. Their mother, a Scottish immigrant, preferred to think he had been infected by another man. Love seemed a nobler cause of death than drugs.

'Then I came to Paris,' Paul said. He sighed and looked out of my open window at the roofs of the Ile St Louis. Like other brilliant young men and women he suspended every solid in a solution of irony, but even he had certain articles of faith, and the first was Paris. He liked French manners, French clothes, French food, French education. He said things like, 'France still maintains cultural hegemony over the whole world,' and pronounced 'hegemony' as '*hégémonie*'. He had done all his studies as an adult in France and French. He asked me what the name of Plato's *Le Banquet* was in English (*The Symposium*, for some reason). He had a lively, but somewhat vain, sense of what made him interesting, which struck me only because he seemed so worthy of respect that any attempt to serve himself up appeared irrelevant.

He was wearing a white shirt and dark tie and military shoes and a beautiful dark jacket that was cut to his Herculean chest and shoulders. He had clear eyes, pale blue eyes. The white tulips he brought were waxen and pulsing like lit candles, and his skin, that rich hairless skin, was tawny-coloured. His manners were formal and French, a nice Georgia boy but Europeanized, someone who'd let me lazily finish my sentences in French ('*quand même,*' we'd say, '*rien à voir avec* . . . '). His teeth were so chalky white that the red wine stained them a faint blue.

His face was at once open and unreadable, as imposing as the globe. He nodded slowly as he thought over what I said, so slowly that I doubted the truth or seriousness of what I was saying. He hesitated and his gaze was non-committal, making me wonder if he was pondering his own response or simply panicking. I wouldn't have thought of him panicking except he mentioned it. He said he was always on the edge of panic (the sort of thing Americans say to each other with big grins). Points of sweat danced on the bridge of his nose, and I thought I saw in his eye something frightened, even unpleasant and unreachable. I kept thinking we were too much alike, as though at any moment our American heartiness and our French *politesse* would break down and we'd look at each other with the sour familiarity of brothers. Did he sense it, too? Is that why our formality was so important to him? I was sure he hadn't liked himself in America.

Speaking French so long had made me simplify my thoughts – whether expressed in French or English – and I was pleased I could say now what I felt, since the intelligence I was imputing to him would never have tolerated my old vagueness. Whereas Jean-Loup had insisted I use the right fork, I felt Paul would insist on the correct emotion.

Sometimes before he spoke Paul made a faint humming sound – perhaps only voiced shyness – but it gave the impression of the slightest deference. It made me think of a student half-raising his hand to talk to a seminar too small and egalitarian to require the teacher's recognition to speak. But I also found myself imagining that this thought was so varied, ocurring on so many levels at once that the hum was a strictly mechanical downshift into the compromise (and invention) of speech. After a while the hum disappeared, and I fancied he felt more at ease with me, although the danger is always to read too much into what handsome men say and do. Although he was twenty years younger, he seemed much older than me.

'Would you like to go to Morocco with me?' I asked him suddenly. 'For a week? A magazine will pay our fares. It's the south of Morocco. It should be amusing. I don't know it at all, but I think it's better to go somewhere brand new –' ('with a lover' were the words I suppressed).

'Sure.'

He said he hadn't travelled anywhere in Europe or Africa except for two trips to Italy.

Although I knew things can't be rushed, that intimacy follows its own sequence, I found myself saying, 'We should be lovers – you have everything, beauty and intelligence.' Then I added: 'And we get on so well.' My reasoning was absurd: his beauty and intelligence were precisely what made him unavailable.

I scarcely wanted him to reply. As long as he didn't I could nurse my illusions. 'That would depend,' he said, 'on our being compatible sexually, don't you think?' Then he asked, with his unblinking gravity, 'What's your sexuality like?' For the first time I could hear a faint Georgia accent in the way the syllables of *sexuality* got stretched out.

'It depends on the person,' I said, stalling. Then, finding my answer lamentable, I pushed all my chips forward on one number: 'I like pain.'

'So do I,' he said. 'And my penis has never – no man has ever touched it.'

He had had only three lovers and they had all been heterosexuals or fancied they were. In any event they had had his sort of *pudeur* about using endearments to another man. He had a lover now, Thierry, someone he met two years before at the club. The first time they saw each other, Paul had been tanked up on booze, smack and steroids, a murderous cocktail, and they had a fist-fight which had dissolved into a night of violent passion.

Every moment must have been haloed in his memory, for he

remembered key phrases Thierry had used. For the last two years they had eaten every meal together. Thierry dressed him in the evening before Paul left for work and corrected his French and table manners. These interventions were often nasty, sometimes violent. 'What language are you speaking now?' he would demand, if Paul made the slightest error. When Paul asked for a little tenderness in bed, Thierry would say, 'Oh-ho, like Mama and Papa now, is it?' and then leave the room. Paul fought back – he broke his hand once because he hit Thierry so hard. 'Of course *he'd* say that it was all my fault,' Paul said, 'that all he wants is peace, blue skies.' He smiled. 'Thierry is a businessman, very dignified. He has never owned a piece of leather in his life. I despise leather. It robs violence of all the' – his smile now radiant, the mainsail creaking as it comes around – 'the *sacramental*.' He laughed, shaking, and made a strange chortle that I didn't really understand. It came out of a sensibility I hadn't glimpsed in him before.

Paul longed for us to reach the desert; he had never seen it before.

We started out at Agadir and took a taxi to the mud-walled town of Taroudant. There we hired a car and drove to Ouarzazate, which had been spoiled by organized tourism: it had become Anywhere Sunny. Then we drove south to Zagora. It was just twenty kilometres beyond Zagora, people said, that the desert started. I warned Paul the desert could be disappointing: 'You're never alone. There's always someone spying on you from over the next dune. And it rains. I saw the rain pour over Syria.'

Paul loved maps. Sometimes I could see in him the solitary Georgia genius in love with his best friend's father, the sheriff, a kid lurking around home in the hot, shuttered afternoons, day-dreaming over the globe that his head so resembled, his mind racing on home-made LSD. He knew how to refold maps, but when they were open he would press his palms over their creases as though opening his own eyes wider and wider.

I did all the driving, through adobe cities built along narrow, palm-lined roads. In every town boys wanted to be our guides, sell us trinkets or carpets or their own bodies. They hissed at us at night from the shadows of town walls: lean and finely muscled adolescents hissing to attract our attention, their brown hands massaging a lump beneath the flowing blue acrylic *jellabias* mass-produced in China. To pass them up with a smile was a new experience for me. I had Paul beside me, this noble pacing lion. I remembered a Paris friend calling me just before we left for Morocco, saying he had written a letter to a friend, 'telling him I'd seen you walking down the Boulevard St Germain beside the young Hercules with hair the colour of copper.' In Morocco there was no one big enough, powerful enough or cruel enough to interest Paul.

Perhaps it was due to the clear, memorable way Paul had defined his sexual nature, but during our cold nights together I lay in his great arms and never once felt excited, just an immense feeling of peace and gratitude. Our predicament, we felt, was like a Greek myth. 'Two people love each other,' I said, 'but the gods have cursed them by giving them the identical passions.' I was being presumptuous, sneaking in the phrase, 'Two people love each other,' because it wasn't at all clear that he loved me.

One night we went to the movies and saw an Italian adventure film starring American weight-lifters and dubbed in French, a story set in a back-lot castle with a perfunctory princess in hot pants. There was an evil prince whose handsome face melted to reveal the devil's underneath. His victim ('All heroes are maso-chists,' Paul declared) was an awkward body-builder not yet comfortable in his newly acquired bulk, who had challenged the evil prince's supremacy and now must be flayed alive. Paul clapped and chortled and, during the tense scenes, physically braced himself. This was the Paul who had explained what Derrida had said of Heidegger's interpretation of Trakl's last poems, who claimed that literature could be studied only through rhetoric, grammar and genre, and who considered Ronsard a greater poet than Shakespeare (because of Ronsard's combination of passion and logic, satyr and god, in place of the mere conversational fluency which Paul regarded as the flaw and genius of English): this was the same Paul who booed and cheered as the villain smote the hero before a respectful audience thick with smoke and the flickers of flashlights. It was a movie in which big men were hurting each other.

Jean-Loup would have snorted, his worst prejudices about Americans confirmed, for as we travelled, drawing closer and closer to the desert, we confided more and more in each other. As we drove through the 'valley of a thousand casbahs', Paul told me about threats to his life. 'When someone at the club pulls a gun on me, and it's happened three times, I say, I'm sorry but guns are not permitted on the premises, and it works, they go away, but mine is a suicidal response.' Paul was someone on whom nothing was wasted: nevertheless sometimes he was not always alive to all possibilities, at least not instantly. I told him I was positive, but he didn't react. Behind the extremely dark sun-glasses, there was this presence, breathing and thinking but not reacting.

Our hotel, the Hesperides, had been built into the sun-baked mud ramparts in the ruins of the pasha's palace. We stared into an octagonal, palm-shaped pool glistening with black rocks that then slid and clicked – ah, tortoises! There couldn't have been more than five guests, and the porters, bored and curious, tripped over themselves serving us. We slept in each other's arms night after night and I stroked his great body as though he were a prize animal, *la belle bête*. My own sense of who I was in this story was highly unstable. I flickered back and forth, wanting to be the blond warrior's fleshy, harem-pale concubine or then the bearded pasha himself, feeding drugged sherberts to the beautiful Circassian slave I had bought. I thought seriously that I wouldn't mind buying and owning another human being – if it were Paul.

The next day we picked up some hitch-hikers who, when we reached their destination, asked us in for mint tea, which we sipped barefoot in a richly carpeted room. A baby and a chicken watched us through the doorway from the sun-white courtyard. Every one of our encounters seemed to end with a carpet, usually one we were supposed to buy. In a village called Wodz, I remember both of us smiling as we observed how long and devious the path to the carpet could become: there was first a tourist excursion through miles of casbah, nearly abandoned except for an old veiled woman poking a fire in a now roofless harem; then we took a stroll through an irrigated palm plantation, where a woman leading a donkey took off her turban, a blue bath-towel, and filled it with dates which she gave us, with a golden grin; and finally we paid a 'surprise visit' on the guide's 'brother', the carpet merchant who happened to have just returned from the desert with exotic Tuareg rugs whose prices, to emphasize their exoticism, he pretended to translate from Tuareg dollars into dirham.

We laughed, bargained, bought, happy any time our shoulders touched or eyes met. We told everyone we were Danes, since this was the one language even the most resourceful carpet merchants didn't know ('But wait, I have a cousin in the next village who once lived in Copenhagen').

Later, when I returned to Paris, I would discover that Jean-Loup had left me for Régis, one of the richest men in France. For the first time in his life he was in love, he would say. He would be wearing Régis's wedding-ring, my Jean-Loup who had refused to stay behind at my apartment after the other guests had left lest he appear too *pédé*. People would suspect him of being interested in the limousine, the town house, the château, but Jean-Loup would insist it was all love.

When he told me, on my return, that he would never sleep with me again – that he had found the man with whom he wanted to spend the rest of his life – my response surprised him. '*Ça tombe bien,*' I said ('That suits the situation perfectly').

Jean-Loup blurted out: 'But you're supposed to be furious.'

It wasn't that he wanted me to fight to get him back, though he might have enjoyed it, but that his vanity demanded that I protest: my own vanity made me concede him with a smile. Feverishly I filled him in on my recent passion for Paul and the strategies I had devised for unloading him, Jean-Loup. It's true I had tried to fix him up a week earlier with a well-heeled, handsome young American.

Jean-Loup's eyes widened. 'I had no idea,' he said, 'that things had gone so far.' Perhaps in revenge he told me how he had met Régis. It seems that, while I was away, a dear mutal friend had fixed them up.

I was suddenly furious and couldn't drop the subject. I railed and railed against the dear mutual friend: 'When I think he ate my food, drank my drink, all the while plotting to marry you off to a millionaire in order to advance his own miserable little interests . . .'

'Let me remind you that Régis's money means nothing to me. No, what I like is his good humour, his sincerity, his discretion. It was hard for me to be known as your lover – your homosexuality is too evident. Régis is very discreet.'

'What rubbish,' I would say a few days later when Jean-Loup repeated the remark about Régis's discretion. 'He's famous for surrounding himself with aunties who talk lace prices the livelong day.'

'Ah,' Jean-Loup replied, reassured, 'you've been filled in, I see' ('*Tu t'en renseignes*').

All sparkling and droll, except a terrible sickness, like an infection caused by the prick of a diamond brooch, had set in. When I realized that I would never be able to abandon myself again to Jean-Loup's perverse needs, when I thought that Régis was enjoying the marriage with him I'd reconciled myself never to know, when I saw the serenity with which Jean-Loup now 'assumed' his homosexuality, I felt myself sinking, but genuinely sinking, as though I really were falling, and my face had a permanently hot blush. I described this feeling of falling and heat to Paul. 'That's jealousy,' he said. 'You're jealous.' That must be it, I thought, I who had never been jealous before. If I had behaved so generously with earlier loves lost it was because I had never before been consumed by sensuality this feverish.

Jealousy, yes, it was jealousy, and never before had I so wanted to hurt someone I loved, and that humiliated me further. A

member of the play-pen dined at Régis's *hôtel particulier*. 'They
hold hands all the time,' she said. 'I was agreeably surprised by
Régis, a charming man. The house is more a museum than a . . .
house. Jean-Loup kept calling the butler for more champagne, and
we almost burst out laughing. It was like a dream.'

Every detail fed my rancour – Régis's charm, wealth, looks ('Not
handsome but attractive').

Everything.

Paul had a photographic memory, and, during the hours spent
together in the car in Morocco, he recited page after page of Racine
or Ronsard or Sir Philip Sidney. He also continued the story of his
life. I wanted to know every detail – the bloody scenes on the steps
of the disco, the recourse to dangerous drugs, so despised by the
clenched-jaw cocaine set. I wanted to hear that he credited his
lover with saving him from being a junkie, a drunk and a thug.
'He was the one who got me back into school.'

'A master, I see,' I thought. '*School* master.'

'Now I study *Ciceron* and prepare my *maîtrise*, but then I was just
an animal, a disoriented bull – I'd even gotten into beating up fags
down by the Seine at dawn when I was really drunk.'

He gave me a story he had written. It was Hellenistic in tone,
precious and edgy, flirting with the diffuse lushness of a pre-
Raphaelite prose, rich but bleached, like a tapestry left out in the
sun. I suppose he must have had in mind Mallarmé's *The Prelude to
the Afternoon of a Faun*, but Paul's story was more touching, less
cold, more comprehensible. That such a story could never be
published in the minimalist, plain-speaking 1980s seemed never
to have occurred to him. Could it be that housed in such a massive
body he had no need for indirect proofs of power and accomplishment? Or was he so sure of his taste that recognition scarcely
interested him at all?

The story is slow to name its characters, but begins with a
woman who turns out to be Athena. She's discovering the flute
and how to get music out of it, but her sisters, seeing her puffing
away, laugh at the face she's making. Athena throws the flute

down and in a rage places a curse on it: 'Whoever would make use of it next must die.' Her humiliation would cost a life.

The next user is a cheerful satyr named Marsyas. He cleverly learns how to imitate people with his tunes: 'Prancing along behind them he could do their walk, fast or slow, lurching or clipped, just as he could render their tics or trace their contours: a low swell for a belly, shrill fifing for fluttering hands, held high notes for the adagio of soft speech. At first no one understood. But once they caught on they slapped their thighs: his songs were sketches.'

Apollo is furious, since he's the god of music and his own art is pure and abstract. He challenges Marsyas to a musical duel:

Marsyas cringed before them like a dog when it walks through a ghost, bares its teeth and pulls back its ears. Anguished, he had slept in the hot breath of his flock; his animals had pressed up against him, holding him between their woolly flanks, as though to warm him. The ribbon his jolly and jiggling woman had tied around one horn flapped listlessly against his low, hairy brow, like a royal banner flown by a worker's barge.

To the gods, as young as the morning, Marsyas seemed a twilit creature; he smelled of leaf mould and wolf-lair. His glance was as serious as a deer's when it emerges from the forest at dusk to drink at the calm pool collecting below a steaming cataract.

And to Marsyas his rival was cold and regular as cambered marble.

Since Marsyas knew to play only what was in front of him, he 'rendered' Apollo – not the god's thoughts but the faults he wedged into the air around him. The sisters watched the goat-man breathe into the reeds, saw him draw and lose breath, saw his eyes bulge, brown and brilliant as honey, and that made them laugh. What they heard, however, was colours that copied sacred lines, for Marsyas could imitate a god as easily as a bawd. The only trick was to have his model there, in front of him.

If Marsyas gave them the god's form, the god himself revealed the contents of his mind. His broad hand swept up the lyre, and immediately the air was tuned and the planets tempered. Everything sympathetic trembled in response to a song that took no one into account, that moved without moving, that polished crystal with its breath alone, clouding then cleansing every transparency without touching it. Marsyas shuddered when he came to and realized that the god's hand was now motionless but that the music continued to devolve, creaking like a finger turning and tracing the fragile rim of the spheres.

The satyr was astonished that the goddesses didn't decide instantly in their brother's favour but shrugged and smiled and said they found each contestant appealing in different ways. The sun brightened a fraction with Apollo's anger, but then the god suggested each play his music backwards. The universe shuddered as it stopped and reversed its rotations; the sun started to descend towards dawn as Apollo unstrung the planets. Cocks re-crowed and bats re-awakened, the frightened shepherd guided his flock back down the hill as the dew fell again.

Even the muses were frightened. It was night and stormy when Marsyas began to play. He had improvised his music strophe by strophe as a portrait; now he couldn't remember it all. The descending figures, so languishing when played correctly the first time, made him queasy when he inverted them. Nor could he see his subject.

The muses decided in the god's favour. Apollo told Marsyas he'd be flayed alive. There was no tenderness but great solicitude in the way the god tied the rope around the satyr's withers, cast the slack over a high branch of a pine and then hoisted his kill high, upside down, inverted as the winning melody. Marsyas saw that he'd won the god's full attention by becoming his victim.

The blood ran to Marsyas's head, then spurted over his chest as Apollo sliced into his belly, neatly peeled back the flesh and fat and hair. The light shone in rays from Apollo's sapphire eyes and locked with Marsyas's eyes, which were wavering, losing grip – he could feel his eyes lose grip, just as a child falling asleep will finally relax its hold on its father's finger. A little dog beside his head was lapping up the fresh blood. Now the god knelt to continue his task. Marsyas could hear the quick sharp breaths, for killing him was hard work. The god's white skin glowed and the satyr believed he was inspiring the very breath Apollo expired.

As I read his story I stupidly wondered which character Paul was – the Apollo he so resembled and whose abstract ideal of art appeared to be his own, or the satyr who embodies the vital principle of mimesis and who, after all, submitted to the god's cruel, concentrated attention. The usual motive for the story, Apollo's jealousy, was left out altogether, as though pique were an emotion Paul didn't know (certainly he hadn't shown any in eight days on the road). His story was dedicated to me, and for a moment I wondered if it were also addressed to me – as a reproach for having abandoned the Apollonian abstractness of my first two novels or, on the contrary, as an endorsement for undertaking my later satires and sketches? It was unsettling dealing with this young man so brilliant and handsome, so violent and so reflective.

At night Paul let me into his bed and held me in his arms, just as he sometimes rested his hand on my leg as I drove the car. He told me that, although Thierry often petted him, Paul was never allowed to stroke him. 'We've never once kissed each other on the lips.'

We talked skittishly about the curse the gods had put on us. I pathetically attempted to persuade Paul he was really a sadist. 'Your invariable rage after sex with your lover,' I declared, melodramatically, 'your indignation, your disgusting excursions into fag-bashing, your primitive, literalist belief that only the biggest man with the biggest penis has the right to dominate all the others, whereas the sole glory of sadism is its strictly cerebral capacity for imposing new values, your obvious attraction to my fundamentally docile nature' – and at that point my charlatanism would make me burst out laughing, even as I glanced sideways to see how I was doing.

In fact my masochism sickened him. It reminded him of his own longing to recapture Thierry's love. 'He left me,' he would say.

'When calls come in he turns the sound off on the answering machine and he never replays his messages when I'm around. His pockets bulge with condoms. He spends every weekend with purely fictive "German businessmen" in Normandy; he pretends he's going to visit a factory in Nice, but he's back in Paris four hours later; he stood me up for the Mister Body-building contest at the Parc de Vincennes then was seen there with a famous Brazilian model . . . He says I should see a psychiatrist, and you know how loony someone French must think you are to suggest that.'

When a thoughtful silence had re-established itself in the car I added, 'That's why you want to reach the desert. Only its vast sterility can calm your violent soul.'

'If you could be in my head,' he said, not smiling, 'you'd see I'm in a constant panic.'

To be companionable I said, 'Me too.'

Paul quickly contradicted me: 'But you're the calmest person I know.'

Then I understood that was how he wanted me to be – masterful, confident, smiling, sure. Even if he would some day dominate, even hurt me, as I wished, he would never give me permission to suffer in any way except heroically.

I drove a few miles in silence through the lunar valley, mountains on both sides, not yet the desert but a coarse-grained prelude to it – dry, gently rolling, the boulders the colour of egg-plants. 'You're right, except so many of the people I've known have died. The way we talk, you and me, about books and life and love. I used to talk this way with my best friend, but that was in America and now he is dead.' That night, in Paul's arms, I said, 'It's sacrilegious to say it, especially for an atheist, but I feel God sent you not to replace my friend, since he's irreplaceable, but . . .'

A carpet salesman assured us the desert was about to begin. We had been following a river through the valley, and at last it had run dry, and the date palms had vanished, and the mountains knelt like camels just before setting out on a long journey. In Zagora we saw the famous sign, 'Timbuctoo: 54 days.' In a village we stopped to visit the seventeenth-century library of a saint, Abu Abdallah Mohammed Bennacer, a small room of varnished wood cases beside a walled-in herbal garden. The old guide in his white robes opened for us – his hands were wood-hard – some of the illustrated volumes, including a Koran written on gazelle skin. Paul's red hair and massive body made him rarer than a gazelle in this dusty village. That night a village boy asked me if I had a 'gazelle' back in Paris, and I figured out he meant a girlfriend and nodded because that was the most efficient way to stanch a carpet-tending spiel.

Paul continued with his stories. The one about the French woman he had loved and married off to the paratrooper, who had already become his lover. The one about the Los Angeles sadist he ridiculed and who then committed suicide. About his second date with Thierry, when he'd been gagged and chained upside down in a dungeon after being stuffed with acid, then made to face a huge poster of the dead LA lover. The one about the paratrooper scaling the mountain at the French–Italian border while cops in circling helicopters ordered him to descend immediately – 'and applauded in spite of themselves when he reached the top bare-handed,' Paul exulted, 'without a rope or pick or anything to scale the sheer rock face but balls and brawn.'

We're too alike, I thought again, despairing, to love each other, and Paul is different only in his attraction to cartoon images of male violence and aggression. Unlike him, I couldn't submit to a psychopath; what I want is Paul, with all his tenderness and quizzical, hesitating intelligence, his delicacy, to hit me. To be hurt by an enraged bull on steroids doesn't excite me. What I want is to belong to this grave, divided, philosphical man.

It occurred to me that if I thought only now, at this moment in my life, of belonging to someone, it was because my hold on life itself was endangered. Did I want him to tattoo his initials on a body I might soon have to give up? Did I want to become his slave just before I embraced that lasting solitude?

The beginning of the desert was a dune that had drifted through the pass between two mountains and had started to fill up the scrub-land. A camel with bald spots on its elbows and starlet eyelashes was tethered to a dark felt tent in which a dirty man was sprawling, half-asleep. Another man, beaming and freshly shaved, bustled out of a cement bunker. With a flourish he invited us in for a glass of mint tea. His house turned out to be a major carpet showroom, buzzing with air-conditioning and neon lamps. 'English?'

'No. Danish.'

That was the last night of our holiday. The hotel served us a feast of sugared pigeon pie and mutton couscous, and Paul had a lot to drink. We sat in the dark beside the pool, which was lit from within like a philosopher's stone. He told me he thought of me as 'gay' in the Nietzchean, not the West Hollywood, sense, but since I insisted that I needed him, he would love me and protect me and spend his life with me. Later in bed he pounded me in the face with his fists, shouting at me in a stuttering, broken explosion of French and English, the alternately choked and released patois of scalding indignation.

If the great pleasure of the poor, or so they say, is making love, then the great suffering of the rich is loving in vain. The troubadours, who speak for their rich masters, are constantly reminding us that only men of refinement recognize the nobility of hopeless love; the vulgar crowd jeers at them for wasting their time. Only the idle and free can afford the luxury (the anguish) of making an absence into the very rose-heart of their lives. Only they have the extravagance of time to languish, shed tears, exalt their pain into poetry. For others time is too regulated; every day repeats itself.

I wasn't rich, but I was free and idle enough to ornament my liberty with the melancholy pleasure of having lost a Bordeaux boy with a claret-red mouth. All the while I'd been with Jean-Loup I'd admitted how ill-suited we were and I sought or dreamed of seeking someone else either tepidly or hotly, depending on the intensity of my dissatisfaction.

Now that Jean-Loup had left me for Régis, I could glorify their love and despise them and hate myself while sifting through my old memories to show myself that Jean-Loup had been slowly, if unconsciously, preparing this decampment for a long time.

When I am being wicked I tell people, 'Our little Jean-Loup has landed in clover. His worries are over. He's handed in his resignation at the bank. He'll soon be installed in the château for the summer and he can fill the moat with his *bandes dessinées*. The only pity is that Jean-Loup is apparently at Régis's mercy and Régis is cunning. He holds all the cards. If he tires of Jean-Loup, the poor boy will be dismissed without a centime, for that wedding-ring doesn't represent a claim, only a – '

But at this point bored, shocked friends laugh, hiss, 'Jealous, jealous, this way lies madness.' Jealousy may be new to me but not to them. My condition is as banal as it is baneful.

And then I realize that the opposite is probably true: that Jean-Loup had always dealt with me openly, even at the end, and had never resorted to subterfuge. As soon as he knew of his deep, innocent love for Régis he told me, I am the one who attributes scheming to him.

He always wanted me to describe his ass, so I'll conclude with an attempt not to sound too wet.

I should admit right off that by all ocular evidence there was nothing extraordinary about it. It wasn't a soccer player's muscled bum or a swimmer's sun-moulded twin *charlottes*. It was a kid brother's ass, a perfunctory transition between spine and legs, a simple cushion for a small body. Its colour was the low-wattage white of a winter half-moon. It served as the neutral support (as an anonymous glove supports a puppet's bobbing, expressive head) for his big, grown-up penis, always so ready to poke up through his flies and take centre-stage. But let's not hastily turn him around to reveal 'Régis's Daily Magic Baguette', as I now call it. No, let's keep his back to us, even though he's deliciously braced his knees to compensate for the sudden new weight he's cantilevered in his excitement, a heavy divining rod that makes his buttocks tense. Concave, each cheek looks glossy, like costly

white satin that, having been stuffed in a drawer, has just been
smoothed, though it is still crazed with fine, whiter, silkier lines.
If he spreads his cheeks – which feel cool, firm and plump – for the
kneeling admirer, he reveals an anus that makes one think of a
Leica lens, shut now but with many possible f-stops. An expensive aperture, but also a closed morning glory bud. There's that
*grain de beauté* on his hip, the single drop of espresso on the
wedding-gown. And there are the few silky hairs in the crack of
his ass, wet now for some reason and plastered down at odd
angles as though his fur had been greedily licked in all directions
at once. If he spreads his legs and thinks about nothing – his fitting
with the tailor, the castle drawbridge, the debs whose calls he can
no longer return – his erection may melt and you might see it
drooping lazily into view, just beyond his loosely bagged testicles.
He told me that his mother would never let him sleep in his *slip*
when he was growing up. She was afraid underpants might stunt
his virile growth. These Bordeaux women know to let a young
wine breathe.

# Sunday Morning: Key West

**ANDREW HOLLERAN**

He was sixteen the first time he went – he drove down from a town in north Florida with the boy next door. They ended up on a beach, a beach he could not identify now, since he now believes Key West has no beaches. There was a beach, at sixteen. He lay down on it, fell asleep in the sun, and got so burnt he had to be hospitalized when he returned home covered with fat yellow blisters. That fall his friend joined the Air Force, and he went north to a university in New York.

The second time he went to Key West, someone yelled 'Faggot!' at him – he was standing beside a fence around someone's garden, straddling a bicycle, when two men in a paint-scraped pick-up truck went by and tossed the word out the window as if it had been a water-bomb or a bunch of garbage. He couldn't remember anything else about that trip. He was astonished by the epithet because, though by now he *was* leading a homosexual life, he didn't think he looked it; but, like being cheated in Naples, it left an indelible impression of the place with him. He did not go back to Key West for fifteen years. He settled in New York and went to Fire Island instead, which had bigger and more beautiful beaches, and met a man there with whom he lived for a while. In other words, like everyone, he had his love. When he went home to Florida during this period, he heard the news of his high-school friend – now stationed at an Air Force base near Frankfurt – and thought: Well, this is my Air Force, my adventure, and that is that. He was content.

Then everything changed. The next time he went to Key West, his first memory – his friend's snow-white body in beige elastic bathing trunks that resembled a woman's girdle – had faded, but one thing still seemed true: just getting there seemed to be the point. Key West had always, he thought, obtained its allure from the fact that it was the end of the road – specifically, A-1-A: the southernmost town in the United States, the last in a string of inhabited islands. The uninhabited islands kept going to the Dry Tortugas. By now he knew New Yorkers who had moved there and opened up shops. But he did not intend to look anyone up. He drove down for the day with a friend he was staying with in Miami. They parked the car, got out, went to see the crowd on the dock poised to applaud the sunset while men juggled coconuts and ate fire, and ran into a friend from Manhattan.

The friend from Manhattan who came up to him on the dock that visit was a good-natured drifter who took jobs only long enough to save money, quit, and then live in places like Key West, a few months at a time. He was the only gay man Roger knew who had temporary-typed his way across the country – living in towns for two months as a New Face; a secretary with a room at the Y., who spent his days in an office, his evenings in the baths, bars, parks, cruising. He looked, in the ruddy light of the big red sun setting behind the Australian pines on an offshore island, as if he'd run out of places to type. Gaunt cheeks, thin forearms, eyes that had a radioactive glow, betrayed his inability to explore much more; Key West was obviously his last stop. They shook hands after a sunset that now seemed heavy with metaphor; he went into a bar with the friend he'd driven down with, and, after one look at the Hawaiian shirts, deep tans, men dancing to canned disco music, they turned to each other, and without a word headed for the car and drove back to Miami.

That was 1981. He left New York that fall to return home to Florida after his father had a stroke. By that time both the man he'd met on the dock in Key West, and the friend he'd driven down with, were dead. The boy next door was still in Germany. Roger listened, at the clothes-line, to his mother tell him the news of her son's trips to Egypt, Turkey, Austria, Sweden (to buy a Volvo), Garmisch (for Christmas vacation) – but when his high-school friend returned with his wife and daughter on a visit that summer, Roger watched him clean his collection of antique rifles at a picnic table in the yard next door, and could not summon the courage or desire to go over and speak with him. The separate paths they'd followed in life seemed to have brought them to such different places.

He kept most people at a distance those years, in fact – even friends seemed to be nothing more than voices on the telephone. He'd return from the nursing home after feeding his father dinner and hear the phone ringing as he got out of the car in the garage. On the other end was one of those friends from New York who now, like himself, lived elsewhere. Some of them had moved to California, some to south Florida. One of them – his former lover – went to Key West one winter to take a job in a restaurant, fell down and cracked his skull while drunk instead, and was taken in by two recovering alcoholics. He ended up staying. He complained, 'You can't have a drink or sleep with anyone in this town without everybody knowing exactly how much you drank or what you did in bed,' but he remained. They spoke on the phone at least once a week. He had no news – nothing happened, at least to him, in his town – but Lee had plenty. The first year, he followed Lee's efforts to stay sober, the second year to persuade a man indifferent to him to be his lover, the third year to start a restaurant, the fourth year to keep the business and love affair from destroying one another. Lee's struggles constituted an on-going soap opera, better than *Dynasty*; he listened gratefully. Some nights, on the telephone, the lure of Key West – that irrational appeal that survived even his knowledge of the place: its drunks, claustrophobia, lack of beaches – was so strong, he could almost hear the rustle of palm fronds beside the porch on which Lee was talking to him. Some nights he needed to be where men cruised one another, had sex, argued, gossiped, talked about the soccer player from Berlin who'd just arrived in town; Instead he followed, on the phone, Lee's move from apartment to apartment, his struggle with the restaurant, the fights and reconciliations with his lover, but declined Lee's invitation to come down. The newspapers said Key West had become a place for men with AIDS to die; it seemed to him the whole world had become that, and the safest place his house.

Then one day, the winter of 1989, a Greek tanker struck a reef off the Keys – spilled oil, damaged the coral, made the evening news. That night while he sat before the television set with his bowl of spaghetti, NBC showed the reef the tanker had hit; a reef already damaged by pollution and the vandalism of tourists. Outside it was a cold, damp, penetrating winter night. His sister had been telling him to take a trip. He decided everything would be all right, if he could just go swimming in that turquoise sea, above that reef – he called Lee.

Changing planes in Miami the next day, he had a sudden longing to fly to Caracas instead. Then halfway along the last leg of the trip – a twenty-minute flight in a small plane – he looked out the window and saw the undulating, white-capped, gelatinous sea. The exhilaration he felt died the instant he stepped through the doorway of the airport terminal, however: he realized suddenly he had not seen Lee in eight years. He need not have worried. Ah, Key West! 'No one comes when they're supposed to,' Lee had complained of carpenters and electricians. Now Lee was not there. He phoned the restaurant; the man who answered said to take a taxi; he went outside and did just that.

The taxi was driven by a skinny, scarred, sunburnt, silent blond who put up the windows and turned on the air-conditioner in the car as they drove into town. His fellow passenger was a man in tasselled loafers, blue blazer and horn-rimmed glasses – a man connected to an art museum or gallery in some northern city, he guessed, on his way to a gay guest-house. They stared out separate windows as the wind-blown, sun-bleached palms went by beyond the glass. A storm was coming. The sky was overcast. The wind was high, the temperature supposed to drop into the fifties that night, the radio said. He got out of the taxi on Duval Street and went into the restaurant.

A short handsome man saw his bag, came up and said, in a Spanish accent, 'Lee is coming. Wait here for him.'

Lee arrived a moment later. 'I was nervous,' he grinned, blushing. 'About seeing you. That's why I'm late.'

'I was nervous, too,' he said.

'The first thing is to rent you a bike,' Lee said. 'Leave your bag here. Ricardo will look after it.'

'Who's Ricardo?' he said after they went out on to the sidewalk.

'My *maître d'*,' Lee said. 'He's a refugee – he came over last year, from Cuba, in a boat.'

'Oh!' he said. 'Is he a hard worker?'

'No,' said Lee. 'All he cares about is dick. He used to work at the dirty bookstore three doors down, so he knows exactly what everyone likes to do, and how big their dick is. It's like living with a government informer in Havana.'

'Well, he was very polite,' he said.

'He drives me nuts,' Lee said. 'He told the tellers at my bank I drank a bottle of vodka last week on my birthday.'

'Happy birthday,' he said.

'I was trying to forget it,' Lee laughed.

With that, he held open the door of a delicatessen they entered to have lunch – in a room where gay men had collected like the grease of a million hamburgers, a million love affairs, he felt, as they sat down. It was the first time in seven years he had been in a restaurant where all the customers were men, sitting alone, in pairs, and quartets. He stared, like a child before an aquarium of sharks at Marineland, at the deep tans, pony-tails, beards, moustaches, tank-tops, backpacks, and Hawaiian-print shirts, as he listened to Lee's stories about his employees ('In Key West, you either wait tables or own the restaurant. There's nothing in between'), his struggle with drink ('I stopped going to the meetings'), his lover ('I had to fire him from the restaurant, he was being so obnoxious to everyone. The next week he was diagnosed with Aids. Now he won't speak to me'), the young German soccer player who worked as a cashier in a health food store ('Wait till you see him, we'll go there after lunch'). Eight years of separation

vanished with their hamburgers. Lee's eyes remained, however –
those azure eyes he'd fallen under the spell of years ago, in the
kitchen of a friend's apartment on Second Avenue. He realized –
with relief, as he ate his Key Lime pie – that Lee was still good, still
kind, still compassionate; which meant more to him now than
years ago, when all that mattered were the eyes.

'You look the same,' said Lee.

'So do you,' said Roger.

They both laughed. The kitchen in which they had met, the
window, the alianthus tree behind the building so close one could
reach out and touch the branches, the two stools on which he and
Lee sat talking till their legs finally touched, came back to him
now, as he watched over Lee's shoulder those who could still do
what he could no longer: eat alone in public. He realized,
watching them, that he was now a recluse. One of those middle-
aged men who, after a parent he was caring for had died, would
go out on a date with another man his age whose parents had also
just died – meeting in a restaurant like this, as fragile as flowers, as
set in their ways as cement.

'Ready?' Lee said, picking up the check. 'We'll go back to the
apartment now, and then hit the beach.'

The beach was the one he must have gone to when he was
sixteen; he remembered the circular cement restroom. The dock
which stretched out from the sand towards the half-submerged
planks of a wooden sea-wall was familiar too, though everything
seemed smaller than he had imagined. He lay down in the shade
of a thatched roof, a few feet from Lee in the bright sunlight, and
said, when Lee asked why he was avoiding the light: 'I have to
stay out of the sun now. I had three skin cancers removed last
summer.'

'I had two taken off last week,' said Lee, pointing to a patch on
his shoulder.

'Then why are you out in the sun?' said Roger.

'I have to look nice for the customers,' Lee said. He laughed.
'My doctor says people have them removed, and go straight to the
beach!'

The beach: beyond the pool of shade, life went on just as he remembered it in the hot sunlight. He and Lee seemed to have picked up, years later, right where they'd left off – with the same artefacts: *New York Times*, box of cookies, jug of water, bicycles. He noted, however, a difference – Lee was cheerful in the midst of troubles: his lover's illness, the hospitalization of a friend. Like everyone in the middle of the fray, he had a vivacity those trying to keep it at a distance did not. Odd, he thought as he listened to the faint sound of voices, waves, passing aeroplanes, how the people who have to deal with it daily seem more alive than those who don't. With that, he roused himself and went out on to the dock to swim. The water felt like ice. He sat there on the slimy steps watching a woman in a bathing cap swim back and forth in diagonal lines across the rectangle of water between the dock and sea wall. She did not seem to mind. Nor did a plump German man, who entered the sea via the steps Roger was sitting on, turned over on his back in front of him, and said, 'Ah! *Schön!*' Finally he went in. He swam fast to get warm, but each time he reached beneath the water to complete his stroke, his hand plunged into the eel-grass growing on the bottom. There's gotta be another beach, he thought, as he got out and walked back through the glare.

There was. Watching Lee negotiate traffic ahead of him as they bicycled across town through narrow streets lined with gardens of grape trees, bougainvillaea and palms, he felt a curious tenderness for the person now taking care of his wants. He looked fragile on the bicycle ahead of him. Odd, how the number of people one matters to in life is small, he thought, and, in the end, the non-renewable resource. When they got to Fort Taylor, two men were lying on their backs on picnic tables in a grove of Australian pines, talking in Hebrew. A group of young men in black bathing suits lay on a pile of rocks near shore, like seals, shining in the sun. They chained their bikes to the trees, and sat down on a picnic bench in the shade. They talked about new friends, old friends, wakes, memorials, blood tests, fear, depression, insomnia, the restaurant, the local gay church, Ricardo, Spring Break, the

invasion of Panama, Manuel Noriega, the drug business, Tennessee Williams, Calvin Klein, Jerry Herman, a memorial service to be
held for a man from Chicago on a dock that evening, the local
newspaper, George Bush, the importance of hats, their parents,
and real estate values, as water-skiers suspended from parachutes
floated by, and an old coast guard cutter returned from the open
sea. Finally Lee mentioned his lover, who would not speak to him
now that he'd been fired from the restaurant, and was dying in a
guest-house in the Old Town, and the friend in the hospital – an
older man he'd met in AA; a man he liked to discuss history and
politics with, whose mail he had promised to take him that
afternoon.

'I won't bring you,' Lee said, standing up, 'because he's too
weak. Let's meet back at the apartment, at five. Unless you meet
one of these beauties,' he said.

Fat chance, he thought. He put his towel down on the sand
between two young men on separate towels of their own, their
lithe bodies simmering beneath a film of sweat and oil. The beauty
of the man on his left – tall, long-legged, curly brown hair, blue
Speedo – grew on him as the afternoon waned, and he began to
feel what he had not felt in a long time: desire. He plunged into the
milky green sea and did his best to catch the attention of the man
in the blue Speedo. When he returned to his towel, the blue
Speedo was saying to the other young man: 'I liked it, but it wasn't
what I'd do with a lamp store. You know? I mean, it was OK for
LA.' And his long-legged beauty disintegrated under the same
banalities that had neutralized desire twenty years ago on the
beach in the Pines. Eventually the two men on separate towels got
up together and left. He imagined their return to a room in a
guest-house: the embrace inside the door, the taste of salt water
on a sunburnt shoulder, the kisses, the undressing, the shared
shower, the water splashing on their backs. He imagined as he lay
there watching the sun descend in the sky the wet footprints on
the floor, the messed sheets, the long, hot afternoon ending,
finally, in sex. Then he took another swim and left the beach. He
looked at the empty porches of the beautiful old houses in gardens

of delicate palms as he bicycled back to Lee's in his bare feet, happy to have swum, to be alone, for the moment, relaxed at last. But all of that depended on his having Lee to return to, he thought. He was just beginning to see the possibilities of the place when he rounded the corner and saw Lee getting off his bike at the gate.

'How was the hospital?' he said, thinking, the moment he said it, it sounded like: *How was your day, dear?*

'He's coming home tomorrow,' Lee said. 'I told him I'd take care of him at home till we need Hospice.' He took out a pack of cigarettes from his pocket and said: 'This is why I keep falling off the wagon. I'm now Barry's main support. The doctor told me he's in the final stages. Sometimes,' he said, as they locked their bicycles to the post, 'I just wish they'd die.' He looked up at him and said: 'Isn't that awful?'

'No,' said Roger. 'I think that about my father, too. It's only normal. On the other hand – '

'What?' said Lee.

'I'm terrified that he will,' he said.

'Why?'

'Because he's my whole life now. What would I be doing if I weren't caring for him?'

'Well,' said Lee, 'I'm not allowed to care for Ray. That's where he is,' he said, as they sat down on the second-storey porch of his apartment. 'Right there,' he said, nodding at the pool house of a pink hotel directly opposite – the shutters of an attic window closed against the sun. 'The weird part is I left some things in his room, and now that he refuses to see me, I can't get them.'

'Like what?' said Roger.

'Like my camera.'

They looked across the street at the pink guest-house, the closed shutters, in the late-afternoon sunlight.

'I keep thinking it must be hot inside,' said Lee. 'I keep thinking a lot of things, since I look right at it, every day.'

'What does he have?' said Roger.

'It went to his brain,' said Lee.

'Toxoplasmosis,' said Roger. 'The thing everybody fears the most.' Together they stared at the closed metallic louvres. Then they returned to the newspaper scattered on the cloth-covered wicker table between them. The palms rustled in the late afternoon breeze. A yellow wagon-train went by half-filled with tourists listening to a man with a microphone at the wheel. Six o'clock plunged the bougainvillaea against the garden wall into shadow. Lee lit a cigarette, and removed his sandals.

'Isn't Panama a mess?' said Lee.

'Yes,' said Roger.

That evening they had dinner in a little Cuban restaurant around the corner whose waiters, Lee promised, were especially handsome. They were. When they got back to the apartment, they began looking at other men – from Fire Island – in scrapbooks Lee took down from the shelf.

'You know, they carry photographs around with them now in San Francisco,' Roger said. 'To show what they looked like before they got sick. A friend of mine out there goes to parties for people with Aids, and sometimes the discrepancy between the photographs, and the people showing them to him, is so great, he starts to cry and leaves.'

Lee shook his head.

'I haven't cried once since this began,' said Roger. 'I don't know why.'

That evening they had trouble sleeping. Lee woke in the middle of the night more than once and lit a cigarette; and Roger, lying awake on the sofa, concluded they were both victims of that malady of middle age – insomnia. Nerves. Something unsettled. Deep down, a discontent. The two questions all survivors faced: What will I do if/when I get sick? And: What will I do at sixty, if I don't? In the morning, Lee said: 'Call the excursion boat.'

There was nothing to take an excursion to – each captain he called said high winds had made the sea so rough, so cloudy, a visit to the reef was impractical. They spent half an hour trying on shorts. Then they went out on to the porch, had breakfast, read the newspaper, till Lee said: 'I have to help Barry check out of the hospital. You go to Fort Taylor. I'll meet you back here at five. Now remember,' Lee said, from the doorway, 'tomorrow you leave town, and you don't have to worry about your reputation. But you do have to leave *me* something to talk about, after you've gone!'

'OK!' he laughed, as Lee went out the door. Instead he washed the breakfast dishes, and went back to the porch and sat down at the wicker table to browse the scrapbooks, and wait out the most intense period of the sun. He became mesmerized by the passage of pedestrians and cyclists in the street below, the emptiness of the garden, the breeze that stirred the pages of the newspaper on the table before him. Time passed. He moved the ashtrays and shells about to weigh down sections of the newspaper as the breeze shifted. What is the point of going to the beach? he wondered. Hidden away here in the shade above the little garden, he felt completely content. Finally, even reading the newspaper seemed too much effort, and he turned his attention to the street below which itself seemed to have expired under the heat of the noonday sun, as everyone lay on the beach. Then he raised his eyes to the shutters, in the pink house across the street, and he wondered if they were not the real reason he was still sitting there.

The shutters reminded him of a church on Good Friday – the hours from noon to three when Jesus was on the Cross, and Catholic children were forbidden to play outside. Now the hours of twelve to three were honoured indoors for a different, purely secular reason. But still the same lesson seemed to obtain: someone was always suffering, while the rest of the world went about its business. He stared at the shutters across the street and marvelled at the fact that, six or seven years after the first people he knew died, unaware of the cause, or the number to follow them, it was all still, in some terrible sense, a mystery – as blank, as impervious to light, or man's cleverness, as those silver louvres layered one upon the other, like the blades of a fan. He sat there thinking of the outrage, the impotence, the deaths past and to come, the denouement no one could have foreseen, like the effect of sun on the skin years after an adolescent sunburn. He sat there wondering why he had not cried till now, not once, and if he would some day. He sat there watching the death-room of someone he did not even know, and was still sitting there hours later when Lee came home from the hospital. He looked up, startled, when the door opened.

'How was the beach?' Lee said.

'I didn't go,' he said, embarrassed. 'I've been sitting looking at these old photographs. It's so cool and pleasant on this porch – I could sit here for ever. You have a very nice life here. Tell me,' he said, closing a scrapbook, 'who are you still in touch with from the old crowd?'

'You,' Lee said. 'You're all I've got, Snookums!'

The words pleased him. They went downstairs together to have an early dinner; they took a long walk to the Truman Annexe and back afterwards. Tourists in cotton clothes, their hair still damp from swimming, were gathering in the streets as twilight deepened. Lee asked him one more time if he wanted to visit the bars, but he declined. They went home and watched a movie on cassette instead, then went to bed, the two of them on the same futon, accustomed now to each other.

In the morning he awoke just as dawn was breaking; a milky blue light filled the garden below, and was stealing through the cracks in the shutters, as if it meant to bathe everything in the splendour and profuse life of the tropics. He looked at Lee – and the pale light surrounding the room – got up quietly, and went out to the porch. The pink house, the silver shutters across the street, were drenched in dew – a dew he imagined as he stood there soaking the bedroom like some miraculous holy water that would dissolve the sickness within. Then he turned and looked back through the open doorway at Lee, asleep on the futon. Next year, he thought, Caracas.

# Suddenly Home

## ARMISTEAD MAUPIN

Tess felt bloated and jumpy, unbelievably PM-essy, when she spotted her brother in the waiting throng at the United terminal. To make matters worse, Will's other half was nowhere in sight. She hadn't expected a welcoming party as such, but she'd counted on Jamie being there to keep things civil, since she knew from experience that Will didn't nag as much when Jamie was around.

Her brother stepped forward with a sleepy, lop-sided grin, hugged her clumsily and reached for her carry-on. He looked tanner than the last time, maybe a little greyer, annoyingly content. 'How was your flight?'

'Not bad.' Already expecting the worst, she fixed her eyes on the distance and strode toward the moving walkway. 'The flight attendant slipped me his phone number.'

Will looked amazed. 'Really?'

She nodded.

'A straight flight attendant?'

She shot him a nasty glance. 'Yes, a straight flight attendant. Where's Jamie? He said he was coming with you.'

'He's at Nordstrom's.'

'Shopping?' She couldn't help but sound cranky about this.

Will shook his head, apparently amused by her reaction. 'They fired a clerk with HIV. There's a big demonstration this morning and . . . You know Jamie.'

She felt a tiny pinprick of anxiety. Outside of the call arranging this visit she hadn't talked to Jamie for at least a month. 'He's OK, isn't he?'

'Fine.' Will looked believably nonchalant. 'His T-cells are way up.'

'Great.'

He glanced at her sideways, narrowing his eyes. 'So, what's going on?'

No way, she thought. Not until we're home and Jamie's with us and you've had *at least* a couple of joints. 'Hey,' she said, feigning jovial indignation, 'Do I require an invitation?'

'No. But this is awful sudden.'

'Well, I do things suddenly.'

'Uh-huh.'

'Look,' she told him, 'I'm going right back to Charleston.'

'Stop. Why are you so edgy?'

'I'm not edgy. You're just in one of your picky moods.' She led the way on to the moving walkway. They cruised past big Lucite boxes, like upright coffins, each displaying a different piece of California 'chair art'. A chair made of Coke bottles, a chair made of cow bones, a Styrofoam chair . . .

'So,' said Will, 'how's the shithead?'

How like him to take the offensive. 'His name is Alec, Will.'

'You called him that first.'

'*Once*,' she said. 'After a fight. You're the one who made it official.'

'Why didn't you bring him along?'

She studied his face for traces of snideness and decided the question was in earnest. Maybe, she thought, Will and Alec would learn to like each other if they spent some time together. 'He's been on business in Philadelphia. I'm meeting him tomorrow, though. In Maui.'

Her brother's face clouded over. 'So this is just a stopover.'

She rolled her eyes. 'We'll have a whole day. I thought we could go to the beach or something, have a nice long talk. In person, for a change.'

'About what?'

'Does it have to be *about* something?'

'No, but . . .'

'God, the men in this city! Look at the arms on that guy.'

This was a cheap diversionary tactic, but it worked. Her brother's gaze swerved and locked on the beauty in question: an off-duty marine, she guessed, with ivory biceps and a shrimp-coloured T-shirt that said SHIT HAPPENS.

'Big deal,' said Will.

'Well, excuse me, Mr Married Man.'

He looked at the marine again. 'He has a tattoo, for God's sake!'

'Really? Is it misspelt? I love it when they're misspelt.'

She hooked her arm through his as they headed toward baggage claim. He was wearing one of his favourite shirts tonight, a pale blue baggy-sleeved thing which he probably thought made him look like Lord Byron. Trini Lopez was more like it.

Gazing up at him, she counted the grey hairs in his moustache, and noticed with affection that his jaw stored fat in the same place as hers.

Will and Jamie's house on Twenty-first Street was not quite the way she'd remembered it. There were two or three new parchment-shaded lamps and they'd put up barn siding – or something meant to look like it – on one wall of the living-room. Over the past decade or so she had watched Will's taste shimmy from rustic to deco to high tech to rustic again.

When they arrived, Jamie was perched on a stepladder in the living-room, wielding a paintbrush. 'Well,' she said, 'home from the wars, huh?'

'Hi, Tess! God, you guys missed something! Three hundred of us took over the escalator at Nordstrom's – this incredible spiral thing that goes on for ever. It was like Tiananmen Square meets Busby Berkeley!'

Will chuckled.

'Really,' said Jamie, 'it was amazing. A whole store full of us chanting, "We're here, we're queer, and we're not going shopping."'

She laughed and held out her arms. 'Can I please have a hug?'

Jamie scooted down the stepladder and embraced her, his fingers climbing her spine until they found the knots at the base of her neck. 'Hey,' he said. 'Tough flight, huh?'

Will said: 'The flight attendant had major hots for her.'

'A straight flight attendant?'

Will shook his head at Jamie. 'Don't.'

Jamie released her. 'I'll give you a good shoulder rub. Soon as I clean up.'

She peered up at the ladder and noticed for the first time that the ceiling above their heads looked dangerously damaged. 'What were you doing up there?'

'Just painting.'

'Shouldn't you fix that huge crack first?'

Jamie seemed proud as a new parent. 'I painted that huge crack.'

'C'mon.'

He shrugged. 'We didn't get any good ones during the earthquake, so we're painting our own. How long can you stay?'

'Till tomorrow.'

Jamie looked crushed. 'Stay till Valentine's Day, at least. It's our second anniversary.'

'She has to be in Maui,' Will announced sullenly. 'For some reason.'

She ignored him, keeping her eyes on Jamie. 'You met on Valentine's Day? You never told me that!'

Jamie smiled sheepishly.

Will said: 'He was passing out condoms at the ACT-UP booth on Twenty-fourth Street.'

'How romantic.'

'Well . . .' Her brother looked affronted again. 'The condoms were heart-shaped.'

She had one hell of a time picturing this.

'The *wrappers* were heart-shaped,' Jamie explained.

'Thank you,' she said.

Jamie laughed with her, and something about the tilt of his

head, the tenor of his laughter, reminded her exactly of Will. He was five years younger than her brother – thinner, blonder and already balder – but on the phone she found it increasingly harder to tell them apart. They claimed not to notice this, of course, pretending to be horrified by what it suggested, but any fool could see what had happened.

Will fixed iced tea, which the three of them sipped on the deck. The air was warm and lemony with a neighbour's verbena, and half-a-dozen seagulls were making languid loops above the little valley. For Tess the scene felt oddly like a homecoming.

'How's the travel agency?' asked Jamie.

'Fine.'

'And Alec?'

Will shot his lover a look.

'He's great,' she said, determined to get on with it. 'He sent you both his best.'

Will grunted, but Jamie ignored him, remaining pleasant. 'Are you guys still . . . together?'

'Oh, yeah. Three or four nights a week.' She smiled at him, grateful for his interest. 'He's still got his own place, but he's not in it much.'

'Awright,' said Jamie.

'Of course,' she added wryly. 'Daddy says I'm a slut.'

'Why?'

'Oh . . . you know, because we aren't married. And Barton and all.'

'Fuck him,' said Will. 'Barton is fifteen years old.'

'Thank you. I know.'

'It isn't any of Daddy's goddamned business whether you're married or not.'

'We live in the same town, Will. I can't just close the door like that. He's Barton's grandfather. He isn't gonna be around much longer.'

'Fuck that. He's been saying that for ever. He was saying that before Mama died.' He fumed silently for a moment. 'When did he call you a slut?'

'It doesn't matter.'

'When, Tess?'

'At Barton's confirmation.'

'At *church*?'

'No.' She smiled at that. 'Afterwards at the party. It was more like a brunch, really.'

'Great. He called you a slut at brunch. Was the shithead there? What did he even . . . ?'

'Will . . .' Jamie was pissed now. 'Stop interrogating her.'

She gave him an appreciative glance before continuing. 'Everybody was full of wine and making these dumb toasts. Daddy didn't mean it. It's just that he likes Alec so much.'

'Figures,' muttered Will.

'He's right, actually. Not about the slut part, but . . . I've been dodging the issue way too long.'

'What issue?'

She shrugged. 'We're getting married.'

The silence seemed interminable. It was Jamie who broke it, reddening noticeably. 'Well . . . that's great, Tess. Congratulations.'

'When?' asked Will.

'Tomorrow. Well . . . day after tomorrow, really.'

'In Maui?' asked Jamie.

'Aloha.'

Will wrote in the air with his finger. 'Mr and Mrs Alec T. Shithead.'

Jamie frowned. 'Will . . .'

'Believe me,' she said, 'I've thought about this long and hard.'

Her brother threw up his hands. 'Fine. Great. Terrific. What do you need us for?'

'I don't know. I thought your blessing might be nice.'

Will sighed histrionically. 'This isn't *Lourdes*, Tess.'

'Tess . . .' Jamie proceeded carefully, measuring his words. 'Do you think you might be . . .?'

'She's obviously made up her mind.'

'You're right,' she said quietly, looking at her brother. 'I have.'

'Fine,' he said, picking up his drink again. 'Go for it.'

She showered off the grime of her flight while Will and Jamie packed a picnic lunch in the kitchen. She could hear their voices dimly through the wall and for a moment tormented herself with what they must be saying. When she returned, though, they were chipper and smiling, absorbed – or pretending to be, at least – in Jamie's bogus earthquake crack.

At Will's suggestion they drove out to Land's End in the VW. They parked in a dust-choked lot above Seal Rocks and, toting their lunches, set off on foot through the gnarled cypresses. A sudden shiver of *déjà vu* made her realize why Will had chosen this spot. He was trying to tweak her memory, to make her nostalgic for the halcyon days of her bachelorhood.

'I know what you're up to,' she told him.

'What?' asked Jamie.

'He brought me here years ago,' she explained. 'After I signed my divorce papers. I was as free as I'd ever been. And I was so . . . intense.'

Will smirked at her. 'More like in heat.'

She smiled at him. 'We came here after the Gay Games. You'd just won a gold medal in something terribly butch.'

'Badminton,' he said.

Jamie hooted.

'We met this guy out here with a pigtail and the cutest butt and Will swore to me he was gay.'

'Was he?'

'Now wait a minute . . .' Will instantly went on the defensive. 'The guy was from LA. It threw me off.'

She and Jamie both got a kick out of this. 'Right,' said Jamie.

'She was shameless,' muttered Will.

Tess remembered every detail of it except the man's name: his baby-blue briefs, his Vangelis tapes, the rust-stained ceiling of his geodesic dome. 'He was so . . . flexible,' she murmured. 'He was an importer.'

'He was a coke dealer,' said Will. 'She disappeared for three whole days. You think I rated so much as a phone call?'

She batted her eyes demurely. 'I was busy.'

As usual, the guys loved this.

They left the noonday twilight of the cypress trees and hiked along a broad, sandy ledge above the sea. The path was hyphenated here and there with makeshift footbridges, and she could see for some distance, watch the picnickers as they made their way back and forth from the parking lot. They were all in pairs, she realized, every last one of them.

'Damn,' said Will. 'I forgot the blanket.'

'Forget about it.'

'We have to have the blanket, Tess. The ground is murder up there.'

'Him and his blanket,' said Jamie.

'You should've seen him when he was three,' she said.

'He had a blanket then?'

'With a *name* no less.'

'Tess!' snapped Will.

She smirked at him and turned back to Jamie. 'Flipper.'

'*Flipper*?' Jamie was enjoying this as much as she was.

'Daddy wouldn't let him have a dolphin.'

Will had had enough. 'I'm getting the blanket,' he said. 'You'll be glad when you have it.'

They found a bench and sat down, awaiting Will's return. 'Do you think I'm making a mistake?' she asked.

Jamie hesitated, clearly uncomfortable. 'That's not for me to say.'

For a moment she pictured Alec in Maui, checking into some amorphous highrise, some soul-deadening place with a Benihana in the lobby and a volcano that goes off on the hour. He'd insisted on booking this one himself, on surprising her, which had seemed romantic as hell at the time, the closest a travel agent could come to being carried over the threshold. Now she wasn't so sure. For all she knew, she was about to be married by a Don Ho impersonator. Alec would think that was funny.

She raked her wind-tangled hair with her fingers. 'He's not such a bad guy, you know. He's always been there for me. And he's pretty nice in the sack.'

Jamie smiled. 'Nothing wrong with that.'

'He's not the world's best conversationalist, but I can always call you.'

He gave her a look of disarming intimacy. 'You'd better.'

Embarrassed, she peered out at the flickering, blue flame of the sea, roughly in the direction of Maui. After a long silence she said: 'I'm scared, Jamie.'

'Why?'

'I don't know. I'm thirty-three and time is running out.'

He nodded thoughtfully. 'Tell me about it.'

She realized her blunder instantly. 'Oh, shit. I'm sorry.'

'Hey . . .' He waved it off.

'You look wonderful, by the way.' She hoped this didn't sound forced or patronizing, because he did look wonderful.

He snatched a pebble off the ground and hurled it down the slope. 'Ever thought about moving?'

'Moving?'

'Sure.'

'Here, you mean?'

'Why not?'

'For starters,' she replied, 'I have this weird thing for straight guys.'

'We have straight guys,' he said, twinkling. 'Especially weird ones.'

She gave him a rueful nod. 'I've noticed.'

Jamie's eyes widened excitedly. 'We could get arrested together. And gang up on Will.'

'Right.' This was much more of a proposal than she had ever

received from Alec. For a moment, she was sure she felt herself blushing.

'He's just like your father,' Jamie added. 'Every bit as pig-headed.'

'Noticed that, huh?' She threw him a quick sideways glance. 'Don't tell me the honeymoon's over?'

He chuckled. 'Let's just say the marriage has begun.'

'Oh, dear.'

'No. We're fine, really.'

She brushed back her hair again and returned her gaze to the water. 'Sure looks that way,' she said.

Another phalanx of couples was plodding toward them up the hill. The ones in the lead were white-haired and ruddy-cheeked, puffed up like a pair of shore birds in purple-quilted polyester.

'These people,' she said.

'What about them?'

'Two-by-two all over the place. You'd think they were headed for the goddamn ark.'

He shrugged. 'Lots of them are just friends.'

No, she thought. They've all go that look. She couldn't quite pin it down, but *lived-with* was how she thought of it. Will and Jamie had it, too, of course.

Jamie slid his arm across her shoulder and gave her a gentle shake, apparently reading her mind.

She mustered a lame smile. 'It's stupid to be jealous, isn't it?'

'Jealous?' Jamie's brow furrowed. 'Of who?'

She abandoned her confession on the spot, uttering a laboured sigh. 'I don't know . . . these people . . . everybody.'

The white-haired couple came to a full stop in front of their bench. The woman was beaming moronically. 'Helloo,' she crooned. Tess just wanted them to go away, to leave her the fuck alone.

'Hi,' said Jamie.

'You look so sweet.'

'Excuse me?'

'The two of you,' explained the woman. 'You make such a lovely sight up here.'

Jamie's lip flickered, but otherwise he didn't betray a thing. 'Thanks.'

'I'm psychic, you know.'

'Really?'

'She is,' said the old man.

'I noticed your aura all the way up here. There's just one, you know. The two of you have one aura.'

Tess cast a quick, sardonic glance at Jamie. Were people here still doing this shit?

'That's nice,' said Jamie.

'You'll have a long life together.'

Jamie gave her a guileless smile. 'Even better,' he said. 'How long?'

'Jamie . . .' Tess realized what he was up to and it made her hideously uncomfortable.

'Now I've embarrassed her,' the old woman said.

'Not really,' said Tess.

'I just thought, maybe you could give me a rough figure.' High on his own private joke, Jamie was milking it for all it was worth.

'Oh,' said the old woman. 'Four or five decades, at least.'

'Hey. Awright.'

'Jamie . . .' Tess rose, brushing off the seat of her jeans. 'We've gotta meet Will, remember?'

He gave her a smile of surrender, abandoning the game. 'Poor thing,' he said, when they were finally out of earshot. 'Not exactly batting a thousand, is she?'

Her depression escalated as the afternoon wore on. By the time they had trekked back to the house, wind-burned and empty-hampered, she was determined to get on with it. Showering again, she changed into clean sweats, then phoned the airline and changed her ticket to a night flight.

Will was a total jerk about it, pacing the room sullenly while she shook the wrinkles out of the green silk cocktail dress she had bought for the ceremony. Beyond the window several long, white fingers of fog had begun to creep across the breast of Twin Peaks.

'Stay for the night at least,' he whined. 'Jamie's out renting a movie and everything.'

'I can't,' she replied as evenly as possible.

He looked at her for a long time, as if weighing his words, as if composing a whole sermon, in fact. 'You know,' he said, 'I spent years looking for somebody and it didn't happen until I *stopped* looking. You've gotta let go a little, Tess.'

She grunted. 'Meaning what? Move here and hang out with the boys?'

'No.' He sounded stung. 'I mean . . . learn to be content in your solitude.'

This was more than she could take. 'Will, that is the biggest load of California crap! You were never content in your solitude. Not once.'

He scowled at her. 'I lived alone for five years before I met Jamie.'

'And you were totally desperate. You were dating devil worshippers!'

She saw him stiffen noticeably. 'If you mean Eduardo, he was a white witch. There is a very big difference.'

She laid out the dress in her suit bag, smoothed the front again and pulled down the zipper. 'All I know is how much you wanted someone. And when Jamie moved in, I sent you champagne and flowers. Why can't you wish me well now that I've . . .?'

'Because the guy is pond scum, OK? Don't you think I know how Alec treats you? Your last five phone calls have been nothing but crying jags.'

This was a rank exaggeration, but she did her damnedest to stay calm. 'I call you when I'm blue, Will. It's not always that way. Alec and I have some rough spots from time to time, but . . .'

'*Rough spots*? You went to a marriage counsellor with him when he was still married to somebody else.'

She reprimanded herself, one more time, for ever having told him about that. 'Look . . . all right . . . I know he's not perfect, but . . .'

'You sound just like Mama. Is that what you want? A lifetime of making excuses?'

She groaned. 'I want to be married, Will. That doesn't make me a doormat.'

'I understand that.'

'Then why won't you say it's OK?'

The look he gave her was infuriating. 'Because I'm not going to be one more man giving you permission.'

She glared at him in glacial silence for a moment, then slapped the bag shut and began snapping the straps. 'Don't flatter yourself.'

'You're not going to marry him anyway,' he said. 'You wouldn't have come here if you were. Why can't you just deal with it? Why does it have to be a man's decision? Why can't it be *you* for once? I haven't got time for this petty shit.'

She dragged the suit bag off the bed. 'Right,' she said. 'I'll remember that. My life is petty.'

'I didn't mean that.'

Suddenly enraged, she flung the suit bag into the hallway. '*Then, what the fuck did you mean?*'

Will regarded the fallen luggage for a moment, then sighed. 'I meant . . . ' He shrugged and turned away from her, gazing out the window. The fog had begun to spill into the valley, tumbling past the Monopoly-board houses, blurring their lights and softening their edges. 'Last week,' he said at last, 'I went out and bought myself a suit just for funerals.'

She sank to the edge of the bed, filled with dread and drained of all energy. It wasn't until she saw her brother's tears that she began to come apart. 'Will, please . . .'

'You keep acting like Jamie and I have some sort of . . . happily-ever-after.' He swiped at his eyes. 'All we have is right now.'

'I didn't . . .'

'That's all anybody's got, Tess. The future doesn't count for shit.'

She picked at a loose thread on the comforter.

'You can't *plan* for happiness ever. You've got to figure out what makes you happy now.'

Her faint, bloodless response seemed to come from somewhere else. 'What if nothing does?'

He sat down next to her on the bed. 'Something will, sweetie.'

When she began to cry, he laid his hand gently on the back of her neck. She curled into his chest, feeling eight years old again, spilling big, ridiculous tears down the front of that ridiculous shirt.

Jamie came loping into the room with a plastic bag. 'Hi guys . . . oh . . . sorry.'

'No problem,' she said, yanking a Kleenex from the bedside table. 'Come on in.' She dabbed at her eyes, blew her nose noisily, cast a quick glance at Will. 'Whatcha got?' she asked Jamie.

'*Lethal Weapon One.*'

'Ugh.'

'I know,' said Jamie, 'but we can always put it on hold and look at Mel Gibson's butt.'

She laughed extravagantly, aglow with relief, giddy from the sudden, miraculous lifting of a terrible weight. 'What's for dinner? Shall I make my lasagna?'

Jamie looked confused. 'Will said you were leaving.'

'He was wrong,' she said.

Will just shrugged at his lover. 'I was wrong.'

After dinner, while Will and Jamie changed into their nightshirts, she skulked off to the bedroom, where she flopped on the bed, kicked off her shoes and phoned the number in Maui Alec had given her. Predictably enough, it turned out to be the Hyatt Regency, another atrium from hell with fiberglass waterfalls and resident flamingos.

There was no answer when they rang his room. She envisaged him down by one of the pools, ordering a Scorpion, hustling the cocktail waitress, bragging to anyone who'd listen about the major deal he'd just closed in Philadelphia. She left a message for him to call her in San Francisco as soon as possible, almost certain he'd know what that meant. For the first time in weeks she felt a little sorry for him.

# Southern Skies

## DAVID MALOUF

*To Judith Rodriguez and Thomas W. Shapcott*

From the beginning he was a stumbling-block, the Professor. I had always thought of him as an old man, as one thinks of one's parents as old, but he can't in those days have been more than fifty. Squat, powerful, with a good deal of black hair on his wrists, he was what was called a 'ladies man' – though that must have been far in the past and in another country. What he practised now was a formal courtliness, a clicking of heels and kissing of plump fingers that was the extreme form of a set of manners that our parents clung to because it belonged, along with much else, to the Old Country, and which we young people, for the same reason, found it imperative to reject. The Professor had a 'position' – he taught mathematics to apprentices on day-release. He was proof that a breakthrough into the new world was not only possible, it was a fact. Our parents having come to a place where their qualifications in medicine or law were unacceptable, had been forced to take work as labourers or factory-hands or to keep dingy shops; but we, their clever sons and daughters, would find our way back to the safe professional classes. For our parents there was deep sorrow in all this, and the Professor offered hope. We were invited to see in him both the embodiment of a noble past and a glimpse of what, with hard work and a little luck or grace, we might claim from the future.

He was always the special guest.

'Here, pass the Professor this slice of Torte,' my mother would say, choosing the largest piece and piling it with cream, or, 'Here, take the Professor a nice cold Pils, and see you hand it to him proper now and don't spill none on the way': this on one of those community outings we used to go to in the early years, when half a dozen families would gather at Suttons Beach with a crate of beer bottles in straw jackets and a spread of homemade sausage and cabbage rolls. Aged six or seven, in my knitted bathing-briefs, and watching out in my bare feet for bindy-eye, I would set out over the grass to where the great man and my father, easy now in shirtsleeves and braces, would be pursuing one of their interminable arguments. My father had been a lawyer in the Old Country but worked now at the Vulcan Can Factory. He was passionately interested in philosophy, and the Professor was his only companion on those breathless flights that were, along with the music of Beethoven and Mahler, his sole consolation on the raw and desolate shore where he was marooned. Seeing me come wobbling towards them with the Pils – which I had slopped a little – held breast-high before me, all golden in the sun, he would look startled, as if I were a spirit of the place he had failed to allow for. It was the Professor who recognized the nature of my errand. 'Ah, how kind,' he would say. 'Thank you, my dear. And thank the good mama too. Anton, you are a lucky man.' And my father, reconciled to the earth again, would smile and lay his hand very gently on the nape of my neck while I blushed and squirmed.

The Professor had no family – or not in Australia. He lived alone in a house he had built to his own design. It was of pinewood, as in the Old Country, and in defiance of local custom was surrounded by trees – natives. There was also a swimming pool where he exercised twice a day. I went there occasionally with my father, to collect him for an outing, and had sometimes peered at it through a glass door; but we were never formally invited. The bachelor did not entertain. He was always the guest, and what his visits meant to me, as to the children of a dozen other families, was that I must be especially careful of my manners, see that my shoes were properly polished, my nails clean, my hair combed, my tie straight, my socks pulled up, and that when questioned about school or about the games I played I should give my answers clearly, precisely, and without making faces.

So there he was all through my childhood, an intimidating presence, and a heavy reminder of that previous world; where his family owned a castle, and where he had been, my mother insisted, a real scholar.

Time passed and as the few close-knit families of our community moved to distant suburbs and lost contact with one another, we children were released from restriction. It was easy for our parents to give in to new ways now that others were not watching. Younger brothers failed to inherit our confirmation suits with their stiff white collars and cuffs. We no longer went to examinations weighed down with holy medals, or silently invoked, before putting pen to paper, the good offices of the Infant of Prague – whose influence, I decided, did not extend to Brisbane, Queensland. Only the Professor remained as a last link.

'I wish, when the Professor comes,' my mother would complain, 'that you try to speak better. The vowels! For my sake, darling, but also for your father, because we want to be proud of you,' and she would try to detain me as, barefoot, in khaki shorts and an old T-shirt, already thirteen, I wriggled from her embrace. 'And put shoes on, or sandals at least, and a nice clean shirt. I don't want that the Professor think we got an Arab for a son. And your Scout belt! And comb your hair a little, my darling – please!'

She kissed me before I could pull away. She was shocked, now that she saw me through the Professor's eyes, as how far I had grown from the little gentleman I might have been, all neatly suited and shod and brushed and polished, if they had never left the Old Country, or if she and my father had been stricter with me in this new one.

The fact is, I had succeeded, almost beyond my own expectations, in making myself indistinguishable from the roughest of my mates at school. My mother must have wondered at times if I could ever be smoothed out and civilized again, with my broad accent, my slang, my feet toughened and splayed from going barefoot. I was spoiled and wilful and ashamed of my parents. My mother knew it, and now, in front of the Professor, it was her turn to be ashamed. To assert my independence, or to show them that I did not care, I was never so loutish, I never slouched or mumbled or scowled so darkly as when the Professor appeared. Even my father, who was too dreamily involved with his own thoughts to notice me on most occasions, was aware of it and shocked. He complained to my mother, who shook her head and cried. I felt magnificently justified, and the next time the Professor made his appearance I swaggered even more outrageously and gave every indication of being an incorrigible tough.

The result was not at all what I had had in mind. Far from being repelled by my roughness the Professor seemed charmed. The more I showed off and embarrassed my parents, the more he encouraged me. My excesses delighted him. He was entranced.

He really was, as we younger people had always thought, a caricature of a man. You could barely look at him without laughing, and we had all become expert, even the girls, at imitating his hunched stance, his accent (which was at once terribly foreign and terribly English) and the way he held his stubby fingers when, at the end of a meal, he dipped sweet biscuits into wine and popped them whole into his mouth. My own imitations were designed to torment my mother.

'Oh you shouldn't!' she would whine, suppressing another explosion of giggles. 'You mustn't! Oh stop it now, your father will see – he would be offended. The Professor is a fine man. May you have such a head on your shoulders one day, and such a position.'

'Such a head on my shoulders,' I mimicked, hunching my back like a stork so that I had no neck, and she would try to cuff me, and miss as I ducked away.

I was fifteen and beginning to spring up out of podgy childhood into clean-limbed, tumultuous adolescence. By staring for long hours into mirrors behind locked doors, by taking stock of myself in shop windows, and from the looks of some of the girls at school, I had discovered that I wasn't at all bad-looking, might even be good-looking, and was already tall and well-made. I had chestnut hair like my mother and my skin didn't freckle in the sun but turned heavy gold. There was a whole year between fifteen and sixteen when I was fascinated by the image of myself I could get back from people simply by playing up to them – it scarcely mattered whom: teachers, girls, visitors to the house like the Professor, passers-by in the street. I was obsessed with myself, and lost no opportunity of putting my powers to the test.

Once or twice in earlier days, when I was playing football on Saturday afternoon, my father and the Professor had appeared on the sidelines, looking in after a walk. Now, as if by accident, the Professor came alone. When I came trotting in to collect my bike, dishevelled, still spattered and streaked from the game, he would be waiting. He just happened, yet again, to be passing, and had a book for me to take home, or a message: he would be calling for my father at eight and could I please remind him, or yes, he would be coming next night to play Solo. He was very formal on these occasions, but I felt his interest; and sometimes, without thinking of anything more than the warm sense of myself it gave me to command his attention, I would walk part of the way home with him, wheeling my bike and chatting about nothing very important: the game, or what I had done with my holiday, or since he was a dedicated star-gazer, the new comet that had appeared. As these meetings increased I got to be more familiar with him. Sometimes, when two or three of the others were there (they had come to recognize him and teased me a little, making faces and jerking their heads as he made his way, hunched and short-sighted, to where we were towelling ourselves at the tap) I would for their benefit show off a little, without at first realizing, in my reckless passion to be admired, that I was exceeding all bounds and that they now included me as well as the Professor in their humorous contempt. I was mortified. To ease myself back into their good opinion I passed him off as a family nuisance, whose attentions I knew were comic but whom I was leading on for my own amusement. This was acceptable enough and I was soon restored to popularity, but felt doubly treacherous. He was, after all, my father's closest friend, and there was as well that larger question of the Old Country. I burned with shame, but was too cowardly to do more than brazen things out.

For all my crudeness and arrogance I had a great desire to act nobly, and in this business of the Professor I had miserably failed. I decided to cut my losses. As soon as he appeared now, and had announced his message, I would mount my bike, sling my football boots over my shoulder and pedal away. My one fear was that he might inquire what the trouble was, but of course he did not. Instead he broke of his visits altogether or passed the field without stopping, and I found myself regretting something I had come to depend on – his familiar figure hunched like a bird on the sidelines, our talks, some fuller sense of my own presence to add at the end of the game to the immediacy of my limbs after violent exercise.

Looking back on those days I see myself as a kind of centaur, half-boy, half-bike, forever wheeling down suburban streets under the poincianas, on my way to football practice or the library or to a meeting of the little group of us, boys and girls, that came together on someone's veranda in the evenings after tea.

I might come across the Professor then on his after-dinner stroll, and as often as not he would be accompanied by my father, who would stop me and demand (partly, I thought, to impress the Professor) where I was off to or where I had been; insisting, with more than his usual force, that I come home right away, with no argument.

On other occasions, pedalling past his house among the trees, I would catch a glimpse of him with his telescope on the roof. He might raise a hand and wave if he recognized me; and sprinting away, crouched low over the handlebars, I would feel, or imagine I felt, that the telescope had been lowered and was following me to the end of the street, losing me for a time, then picking me up again two streets further on as I flashed away under the bunchy leaves.

I spent long hours cycling back and forth between our house

and my girlfriend Helen's or to Ross McDowell or Jimmy Lar-
wood's, my friends from school, and the Professor's house was
always on the route.

I think of those days now as being all alike, and the nights also:
the days warmish, still, endlessly without event, and the nights
quivering with expectancy but also uneventful, heavy with the
scent of jasmine and honeysuckle and lighted by enormous stars.
But what I am describing, of course, is neither a time nor a place
but the mood of my own bored, expectant, uneventful adolescence. I was always abroad and waiting for something significant
to occur, for life somehow to declare itself and catch me up. I rode
my bike in slow circles or figures-of-eight, took it for sprints across
the gravel of the park, or simply hung motionless in the saddle,
balanced and waiting.

Nothing ever happened. In the dark of front verandas we
lounged and swapped stories, heard gossip, told jokes, or played
show-poker and smoked. One night each week I went to Helen's
and we sat a little scared of one another in her garden-swing,
touching in the dark. Helen liked me better, I thought, than I liked
her – I had that power over her – and it was this more than
anything else that attracted me, though I found it scary as well.
For fear of losing me she might have gone to any one of the
numbers that in those days marked the stages of sexual progress
and could be boasted about, in a way that seemed shameful
afterwards, in locker-rooms or round the edge of the pool. I could
have taken us both to 6, 8, 10, but what then? The numbers were
not infinite.

I rode around watching my shadow flare off gravel; sprinted,
hung motionless, took the rush of warm air into my shirt; afraid
that when the declaration came, it too, like the numbers, might be
less than infinite. I didn't want to discover the limits of the world.
Restlessly impelled towards some future that would at last offer
me my real self, I nevertheless drew back, happy for the moment,
even in my unhappiness, to be half-boy, half-bike, half aimless
energy and half a machine that could hurtle off at a moment's
notice in any one of a hundred directions. Away from things – but

away, most of all, from my self. My own presence had begun to be a source of deep dissatisfaction to me, my vanity, my charm, my falseness, my preoccupation with sex. I was sick of myself and longed for the world to free me by making its own rigorous demands and declaring at last what I must be.

One night, in our warm late winter, I was riding home past the Professor's house when I saw him hunched as usual beside his telescope, but too absorbed on this occasion to be aware of me.

I paused at the end of the drive, wondering what it was that he saw on clear nights like this, that was invisible to me when I leaned my head back and filled my gaze with the sky.

The stars seemed palpably close. In the high September blueness it was as if the odour of jasmine blossoms had gathered there in a single shower of white. You might have been able to catch the essence of it floating down, as sailors, they say, can smell new land whole days before they first catch sight of it.

What I was catching, in fact, was the first breath of change – a change of season. From the heights I fell suddenly into deep depression, one of those sweet-sad glooms of adolescence that are like a bodiless drifting out of yourself into the immensity of things, when you are aware as never again – or never so poignantly – that time is moving swiftly on, that a school year is very nearly over and childhood finished, that you will have to move up a grade at football into a tougher class – shifts that against the vastness of space are minute, insignificant, but at that age solemnly felt.

I was standing astride the bike, staring upwards, when I became aware that my name was being called, and for the second or third time. I turned my bike into the drive with its border of big-leafed saxifrage and came to where the Professor, his hand on the telescope, was leaning out over the roof.

'I have some books for your father,' he called. 'Just come to the gate and I will get them for you.'

The gate was wooden, and the fence, which made me think of a stockade, was of raw slabs eight feet high, stained reddish-brown. He leaned over the low parapet and dropped a set of keys.

'It's the thin one,' he told me. 'You can leave your bike in the yard.' He meant the paved courtyard inside, where I rested it easily against the wall. Beyond, and to the left of the pine-framed house, which was stained the same colour as the fence, was a garden taken up almost entirely by the pool. It was overgrown with dark tropical plants, monstera, hibiscus, banana-palms with their big purplish flowers, glossily pendulous on stalks, and fixed to the pailing-fence like trophies in wads of bark, elk-horn, tree-orchids, showers of delicate maidenhair. It was too cold for swimming, but the pool was filled and covered with a shifting scum of jacaranda leaves that had blown in from the street, where the big trees were stripping to bloom.

I went round the edge of the pool and a light came on, reddish, in one of the inner rooms. A moment later the Professor himself appeared, tapping for attention at a glass door.

'I have the books right here,' he said briskly; but when I stood hesitating in the dark beyond the threshold, he shifted his feet and added: 'But maybe you would like to come in a moment and have a drink. Coffee. I could make some. Or beer. Or a Coke if you prefer it. I have Coke.'

I had never been here alone, and never, even with my father, to this side of the house. When we came to collect the Professor for an outing we had always waited in the tiled hallway while he rushed about with one arm in the sleeve of his overcoat laying out saucers for cats, and it was to the front door, in later years, that I had delivered bowls of gingerbread fish that my mother had made specially because she knew he liked it, or cabbage rolls or herring. I had never been much interested in what lay beyond the hallway, with its fierce New Guinea masks, all tufted hair and boar's tusks, and the Old Country chest that was just like our own. Now, with the books already in my hands, I hesitated and looked past him into the room.

'All right. If it's no trouble.'

'No no, no trouble at all!' He grinned, showing his teeth with their extravagant caps. 'I am delighted. Really! Just leave the books there. You see they are tied with string, quite easy for you

I'm sure, even on the bike. Sit where you like. Anywhere. I'll get the drink.'

'Beer then,' I said boldly, and my voice cracked, destroying what I had hoped might be the setting of our relationship on a clear, man-to-man basis that would wipe out the follies of the previous year. I coughed, cleared my throat, and said again 'Beer, thanks,' and sat abruptly on a sofa that was too low and left me prone and sprawling.

He stopped a moment and considered, as if I had surprised him by crossing a second threshold.

'Well then, if it's to be beer, I shall join you. Maybe you are also hungry. I could make a sandwich.'

'No, no thank you, they're expecting me. Just the beer.'

He went out, his slippers slushing over the tiles, and I shifted immediately to a straight-backed chair opposite and took the opportunity to look around.

There were rugs on the floor, old threadbare Persians, and low down, all round the walls, stacks of the heavy seventy-eights I carried home when my father borrowed them: sonatas by Beethoven, symphonies by Sibelius and Mahler. Made easy by the Professor's absence, I got up and wandered round. On every open surface, the glass table-top, the sideboard, the long mantel of the fireplace, were odd bits and pieces that he must have collected in his travels: lumps of coloured quartz, a desert rose, slabs of clay with fern or fish fossils in them, glass paperweights, snuff-boxes, meerschaum pipes of fantastic shape – one a Saracen's head, another the torso of a woman, like a ship's figurehead with full breasts and golden nipples – bits of Baltic amber, decorated sherds of pottery, black on terracotta, and one unbroken object, a little earthenware lamp that when I examined it more closely turned out to be a phallic grotesque. I had just discovered what it actually was when the Professor stepped into the room. Turning swiftly to a framed photograph on the wall above, I found myself peering into a stretch of the Old Country, a foggy, sepia world that I recognized immediately from similar photographs at home.

'Ah,' he said, setting the tray down on an empty chair, 'you have discovered my weakness.' He switched on another lamp. 'I have tried, but I am too sentimental. I cannot part with them.'

The photograph, I now observed, was one of three. They were all discoloured with foxing on the passe-partout mounts, and the glass of one was shattered, but so neatly that not a single splinter had shifted in the frame.

The one I was staring at was of half a dozen young men in military uniform. It might have been from the last century, but there was a date in copperplate: 1921. Splendidly booted and sashed and frogged, and hieratically stiff, with casque helmets under their arms, swords tilted at the thigh, white gloves tucked into braided epaulettes, they were a chorus line from a Ruritanian operetta. They were also, as I knew, the heroes of a lost but unforgotten war.

'You recognize me?' the Professor asked.

I looked again. It was difficult. All the young men strained upright with the same martial hauteur, wore the same little clipped moustaches, had the same flat hair parted in the middle and combed in wings over their ears. Figures from the past can be as foreign, as difficult to identify individually, as the members of another race. I took the plunge, set my forefinger against the frame, and turned to the Professor for confirmation. He came to my side and peered.

'No,' he said sorrowfully. 'But the mistake is entirely under-standable. He was my great friend, almost a brother. I am here. This is me. On the left.'

He considered himself, the slim assured figure, chin slightly tilted, eyes fixed ahead, looking squarely out of a class whose privileges – inherent in every point of the stance, the uniform, the polished accoutrements – were not to be questioned, and from the ranks of an army that was invincible. The proud caste no longer existed. Neither did the army nor the country it was meant to defend, except in the memory of people like the Professor and my parents and, in a ghostly way, half a century off in another hemisphere, my own.

He shook his head and made a clucking sound. 'Well,' he said firmly, 'it's a long time ago. It is foolish of me to keep such things. We should live for the present. Or like you younger people', bringing the conversation back to me, 'for the future.'

I found it easier to pass to the other photographs.

In one, the unsmiling officer appeared as an even younger man, caught in an informal, carefully posed moment with a group of ladies. He was clean-shaven and lounging on the grass in a striped blazer; beside him a discarded boater – very English. The ladies, more decorously disposed, wore long dresses with hats and ribbons. Neat little slippers peeped out under their skirts.

'Yes, yes,' he muttered, almost impatient now, 'that too. Summer holidays – who can remember where? And the other a walking trip.'

I looked deep into a high meadow, with broken cloud-drift in the dip below. Three young men in shorts, maybe schoolboys, were climbing on the far side of the wars. There were flowers in the foreground, glowingly out of focus, and it was this picture whose glass was shattered; it was like looking through a brilliant spider's web into a picturebook landscape that was utterly familiar, though I could never have been there. *That is the place*, I thought. *That is the land my parents mean when they say 'the Old Country': the country of childhood and first love that they go back to in their sleep and which I have no memory of, though I was born there. Those flowers are the ones, precisely those, that blossom in the songs they sing.* And immediately I was back in my mood of just a few minutes ago, when I had stood out there gazing up at the stars. *What is it,* I asked myself, *that I will remember and want to preserve, when in years to come I think of the Past? What will be important enough?* For what the photographs had led me back to, once again, was myself. It was always the same. No matter how hard I tried to think my way out into other people's lives, into the world beyond me, the feelings I discovered were my own.

'Come. Sit,' the Professor said, 'and drink your beer. And do eat one of these sandwiches. It's very good rye bread, from the only shop, I go all the way to South Brisbane for it. And Gürken. I seem to remember you like them.'

'What do you do up on the roof?' I asked, my mouth full of bread and beer, feeling uneasy again now that we were sitting with nothing to fix on.

'I make observations, you know. The sky, which looks so still, is always in motion, full of drama if you understand how to read it. Like looking into a pond. Hundreds of events happening right under your eyes, except that most of what we see is already finished by the time we see it – ages ago – but important just the same. Such large events. Huge! Bigger even than we can imagine. And beautiful, since they unfold, you know, to a kind of music, to numbers of infinite dimension like the ones you deal with in equations at school, but more complex, and entirely visible.'

He was moved as he spoke by an emotion that I could not identify, touched by occasions a million light-years off and still unfolding towards him, in no way personal. The room for a moment lost its tension. I no longer felt myself to be the focus of his interest, or even of my own. I felt liberated, and for the first time the Professor was interesting in his own right, quite apart from the attention he paid me or the importance my parents attached to him.

'Maybe I could come again,' I found myself saying. 'I'd like to see.'

'But of course,' he said, 'any time. Tonight is not good – there is a little haze, but tomorrow if you like. Or any time.'

I nodded. But the moment of easiness had passed. My suggestion, which might have seemed like another move in a game, had brought me back into focus for him and his look was quizzical, defensive. I felt it and was embarrassed, and at the same time saddened. Some truer vision of myself had been in the room for a moment. I had almost grasped it. Now I felt it slipping away as I moved back into my purely physical self.

I put the glass down, not quite empty.

'No thanks, really,' I told him when he indicated the half finished bottle on the tray. 'I should have been home nearly an hour ago. My mother, you know.'

'Ah yes, of course. Well, just call whenever you wish, no need to be formal. Most nights I am observing. It is a very interesting time. Here – let me open the door for you. The books, I see, are a little awkward, but you are so expert on the bicycle I am sure it will be OK.'

I followed him round the side of the pool into the courtyard and there was my bike at its easy angle to the wall, my other familiar and streamlined self. I wheeled it out while he held the gate.

Among my parents' oldest friends were a couple who had recently moved to a new house on the other side of the park, and at the end of winter, in the year I turned seventeen, I sometimes rode over on Sundays to help John clear the big overgrown garden. All afternoon we grubbed out citrus trees that had gone wild, hacked down morning-glory that had grown all over the lower part of the yard, and cut the knee-high grass with a sickle to prepare it for mowing. I enjoyed the work. Stripped down to shorts in the strong sunlight, I slashed and tore at the weeds till my hands blistered, and in a trancelike preoccupation with tough green things that clung to the earth with a fierce tenacity, forgot for a time my own turmoil and lack of roots. It was something to *do*.

John, who worked up ahead, was a dentist. He paid me ten shillings a day for the work, and this, along with my pocket-money, would take Helen and me to the pictures on Saturday night, or to a flash meal at one of the city hotels. We worked all afternoon, while the children, who were four and seven, watched and got in the way. Then about five-thirty Mary would call us for tea.

Mary had been at school with my mother and was the same age, though I could never quite believe it; she had children a whole ten years younger than I was, and I had always called her Mary. She wore bright bangles on her arm, liked to dance at parties, never gave me presents like handkerchiefs or socks, and had always treated me, I thought, as a grown-up. When she called us for tea I went to the garden tap, washed my feet, splashed water over my back that was streaked with soil and sweat and stuck all over with little grass clippings, and was about to buckle on my loose sandals when she said from the doorway where she had been watching: 'Don't bother to get dressed. John hasn't.' She stood there smiling, and I turned away, aware suddenly of how little I had on; and had to use my V-necked sweater to cover an excitement that might otherwise have been immediately apparent in the khaki shorts I was wearing – without underpants because of the heat.

As I came up the steps towards her she stood back to let me pass, and her hand, very lightly, brushed the skin between my shoulder blades.

'You're still wet,' she said.

It seemed odd somehow to be sitting at the table in their elegant dining-room without a shirt; though John was doing it, and was already engaged like the children in demolishing a pile of neat little sandwiches.

I sat at the head of the table with the children noisily grabbing at my left and John on my right drinking tea and slurping it a little, while Mary plied me with raisin-bread and Old Country cookies. I felt red, swollen, confused every time she turned to me, and for some reason it was the children's presence rather than John's that embarrassed me, especially the boy's.

Almost immediately we were finished John got up.

'I'll just go,' he said, 'and do another twenty mintues before it's dark.' It was dark already, but light enough perhaps to go on raking the grass we had cut and were carting to the incinerator. I made to follow. 'It's all right,' he told me. 'I'll finish off. You've earned your money for today.'

'Come and see our animals!' the children yelled, dragging me down the hall to their bedroom, and for ten minutes or so I sat on the floor with them, setting out farm animals and making fences, till Mary, who had been clearing the table, appeared in the doorway.

'Come on now, that's enough, it's bathtime, you kids. Off you go!'

They ran off, already half-stripped, leaving her to pick up their clothes and fold them while I continued to sit cross-legged among the toys, and her white legs, in their green sandals, moved back and forth at eye-level. When she went out I too got up, and stood watching at the bathroom door.

She was sitting on the edge of the bath, soaping the little boy's back, as I remembered my mother doing, while the children splashed and shouted. Then she dried her hands on a towel, very carefully, and I followed her into the unlighted lounge. Beyond the glass wall, in the depths of the garden, John was stooping to gather armfuls of the grass we had cut, and staggering with it to the incinerator.

She sat and patted the place beside her. I followed as in a dream. The children's voices at the end of the hallway were complaining, quarrelling, shrilling. I was sure John could see us through the glass as he came back for another load.

Nothing was said. Her hand moved over my shoulder, down my spine, brushed very lightly, without lingering, over the place where my shorts tented; then rested easily on my thigh. When John came in he seemed unsurprised to find us sitting close in the dark. He went right past us to the drinks cabinet, which suddenly lighted up. I felt exposed and certain now that he must see where her hand was and say something.

All he said was: 'Something to drink, darling?'

Without hurry she got up to help him and they passed back and forth in front of the blazing cabinet, with its mirrors and its rows of bottles and cut-crystal glasses. I was sweating worse than when I had worked in the garden, and began, self-consciously, to haul on the sweater.

I pedalled furiously away, glad to have the cooling air pour over me and to feel free again.

Back there I had been scared – but of what? Of a game in which I might, for once, be the victim – not passive, but with no power to control the moves. I slowed down and considered that, and was, without realizing it, at the edge of something. I rode on in the softening dark. It was good to have the wheels of the bike roll away under me as I rose on the pedals, to feel on my cheeks the warm scent of jasmine that was invisible all round. It was a brilliant night verging on spring. I didn't want it to be over; I wanted to slow things down. I dismounted and walked a little, leading my bike along the grassy edge in the shadow of trees, and without precisely intending it, came on foot to the entrance to the Professor's drive, and paused, looking up beyond the treetops to where he might be installed with his telescope – observing what? What events up there in the infinite sky?

I leaned far back to see. A frozen waterfall it might have been, falling slowly towards me, sending out blown spray that would take centuries, light-years, to break in thunder over my head. Time. What did one moment, one night, a lifespan mean in relation to all that?

'Hullo there!'

It was the Professor. I could see him now, in the moonlight beside the telescope, which he leaned on and which pointed not upward to the heavens but down to where I was standing. It occurred to me, as on previous occasions, that in the few moments of my standing there with my head flung back to the stars, what he might have been observing was *me*. I hesitated, made no decision. Then, out of a state of passive expectancy, willing nothing but waiting poised for my own life to occur; out of a state of being open to the spring night and to the emptiness of the hours between seven and ten when I was expected to be in, or thirteen (was it?) and whatever age I would be when manhood finally came to me; out of my simply being there with my hand on the saddle of the machine, bare-legged, loose-sandalled, going nowhere, I turned into the drive, led my bike up to the stockade gate and waited for him to throw down the keys.

'You know which one it is,' he said, letting them fall. 'Just use the other to come in by the poolside.'

I unlocked the gate, rested my bike against the wall of the courtyard and went round along the edge of the pool. It was clean now but heavy with shadows. I turned the key in the glass door, found my way (though this part of the house was new to me) to the stairs, and climbed to where another door opened straight on to the roof.

'Ah,' he said, smiling. 'So at last! You are here.'

The roof was unwalled but set so deep among trees that it was as if I had stepped out of the city altogether into some earlier, more darkly-wooded era. Only lighted windows, hanging detached in the dark, showed where houses, where neighbours were.

He fixed the telescope for me and I moved into position. 'There,' he said, 'what you can see now is Jupiter with its four moons – you see? – all in line, and with the bands across its face.'

I saw. Later it was Saturn with its rings and the lower of the two pointers to the cross, Alpha Centauri, which was not one star but two. It was miraculous. From the moment below when I had looked up at a cascade of light that was still ages off, I might have been catapulted twenty thousand years into the nearer past, or into my own future. Solid spheres hovered above me, tiny balls of matter moving in concert like the atoms we drew in chemistry, held together by invisible lines of force; and I thought oddly that if I were to lower the telescope now to where I had been standing at the entrance to the drive I would see my own puzzled, upturned face, but as a self I had already outgrown and abandoned, not minutes but aeons back. He shifted the telescope and I caught my breath. One after another, constellations I had known since childhood as points of light to be joined up in the mind (like those picture-puzzles children make, pencilling in the scattered dots till Snow White and the Seven Dwarfs appear, or an old jalopy), came together now, not as an imaginary panhandle or bull's head or belt and sword, but at some depth of vision I hadn't known I possessed, as blossoming abstractions, equations luminously exploding out of their own depths, brilliantly solving themselves and playing the results in my head as a real and visible music. I felt a power in myself that might actually burst out at my ears, and at the same time saw myself, from *out there*, as just a figure with his eye to a lens. I had a clear sense of being one more hard little point in the immensity – but part of it, a source of light like all those others – and was aware for the first time of the grainy reality of my own life, and then, a fact of no large significance, of the certainty of my death; but in some dimension where those terms were too vague to be relevant. It was at the point where my self ended and the rest of it began that Time, or Space, showed its richness to me. I was overwhelmed.

Slowly, from so far out, I drew back, re-entered the present and was aware again of the close suburban dark – of its moving now in the shape of a hand. I must have known all along that it was there, working from the small of my back to my belly, up the inside of my thigh, but it was of no importance, I was too far off. Too many larger events were unfolding for me to break away and ask, as I might have, 'What are you doing?'

I must have come immediately. But when the stars blurred in my eyes it was with tears, and it was the welling of this deeper salt, filling my eyes and rolling down my cheeks, that was the real overflow of the occasion. I raised my hand to brush them away and it was only then that I was aware, once again, of the Professor. I looked at him as from a distance. He was getting to his feet, and his babble of concern, alarm, self-pity, sentimental recrimination, was incomprehensible to me. I couldn't see what he meant.

'No no, it's nothing,' I assured him, turning aside to button my shorts. 'It was nothing. Honestly.' I was unwilling to say more in case he misunderstood what I did not understand myself.

We stood on opposite sides of the occasion. Nothing of what he had done could make the slightest difference to me, I was untouched: youth is too physical to accord very much to that side of things. But what I had *seen* – what he had led me to see – my bursting into the life of things – I would look back on that as the real beginning of my existence, as the entry into a vocation, and nothing could diminish the gratitude I felt for it. I wanted, in the immense seriousness and humility of this moment, to tell him so, but I lacked the words, and silence was fraught with all the wrong ones.

'I have to go now,' was what I said.

'Very well. Of course.'

He looked hopeless. He might have been waiting for me to strike him a blow – not a physical one. He stood quietly at the gateway while I wheeled out the bike.

I turned then and faced him, and without speaking, offered

him, very formally, my hand. He took it and we shook – as if, in the magnanimity of my youth, I had agreed to overlook his misdemeanour or forgive him. That misapprehension too was a weight I would have to bear.

Carrying it with me, a heavy counterpoise to the extraordinary lightness that was my whole life, I bounced unsteadily over the dark tufts of the driveway and out on to the road.

# The Changes of Those Terrible Years

## ADAM MARS-JONES

Nobody believes I've really put the house on the market. Someone even said it was a monument. People seem shocked, and it doesn't seem to occur to them that I might have had enough. I'm not allowed to have any doubts or weaknesses, that's what it amounts to. People ask me what I'm going to do now, but they think I'm joking when I say that I used to share a small flat with a friend in Bloomsbury, and what I'd really like to do is move back there.

I'm not joking, though of course it's a silly idea. My flatmate – that's all he was, it was simply a convenient arrangement – wasn't phased when I moved out, and we haven't kept in touch. But his habits were so regular that I have the feeling I could plot his progress from year to year.

Every Saturday he would tackle a new classic of French provincial cookery for a dinner party, working methodically through the regions. He liked to work alone, though if he had chosen a really ambitious menu he might ask me to do some simple preparation. And now I have the idea that with a calendar, a map and a copy of his chosen cookery-book, I could bring myself up to date, and arrive at what used to be our front door one Saturday night, bringing wines that would perfectly chime with each intricate course.

It's odd to have this little pang of missing a nest that didn't suit me all that well, and that I left with hardly a second thought. But

I've learned to indulge myself when little fantasies like this occur to me, and not to mistake them for real needs. When I need help, I will ask for it.

It's three weeks now since Anthony died. I seem to be going through a phase where I need to go out a lot, which you'd think would mean that I want to be with people. But if anyone tries to talk to me, I go all charming for a few minutes, and then I find some way of putting them off.

Things have changed since the last time I was in the habit of going out – long ago, before I had found myself a circle of friends. I remember a time when with a little effort you could look as if you'd put on the first thing that came to hand. Not any more. There used to be *sweaters*, pubs full of sweaters. Now you have to get everything right before people will even ignore you properly.

People do come up to me, and I should be grateful for that, even though they always ask about the house, and tell me how much they admire me. They tell me I look well, and that what I'm doing is marvellous. I suppose what I'm really looking for when I go out is someone who will give me permission to collapse, someone who will say, you're killing yourself, put your own needs first for a change. It never happens. Even when they know me hardly at all, people have a vested interest in my ability to cope.

One young man even asked me about Anthony. He was wearing a baseball cap and a sort of anorak, with a row of fluorescent green bicycle clips all up one arm. It was a shock to hear the name mentioned, of course, but it was worth it if this was a friend of Anthony's – though of course he wasn't, just someone who had heard about what had happened. He was roughly the same age as Anthony, I suppose, and I tried to take an interest in him, but it was an effort. Illness had taken Anthony out of his age-group somehow. It often seems to do that. This young man seemed shallow by contrast, politely aware of an epidemic that had always been there in the background of his young world.

He wanted to know how I felt about Anthony dying in hospital and not in the house. It's no secret that I wanted to nurse Anthony to the end, and I expect he was only trying to be sympathetic, to draw me out, but I found myself getting angry. Every time he asked a painful question – and all his questions were painful – he took a long sip of his beer, looking down into his glass so he wouldn't have to look at me while I answered.

Then he asked me if it was true I was selling the house, and this time he looked at me squarely. He told me he thought it was out of character – as if he knew what my character was – and that I'd regret it. It's only a house, I told him, and it's *my* house. And who'll help when I can't cope? Maybe I will, he said, and he wrote down his telephone number on the back of a book of matches.

I dare say the urge to flirt was there at the back of my mind all the time we were talking, shamefully enough, but if so I soon suppressed it. I started talking about what Anthony had gone through with CMV – that's cytomegalovirus – and after that the conversation could only fizzle out.

I took the tube home. I used to find public transport exasperating, but I've spent so much time since then as a sort of amateur ambulance driver that riding on a bus or a tube is a real pleasure. I enjoy not being responsible for anyone but myself; if I'm late, that's my business. Let someone else take the responsibility. But it was also a tube journey, once, that changed my life. It was on a tube train that I started to face the changes of these terrible years.

I was going on holiday, not because I needed one but because it was time to take one. I worked for a well-established agency that specialized in representing musicians. We had a number of successful performers on our books, and even one or two outstanding ones. I enjoyed my job. I believe I was the only partner with no musical ambitions of my own. Certainly at the firm's Christmas party each year two of my colleagues would be led protesting to the piano to attempt some Schubert four-hands. Despite their protests at the stiffness of their fingers and the limited time they had had for practice, they were really not very good.

I think my being free of that kind of self-deception made me good at my job, although it also made it easy for me to leave it when the time came. What I most enjoyed, and what became my professional speciality, was overseeing the beginning of a young singer's career. When I heard a young voice for the first time, I seemed to take a photograph of it, but a photograph that was also an X-ray and a clairvoyant's reading.

I closed my eyes and I could see the characteristics of a voice, its strengths but also its temptations. I knew which singers were basing themselves on the wrong models, dreaming of a sound that was impossibly big or pure. The limitations of the physical apparatus must be faced squarely, but then transcended. It's actually the limitations of the voice's owner, rather than the voice itself, that most often impose artificial boundaries on a singing career.

I got on exceptionally well with the singers I represented, although our priorities were a little different. They thought that The Voice made them important. To me, it was The Voice that made them unimportant as people. Nothing in their personalities must be allowed to impede its development. But in practice our approaches were compatible. With as much tact as I could muster, I set myself to reveal the musical self that their selfishness would otherwise hide from them.

Why would I need a holiday from that? Well, perhaps I did. Since then I have discovered that people can be exhausted, and keep the fact a secret from themselves. At any rate, a holiday was not what I got.

I struggled out to Heathrow on the tube, leaving what I thought was plenty of time before my flight, though admittedly not the absurd stretch of hours that the airlines stipulate so solemnly. I had never had any trouble before. At Heathrow I was told that economy was overbooked, which sounded like good news to me. I'd heard from friends how much more pleasant a trip they'd had when they were bumped up into business class. Except that it turned out that business was full up by now, and they weren't going to start a revolution by bumping me all the way up to first. The woman at the check-in counter offered me the use of a tatty lounge until she could secure me a seat, and that was as far as she was prepared to go.

The tatty lounge was full of mood music, but it wasn't the music for my mood. Friends were expecting me in New York, but there was no urgency to that. I couldn't claim that I was being kept from some urgent appointment. I couldn't work up my irritation into something magnificent, but nor could I bring it down into evenness of temper.

I had also left behind my fancy camera, newly bought, in the flat, but I like to think I wasn't just going back to fetch it by getting back on a tube heading eastwards, and I don't mention the camera when I tell people the story. If I was sure I was coming back to Heathrow, would I have carried all my luggage back to town, when I could have checked it in or left it in a locker?

At Earls Court a man got on the tube, sat in the seat next to me, and burst into tears. I recognized him. He had been a guest at one of my room-mate's regional feasts, though I didn't exchange more than a few words with him. I was on *bain-marie* duty that night, tending a beautiful smooth sauce over a flame so low it was more an idea than a fact, and ready to shout for help at the first sign of curdling. Then at dinner we were seated far from each other. I can't say I minded too much; I didn't find him immediately attractive. He wore his hair at a sort of compromise length, wanting to look smart and conventional in the office by day, and all bristly and animal in the clubs at night. Of course it looked silly both ways, whether he was dressed casual–smart, the way I first saw him, or in office drag as he was now, his narrow shoulders heaving beneath the pinstripes.

No one in the carriage was looking at the crying man. Why are the English so terrified of tears? Perhaps my upright fellow citizens were afraid that if they paid the man any attention he might tell his sob-story, or even produce a banjo, sing some show tunes and pass round a hat.

Since that time I have shed tears in public often enough myself, and have found that I am suddenly invisible. Once, in a café, I cried enough to feel better, and I wanted another cappuccino, but I couldn't attract the waitress's attention. I couldn't get out of the well-mannered pit that had been dug for me.

Now, in the tube train, I put my hand on the man's knee. 'Hello
. . . Dougie, isn't it? What's the matter?'

Then it all came out. He was on his way to visit an ex-lover of
his, who had Aids. He didn't need to explain what Aids was. The
newspapers had just started to go mad about it all. This ex-lover,
Shawn, had discharged himself from hospital early after a bout of
pneumonia, because the ward he was on was the same one where
*his* lover had died three months before. Now he was at home
alone, which didn't sound a lot better psychologically, and in
need of looking after. Meanwhile Dougie's current lover, terrified
of infection, had forbidden him to do any visiting, and said he
would lock Dougie out if he was stupid enough to go anywhere
near the sick man. So Dougie was taking days off work, without
telling his lover, to do what he could for Shawn, but he knew he
couldn't go on for ever, or he'd lose his job.

I couldn't believe there was no help to be had. 'Isn't there
anything the council can do?'

'I keep on phoning. But the moment they hear what the matter
is, they say they'll phone back, and then they don't.'

'Isn't there some sort of charity?'

'There's one just starting up. They hope to have some volunteers trained soon. In a month or so. But I can't do much more for
Shawn, ex-lover or no ex-lover.'

I squeezed his knee. 'It must be very distressing for you.'

'Oh, it's not that,' he said. 'But he treated me like shit when we
were together, and he treats me like shit now. Sometimes when
I'm making up some Build-Up for him, he's just so horrible that I
want to pour it down the sink, and let him stay just as skinny as he
is.'

I don't normally have much patience with messy lives. Does it
sound smug if I say that I saw through the seventies and its
morality before most people? I can't help that. I tired fairly early of
people boasting about their open relationships, and then complaining when that same openness let everything they could have
valued trickle away. The word *open* began to sound warning bells
long before it became apparent that people were leaving them-

selves open to more than bad behaviour. I would almost flinch when I heard the word.

Perhaps it was necessary for me to be out of step with the old habits to find my place in the world that came afterwards. I can live with that. I don't think it was any more sensible to have a different man in your bed every weekend than, well, to recreate a new masterpiece of French cooking every Saturday night.

But of course I didn't judge Dougie, as the tears dried on his face in the seat next to me on the tube. I felt for him very much, and for the situation he was in. This all happened a long time before there was such a thing as an antibody test, and Dougie's life, like the lives of everyone like him, would have been a nightmare of anxiety even if no special demands were being made of him.

But I wasn't considering Dougie's position so much as my own. Looking down, I could see arranged round me, properly tagged and labelled, all the burdens of leisure. On a hanger inside one of my cases, I remember, visible through a sort of cellophane window, was a navy blazer with gold buttons that made me look smart and even slim, but somehow never seemed right for London. I had turned my back on London, but New York wouldn't have me. The rejection was only temporary, but it lasted long enough to make me reconsider my trip. A few phone calls would dispose of the welcoming committee, and I would be free, if I dared, to meddle with a stranger's destiny.

I told Dougie that I would do what I could for his friend Shawn, for a few days at least, but only if Shawn agreed. I wasn't going to foist myself on anyone. We arranged that I would wait in a coffee shop round the corner from where Shawn lived, in Pimlico.

Dougie was back in a few minutes, and just watching him through the coffee shop window, as he walked purposefully down the street, gave me my first dangerous taste of feeling useful. He talked non-stop as we covered the short distance. He led me up some steps to the entrance of a large wedding-cake house, with eight buzzers by the front door, and showed me into a spacious ground floor flat, the walls thickly covered with modern paintings.

I had a moment of belated panic, at the idea that my body might harbour some final resistance I was unaware of, which would make me spin around in spite of myself and march back down the steps. But Shawn's hand as I shook it conveyed only the usual neutral human messages.

Shawn had put on a bow-tie in my honour, a task that had clearly exhausted him. I found my eyes drawn irresistibly to his Adam's apple, making its reflex journeys up and down an unrefreshed throat. He leaned heavily on a beautifully carved stick which might otherwise have seemed an affectation.

There were in fact, as I found out, traces of dandyism about him even in illness. He liked to wear a kimono during the day, if he was well enough. He had several, of an antique silk almost as fragile as himself, so that an awkward elbow-movement while he was putting it on could easily rip the luminous fabric.

Dougie took a couple of dirty glasses into the kitchen, and left. Then we were alone.

With the experience I have now, I'm sure I would handle that meeting differently. I would mentally set a time limit, for one thing – an hour, an hour and a half at most – so that I didn't unduly tax someone who was forever paying off an overdraft of energy. And I would find some tactful way of stopping him from playing the host, struggling to show me where the sheets for the spare bed were, when I could have found them myself with the minimum of guidance. But at the time we were both unwilling to give up the habits that defended our identities. We were in no hurry to mix our lives in together, by chance and in crisis.

It was only later that I realized how unusual it was for Shawn to strike up such an immediate rapport with someone. When Dougie paid his occasional visits, taking half-days off work or hurrying across in his lunch hour so as to keep his lover in the dark, he turned out to be telling no more than the truth. Shawn treated him like a dog. Shawn expected him to read his mind, and was always tetchily interrupting. I had beginner's luck. But I was also shrewd enough to realize that Dougie brought out all the sourness in Shawn, leaving me to deal with a character surprisingly sweet. I made it clear to Dougie that his visits were necessary to the running of the household, although he might think that his attention was repaid only with scorn. I don't know how long I could have gone on dealing with Shawn, if he had turned the sharpness of his tongue on me.

Shawn and I soon slipped into a rhythm and a routine. Though I had sacrificed my trip to New York, there was a stubborn atmosphere of holiday about those first weeks of knowing Shawn. Perhaps it was just the fact of sleeping in a strange bed and living out of a suitcase that made the experience perversely refreshing. I was being tested, certainly, but tested in unfamiliar ways. Oh God, am I really only saying that a change is as good as a rest? I was under a strain, but I felt it to be a beneficial one, as if lazy muscles were protesting against being used in the way for which they had, after all, been designed.

I went on paying rent for the Bloomsbury flat, but I was pretty much an absentee tenant. After my fortnight's holiday was up, I took another two weeks' leave that was owed me, and after that I explained the situation to my colleagues. They agreed with reasonable grace to let me work part-time. I stopped taking on new clients, and even passed one or two of my current ones on to other agents in the firm, but I didn't stop representing anyone I really cared about.

Life in the flat in Pimlico was surprisingly peaceful, even if it was the deceptive peace of physical decline. One day I remarked to Shawn about how quiet the building was. Wasn't that lucky, seeing he spent so much time there?

'Yes and no,' he answered. 'It doesn't have much to do with luck, actually. But yes, it is nice.'

'How do you mean?'

'Everybody's moved out but me.'

'Why? Is the house being sold? Will you have to move?'

He smiled. 'Hardly. But my neighbours didn't take to having Aids on the premises. Ideally they would have liked me to move out. As it is, they've all made other arrangements. The last one left two weeks ago.'

'But that's appalling. Couldn't you explain to them that they're not at risk?'

'My lover tried that, last year. He tried phoning round, and people hung up. So he visited the flats one by one. The whole building stank of disinfectant for a week.'

If I had been in Shawn's shoes I would have found it hard to live in a building so full of recent hostility, and in a flat so full of associations. His lover's clothes still took up one of the wardrobes in the master bedroom, and there were reminders of him everywhere.

Stacked above the wardrobe in the spare room, where I slept, I found a large number of paintings which I realized must have been done by Shawn. He had gone to art school, though his job had been running a gallery. He always referred to himself as a parasite, a fussy parasite but a parasite just the same. But the paintings in the spare room were not quite the standard art-student productions. They were in a wide range of styles and mediums, and the most recent of them had been done only a couple of years before.

Half-playfully, but also with a more serious intention, I started taking the pictures off the walls – starting with out-of-the-way places, in corners or above doors – and replacing them with Shawn's own. He caught on almost right away, of course, but I think he enjoyed watching in his quiet way as gradually the flat played host to his first and last one-man show, a private view – and in the West End at that, if you stretch a point.

More than anything, Shawn wanted to die at home. I wanted to help, but there was a limit to what I could do. I didn't have the skills or the facilities to make more than a little difference. At best I could make it possible for him to leave hospital a day or two earlier as each infection began to give ground, and to stay at home a day or two longer as the next one began to hold court among his ruined defences.

But even when Shawn was in hospital he wasn't a difficult patient. Our relationship still had texture and unpredictability. I

have a vivid memory of him looking up at me from a bowl which
he had already more than half filled with bright yellow vomit, and
saying, 'This must be very hard for you.' I didn't know what to
say. If his idealization of me made it possible for him to project
himself beyond the confinement of his illness, it was best to say
nothing. But why would he think his illness violated my nature, in
a way it didn't violate his?

I just thanked my lucky stars that Dougie visited whenever he
could to maintain the balance of our relationship, bringing his
flowers to be disparaged and his cards to be tucked away in a
drawer, or have orange juice spilled on them.

One day just before the end, Shawn rang for a nurse and asked
her, 'When is D-Day?'

She blushed and said, 'I don't know, I'm afraid, June sometime,' thinking for some reason that Shawn was testing her
general knowledge, when in fact he was asking in a veiled way
about his death. Then he put his hand on her arm and repeated
the question – I have a mental image of his kimono sleeve against
her uniform. When she understood what he meant she tried to
reassure him, saying that although he had been very poorly they
were sure they could break this most recent infection. But of
course he was right.

I don't know whether I was surprised or not when I learned
Shawn had made me the beneficiary of his will. On one level, I
couldn't imagine him leaving property to anyone else. I knew his
parents were dead, and there was a brother in South Africa that he
didn't have anything to do with. If there had been particular close
friends I would have been sure to hear about them in the time I
lived with him. I wouldn't have been surprised if there had been a
conscience-money payment to Dougie, after the way Shawn had
treated him, but there wasn't even that.

At the same time I did find it shocking to think that Shawn had
summoned his solicitor to attend him in hospital, had dictated a
will, and had had two nurses witness it. There seemed, irratio-
nally, something hurtful about that, I suppose because it was
exactly the sort of thing I used to arrange for him. I had got used to

the idea of being indispensable. But there's no doubt Shawn did right not to tell me what he was doing.

I had never mentioned the matter of a will to him myself. It's realistic to make a will, of course, and it's downright stupid to die without one. But there seemed to be quite enough realism in Shawn's life to be getting on with.

What really did shock me, though it took a while to take it in, was just how much I had inherited. It had never occurred to me that Shawn might own the whole building in which he lived. His parents had bequeathed it to him. It made sense in retrospect that the tenants in the building had had no prospect of forcing him out, no alternative but to leave a situation that they in their ignorance found intolerable. But now I was puzzled by something else.

If Shawn was capable of summoning a solicitor to do his bidding, he could have done the same with an agent. Come to that, he could have asked me to find new tenants, if he had wanted them. All he would have had to do was fill me in about the true state of affairs in the building. So why had he left those flats empty? It couldn't really have been that he valued the peace and quiet.

It would be flattering to think that only the desire to reward me could make him bestir himself in his weakness – flattering, but not really convincing. I began to be haunted by the idea that Shawn was somehow freeing up the building, for me to do what I wanted with it. Then the horrible thought struck me that by taking his valuable collection of modern art off the walls, and replacing it with his own work, which had no market value, it must have looked to him as if I had already cast a beady, valuing eye over the contents of the flat.

I was able to suppress the second thought, clearly rooted in guilt at having been found worthy of the profound emotion that an inheritance represents. But the other thought persisted, the thought that Shawn had plans for me that involved the whole house. It even occurred to me that he might have evicted those tenants; for a resident landlord that would have been relatively easy.

I didn't take any decision in a hurry. I gave my room-mate in Bloomsbury notice, and I kept on working on a part-time basis. I noticed that I wasn't enjoying the work as much as I had used to, but didn't know what to put it down to, exactly. Was it that after nursing Shawn, merely nursing a voice and its owner seemed rather an inconsequential business? Or was it that because of my new financial status I lost the reflex of deference? Though in the past my deference had often been tactical.

It was Dougie who intervened in my life again, Dougie who made the decision for me. He had a persistent fever, and lost a lot of weight, and after that his lover kicked him out. I had room – good God, did I have room! – and I took him in.

Dougie was the house's first inmate under the new dispensation, but he turned out to be an uncharacteristic one. When he got better he stayed better. Away from the influence of his lover, and away I must also say from Shawn, who had hardly given him a flattering image of himself, he came into his own. When an antibody test for what was then beginning to be known as HIV became available, he took it, with what seemed to me to be astonishing courage. His test came back negative, and in fact he came through his ordeal with his health intact and his heart mended. He started a relationship with the male nurse, of all people, who had given him counselling before his test, and who really seemed to appreciate him – which must have made a change. In due course he moved out of the house to live with him. They still pay visits, from time to time.

But by then the house's new identity was well established. My first move was to install an industrial washing-machine and a drier in the basement. I remembered all too well the indignities that Shawn had suffered with night sweats, and how much difference it made to him to have fresh sheets, even though he would soak them through in a couple of hours. The house was a long-standing conversion, full of awkward passages and wasted space, but at least there were plenty of facilities. I installed handrails in the bathrooms and the lavatories. Later it seemed a good idea to buy a special sort of trolley that made bathing someone easier. I invested what seemed like an absurd amount of money in a proper hospital bed, and eventually I bought quite a few of them. The minibus is a relatively recent acquisition.

By this time, every gay man in London knew of someone who was in need of looking after, without quite being a hospital case. I realized that I would need to pick up some practical skills, and fitted in some paramedical courses where I could. Of course, by the time I'd learned how to lift a person safely, to give bed baths and so on, I'd done a certain amount of damage to my back, but at the time it was either that or leave people unturned or dirty.

I had to make an iron rule, early on, that I could only take on unattached men. This wasn't an arbitrary decision, and there were times when I had room to spare, and still turned people away, that it seemed like an unreasonable one. But if there is one thing I can say about myself it is that I have learned from my mistakes. Early on, I offered the hospitality of the house to a young man recently discharged from hospital, and although I have nothing to reproach myself with as far as physical care goes, I know that he sustained psychological damage during his stay.

His lover had visited him devotedly while he was in hospital, but although I had made it clear to him that he was to make himself at home without reservation, his visits to the house became less and less frequent.

I was changing the flowers on the sick man's bedside table one morning, when without a word of warning he said, 'I know what you're doing.' He solemnly informed me that I was trying to drive his lover away, so that I could keep him – in some unspecified and barely imaginable way – for myself.

I was astonished. 'What on earth makes you say that?'

His voice took on a paranoid harshness. 'You said his washing-up wasn't good enough.'

This was perfectly true, but it hardly seemed an unreasonable remark in context. There are few things more irritating than reaching for a clean glass or plate from cupboard or drying-rack, and finding it stained or even encrusted with dirt. And while I'm quite happy to do the washing-up myself, I do resent having to wash things a second time to put things right after someone else. If this young man's lover wanted to make himself useful, as he said, then he should do exactly that, and if washing-up wasn't in his line I'm sure we could have agreed on something else.

It was a horribly difficult situation, and of course I couldn't explain what was really going on. The last thing an invalid, freshly discharged from hospital with a purple cancer lesion on the end of his nose, needs to hear is that his lover is terrified at the prospect of having to look after him, and after appeasing his conscience that everything possible is being done by other people, is running away just as fast as he can, using any flimsy excuse that comes to hand to cover his retreat.

But of course I couldn't say that. I had to bite my tongue and go on with the business of caring as usual, changing the sick man's sheets, bathing him, trying to get him to eat, while all the time being told in this perfectly mad way that I had got what I wanted, now that I had destroyed my patient's emotional life.

Even with unattached men, of course, I made mistakes. I hated the idea that my hospitality was conditional in any way, but after one particular bad experience I had to set up a rudimentary sort of admissions procedure, some elementary cross-checking. I welcomed into the house a man exemplary in his lack of attachments, who had clearly been having a terrible time. He seemed to be carrying a little extra weight all the same, and I remarked that at least he showed no sign of wasting away. He replied dogmatically, 'I have sustained a considerable and irreversible loss of weight.' I said I was sorry to hear that.

But in fact he ate heartily, and it seemed to me after a while that he was getting positively plump. He claimed to be exhausted, and spent most of the day in bed. Eventually I became suspicious enough to contact the hospital where he had claimed to be treated, and they told me he was always telling them about some nightmare infection he had suffered the week before, but there was never anything actually wrong with him when they examined him.

Even before then, I was beginning to suspect he was reeling off sets of symptoms memorized from medical pamphlets and Government circulars – the line about the weight loss, for instance, was reproduced word for word. In a sense, he wasn't even faking, since he had genuinely convinced himself he had Aids. But even on a good day I was often out of my depth – I can admit that now – and I couldn't deal with mental illness on top of everything else. I had to get him out.

I tried to persuade him that he was getting better, and could for instance begin to help around the house. But he clung fast to his bed, and to his fatigue. Finally I had to cut his rations, saying that we needed to starve the organisms that were infesting his digestive tract. Then it was only a matter of waiting until he raided one of the fridges, and catching him red-handed with a bowl of rice pudding and a spoon.

I told him that he had broken the house rules by stealing food, and must go. He pleaded for forgiveness just as if the house was his only hope, and I'm sure he thought it was so. But I couldn't let him take up a valuable bed, and I had to see through what I had started, whatever I felt about it.

I don't want to give the impression that I had no help in what I did. The staff at the major hospitals were only too aware of the limitations of their resources. They were forced to rely on voluntary agencies of one sort or another to make up the difference, and over the years they learned to do so with a good grace. If I had medical questions, or needed advice on the practical matters of nursing, there were numbers I could call. I could rely on getting a good hearing from people who knew that we were basically on the same side. However busy they were, they could be sure that I too had a lot on my plate, and I wouldn't be troubling them if it wasn't important.

There were even doctors on the HIV wards at St Stephen's and the Westminster who would pop by in their own time. Relationships between doctor and patient tended to be much more personal on those wards than in more conventional ones, and the doctors liked to keep an eye on how their ex-patients were doing.

But we also had a common interest – emotional on my part, more practical on theirs – in people spending as little time in hospital as was possible. This was particularly true when the HIV wards were full, which happened in strange cycles. For a long time there would be empty beds, and then suddenly there would be a wave of admissions. At peak times, it sometimes seemed that my house was actually a hospital annexe, with nurses delivering medication to the less acute cases, or else strong analgesics to those for whom nothing could be done. The house was large, but once or twice I and a couple of helpers ended up sleeping on camp beds in corridors.

Does it sound pathetic if I say that one of the great achievements of my life was to feed a young man, on his last day, a full portion of steak-and-kidney pie? I hope not. I encouraged him through the meal, mouthful by mouthful, knowing perfectly well – who better?, since I was nursing him – that he was profoundly incontinent, his poor ruined system retaining only the barest memory of how to extract the virtue from food.

But I don't want to give the impression that I was running a one-man-show. I didn't actually cook that steak-and-kidney pie, though I did put in a fair amount of time in the kitchen. I had plenty of helpers, and there were always tasks for them to do, God knows, whatever their particular skills or willingnesses. Helpers with any sort of medical training were of course a godsend, but naturally enough they were much in demand elsewhere, and I can understand that it would be more satisfying for them to put their expertise at the disposal of a more orthodox establishment.

It was particularly gratifying when the lovers or friends of people to whom I had given hospitality repaid their debt in kind, by offering their services as cooks, cleaners or drivers. Sometimes even former guests did so. It's only fair to say that my helpers didn't always stay very long, and often left before they completed the spell of duty they had set themselves. But until they try it, people don't realize quite how intense an experience it is to be faced with the continuing crisis of Aids. The atmosphere at my house could be very elevating, but it could also be taxing. I only hope that those who moved on before they had planned to don't feel they have let me down, or let themselves down.

Long before this time, of course, I had given up my job. The artists I represented said they would miss me, but what they really meant was that they couldn't imagine how I would manage without them. They paid lip-service to the idea that there might be some value in what I was doing, but they couldn't form a very clear mental picture of a life that wasn't focused on them. I get Christmas cards from one or two.

I gave up my career with good grace, and without agonizing overmuch over the decision. It was only a year or two later, when I met a French-Canadian who was touring the world in an aimless sort of way after his lover had died, leaving him with two cars, two motorbikes, a large apartment, a house in the country and considerable savings, that I found myself venting in front of this sympathetic listener an unsuspected rage against Shawn for his legacy. People forget that there are the Aids rich as well as the Aids poor, people whose lives have been wrenched out of shape by an unwanted affluence just as surely as others by poverty. I had my little rant of resentment against Shawn, and then returned meekly enough to the house and what it demanded of me.

Friends have always tried to persuade me that I should set up the house as a charity; I've always resisted the suggestion. I've barely been able to manage with things as they are, and the idea of making things permanent fills me with terror. I appreciate that after an initial period the burden would actually become lighter, once a structure was established that didn't depend so directly on me. But I know I wouldn't be able to keep going that long. I can only cope by living from day to day, not looking further into the future than the next small improvement in the house's running or equipment, a bigger microwave, a sterilizer, a hot-drinks dispenser.

It's certainly not that I'm awed by the Charity Commissioners. If I can handle undertakers, I can handle Charity Commissioners. I can hardly remember the time when my idea of a tough negotiation was trying to persuade the management of a concert hall to

book an untried talent, or a young singer not to attempt the
impossible cliffs of the repertoire. But soon after the house became
a place of caring I found myself delivering an ultimatum to an
undertaker.

I can see no good reason whatever for a person, from the
Pharaohs on down, wanting to be embalmed. But if people want it
done, or more likely their families want it done, then it should be
done without question. That the deceased had Aids doesn't come
into it. If the undertaker can't protect himself from infection, he
should consider a different line of work. It's as simple as that.

I rehearsed various approaches, all of them heavily sarcastic.
*You can't offer an embalming service, and then say you've changed your
mind. Embalming someone isn't a compliment, you know. It's a business
arrangement. It isn't a favour you can decide you don't mean after all.*

Then it occurred to me that sarcasm was the wrong way to go
about it. I didn't need to be wounding, because in a strange way I
had power. I represented a sort of trades union of the dead. I had
to be their spokesman, and make claims in their name. If I had to, I
could boycott any funeral director who made difficulties, and I
could make sure that the world heard about it.

In the end, I didn't even need to threaten this particular
undertaker with a boycott. All I had to do was threaten him with
complaints to his professional body (whatever that might be) and
with the revoking of his licence (there had to be a licence of some
sort). And I got my way. In fact the question has hardly ever arisen
since then. But it was in its horrible way a point of principle, and a
turning point. I don't think I was weak before, but I was strong
after.

If the house was run as a charity the money side of things would
certainly be easier. My desk with its wilderness of bills is a
terrifying place for me, in a way that no sickbed will ever be again.
I still have a few items from Shawn's art collection left over, but
the minibus gobbled up an awful lot of paint and canvas, and I'm
keeping what's left for emergencies. As it is, I'm not above
accepting small contributions from various charities to help with
my running expenses.

After a death I'll sometimes be sent a cheque by the dead man's parents. I wish I could afford not to cash it, on those occasions when I feel that the cheque is being used to pay me off, to let the bereaved parents wash their hands in some way of their son's dying. I feel much more comfortable with a financial contribution when the parents in question have actually paid a visit to the house. I know it has made all the difference in the world to those parents who have nerved themselves to it, and have found that their son's last real home was a place both of peace and of a paradoxical excitement.

Often it has been a mother who has come on her own; never a father, on his own. There is something peculiarly painful about watching a family that is unable to settle its differences. I have had to watch many failures, not of love but of courage.

So if it happens that I open the front door of the house to a woman unaccompanied, I'm always careful to ask how she has travelled. Often it turns out that her husband has driven her to the house, but refuses to go any further, and is staying in the car. In that case I ask the mother to tell me the model and colour of the car, just in case, and I escort her to her son's bed, or if he is well enough, to one of the dayrooms. Then I go down to my kitchen and brew a nice pot of tea.

When it's ready, I pour out a cup, balance a couple of sugar lumps and a biscuit on the saucer, and go out into the street with it. Once I've located the right car, I go over and tap on the window. Maybe the man in the car has seen me coming in one of the mirrors, maybe he tries to bury himself in the newspaper he is reading, but sooner or later he has to acknowledge me and wind down the window. Then I smile pleasantly and pass the cup of tea across, without a word.

The first time I tried this little manoeuvre I had no idea what tremendous pressure it placed on the man in the car. It happened that he had driven a long way, it was a hot day, and I felt sorry for him, sorry mainly for the way he was impoverishing himself by disowning his son, in a way he would find hard to forgive himself for, later on. But now I recognize the deviousness behind my tea-making. I can almost say I glory in it.

By taking tea out to the father in the car I am acknowledging his right to keep his distance – which disarms him – while also making him feel foolish. Why is it, I wonder, that a cup should administer so much more effective a rebuke than a mug? I don't know. But at all events I prove to him that he has not been able to put himself outside the range of my welcome. Every father to whom I have brought tea has come into the house, and more than once I have hardly turned my back before I hear the sound of the car door opening, and the sound of the first footsteps on the way towards acceptance.

I think I can claim that my teapot has brought more families together than all the counselling services in London combined.

After a death, though, it isn't the families who dispose of the dead man's possessions. That falls to me. I have learned to do it quickly and efficiently, not letting myself think too much about the associations of each little hoard. I'm not going to linger over the task the way I did with Shawn's things. It was months before I managed to clear everything away. I had to steel myself to get rid of the kimonos, hearing Shawn's voice saying with reflex pedantry, 'the plural of *kimono* is . . . *kimono*'. He always gave the word invisible italics and three short syllables.

I left only the paintings that I had promoted to the walls. Oddly enough, I have never managed to disturb the wardrobe in the master bedroom, where the clothes of Shawn's dead lover are stored. Not having known him, I don't feel I have the right. That wardrobe is probably the only part of the whole building that has been left untouched in the quiet overturning I have visited on the house that Shawn left me.

It would have been good to hear from the families of our guests, after they had left us. But that may be rather a lot to expect. Families have their own way of saying goodbye, as we in the house have ours.

I've been careful to cultivate a good relationship with television and the newspapers, in the years since they first showed an interest in what I was trying to do at the house. There's only one aspect of the house's life that I prefer to keep private. I'm always aware that the media have their own priorities, and that I can't expect them necessarily to see everything the way I do. After all, the house has featured in documentaries about both the triumph of private enterprise and the breakdown of the health service, as a glorious example and a terrible warning. And there are some things that I simply don't trust them to see.

It sounds stupid to say that the first time someone died in the house, I was unprepared. Of course I had imagined the fact of death, but I hadn't given any thought to what I would do when it happened. What seemed more important than anything, though, when it did happen, was avoiding any feeling of taboo. So I simply gathered together everyone who was in the house at the time, and we sat round the bed and talked. I said a few words about the dead man, and then someone brought in a bottle of wine. Someone else put on some music. Nothing could have felt more natural. It would have been ridiculous to have covered our friend up, as if he had done something wrong. I think all of us in the room that night felt the strength that comes from facing things – and not just facing them for a few moments, by an effort of will, before turning away.

That was the beginning of our tradition. A farewell could never again be a spontaneous event in quite that way, but our farewells have become central to what we do at the house. I think the hospitals understand that. When medical complications or special circumstances mean that we haven't been able to take care of someone to the end, the hospitals know that he belongs with us all the same, and they release him to us so that we can take our leave in our own way.

A ritual like our farewell is important because it standardizes the emotions. It makes us express a uniform grief for those we have lost, when the truth is that we discriminate brutally from person to person.

Anthony was always different. Anthony was special. He had only been down from Durham for a few months before he became ill. In that time of accelerating weakness, he had made few friends. He was a bright boy, well-spoken and serious-minded, but he hadn't known what was happening to him, and things had gone pretty far by the time anything was done for him. To the house he brought only a spare pair of running shoes, a rucksack with a few clothes, and his personal stereo. He had four tapes to play on it, which he seemed to listen to, when he was well enough, in strict rotation.

Anthony wore his hair in a style that was severe but also rather complicated, and I had seen at once that it would be beyond the skills of our normal hairdresser, a volunteer who had mastered only the basic techniques, to maintain. So I bribed a hairdresser from Warwick Way to come in every now and then to attend to it.

I made sure Anthony was put in a bed near where I slept, so that I could hear him if he cried out in the night – which sometimes happened – whether or not I was officially on duty. Meningitis isn't exactly a novelty in the house – fungal, bacterial, we've had all kinds – and I'd always known that extreme sensitivity to sound was a common symptom. But only now did I set myself to keep the noise level in the house down, and I snapped at a volunteer who was singing, which I much regret. Singing is not something you can have too much of in a house like mine.

I could see how things were going with Anthony. After a time, you develop an instinct. Finally, one morning, before anyone else was awake, I took his hand, and held it. Anthony ran his other hand, almost dreamily, back and forth along the line between zones of his haircut. The line was as crisply maintained as it had been the day he arrived at the house, and I allowed myself to feel a little satisfaction at that. I had seen that in its own way it mattered, and I had done what I could to help.

I said: 'Anthony. If you want to fight this thing, I'm right with you. We'll fight it every step of the way. But if you've had enough, don't be ashamed of it.' I squeezed the hand I was holding. 'I can let you go now.'

When he spoke, his voice was thick with thrush, and he left long pauses between his phrases, but I could make out clearly what he said. He said, 'It's not up to you, old man. Where do you get off telling people when they can die? Look at yourself. You've grown fat on other people's misery. With your television modesty, and your obscene birthday parties for corpses. But you're not going to get me.'

It was strange that he told me to look at myself, because he himself can only have been aware of my voice. The CMV had reached his eyes by this time, and he was blind. Strange, too, to hear him talking that way, when his temperature had come down so substantially since the meningitis.

On my way from the tube I try to slow my steps down, but when my thoughts wander my natural brisk pace reasserts itself – my health, with all its obligations, reasserts itself – and soon I am home. I must call it home. I open the door of the house gingerly, as if I might wake someone, the slightest noise magnified into pain in the roaring ears of the sick. But in fact this is one of those in-between times when no one is positively in danger. There's no one in the house at the moment who couldn't be moved, if it came to that. There have been one or two hiccups in the property market just lately, but I can't imagine that a large freehold like this, conveniently subdivided, would wait long for a buyer.

I used to think that the house wanted to throw off its partitions, its ungainly conversions, and start functioning again as a unit. I expect it's quite common for house-owners to have ideas of that sort, as if their property harboured plans for itself. Now I have different ideas. Now I think that the house can't wait to be properly broken up again, given over to people who will close their individual front doors, and not think too much about what happens on the other side of them.

## *From* The Swimming-Pool Library

### ALAN HOLLINGHURST

No headaches, painless breathing; bruises, with all their touchy, indwelling tenderness, mysteriously fading out: I felt well again, whole, and wholesome. I didn't need the decadent secrecy of Charles and his pals – and as I had left Staines's house I had thought of putting the whole thing behind me. Why be encumbered with the furtive pecadilloes of the past, and all the courteous artifice of writing them up? I wasn't playing the same game as that lot. I looked forward to clear July days, days of no secrets, of nothing but exercise and sun, and the company of Phil. I was enthralled, almost breathless, at the very idea of men, the mythological beauty of them running under trees and sunlight in the Avenue or in the long perspectives of Kensington Gardens. But I was pure and concentrated as well. No longer loathing myself I was once again in love, and turning the full beam of my devotion upon Phil. I dreaded somehow to find that he had grown complicated, that my hatefulness of the past few weeks had left a stain on him, or eroded that ingenuousness which struck me almost as a property of his body, residing speechlessly in his palms and wrists, in his strong calves and ridged stomach, in the crisp hair above his cock, in the pumping heart I laid my ear to, the neck I kissed and bit, the glossy, speckled darkness of his pupils in which I looked and looked and saw myself, miniature, as if engraved on a gemstone, looking.

But no. He was surprised, relieved – like a child released at last from some unfair and arbitrary penance. But there was no resentment in him – and he had I suppose the further relief of finding me pretty again, with only the knotty broadening of the bridge of my nose and the too American whiteness of my ingenious new tooth to remind him of our little season of misery. Unlike recovery from a cold or a hangover this took me forward, not merely back to the old unthinking well-being. It made me romantically ambitious for sweetness and strength, and for the moment I felt all over some seasonal convulsion, quite exhilarated by that grand illusion, that I could make myself change. It was the return of physical strength – and at just the time when, sitting apprehensively, watching those two stoned boys and that beautiful scarred stitched-up man, I had seen myself, with weird detachment, in the society of corruption: the baron, the butcher, the boozed-up boyfriend, and most corrupt of all the photographer.

I went straight to Phil that night, though he was not expecting me. I had not been at the Queensberry for weeks, and as I got out of the taxi a new boy on the door – very thin and formal, not at all my kind of thing – asked me if he could help. I looked in on the staff TV room, where one of the receptionists was watching the news and a commis chef, fast asleep, had fallen half out of his chair. In the corridor I ran into Pino, who was fantastically pleased to see me and shook my hand between both of his, insisting on a complete account of the injuries Phil had told him about. He was keen too not to keep me from my friend. 'You go to see Phil? Is upstairs. Is gettin is beauty-sleep.' We shook hands again before he left me, and I heard him laugh aloud with pleasure as he went on his way.

Up under the roof, in the hot, shadowy corridor, outside Phil's door . . . distant traffic and a creaking floorboard making no impression on the silence, residual, anticipatory . . . dream echoes of childhood evenings, going up to fetch a book, drawn to the open window and the stillness of the elms . . . or at school, waiting for Johnny, knees under my chin on the sill of a gothic dormer, heart thumping, swallows plunging into the darkening

court below . . . pushing open the rattling, leaded panes at
Corpus Christi, the sky precipitating its blues, its darker blues . . .
the surprising, secret moistness of the twilight, sloping down to
the Swimming-Pool Library, the faint, midsummer-night illumination of a glowing cigarette . . . exquisite, ancient singleness in
moments just before whispers, the brush of lips and love . . . I felt
it all again, the romance of myself, for three or four seconds
squeeze urgently about me, and my mouth went dry.

I barely knocked, tapped with the backs of my nails. It seemed
like a cowardly knock, hoping not to be heard. If he were awake
he might just hear, and I listened for an answering rustle or call.
But what I wanted was to come upon him as he was, to stream
through the keyhole, to be with him without any prosaic ado. One
morning, weeks before, when he was asleep I had pinched his key
and had it copied in a heel and key bar at the station. Phil was so
orderly and cautious that he always dropped the catch, and I
envisaged some picaresque occasion when I might need to get in,
some about-turn in a sex comedy that called for a surprise entry.

I slid the key into the lock notch by notch and opened the door a
fraction. There was no light on, though the last of the day still
lingered and without yet going in I could see the room in the
dressing-table mirror, Phil lying on the bed, the white of his
underpants. He didn't move as I came forward, silently closed the
door, and stood at the end of the bed. His breathing was extremely
slow and distant and he was clearly deeply asleep. He was lying
face downwards, but slightly turned to one side, his left leg half-
drawn up, his mouth squashed open on the pillow, his thighs
apart but not widely apart, his ass slewed a little to the right. I
wanted X-ray eyes for that, though the barrack-room modesty of
his sleeping in his knickers was beautiful too. Beside the pillow,
trapped under a slumberous arm, was *Tom Jones* – the fat, squashy
Penguin redolent of O levels and essays on virtue.

I could hardly bear to look at him any longer, and shook him
roughly to wake him up, falling on him before he knew what was
happening and bothering him with kisses.

I hadn't made love like I did then since I was a schoolboy. It was extraordinarily innocent, fervent and complete. By the time Phil had to get to work it had begun to rain, and after he had gone I lay in the dark with the window open and listened to it pattering on the leads. Falling asleep I slid briefly through a zone of luminous happiness, a vision as clear as summer – not the omnious clarity of Hampshire or Yorkshire summer but a kind of desert radiance where rocks and water and scrawny shade, lying by chance together, seemed divinely disposed and glowed in their change-lessness.

I more or less forced Phil, who did it with a certain comical reluctance, to take the following night off in exchange with Celso. Celso, it transpired, was anxious to have Friday off to treat his wife on her birthday – a musical and dinner and then, one assumed, some especially Spanish and honourable congress. I'd hoped for a high noon of sunbathing, back on the roof, but it was one of those close dark days when one can never get dry and longs for a thunderstorm that never comes. We went back to my flat and lounged about and I came on rather fierce about wanting sex several times, at which Phil showed at first a demure disbelief though clearly, when it came to it, he wanted it just as much himself. Later we went up to the Corry, which was unmomen-tous, no one seeming to have noticed that I had been away and the virulent strains of exercise going on much as normal.

It was wonderful though, additionally hot from weights, to plunge into the sombre coldness of the pool. No discipline made me feel more free, or contained me and delighted me within its own element so much as swimming. Even so, when Phil came down the spiral stairs – displaying (some well-judged vanity of his own) new trunks cut high on the hips, black behind and gold in front – I was happy to do things I normally deplore, getting in people's way, doing handstands or swimming between his splayed and sturdy legs. For a while we gloomed Cousteau-like in the depths of the deep end, swivelling our goggled heads from side to side, searching for our locker keys which we had thrown in and left to settle, buffeted and wandering in the choppy water. Where the end wall met the floor of the bath Phil pointed out to me with slowed, speechless gestures the melancholy aperture where the water escaped, and, gathered round it, dozens of sticking-plasters, bleached clean by their long immersion and waving over the filter like albino, submarine plants. Then I saw him give out his breath, the bubbles crowding from his mouth, flooding around his head and up towards the light with baroque exuberance. He himself shot up then and I followed a second or two later. We hung on our elbows to regain our breath.

The plan was to go later to the Shaft and dance and get drunk and have a wonderful time. Phil had never been there with me: our funny routine isolated us from the normal gay world, and what with one thing and another I had not been there myself for a couple of months – though for a year or more before that I was impelled towards it, without any power to resist, every Monday and Friday night. I had been an addict of the Shaft. If I was out to dinner I would grow restless towards eleven o'clock, particularly if I was away in the western districts and had several miles to travel. I would go to the opera very inappropriately got up, and had more than once exploited the privacy of the Covent Garden box to slip off during the last act as the anticipation of sex welled up inside me, rapidly distancing and denaturing the carry-on on stage into irksome nonsense. The Shaft itself I hardly ever left alone, and I had made countless taxi-journeys down the glaring, garbage-stacked wasteland of Oxford Street and along the great still darkness of the Park, a black kid, drunk, chilled in his sweat, lying against me, or secretly touching me. I took home boys from far out – from Leyton, Leytonstone, Dagenham, New Cross – who like me made their pilgrimage to this airless, electrifying cellar in the West End, but had no way, if they failed to score, at three or four a.m., of getting home.

Phil took a practical attitude to his initiation, and we walked from the Corry through dusky, cooling Bloomsbury to have supper at the hotel. In Russell Square, under the planes, there was at last a perceptible breeze. The immense, leafy twilight shivered, and the three fountains, shooting up their forceful jets, reckless and almost invisible, splattered down across the path and caught us in their spray. Phil put his arm round me, remembering too, I suppose, our first terrifying walk here.

The kitchen at the Queensberry was a high, white-tiled hall into which plunged a series of writhing air-ducts, tubes of aluminium, riveted along their joints, and opening out into wide, battered hoods above the loaded and archaic gas-ranges. Even so, it was wearyingly hot in there, and the team of chefs, in their crumpled white jackets and hats and their blue and white checked bags, were testy and pink-faced, shying the portions that were ordered along the metal counter beyond which the waiters waited. As 'staff' we had to wait there too, until there was a convenient pause. I felt awkward, ready to be resented, whenever we visited the kitchen. Its incessant toil, unadorned by the servility and charm of the public parts of the hotel, made me feel a frivolous observer of some truly serious industry.

Tonight Phil got us some whitebait – dull, Rotarian starter – and then excellent beef olives, the fat tongue of veal juicy in its meaty sheath. We ate it in the staff dining-room, keeping to ourselves whilst two of the washing-up women and a leathery old porter smoked fanatically through the last minutes of their dinner-hour.

'Off out tonight, then, young Philip?' enquired the porter, preparing to go, hoisting up his waistband and buttoning his hot jacket. There seemed to be some hint of contempt in his voice, a sarcasm in his civility which showed it to be a challenge, even an insult. As he drew himself up, he was somehow shielding and shepherding the two women – though they themselves betrayed no sense of danger.

'Yes, I'll probably go out for a drink or two.' A subfusc, minimal answer.

'Don't stay in this fucking shithouse anyway,' said one of the women kindly.

'I won't.'

'Don't go breakin' too many 'earts, neither,' said the other with a chuckle.

I said nothing until they had gone. They probably thought me very stuck up, but I felt a kind of duty not to incriminate Phil. It was hard to believe they didn't see me for what I was, but a pretence, a performance, was sustained that we were just pals. Rather like James, Phil cultivated a reserve that grew into a sort of authority. I must have needed their discretion just as they were freed by my lack of it.

I finished eating and laid my knife and fork side by side. 'Am I a frightful liability to you, darling?' I said, conceitedly and solemnly.

In a swift, unconscious convulsion he clutched together the bevelled glass salt and pepper pots. 'Of course not. I love you.' He looked up for a split second and then went on very quickly and quietly, pushing the last French beans around his plate with his fork, 'I really love you, I don't think I could live without you. I couldn't bear it when you were ill, and . . . I don't know . . .'

It was much more of an avowal than I'd asked for, and the tears came to my eyes and I grinned at the same time. I covered his hand that was coupling the cruet with my own, and looked anywhere but at him – around the horrible, narrow but dispro-portionately tall room, which had obviously been made by splitting some more generous space in two.

Afterwards we got changed upstairs and shared a tooth-mug of vodka, which made me if anything more amorous, though in a generalized way, as if it were not just Phil but the whole world that was in love with me. I put on some very old, faded, tight-loose pink jeans and a white T-shirt with no arms and side-seams ripped open almost to my hips. Phil squeezed into other new acquisitions – some hugging and rather High Street dark blue slacks with a thin white belt, and a gripping pale blue T-shirt.

When we were clear of the hotel I took Phil's arm. It moved me to do this, to insist out loud that he was mine (he himself, keen to be so claimed, didn't quite flow with it, butchly somehow held himself apart – though I locked my fingers through his). At Winchester one summer day I had run across a couple of queens – one perhaps an old Wykehamist showing his friend the places where his honour died. They had wandered over to Gunner's Hole, that curving canal-like backwater, drawn off and returning to the Itchen, where in Charles's day swimming had taken place. Now, of course, there was a beautiful indoor pool – where I was soon to establish my freestyle record – and the Hole had surrendered, as it must always have promised to do, to crowding cow-parsley and heavy seeded grasses, while in the water itself long green weeds curled to and fro in the current. I came scuffing past through the meadow, hot, shirt undone, and saw them gazing, one pointing at the rioting May-time flowers, then spotting me, giving me a glance – very brief but I felt it – and then the two of them turning back towards College, arm in arm. I mastered a frisson of shock into pleasure – not at them individually (they seemed hopelessly old and refined) but at the openness of their gesture. I wanted men to *walk out* together. I wanted a man to walk out *with*.

Well, I had one. My heel was suddenly tacky, and I stopped – though Phil kept going and almost pulled me over. I hopped forward, supported by him, and turned my sole upwards under the yellow street light. A tongue of white chewing-gum, rough with grit, had welded itself to the rubber and squelched into a curl under the step of the heel. It was surprisingly difficult to detach – and I had a certain revulsion from it, and reluctance to touch it. So with drunken insouciance I remained, leaning on Phil's bunched shoulder, one flamingo leg drawn up, and spoke quite seriously about the British Museum, outside whose bleak north entrance we were standing. On a huge pillar above our heads a poster advertised the Egyptian galleries, with a number of aproned, broken-nosed pharaohs standing stonily, but rather pathetically, in a row. As I spoke of Charles's relief of Akhnaten Phil actually started giggling, and only giggled more when I told him to fuck off.

'If you really cared you'd get this stuff off for me,' I said. 'At the one time I need help, you refuse it to me.'

He was not quite sure of the rhetorical conventions now, but muttering 'Oh give it here' grabbed my foot and jerked it upwards, so that I hopped round involuntarily and hung on his neck. I don't know how slow I was to realize that we were being watched. Certainly my eyes dwelled incuriously on the far pavement for several seconds and though I took in a figure waiting under one of the gently stirring young trees I did so abstractly, and focused all sensation in my hands on Phil's cropped neck. To the watcher we must have been a well-lit and enigmatic group. I looked away as Phil flung down my foot, but still embraced him while he groped for a handkerchief, a quiver of protective anxiety ruffling my sexy, complacent mood. Two seconds later, the figure had moved. I was slow again to spot him, now further off, under the next tree, and screened to chest height by cars parked at meters along the middle of the street. His act was to be going away, disarming the suspicion he had aroused in me. Or perhaps he did not know he had been seen. He was looking back again now, but still moving, sidling inexpertly under a street-lamp. Then I quickly led Phil away, keeping him turned in towards me, my arm and hand oppressively around his shoulder, so that he was squashed and stumbling against me. But there could be no doubt who it was.

It gave me a shock but also the pleasure of a bitter little nodding to myself in recognition of what was afoot. 'Right!' I thought, and then, after turning quickly at the corner to look back – but there were other people on the street now, and the distance was all a pattern of shadows – more or less forgot about it for the rest of the night. I was too taken up with the honest but slightly unworthy excitement of coming back to my old haunt with such a luscious piece of goods as Phil.

It was the half-hour after closing time and the narrow grid of Soho was rowdy with people, some shutting up shop, some stumbling from pubs, and others performing the awkward, drunken transition from one place of amusement to another, where money would pour off them into the early hours of the morning. There was a small crowd outside the Shaft, a gaggle of excited boys, and others waiting, staring challengingly at the arrivals. The thump of the music, like some powerful creature barely contained, came up out of the ground and gathered around us as we went in at the door. On the stairs it began to be really loud, the whole foundations humming with the bass while a thrilling electronic rinse of high-pitched noise set the ears tingling. From now on talk would be shouting, or confidences made with lips and tongue pressed close to the ear: we would be hoarse from our intimacies. The medium of the place was black music, and even the double-jointed spareness of reggae came over the dance floor like a whiplash.

At the foot of the stairs, in his pink-bulbed cubbyhole, Denys took our money. 'Hey Willy, I thought you was dead, man.'

'I've been resurrected, just for tonight.'

He grinned. 'Whatever did happen to your nose, eh?'

I pinched the broken bridge with my fingers. 'Ooh, a bit of trouble with some boys – a bit of rough, you might say.'

'Well you take care man – because you, are, *pretty*.' He fluttered his long lashes, but kept the straightest of faces. 'And I hope you will have a pleasant evening too sir,' he said to Phil, who thanked him apprehensively. So we passed on, waved in to the pounding semi-darkness by the impassive Horace, whose twenty-stone bulk, toiling and yet stately in a Hawaiian short-sleeved shirt, was reflected in floor-length mirrors that flanked the door and repeated him *ad infinitum*, like exotic statuary surrounding a temple.

The mirrors and pink lights were reminders that this place, which to me was purely and simply the Shaft, was other things for other people on the intervening days and nights. Indeed, the club went back a bit and under different names had been a modish sixties dive and before that a seedy bohemian haunt with a pianist and alcoholics. The décor, of what was essentially an arched, brick-walled cellar, was correspondingly eclectic, the bar over-hung by a thatched roof, and the sitting-out area screened from the dance floor by a huge tank of flickering tropical fish. On first acquaintance these features seemed hideous or absurd, and gave me the sinister feeling that nightlife was still run by an elderly, nocturnal, Soho mafia who actually thought such details were smart. Soon, though, they became camp adornments to the whole experience, and I wouldn't have had them changed for the world.

The heavy hotness of the day, which had begun to drain from the streets, was redoubled in the thickly crowded club. Some people had come all innocently in shorts, and on the floor a trio of black boys had already removed their singlets, which swung, like waiters' towels, from the loops of their jeans. I propelled Phil to the bar for the sharp, gassy lager, not in itself pleasant, which was the economy fuel of the place. We leant together at the counter, his arms bulgingly crossed, and I splurged my tongue up his jaw and into his ear – he turned to me with a grin and gave me, too close to be in focus, a look of the tenderest trust.

We perched for a while by a little shelf, drinking quite fast, feet rocking to the music, more or less silent though I pointed people out to him and he looked and nodded in a factual sort of way, not feeling, perhaps, that it was quite right to rave adulterously about other men. Even so, he was enthralled when Sebastian Smith moved through the crowd at the heart of his own little crowd, who touched, supported and congratulated him. He had come fresh, exhausted, from Sadler's Wells, was still on the serene, unpunctured high of adoration and acclaim, still sustained, as in some sugary Spanish Assumption, by the pink clouds of triumph and the tumbling black putti of his entourage. Still wearing, too, his leotards (though now with little patent, winking pumps), his torso rising in a naked black triangle to the glitter-sprinkled, ballerina-hefting shoulders. Everyone wanted him to dance, and he came forward, considering it, to the floor's edge – one foot set before the other as if on a gym bar, the long, taut thighs chafing, all the effort instinctively keeping his body steady, as though it were his discipline to carry a glass of water on his head or to propel without obscene lurching the contents of his high, prancing basket. But he decided against it, paced back to a darkened corner, leaving me with a faint ache of adulation and inadequacy.

Phil I found had that look of relished, vulgar curiosity which from time to time reminded me that he was as prone to sudden lusts as the next man. Not for you, dear, I thought, as I gestured 'Let's dance', he carefully finished his drink, and we felt our way through the gay throng. I turned, we sculpted out a little area on the edge of the mass of dancers, and were drunk enough to be dancing already, Phil too (who I thought might selfconsciously jiggle), going into a kind of mood, hardly looking at me and swivelling chunkily to left and right in a tight, fashionable style he must have picked up somewhere. I sprang about in my own reckless way. In a sense we had nothing to do with each other, though I kept an eye on him and grinned with pleasure when his shy dark gaze held mine. Then I would whirl him round once or twice, and hold his handsome head and kiss him clumsily, bumping noses.

I kept him at it for about an hour, never stopping as, under the DJ's gurgling patter, the rhythms of one track, clean and fierce, cut across and then went under the rhythms of the next. It was a sport, where exhaustion was only a spur to more effort, the blood-opiates sang through the system, lap succeeded lap. On the floor there was competition, more athletic than sexual, and I would find myself challenged, magnetized by strangers, drawn into faster and faster action, though no words were said, we affected not even to look at each other. And some of the kids there could dance. Sometimes a ring would suddenly form around one or two of them, and we hung on each other's shoulders to see them – their brief, fizzy routines of backward handsprings, jack-knife jumps and other crazy things. Boy after boy would follow, explode in action, stumble back into obscurity; and then the ring would dissolve, the crowd would repossess the floor.

At last Phil rocked to a stop and gestured for drink. I gasped 'Lager' in his ear. Both of us were parched – and all wet outside, so that his hair, when I roughed it and sent him off, stood up, and the bristly back of his neck glistened as if it had been dressed. I lurched off the dance floor and into Stan.

Stan was a colossal Guyanan bodybuilder, not only gigantically muscular but six feet six inches tall. 'Love the arse on your chum,' he said. 'I've been watching him.'

'Heaven, isn't it?'

'Yeah. Where d'you find that then?'

'I took him under my wing at the Corry.'

He craned to see where Phil had got to in the further spotlit half-dark. 'Still go there then?'

'Daily. You should come back. We all miss seeing you.'

Stan smiled sweetly and said, 'I bet you fucking do.' His mouth, like the rest of him, was vast, so that when he laughed it seemed his whole head would open up like a canteen of cutlery. I had met him at the Corry during my first Oxford vac and fooled about with him rather unsatisfactorily in an alley off the Tottenham Court Road. I remember how struck I was by the contrast of his rocky physique and the beautiful, almost smothering softness of his lips. A term later he had left, for some north London gym more suited to his championship needs. But I would run into him from time to time in clubs and bars, and though we had nothing much in common I seemed to charm him somehow, so that despite his superhuman body he was slightly in awe of me. I rested a hand on the side of his neck, whose shaft, thicker than his head, was buttressed by the gathered, sloping muscles of his shoulders.

'You're looking very big, Stan,' I said, smiling at him teasingly. He was a hard man to clothe and at night often went out as he was now, his torso draped in the tatters of some sweat-scorched singlet, a broad leather belt (which he assured me *came in handy*) needlessly supporting pale old jeans rubbed thin under his bum and along the thick bolt of his cock. He once showed me a picture of how he looked at fifteen – tall and uncertain, and indifferently built. I think some sort of crisis about being gay had got him to the gym, which gave him both lovers and a new body. An element of defiance had made him a now almost unconscious exhibitionist. A lot of sex went on in the lock-ups of the Shaft, but one evening I had stumbled in for a piss to find Stan fucking a boy just inside the door. He had him with one leg cocked up on a washbasin and as he laid into his ass the bracket of the basin was breaking free of the wall, and the kid, who looked the younger and slighter in his giant grasp, rode up and down against his own breath-smeared reflection in the mirror. An ever-growing group of admirers deserted the dance floor and stood around feeling themselves and muttering encouragement.

Phil was back with the much-jogged pints of beer. I craved liquid, and as I drank my dry palate seemed to admit the alcohol straight to my brain. 'See you, sweetheart,' said Stan, realizing we would be no good to him – the endearment, as always when spoken by a real man, a virtual stranger, moving me for a few seconds intensely.

Phil watched him amble off. 'Some bloke grabbed my cock, at the bar,' he said, in a tone which strove to combine pleasure and resentment and came out, neutrally, as a statement of fact. I drank and then kissed him, squirting cold lager into his mouth, though much of it, in his surprise, ran back down his chin. As I held him I could squeeze the sweat from his shirt where it clung down the channel of his back – so I took his drink from him, and helped him tug the wet garment off. The atmosphere was more and more liquid. Everyone was stripping off, and those who touched each other could cream off the sweat with a finger.

I took his hand and led him away. There were corners of the club, removed from the dance floor, dead-ends of cellars, crypt-like areas, dimly lit, faintly damp, with a limey dampness quite distinguishable from the tropical humidity the weather and the dancers made. We ran into John and Jimmy, a sweet black and white couple who had been together for years, John a cuddly blond, Jimmy handsome to tears, with lingering, ironical eyes. We stood and shouted some banter, Jimmy as usual hugging his friend from behind: they would shuffle around for hours like that, coupled and domestic and yet giggling, party-going. They might have been the beginning of a conga, ready to sweep everyone away in silliness and fun, but their devotion to each other made them at the same time inaccessible. I knew they had something which I had never had. They felt Phil a bit, ooing as he looked bashful but knew he couldn't object, and Jimmy lifted up his hand as if he'd won a fight and made him flex his biceps and triceps, and then in a little showery cadenza of laughs and nonsense they were on their way.

We went into the section beyond the fishtank, with a comfy bench running along the walls, very low, with knee-high tables crowded with beer glasses. From where we sprawled the fishtank formed an unreliable window on to the dance floor, its water threaded by bubbles up one side, and the tiny fish, neurotically it seemed, twitching from one direction to another as the music shook the thick glass. The floor of the aquarium was at eye level, and laid out like a miniature landscape, with picturesque rocks tilting up out of the pinky-brown sand, and a little pink house like a French country railway station with gaping doors and windows which the fish never deigned to swim into. The subdued lighting made the surface gleam when one looked up to it, and gave the water an unnaturally thick appearance, like a liqueur. Through this entranced, slowing medium the dancers could be seen spinning, rocking and bouncing, freakishly fast and disconnected.

'All right darling?'

Phil nodded. 'Bloody hot,' he said, running his hand over his chest and stomach and then looking at it admiringly. It was one of those occasions when I couldn't think of much to say to him: we lolled stickily together and slurped our lager. They kept the lager so chilled that the glasses were slippery with their own cold sweat. When Phil slid his hand through the slit side of my vest I gasped at the shock – like cold water thrown in horseplay in the showers, or the touch of hands under clothing in winter out of doors.

A short way off I made out a couple talking about us in a way meant to be noticed, heads together, with long glances and point-weighing smiles and nods. I raised an eyebrow, recognizing the boy, Archie, whom I'd taken home a few months before. He had one slightly sleepy eye, which gave him a lewd and experienced air, though he was only a kid, sixteen or seventeen, illicit and the more queenly for it. He had trashed up his appearance since he'd gone with me: hair slick with a jar-load of gel, black lips queerly glossed with lilac lipstick. He said something to his companion, then got up and came over to us, surrendering himself confidentially to the seat beside me.

'Hello dear!'

'Hello Archie.' We looked at each other for a moment with that strange disbanded intimacy of people who have once briefly been lovers. 'This is Phil.'

'Mm. I'm with Roger. He says he's seen you in the gym. He was well jeal when I told him about you and me.' I glanced over to where Roger was affecting an interest in some men in the other direction. He was someone I was half-aware of, a morose middle-aged fellow who appeared at the Corry in a suit on weekday evenings but on Saturdays and Sundays was transformed by heavy boots, jeans and biking jacket, the ensemble looking just a trifle too much for him.

'I'm not sure that I'm not jealous of him,' I said with arch courtesy. 'Are you seeing a lot of him?'

'Yeah, last couple of months I've been stopping over at his place, Fulham, quite posh it is. He's got a video and that.'

'I can imagine.'

'No, he's really sweet though.'

'I think he's perfectly hideous, but I suppose it's nothing to do with me.' He might have been hurt by this remark, but he seemed to quite admire me for it.

'Yeah – still it's nice having someone to look after you, know what I mean?' He slid his hand between my legs, and I felt Phil go tense on the other side of me. I said nothing, but stared at Archie in an existential sort of way, my cock quickly thickening under the light pressure of his fingers.

'Not today dear,' I murmured, shifting away and slipping my own hand on to Phil's thigh.

'P'raps you're right,' he said, with his typical experimenté air, and looked round to find out what had happened to Roger. Roger was smoking a cigarette and gazing at the ceiling, a model of tense insouciance. 'Your mate looking for a friend, is he?' Archie asked, as if it were the 1930s.

'Phil you mean? No, no: he has a mate.' Archie looked at me, expecting me to say something else as it sank in.

'That's not like you,' he said. 'I thought you only went with black boys. Sorry love,' he said to Phil, needlessly enlarging on his error; 'I thought you must be down here after a bit of beige. That's what most of the white guys come here for.'

'That's all right,' said Phil gruffly.

'D'you hear about Des?' Archie asked in tones of gossipy shock. I had to think for a second. There was a Desmond at the Corry; but he must mean 'little' Des, dancing Des. It was yet another sentimental history salvaged from the nightclub floor.

'You mean little Des?'

'Yeah, you know. You had that threesome with him and that bloke from Watford.'

'You seem to know a lot about my sex life.'

'Yeah, well, he told me. Anyway, he got involved in some other really heavy scene. This taxi-driver that tied him up and whipped him. Anyway, one night things got well out of hand and this cunt goes off and leaves little Des tied up in some garridge, with rats and stuff, and he's got burns all over him. He was there for three days till some old bird found him. He's in hospital now, and he don't look good.'

Archie was pleased to be able to tell me this horrible news, but I saw him swallow and knew he was as shocked in the retelling as I was, hearing it for the first time. While he was speaking the lighting system had gone over to ultra-violet, so that the dancers' teeth and any white clothes they were still wearing glowed blueish white. Seen through the tank these gleaming dots and zones themselves seemed to be swimming and darting in the water and to mingle with the pale phosphorescence of the fish.

There were two or three sickening seconds. The vulnerability of little Des. The warped bastard who had hurt him. A face passing beyond the glass, turning to look in, mouth opening in a luminous yawn.

I got up with such suddenness that Archie and Phil, leaning on either side of me, tumbled together. 'Must have a piss,' I said. But I was hardly thinking of them: my heart was racing, excited relief rose in a physical sensation through my body, I felt angry – I didn't know why – and frightened at my own lack of control. Over

and over, under my breath, or perhaps not even vocalized, just
the shouting of my pulse, I said, 'He's alive, he's alive.'

I caught up with him on the far side of the dance floor, was on
him even before he recognized me, and flung my arms round him;
we fell back against the wall, where he held me off a moment to
look at me. 'Will,' he said, and smiled only a little. I was kissing
him and then bundling him down the passage and through the
swing door. A couple of guys were rolling joints on the edge of the
washbasin and looked up nervously. A lock-up was empty and I
pushed him in in front of me, falling back with amazement against
the door when I had bolted it. I had almost no idea what I was
doing. I prised open the top stud of his trousers – maroon cords,
just as before – yanked down the zip, pulled them round his
knees. Seeing again how his cock was held in his little blue briefs I
was almost sick with love, fondled it and kissed it through the soft
sustaining cotton. Then down they came, and I rubbed his cock in
my fist. I knew it so well, the thick, short, veined shaft. I weighed
it on my tongue, took it in and felt its blunt head against the roof of
my mouth, pushing into my throat. Then I let it swing, went
behind him, held his cheeks apart, flattened my face between
them, tongued his black, sleek, hairless slot, slobbered his asshole
and slid in a finger, then two, then three. Long convulsions went
through him, indrawn breaths. Tears dripped from his chin on to
the stretched encumbrance of his trousers and pants. He was
sniffing and gulping.

Slowly I came to my senses, slid my wet fingers from his ass,
stood up behind him and pulled him gently to me. 'Baby . . .
Arthur . . . sweetest . . . love . . .' I kissed the back of his neck,
half turned him against me and kissed the submerged pale
filament of his scar, cool tears over a burning face.

He was reaching down, tugging up his clothes again. I helped
him maladroitly. He said nothing; sniffed. I felt abjectly unhappy.
We leant awkwardly together in the narrow, stinking box of the
lavatory, and I ran my hand soothingly up and down his back.

'Will . . . I got to go. My brother's here. He's waiting. I got to go with him.' He looked at me with unspeakable sadness. 'To do stuff for him. I got to go.'

He let himself out of the lock-up and left me standing stupidly in it. Someone else was hovering to get in, saying, 'Have you finished?' I almost fell past him, wandered out in a torment of confusion and self-disgust into the flashing darkness of the club – and then stood, looking on, but drowning in a world of my own.

This must have taken several minutes, until some outcrop of objectivity rose again from the flood. Out on the street it was surprisingly cold, and I ran a little way in both directions. There was no sign of Arthur. I was loitering, dithering, craning around at the nothing that was going on. It was nearly two o'clock. A taxi came slowly past, its yellow light burning – and then just behind it a yellow Cortina, with tinted windows and the wheel-arches flared out over gigantic customized tyres. It came almost to a stop at the entrance to the club and as I walked up quite fast a thick-set black man stepped out from the pink glow of the doorway, the car's rear door was flung open for him as a voice inside said 'Come on, Harold.' Then the door slammed, and the car surged away past me and down the street. I saw its bank of rear lights glare on as it braked at the crossroads, and then it swung to the right and was gone.

# The List

## PATRICK GALE

'Mother will have a fit,' I told her.

'Polly,' she said, taking my hand in hers beneath our discarded coats. 'Calm down. It'll be fine. It's not as though it will be any great surprise for her. She knows about us and everything.'

'Yes,' I said. 'At least she should do by now – she can be evasive. But I'm her baby. Her littlest.'

'Even littlests have to fly the nest some time. You're twenty-six for Christ's sake.'

'Twenty-five.'

'Is that *all*?'

'Twenty-six next birthday.' I smiled. The taxi pulled over. Mother's street. Holy Mary, Mother of God.

'You make me feel so old,' Claudia complained.

'Mother will think you're a cradle-snatcher.'

'She won't, will she?' A moment of panic from Claudia.

'Just teasing.' Now it was her hand's turn to be pressed.

'Anyway,' she went on, 'with you having lived it up in Rome for the last year she can scarcely accuse me of ripping you untimely from the maternal bosom.'

'Mmm,' I said, thinking of Rome, of Claudia's enormous bed in Rome, of the old pewter plate of figs and nectarines on the bedside table and the buzz of afternoon scooters beneath the shuttered window. 'But that didn't count. Abroad doesn't count as long as your mother has a room full of your things.'

'What things?' She withdrew her hand to push some hair back, exposing a silver earring in the shape of a shell. She saw me look. Renaissance silver. I had the other one but was not wearing it today. Mother had superstitions about wearing odd earrings. Like so many younger habits, she found it spiritually unhygienic.

'Oh, just things,' I said. 'Books. Boxes of letters. Clothes I never wear. Winter coats. My bears.'

'Bears?'

'Teddy bears. You know; toys. I have several. They were my grandmother's. They get passed down.'

She smiled discreetly and looked out of the window.

'We must adopt a baby *subito*,' she said.

The cab-driver was counting the numbers on the white-painted porticos. Forty-six. Forty-eight. Now and at the hour of our death.

'Just stop right here.' I tugged his little window open. Claudia had shut it earlier to give our conversation privacy.

'But I thought she lived at eighty-something?' she protested.

'Yup. Right here's just fine. Thanks,' I told the driver. 'I want to walk a little,' I told her. 'Fresh air will do us good.'

'Sorry we're in the dark,' Mother said. 'Mrs Sopwith's polishing silver.'

All the thick downstairs curtains were drawn. The dining-room table had been opened out and covered with several old flannel sheets. The family silver, which was kept in a broken twin-tub in the basement, was spread out on it, its variety of impractical or impenetrable shapes glistening in the light of a single, low-wattage lamp. Mrs Sopwith was hunched over a coffee pot, scrubbing at it with the brush my late father had used on his false teeth.

'Come up, come up,' sang Mother, mounting the stairs, 'and let me have a good look at you. Both of you.'

Claudia slipped a hand between my legs as we followed. Mrs Sopwith saw. I know she did.

Mother led us into the morning-room. It was full of things. Even without her silver knick-knacks (which Mrs Sopwith was polishing along with the bulkier stuff) its tabletops were cluttered. Family photographs smiled equally over one another's shoulders. Pot pourri mouldered in assorted Chinese containers. African violets and small begonias thrived on several surfaces and a vase of lilies sent out scarves of scent from the mantelshelf. New, unread novels, freshly delivered on account, caught the autumn sunlight on her desk-top. A sheaf of well-thumbed magazines had been painstakingly fanned out on the low, rectangular table between the sofas. A coffee table in any other house, it had always remained nameless in ours, scorned by Mother for its blameless lack of antique charm. I wished myself in Rome, furled in Claudia's matchless bed linen.

'I do wish Mrs Sopwith wouldn't do that,' said Mother, sweeping the magazines back into a vertical pile. 'Makes the place look like a chiropodist's waiting room.' With a few soft pats to the sofa cushion, she gestured to Claudia to sit beside her. I sat on the sofa before them and saw with a shock that they looked almost the same age, although Mother was the older by at least ten years.

Mother was what I had always thought of as a Chelsea blonde. I was blonde too, but to qualify for Chelsea blondedom one's hair had to be dead straight, hanging just to the shoulder, and preferably with the subtlest hint of who-gives-a-damn silver. Seen at its best oiled sleek on a beach or revealed *après ski* by the removal of an unflattering woolly hat, it was worn around town as occasion demanded. The severity of the look could be (and usually was) offset with all manner of frills and flounces down below and had the advantage over the dowdier Mayfair perm of conveying an unerring purity and youthful vigour.

'So,' Mother said, fatuously. 'You must be Claudia.' Thoughtlessly I corrected her pronunciation. 'Thank you dear. Claudia. Claudia.' She turned to Claudia for confirmation. Smiling girlishly. 'Claudia? To rhyme with "rowdier"?'

'That's right.' Claudia gave her a slow smile.

'Claudia.' Mother tried it again. 'But it sounds so much more attractive that way; quite fresh!' She laughed. I slipped off my shoes and drew my feet up on to the sofa, retreating. 'Polly's told me so much about you in her letters: Claudia this and Claudia that.'

'I hope she didn't bore you too much.'

'On the contrary. What an enchanting earring that is.'

'Thank you.'

'May I?'

'Of course.'

Mother was actually lifting Claudia's hair for a closer look. How dared she? Her liver-spotted digits on Claudia's silky darkness! She would never have shown such intimate interest in the few boys I had ever brought home. Smiling at the thought of her stooping to fondle Jeremy's belt buckle or Simon's latest loafer, I feigned interest in some new photographs of my cousins.

'I've given the other one to Polly,' said Claudia. 'They're pretty, aren't they? Mamma always swore they were seventeenth century but fakes are so clever nowadays, it's almost impossible to tell.'

'Good lord! Polly, have you got yours on now?'

'No. It's . . . It's back with my things.'

'Well I hope your things are somewhere safe.'

'Oh yes.'

'My brother's flat has more security than Fort Knox,' put in Claudia. 'Quite absurd because Enzo seems to spend his every daylight hour at the bank and has nothing to steal.'

'Is he married?'

'Enzo? No. Only to his bonds and his little screens. He does drive an absurdly powerful car though, so I suspect he may yet surprise us all.'

'Like our Polly,' said Mother and giggled. 'But you won't be living at his place indefinitely, surely?'

'We're flat-hunting already,' I broke in.

'We?' Mother queried.

'Claudia and I.' I crossed my fingers. 'We're going to live together.'

'But surely you have to get back to Rome for your studies, darling?'

'The course is over. I must have told you several times in my letters. It finished in June. I was thinking of staying on for a bit but then Claudia's partner had this idea of opening a London office so we decided to come and set up house over here.'

In the space of a few, sunlit seconds a miniature drama of reaction and snatched understanding was played out across Mother's greyhound features.

'Oh!' she said. 'Oh,' (this with an undermining smile of self-mockery), 'I see.' She stood quickly and came to sit beside me. 'Darling, I hadn't realized. It'll be so lovely having you back for good. It is for good, isn't it?'

'Fairly good,' I said, 'Yes.'

She kissed me then pushed my hair back to reveal where the other earring should have glistened. She was showing all manner of unfamiliar emotions and I was not sure I was altogether happy with any of them. She kissed me again.

'I'm so glad for you,' she said then turned to Claudia. 'And Claudia, too,' she said, holding out her hand which Claudia, bemused but smiling, took. 'I'm so glad. We must have a party.'

'Why?' I asked.

She prodded me in the ribs and scoffed, 'You're so like your father, darling. "Why?" To celebrate. To welcome you back, to introduce everyone to Claudia and to *celebrate*! Have you found somewhere to live yet?'

'Well as a matter of fact,' Claudia admitted, 'we looked over somewhere yesterday which was perfect. Right on the park with a roof-terrace and some good-sized rooms which would be convenient for showing off pieces to clients, and a quite extraordinary bathroom . . .'

'But they were asking the earth for it,' I said. 'It was fairly huge.'

'. . . and I wasn't going to tell Polly until I'd had some confirmation, but I rang them this morning and made an offer which they accepted.'

'Claudia!'

'Are you cross?' she asked me.

'No, I'm thrilled. But . . . you didn't tell me.'

I was thrilled. I was very, very happy. The flat was indeed perfect for us. Somehow the whole treat had been spoilt, however, by being revealed in Mother's presence. Our new love-nest was twenty minutes' or more drive from where we sat but suddenly I felt as though its newly painted, spectacularly empty spaces were merely a previously undisclosed annexe to Mother's over-furnished domain. No sooner was the precious territory offered me than the Kingdom of Knick-Knack absorbed it.

Excited, Mother clapped her hands.

'Now, you mustn't say no. As my only daughter you can't escape a proper send-off. Your father set aside a tidy sum for just such an eventuality – well, maybe this wasn't quite the eventuality he'd had in mind, but still – so it won't cost you a thing. By rights we should put an announcement in *The Times*.'

'Mother!'

She pointed at my face and laughed at its expression. '*Just* like your father! Don't worry. No announcements. I'm not utterly grotesque. But I do insist on giving you both a proper reception with invitations and I'm damned if I see why all your dreary brothers should have got married and had lists and you shouldn't.'

'But I'm not getting married.'

'Well you're not going to marry anyone else, are you?'

'No, but . . .' She was breaking every rule. She was quite mad. I looked to Claudia for help but she was sitting back, stroking her gentle smile with the back of a forefinger and looking to see what Mother would say next. She was charmed. I could tell.

'There we are then. Why don't we go round there now? It would be such fun.' Mother uncurled herself from the sofa and stood, giving her Chelsea blondeness a quick flick as she glanced in the looking glass. 'Have you got much to do this morning?'

'No. Not really,' said Claudia, still smiling to herself. 'But tell me, Mrs Reith . . .'

'Prudie, please.'

'Prudie.' Claudia's pronunciation was right first time, although the pout it lent her lips was perhaps unnecessarily seductive. 'I don't quite understand. What is this list?'

'When you set up house together . . .'

'Get married,' I broke in.

'Same thing,' Mother snapped.

'But it's meant to be a reward,' I said, astonished, 'for doing the right thing.'

'Just like her father,' she told Claudia again, shaking her head in mock sorrow. 'Such a shame you never met him. Anyway, when you set up house together – or marry,' she added, with a bow in my direction, 'you run up a list at your favourite shop of all the things you need to make domestic bliss complete, and your friends and well-wishers call in there and buy them for you. If you get your timing right and don't go living in sin for too long beforehand, you don't have to buy a thing. You'd be amazed at people's generosity. You shall be.'

We drank a quick celebratory gin while Claudia met Mrs Sopwith and was asked to cast a charitably professional eye over some of the more outlandish family silver. The few excuses I could drum up were quickly quashed by both Mother and Claudia, and soon the three of us were walking down the road to Sloane Square.

'It's an inexplicably dull shop,' Mother explained as I held open a swing door for them both. 'But utterly trustworthy. You could leave a child in its care. I quite often did.'

The 'Bride's Book' was still appropriately close to the department selling prams and pushchairs. The only apparent concession to modern living was the computer on which its lists were now maintained. Twisted with embarrassment, I dawdled by a shelf of soft toys and succeeded in making Claudia drop back to find me.

'What's wrong, Polly?' she asked. 'You look quite grey. Do you want to go back into the fresh air?'

'Quite right I do. She's only doing this to embarrass us. She wants to punish me for not bringing home some dull man she can approve of and tease.' I snatched a donkey and pulled on its pink felt ears. 'She's going to make a huge scene, I warn you. And so will the shop. They only do lists for nice young girls with fiancés. Not . . .' I hesitated.

'Not what?'

'Not not-so-nice young girls with elegant, titled but undeniably female partners.'

'So?' Claudia purred, setting the donkey back on its shelf and taking my hands in hers, 'Let Prudie have her joke. Let her show her feelings. Maybe its easier for her this way. After all, it's only a shop, not the *Castello* Windsor.'

The precision of her pronunciation of Windsor made me smile through my mortification. I called to mind the beauty of the flat she was buying us. I let her lead me forward.

The woman behind the counter was old enough to have granddaughters. Unable to meet her eye, I fell to examining her uniform, wondering how something so ill-tailored could convey such irreproachability in the wearer. She would be scandalized.

'Good morning,' she said.

'Hello,' said Mother.

'Have you come to choose something from a list?'

'Not exactly,' said Mother. That was my cue. She was smiling at me and the woman behind the counter was waiting with her head at a politely inquiring angle.

'We've come to make one of our own,' I confessed.

'Lovely,' said the woman, her face impassive the while. 'Congratulations. I'll just open a file for you.' She tapped away at the computer keyboard. 'Your name, please.' Now she smiled at me briefly.

'Polly Reith,' I told her. 'Miss Polly Reith.'

'And the gentleman's name?'

'Er . . .' I faltered and looked to Mother for help.

'Not a gentleman,' Mother told her. 'Not a male, that is. Is there a problem?'

I noticed that the woman wore an unusual jet ring. She turned it briefly on her finger.

'Not at all,' she assured us. 'The lady's name?'

'Claudia Carafontana,' said Claudia.

'Contessa,' Mother added. I saw her eyes glitter with vulgar pride. The woman behind the counter tapped in Claudia's title.

'Contessa,' she repeated under her breath. 'And will you be wanting the gifts delivered as they are bought,' she asked, 'or would you rather arrange for collection at a later date?'

'Oh, delivery would be better, I think,' said Claudia, evidently entering into the spirit of the occasion. 'Don't you think so darling? Of course, the address is not quite certain as yet.'

'That's not a problem. If I could just have a phone number in case of queries.'

'Of course,' I said, anxious not to be quite passed over, and I gave her Lorenzo's number and address.

'Fine,' we were told. 'Walk around the store at your leisure and when you see things you'd like just write their details on this form. Here, I'll fix it on a clipboard to make writing easier.'

'Not a perambulator,' said Claudia as we headed towards the household appliances department, 'not just yet.'

Claudia's solicitors and those of the property developers who sold her – who sold us – the flat, worked fast. We were able to take possession within a month of her offer being accepted. In the interim I discovered Claudia to be far richer than I had imagined. In Rome she had existed within a *mise-en-scène* completed long before my arrival. Her chests, mirrors and portraits, her rugs, pewter plates, even her vast bed with its carved headboard, were so encrusted with Carafontana family history that they seemed an extension of her personality, barely material and certainly nothing one could buy. It was something of a shock, therefore, to see her cut adrift from her historical moorings, free to create a new setting of her very own. Of our very own. She dedicated her mornings to setting up the new branch of her antique business. Claudia and her cousin Maurizio did nothing so sordid as buy and sell. Rather, they found antiques for clients too busy to shop themselves, discreetly arranging purchase and well-insured delivery for a large commission. She swiftly found a clutch of London clients who were either eager to buy the kind of Italian antiques that rarely found their way into auction houses or keen to sell their English furniture for the inflated prices Claudia could easily persuade her Italian clients to pay. I spent my mornings sustaining the illusion that I was searching for gainful employment.

Claudia devoted her afternoons to Mammon and Mother in equal proportions. Trailing me, astonished, in her wake, she bought paintings, mirrors, Bokhara carpets, candelabra and vases. We pored over whole epics of fabric samples and she ordered curtains and drapes of a luxury that rounded even Mother's bridge-table eyes. She was dissatisfied with much that the property developers had done, and painstaking hours were spent planning the undoing of their costly work and choosing replacement doorknobs, windowcatches and taps. Until then I had no idea that taps could be so expensive. This booty was stored in what had once been my bedroom which was, as Mother pointed out, only twenty minutes' drive from the new flat. Mother would admire each new purchase judiciously, robbing it, as she did so, of the charms that had briefly seemed to distinguish it from others of its kind. She would then invariably take Claudia on some social excursion.

'You don't mind my borrowing her, do you, darling?' she asked the first few times, making it plain that I was surplus to her requirements. 'Just silly old friends who bore you rigid, but they will insist on laying eyes, if not hands, on dear Claudia before the reception.'

Claudia's capacity for such socializing astonished me. In Rome she had only met people in the evenings and then only in strictly monitored doses. She regarded her own mother and her fustian social rounds with undisguised contempt, which made her unlooked-for charity towards mine and her no more interesting bridge cronies doubly curious.

Left to my own devices I indulged in cinema matinées, enjoying the excuse some of the more far-flung repertory houses gave for lengthy taxi rides. A cinema in Hampstead was showing *Rose-*

*mary's Baby*. I had missed it first time around and found the plot oddly compelling. I saw it three times in one week. Like *Othello* (which Claudia claimed had one of the theatre's richest histories of audience interruption), the more one saw it the more maddening it became.

'Open your eyes!' I wanted to scream at Mia Farrow. 'Put down that milkshake, pack your bags and run!' But I never did.

We moved into the flat only two days before the reception was to be held there, but the process was remarkably unstressful. Claudia and Mother between them had scheduled the delivery of her larger purchases with the precision of a military campaign. Unfortunately my half-hearted trail through the job market had proved successful and I found myself committed to a mornings-only post as a researcher.

'Never mind, *cara*,' Claudia told me, 'you can come for lunch and have a lovely surprise.'

So I set off to work from Enzo's flat as usual then came home to our own, for lunch.

Two men had been to remove taps, knobs and windowcatches and Claudia's choices were now in place, as were her rugs, the booty briefly stored in my childhood bedroom, and a Jacobean bed that was almost as big as the one we had shared in Rome. I stood in the doorway looking around me over the wall of cardboard boxes. Claudia shut the door, stooped to remove my shoes, kissed each of my stockinged feet then led me to the bed.

'And so,' she said, unbuttoning my suit, 'begins our new life together.' She made her habitually subtle love to me on new, matchless, bed linen after which she fed me champagne and, *in memoriam*, figs. 'Mmm,' she sighed contentedly, 'Prudie was right to have the bed delivered first. I was all for concentrating on the pictures.'

'This was *her* idea?'

Claudia laughed nervously at my tone. 'Well, only the bed. I thought of the figs myself.'

'Glad to hear it.'

'Polly, don't sulk. It's childish.'

'Well maybe, but spending so much time with old women is unnatural.'

'*Unnatural?*'

'Yes.' I sat up and swung my legs off the side of the bed. 'Anyway, they're only interested because you're a countess.'

'Hardly,' Claudia snorted. 'Prudie's circle is a lot more sophisticated than you seem to realize. They haven't batted an eyelid about you and I living together and if the way that wedding list is being ticked off is any indication, they're giving us a substantial blessing.' She rubbed my shoulder. '*Cara.*' She hesitated. 'You really don't see it, do you?'

'See what?'

'When did your father die?'

'When I was about three.'

'And how many boyfriends has Prudie had since then?'

'I don't know. She's always been very discreet. Several, I should think.'

'None, Polly. She's had none. And she's still an attractive woman. Does she cherish his memory?'

'Not exactly. He was much older than her. There's a photograph of him somewhere.'

I turned at last. Claudia was leaning on one elbow, dark hair swept back to reveal silver earring. She raised her glass to drink and her ivory bracelets slid with a clatter to her elbow. She smiled slowly.

'No!' I breathed.

I dressed fast, left the flat and caught a taxi to Sloane Square. My mind was filled, as in some Satanic slide-show, with images of Mother and her 'nearest and dearest', Heidi Kleinstock, Tricia Rokeby, Daphne Wain, the Crane sisters (about whom I had always had my suspicions) and even Mrs Sopwith, in a fast-changing circuit of sexual arrangements. The editrix of the Bride's Book greeted me with a knowing smile and twiddled her ring. I realized why it had first caught my eye. Daphne Wain had a jet ring too, though larger, of course, and so did Heidi Kleinstock and, when blowsy peasant fashions had held sway, even Mother had sported one, with large jet earrings to match.

'Good afternoon, Miss Reith,' said the woman. 'Come to make a progress check? I'll do you a print-out to take away with you.'

She pressed a button then, somewhere beneath her desk, a printer hummed into action. When it came to rest she handed me a sheet of paper. There were all the plates, bowls, cutlery, glasses, salad bowls and napkin sets chosen, as I had then supposed, merely to humour Mother's fantastic game the other day. And there, beside most of them, were women's names. Numerous women's names. Many of them were quite unfamiliar and all of those I recognized were single by death, solicitors or choice. Half in jest, Mother had suggested I set down the name of a highly-developed dishwasher. A chronic exhibitionist, Tricia Rokeby had bought it for us. I pictured it being delivered wrapped in a large jet-black bow with a card attached, swirled over with her jet-black greetings and unwanted solidarity.

I drank a cup of strong tea, not because I wanted it but because the store's top floor café, The Coffee Bean, carried unfailing associations with the well-buttoned certainties of childhood. I drank a second cup because I had begun to realize that I was, perhaps, a little disorientated from drinking champagne with no more substantial accompaniment than a few figs. Two walls of the café were taken up with windows on to the square and one of the bustling roads that fed it, a third, which I was facing, was panelled with mirrors. I stared at myself long and hard, stared at the long, unChelsea curls of my hair, at the unmade-up face which Mother had once called 'quiet' in my hearing, at my small, ringless hands. I had bought my navy coat on a trip to Milan and it had done its best to look too big for me ever since, dissociating itself from my neck and shoulders at the least opportunity. I sat up straight and tugged it slightly at the lapels. Obediently, it fitted me once more. I had taken shelter from a downpour – unprepared as usual – although Claudia was waiting for me in a restaurant on the other side of the piazza. It was the only important garment I had bought on my own since meeting her; normally she was at my elbow purring, 'Or this, perhaps?'

I paid for my teas and hurried down the stairs to street level. There was a hair salon a few doors away, far too fashion-conscious and young for Mother, whatever her proclivities. I let myself in. Its atmosphere was stridently chemical; bubblegum and bleach. The music was loud – Claudia tended to listen to Baroque productions performed 'authentically' – and gave me back the strength the mirrors had sapped. I would have my hair cut to within an inch of my scalp and dyed red. Traffic-light red. It was what my coat had always needed. Mother too, perhaps.

'Hello there. What can we do for you, then?' asked a stylist, picking incuriously at my hair. The words sounded like a challenge but her mind was plainly on other things.

'Oh,' I said, 'just a trim, please. And a wash.' I offered her my quietest smile.

## *from* The Novice

**TIMOTHY IRELAND**

'Do you want a buttermilk bedroom? Or would you prefer a Harmony or a Misty shade?'

Davy smiled.

'You choose,' he said.

We were standing inside a high street do-it-yourself store in front of a bright display of paint colours.

'You found the flat,' I said carefully.

Davy turned to me.

'It's for *our* bedroom.'

Our. The word was somehow comforting. I ran my eyes once again over the colour cards.

'Perhaps we ought to get paint that fits in with the carpet and curtains.' I turned my attention back to Davy. 'What colour are they under all the dust?'

For a moment I thought Davy hadn't heard me. His face was suddenly blank as though he were somewhere else. Perhaps it was the strangeness of these last days, the suddenness of the changes . . .

Davy had discovered the flat tucked away at the bottom of a tall, crumbling Victorian house in Queen's Park. It was a decent size, having a large lounge, a double bedroom and a separate kitchen and bathroom. There was even a small garden at the back. The reason we could afford it was because of the run-down condition it was in.

As you entered the dim hallway the smell of damp and cats almost knocked you over. In the narrow kitchen the crooked cupboards were coming away from the walls covered with dirt and grease. The gas-cooker, practically an antique, looked as though a hundred saucepans had boiled over and still no one had cleaned up.

Although the previous tenant, a Mrs Wheeler, was no longer in occupation, she'd left traces of her life behind her. The stick she'd used, perhaps to support her stumbling walk, still stood in the corner of the living room beside the heavily indented armchair which must have been her favourite resting place. On the mantlepiece above the old-fashioned gas-fire pranced a set of brown and white china dogs grey with dust.

But dust was everywhere. The windows were grimy and the veiled curtains discoloured. Faded floral wallpaper was coming away from the walls and spider-webs had collected in the corners of the ceilings. Everywhere bore the marks of the helpless neglect of an old woman too frail or infirm to make the necessary practical changes and repairs. It was difficult to believe that the flat would ever feel like home.

Coming out of his own private reverie. Davy seemed to read my thoughts.

'Once we've decorated the bedroom, it'll be all right,' he said. 'Then we'll have at least one liveable room to sleep in.'

That night we slept on a mattress on the living-room floor. We had worked together all afternoon and evening in the bedroom, stripping away all the old wallpaper.

Weary, we undressed for bed in darkness, lying down on the wide mattress without an embrace. With the two wardrobes towering over me and the walls of boxes and bags we still couldn't unpack, I felt as though I were sleeping on the floor of an old junk shop.

Restless, for a long time I lay awake, listening to the tick of Davy's old clock set on the mantlepiece where once the china dogs had been. It had taken four black dustbin liners to clear the flat of old Mrs Wheeler's personal possessions. Thinking of the old lady, imagining her sitting in the sagging armchair, I reached out to touch Davy who was sleeping with his back to me. But his body seemed to reject even the thought of a caress.

We'd argued that afternoon, irritated by the dust and dirt, sensitive to the fact that now we had to try and make it together: that neither of us had a separate space to escape to.

So began a routine. Every evening we came home from work and changed out of our working clothes into our oldest jumpers and jeans. After a quick cup of tea, we'd go back into the bedroom to continue our decorating.

First we had to finish stripping the peeling wallpaper off the ceiling and walls using solvent and metal scrapers. Then we sanded down all the woodwork; the window frame, the curtain rail, the door and the skirting boards. We'd left the calor-gas heater on full for days to try and dry the walls out, but in the end Davy had to chisel out the worst of the damp patches, damp-proof the walls and then replaster. Then we wallpapered everywhere and overnight the room was as white and bright as a room in a hospital.

Weary, hardly able to believe we would ever finish, we began the painting, undercoating the walls ready for two coats of the pale lilac paint Davy had chosen because it was a soft enough colour to encourage sleep.

Lilac dreams, I'd teased, and it became a catchphrase between us; something to make us smile when the dust, the plaster, the glue, the paper and the paint made us want to run out of the flat screaming.

*Lilac dreams.*

All we seemed to do was work on the flat.

Perhaps they were happy days? The sense of labour drew us closer, but also wore us down to the point of sadness. Tired, neither of us could hide our doubts. Had we done the right thing in living together? Since we'd moved into the flat we hadn't made love once, seldom ever kissed. Never have I understood why it was like that.

The evening after we'd finished painting our lilac walls Davy came home with a large brown paper parcel. Inside the package were new curtains: the palest cream background with feathery green leaves interlaced with lavender and pale blue flowers.

Still nervous of kissing me Davy stepped away. I held the curtains up between us, soft in my hands.

'They're beautiful.'

'I chose the material specially. You're always going on about flowers, and I've hardly bought you any.'

Not knowing what to say, I took his hand.

'You'll see the blue and purple blooms,' Davy whispered, 'Last thing at night and first thing in the morning. All year round.'

At last the day came when everything in the bedroom was done. Scarcely able to believe we'd finished, we took it in turns to soak in a hot-scented bath. Sitting up in bed with tall glasses, the room warmed by the gas-fire, we shared a bottle of red wine.

For days we hadn't touched, but when at last he held me I was happy. At the keenest moment of shared pleasure there was for once no ending. Wet in our embrace, still we lay in each other's arms.

Davy kissed me.

'I love you,' he whispered.

It was the only time he ever used those words. But I cannot forget.

Living together involved unforeseen changes and compromise, and the loss of what we both called our independence. We argued, sometimes bitterly. Perhaps love, if it endures, makes us responsible. But it takes time to get used to, this business of considering someone else's needs.

I was often afraid, but gradually the fear faded and there were times when I felt more content and secure than ever before. At the end of the day I lay down to sleep with my lover beside me. And when I woke in the morning and reached out, he was there.

In the moments of doubt, it was strangely the small routine things which helped reassure me. Cooking for the first time became satisfying now I was preparing a meal for both of us.

Ironing, previously so tedious, had a relaxing even theraputic quality, now my life had a calmer home base. And of course, if I ironed his shirts, then a week later I could sit and watch him take his turn at the ironing-board.

Even shopping for groceries, a chore I'd always disliked, was almost enjoyable now we wheeled a trolley round Sainsbury's together, treating ourselves occasionally to favourite cheeses and biscuits, selecting a joint of meat for a shared Sunday roast.

My one regret was that we didn't spend Christmas together that year. I went home to Mum and Dad and Davy took the train back to Wales, spending the festive season with his Da and his brother's family in Blaengarw. 'There'll be other Christmases for you and me,' Davy said.

The New Year came and went. The winter weeks slipped by and gradually the darkness didn't draw in quite so soon. I was able to walk about the flat in one jumper instead of two. When March came, I turned my attention out of doors.

The garden of our basement flat was small and U-shaped; overgrown flowerbeds around an oblong of rakishly tall grass.

'There's some shears in the hall cupboard,' Davy said, one Sunday afternoon. 'I could cut the lawn back.'

'It's better if we clear the beds, first. Uproot all the weeds.'

Davy nodded.

'Right then.'

Several mugs of tea and six black dustbin liners later, the flowerbeds were two-thirds clear of weeds, bramble and dead plants.

'We'll save the smelly part till next week.' I said. 'Digging in the horse-manure.'

Davy grinned.

'Are you sure you know what you're doing?'

'I've seen my mother put manure in the ground for roses. It must enrich the soil.'

'Feeding the earth before the plants feed themselves.'

'That's the logic of it.'

Standing close to him, I reached out a hand to touch his cheek, then stopped, remembering the neighbours. You only had to step out into the backyard before the curtains twitched.

Davy winked at me.

'We deserve a rest and a cup of tea,' he said.

'Sounds good.'

We smiled at one another and I was aware of Davy standing close behind me.

'I'll run the hot water,' he whispered. 'If you'll share a bath with me.'

As I began to trust Davy, so the sex between us grew better and better. Secure in his arms, at last I could relax completely, put aside my fear of being held, my body at another's mercy. Whatever anyone says, being fucked by another man can be the most miserable of sexual experiences. But it can also be an experience which is profoundly pleasurable. Being able to satisfy each other in this way deepened our sense of sharing, as though now nothing was being held back.

Of course at the time when Davy and I shared this – not even a decade ago – relatively few people in the United Kingdom had heard of Aids. Even though a number of men had died in this country, it was still perceived very much as a North American disease. There was not yet the panic for Immunity, and Safe Sex meant only steering clear of the Yanks.

In so little time things would change.

For Easter we bought each other chocolate eggs. 'The first I've had since I was a kiddy,' Davy said.

I ruffled his hair.

'It's not Easter, not properly, without an egg.'

Davy grinned.

'You're a weird one, boy.'

Shrugging, I sat up.

'Why should we give things up just because we're adults? If we had children of our own we'd be playing at Christmas and Easter for years.'

'You want babies now?'

I laughed. 'Despite even your ingenuity, Davy, I don't think we could manage that.'

Davy dipped his head, teasing. 'Wait till we're married.'

'Aren't we married now?'

'We're living together . . .' Davy made a face.

'It feels like being married.'

'Being married is Church and Weddings, Don. Family celebration. It's different from this.'

'But it comes down to living together.'

'Maybe.' Davy shook his head, smiled. 'Next thing I know you'll be asking me for a ring.'

The following Saturday morning I woke to discover a freak fall of April snow. Clearing a space on the cold frosty glass of the bedroom window, I looked out to see a thin white blanket covering everything in the backyard. In a sudden shaft of sunshine the snow glittered crisp and brilliant, making even our small garden beautiful.

I woke Davy with a kiss high on his forehead. He blinked, turning over playfully and hiding his head under the bed-covers.

'Davy, I've brought you tea.'

Making doggy growling noises, he burrowed deeper under the blankets. Smiling, I slipped off my dressing-gown and crept under the covers to join him, feeling him move close and wrap his arms around me, press his face into my chest.

'Mind where you put your cold feet,' he whispered.

'You're as hot as toast.'

'I want to stay that way.' There was a laugh in his throat.

'Cuddle me,' I asked.

'Cuddle me says the Ice-Box. Where did you get such cold hands?'

'There's snow outside. The kitchen's like a refrigerator. Frost on the window. I made us both a cup of tea.'

'You deserve a hug then.'

'Mmmm.'

The snow disappeared as quickly as it had come. Spring was firmly settled in. Davy watched me fill the lightweight plastic trays with earth from the garden. Using a pencil to dig small holes, I painstakingly sowed one by one the seeds from the packets: night-scented stocks, lavender, pansies, lupins and mesembryanthemums. Watering the trays using an old milk-bottle, Davy solemnly promised to buy me a watering-can. We covered the trays with wedge-shaped shards of glass left over from a once-broken window.

'If we leave these in the light and remember to water them,' I said. 'They should be all right.'

Davy nodded.

'So all we need now is luck.'

Now the days called to summer. The evenings grew lighter, drawing people out on to the streets. Everything was taking shape now. Davy had cut the grass back and raked out even the most persistent weeds. The seeds we'd planted under glass in the plastic trays, sprouted green tendrils and miniature curls of leaf. Two weeks later the seedlings stood tall enough to plant out into the garden.

'It will be fair splash of colour,' Davy said, contemplating the flowerbeds, imagining how it would be.

'We can sunbathe out here,' I smiled at him. 'Get a tan while we watch the flowers grow.'

'And next year, roses.'

'Yes.'

We looked at one another, as though we were still surprised at our closeness. It was strange that sense of maybe having a future: the two of us together sharing a life.

In May we decorated the living-room, painting the walls white-with-a-hint-of-apricot. It made the flat brighter, gave us the feeling of having more space.

And the summer came.

In the warm evenings the air in our garden was sweet with the perfume of white and purple night-scented stocks. The sweet peas, delicate shades of red, blue and mauve, climbed the strings between the bamboo canes, became a wall of soft warm colour.

The pansies were cheerful clown-faces and the common stocks stood sturdy cream and gold. Even the lavender flourished. The fiery mesembryanthemum closed their daisy heads in early evening and opened again bright in the dawn.

In the hot July days the earth dried out and cracked and we feared the flowers would perish. So every evening, when the heat of the day had died away into an exhausted thrumming, Davy and I watered our garden. I'd stand in the kitchen and fix the suction end of the hose over the cold-water tap. The long hose snaked out through the kitchen window down to where Davy stood, waiting for the first jet of water. The flow of the water could be adjusted and Davy took great care, making sure that the frailest flowers were dampened by the finest spray.

Wandering out to the garden in light clothes, I'd stand close to him in the cool dark, caught in the long drawn cry of summer. As the droplets of water fell onto the flowers we'd tended, above us were the stars, brilliant in the night sky. I'd shut my eyes and just listen, aware of him there. Never have I known such peace.

# Three Wedding Ceremonies

## NEIL BARTLETT

*I was perfectly agreeable to be his wife or husband,
whichever he preferred.*

Anon, *Confessions of a Maryanne*, London 1881

### ONE

That summer of their courtship they were, as we said, *living
together*, but with the accent on the first word, to indicate not that
they were sharing the same premises, for they had not yet moved
into the flat, but to indicate that they were indeed *living*, living a
fine life together, a life of quite scandalous sexual happiness and
promise. We talked about them all the time; we felt that their
coupling was somehow different, that they were somehow, for
the duration of that long summer, our mascots, our perfect pair,
the sign of all our hopes. Each time they appeared in public we
would note how well they looked, or how tired, and speculate on
what made for such happiness, or what indeed made a young
man like Boy look so tired on a midweek evening, and especially
we would speculate on when, oh when would O. and his Boy
declare themselves, and become a real couple and not just an
affair. When, we wondered, would they first be heard or over-
heard to use the word 'we'.

We had no shortage of occasions for speculation; they appeared
in public together several times a week that summer. They had, as
so many had at that time, a great hunger for entertainment.

Night after night they would dress elaborately and late and set
out for the part of town where all the theatres were. They never
paid for these visits, because O. would always time their arrival to
coincide with the first interval, and no manager or usher ever
queried the right of such a handsome and proud-profiled couple
to pass unhindered to their seats. Besides, they were so well-

dressed. There always seemed to be two empty seats in whatever theatre they attended (O. liked them to sit where they could see everything) and O. would lead his Boy confidently to them and they would take their seats and then sit there surrounded by people who all looked much like each other, reasonably happy and well-dressed and well-coupled people, would sit there invisible in the particular, comfortable darkness of a theatre whose tickets are expensive, a darkness smelling of chocolates, hair and expensive fabrics, fans, the fresh gilt of restored cherubs, velvet, even furs, real leather, the perfume of wives, the heavy breath of a sleeping husband.

They themselves never ate chocolates or ordered drinks, since they came out with only their bus fares in O.'s pocket. Sometimes they felt that they had to go out every night of the week, sometimes O. even wanted to see the same show three times in the same week. Boy always accompanied him, of course, and all day for days would be spent in bathing and resting and ironing so that even though they had few outfits in those days they would always be gorgeous, so handsome; as good to look at, in fact, as all those married people.

They never discussed what they saw. In fact they hardly talked at all on these evenings. Boy was holding his breath with the effort of being beautiful (Boy himself would have said; *as handsome as he is*) most of the time, and knew that O. preferred them to be silent in public anyway, very strange and well bred; he wanted married women to look at them as they passed and ask themselves the question, *what is their story?*

The shows they saw never, of course, quite made sense, since they had always missed the first hour of whatever story there was. Boy guessed and guessed correctly that it did not much matter to O. what it was they watched, although he noticed that O. avoided the family comedies and preferred tragedies, operas and farces, any genre in which the male characters are reduced or elevated to tears. Boy himself wanted shows full of loud music, expensive lighting, punishing dance routines executed by desperate and expert boys and girls, astonishing stages which rose and fell to reveal deep black spaces (Boy thought; *that's how my heart works*) where moments earlier metal walls had risen, or staircases of coloured glass. But in every show they watched what they both truly wanted (and they would sit together in silence, would travel all the way there in silence waiting just for this to happen) was for there to be a single moment, a very special moment in which a woman would be caught in a spotlight and would sing, well, would just sing her heart out, about what they never exactly cared, but they knew it was for them, somehow, that she sang, for their condition; and they knew that it was for this moment that they had waited in silence each night, through the crowded streets, and through the foyer and then silent amid the eager conversations before the second act curtain. It was this moment that they wanted, this moment when the woman turned and sang, sang for them, and they would sit there together in the dark and listen to her and let the tears come and let them roll down their faces and drip with no one to see them and no one to ask them why they needed this moment or what they were feeling.

Waiting for this moment, this moment whose arrival could never be guaranteed, they would sit through as many as seven shows in a week. In the eighth week of their courtship and the tenth week of that especially hot summer – when all of the city, especially late at night and especially wherever we had gathered to flirt and sweat, seemed suspended in a state of strange anticipation, as if things were about to happen – they watched many extraordinary things.

They watched shows in which a moaning chorus of giant gibbons took the curtain with their artificial and elongated arms brushing the mirrored stage floor, each furred body topped by a tiny, sweating human face. They watched women in cages hoisted by bare-torsoed and grinning men; they watched shows in which entire cities slid mechanically to their ruin, each yellow-lit skyscraper leaving a slick of blood in the snow as it went. On the Thursday night they watched the demolition of smoking barricades manned by child-actors (their small and exposed limbs making the timbers that fell on them seem larger than they really were) – the ruined streets swung up on wires to reveal an inexplicable black lake in which the reflections of artificial stars were made to shimmer by the waving hands of white-gloved and singing swimmers. On the hottest Friday of that year they sat, surrounded by women, through a musical in which sixty-year-old actresses sang the songs of forty years ago, and were wildly applauded for exposing the ruins of their voices. Their legs were still worth seeing, if not for their elegance then for their strength, braced on sequinned shoes, flashed from the sequinned sheaths or spangled gauze ballgowns that they wore. The audience seemed to know all the words of all the songs – Boy and O. knew them too, but they did not mouth them under their breath as the others did, neither did they applaud at the end of each number. They were waiting. They were waiting for the moment when, at last, a single woman walked on to a stage suddenly cleared and darkened and bared (the scenery took flight in every direction), walked into a single light and stood there alone, in a dress as black as O.'s eyes and with arms as white and strong as Boy's. The woman turned her exposed back for a moment, then with the violins she turned again, she turned to them and she sang, sang her heart out, sang words no woman in her right mind would say.

On the seventh night the show which O. had chosen did not give them what they wanted. On this, the final night of a week of silent and elaborate revels, the tears did not come. They sat and waited as on the other nights, but on this night they had to leave the theatre unsatisfied. And it was on this night, Boy later told us, it was on this night that O. had finally, in his own way, proposed. It was on this strange night that they declared themselves to each other – although it was not until later, you understand, that the engagement was made public, and was publicly celebrated.

The show that night was an historial epic entitled 'By Night; or, The Dark Side of Our Great City'. Its final number was a famous spectacle at that time; a reconstructed Victorian pantomime, in whose transformation scene ludicrously winged fairies hung on wires above the smouldering jewels of a lime-lit diamond mine. The touch of a wand, a swing of Harlequin's bat, and the jewels began to spit and sparkle in a display of synchronized fireworks. It was so beautiful that everyone, O. and Boy as well, was jolted into applause. They stared and applauded as the sparks drifted upwards, applauded as one caught the gauze skirt of the fourteenth hanging fairy, applauded still as she hung there and burnt, twitching. They applauded out of simple shock as her hands brushed her skirts free of flames, as the glazed paper of her wings burnt especially brightly.

The reviews of the show reported (this was a clipping Boy long kept in his box of papers and would often read when O. was out of the flat), that in the original version of the scene, staged in a pantomime of 1867, thirteen women had burnt to death in front of an audience that had included the Queen and four of the Royal children. In fact, such incidents were common in those days. An eyewitness account of the deaths noted that the morning after Boxing Day there was a queue of women at the stage door, frightened but hopeful. After all, all you had to do was hang on a wire and grin. It must have been terrible of course for those girls, and terrible for all the people watching, just sitting there watching, but it was a terrible job anyway. Terrible just having to hang there. Terrible. *Terrible money of course. The worst thing was if you were hanging there and you felt a bit sick, and of course I did feel a bit sick, it was sickening, oh dear when Jenny was three months gone oh fuck it was halfway through the hellmouth scene and that bloody woman was singing and up it all came, all down her dress and all over the stage, bread and beer all nicely warmed up and spilt all over Johnny in his devil outfit, but of course you mustn't laugh because then the harness cuts into you when you jiggle up and down. Oh and the worst, Jenny the worst is when you come on, it's terrible, there you are, hanging up there trying to keep still during the sea-ballet, and you can feel the blood trickling down your sea-green, and you think, how are you going to get them home to wash them, because he checks your baskets when you leave because of course so many of the girls try and sell their other tights and then wear the same pair for the first three scenes, you can't really tell if they're yellow or red under those flower-girl outfits after all (I hate that fucking scene, red cotton roses, red silk and red wax and you have to kick the skirt forward and up with every step, I don't know how those poor girls managed in those days when they had to do it all day for a living), and there you are hanging there dripping blood, it went all the way down on to her shoe. The funny thing of course is the having to grin all the time no matter what's happening, that's all he ever says, Smile Jenny, smile, and when you're having a break, or after, you walk home, and it's not the feet, it's not the shoulders, it's the face, your face hurts, your lips crack with all that smiling, smiling all night, and I'm so embarrassed about my teeth, it's awful, I don't mind showing my bits but I do like to keep my lips closed if you know what I mean, though of course those costumes don't half show off all your legs (of course, that's what they're paying for) I get so hysterical if I see some Johnny I fancy, they think you can't see them, there you are hanging on a wire with the footlights right up your fucking frock and you get all hot and you see him talking to his friends about you and you think Oh God don't let there be a damp patch, he can see everything from down there and all for fucking four and six, it's hysterical really, but you mustn't start laughing of course because if one of you kicks off that's it there you all are up there laughing and jiggling and Jenny drops her wand and it just makes me want to piss. I never have pissed up there but I'd like to. Imagine that, a bunch of fairies hanging up there, Fairy of Piss, Fairy of Shite, Fairy of Bleeding, Fairy Up It Comes, Fairy of Hysterical Laughter, Fairy Fairy, Fairy Cunt, Fairy Fairy-Fucker, and as the centrepiece, with tears of crystal, Fairy of Public Weeping, that would be something to see, imagine us all up there in a row, each with her gimmick, that would give them something to grin at. I'd like to see that on the programme tonight. Tonight a Foreign Country with all its scenes and features, and at the Grand Finale the Fairies will weep, Fairy of Come-Dripping-Out, Fairy of Excuse-me (that's the new girl, she must be desperate for work!) and on the lead wire the Fairy of Dead Children, an entirely new feature; glycerine tears, a headdress of India Pearls and white Paris sequins, her dress stitched entirely with teardrops and the chiffon hand-dampened with rose-water by The Girls, and in her left hand the Tear Wand, that drips when you squeeze it, it doesn't half do your wrist, and we all sing:*

It only hurts me when I cry;
I couldn't ever tell you why

My foot's got no shoe on it : I've lost me stockings too;
I've sold me feather bonnet and I don't know what to do –
But my Boy he's a Butcher, he smiles and says to me;
'I'll give you good fresh meat Girl, I gets it all for free.' –
Oh! That won't hurt you
(That can't hurt me!)
This won't hurt you
(Go on, hurt me!)
Does it hurt you?
(Does it hurt? – OOOh!)
Does it hurt you?
(Tell me please do – )


CHORUS: Only when I cry, Johnny,
         Only when I cry!
         Only when I cry, Johnny,
         Only when I cry!

*Everybody off and change. Change please!*


## TWO

And so amidst all that they made their choice, and they were
finally married. Everyone was there, everyone.

And after the wedding there was the reception in their flat, and
when that was over we all went home, for there was nothing more
we could do to make them happy or bless their union except leave
them alone together to get on with it; and as we left we left slowly
and wondering, most us, half of us wishing that it was us left
behind and not doing the leaving, imagining the night to come
and then the days to come.

And so O. and his Boy saw the last of us out of the door and
then they shut the door, their front door, and they were finally,
after all the plans and rehearsals and new outfits and best wishes,
finally left alone at five o'clock on the last hot day of summer, left

alone with the cigarette ends and the plastic cups everywhere and nowhere to sit, no chairs, not a stick of furniture in the whole flat except the bed, and the records and the stacks of books, for they were real newlyweds in that way. All they had on that first afternoon alone together as a properly married couple in their flat was a bed and plenty to drink; and everywhere the great big bunches of flowers, dying already, some of them wild flowers, seeding and smelling of fields; and the early evening sun coming in and turning the walls yellow.

When everyone was gone they didn't want to talk much or even move much, they just wanted to be alone and taste this novel sensation of being left alone as a couple in their flat, to be quiet; but they were both so happy that every now and then they had to say something to each other or touch each other, so O. would come up to Boy for a kiss and Boy would pull away and smile and say *Do you really want to hurt me, do you really want to see me cry?*, and then O. would play looking very serious and say *Babe I'm going to show you that a woman can be tough, so come on, come on*, and then he would pull Boy to his feet and into his arms and say, *Take it, take another little piece of my heart now baby, break it*, and they'd slow dance in the middle of the empty room for a while with no one to watch them and no music playing except what they imagined they could hear. Then O. left Boy leaning against a bare wall in the sun, watching him, and he lit a cigarette and opened another beer and he sat in the middle of the floor and he wired up the stereo which had been our collective wedding present to the happy couple. This was the first truly domestic act of their married life, prior to making a cup of tea or making the bed. And then he opened one of the big cardboard boxes and he took out a set of records from the pile that was in there. Boy watched him smiling while he took the second record in the set out of its sleeve and carefully selected the right place on the second side for the needle to go down, but before he put the needle down O. went over to the window and threw it full open, and Boy knew as he watched him that this was not just to let in the sun, which was now turning to real solid gold along the walls, making the flowers, even the dead ones, shine in strange high-summer colours, but also because he wanted all the neighbours to hear this song. Then O. turned the volume up and he put the needle down and it started to play. It was a man singing in Italian, a man now forty years dead singing the aria called 'Dalla Sua Pace' from Mozart's opera of *Don Giovanni*, although Boy did not know these details until much later, when they had been living together for some time and O. had explained to him where all his records had come from and why. All Boy knew for now was that the voice was high and strong and beautiful, and as he listened to it he knew that this song was for him and for all the neighbours, knew that it was O.'s public and very special gift to him on the occasion of their wedding, more precious than the ring and more personal somehow. O. looked up at Boy from where he was crouched by the record player in the middle of the floor, and then he came back to where Boy was standing and leaning against a wall in the sun, and he reached out and he ran his fingers into the hair on both sides of Boy's head, and pushed him hard back against the wall, and pushed one knee between Boy's legs and brought his face right up close to Boy's. Boy thought he was going to get kissed. Instead what happened first was that O. just filled his hands with his beloved's hair like it was a breast or a bird, then took hold of it harder, as if the bird was struggling, and he began gently knocking Boy's head back against the wall, staring all the time right into his eyes. Boy put his hands up on O.'s shoulders and returned his gaze and let him do what he was doing, seeing that O. wanted to speak, but couldn't, and that he was biting his lip and that his eyes were beginning to fill with tears. Then Boy did get kissed; O. drew his left hand out of the black hair and let his fingers go down over Boy's temple and then his cheek, and then he brought his face even closer and kissed him, kissed him gently under the eye. Then he bit him over the cheekbone, and Boy was crying now too, silently, and his cheek was wet and his head swam from all the drink and the kisses that there'd been that afternoon, and from the hair pulling which began to hurt, and his face was sore from O.'s stubble and from his teeth, and O.'s knee was hurting him between his legs, and the music was playing, and

his heart was so full that his ribs heaved and ached on the left side
and he couldn't speak at all but he was thinking this is love, this is
love, this is love, this is my lover; and O. didn't think that he could
speak either what with the music and the sunlight and holding
Boy so loving and handsome in his hands, but after a time he did
find a voice; the music on the record dipped to a sweet hush for a
moment and looking Boy right in the eyes, still with his right hand
full of hair and with his voice brought low and gentle and broken
by his feelings he said

'Do you know what this means'
meaning the music, meaning the words the man was singing,
since he was singing in Italian, and Boy said, he wanted to say yes,
but instead he said

'No'
and at that point the voice on the records soared up again and all
the neighbours could hear and even see through the open
window, and O. put his mouth close to Boy's ear and sang the
lyrics to Boy, or rather half sang them, for he did them in English
so that Boy could understand every word of what he was saying as
they leant together against the yellow wall. By way of introducing
his translation he said, in a voice close to breaking as the voice on
the record rose,

'Let me tell you the meaning of this'
and then he did the aria itself, and what he said was

*On your peace of mind, mine depends,*
*When you sigh, I feel my own chest heave.*
*Your joy is my joy; you know that when you come that makes me come too.*
*I can't see you weep except through tears of my own,*
*And when I can't see you, I worry about you;*
*Take good care of yourself.*
*If you're not free, I'm not free*
*If you can't walk the streets in safety, then I can't walk either.*

Boy had never had a man sing to him before, and he had never
heard one man telling another that he loved him before, and so it
did not occur to him that this was at all a strange way of doing it.

### THREE

Even though they had of course been sleeping together since they first met – indeed the first thing they did on the very night they met was to kiss deeply right in the middle of the bar, the kind of kiss you more usually exchanged only after, immediately after, an especially passionate encounter – , that first night of their married life was still, Boy said, different. The sex was different. It felt new, he said, and we certainly knew what he meant even if we couldn't quite believe him.

That honeymoon night of all nights O. gave his boy a real hard time. He gave him real dirt. He talked real dirty to him. He didn't touch him too much at first. He made him bend over and spread his buttocks with both hands. He made him display the marks on his back, display his armpits, the insides of his mouth, the soles of his feet and the roots of his hair; as if he was deciding whether to buy an animal or not, O. made Boy pull back his eyelids, his lips and his foreskin. And all the time O. kept on talking, talking very low so that Boy had to listen very hard even when he didn't want to (didn't quite want to hear what he was in fact hearing his lover say), listen so hard that Boy couldn't think any longer about what he himself was doing, couldn't keep up, couldn't keep his balance, couldn't keep his feet on the floor, couldn't answer the quiet questions which demanded to know the most humiliating details, questions about his body, about what he wanted, where he hurt, what he was thinking, what he really wanted to do next, couldn't even think about which way up he was because O. talked so low, talked so bad, said things you never heard one man say to another before, he said such dirty things, said *Baby take care of yourself*, said *Baby you hold on to yourself, don't give yourself away, don't give up the ghost, don't give it away, don't give me that shit*, and then without stopping, without stopping talking he took hold of Boy right down there real hard with both hands, one hand round his balls and three fingers up his arse and he pushed so hard that the two sets of fingers almost met through Boy's skin and then he said, this was the worst of all, he got so close to Boy's ear that it was more like biting than whispering and he said *Do you want me to hold on to you, want to get held tight honey, Do you want me to hold you, do you want me to take care of you, will you let me put you in the bath, can I give you the bottle, do you need the toilet, do you want me to make you cry, can I dry your tears, stand over you, can I stand by you, can I stand up for you can I promise you I won't die because you see you're my boy, you're my body, you're my woman, you're my pussy; you're my dog with a bone, you're my bruised and broken darling, you're the song in my heart, you're my sky at night, you're my little brother, you're my river through the city, you're the bird in the bush, you're my lover in my arms, you're my daddy home from work. You're my fucker, fucker, fucker, fucker what are you?*

Boy had got used to the idea that O.'s mouth could do just what it wanted, could lick, open or bite him anywhere. Since he had been covered in spittle, he didn't see why he shouldn't be covered in words as well.

When all that, the violence, was over, O. and his Boy made love just like a married couple for the first time. They did it with a tender concentration and a complete lack of fear that surprised them both given the way they lived and what had just happened, but I would say myself that they looked just like several other hundreds of men in similar beds in that city and that particular hour.

They were both so eager to mark and use each muscle and joint of the other that neither looked up from the bed during their lovemaking. Neither of them looked up and saw, hovering over that white and isolated bed, or rather not hovering but crowding, pressing and stretching up on their toes some of them so that they could see, a crowd of fifty or sixty men, all of them naked. All of them were white skinned and dark eyed; they were the army of lovers, the ones who had come before, the men whom O. and Boy never knew or had never even heard about, their witnesses and peers, the attendants and guests of honour at this ceremony, this great labour of love. All of them were quite still, and all of them smiled; all of them cast down their eyes to behold the slow-moving wonder on the bed. Some were frankly fascinated, watching two handsome men engage in sexual practices which had not been invented in their own century; their eyes opened wide. One older man's eyes wrinkled in a great grin and then slowly brimmed over with fat tears of admiration. The room was so full that those at the front of the crowd were pressed against the bed, and some even knelt at the edge of it; they appeared to have dropped to their knees like attendants in a painted Adoration. One even held up both hands open-palmed, and his face, open-mouthed with delight at the beauty of what he saw, was lit gently from below by the single candle which O. had placed in a saucer by the bed to light the scene. Some of the men held hands, or seemed to be lovers themselves, for they stood pressing themselves against a thigh or the small of a back, or just constantly, idly touched or stroked each other's hair or shoulders with the tenderness of habit. Some were themselves sexually excited, perhaps by being in such a crowd, or perhaps by what they were watching. One young cock was upright, beating slowly against a black-furred stomach, until the four fingers and thumb of an older hand closed around it and held it still. The young man did not turn to see whose hand it was; indeed no one looked away or talked; apart from these few small, occasional, emblematic gestures of contact and love the crowd was quite still, as still as the Kings and the Shepherds always are in such scenes, as still even as the Angels whose very draperies hang quiet and immobile in the night air for sheer wonder.

Had O. or Boy looked up, they would have seen that some faces appeared in the crowd several times. Each time the face appeared, it appeared with a different body, the nakedness of the limbs set off by the hairstyles and accessories of different centuries – a seventeenth-century betrothal ring in which two chased-silver hands clasped a chipped and crowned garnet heart; a badly hennaed auburn wig, burnt by the curling tongs; a regulation moustache clipped by a forces' barber. One man, a sixty-year-old with white hair on his fat stomach and across his shoulders, was holding, wrapped in his huge arms, a smiling butcher's assistant whose neck and chest were red and sore and covered with bites and bruises. The boy's features were strangely like those of the older man, as if they were related – though his hair was black and his stomach flat, and his eyes were not red and clouded like the ones that gazed over his shoulder. The old man was in fact holding his younger self in his arms, holding him tight; and the young man looked glad to be held.

When O. and Boy had both come, and curled up together, and drifted apart and fallen asleep with no sheet to cover them, the candle was not extinguished, and seemed not to burn low or even gutter, but to burn for several hours more, and the crowd of men stayed quite still and silent around it, quite still and all of them, all of them, smiling. In time a few, at the back of the crowd, seeing the sky beginning to lighten through the window and finding that they were not able to see the tableau that the sleeping bodies made, turned away and began to look around them, leafing through O.'s half-unpacked collection of books just like you do when you're alone in a strange apartment for the first time. The rest remained watching the lovers, watching them and watching over them on this the first night of their marriage, so that anyone walking home late that night could have looked up at the bedroom window at four a.m. and seen an inexplicable sight; framed by a bedroom window on the fifth floor, lit by a single candle flame, a silent crowd of fifty or sixty smiling, naked men, pressed close together, fifty or sixty of them together in a single council-flat bedroom.

In the morning the lovers did not notice that the clothes they had left lying on the bedroom floor had been walked on, rearranged, or that their jeans were slightly damp. They were too busy clearing up the party for such details. They know nothing, nothing, nothing.

Years later they found a single baroque pearl which had dropped that night from a white-leaded ear, but they assumed it

was fake, and they put it in the dressing-up box with the rest of
their spare jewellery.

These fragments appeared in a different form in Neil Bartlett's novel,
*Ready to Catch Him Should He Fall*, published in 1990 by Serpents Tail,
London.

# When You Grow to Adultery

### DAVID LEAVITT

Andrew was in love with Jack Selden, so all Jack's little habits, his particular ways of doing things, seemed marvellous to him: the way Jack put his face under the shower, after shampooing his hair, and shook his head like a big dog escaped from a bath; the way he slept on his back, his arms crossed in the shape of a butterfly over his face, fists on his eyes; his fondness for muffins and danishes and sweet rolls – what he called, at first just out of habit and then *because* it made Andrew laugh, 'baked goods'. Jack made love with efficient fervour, his face serious, almost business-like. Not that he was without affection, but everything about him had an edge; his very touch had an edge, there was the possibility of pain lurking behind every caress. It seemed to Andrew that Jack's touches, more than any he'd known before, were full of meaning – they sought to express, not just to please or explore – and this gesturing made him want to gesture back, to enter into a kind of tactile dialogue. They'd known each other only a month, but already it felt to Andrew as if their fingers had told each other novels.

Andrew had gone through most of his life not being touched by anyone, never being touched at all. These days, his body under the almost constant scrutiny of two distinct pairs of hands, seemed to him perverse punishment, as if he had had a wish granted and was now suffering the consequences of having stated the wish too vaguely. He actually envisaged, sometimes, the fairy godmother shrugging her shoulders and saying, 'You get what you ask for.' Whereas most of his life he had been alone, unloved, now he had two lovers – Jack, for just over a month, and Allen for close to three years. There was no cause and effect, he insisted, but had to admit things with Allen had been getting ragged around the edges for some time. Jack and Allen knew about each other and had agreed to endure, for the sake of the undecided Andrew, a tenuous and open-ended period of transition, during which Andrew himself spent so much of his time on the subway, riding between the two apartments of his two lovers, that it began to seem to him as if rapid transit was the true and final home of the desired. Sometimes he wanted nothing more than to crawl into the narrow bed of his childhood and revel in the glorious, sad solitude of no one – not even his mother – needing or loving him. Hadn't the hope of future great loves been enough to curl up against? It seemed so now. His skin felt soft, toneless, like the skin of a plum poked by too many housewifely hands, feeling for the proper ripeness; he was covered with fingerprints.

This morning he had woken up with Jack – a relief. One of the many small tensions of the situation was that each morning, when he woke up, there was a split second of panic as he sought to re-orient himself and figure out where he was, who he was with. It was better with Jack, because Jack was new love and demanded little of him; with Allen, lately, he'd been woken up by thrashing, by heavy breathing, by a voice whispering in his ear, 'Tell me one thing. Did you promise Jack we wouldn't have sex? I have to know.'

'No, I didn't.'

'Thank God, thank God. Maybe now I can go back to sleep.'

There was a smell of coffee. Already showered and dressed for work (he was an architect at a spiffy firm), Jack walked over to the bed, smiling, and kissed Andrew, who felt rumpled and sour and unhappy. Jack's mouth carried the sweet taste of coffee, his face smooth and newly-shaven and still slightly wet. 'Good morning,' he said.

'Good morning.'

'I love you,' Jack Selden said.

Immediately Allen appeared, crushed, devastated, in a posture of crucifixion against the bedroom wall. 'My God,' he said, 'you're killing me, you know that? You're killing me.'

It was Rosh Hashonah, and Allen had taken the train out the night before to his parents' house in New Jersey. Andrew was supposed to join him that afternoon. He looked up now at Jack, smiled, then closed his eyes. His brow broke into wrinkles. 'Oh God,' he said to Jack, putting his arms around his neck, pulling him closer, so that Jack almost spilled his coffee, 'now I have to face Allen's family.'

Jack kissed Andrew on the forehead before pulling gingerly from his embrace, 'I still can't believe Allen told them,' he said, sipping more coffee from a mug which said WORLD'S GREATEST ARCHITECT. Jack had a mostly perfunctory relationship with his own family – hence the mug, a gift from his mother.

'Yes,' Andrew said. 'But Sophie's hard to keep secrets from. She sees him, and she knows something's wrong, and she doesn't give in until he's told her.'

'Listen, I'm sure if he told you she's not going to say anything, she's not going to say anything. Anyway, it'll be fun, Andrew. You've told me a million times how much you enjoy big family gatherings.'

'Easy for you to say. You get to go to your nice clean office and work all day and sleep late tomorrow and go out for brunch.' Suddenly Andrew sat up in bed. 'I don't think I can take this any more,' he said. 'This running back and forth between you and him.' He looked up at Jack shyly. 'Can't I stay with you?' he asked. 'In your pocket?'

Jack smiled. Whenever he and his last boyfriend, Ralph, had had something difficult to face – the licensing exam, or a doctor's appointment – they would say to each other, 'Don't worry, I'll be there with you. I'll be in your pocket.' Jack had told Andrew, who had in turn appropriated the metaphor, but Jack didn't seem to mind. He smiled down at Andrew – he was sitting on the edge of the bed now, smelling very clean, like hair tonic – and brushed his hand over Andrew's forehead. Then he reached down to the breast pocket of his own shirt, undid the little button there, pulled it open, made a plucking gesture over Andrew's face, as if he were pulling off a loose eyelash, and bringing his hand back, rubbed his fingers together over the open pocket, dropping something in.

'You're there,' he said. 'You're in my pocket.'

'All day?' Andrew asked.

'All day.' Jack smiled again. And Andrew, looking up at him, said, 'I love you,' astonished even as he said the words at how dangerously he was teetering on the brink of villainy.

Unlike Jack, who had a job, Andrew was floating through a strange, shapeless period in his life. After several years at Berkeley, doing Art History, he had transferred to Columbia, and was now confronting the last third of a dissertation on Tiepolo's ceilings. There was always for him a period before starting some enormous and absorbing project during which the avoidance of that project became his life's goal. He had a good grant and nowhere to go during the day except around the cluttered West Side apartment he shared with Allen, so he spent most of his time sweeping dust and paper scraps into little piles – anything to avoid the computer. Allen, whom he had met at Berkeley, had gotten an assistant professorship at Columbia the year before – hence Andrew's transfer, to be with him. He was taking this, his third semester, off to write a book. Andrew had stupidly imagined such a semester of shared writing would be a gift, a time they could enjoy together, but instead their quiet afternoons were turning out one after the other to be cramped and full of annoyance, and fights too ugly and trivial for either of them afterwards to believe they'd happened – shoes left on the floor, phone messages forgotten, introductions not tendered at parties: these were the usual crimes. Allen told Andrew he was typing too fast, it was keeping him from writing; Andrew stormed out. Somewhere in the course of that hazy afternoon when he was never going back he met Jack, who was spending the day having a reunion with his old college room mate, another art history graduate student named Tony Melendez. The three of them chatted on the steps of Butler, then went to Tom's Diner for coffee. A dirty booth, Andrew across from Jack, Tony next to Jack, doing most of the talking. Jack talking too, sometimes; he smiled a lot at Andrew.

When one person's body touches another person's body, chemicals under the skin break down and recombine, setting off an electric spark which leaps, neuron to neuron, to the brain. It was all a question of potassium and calcium when, that afternoon at Tom's, Jack's foot ended right up against Andrew's. Soon the accidental pressure became a matter of will, of choice. Chemistry, his mother had said, in a rare moment of advisory nostalgia. Oh, your father, that first date we didn't have a thing to talk about, but the chemistry!

At home that evening, pottering around while Allen agonized over his book, Andrew felt claustrophobic. He wanted to call Jack. Everything which had seemed wonderful about his relationship with Allen – shared knowledge, shared ideologies, shared loves – fell away to nothing, desiccated by the forceful reactions of the afternoon. How could he have imagined this relationship would work for all his life, he wondered. Somehow they had forgotten, or pushed aside, the possibilities (the likelihoods) of competitiveness, disagreement, embarrassment, disapproval, not to mention just plain boredom. He called Jack; he told Allen he was going to the library. The affair caught, and as it got going Andrew's temper flared, he had at his fingertips numberless wrongs Allen had perpetrated which made his fucking Jack all right. He snapped at Allen, walked out of rooms at the slightest provocation, made several indiscreet phone calls, until Allen finally asked what was going on. Then came the long weekend of hair-tearing and threats and pleas, followed by the period of indecision they were now enduring, a period during which they didn't fight at all, because whenever Andrew felt a fight coming on he threatened to leave, and whenever Allen felt a fight coming on he backed off, became soothing and loving, to make sure Andrew wouldn't leave. Andrew didn't want to leave Allen, he said, but he also didn't want to give up Jack. Such a period of transition suited him shamefully; finally, after all those years, he was drowning in it.

In cryptic or self-critical moments, Andrew perceived his life as a series of abandonments. This is what he was thinking about as he rode the train from Hoboken out towards Allen's parents' house that afternoon: how he had abandoned his family, fleeing California for the east coast, wilfully severing his ties to his parents; then, one after another, how he had had best friends, and either fought with them or became disgusted with them, or they with him, or else just drifted off without writing or calling until the gap was too big to dare crossing. There were many people he had said he could spend his life with, yet he hadn't spent his life with any of them, he saw now – Nathan and Celia, for instance, who it had seemed to him in college would be his best friends for all time – when was the last time he'd seen them? Five, six months now? Berkeley had severed Andrew from that ineradicable threesome of his youth, and now that he was in New York again it seemed too much had happened for them to fill each other in on, and in the course of it all happening their perceptions and opinions had changed, they were no longer in perfect synch, they weren't able to understand each other as gloriously as they once had because, of course, their lives had diverged, there was no longer endless common experience to chew over, and on which to hone shared attitudes. After those first few disastrous dinners, in which arguments had punctuated the dull yawn of nothing to be said, he had given up calling them, except once he had seen Nathan at the museum, where they stood in front of a Tiepolo and Nathan challenged Andrew to explain why it was any good – a familiar, annoying, Nathan-ish challenge, a good try, but by then it was too late. All of this was guilt-inspiring enough, but what made Andrew feel even guiltier was that Nathan and Celia still saw each other, went to parties together, lived in the clutch of the same old relationship, the same old dynamic, and presumably the same glorious synchronicity of opinion. They were going on ten years with each other even without him, and Andrew felt humbled, immature. Why couldn't he keep relationships up that long? As for leaving Allen for Jack – wouldn't it amount to the same thing? In three years, would he leave Jack as well?

Perhaps it was just his nature. After all, he had lived for the entire first twenty-two and most of the next six years of his life virtually alone, surviving by instinct, internal resources. This was not uncommon among gay men he knew; some reached out into the sexual world at the brink of puberty, like those babies who, tossed into a swimming pool, gracefully stay afloat; but others – himself among them – become so transfixed by the preposterousness of their own bodies, and particularly the idea of their coming together with other bodies, that they end up trapped in a contemplation of sex which, as it grows more tortured and analytic, rules out action altogether. Such men must be coaxed by others into action, like the rusty tin man in Oz, but as Andrew knew, willing and desirable coaxers were few and far between. For him sexual awakening had come too late, too long after adolescence, when the habits of the adult body were no longer new but had become settled and hard to break out of. Chronically alone, Andrew had cultivated, in those years, a degree of self-containment which kept him alive, but was nonetheless not self-reliance, for it was based on weakness, and had at its heart the need and longing for another to take him in. He remembered, at sixteen, lying in his room, his hands exploring his own body, settling on his hip, just above the pelvis, and thinking, no other hand has touched me here, not since infancy, not since my mother. Not one hand. And this memory had gone on for eight more years. Had that been the ruin of him, he wondered now. Doomed by necessity to become self-contained, was he also doomed never to be able to love someone else, always to retreat from intimacy into the cosy, familiar playroom of his old, lonely self?

Outside the train window, the mysterious transformations of late afternoon were beginning. It was as if the sun were backing off in horror at what it had seen, or given light to. The train Andrew was on had bench seats that reversed direction at a push, and remembering how impressed by that he had been the first time Allen had taken him on this train, he grew nervous: suddenly he remembered Allen, remembered he was on his way to a man who considered his life to be in Andrew's hands. Already he recognized the litany of town names as the conductor announced them: one after another, and then they were there, they had arrived. By the crossing gate Allen sat in his father's BMW, waiting.

He smiled and waved as he stepped off the train. Allen didn't move. He waved again as he ran towards the car, waved through the window. 'Hi,' he said cheerily, getting in and kissing Allen lightly on the mouth. Allen pulled the car out of the parking lot and on to the road.

'What's wrong?' (A foolish, stupid question, yet somehow the moment demanded it.)

'This is the very worst for me,' he said. 'Your coming back. It's worse than your leaving.'

'Why?'

'Because you always look so happy. Then you fall into a stupor, you fall asleep, or you want to go to the movies and sleep there. Jack gets all the best of you. I get you lying next to me snoring.'

He was on the verge as he had been so many times in these last weeks, of saying inevitable things, and Andrew could sense him biting back, like someone fighting the impulse to vomit. Andrew cleared his throat. A familiar, dull ache somewhere in his bowels was starting up again, as if a well-trusted anaesthesia were wearing off. It felt to him these days, being with Allen, as if a two-bladed knife lay gouged deep into both of them, welding them together, and reminded anew of its presence, Andrew turned futilely to the car window, the way you might turn from the obituary page to the comics upon recognizing an unexpected and familiar face among the portraits of the dead. Of course, soon enough, you have to turn back.

Andrew closed his eyes. Allen breathed. 'Let's not have a fight,' Andrew said quietly, surprised to be on the verge of tears. But Allen was stony, and said nothing more.

As they pulled into the driveway the garage doors slowly
opened, like primaeval jaws or welcoming arms; Sophie, Allen's
mother, must have heard the car pulling up, and pushed the little
button in the kitchen. A chilly dusk light was descending on the
driveway, calling up in Andrew some primaeval nostalgia for
suburban twilight, and all the thousands of days which had come
to an end here, children surprised by the swift descent of night,
their mothers' voices calling them home, the prickly coolness of
their arms as they dropped their balls and ran back into the warm
lights of houses. It had been that sort of childhood Allen had lived
here, after all, a childhood of street games, Kickball and Capture
the Flag, though Allen was always the one the others laughed at,
picked last, kicked. A dog barked distantly, and in the bright
kitchen window above the garage Andrew saw Sophie rubbing
her hands with a white dishtowel. She was not smiling, and
seemed to be struggling to compose herself into whatever kind of
studied normalness the imminent arrival of friends and relatives
demanded. Clearly she did not know anyone could see her, for in
a moment she turned slightly towards the window, and seeing the
car idle in the driveway, its lights still on, started, then smiled and
waved.

A festive, potent smell of roasting meats came out of the porch
door. 'Hello, Andrew,' Sophie said as they walked into the
kitchen, her voice somehow hearty yet tentative, and she kissed
him jauntily on the cheek, bringing close for one unbearable
second a smell of pancake make-up, perfume and chicken stock he
almost could not resist falling into. For Jack's sake he held his
own. Of all the things he feared losing along with Allen, this
family was the one he thought about most. How he longed to
steep for ever in this brisket smell, this warmth of carpeting and
mahogany and voices chattering in the hall! But Allen, glumly,
said, 'Let's go upstairs,' and gestured to the room they always
shared, his room. Even that a miracle, Andrew reflected, as they
trundled up the stairs: that first time Andrew had visited and was
worrying where he'd sleep, Sophie had declared, 'I never ask
what goes on upstairs. Everyone sleeps where they want, as far as

I'm concerned it's a mystery.' It seemed a different moral code applied where her homosexual son was concerned than the one which had been used routinely with Allen's brothers and sister; in their cases, the sleeping arrangements for visiting boyfriends or girlfriends had to be carefully orchestrated, the girls doubling up with Allen's sister, the boys with Allen himself – a situation Allen had always found both sexy and intolerable, he had told Andrew, the beautiful college boys lying next to him in his double-bed for the requisite hour or so, then sneaking off to have sex with his sister, Barrie. Well, all that was long past – Barrie was now married and had two children of her own – and what both Allen and Andrew felt grateful for here was family: it was a rare thing for a gay man to have it, must less to be able to share it with his lover. Their parents had not yet met *each other*, but a visit was planned for May, and remembering this Andrew gasped slightly as this prospect arose before him – yet another lazily arranged inevitability to be dealt with, and with it the little residual parcel of guilt and nostalgia and dread, packed up like the giblets of a supermarket chicken. His half of the knife twisted a little, causing Allen's to respond in kind, and Allen looked at Andrew suspiciously. 'What is it?' he asked. Andrew shook his head. 'Nothing, really.' He didn't want to talk about it. Allen shrugged regretfully; clearly he sensed that whatever was on Andrew's mind was bad enough not to be messed with.

'Well,' Allen said, as they walked into his room, 'here we are,' and threw himself on to the bed. Andrew followed more cautiously. The room had changed hands and functions many times over the years – first it had been Allen's sister's room, then his brother's, then his, then a guest room, then a computer room, then a room for visiting grandchildren. It had a peculiar, muddled feel to it, the accretions of each half-vain effort at redecoration only partially covering over the leavings of the last occupant. There was archaeology, a sense of layers upon layers. On the walnut dresser, which had belonged to Allen's grandmother, a baseball trophy shared space with a Strawberry Shortcake doll whose hair had been cut off, a two-headed troll and a box of floppy disks. Ill-fitting clothes suggesting the worst of several generations of children's fashions filled the drawers and the closets, and the walls were covered with portraits of distant aunts, framed awards Allen had won in high school and college, pictures of his sister with her horse. The bed, retired here from the master bedroom downstairs, had been Sophie and her husband Ed's for twenty years. The springs were shot; Allen lay in it more than on it, and after a few seconds of observation Andrew joined him. Immediately their hands found each other, they were embracing, kissing. Andrew was crying. 'I love you,' he said quietly.

'Then come back to me,' Allen said.

'It's not that simple.'

'Why?'

Andrew pulled away. 'You know all the reasons.'

'Tell me.'

The door opened with a tentative squeak. Some old instinctual fear made both of them jump to opposite sides of the bed. Melissa, Allen's five-year-old niece, stood in the doorway, her hand in her mouth, her knees twisted one around the other. She was wearing a plaid party dress, white tights and black patent leather pumps.

'Hello,' she said quietly.

'Melly! Hello honey!' Allen said, bounding up from the bed and taking her in his arms. 'What a pretty girl you are! Are you all dressed up for Rosh Hoshanah?' He kissed her, and she nodded, opening her tiny mouth into a wide smile clearly not offered easily, a smile which seemed somehow precious, it was so carefully given. 'Look at my earrings,' she said. 'They're hearts.'

'They're beautiful,' Allen said. 'Remember who bought them for you?'

'Uncle Andrew,' Melissa said, and looked at him, and Andrew for the first time himself remembered the earrings he had given her just six months before, for her birthday, as if she were his own niece.

'Look who's here, honey,' he said, putting Melissa down, 'Uncle Andrew's here now!'

'I know,' Melissa said. 'Grandma told me.'

'Hi Melissa,' Andrew said, sitting up on the bed. 'I'm so happy to see you! What a big girl you are! Come give me a hug!'

Immediately she landed on him, her arms circling as much of him as they could, her smiling mouth open over his face. This surprised Andrew; on previous visits Melissa had viewed him with a combination of disdain and the sort of amusement one feels at watching a trained animal perform; only the last time he'd been to the house, in August, for Sophie's birthday, had she shown him anything like affection. And it was true that she'd asked to speak to him on the phone every time she was visiting and Allen called. Still, nothing prepared Andrew for what he saw in her eyes just now, as she gazed down at him with a loyalty so pure it was impossible to misinterpret.

'I love you,' she said, and instantly he knew it was true, and possibly true for the first time in her life.

'I love you too, honey,' he said. 'I love you very much.'

She sighed, and her head sunk into his chest, and she breathed softly, protected. What was love for a child, after all, if not protection? A quiet descended on the room as Andrew lay there, the little girl heavy in his arms, while Allen stood above them in the shrinking light, watching, it seemed, for any inkling of change in Andrew's face. Downstairs the dinner smells and dinner sounds, and Sophie's voice beckoning them to come, but somehow none of them could bear to break the perfect eggshell membrane which had formed over the moment. Then Melissa pulled herself up, and Andrew realized his leg was asleep, and Allen, shaken by whatever he had or hadn't seen, switched on the light. The new, artificial brightness was surprisingly unbearable to Andrew; he had to squint against it.

'We really ought to be going down now,' Allen said, holding his hand out to Andrew, who took it gratefully, surprised only by the force with which Allen hoisted him from the bed.

Chairs and plastic glasses and Hugga-Bunch plates had to be rearranged so Melissa could sit next to Andrew at dinner. This position, as it turned out, was not without its disadvantages; he

was invariably occupied with cutting up carrots and meat. The
conversation was familiar and soothing; someone had lost a lot of
money in the stock market, someone else was building a garish
house. Allen's sister sung the praises of a new health club, and
Allen's father defended a cousin's decision to open a crematorium
for pets. All through dinner Melissa stared up at Andrew, her face
lit from within with love, and Allen stared across at Andrew, his
face twisted and furrowed with love, and somewhere miles away,
presumably, Jack sat at his drafting table, breaking into a smile for
the sake of love. So much love! It had to be a joke, a fraud!
Someone – his mother – must have been paying them! Wait a
minute, he wanted to say to all three of them, this is me, Andrew,
this is me who has never been loved, who has always been too
nervous and panicked and eager for love for anyone to want
actually to love him! You are making a mistake! You are mixing me
up with someone else! And if they did love him – well, wouldn't
they all wake up soon, and recognize that they were under an
enchantment? Knowledge kills infatuation, he knew, the same
way the sudden, perplexing recognition that you are dreaming
can wake you from a dream. He almost wanted that to happen.
But sadly – or happily, or perhaps just frustratingly – there
appeared to be no enchantment here, no bribery. These three
loves were real and entrenched. His disappearance from any one
of them was liable to cause pain.

Even with Melissa! Just an hour later – screaming as her mother
carried her to the bathrub, screaming as her mother put her in her
bed – no one could ignore who she was calling for, though the
various aunts and cousins were clearly surprised. Finally Barrie
emerged from the room Melissa shared with her on visits, shaking
her head and lighting a cigarette. 'She says she won't go to sleep
unless you tuck her in,' Barrie told Andrew. 'So would you mind?
I'm sorry, but I've had a long day, I just can't hack this crying shit
any more.'

'You don't have to, Andrew,' Sophie said. 'She has to learn to
go to sleep.'

'But I don't mind,' Andrew said. 'Really, I don't.'

'Well, thanks, then.'

Sophie led him into the darkened room where Melissa lay, rumpled-looking, in Cabbage-Patch pyjamas and sheets, her face puffy and her eyes red from crying, then backed out on tiptoe, closing the door three-quarters. Immediately upon seeing him Melissa offered another of her rare and costly smiles.

'Hi,' Andrew said.

'Hi.'

'Are you all right?'

'Uh-huh.'

'You want me to sing you a bedtime song?'

'Uh-huh.'

'OK.' He brushed her hair away from her forehead, and began singing a version of a song his own father had sung to him:

> Oh go to sleep my Melly-o
> And you will grow and grow and grow
> And grow and grow right up to be
> A great big ugly man like me . . .

Melissa laughed. 'But I'm a girl,' she said.

'I told you honey, this is a song my Daddy sang to me.'

'Go on.'

> And you will go to Timbuktu
> And you'll see elephants in the zoo.
> And you will go to outer space
> And you will go to many a place.
> Oh think of all the things you'll see
> When you grow to adultery.

This last line, of course, caught him. It had always been a family joke, a mock-pun. Had his father known something he hadn't?

'That's a funny song,' said Melissa, who was, of course, too young to know what adultery meant anyway.

'I'm glad you liked it, but since I've sung it now, you have to go to sleep. Deal?'

She smiled again. Her hand, stretched out to her side, rested lightly now at that very point on his hip he had once imagined no one would ever touch. Now her tiny handprints joined the larger ones which seemed to him tonight to be permanently stamped there, like tattoos.

Though he'd left the light on, Allen was already tightly encased between the sheets by the time Andrew came to bed. He lay facing rigidly outward, and Andrew, climbing in next to him, observed the spray of nervous pimples fanning out over his shoulders. He brushed his fingers over the bumpy reddened terrain, and Allen jumped spasmodically. Andrew took his hand away.

'Don't,' Allen said.

'All right, I won't, I'm sorry.'

'No, no. Don't *stop*, don't stop touching me. Please, I need you to touch me. You never touch me any more.'

Andrew put his hand back. 'Don't,' he said. 'Stop, Don't. Stop. Don't stop, don't stop, don't stop.'

'Thank you,' Allen said. 'Thank you.'

'Switch off the light.'

'You don't know,' Allen said, 'how much I've missed your hands.'

'Allen, I've been touching you plenty,' Andrew said.

'No you haven't. You really haven't.'

'This really is a stupid topic for an argument,' Andrew said, not wanting to let on the sensation he was just now feeling, of a spear run through him, the whole length of his body. He reached over Allen's head and switched off the light. 'Just relax,' he said, and settled himself into a more comfortable position against the pillow. 'I won't stop touching you.'

'Thank you,' Allen whispered.

In the dark things broke apart, becoming more bearable. His hand travelled the mysterious widths of Allen's back, and as it did so its movements slowly began to seem as if they were being controlled by some force outside Andrew's body, like the pointer on a Ouija board. He had the curious sensation of his hand detaching from his arm, first the whole hand, at the wrist, and then the fingers, which, as they started to run up and down Allen's back in a scratch, sparked a small moan; this too seemed disembodied, as if it were being issued not from Allen's mouth but from some impossible corner or depth of the room's darkened atmosphere. Allen's back relaxed somewhat, his breathing slowed and Andrew, with his index finger, scratched out the initials 'J. S.' My God, what was he doing? For a moment he lifted his hand, then thrust it back, ordering his fingers into a frenzy of randomness, like someone covering up an incriminating word with a mass of scribbling. But Allen didn't seem to notice, and breathed even more slowly. Andrew held his breath. What was possessing him he couldn't name, but cautiously he wrote 'Jack' on Allen's back, elongating the letters for the sake of disguise, and Allen sighed and shifted. 'Jack Selden', Andrew wrote next. 'I love Jack Selden.' His heart was racing. What if those messages, like invisible ink, suddenly erupted in full daylight for Allen to read? Well, of course that wouldn't happen, and closing his eyes, Andrew gave himself up to this wild and villainous writing, the messages becoming longer and more incriminating even as Allen moved closer to sleep, letting out, in his stupor, only occasional noises of pleasure and gratitude.

## *from* Native

WILLIAM HAYWOOD HENDERSON

The wind, ripe with sage, rolled particles of mountain down each spine of
the badlands, through gullies of flat washed rock, along trails scratched
into the crust. From the highest parapet of badland, an antelope watched
the moon fall from the zenith. Below him, the earth plunged. Behind him,
the bench rose across dark jumbles of sage, across open fields pocked with
clumps of stiff grass and tundra slick at the edge of snowfields, and reached
for pinnacles feeding on stars. The antelope lowered his head and rubbed
his foreleg with his pronged horns. Then he raised his head, and his ears
drew in sounds of wind, nothing else.

But there was something below the wind, something keeping him from
turning away from the edge and joining his mates in the risings toward
the peaks. He knew the trails laid out below him – the escapes down over
the edge, the straight lines along wire to gaps, the passages through
abandoned creek bed, along flowing water, across an open hillock where
soil is white, licked for salt. He always skirted the wide trail dug hugely up
the valley floor, a strip of ruined grass at its centre, the trail that ate a
steady swathe of sage, that led only one direction, regardless of the
delicacies or wanderings to each side, the trail that troubled him, though
he wasn't always sure of the reason.

But now, as the sound below the wind came clear, he felt the reason
quiver down his limbs. A truck, with stars at the front and fire behind,
followed the wide trail. It wasn't fast – he could easily outrun it. It wasn't
smart – it rarely left the trail, but usually lumbered up the valley on its
black wheels in stupid pursuit of nothing, leaving the antelope to pause in
his escape, safely up a ridge, and watch it disappear, seemingly unaware

*that its quarry had been left behind. He feared it because it moved
unpredictably, sometimes unloading a man who'd shoot a rifle, bring
strange luck – rocks would jump at the antelope's hooves.*

*The antelope watched until the truck's fire had burned away around a
curve of the valley, and then held his head high and cried – a sharp whistle
that reclaimed the valley below and echoed as he sprang away to join his
mates.*

Severed heads – antelope, deer, moose – and the moving heads, I
couldn't place them, not from outside with the red neon flashing,
drawing lines through couples dancing. It surprised me, so many
people. Clarence sat back there on the stage, one hand on his
trumpet, the other on the piano – he'd accompanied the couples
for years on Saturday nights. I pushed the door open and the
sprung hinge creaked, a strained scraping sound, something I'd
heard from the outside, passing on the sidewalk – it had been
years since I'd heard it from within the doorway. But I stepped
straight through as if I'd done it every Saturday night of my life, as
if Mother's stories stepped with me.

Max pushed off from Sally and greeted me, 'Hey, Blue.' His
scarred ear came around as he turned away, the ear scarred from
that old, sad football team back then. Hardly worth a scar.

Albert took my hand, pulled me toward him, gave me a hard
shake, and said, 'How can you stay so invisible and still run that
Fisher place?' He leaned closer to say, 'I wish I could convince you
to manage *my* place, young man.'

'Thanks, but I'm pretty much set already.' I returned a good,
solid shake, the proper gesture, pulled back out of his grip, and
tried to find a way through the crowd.

The Talbots blocked me. Mrs Talbot kicked her leg back on each
spin; her skirt twisted and bunched and then flew out full again.
They held their clasped hands straight out toward me in a large fist
and smiled, broke their step, and as Mr Talbot acknowledged me
and headed for the bar, Mrs Talbot approached, smoothing her
skirt with her white hands. 'Hi, dear,' she said. Her fingertips
landed on my hip. 'Heard anything from that father of yours?'

'No, ma'am.'

She rose up on her toes and pressed her lips to my ear in a soft kiss. 'It's so good to see you out.' Clarence, who had put his trumpet on top of the piano, set to playing more seriously, and his drummer took up his sticks and started to beat. 'I love it, this song,' Mrs Talbot said, and she wheeled around, looking for her husband. She reached back, touched me on the arm. 'Call me sometime about dinner, Blue. We'll have you over. I've missed you. I've missed your dear mother, all these years.' She wandered away into the crowd. Everyone danced the same dance, the two-step – the women spun to the farthest reach of an outstretched arm and then snapped back close again.

They all grinned, kept their backs straight. I took a few more steps, paused, looked over the bobbing heads. Then I spotted Sam at the bar, standing with Derek – Derek of repaired rifles and swapped snowmobiles, planned wilderness trips, the memory of a single poached cougar still darkening what everyone thought of him. Sam was too close to him, should not have been talking to him, had maybe spent the day with him picking up who knows what kind of angry habits. But Sam seemed unchanged, calm, as if he'd forgotten what he'd said last night, that he might drop by to see me today, Saturday, first day of a free weekend. There'd been no sign of him. I'd spent the day up on the windmill, replacing the mechanism, watching each car pass on the road at the base of the red badlands across the valley. The grass waved in the fields, dark green and then suddenly a greenish silver. The cows lay in the sun like black rocks, and the calves ran in circles. No Sam.

Last night he'd told me about where he was heading, his voice strong, eager. He talked on and on about the places he'd worked, starting in the hot box of a factory making knives. He was glad to be in a mountain town, six months now and settling in, glad to be working on a ranch large enough that he could get far away, duck through a fence, walk to the shadow of trees, cool his feet in a creek, lie out in a patch of sun on a padding of pine needles, and feel the heat on his skin. He'd been heading higher, up off the plains, and he was getting closer. As soon as he had a chance, he'd be out on the trails he'd plotted on his maps, getting up to where he could see maybe all the way back home.

I'd thought, as I waited for him, that he might have already made up his mind to quit and move on. But I could give him something that would keep him around, an assignment I hadn't offered anyone yet. I'd phoned him – no answer. After dinner, I went out looking, wound up there in the bar. It was part of my job, to set things up. He could help me.

Now I came up beside them, said, 'Derek,' smiled down at Sam, thinking of the cow camp, twenty miles up at the first lush edges of altitude after all that dry road.

Sam grabbed my arm and shouted over the roar of voices, drums, piano, 'Derek and me are buds.' Sam, my young hand with his mind on the wilds, just legal enough to drink. He waited for me, his round flat face without concern or humour, just open and pale, looked at me with dust in the creases around his patient grey eyes.

The cabin at the cow camp was unpowered, complete and rustic and far removed, isolated from unnatural sound. The barest thread of water flowed from the spring in the willows and carved a straight line behind the cabin, with a wooden box built over the water in which to cool cans of fruit, beer, a stick of butter in that iced water drawn straight from a wound at the base of the Ramshorn. The peak and spring snow hung like solid clouds over the cabin, the green roof. The view from the porch opened down to where the thread of water split and wove a marsh of tangled roots, where skunk cabbage leaves cupped white flowers beneath explosions of young willow branches.

Derek had hold of my other arm, and he shouted, 'This here greenhorn shithead you hired is all right, Blue. He's keeping me company till Janeen gets here.' They leaned toward each other and bumped foreheads.

The jolt of their butting bone went down through their arms and into their grip on my muscle, and I said, 'Yes, he's fine.'

'Bullshit – he's a bigger asshole than you, Blue,' Derek said.

'Where the hell you been? I ain't seen you out for years, you fucker. You looking for a babe?' He shook me.

Sam said, 'Boss man,' and he also shook me.

They laughed and swore at each other and butted foreheads again while I tried to back out of their grips, saying, 'If you have a minute, Sam, I'd like to talk to you about something.'

Derek mocked, 'I'd like to talk to you.'

Sam said, 'Boss man wants to talk to me,' staring up at me blank for a moment as if he were waiting for me to do something, to order him, but then he released me, both of them released me, and they bought me a beer as I waited.

Sam forced the bottle up against me, the glass cold through my shirt. I followed him away from the bar, through the dancing couples. Max and Sally whirled past. David danced with someone new, or maybe it was still Betty but with different hair, and he shouted, 'Blue, I got the truck running. I'll move those bales tomorrow.' His arm came up off his partner's waist, it was Betty, and he slapped me hard on the back as I passed. 'Trust me, Blue.' He hooked my arm and turned me back toward him.

'I trust you, David.' He laughed, eyes snapping back to Betty as she lowered her chin to his shoulder and got his free arm back on her. 'You know I trust you.'

We found the other wall and the booths, slid in, and Sam was straight across from me. I raised the bottle to my mouth, placed my lips over the open circle, and sucked liquid down into my throat, feeling the cold reach through me. I said, 'Sam, I want you to man the cow camp up at the Ramshorn this summer.'

Sam rocked his bottle back and forth, lifted it, tapped it on the tabletop. Then he glanced up at me, opened his mouth to speak, shut it. I took a long swallow of beer, thinking it might be best if I finished and got going – he could give me an answer later when his mind was clearer. But he snapped his fingers at me, smiling broadly, pointed toward a small, square sign at the far end of the room, got up, and walked away to piss, left me alone. I could wait.

There were many more people than I'd thought I'd see, and I

ran through their names, watched their faces, wondered if they were surprised to see me. They all kept dancing.

Mrs Hudson, the high school music teacher, slid in across from me. Her throat flushed red, and her tortoise-shelled, magnified eyes ran over me and out into the crowd as she chuckled. 'Leslie Eugene Parker, your eyes are blue as ever,' she said. She reached across and patted the back of my hand, and her heavy fingers made my bones feel thin. 'It's so good to see you out and around and getting so handsome. Smile for me, darling. I always liked your smile.'

'I just dropped in to check on my new hand, Mrs Hudson.'

'You're working? Shame. Let's dance.'

'Thanks, but I want to finish my drink.' I held my beer out toward her and then took a swallow.

'Come on.' She took my hand, pulled my arm out straight, and lolled her head from side to side with the music. 'I'll get Clarence to play something younger.'

'I'm fine, really. Maybe later.' I pulled my hand back and clamped it under my thigh on the bench.

'OK, dear, but there's a lot of fun you're missing.'

She started singing quietly with the music as she watched the couples churn past, their hips shifting with the beat. Mr Kroeber held tightly to someone else's wife, and I knew the words he whispered with cheek pressed to temple. Paulie, just out of high school, followed the lead of his taller sister, his arms held stiffly. Derek swung by with Janeen, her unusually blonde hair shining down over her sweater, and he paused long enough to look back over his shoulder and say, 'Get a load of the fucking squaw if ya got a chance.' I roused myself and looked around to see what he meant, but then Sam slid in against me, and with the jolt of his body I pushed myself back into the corner, giving him room.

'Is this the business you can't set free for one Saturday night?' Mrs Hudson said.

'Mrs Hudson, this is Sam.' They shook hands quickly across the table.

'Sam, sweetheart,' she said, 'you make sure Blue has some fun, OK? I leave him in your hands.' She got up and left us, took a young man from the next booth, and danced out into the crowd.

'Nice old lady,' Sam said, sitting at my side. He stretched across the table to get his beer, took a sip. 'Tell me more about this cow camp, Blue.' He looked straight ahead, down the row of booths as he spoke. 'How far up is it?'

'Twenty miles off Horse Creek. Just below the Ramshorn.'

His face came around toward me, and he said, 'I'd like to do whatever you want me to do, Blue. What would I do up there?'

He sat close to me in the booth, his roughness softened by beer or something, his small sharp nose flushed pink. 'We take the herd up there. For the summer. You'd stay in the cabin.'

The night before, Sam had complained of his old factory job, saying, 'All that dull shit just to make *these*,' and then he unbuckled his belt. The tang chimed, the long end slapped leather down against his leg as he slid the sheath off and held it out toward me, wanting me to inspect a knife he had made in that factory. I took the sheath from him and turned it over, unsnapped it, pulled the blade from the leather, and the light of flames from the fireplace licked the edge. It was sharp, I could tell, liable to cut by accident.

Sam leaned his shoulder into my upper arm, and his voice cracked and rose. 'But what would I do?'

'You'd ride lines.' I wanted to place him up there against the Ramshorn, place him in that green space above the marsh.

'Which horse would I have?' His weight rushed my pulse through my arm.

'Starwood. She's good on the rougher trails. You'd just keep an eye on things, watch out for strays and sickness.'

He'd sit on the porch, hear the water running in the narrow channel behind the cabin, smell the tart funk of skunk cabbage, keep track of the herd in its high country grazing, release a calf from barbed wire, but mostly lean back in a chair. The heat of late evening would evaporate in empty sky, walls of green discs would shiver above the ribbed white leggy aspens.

'Blue,' Sam said, and he poked me with his elbow. 'Blue, we have a guest.'

A figure stood at the booth, fleshy, dressed in black jeans, turquoise buckle, baggy white shirt, obscuring the crowd. Squaw. This man stood there and looked down at us. His black hair was straight, long, and slick, and it played along his shoulders as he moved with the music, but it wasn't a movement I had seen, not like the couples two-stepping behind him.

His shoulders rose and fell, his hands came up. He descended into the rhythm, hips revolving. His head fell forward. He flipped his hair back over his shoulders and danced with eyes on us. He was a man without joints, loose and snaking. His smile pinched. He didn't know to turn his black eyes away, to act as if he weren't watching us.

He said, 'Cosy,' and we didn't move. I didn't look away from those black points. His eyes made the little shift back and forth between Sam and me. 'Boys. Cosy.' Then Sam seemed heavy against me, as if he'd been sleeping against me. 'Someone needs to dust you two off and you'd be a fine pair.' He laughed, a deep rumble, a laugh I didn't know, as if it were choked with honey. His face was brown and smooth as clean carved clay, his lips big, eyes Asian like the Indians get, and hair that moved down across his cheeks as if it were laughing with him. 'It's the sugar in the alcohol that gets me every time. We don't break down sugar the way you white boys do.' Then his laugh rose into a little chant, something I might have heard from the Indians in the ceremonies. His eyes closed for a moment. Arms over his head, he shook, spun, stopped dead where he'd started. He gave us a last look. 'Fine pair.'

He stepped away, turned his back to us, and people made room for his walk through their dance – Mrs Hudson pulled her partner back with a hard manoeuvre of her elbow, the Talbots spun off in another direction. I watched the people watch him, saw their smiles flicker or go flat, and then I watched the man. He shadow-danced in imitation of each couple he passed, taking his time. He held his arms up in a feminine echo of each woman whose back came around to him. He might have been moving in those lines of Indian women, shuffling through those ceremonies down on the reservation. The old Indian women would come up maybe once a year to buy something at the Mercantile, but they all had better places to go. It was rare to see a man, an Indian man, in this town. I couldn't remember an Indian ever talking as if he didn't know he could get hurt, as if he'd never heard the way a guy like Derek could say 'Squaw.'

And now Derek, it was his turn, Derek let go of Janeen and stood face to face with this man, mouthing something angry. The man should have known enough to turn away, should have known better than to sink into his loose dance, to let his chant slice through the music, should have known better than to reach out for Derek, take his wrists, and tug him around in a circle, a close circle, too quick for Derek to stop his steps. Then the man freed Derek's hands, held his own hands over his head, and closed his eyes, chanted again.

Derek clenched his hands across his chest, shouted something and whirled, stumbled against his girl friend, pulled her arms around him. The Indian, whose chant had stopped with Derek's shout, shook his hair back and continued toward the bar. The couples moved in behind him, everyone whispering with lips close to ears, before returning their full attention to the dance.

'Funny guy,' Sam said as he held up his bottle, took a swallow. Bubbles rose through the liquid and burst. 'Do you know him?'

'No, I don't.'

'He can dance.'

'He'd do himself a favour if he stood still.'

'Beats me.' Sam laughed. 'I think he can dance.'

'Not here.'

But I could imagine the reservation, the cottonwood's big green clouds along the river, the earth dry. The stony men around the one big drum would pound, start the chanting, deep and wandering as if they were on their way somewhere. The women in white deerskin, fringe, beads, would begin to move out like a line of sadness, shuffling, hands clasped at bellies, heads down, shuffling and bobbing, as if something moved them all at once forward, then pushed them back a little, bobbing, playing with the beat, then forwards again, in no hurry, never stepping off to the side, all moving directly into the steps of the one ahead. I could see the man moving with them, hear the chant, his hair down his back, hot black in the dry sun along the river, his feet in the footsteps of the women, his voice on the beat with theirs, his black eyes bold as a man's, his soft moves amplified and strange.

'So, what, I'll be riding lines?'

I leaned into the corner of the booth. The squaw was out of sight, over by the bar, or maybe he had come to his senses and left. Sam's fingers drummed, travelling across the tabletop, closer to me, away from me. 'Yes. Riding lines.'

'Any lakes up there?'

'Sure. Lots of water. Snowfields. Waterfalls. Anything you could want.'

'But what else will I do? The day-to-day stuff?'

'Just watch the herd, like I said. I did it myself a few years ago.'

'You'll teach me what I need to know?'

'Of course.'

He nodded slowly and took another swallow of beer. 'It's a deal, then,' he said, and his lips tightened.

'Deal.'

He reached below the tabletop, took my hand from my lap, pulled it up between us, and shook it. 'Good.' He smiled broadly and released me, leaned his shoulder into my upper arm, laughed. 'You're a good guy, Blue. I mean it.' His head came around and his nose brushed my sleeve.

'It's nothing.'

He tipped his head away and looked up at me, his brown lips moved a little, a second of limp hesitation. But his shoulder bore harder against me when he said, 'A good guy. Setting me up in a place, way up high.'

I could have left him there against me – he seemed drunk enough to be leaning like that – but Clarence stopped and people turned around, looking for seats. I sat up and Sam shifted away from me, went back to his beer. I sat there with my new ranch hand, and I drank from my own beer. 'It's not easy work,' I said. 'It takes a strong guy.'

'Don't worry.' Smiling again, he leaned a little, and I pressed my shoulders square against the back wall. He finished his beer, started to peel the label, and recited some names he'd learned from his maps – 'Battram Mountain, Pony Creek, the DuNoir.'

We started in on new beers. A few people danced to the jukebox. After a while, Clarence started playing again, going from a long note on the trumpet to a fast riff on the piano, and the crowd filled the floor. I could have fallen asleep there, watching people dance. Sam held himself upright on his elbows, drank from his beer in silence, nodded slightly with the music or smiled when he caught my eyes.

From down along the line of booths, the Indian approached. It's one thing to play a game once, but I couldn't figure why he would play it again when it could get him hurt. He had something to say to the people in each booth, and I watched his lips move, tried to catch his voice, tried to catch reactions, shouts, whatever, but the music drowned all but his movement. He laughed. He approached. Two more steps.

He danced at the end of our table, blocking things. Chanting at us, he tapped Sam on the shoulder. Sam sat up, looked at the man, turned his head slowly, loosely, toward me, and said, 'Hey, who is this guy, anyway?'

'I don't know.'

Sam turned back toward the man. 'Hey, buddy, who *are* you?'

The Indian raised his arms, snapped his fingers out in front of his forehead, and spun himself around once with churning steps. 'Gilbert.' He slowed, leaned forward and supported himself at the end of the table on straight arms, his hips tilting and grinding, and his lips, tongue, worked around his words. 'Gilbert fucking Richards. Some white guy's name. I'm changing it. Wagonburner, eh? Something with some guts. I'm gonna set something on fire, boys.' Then he just stood there inspecting us for a moment as if he were waiting for a truck to run over his feet before he'd move. His face twitched with smiles, his eyes worked back and forth across us.

'Ha.' Sam's head fell back, his face to the ceiling. 'Isn't he funny,' he said, and then he righted himself, watched Gilbert.

Gilbert started dancing again, kept his eyes on Sam. 'You, boy,' he said, his arms surging out toward Sam, pulling back. 'Who are you, boy? Tell me.'

'Sam.'

'And him?'

'Blue.'

'Sad? Baby. Sweet baby. Smile for mama.'

'My *name* is Blue,' I said.

I pushed Sam's beer into his hand and he took a few swallows, lowering the liquid, his shoulder drifting again toward me. I drank from my own bottle. This Gilbert character danced and watched us. He tossed his hair back. Sam watched him. Sam's head swayed with the same rhythm.

'Sam,' I said, 'are you all right?'

'Fine.' He didn't look at me.

'Sam, maybe you should slow down.' I grasped the neck of his bottle, but he held on to it, forced the opening to his mouth and took a swig.

'I'm fine, Blue. Trust me.'

'Boys. Boys.' Gilbert frowned and shook his head. 'Tired? Cranky? Be good. Good boys. White boys. What's in store for you two?'

Sam laughed, and he waved Gilbert off. I watched the tendons shift in the side of Sam's neck as his jaw worked. I watched the back of his neck, his hair cropped in short whorls. 'Blue here is setting me up in a place. Real rustic. Way up high.'

'Lovely.' Gilbert reached out and took Sam's hand, pinched it between thumb and index, and pulled it up into his dance for a beat before letting it fall. 'You've done well. Mama's proud.' Then he looked at me, ran his hands up through his long straight hair to clear it out of his face. I got it all, the black eyes, the thick lips pursing and working around his deep voice, the woman's skin on his sharp chin as if he'd never had to shave. 'You, Blue. Lovely. What about you?'

Then Sam watched me too, he turned back to me, finally, for a static moment. His lips were wet with beer. I imagined him pulling his jeep off the highway, under the crossbar of the main gate, down the dirt road past the Fisher's stone house, a sharp turn with tight elbows and the jeep slides to a stop in the lot among the outbuildings, windmill, my cabin. Dust settles.

'I'm set fine,' I said, and Sam nodded sharply and looked back to the Indian for his response, wouldn't stop looking.

'You are,' Gilbert said. 'Set fine. Yes. Envy's a foul thing. I envy.' He leaned far forward over our table, grasped my hand quickly, his skin rough, his grip strong, tugged at me for a beat, too strong for me to pull away without obvious force, without seeming that I had something against Indians, something against any normal Indian. He squeezed my hand – the unpleasant feeling of pressure on bones so close to the surface they're almost visible through skin. But he let go, leaned away unsteadily and grabbed the back of the booth behind Sam's head for support. His fingers twitched on the maroon vinyl, nearly brushed at the skin on the back of Sam's neck, the skin above Sam's collar burnt lightly by days in the intense, high altitude sun. Gilbert leaned down, and from what I could tell, his hair might have fallen across Sam's face. My hand rose, maybe to pull Sam back, maybe to push Gilbert's fingers off the vinyl. But Gilbert stood away, laughed, and looked at me hard. 'Don't be frightened, white boy. You want to hide out? I got a room at the Pinewood Cabins. Number seven. I've got one night in you white boys' town, then it's fuck-you-all-to-hell and on to better parts. I've got high standards.'

He made no sense. I'd never seen anyone go so soft, as if he had no bones to hold his shoulders square. He might have gone on forever it seemed, he might have babbled on until I could finally wrestle Sam to his feet and help him to his jeep, load him in the passenger seat, drive him back to his trailer.

But Derek came up to Gilbert and stood a foot away. Gilbert

didn't retreat, didn't turn, just brought himself up and waited. Gilbert had an inch on Derek and more bulk. He seemed to be waiting for Derek to speak, as if he couldn't guess from the look on Derek's face what the message would be. But Derek didn't speak to Gilbert – he broke his stare away from the Indian and turned to us, to Sam and me, and his voice twisted out of his face as if it were hard for him to move. 'What the hell are you assholes doing with yourselves? If you're not going to act right, why don't you go home?'

I would have gladly gone home, would have put an end to the game, would have given Derek a friendly fist in the gut if he'd pursued his anger any louder, but now three people were blocking my exit. I had to wait for an opening, for things to take their rapid course.

'Hey, bud. Hey, Derek,' Sam said, motioning for Derek to slide into the seat across from us. 'Have a beer. Sit. We're having a rip.'

Derek didn't move. 'Why don't you get out of here? Get some air? There's got to be something better for you fuckers to do with yourselves.'

As Derek spoke, his voice harsh and tight, Gilbert watched him closely, watched his mouth move, darted his eyes to follow the descent of a dot of spittle forced out with the words. Then Gilbert's hand started to rise slowly, a finger extended, the nail flesh-pink at the tip. That pointed finger rose past Derek's shoulder, rose even with his jaw, and as Gilbert whispered, 'There's nothing better for these boys,' and as Derek snapped his head sideways to face Gilbert, he forced that finger straight at Derek, pressed against the lower lip, the nail sharp against the upper lip, pushed in. And Derek was gone, suddenly out into the crowd, walking with shoulders jerking up against his neck, with hands snapping out to the side as if he were trying to shake off water. He left Gilbert standing, unmoved, with white spit on the tip of his outstretched finger.

My own fingers are slender and long. Sam's are squat. Gilbert's are dark with blue veins obvious beneath the surface, and I couldn't be sure if the veins were from real muscle or if they were just tangled decorations, something fancy and untrue. Who could tell if he had any real strength, or if he was just art, a dark design on a clay pot. Designs are born out of something. I listened to him. Sam listened to him. Derek was invisible, silent, gone.

'I have things to give you, boys.' He danced, soft and spinning, dead still, chanting, silent. 'See me? You think I'm drunk? No. Magic.' Sam tapped his fingers with Gilbert's beat. 'Screw. Screw up your courage.' Sam leaned back toward me, leaned away, his shoulders starting to tilt with the music. 'You can hear the music. Smell the sweat stirred up by firelight. Some young warriors. Screw the berdache. Make the rain. Luck. Heal something. Berdache.' He did a fancy turn, arms out, one hand up, one hand low, like a bird. He chanted at us. He blocked everything behind. 'Tell me I can't dance.' Sam rocked harder. 'Tell me I'm not something you could prize.'

No one had to tell me that this man hadn't been in town before. What was to keep trouble away if he wouldn't get out quickly? What was to keep Sam out of trouble if all he could see was Gilbert, blocking everything behind? But I too watched Gilbert as if there weren't anything else to see, as if the faces I knew weren't where they could see me, as if his words had closed in over me.

'A real honour,' Gilbert said. He danced, his moves fancy and loose. I wanted to figure him out, figure what would push him away. Sam leaned toward me, the back of his head brushed me, and then he leaned toward the dance. Gilbert put out a finger and pushed Sam back toward me, frowned, said, 'I want to dance. *Tell* me I can't dance.'

His fingers snapped over his head. He lifted Sam's hand and tugged. Sam lurched, his head flopped, his eyes came around toward me sleepily, he gave a limp grin, said, 'Blue. I've been drinking.' Gilbert pulled harder on Sam's hand and got him to his feet and took him away.

I thought of Sam below the Ramshorn – black rosy finches passed through to the cliffs above timberline.

Lots of hands pressed on asses, the two-step, like before, and it didn't seem much different, except for an odd leaning, a swaying off the rhythm, as if they were all being pushed away from something dangerous, a wounded dog. Joanne Miller, her eyebrows skewed, lost a step as she snapped out, one-armed, from her partner. Jason Woodburn moved his wife away, keeping her back to it. The couples shifted, and I saw long black hair, straight, moving dead on the rhythm, snaking over shifting shoulders. Sam was supported and pulled through the steps by Gilbert's large hands. Sam's face drew up serious above his eyes, his forehead wet, and he danced with Gilbert as if it were something to learn – a small rough hand, fingers spread, on the ass of a guy a foot taller with long hair and eyes half closed making a high chant like a woman in a ceremony we didn't know anything about.

I didn't get up to help Sam then. No one watched me. Sam would have done whatever I asked, whatever I ordered him to do. I could have taken him by the arm, said loudly that he'd had too much to drink, led him away, and then in a few days he'd have been at the cow camp, out of sight.

But then Derek was beside them. He reached out and took Sam by the belt loop and pulled him away from Gilbert, who reached to bring Derek into the dance too. Derek twisted his arm away and led Sam toward the door.

Space opened through the moving people, and I thought I heard the scrape of the door over the noise of the piano, drums, voices.

Sam was outside now. Sam would be reaching into his pockets for his keys, in no shape to drive. But he was safely free from that dance. My way was clear to stand up, get out, help him home.

Gilbert stood alone, letting his movements slowly stop. I blinked hard to focus. The couples continued their dance, watching the floor, watching Gilbert, no one watching me yet. They were careful to leave a space for Gilbert, whatever direction he might turn, but while I watched for an opening toward the door, he walked toward me, toward the booth. People moved in behind where he walked, twisted their heels over where he stepped, John and Alex and Betty and Mrs Hudson, all with a glance at me.

I didn't wait to see if their faces would calm, because I was on my feet and moving. I thought people might have been reaching for me as I pushed through, might have been trying to talk to me, but I was out the door and on the sidewalk. No one to touch me. The dead street, parked trucks, the bar noise muffled by the cool silence. I watched my feet through the red flashing on the sidewalk and stepped past the end of the bar building. The narrow empty lot opened out on my left and I heard voices. I looked over and saw two men circling, grappling, not a dance, a fight, every move falling into blurred shadow, a hollow sound, dust, not clear, but understood, like a knife cutting – at first you see it cut, then you feel it, then you realize what it is you feel, and then you don't believe it, as if it's a mistake, and you run back through things, run to your truck, slam it into motion, drive away, off to somewhere high up.

# Denny Smith

## ROBERT GLÜCK

Something painful encloses something joyful and now I am enclosing that painful thing as a way to assert my joy. Last June you said we had to have a talk. I hate the word relationship, a sheep bleats in it. We sat at a metal table under a red and blue umbrella, you in the bright sun, I in the shade, in the middle of the day, in the de Young's walled garden café – your sparkling water, my coffee lifted to lips, poured on to cells a little hot from thirst. I was leaning forward on an elbow so my shirt would clear my right nipple – it ached quietly from the rough pleasure dispensed a few hours before – but I sat back when you said our relationship was over. My face tightened around a precise smile: you were the one who needed to say 'I love you'. We'd spent four years together, planned to spend the rest of the day together . . . You nodded and blinked, deferring, but I felt you were exposing me, as though my life collapsed on the scale of hidden/exposed. How to protect myself from this conflict without benefit of a rehearsal? Next to our table a huge bronze cherub blew a conch; the boy was the same dark grey as the garbage-can in front of him. And now how to remember the conflict without supplying that rehearsal? Something joyful encloses something painful. I thought it was the fluttering of a butterfly, but it was just a man walking by with a white cup.

First our talk lacked any exchange; then suddenly I was no longer your business. I was alone, waked from a spell. I wondered if this would be as gruelling as my loneliness before I was detained by you four years ago. We didn't grow old and night never fell. I didn't write about us. I couldn't use your hazel eyes or wry endorsement. I was working on something else. When it needed sweetness, I just cannibalized a tender moment. My book improved when I pulled back the sheet and ran my hand along your hip – then everything shifted, your thigh moved with my hand, your buttocks shifted down and towards me voluptuously and at the same time you sighed as your hip tipped sideways like an Indian god, your balls slipped over each other and your cock slid across dark curls. So in a way both of us took without putting back, and now with a wave of your hand our relationship vanished as though it were a normal surprise for everything in the garden to disappear.

You said, 'I know what you're doing. I know that look – you're composing this in your head.'

'Oh, don't worry, I already promised not to use your name.'

'*Mon ami*, I was only being flippant.'

'For four years?'

'People have been flippant for four years.'

I laughed merrily, then suddenly, like the mentally ill, became despondent. You cleared your face with the heel of your palm and discarded the features; it was your mother saying, 'Go on without me, I'll just stay here in the trailer and wash my hair.'

I was alone; to the degree I didn't feel pain I felt a greater pang; in four years we never reached a point of no return. Until this moment there was nothing irreversible between us. I debased the time of my one and only life watching *Wild Kingdom* with you on listener-sponsored TV, to feel awe when the lean coyote eats the rabbit, the brine-shrimp drifts into the jellyfish, the leopard brings down the wildebeest, and then to feel justified, as though I'd learned something. We were never admitted into the story.

The End: a dialect was lost – no more Nadia Comaneci in bed, no more 'Four Last Songs'. You replied, 'What's Nadia Comaneci?' I tried to seize a last opportunity to be who you are. What do you ask people to recognize when they see you? I could only proceed by subtraction: your lack of cruelty. Had I failed to be amazed that no one in the world is afraid of you? Even your penis averts its eye. In the café, I tried to sit behind your hero's jaw, an exclamation point in resolution but small, therefore to be treasured – your hero's face, the miniature grandeur of a chess knight portraying old-fashioned heroism, sincerity rather than prestige.

There should be a word for a reversal that occupies me like an invading army – takes me over – while in the same gesture I become that army, that change of plans. We sat in silence for a while and when that became too much we talked. Pansies and geraniums bloomed in metal pots; behind a boxwood hedge the ubiquitous agapanthus held blue-purple aloft on slender stems, and the last of the white camellias browned.

You treated me well, we were happy, I believe it. I also wanted this separation, but I wanted to stay together more. We had no expectations and sometimes I was ashamed for degrading my time with such well-crafted entertainment. Mr Pitch and Mr Catch are wry, conscious characters, charming, humiliated by mortality, more prudent than nuts and seeds, trapped in a story smaller than themselves which illuminates a truth too shiftless to get out of bed and meet demands. Say it ignores cause and effect and probability in favour of a quick-sketch of its own existence. Catch thinks, My life my life my life my life as a novelty act, and I am afraid. Then he comes quickly and easily, no one the wiser, but does this sex keep the world from slipping away or is it an image of that disjunction? It never slowly dawns on Pitch that by not knowing Catch he doesn't know himself. It never slowly dawns on Catch that he oppresses them both by regarding himself as a problem and Pitch as a solution.

Like Pitch and Catch, I couldn't find my grievance. 'This is the wrong time and place, Bob, I don't want you to be upset.' You pushed your glass, which was this time and place, a few inches away. I knew just what you meant. For you personal drama was like bragging. Once you observed that birth is merely a change of location, death a slight breath, then the lack of a slight breath. Your mildness subdued me and your steadfast gaze exasperated me – it made me more aware of your suffering than my own. I studied my blue cup to punish you. It took me a while to wonder if the murder of an impala would follow a raised voice. To cry in the wilderness you need tears and a wilderness – we were breaking up in a walled garden more real than the battle it surrounded. I could say nothing true to convince myself, to prevent anger from weaseling out of its trajectory. The first of a series of duels tumbled through the floating conference room. The self seems deep because it can use two vanishing points. I couldn't hate you or condemn you – I vented my indignation on the enemies of all mankind. In that conflict truth takes the form of the words it is spoken 'through' and a word of truth outweighs the entire world. Into that word of truth I was born – in a generation – that's where I stay – in a body – in a life – unequal – in a personality – forward motion – a language – country – no getting around that – in my country's century.

So Marcos is introduced to me. His face, turning from the reporters, retains for a moment its blaze of delight, mid-air, before subsiding like a flare in empty night. His lei of white plumeria weights the air with pepper and vanilla. My finger is in his face. He replies, 'You have been wrongly informed, and I intend to see that the correct information reaches you.' I feel some doubt – my hazy understanding of corruption in the Philippines may be responsible for its continuation. I counter with, 'The election was a joke.' He protests, 'I have three dozen books on democracy.' But I keep listing the secret bank accounts, the murders, the real estate. Finally I shout the irreversible. 'You are a murderer, a liar and a murderer!' He reddens – 'I am a patriot and –' I cut him off – 'Liar! Liar and murderer!' In his fox-face I see the dawning consciousness of a misfortune beyond remedy, the teeth of my words pinning him for ever. The words hold and he writhes with hatred and despair. His mouth gapes and his pupils shrink to pinpoints. I move to spit in his face but even in my imagination I'm frightened of his shadowy might – what if he takes a punch at me?

'The Egyptian Room?' you asked hopelessly, as though we

could finish the coffee and Calistoga and re-enter suspended animation.

The skin of my elbows and knees itched with exasperation. Rejection coincides too well with a tired romantic song of who I really am, some cancelled trip, some mix-up of modes of transportation, stone steps descending into a lake. I have already demonstrated contempt for those who sail away: morons. *I* never left anyone. Dogs and I understand each other, guarding the kennel. Also, I have too much dignity (arf arf). Already our break-up seemed like a memory, a remembering where everything is recycled, suspended in one or more versions of the present without being entirely alive.

So I summon Imelda, exuberantly corrupt as Vice in a morality play. I could spit at Imelda; because she's a woman I'm not physically afraid of her, and I feel that something inside her can be reached. She is very beautiful, her hair a glossy helmet above the succinct features. 'Imelda, what about the shoes?' She teases, 'And the Gucci bags? I think you are a momma's boy?' She touches her earring and polka-dot scarf. 'I am my little people's star and slave. The trouble is that we are out of fashion.'

I'm flabbergasted. I demand an explanation for the tribal murders. She picks a thread off my jacket and gives my shoulder a familiar pat; she touches me as though she were my mother. 'Liar!' I say this directly and levelly. She's confused; then she removes the mask of luxury to reveal the fanged mask of power. She literally bares her teeth. My jaw drops – her expression is more frantic, less comprehending than Marcos's. I jump back, my heart pounds, but I shout, 'Liar and murderer! Liar and murderer!' Imelda moans; her face convulses; she finally sees that language is refusing to lie. The truth has snared and exposed her. Marcos agrees, 'Yes, we were malicious, yes we were criminals.' When I convince them to disappear they are most truly dead, united with their absence and bound to an irreversible language. One way to describe this language is, It can't be so.

The End: It's the Last Judgement, when secrets are revealed and the story is over, when language is real so the self can continue after death, when the description of that self is the final truth. Liar and murderer! Then you and I might as well go to heaven and real life might as well be on the other side in the kingdom which is to come. Secrets are known and the dead speak – what do they say? They don't sing about decay or about the next venture in the chequered career of individual life – same soul, new form, king me – but the song of their character in order to arrive at new subject matter more crystalline.

I felt abandoned in both senses – lonely and wild. It's as impossible for me to understand the withdrawal of love as it is to understand my death – simply a gap – a romantic failure of the world to love me. Still, I felt a tickle of joy at leaving this nest of limitations, and a validation. It was a life-after-death experience where I look down and suffer the savage regret of not having climbed past the lid of a particular ignorance, not having climbed five or ten feet higher, whatever, beyond the two abandoned selves in a garden café muted by sunshine, the walls of lattice and grey stucco, the enormous bronze putti straddling swans at the corners of an uneventful pool that sends into the air one faltering needle, tree of knowledge, little flight of stairs that flares up out of nowhere. Then I actually climb those five or ten feet into infinite space - climb into a ticklish joy and expectation without pulse. Life after death gives my self the authority that nothing else does. I exist as unattached reality; I no longer need to win or lose or mediate the cultural and biological. One of the ways to describe my horizonless self is, It can't be so.
    I noticed your glass of Calistoga. The water contained two sapphires of light and its surface jumped with fizz. An irreducible object stands next to the impossible as though to lend it some objectivity. I jiggled the glass a little – the sapphire on top rocked back and forth, the one on the bottom stayed put. The one on the bottom, really the sun, was hard to look at, a star caught in the flux of two layers of lazy spirals and enough horizons for none to obtain, so that the slight figure with melted wings tumbles over and over not even knowing which horizon to crash on. The

horizons reflected concentric arcs into the glass's shadow on the black table. The bubbles near my side of the glass were smaller than the ones on the distant side, crisp and prismatic, and the water's surface jumped, animated, the bubbles going about their own business.

'No, I don't want to see the museum.' You raised your eyebrows. Was I over reacting? I had waited a long time for this June – to be happy in spring, happy in summer. It seemed my duty to prolong our conversation, and I did not intend it to end until I finished my blond brownie. I could not go on without its muddy butterscotch and dark nuggets, so I pretended that we might have a future. That was the only way I could talk and you went along with it.

'If we stay together,' I said with effort, 'I want you to take more control of your life.' My voice carried no weight; there you were, taking control for once, getting rid of me. You were giving me puppy-dog looks, urgent endearment, guilt in quotes.

'Bob, I want you to know I always thought you were a handsome man.' The words gave me a chill. I was beginning to be recast in the past tense. I wondered how long it was going to take.

The coffee started up, or revealed, a hum of pleasure.

I keep sifting through our conversation looking for the drama that demands all our resources, the course of obstacles that reveals the imminent. I jiggled the glass a little – the sapphire on top slid back and forth. Even an affirmation distracts from the tickle of that reflection. It floated against the far shore, actually dividing and rejoining, as though pushed together by the bubbles, so really the sapphire had no centre at all, breaking up and reforming, and not inside the actual circle, but inside a slightly smaller circle of light, the image of the glass bottom reflected upwards. The star pinged and returned, pinged and returned, as though hit by billiard balls. Then a bubble formed a dome that travelled across the surface to eclipse it. When the bubble popped, light streamed in to replenish the sapphire – the bottom light a sun slipped into the underworld, the top one floating like a nineteenth-century symbol, one sub-stance which is a reflection of a reflection, light streaming towards it. But its story is the shallow one of probability, of matter making quantum leaps, jumping in and out of existence so chance can have its role to play.

A few nights before, in bed, I felt something travel over my ear and fall across my eyes. I opened them and organized the information of all those legs into a spider and flung it away with a shout. But I retained the memory as an auspicious moment, part of my allotment of good luck, and I thought about it at the café, the dry delicacy of the spider, as though a dry leaf had the will to move, a small lament, and how it fell across my eyelids as though to resemble their delicacy. Nothing uncanny could be more elegant, a ghost. The spider was on the side of the sapphires. Their witty joy turns the world upside down. I felt in our break-up the same possibility, the same tickle.

I was getting high on coffee and beginning to sweat a little; the buzz gave my speech pattern an inappropriate lift, pleasure starting up in my tongue, lips and chest. I felt like a good deal had come to an end, cheap rent or free food.

'If we stay together,' I asked, 'what conditions would have to be met?'

'Well, I'm not saying we have to break up, just that we won't be having any more sex.'

'This is the end,' I thought with relief and hysteria. No one to witness my orgasms, no one to wring pleasure from me for his own ends. I pictured another big helping of American suffering, pointless and abnormal, a case history rather than a myth, leading nowhere. Well then, I'm never sleeping with you again. I tried to measure your Deco symmetry: bedroom eyes, a face as true as architecture. Already my unconscious was sending dreams to the rescue like the cavalry. I saw us meeting at a bar one night a few months away. You say, '*Mon ami*, I've missed you,' and so directly asked to be with me, as you did in the first place, that your candour is more compelling than any difficulty. You take my elbow, and once again you arouse me and make me happy. We get together – live together – but my imagination cancelled that, was not free to think that.

No more sex. That shut me down just as I reached for the lift fuelled by the coffee. The self is a wave, it needs some forward momentum to stay organized. I broke into parts; I felt bad and I was very happy. You were the answer to a wish for safety; it's my fault for getting what I wanted. You don't want anything; you have a fairy-tale Jane Eyre integrity that's close to a death wish, eager to go down with any ship rather than scramble like that rat, the ego.


Sitting at a café, degrading their time, their names are Pitch and Catch. Across his forehead Catch wears a high platinum wave whose momentum never breaks so that he looks amazed. Its duplicate stands rigid above his mother's face and also in other respects she is a loaded gun in him. Catch is sometimes handsome; it becomes apparent that behind his glasses his eyes are, I don't know, blue; his body is . . . so desirable only vague words like 'amazing' convey a true impression. The real wars in his life have been fought over commitment in relationships. Pitch is six years younger, his face a handsome Irish box, antique, charming, slight, scrubbed, regular, bleak, an exclamation point, and the whites of his eyes can be red after a good night's sleep. Pitch is so modest that singing on key is too much of an assertion although, like Jane Eyre, he loves the common welfare and maintains he's as tall as his beloved, overriding the evidence of the mirror. Catch is as simple as Pitch but also more complex, as self-effacing but also more ambitious. Put another way, Pitch can abide the incomplete while Catch has a horror of being wrong.

Pitch loves Catch even as he rejects him. 'Why do you make a big deal about everything? You should get over yourself.'

'That would be quite a hurdle,' Catch observes. He thinks, There should be a word that means: At my feet emptiness yawns, bottomless as far as I can see. I *am* the emptiness and I'm the mountain-top hidden in night.

Pitch mentally replies, 'I love Catch and always will. I make a vow always to take care of Catch, always to drive him to the

airport, watch his dog.' Pitch loves Catch and always will. The two
men share a saintly belief in the existence of the world, including
the garden gate, the stunted acacia and the unwilling street that
goes up and over the volcano. Pitch will help Catch out of trouble
with the same goodwill he deploys painting signs at the Union
Hall for the next demo. Being lovers is a fine point, sex is a fine
point, why get excited? Can Catch, by deferring and exerting, cut
and nullify the prerecordings?

Pitch crosses his slender arms; he is aware of the sound of traffic
and the fountain's bland hiss, the scent of the boxwood hedge and
the tiny sigh of a squeaking hinge, and from where he sits he can
see eucalyptus and cedar behind the stage-set façade, the surveil-
lance and security mechanisms visible on the roof-line, the
sunlight reflecting off the inside of Catch's frames, and the red
camellias behind Catch which Catch, being colourblind, couldn't
find in the green foliage anyway. Pitch is smooth, slight; he
pursues men who are hairier, more substantial; he is a waif except
he dominates in bed. Catch learned exactly that. He acquired the
patience to be ravished – knowledge of the bridgeless gulf
between supine (without muscle and without will, where mem-
branes are caressed so that pleasure can be exposed) and upright
(muscular and wilful). Catch learned about hoisting himself up,
the tremendous exertion needed to undertake change without
belief: there can be no new faith until the pleasure of the new
position convinces and becomes normal. With every caress insight
was *given* to Catch; he experienced himself on his big cedar bed to
the degree he could, to the degree he was not unreachable but
reached, on a plateau where meaning equals animal pleasure,
simple and orderly.

Pitch loves Catch, true to the end. Catch will learn this
eventually, everything will be fine. Why do Catch and Catch's
friends get so worked up? They are all writers and, well, drama
majors at heart. Pitch thinks, Aesthete is misfit spelled backwards.
He'd like to try this joke on Catch and longs for a happier mood.
Catch takes a drink of Pitch's Calistoga and when he sets the glass
down the top sapphire is gone. His gaze settles on the other. The

eye always settles on the brightest and likes it, he thinks infor-
mationally. How does some mechanical impulse become aesthetic
and moral?

Pitch keeps things simple on a slightly ironic principle. Can he
subdue the cipher of his destiny by his insistence on the fresh-air
smell of a cucumber or on self-effacing vegetables like celery and
carrots? He's so slight he resembles a puppet, the empty body and
expressive face. 'How many times did Catch make trouble by
raising expectations I couldn't fulfil? Who could win his race? I'm
sick of fretting, but I will always love him,' Pitch recites restfully,
'because Catch is always afraid, with a pleading look in his eyes.
He is shy which means fearful, too good which means fearful, he
is a comedian which means fearful, he is a gay man which means
fearful, a collector of small souvenirs which means fearful, he is
full of grievance which means fearful, he must always be right
which means fearful, he is a heavy judge which means fearful. I'll
always love him, he arouses my humanitarian instincts.'

Catch gazes at the Calistoga bottle – the image on its label is
supposed to be a geyser but he thinks it's more like a brain on its
stem: a misfortune beyond remedy. He allows himself the thought
that he needs to be touched to be himself because during his ten or
twelve years of childhood which began thirty-nine years ago his
mother didn't touch him. I love my mother, Catch reminds
himself in a prayer. I only want nothing upsetting to happen. He
holds his bleeding palms aloft: that's his mother and father and
forebears holding up their palms – that's the righteous one who is
harmed.

He looks up: a surprisingly precise cloud stands white and
alone, solid as a brain in the deep sky; when he returns the garden
is completely arrested and seems to have jumped forward in
intensity. Everything has found its place poised at the brink.
Customers at other tables uphold this saturation. Catch gazes in
estranged wonder as the moment subsides, yielding in stages to
the chime of a glass, a woman's head turning, a door swinging,
laughter, branches tossing. Time passes. It's strenuous and finally
impossible to keep the gravity of the occasion in mind. Catch is

distracted by a gaiety that underlies even the most solemn funeral, as though at bottom they were only children burying a mouse.

He's rather bored; while producing minimal small talk he daydreams this story to himself: My attitude towards insects changed when I resisted the impulse to squirm and learned to remain absolutely still when they landed or walked over me. They thought I was inanimate. I thought they did. Once when I was in bed a large spindly spider, the kind that isn't frightening, not fat or hairy, walked over my shoulder. Then it lowered its mouth onto my skin and bit me! I certainly thought that the spiders who bite are smaller, flea-like. First it felt itchy, then it hurt, then really hurt. Some poison, because my arm felt pins and needles and I smelled dry-cleaning odour. I started swiping but couldn't detach it – some kind of ghastly aberration – but my swipes kept knocking off its legs until there were none left. They were spindly and loose and I recoiled from their being on my skin. I ran and got the tweezers to pull off the head but it wouldn't come, it was like wood, and the pain continued. I went to the doctor and he said it was a mole! What an idiot! The pain has continued and I can't get it off – it's there for keeps – and I think I am even beginning to feel some sensation in it.

The listlessness of Catch's story irritates him; he chooses this moment to regain some tension; he sits forward and tells Pitch about the man in the yellow Triumph who exchanged glances with him and then parked. After a quick appraisal and a whiff of Aqua de Silva, Catch led him upstairs. Pitch is upset, but not too much. 'Mon ami,' he volunteers, 'I've had a few accidents myself.'

'How many?'

Pitch looks up. 'Oh I guess one every few weeks for the last two years.'

Catch whistles. Now that is an ugly and impressive surprise. He didn't want Pitch to be unfaithful, but never liked fidelity per se. Pitch already confessed to some of these accidents, as he calls them. Catch was, Pitch thought, inappropriately aroused by the details he kept wheedling out of Pitch. 'What kind of sheets did he have?' 'What colour was his pubic hair?' Catch scandalized the repentant criminal, who felt so exploited he changed roles and became the victim. Still, Catch is wounded by the size of the two-year statistic. He understands for the first time that they are breaking up, that Pitch continues beyond him.

'Safe sex?' Catch inquires.

'Of course,' Pitch replies, 'except for when some sperm got in my eye, but my doctor said . . .'

Like most revelations, it makes a lot understandable and a few things more mysterious. Evidently Pitch augmented their narrowing agenda in bed with variety in partners, but how to explain his steadfast passion? Catch's right nipple hurts, testifying like a bell that still vibrates. But Catch also suffers the hurt of the under-utilized. 'It's just a waste – I'm so interesting – like he attended Harvard and only took woodshop. He didn't get the best of me.' It's a final statement, true in no instance. They don't know how to act or react. Catch began every day for the last four years with the name Pitch. That's not true, although it portrays Catch's mood. The coffee is making Catch need to use the toilet; he feels hemmed in and vexed – he moves from side to side as though he were in a crowd instead of containing one; actually there are only five or six people in the garden. Pitch wants Catch to be playfully angry; Catch wants to blame Pitch for the sheer time promiscuity takes. Catch gazes at Pitch, his face, his lack of ambition. Pitch thinks, I'm tired of being his source of disappointment, but Catch is just being amazed that one person is one way and another person is another – this is the romance of personality but also the mystery of form, which deepens in a climate of separation and longing.

Catch tried to corrupt Pitch by teaching him to want. 'Catch, I'm a blue-sky person.' Their drinks grow distant as the Calistoga loses its chill and the coffee its heat. The strongest contrast is not between the state of satisfaction called Pitch and the state of dissatisfaction called Catch, but between the full sun and the flat ovals of shadow under the seven umbrellas.

Catch allows himself to think, My mother never touched me; now I believe that only familiar touch counts, and that death is a romantic failure of the world to love me. Catch had shelved this mother-thought long ago, but behind him there is a second Catch permitting and disallowing. Catch remembers being startled and impressed when he learnt he could have problems of his own, could claim possession of an unconscious, he was at least that much a member of the human club. Pitch and Catch search each other's eyes for an assumption. They are motionless; they dread complicity with a brutish reduction of their experience; they know that they don't know how to act; they know the uncertain choice they make will determine the reality of their break-up, will peg it in their memories. The memory is attracted to motion, what is still becomes background. They are tamer than the fountain, weaker than birdsong.

How to explain Denny Smith's steadfast passion? I followed him towards the circumscribed, with less touch but more revealed. I resented each subtraction as it happened, then the eroticism of the remove gratified my imagination with a shorthand for intensity – say an instant of pain stands for a tender life – and I insisted on limits while resisting them. A few hours before, Denny had produced in me an orgasm so absolute I was shaken; in victory I was one with the self's strategies, and the forward momentum carried me up and out to walk my dog. I was so ravished and full of wonder I had an impulse to tell the people in my neighbourhood about my orgasm as though it were a flying saucer.

That impulse to speak turned back on itself, became a language created on top and destroyed from underneath. On top was a tropical paradise. I had always wanted to be happy and to believe in the world. Suddenly a world appeared that required little faith: work OK, boyfriend, money OK, affection, friends. It was an immaculate morning and I'd risen from the strict configuration of Denny's body. Things were going well in general and I felt united in myself and perfected under the banner of his 'I love you'.

When I told Denny about my orgasm he said, 'Really?' – neutral surprise noted and retained by my imagination, expert at familiar touch as a prisoner at weather. But romance closed the interval before I could perceive it. Now I realize the exact fierceness I'd taken for Denny's passion was exasperation. So there *was* cruelty in our garden. Liar and murderer! I'm grateful that anger and hunger at last have a shape; I'm humiliated to have felt such rapture under the wrong circumstances. His I-love-you's weren't lies, I think, so much as incomplete statements and accommodations. My pleasure is cast in doubt by hands that dispatched me rather than brought me to life. Yet the physical rush was undeniable, and the joy. I think these thoughts with a growing, marvelling sorrow. I consider the sapphires of light parting the future from its shadow in the garden. Hidden and exposed, captured and free, held aloft between equal magnets, I can't even argue or assign pain to a wrong. I consider the pleasurable breakdown of assumptions and the unwelcome days ahead.

# BM

## JAMES M. ESTEP

'Is it clear?'

'Go on whore.'

'Johnbouy, don't call me that. I'm free and easy, but not necessarily a whore. Do you want one?' I asked, emptying a third miniature bottle of vodka into my water glass.

'No. Hurry up, girl. Pumpkin Cow's comin' down the steps.'

Johnbouy stepped out of the waiter's station and into the corridor to stall 'Pumpkin Cow' and keep me covered. I raised the glass to my lips and drained the fiery liquid. That tingling in my toes – the one that eased my pain, calmed my fear, induced courage and gave hope and purpose to my life – was now in progress. I put the empty glass, mouth down, back on the bar rack with the clean ones, burped and hurried out of the waiter's bin with a tray full of silver and a towel slapped over my shoulder.

'Why, good evenin', Pumpkin. I d'nt hear ye come in.' This was the owner greeting Johnbouy. You could watch the blood drain from his face and the stiffening of his muscles every time she spoke. Calling him 'Pumpkin' only made matters worse.

Pumpkin Cow was a displaced, over-stuffed, discreetly pickled southern belle with the congeniality of a Melony Wilkes that no one trusted and the cunning lash of Scarlett O'Hara that everyone was afraid of. Nobody liked the heifer. Even her eighty-year-old, blatantly pickled, boyfriend openly despised her. Often after his second bottle of bourbon had been uncorked, you would see him stumbling around the old mansion in a daze, mumbling a distinct 'cunt' with each sip.

As she passed by Johnbouy, she flicked a piece of lint from his jacket, then patted the spot and said, 'Now, don't you look handsome!'

I choked on my chuckles as Johnbouy's face went scarlet and his fists clenched into little angry balls. Nobody hated her as much as he did.

'Evenin' darlin',' she said to me in passing. Then her brow knitted up in the shape of an anus (she never would have done that if she knew), she took the towel from my shoulder and placed it over my forearm, smirked a smile, sniffed twice as though suspicious of I-don't-know-what! and went off to the kitchen

'Hey Pumpkin!' I snickered.

'Bitch wants it so bad, she's spottin' the rug,' Johnbouy growled.

He stalked off to the terrace and I went back to my water glass. My toes tingled so good already, I didn't think twice about getting caught.

By the time Johnbouy walked back into the room even my ears were tingling and little glee-filled beads of sweat were gathering on my brow. He was grinning from ear to ear and I could literally smell that perverted brain of his overheating.

'You'd best chill out, *darlin'*; we gotta new boy workin' with us tonight.' And then he added the 'Umh, umh, umh!' that defined that smell.

'Umh, umh, umh?'

'You'll see. It's the best little butt I've seen since we been in Florida.'

Just at that moment the swinging door flew open and Barry Best Butt whizzed past us and into the kitchen. He flashed a cheeseburger, Hollywood grin from beneath his bushy moustache and left a heavy scent of Brut trailing behind him.

'He's cuuute!' I wailed.

'That one's mine,' Johnbouy warned.

'That one ain't *your's* – that one's his, you silly queen. And who's to say he won't choose to make his *mine*!'

'I got five that says it's mine first,' Johnbouy answered. His nostrils flared when he said it and that lewd scent came back into the room.

The swinging door slammed up against the wall and the grinning little Italian swished his bun-perfect corps past us again. But this time, for just one split-second, his woppy brown eyes locked up with mine and somewhere among my tingling parts a flutter was born.

'OK, Johngirl! You're on! But I think you just lost!' I cried.

'I saw it, whore. What a waste.'

'Whatda you mean, "What a waste?" ' I said, going back to my water glass to celebrate the upcoming nuptial.

'I mean, you'll never make use of that glorious caboose,' he said. 'And slow down, lush. I ain't goina port your tables for you.'

'You've never "ported" my tables, bitch!' I downed my drink, patted my crew-cut with the palms of my hands, puckered-up my lips and tingled back out to the dining-room.

After work that evening the three of us piled into Johnbouy's Toyota and skirted off to The White Lion for a *drink*. Barry and I had already laid the ground for the consummation of the 'goo-goo' eyes we'd passed back and forth throughout the evening, so there was no more competitive heat going on between me and Johnbouy.

I pulled my Southern Comfort bottle from underneath the back seat and offered it to Barry.

'Straight?' he asked and twisted his face up like Pumpkin Cow's.

'Don't do that,' I said drily. 'You'll get wrinkles.'

'Mike likes his liquor in a pure way,' Johnbouy volunteered, drawing on those long southern I's.

By this point in any evening, most of my tingling parts had already tingled themselves numb, and I could not have cared less whether Miss Best Butt approved or disapproved of my acquired tastes.

'I'll buy you one with some Seven-Up in it when we get to the bar,' I said and then smiled too big.

'Gimme a swig.' Johnbouy reached back for the bottle, took a swig, snarled, said 'N-a-s-t-y!' and shoved the bottle back.

I've tingled too much, for too long, to be able to give a true account of what happened after that. I remember quite distinctly drinking. Otherwise I have a vague recollection of playing with Barry's leg under the table while we were at the bar and somebody was playing with mine. Couldn't possibly have been Johnbouy, so I assume it was Barry. Then we went home to the Saint Augustine Motor Inn (John and I lived there). Barry came with us and the following day he came back with his suitcase and an intent to stay. I guess I did something right that evening.

Two weeks later, after a delightful chilliburger at Sambo's Drive Inn, Barry and I had our first serious talk.

'I can't do it,' I mumbled, my head tucked and shoulders slouching in timid fear. We were shuffling along the highway on our way back to the motor inn.

Barry burped, filling the air with garlic-chilli stink and then said, 'Why not?' But I couldn't tell whether the tone of his voice was verging on a growl or a sob. (I was to find out later that both could be employed within the same minute depending on what effect he wanted to elicit.)

'You wouldn't understand,' I mumbled firmly.

'Try me.'

'OK.' I stood up straight and raised my volume. 'I'll try. It's because it's against the Church.'

'The Church!' A definite, uncontrollable growl.

'I told you, you wouldn't understand.' I went back to mumbling.

'What's the fuckin' Church got to do with you lovin' me?'

'Nothing against loving you.' I was all humped over now. 'It's living with you sexually that's wrong. You were married and never annulled it. It's already bad enough that we're both men.'

'Fuck an A!' he cried out and kicked the gravel on the side of the road in such a fury that I froze, humped-up in terror.

'What's an A?' I whispered.

'You wouldn't understand!' And he shot off ahead of me leaving me alone with my morals.

I didn't chase after him. Instead I took the long way home to think over what I'd done. Sadness overwhelmed me in dread of what might happen, but self-righteousness equalized it. So I said a rosary while walking and imagined my morals strengthened.

Once back at the Inn, I witnessed my good wholesome ethic go like ice on the fire. Barry had left, leaving behind him a 'Dear me' note and a phone number in Allentown.

Those tragic moments . . . lost love, jealousy, the I-can't-live-without-hims . . . were never again to be so disastrous as they were in my tingling youth. I see now that they were indeed great indulgences deserving of many merits in that illusory paradise of great moral souls. Hail Mary! – Barry came home.

'I think we should get outta here,' he said.

I wrapped by legs tighter around his back. 'I missed you so much, honey! I'm sorry! Nothing will ever take us apart again.'

'Promise?' (He took advantage of that one.)

'Oh, honey . . .'

'Then, let's get outta here,' he said again and popped his now limp love-stick from my throbbing hole and plopped himself down at the foot of the bed.

'And go where?' I asked.

'Anywhere – everywhere! We're young. Let's take advantage of it.'

'Yeah!' I jumped up. 'Let's do it! Where do you wanna go?'

'Miami,' he decided.

'OK, Miami. When do we go?'

'Now.'

'Now! On what?' I got a nervous twitch and reached for the Dewers on the night-stand.

'You've gotta cheque book and so do I.'

'True, but as far as I know, they're both empty.' He was really making me twitch.

'That's not important,' he assured me. 'You're gonna give me a cheque for five hundred and I'll give you one for five. You go to the branch on the highway and I'll go to the one on the island. We'll write a cheque for the plane tickets and by the time the downtown branch figures it out, we'll be in Miami with a thousand bucks.' A smile played on his lips and those dark, woppy eyes gleamed at me from behind a veil of the madman's euphoria. It was evident that the prospect of a felony was more appealing to him than the move itself. However, as my twitch began to tingle, I started to share in his deviant thrill.

Everything worked out just like Barry said it would and we began to adopt this method of banking on a continual basis. Whenever times got tough or just too monotonous, we robbed the bank and left town.

Miami Beach didn't hold us long. Two months after our landing, it lost its charm – Barry suggested we stage a mugging. We did. I pushed her and he grabbed her bag. A quarter of a mile later we could still hear her yelping. I felt real bad over that one, but then we counted up the money and found over a hundred dollars . . .

While I was packing, Barry left the room and returned five minutes later with another hundred. The waiter in the room next to ours had fallen asleep with his door open. Barry was on a roll. Since we hadn't paid the rent that week, we tossed our bags out of the window and shimmied down the drain-pipe. We took a cab to the Greyhound, wrote a cheque and moved to The State Street Hotel, State Street, Colombus.

'Do you know what tomorrow is?' he asked grinning. He was sitting in the easy-chair next to the window of our State Street room.

'Friday?'

'The eleventh of April . . . Our first anniversary.'

'Oh, honey!'

'We gotta do somethin' special,' he gleamed.

Loving, passionate sex – backed for me by ludes and Scotch – was our speciality.

Barry, a true Italian, found nothing more exhilarating than burrowing himself up in a hole and staying there for hours on end . . . namely, my hole. At first I found these unions painful (he was well endowed and my hole was still a teenager's). Therefore, I insisted that the burrowing time be limited and his drilling gentle.

But Barry only pretended to agree to these conditions.

'Relax, Shunkums . . . just relax. Here, I'll put some more spit on it. There, ain't that better. I got the head in. You're so warm. I love you baby. I wanna be one with you. I wanna keep it in you for ever.' Then, right in the middle of an 'Ooohhh, baby! You're sooo . . .' he would pull it out and shove it up my ass again, bulldozer style – full force – leaving me breathless and needing to pee.

But, I believed him anyway.

Even later, when he became more and more sadistic . . . I still believed him. Of course, I was begging for it by then.

Colombus became a memory of misery for me. The booze, along with our 3 a.m. pig-outs on White Castle onion-burgers, started to create a thick coat of blubber around my middle and bottom. This blimpy condition in conjunction with my increasing lethargic state of being, made Tim – some blond bumpkin Barry had picked up at work – all the more desirable to him.

It's maddening, that gut-wrenching pain that seems to suck life-breath-soul from beings and leave them comatose and lobotomized . . .

I sat on the floor of that barren State Street room, rocked back and forth, cried, wailed and drank. It was 4 a.m. There is no other excuse but another man at 4 a.m.

'Where were you?' I choked. It was 7 a.m.

'Out.'

'Oh, Bar . . . Wah! Wah! Wah!'

'You're drunk!'

That startled me. I thought about it for a minute and then decided that it wouldn't do. I was most surely drunk. However, he had sinned in a much bigger way.

'Wah! Wah! Wah!' There was no pride or shame; just Scotch and excruciating pain.

'You're disgusting!' And with that he went to bed.

This lasted for seven whole days. From noon till four I'd serve cocktails to the uppity drunks at the Colombus Athletic Club. Then I'd go back to that frayed and sombre room on State Street, cry and wring my hands. I'd stopped eating and switched to 151 proof rum. Ludes, Camels and Bacardi kept me alive. I did sit-ups for hours and said many rosaries. But most significant to me was the hardening process of my internal being which began at this point in my life . . . ever so lightly and ever so slowly. With this came my firm resolve to remain as dignified as possible through-out this nightmare. I was *not* disgusting! This dignified stance, of course, required that I pass out by nine o'clock sharp.

I suppose the bumpkin must have been boring or else he petered out. On the evening of the seventh day, Barry came home early. I remember well that it was before 'dignity hour', because I was still lying on my back nipping rum and still conscious enough to be doing those incessant sit-ups.

'Let's go back to Florida,' he said.

Worn from pain and loneliness, I was sceptical this time. But I said 'OK.' anyway and started twitching again. We left the next day.

Two weeks of separation had its end at the Sea Lodge Motel on Daytona Beach. I came to one night about 3 a.m. with the most incredible urge to take a dump. When I opened my lids and tightened my sphincter, I realized that the urge was being induced. Barry was ploughing up the dirty back road in high gear.

I was sooo pleased!

One of the things that used to excite him the most was sticking his finger up there. 'You like that?' he'd say, wide-eyed and breathless, his own pleasure exhibiting itself in his stone-hard, dripping, wop dick. Little beads of sweat would cover his body and the head of his dick would swell to an as yet unseen proportion, without any aid whatsoever. Then he would inform me in a triumpant air, 'I've got three in! Relax, baby, I'm gonna give it all to you! And you're gonna love it!'

What I 'loved' was that air of *taboo*, that sadistic ring in his voice and above all, his rock-hard, dripping, wop dick. The ache in my anus seemed a fair price.

I don't *think* he ever got it all in. I always seemed to object after 'I got four in!' Of course, persuading him to exit meant suffering through several now-or-never last attempts to 'give it all to me'. Eventually he'd give up, sit on my face while he yanked his rod and then back off just in time to waste his garlic-flavoured drippings 'all over my pretty face'. (He said that once: 'I'm goin' to waste it all over that pretty face!' Then he growled, snarled, smacked my ass and did it.)

I loved Barry.

After hours of mad passion such as this, we would cuddle up in bed like two kittens. I would lie behind him – both of us curled up – wrap my arm around his furry chest and he would hold on to me to secure the lock. Before sleep each night we had to kiss three times. 'I love you, honey,' I'd say. And he would have to answer, 'I love you too, Shunkums.' This was the nightly code and one or the other of us always insisted on it.

He had a four-by-four-inch patch of hair just below the razed part of the back of his neck. I'd bury my nose in it each night. He was always self-conscious about it and I was forever begging him not to shave it off.

He also hated his big nose and the fact that he was only 5' 8" tall – two more of his characteristics which I loved. The nose was a constant reminder to me of his ten-inch dick and his height gave me a false sense of supremacy. I was constantly reassuring him that these were great assets, except of course, when we were at war, which was often. At these times, that 'fuckin' wop nose' was the first to go.

Daytona was difficult at first. Barry finally got a job in an amusement park, handing out teddy bears to the best marksmen. I was to begin waitering at a Steak'n'Ale three days later.

The first night he went off to Cotton Candy Kingdom by the beach, I went out 'sightseeing'. I had spotted several interesting-looking cinder-block cottages along the beach, inscribed, 'MEN'. That's where I went.

I should have noticed that the guy occupying the pisser next to mine wasn't making any of the right moves – but I didn't. I should have noticed when he went out and then came in the second time that he wasn't wacking on it at all – but I didn't. Instead, I nearly broke my neck trying to get a peek on it. I got to peek his silver badge; and I went in.

'Wah! Wah! Wah!' But it didn't do any good.

'I gave you a chance buddy,' the plainclothesman said as we zoomed down Daytona's drive-on beach in the patty wagon. 'You should have left the first time. That ain't no place to be playin' with it.'

'Wah! Wah! Wah!' How would I ever explain this one to Barry?

I didn't even get a chance; the police told him the truth. Then he called my mother and told her the truth! Mortified!

'You're charged with lewd and licentious conduct: masturbating in a public place. How do you plead?' The judge's voice echoed off the walls of my brain and was followed by a series of gasps and snickers from the audience in the overcrowded court room. I knew *he* was out there. But, I couldn't look.

I followed the counsel of my fellow inmates and pleaded 'g-u-i-l-t-y' with a sixty-second stutter.

'One hundred and eighty dollars or sixty days' detention. Next!'

I twitched off stage.

My mother's bail hadn't reached me yet so they took me off to the farm. Then the money came and they let me out the same day. (I've always regretted that, having had so many fantasies about prison rape . . .)

'You're disgusting!' with an emphasis on the 'gusting' was Barry's response. I should have already become used to that label, but I hadn't. My humiliation, topped with his cold, heartless disposition, convinced me to kill myself.

A bottle of Sleep-Ease and a quart of vodka later, I lay on the floor of our motel with a dead look on my face: eyes rolled back, open just a slit so you could see the whites: mouth open wide and head tilted back to create a rattle; breathing minimized with the chest rising and falling no more than twice a minute; right hand clutching the neck of the vodka bottle and the left one lying next to the empty pill bottle. *I* thought I looked good and dead . . . until Barry came in.

'Good God! You fucking pig!' he screamed. Then he slapped me. I let my head roll in the direction he hit me, as though there was nothing connecting it to my shoulders. Inside, the rattle was becoming more distinct as I choked back my sobs. How could he be so mean?

He called the ambulance; they slapped me too, but I let the head flop like a cooked noodle. They ended the act with those little amyl capsules – it seems to me that even a real dead one would have a hard time resisting those. They took my vitals and then told Barry that I was fine; did he want to commit me? I froze. No, he didn't. The next day we were evicted.

We sat up housekeeping at the Ocean View Motel a few miles further down the beach, right across from one of those 'MEN' museums.

'Let's just go look,' Barry said one night. My jealousy and cock rose in perfect synchronization with each other.

'Nobody just *looks*.'

'If we do it together, it'll be OK.'

'Admit it! You're tired of me! Just admit it and I'll leave!' I still had this need to show off my morals.

'OK. We won't go. Forget it. I've never done it alone. I just thought, together . . . forget it.'

Shit! Me and my ethical misconceptions . . . 'Look,' I changed positions, 'We could. I mean, if we really did it *together* and we promise never, ever to do it alone.'

'OK.' He agreed quick enough. 'We'll share everything, but they can't fuck you, that's mine – ours.'

'OK. But then you can't plug them,' I decided.

We crept into the little cinder-block building about 4 a.m. Sand covered the tile floors and the stench of urine was overwhelming. There was a shuffle and someone murmured, 'Somebody's coming.' But when we entered, the dim lighting from the street lamp outside showed one man standing at the urinal and the feet of another sitting on the toilet behind the divider wall, pants and white briefs wrapped around his ankles.

There were three urinals and the guy was on the end next to the toilet. I zoomed into the middle pisser, completely forgetting about Barry. Barry moved in beside me. The guy backed up to show me his boner and Barry whispered, 'Suck it!' I fell to my knees in obedience and Barry moved around to his back side. 'Remember!' I warned him with my mouth full. He gave me the evil eye, but I wouldn't relent. He'd promised!

I put my hands on the guy's butt while I blew him. Each time Barry tried to stick it in him. I pulled the guy further into my mouth, throwing off the fucking alignment. Barry finally gave up. 'Let me suck him,' he said. But it was too late. The guy started to shoot off, so I greedily consumed the wad. Luckily, he was of the type who enjoyed a prolonged lick after ejaculation. So, I jerked Barry's head down to the guy's dick, already wiped clean and said, 'Go for it. He's gonna' come.'

Meanwhile, I scooted off behind the divider wall to the fellow on the toilet, serviced him in a matter of seconds and came out just in time to see the first guy leaving and Barry ramming it up some little blond number.

He glared up at me and then growled, 'Don't say a word! Fuckin' lyin' pig!' He must have tasted the residual come on that going-limp-quick dick I'd passed him.

I glared back and vowed silently that he would pay and pay dearly for his breach of contract. But for the moment, I wasn't going to be cheated out of blondie. I took his little boyish prick from his grasp and swallowed it. Not a minute too soon either. He popped immediately. My third mistake of the evening, for this one wasn't in to any prolonged effects or Christian charity. He uncorked Barry's raging, wop dick from his hole, pulled up his pants and ran out the door – race against guilt I presume.

Barry's anger boiled in silent looks of death, promising my upcoming extinction. We got back to the room, both of our crotches still burning for it. I was afraid to approach him. I poured a long Scotch and drained it. He walked past me on his way to the bathroom and shoved me up against the desk. Pissed, pickled and now endowed with eight-year-old, eighty-proof courage – I slapped him.

'*Bitch!*' he yelled and the tempest raged. Lamps, glass, furniture and resistant body parts flew around the room. Though I was stronger than him, his insane anger always topped me and my eight-year-old, eighty-proof courage.

Straddling my chest with his legs, he wrapped his hands around my neck and banged my head against the floor in tune to a drum-roll. The grip tightened; my head began to burn, ears ring and eyes tear from the pressure. I decided that my only hope was to play dead. (I thought I was good at this.) I went limp and faked dead. Seconds later he relaxed his grip. But then I must have flinched or breathed or something. '*Bitch!*' he screamed and slapped me again full force across the face.

Throughout the whole of this homicidal outrage, I was fully confident that my saviour was pinned up in the throbbing bulge pressed into my chest. I was right.

He ripped my shorts off in one brutal snatch and plunged in full force, full speed and no spit. I screamed in pain.

'Fucking pig! *PIG!*' and rammed it in again. 'You slimy slut. You love it!'

And I did.

Afterwards, we cuddled all night, apologizing and promising undying love and foreverness.

'Ah, honey!'

'I love you, Shunkums!'


Both of us broke and bored one weekend, Barry had an idea:

'I gotta idea.'

'Yeah?'

'Let's go hustle some money and get outta here.'

'Hustle?' I was forever being a virgo.

'Like this,' he explained. 'We'll go to the bar and pick up somebody – anybody pussy enough or drunk enough. We'll lead 'em on, get them to take us back to their place, do 'em in and then rob them.'

'What?'

'I don't mean kill 'em, idiot! Just rough 'em up a bit.'

I thought about that for a minute, I liked the idea, specially the insinuated sexual overtones. But I didn't want to do it with him. 'Three ways are hard to come by,' I said with caution.

He didn't hesitate (probably had some kinky plan of his own). 'OK. We'll go separately.'

Twitching and giggling at the same time, I reached for my bottle.

'Don't get drunk!'

'I'm always drunk, you bozo! Besides, you don't have to worry about me – I'm taking the club. One wack with this and all will be calm.' I pulled out a seven-inch leather strap with lead in the end of it. Excited, I giggled some more and stuck it in my sock.

Thirty minutes or so after we got to the club, Barry came up to the bar and pulled me away from my 'Marine' target.

'Let's quit,' he said. 'There's nobody here and besides I don't wanna do it any more.'

'Oh, no! You quit if you want. I'm goin' through with it.'

'You're drunk!'

'We gotta find you a new line, *Honey*.'

'OK. Go on.' He left. Even in the tipsy tingles I knew he was up to something. 'OK.' was not Barry's style, nor did he ever give in.

Shortly after he left, that hot, blond, burr-headed, manly marine and I staggered off to his mobile home.

We toked on a joint on the way and he gave me a lude. By the time we reached his one-room trailer, the only thought that remained in my pickled brain was to get laid by this humpy soldier.

'You want another lude?' We were lying on his bed with our hands shoved down one another's jeans.

'Yeah,' I said.

'You like poppers?'

'Yeah.'

'How 'bout toys?'

'Yeah.'

He pulled out a brown bag full of dildos, vaseline and various cock rings. He took his clothes off. He was Marine from head to toe; muscle-bound and beautiful with a mushroom head on his penis the size of a golf ball; beet-red and glistening with pre-come.

'God, you're hot.' I muttered, taking another whiff of poppers.

'So are you, cutie.' And it was true. I was blond, bombed and beautiful in my eighteenth year.

He struggled to undress me. (He was just barely in touch with his own motor section.) When he got the pants off from around my ankles, he pulled the lead piece from my sock, wacked it a couple of times into the palm of his hand and said, 'What's this for?'

'That?' I snickered. 'I'm supposed to hit you over the head with that and take your money.'

He frowned. I roared with laughter and told him the whole plan. He seemed to find the whole thing as funny as I did, however, I distinctly recall him sliding the black jack under the bed, far from reach.

'Can I stick this up your ass?' he asked politely, greasing up the biggest of his dildo collection. I put my feet on his shoulders and smiled.

While he rotated it in and out he hung over me and drained a steady flow of spit from his mouth into mine. He changed positions, stuck his ass on my face and sucked me. 'Come on baby, eat daddy's ass.' I tried to digest the whole bottom rump.

Meanwhile the dildo turned into his fist. He went back down to the foot of the bed so he could ram it in a little further. 'I wanna drink your piss,' he said. I quenched his thirst and then he quenched mine.

Two hours or so later, my hands were tied to the headboard and he was sitting on my cock, riding it raw. 'Come with me,' I said: I couldn't hold it any longer.

'OK, baby,' he answered. 'Open your mouth; I wanna shoot it in from here. You fill my hole up, OK?'

When the first white drop shot out of the mushroom, I exploded. He licked his come off my face and spit it back in my mouth. 'I got yours, and I want you to have all of mine, pretty boy.'

That was one morning I didn't see the sun nor feel the heat consuming my wraught being as I walked along the black top back to the Ocean View Motel.

Ecstasy had never before been so ecstatic. Barry who? Fuck him. I'll tell him the guy beat me up . . . who cares?

A half a block from the motel, I saw him standing in the doorway of our room. He saw me. He went off.

*'Fucking whore!'*

The neighbours' heads came out of the windows. Barry had no inhibitions.

*'Bitch pig!'*

He had that crazy-man look on his face this morning. I guess his own kinky plan, whatever it was, hadn't come off.

But this was one time he went too far. He turned and picked something up. Then I saw my luggage flying out of the doorway. I started to boil, partly because he was ruining my euphoria, but mostly because I was paying the rent.

I was a foot from the door when my train case came flying out and caught me in the right eye.

*'Good! You fuckin' drunk!* I hope it *hurts!'*

I stuck my foot in the door just before he slammed it. This time, *I* got the shot of adrenaline. I knocked him backwards, pushed him over the night-stand and before he got up, I jerked the black jack out of my sock and with sheer luck I planted the lead end full force to his left temple. He went out, but I couldn't stop. I just kept banging him on the head with it. Finally I quit and took his pulse. He had one. I gathered my things from the driveway, smiled and nodded politely at the neighbours, locked the door, pulled the shades and poured a Scotch. Now what?

BM. Barry loves Mike. Bowel Movement.

   'Ah, honey . . .'

   'Ah, Shunkums . . .'

We made four years of mad passion. I loved him and he loved me, even though we had a few 'problems' now and then.

   I used to run away a lot. Every six months or so I'd go . . . two days, two weeks and once for a whole month. Yet, nothing could soothe the yearning, the longing, the void, the black hole that ate at me from the inside out – nothing except the inevitable reunion of BM.

   Memories would eat at me like a raging cancer: that four-by-four-inch patch of hair on his back; 'Shunkums – Honey'; the night we huddled against the cold under that viaduct in Wyoming on a hitching tour from San Francisco to New York; making love on the back seat of a Greyhound carrying us to the next Emerald City; the gang bang at the CBC in Key West; the star-filled southern sky, blanketing us as we slept on a hay cart next to the railroad tracks in Georgia; breaking and entering; fraud; theft; embezzlement; doing it in the john of a 747 Pan-Am charter on the way home from Oz . . . The passion burned and the love paralysed.

   And then? M. finally gave in to his bottle. B. found a younger, less-intoxicated blond. We tried for a while to be 'friends'. Then we fucked – that's the best thing we ever did, fuck. We had to stop that too.

   Two months had passed that we had been living in separate hotels. The passion, I thought, had been reduced to a tolerable state.

   I was pouring drinks that night to an élite crew of drunks from behind the bar of Philadelphia's finest. The bar phone flashed.

   B: I wanted to call and tell you bye.

   M: Where are you?

   B: At the Greyhound. They're calling my bus; I gotta go. I love you, Shunkums!

   M: *Honey!*

Click.

# Another Life

## LEV RAPHAEL

*Send me out into another life*
*Lord because this one is growing faint.*

W. S. Merwin, 'Words from a Totem Animal'

Nat had not started coming to Michigan State's small Orthodox congregation two years ago to look for a man. He expected to feel safe there, hidden, because it was not like his parents' huge suburban synagogue outside Detroit – all gleaming polished oak, a theatre, a social hall, a stage. In the Jewish Students' Centre at the end of campus, they prayed in a bare, high-ceilinged narrow room that was like an exercise in perspective, drawing your eyes inexorably to the plainly-curtained Ark in front. His first time, he'd sat in the last row, on the men's side, alone, after putting on his prayershawl and slipping a prayerbook from the crowded chest-high bookcase behind him. At the small slanting-topped lectern, a man was praying aloud wrapped in an enormous black-barred wool prayershawl as large as a flag. Nat's little polyester one, gold-embroidered like a sampler, seemed incongruous, almost ugly – though it was what he'd always used since his *bar mitzvah*. The man came back to shake Nat's hand at the point where waiting for enough men to continue with prayers began, and got Nat's Hebrew name for when he would call him to the lectern. Nat always regretted just being a *Yisroel*, one of the vast majority of Jewish men. *Levis* claimed descent from the Temple functionaries who sang psalms and were entitled now to the second Torah blessing at services. *Cohens* were descended from the priests and had the first Torah blessing in synagogues; Nat liked this remnant of the Temple hierarchy even though he was at

the bottom (his sister Brenda said, 'Well then, that leaves *me*
underground!').

Only six of the thin-seated black plastic and chrome chairs were
filled that first morning, by guys who would have been unex-
ceptional on campus or in town but here looked costumed and
exotic in prayershawls and skullcaps. They all chatted for a while.
Most were graduate students, but for Nat they had the authority
of much older men, because of their deep Jewish knowledge and
the way they prayed.

The few women – wives, a girlfriend – were pale, plain,
undemanding. Nat was glad they were on the other side of the six-
foot-high wooden barrier – the *mehitzah* – separate, even after
services, even talking to the men, still as private and inaccessible
as ducks brooding by the river on campus. They came to consider
him shy, he knew, because he seldom initiated a conversation.

Nat had always watched other men pose, lean, grin and
entertain women, as if from a distance, thinking they looked like
clownishly intense animals in mating desperation, all puffed up
on display. Nat couldn't mimic the flattery and ogling because
women had never stirred a desire even to pretend in him. They
were merely figures in a landscape.

The Orthodox service on Saturday mornings was very long,
almost four hours, and some of the prayers and melodies were
unfamiliar at first, but the direction and sequence was similar to
the services he'd grown up with, and coming every week, he
began to fit inside this new structure for belief. Nat's Hebrew,
always better than Brenda and his parents knew, blossomed until
he felt confident enough to offer to do part of the service. It was
such a small congregation, usually less than fifteen except on
holidays, that praying here was intensely private for him, thank-
fully not a time to see relatives, friends from high school, or be
shown off by his parents as a faithful son. Sometimes he was so
moved, he covered his head with the new, large prayershawl he'd
bought in Southfield, shutting the world and everyone out as the
truly Orthodox did.

The singing, the absence of English, the spiritual concentration

– *kavannah* – seemed beautiful to him, as if they were all, at the most powerful moments, the fabulous gold cherubim on the Ark of the Covenant, over which hovered God's presence. Sometimes he felt *that* holy, *that* moved beyond himself – but who could he tell? The few Jewish acquaintances he had at State weren't interested in hearing about his discoveries. Most people would just class him as a fanatic, like his parents seemed to (Brenda listened, but not with enthusiasm), and even the congregation's regulars stayed away from talking about feelings or anything verging on mysticism. For them, the service was simply the right and only way to pray.

Yet he welcomed their self-absorption. He had really come here, at first, before he was seduced by the service itself, hoping that the Orthodox congregation, the *minyan*, might be a bath of acid in which he could burn away, like verdigris from a bronze, his obsessions about men. He'd heard about druggy friends saved by joining Orthodox communities in Brooklyn, lazy and almost criminal 'trouble' students at his high school straightening out in Hasidic enclaves of Jerusalem, and had hoped for a similar miracle. Nothing else had worked.

Acting had not helped him lose himself, but brought him into a terrifying world of men who blared their availability and were always making reconnaissance raids on guys who didn't. Learning French and starting on Russian had only given him new words, not a new identity. Running did make him fit, supplied a hobby and completely new range of conversation – shoes, tracks, breathing, diet, shin splints, marathons, stars, books and magazines – but he was still only Nat for all those miles. And he only admired other runners more, became a connoisseur of those wonderful high round asses, those long and heavy thighs. When he watched track and field events on TV he waited for close-ups or slow-motion shots to see the heavy weight inside a favourite runner's thin and clinging shorts whip and swing from thigh to thigh.

Even at services, alone with the other men, trying to stay deep in prayer, his thoughts sometimes wandered: to a barefoot guy in cut-offs hosing down his car across the street, who'd glanced at him one morning as Nat entered the building; or two wide-backed, tanned bikers damp with sweat and exhaustion shouting to each other as they cut down the street; or even Italian-looking Clark, who helped run the *minyan*, Clark whose weight-lifting had left him as bulging and tight as a tufted leather sofa. Nat's private gallery. He felt then lonelier than ever, tracing the path of his unquenched thirst for men, to be a man (was that different? the same?) back to childhood. When had he not felt this way? And what would it be like never to look at men but only *see* them: pure registration without excitement, interest, pain? He was always feeling helpless, like turning a corner in town to almost bump into a guy in sweatpants with those seductive grey folds, whose belly seemed harder, flatter over the shifting jock-rounded crotch, or watching someone's tight jutting ass in the locker room at the gym as he bent over to pull up his shorts.

Still, he could lose himself in prayer often enough, long enough. And then his sister Brenda, doing her Ph.D. at State, began to join him at services after he'd learned the cantillation for reading the Torah. With her, he felt more anchored, sure this might be an answer if only he waited. Brenda wasn't pleased with sitting on the women's side at first, but she respected what he'd learned, or at least all the weeks of practising at her apartment with a tape recording, chanting to himself there because it drove neighbours at the dorm crazy. And *he* was pleased that his pretty sister drew attention from the men, as if her presence made him less of a shadow or a blank, less suspiciously alone. With Brenda at services he felt he could be normal – or seem that way – and sometimes it was easier to concentrate. Thoughts of men were not so intense; she was like a powerful signal jamming pirate broadcasts.

'I didn't think I would, but I like the service,' she admitted after a few months. 'I don't even mind the *mehitzah* any more. I don't get distracted looking around, like back home.'

At men, he thought, wondering what she had guessed about him.

Perhaps she knew everything and didn't want to mention it, like the Jews in polls done by national Jewish magazines who overwhelmingly supported civil rights for homosexuals, but didn't want to have to *see* what that meant in their own lives. This unspoken demand for invisibility was more enlightened than Judaism's traditional distaste for homosexuality, but Nat could not find the difference very comforting.

Nat watched Mark's strong shoulders inside the black-striped prayershawl on Mark's first *shabbos* at the Orthodox congregation. Mark read Torah with a slow persuasive rise and fall, beautiful large hands flat on the lectern, rocking softly, and Nat found himself staring at Mark's smooth thick lips when Mark brought the Torah around and he touched his prayerbook to the velvet-sheathed scroll. Mark nodded.

Mark was a Levi, and Nat imagined him in the Temple, strong feet bare, curly hair and beard fragrantly oiled. With those deep set blue eyes and beard growing high on his cheeks, and the muscular frame, he looked distant, romantic, like someone's burly wild grandfather in an old photograph: a man who had disappeared on an adventure in Australia or Brazil. Nat drank and drank Mark's every movement on that brutally hot and dusty June *shabbos* Mark first came to services. When Mark kissed his prayerbook on closing it, or bowed during certain prayers, the gestures were smooth and authentic expressions of a certainty Nat found seductive, and that made Mark unlike anyone else he knew.

In the little crowd after services, they discussed Mark doing part of the service next week. Mark talked briefly about having just taken an administrative job at State, after a similar position at New York University, and Nat told him about being raised Reform. He described their invisible choir and organ, the three gowned rabbis who had seemed like Hollywood extras, watching them high on their stage from a sharply-raked auditorium. It was theatre to him back then, distant and boring.

Mark smiled. 'So how'd you wind up here?'

Nat hesitated.

And Mark invited him back for *shabbos* lunch after they chatted with Brenda, who assured Mark she had other plans.

They walked the mile or so from the Jewish Centre in an almost incandescent heat – even Nat's skullcap seemed too warm and heavy to wear.

Nat did most of the talking, and felt very young again, excited, as if he were on the verge of a birthday present, or a longed-for trip.

The air-conditioning had left Mark's place blissfully cold. 'This is just temporary,' Mark said, explaining the boxes all over his featureless apartment. 'I'm looking for somewhere nice.'

They set the table and Nat tried not to falter when he handed Mark the silver laver at the sink after washing his hands and drying them while saying the blessing. Sitting opposite Mark, Nat watched him say *Hamotzi* – the prayer over bread – long hands on the swelling shiny challah. Mark sliced a piece, salted it and gave Nat half.

'This is beautiful.' Nat fingered the linen cloth, the silver.

'Wedding presents.' And then he shrugged. 'That was a long time ago – it's not important.'

After lunch of a traditional *shabbos* cholent – the meat and beans stew that baked overnight – and singing the prayers, they played Scrabble and read the Detroit newspapers in a silence so comfortable Nat felt as purified and free as after an hour in the campus steamroom.

'Why don't you stay?' Mark said near six o'clock.

'For dinner?'

Mark smiled and slipped off his skullcap, then shook his head.

'Stay with *me*. Aren't you gay?'

Eyes down, Nat said, 'I've never done this.'

'But don't you want to?' Mark came to hold him tightly, stroking his hair, his arms and face, taming the wild beast, fear, and then led him into the bedroom. Mark stripped. His body was statue-hard, blazingly dark and public – as if all the men Nat had ever gawked at padding from the showers to their lockers; or lifting weights, shoulders and face bulging as if to hurl themselves up through the roof; or lounging near the pool in bathing suits no larger than index cards – as if their essence had been focused like a saving beam of light into this room, for him.

He pulled off his clothes and moved to hug Mark, entering that light which seemed now to blaze up inside of him as he rubbed himself against Mark.

'Wait.'

Mark led him close to the mirror on the closet door, slipped behind him. 'Look. *Look.*' With one hand he held Nat's head up so that Nat was forced to see his own wide eyes, and Mark's guiding him. He leaned back into Mark as if cushioned by water in a heated pool, floating, hot, abandoned, as Mark lightly ran fingers along his sides, down to his thighs, and back up, circling, teasing, calling up sensations from his skin like a wizard marshalling a magical army from dust and bones. Nat watched his body leap and respond as if it, too, were urging him to keep his eyes open and unashamed. Mark slipped one dark and hairy hand down from his waist to grasp him; the other stroked his chest. Mark kissed his neck, his ears, his hair.

'Don't look away.'

The words came to Nat as if in a dream in which he was a solitary tourist lost in some vast but familiar monument whose history and meaning he strained to understand in a shower of pamphlets. He struggled, he gave in, staring into Mark's eyes watching *him* watch an incomprehensible act that ended – for now – with a savage rush as he came, and Mark grinned, laughed, right hand wet and white.

Later that night they took a walk to campus, and it was a bit cooler where they sat by the river.

'Sometimes I feel transported, completely,' Mark told him, explaining why he was often intoxicated by *davening* – prayer. 'Once on Rosh Hashonah I saw my shadow on the wall in *shul*, *yarmulkah*, beard, and it didn't look like me. It could've been anyone, any Jew, who knows where, how far back.'

Ducks, white and startling in the dark, idled against the river's current. Nat breathed in the faint sweetness of Mark's skin and hair, wanting to brush a hand in his beard.

'You know,' Mark began, 'there's a legend that Torah is written in letters of black fire on white fire. Sometimes I can almost see it.'

Nat admired how for Mark, being Jewish was home, not a foreign land to be approached with guide books and a map.

He thought about black and white fire the next *shabbos*, and found himself crying when they sang '*Av Harachamin*', Compassionate Father, before the Torah was taken out of the Ark, their voices blended and thoughtful, not loud as usual. As Mark's soulful voice rose above the others Nat felt open and faint, wanting to rise, enter, disappear.

When Mark blessed the wine after services, he was beautiful in his brown slacks and beige shirt, brown and beige Italian silk tie, not at all like the other guys in the *minyan* whose shabbiness was almost boastful.

'Are you OK?' Brenda asked Nat. 'Are you getting a cold or something?' She was their family's smart one *and* the beauty – slim-hipped, grey-eyed, magnetic in a bikini, with curly long almost red hair, face wide and kind and striking, with Dad's strength and Mom's charm – but Nat no longer felt like her tagalong, plain and unimpressive little brother.

'I'm great,' he said.

Nat helped Mark move to a larger apartment further from town. It was splendidly cool, neutral-toned, all gleaming glass and brass, a construction, perfect and complete. And with its balcony view of a man-made lake it was like a brand new eraser wiping Nat's ugly dorm room from a board like a hopelessly misspelt sentence. He hated leaving Mark's place, which felt like his first real home.

At the dorm he had to laugh at the jokes about getting laid, about faggots, had to be careful not to stare at anyone getting out of the shower or even stare into the mirror at the reflection of someone half-dressed, or nude under an open robe, shaving, spitting, scratching, praying for consciousness. Here he felt safe, could shower with Mark, stroke his back, go nude, bite Mark's ass in the kitchen, be completely free, or at least *grow* towards that freedom. Because even when they just went out for dinner, or to a movie, he was not relaxed. He felt stared at, wondering if they looked like more than friends.

Mark insisted that here in a college town it was different than in New York; most people wouldn't assume two men together were *together*. 'Look at all those jocks, and the fraternities.' But Nat disagreed, worried about the ten years between them, wishing that he too were big, broad and dark, bearded, blue-eyed, hairy, so that they could look like brothers or cousins.

Nat's fear led to their first explosion. Mark had bought them expensive seats for an upcoming Chicago Symphony performance on campus – an all-Russian programme of *Ruslan and Ludmilla, Le Sacré du Printemps* and Prokofiev's Fifth Piano Concerto. But Nat just set aside the card with the tickets and didn't smile at his surprise that came with dessert.

'That's a *date*,' he said. 'Everyone will see us.'

Mark was silent after that, rinsing off the dinner dishes in their sink of soapy water, starting the dryer, wiping the counter. He hung up the dishtowel, his movements heavy, admonishing.

Nat sat at the table, waiting out the silence, feeling like he'd entered a room of celebration with news of someone's death – important but guilty.

Leaning back against the sink, thick arms crossed, not even looking at him, Mark almost spat out 'What is *wrong* with you? Why is everything so fucking secret? You won't even tell your *sister* about us!'

'We're not in New York, this is Michigan, and we're Jewish, and it's wrong.'

'Sure! And tell me you voted for Reagan! Is it wrong for *you*, does it make you a monster? Will you stop lighting candles, stop being a Jew?'

'Sometimes at services I feel like I shouldn't *be* there, shouldn't kiss the Torah or do anything.'

'That's what your *parents* would say, your *Rabbi*, not you! You don't believe that, you *can't*. When are you going to stop *hating* yourself?'

Mark went on, and Nat hardly listened, but he felt the passion in Mark's voice and felt near tears, wishing Mark's message of acceptance was not like the anguished cry of someone aboard a ship that was pulling out to sea calling back to the dock, 'Jump in, hurry, *swim!*'

And then he *was* crying, and Mark handed him a napkin, and said, 'Oh *fuck* the concert.'

'No,' Nat said. 'Fuck me.' When Mark had first wanted to fuck him on their first night together a month before, Nat had pulled away as if slapped. It seemed impossible – too brutal and strange – and painful proof of how far he would have travelled from his incoherent fantasies of being with a man. He said no then, and had kept saying it, but now his fear or what it meant, what it would feel like fell from him in a rush, like the fan-shaped leaves of his parent's gingko tree which could drop in one cool fall day. He smiled: 'Fuck *me*.'

With Mark's weight around and inside him, Nat felt like all those characters he'd never understood in *The Rainbow* and *Women in Love* – annihilated by sex, transformed beyond words.

When Mark was finally asleep, Nat imagined his parents bursting in on them, Brenda horrified, old friends nodding, 'Sure, I always knew.' What could he tell them?

It was oddly like the first time he had prostrated himself on Yom Kippur at the Orthodox services during the service of the High Priest, the only time Jews ever did that in prayer. The service described in lavish detail the High Priest's preparation for entering the Holy of Holies and everyone, many *thousands* of people at the Temple Mount throwing themselves to the ground when the Priest pronounced the Name of God in a way lost to history and the multitude crying 'Praised be His glorious sovereignty throughout all time! – *Baruch shem kavod malkuto layolom va'ed.*' With his forehead touching the floor, tired, hungry from fasting, intent, awed by the moment kept intact through two thousand years, Nat had known that his final, unexpected willingness to surrender to something beyond his understanding was a border, a crossing that would always mark him as different from what he had been.

# My Mark

DENNIS COOPER

Mark stands in the windy darkness outside a nightclub. He teeters, bracing one hand on the wall at his side. He slurs a few swear words, pressing the other hand to his head which is covered with sweat. He wipes it off on the front of his T-shirt and leaves his palm there, feeling the rise and fall of his chest, the word Maxell, his heart. One of his knees gives out, but he catches himself on a drain-pipe.

The coke he's snorted and Scotch he's been swigging all night make it seem unimportant. Mark wants to wander back into the club, but he's sure he is going to puke. In a matter of seconds, in fact. The front door swings open. A few strangers shove their way past. He bends suddenly at the waist, throws up, getting some on the wall before he can lunge to the left and heave the rest in some bushes.

He drops to the pavement, rests his elbows on his knees and puts his face in his hands. It's a decent one. Its decency lies in its lack of incentive, the blank kind of face which one finds on the inbred boys of the South, those backwoods he'd hitchhiked from. Looking at it, one couldn't glean his intention, the mood he is in. 'I couldn't say,' Mark's face would mutter if it could speak for itself, like the moon's almost might, if it wasn't so cold and decrepit.

Colour is back in his face. His breath is quieting down. A few pedestrians stop, seeing he's ill. When they're sure that he'll live, they rush off. Mark glances around. No one's looking at him, but the scenery's getting in focus: a run-down hot spot, several patrons, their nondescript clothes. Their faces are low burning lanterns that stoned bodies carry. Such faces show off the ideas inside with an undermined light, at least to his taste.

A man meandering by decides that Mark's hot. Mark notices this. A place to sleep and some money: his second, third thoughts. He gazes back, hoping that sweat hasn't given him up. Said man walks over, crouching in front of him. They stare at each other up close. The man isn't much, has a hard-on, looks gay. 'Can you walk?' Mark doesn't know. It's a good question.

'Try.' Mark puts his hand on the man's back in order to keep his balance. He feels drunk but hardly spectacular, wobbly in other words. The man caresses Mark's ribs, spinal cord. He fans out over the hip bones. They're broad and sculptural, barely padded by flesh. And in the boy's face, the man sees the skull which is propping it. Mark's eyes roll back in his head. He pulls away, falls down and, holding on to a bumper, vomits into the street. The man waits until he has finished, then hoists him back up.

Mark really stinks now. He's sure about that. He's glad this guy's indiscriminate. He hasn't stopped groping Mark all the way to the door. Mark's bones, actually. A duplex. It's dark inside. Mark trips on the rug but catches himself on an end table, brings it crashing with him to the ground. A lamp just misses his head and shatters against a wall. He has to piss but the man has already toppled on him. His T-shirt is over his head. His jeans are folding up, like accordions at his feet. His ass may as well be a new best-seller, the way the man thumbs to its dirty part.

Mark's on his knees and one cheek is against the carpet. The man puts his head by Mark's ear, muttering less than a stream of consciousness, more than a string of clichés. Mark reeks of sweat, vomit, and what he's been drinking. He wants to piss, sleep, and that's about it. *It* is the best that could happen right now. The man settles back on his haunches. Mark's ass hunches up in the air, courtesy of its skeleton, which the man has envisaged inside.

The man grapples forward and locates a skull in Mark's haircut. He picks out the rims of caves for his eyeballs and ears. The lantern jaw fastens below them, studded with teeth. He comes to the long shapely bones of Mark's shoulders, toying with them until two blades resembling manta rays swim the surface. He clutches his way to both elbows. Ribs ride short breaths to the touch. He grasps Mark's hips and their structure floats up to him. He strokes through a reef of wild femurs which keep up the ass. He lowers, hand over hand, down each thigh bone, past knees, negotiating sharp ankles and finishes off with an inventory of feet.

Mark hears the man cum, OK, so that's over. He raises up and glances over his shoulder. The skeleton turns to stare at its lover. Whatever it's thinking, it always looks like it's laughing at the expense of a boy who's in sparkling focus. The man's eyes are spooked when they look at him. The man grabs and kisses the apparatus on its lips. Then he lowers his bony companion to the floor. It just lies there. The sound of a shower goes on in another room.

Mark combs his hair in a mirror. The man comes out dripping, puts on a robe and starts straightening up. Mark asks for money. The man shakes his head. The boy's face blurs as he does. Then it clears, but he still sees the skeleton there. It's a premonition. Its glee is the the truth behind Mark's bored expression. Mark puts his hands in his pockets. A light through the open door sil-houettes him in his last few seconds. He lowers his eyes. 'Bye.'

Mark goes alone to the top of the hill and stretches out on his back, looking into the sky where an endless succession of darkening clouds drift over shadowing him for a second or two at a time. Sure, it feels peaceful, but after a few minutes that shit gets boring. He stands up, brushes the dust off, and heads back down.

At the foot of the hill is his parents' new condo. He puts on the brakes, slowing down to a jog as he reaches its steps and strolls up. Nobody's home. There's a drawer in his mom's bedside table that is as low to the ground as a doll's, with two tiny knobs which Mark's fingers can barely keep hold of when sliding it open. It's longer inside than you'd think, and his dad's .45's hidden there.

His mom has a floor-length mirror. He stands a few feet from it, holding the skinnier end of the cold, blue-black barrel crosswise under his nose as a moustache. His father shoots antelope in the eye, then ties them on to the car trunk. 'Heil Hitler,' Mark says in a soft Southern accent.

Mark's face is supple, secured to his bones in slight ways, and thin-skinned, so he reddens or pales with different expressions. Guys think he's handsome and talk up his fleshtones. But, as an older friend tells him, 'Anyone's cute at your age,' although Mark looked around and saw that was shit. His friend's just attracted to 'youth'.

Mark's dad was once a hapless farm boy in Georgia. Mark was a crazy idea in his head – one more squabbling, lightly flushed blob indistinguishable from the rest of his first grade class. Mark sat in back by the windows because it was furthest from anyone, though he was told they would shatter and snow in his eyes when the bombs hit. He'd be found centuries later, crouched under beams which had beaned him, surrounding his head with stars.

This room is lit poorly, designed to look just like its twin in their old house, where Mark had been born. Bulldozers crushed the original last Wednesday. That hurt, but it fell without anyone trying to save it, while Mark stood around on the sidewalk eyeing the hard hats and fussing with what he was wearing.

He met the eyes of one worker, filled his own with something bordering on longing, and managed a few similar words of encouragement. 'Hi there,' for instance. He and the fellow met up in a bar late that evening. Sometime next morning Mark let his jeans be unbuttoned. It took thirty seconds. He watched his face in the skylight. He'll never forget how impressive he looked as long as he lives.

He lives for moments like this, being totally calm in his own way, seeing himself in a mirror, or the more distant reflection of him in the face of a man who is trying to give him an orgasm he doesn't want in the first place. Mark puts the gun to his head, but would never pull the trigger. He likes the people he sleeps with, but hasn't gone overboard. He's bored when he thinks about anything else but sex.

Mark leaned back on the wall, his black curly hair closely shorn. Last year it was long. He still seemed angelic, a bit more mature, though his eyes hadn't lost their inviting look. *I* felt like I was on something, but had a hard-on; the best of both worlds. Mark's words were all slurred.

He wore a tweed coat which somebody who'd rimmed him had bought. 'Nothing romantic,' he said. I signed my name in his copy of my book. I scribbled his number on half of a sheet of loose paper. I wrote his name in my tiny black booklet where poems start out lines of words dreamed up when coming on people like him. We shook hands. Now it's weeks later.

Mark's on his hands and knees in Marina Del Rey being rimmed by some man who is paying his way around town at the moment. He's stoned on excellent acid. His cock isn't hard, but once was. His ass is pink from a few light slaps, more on the way. He's ten storeys up in a high-rise. A window looks over the ocean.

The man has his face in Mark's ass. It smells like a typical one, but belongs to a boy who's a knock-out, so it's symbolic. It's sort of like planting a flag where no human has been. Well, maybe a few old explorers. It's sort of like putting on make-up in front of a small, fogged mirror. It's an expression of caring.

The seat of Mark's pants is draped over a TV set, undies kicked under the bed in the hope he'll forget about them. It's the end of their day, the beginning of mine. He'd just be spreading his ass with his hands and fitting it over my face about now, if he were smart and didn't need money, would settle for gold in the eyes of a guy who is gaga for him.

The man screws his eyes up. Mark's anus is wrinkled, pink, and simplistically rendered, but nice. All that licking has plastered its hairs to their homeland, smooth as a snow-covered countryside seen from a distance, at sunset. Closer, the ass has pores much like anywhere else, only more refined.

On TV some cowboy is shouting, '*Arriba!*' It sounds like 'I need you' to Mark and he smirks for a second. It sounds like 'amoebas' to the man rimming. He's risking them, so he can find out what makes this boy happy. He leans back and takes a flash picture. By the time it's developed, the sight of this asshole will sicken him.

Mark falls asleep and the man has his face in a wash rag, in which soap smells heavenly after that last place. Mark has crashed out on his stomach, the usual pout on his lips, his ass crack reflecting moonlight. It looks like a blaze in a faraway valley. 'Not far enough,' thinks the man in the bathroom. He dresses and goes for a walk on the small man-made beach near the harbour.

He looks up at the window. It's low lit. I like how it is now. It makes me seem less like a ghoul when I am, dreaming of someone I barely know. Mark sleeps his way through the rest of this story, face down, like someone who just shot himself in the temple. Spray flies on the man who is thinking things out. Has Mark been worth it? What did he want from the boy in the first place?

He wanted the same ass I do, their eyes met, and they danced to a Gloria Gaynor number. Mark saw the cut of the older man's clothes and thought, 'Money'. The man saw the ass in Mark's corduroy pants, connected it up to his Caravaggio face, and thought, 'Bullseye'. He hadn't pictured the odour, which he got used to, then paid for.

One evening Mark shared a joint with me in the men's restroom. I came back smacking my lips like a demon, friends tell me, which is the story that led me to make this concoction, which I'd like to blow up in Mark's perfect face like a poorly planned chemistry project. I wish it was like in the movies where this would backfire and I'd end up wiping my eyes, face black with soot. Wish I could be there.

The man walks out on to the jetty, all the way to its end. From there, his building looks less functional and prettier. The boy in his slumbers, stretched somewhere therein, is as small as a doll that the man couldn't play with. He'd feel too embarrassed. Mark's long white body is warm where it is. The man shivers thinking of it. It's a godsend, granted, that's leading him back to the shore again.

The black ocean rolls on for ever. A boy being tucked in, that's easy to figure. Mark's ass is a moon to the moon. One dripping wet man stands around in its low light, putting it out with a sheet, blanket, coverlet. He goes to the window and looks at the jetty whose top seems too small to have walked on. But he knows an illusion when seeing one.

I see myself in the man's position, though more on a level with Mark in the sense that I'm brighter and less prone to unbridled worship. I'd ask Mark to stop if he yelled at me. I don't have the money to pay for him. But here I am blocking the view of this simple scene, like a director who accidentally walks in front of his own projector, then stands there, oblivious to the snoring around him.

A pretty boy and a wealthy man sleep together. Their body types can't be made out from the heavy bed clothing. The lamp's off, which buries them deeper, then my eyes adjust and I find them. Man on the left, boy on the right. No sign of struggle, except in my voice as I try not to care for them, feelings I've slipped from this body of work like a boy steals a richer man's wallet.

What's left behind is Mark's beauty, safe, in a sense, from the blatant front lighting of my true emotion, though it creeps in. I'm moving stealthily closer, I think, to the heart of the matter, where Mark's body acts as a guide to what he has been feeling. That's his, like great art is the century's it was created in, though still alive in the words of a man who speaks well of him. 'Mark keeps me going.'

Mark was on drugs a friend said, so he must have been really beautiful. He lived by the ocean two hours south of here, with Preston Adams, a rich older man who was trying to start an affair with him. Mark said, 'No way, man,' then came back to earth minutes later, a little bit wealthier, to shake his friend's hand and start undressing.

When Mark was older and thought I was someone important, he used to motorbike over, listen to records with me, go get Mexican food, smoke a joint, stand around with his hands in his pockets, look at my books, say how stupid love was, then ask if I loved him. I guess at the time it was sexy. Now it's just more of what gets to me.

These thoughts are more about me than my friend because when I was with him his looks left me speechless. That kind of beauty is insular, fills all my words anyway. What I construct must divide him from them in slight ways, such as placing the warmth of his skin against clinical language, like flesh of a man who lies down on a sharp bed of nails and is saved from real pain by the evenness of the impression.

Mark held his liquor. I'd get undressed in the bathroom. He'd be in bed with the covers up to his nipples. His hands and his feet would be cold until I warmed their details. He'd lie there fumbling for words in a shy way. We'd talk, and when one particular sentence ended his mouth would stay open. We'd french. I'd slobber down to his cock, making several stops on the way, bend his legs back and fuck him. He'd do something similar to me, and etcetera.

If you need to know what Mark looks like, see the gay porno film *Give Me A Hard Time*. There's a guy in it named 'Sandy', a box boy who's picked up hitchhiking by sailors and raped in a ship's hold, then disappears from the movie. He's skinny, dark haired, very pale, smooth, and about 5' 7''. He's listed in the credits as Steve Getsuoff and, in close-ups, his eyes are too serious.

I have a note which Mark scribbled when he got up in the morning several years ago. It isn't much but it came at a time when his body was near me, so I unfolded it hopefully. It said, 'Dear Dennis, I wish I could stay but I couldn't. I took a peach and borrowed a book. Don't go to see *Love and Death* and I'll see it with you tomorrow. I'll call from the bus stop.' Part of it's faded, then . . . 'your Mark.'

That's just one semi-articulate fragment of what's still important. I found it deep in my file cabinet under 'Mementoes' along with a few other stragglers. It's strange how something tossed off could have been so impressive, like the graffiti that piles up on neighbourhood walls, which I stopped looking at after a few months, but which I've heard has been raised to the level of Art by the experts, simply because it's expressive of one human being.

One morning I took Mark's face in my hands, having unfastened the front of his outfit, once we'd begun kissing. I hoped to see why I'd read so much into it that summer. His skin was cool and expressionless. His eyes looked warm, but were clearly kidding, and, with all that distance between us, he may as well have been gazing into my camera lens like he did several weeks later, standing in his doorway. That photo's propped up in front of me this evening.

A head that has power over me. A globe lightly covered by pale flesh, curly black hair, and small, dark eyes whose intensity's too deeply meant to describe or remember the colour of, seemingly smeared and spiralling.

I fill a head with what I need to believe about it. It's a mirage created by beauty built flush to a quasi-emotion that I'm reading in at the moment of impact: its eyes on mine, mine glancing off for a second, then burrowing in.

Its face is pale and unmemorable. My eyes give off fear or indecision. Its face is lit from below. My fear is lit by my face. It's scary but warming, like some long lost pumpkin set on a darkened sill. It had two poorly made, gentle, and endlessly flickering eyes which would scare me when I was innocent, although I'd carved them myself.

It couches itself in expressions which value a force past its flesh, fit very tightly to delicate bones whose eyes reflect what they intend in illusory ways, with some sort of murky belief held so many levels below that they can't be described for the beauty of what's keeping it.

My eyes are warm in the middle of this. They hold my body out, which I offer free of restraints: these flimsy blue nothings I'm wearing. But its eyes are cold, have been out in the open too long, got carried away. What's left is ice where love lay such long hours when younger, covers the idea of something under their forgotten colour, like the representation of life that a prisoner leaves in his bunk at a jailbreak, seemingly sleeping away.

It eyes the reward of a power greater than loving, that stormy opinion which simply erupts in smudged irises, leaving this holiest look in its path. I want to slap it. It wants to soften my blow with the more heady vision of what lies below: its hairless body, the sense of which can't slip past well-tailored clothes meant to colour a head which has some wits about it.

It rests on its hand, and it stares into space like the head of a dying boy, vaguely aware of somebody he loved or despised in his lifetime, but hollowed out now with a whittler's patience, which leaves these black slits for its eyes and the sign of some thinking around them: a mask that's been saved for all year, then shoved on the skull of a friend, to affect me.

I'm here alone. Mark is in Washington, DC. Craig is in Downey. Julian's in Paris. Robert, David, and Shaun are at work. They were my lovers. Now they sound more like the names you hear paged in an airport and sort of wonder about. All of the fingers on my hands extended mean 'presto change-o,' which, aimed at somebody important, can't make him love you but, used on Mark's shoulders, seemed to relax him a little.

There's an odour inside the body I can't figure out, unlike a crotch's, and worse than the ass's reminder of brunch, snack, or dinner. I've read about it in novels: the madman poised over an innocent victim, his knife at the end of its trudge down the teenager's chest which, like the earth in some scared Californians' opinions, splits open upon the least provocation. The murderer, thinking of rummaging inside the torso, is driven back by a frightening stink which writers leave in obscurity, stumped as to how to describe it, not having smelt it.

Without it Mark's not complete, but it lies slightly out of my grasp like the big ring of keys to the door of the jail cell where somebody somewhere is probably locked up for strangling some kid he couldn't get love from. He'll reach as far as he can through the bars and never get near it. I mean the truth about anyone.

Mark's still a mystery to me. He was, in part, a young man who happened to wind up with well-balanced features, knew what to do with his eyes, and I exaggerated his power, as it was a time in my life when I needed to feel very strongly. Mark filled the bill. Seeing his face on first meeting, I was so speechless that friends had to turn me around and shake my shoulders.

When I was younger and met a boy who I wanted to sleep with, I was too embarrassed to say so. I'd lie there wishing that he was in trouble or dying, so that my feelings about him were justified, then I could say it to him on his death bed – *it* being 'I'll always love you' – and he would die thinking of me. Now I'm too embarrassed to think of the people I care about dead, and those who I love may as well be starring in their lives around me, and I one of tons of admirers breezing by.

Once Mark took me to a magic show. I was called onstage to assist the magician. I was amazed by how phoney his sparkling tubes looked. He pulled something out of my ear. I felt stupid, was famous for weeks in a vague way. We saw a man with a partially paralysed face who did some pretty good card tricks, but all the magic was ruined by having to watch him perform. Later we heard he had died.

I miss Mark. I aimed my feelings right at him. He moved back to Georgia, left no address or phone number, and was 'lying nude in the dark listening to music' the last time I heard from him. I loved him. I should have said so less often. It got so his eyes wouldn't register that kind of input. He'd lie there thinking of something or somebody so far away that he seemed dead, and I'd have to rub his skin like a frostbite victim's until he knew I was home. That's an exaggeration.

This is a time when independence seems important. I keep my guard up. I've got a dim trace of wit where my heart would be turned up full volume and pointed at someone. I have less sex with more people. I should just say things are OK, I guess, like I would if questioned by cops about it. Once they impressed me, but so did the bullies who hit me with math books and left me prone on the ground. My father found me asleep at my train set and carried me up to my bed.

'Wake up,' Mark yelled at me. 'Look around you. Get your fucking life into gear.' My life was great and that wasn't what he was trying to say. He'd walk around in the evening slamming doors rather than say what he meant, which was what I had asked for. I was probably drunk, hoping I'd die or he'd stop me, one or the other. I couldn't speak my mind either, so I emptied a fifth of tequila into it.

I have a photograph of Mark and me against a white wall which could be anywhere in the world. We look incredibly happy, having been drunk on our asses seconds before. We have our arms around each other's shoulders. I'm more ecstatic than Mark, and he's more determined to look great on paper. It was a luminous moment. My line to friends upon showing it is 'We'd have made some great babies together.' Their eyes roll upward.

'In blindness that touches perfection a hearse is like anything else.' Ian Curtis wrote that. He sang with a rock band called Joy Division. Hearing him sing such things in his deep quavering voice, I had the sense that he couldn't get close to his feelings, and his embarrassed attempts were the subject of what he was doing. He killed himself before getting respect for that.

'I knew this would happen. I remember the first day I met him. He said "Hi, my name's Ritchie White. I'm on probation." ' I stole that line from a movie because what the young boy pronouncing it really wanted to say was, 'I liked him.' He felt too stunned to. The fellow named had been shot by police when he pulled out an unloaded pistol. Ritchie was brown haired, brown eyed, smooth skinned and bored, then he rotted away in the ground. His friends set fire to their school to feel better.

I'm trying to get to the truth, just like they were, so that even when looking into the eyes of somebody who doesn't care about me any longer, or never did, I'll be strong. Mark used to make me seem helpless. Back then I wrote in my journal, 'When I'm with him I feel perfectly calm and when I'm not I want to jump off a building so he'll never stop thinking of me.' Now I've added in a steadier hand, 'I couldn't have meant that.'

Certain things mean a great deal to me. Mark did. My father does. Sex does. Being a friend to a great person does. So does the knowledge that I'm alone, although praised to the hilt by some people, even when loved so intently I don't have to think about concepts like love any longer, which I've never been, nor would have realized if I was, which doesn't matter, or has been hopelessly screwed up by me and won't come back.

Once I held high hopes. I'd loved Mark, found that emotion was possible. He was a small human shape climbing into a car at the end of the driveway. I knew that he'd become much less important to me, but there I was writing a letter, so he'd at least understand things a little. He called me up when he got it. We talked for hours, and when there was nothing but awkward silence left, he said, 'Then let this be it, OK? Promise me.' I promise.

# Forced Use

## ALLAN GURGANUS

*A naughty story for David Del Tredici*

Three brown beetles – meeting windshield at 61 mph – smeared green paste three ways: I took this as a sign to finally stop and phone my wife.

I pulled into a rest area on 87 South – a grassy stretch without bathrooms, just six picnic tables, one dempsy dumpster, tall anchor fencing stretched all around and keeping back the woods. I reversed charges and noticed a young man sunning on one table. 'Darling,' I told Alice, 'I survived.' Big arms were interlocked across his forehead. He wore only shorts, no shoes, no shirt. Good legs dangled off the table's end, the kid's toes kept flexing, pointing, bobbling as he thought his thoughts; otherwise he looked asleep. To my wife, I described the convention. I reported who'd inquired about her; I repeated their compliments: Alice's charm, her brightness. She asked how my paper was received; I admitted Wilkinson claimed it was the first *new* thing he'd heard since discussing the subject with Berenson once in Rome.

'*Wilkinson* said that?' My loyal wife reads all the journals in my field and her own. Alice's voice was elated, lovely, 'So, a triumph, right? You must be feeling very smug.'

'I guess,' I said; his hair was brown, (some blue, some copper in it) tangled ringlets full of light. Behind me, the highway sounded sickening: I'd driven since dawn; it was nearly noon now, it was mid-July, pure humidity, pure heat. I told Alice when I would arrive this evening. I asked if she had mailed the tuition cheque to our young son's day school. As I talked I wondered if the table underneath him – flecked with picnic drippings, gouged with lovers' carved initials – if it weren't sticking to the fellow's skin, didn't wood cut into his fine wide back? Driving, I'd been feeling wasted, old. Nothing I did ever called for total energy.

Of all my strengths, I utilized maybe thirty per cent at a time. The career, I thought, it's been too easy. After my success at the convention, after getting every possible rave from the people I respected most, I felt oddly let down. Thirty-one years old, too soon at the top of my profession, secure, in good health – and yet, nothing, nothing whatsoever had ever really *happened* to me. I was in my prime, or rather it was in me, a vat full of goods but wasting, like surplus food – curdling due to some silly hold-up in paper-work – spoiling while the whole world starved.

Standing here, all nerves and worries, I longed to feel drained, to know I'd given something absolutely everything. Oh, to be used up so perfectly – it would feel like getting understood!

The only others in the park – a family – sat eating at a distant table in the shade. Nearer, he was belly-up in the light. I studied him, unable to say exactly why he interested me so. Did he look like a friend of friends? – I hadn't seen his face yet. Did he remind me of myself at twenty-two or -three, making those long cross-country drives (gas twenty-nine cents a gallon) napping in the sun along the way? Just now, as I listened to my wife (her argument with a boss' secretary, our son's latest funny saying), the well-made boy lowered his arms, displayed a squarish jaw, opened his eyes, then stretched. It was a simple and effective and profound animal stretch. Big toes curled under as both legs lifted, hovering – effortless – level with the tabletop. Seeming to wake, he looked to where I stood – me, all awkward and exposed in the glass booth, me, caught gawking at him.

The kid propped one cheek on one fist and stared over here in a bored unembarrassed way. When I didn't turn my head at once, he lazily reached down with his free hand and, index finger crooked, tugged at the groin of his cut-off khaki shorts; he kept his thumb and forefinger nuzzling around up under the fabric,

testing, pinching loose skin there. He gave me this steady
noncommital smirk. His bearing was a smart alec's. His dark face,
oval like some boy saint's. The body was wide, valuable with use
as a seasoned stevedore's – only, his looked newer.

I turned my back on him. He was a kid, some punk. I faced
interstate but – counting cars parked in the lot here – tried
guessing which was his. My wife announced that the food
processor had arrived at last and was working like a whizz.
'Good,' I said. She'd made watercress soup just this morning and,
served cool later, it would be fantastic in weather as brutal as this.
'Great,' I said. I chose an old red Jaguar convertible, its front end
so bitten with rust, the grill hung half dislodged. I invented a
story: he was from a poor working family, second generation,
seven brothers and sisters, his father – a plasterer – drank, kept an
expensive mistress. The boy had saved to buy this used car, he
bagged groceries and cut people's yards; he repaired the car
himself but, when he saw it wouldn't do what he hoped for his
local reputation (on the street, everybody knew him) he lost
interest in it. He just drove it now – to hell with maintenance. He
drove it out to rest stops on the interstate where strangers were.
Dressed in next-to-nothing, he stretched out on tables at the rest
stops, hoping to get noticed by these strangers. He got noticed.
The Jaguar, still sleek, was pocked with lacy excremental rust, gills
and flecks and finger-length brown holes of it. The ruined car
looked expensive and disreputable, both. Like him. Like him.

'What?' my wife asked. Alice knows me.

'Nothing. Just tired from driving and the heat.'

'Stop somewhere. Take a break, take one of your famous ten-
minute naps.'

'I will. I think I will.'

I turned around and watched him stand, uneasy as a child on
his bare feet, both arms out, balancing. In one fist, he held a pack
of cigarettes; from the other, car keys dangled. He meandered
towards the woods that started, one lush surface, just where the
clearing ceased. Since there were no bathrooms here, some
merciful planner had left a few high bushes before the fence and

you could see well-worn foot paths slipping around behind them. The kid stepped into leafy shade then, leaning against fence, turned to face me. Alongside either hip, his fingers jammed through metal mesh. In shadow, he looked even browner. He just stood there, waiting.

Only I could see him. At a far table, the small family ate, glum, overheated. Skinny little twin girls, shirtless in seersucker shorts, tied motel handtowels around their necks as capes. They modelled these for one another. Parents – red-faced, silent – watched their own fast-moving, witty kids. The twins kept stooping, talking to an animal's carrying case – its roof was all polka-dotted, holes pierced for something's breathing. The boy simply looked towards me. I did not know what he wanted. Still, anyone could guess. I'd been around. I knew human nature, that all is possible. Myself, I couldn't do that sort of thing. But anybody could figure why he eyed me in that steady, breathing way.

Alice: 'Laura had the piece in the *Times* on Tuesday, see it? I told her to cut out all the sociology double-talk and she did drop some. I do think it's better than when she showed it to me first. Kevin's school is going to the Planetarium and he's impossible with quasars and black holes and all that mess. His teacher said . . .'

Shouldn't the ordinary matter of your own life interest you? Today it did not. Today, in this humidity, in this young thug's gaze, I and my wife and our gabby little prodigy seemed monotonous and greedy, trivial. I thought, the best part of me will go wholly wasted. It'll die untapped, unknown. The sweetest secret energies will never once get used, never even hinted at or touched.

Alice said, 'You know it really *is* amazing about these gaps in outer space, ones our encyclopaedia claimed nothing could withstand, raw holes that use up everything as temporary heat, vacuums snorting in whatever meteoric junk drifts near. Scientists call such pockets anti-matter.'

'That's how I feel,' I said. 'That's what *I* need.'

Maternally, Alice ignored this grumpiness, sped right along with household news.

He was hidden from the others. Above him, 'Trespassers Will Be Prosecuted Beyond This Point. State Land Ends.' The sign was clamped to fence, along its top, a crown and garland of barbed wire. He tipped back and, fingers in its gaps, rocked fencing some; three birch branches, growing through it, moved. He simply stared. His feet spread wide apart. His head kept tilting slightly left. I could look him over. I thought he wanted me to. I did . . .

He wasn't quite grinning, wasn't quite frowning either but offered me this wry half-secretive expression as if waiting to be recognized. His face – sulky, sour, pretty – was anything but neutral. A dimple cut the right side of his mouth. He squinted at me knowingly then turned and, knuckles locked within steel webbing, did some angled push ups – lumpy back expanding. He flipped around to watch me noticing.

He was somewhat stubbily constructed, built with a smooth round chest. The brown torso was halved then quartered; lower fourths, across a flat belly, were quilted into separate eighths. One dark strip of hair, growing in herringbone pattern, kept pulling sight down towards and into his green shorts. The brass buckle, like the ones they sell in tourist traps, advertised a local beer. To me, it looked cheap. Even as a joke, I'd never wear a thing like that. It made you feel sorry for the kind of jerky kid who'd go out and pay good money for that. But, on him, somehow, it did look sort of good. The longer I stared, the better it looked. By now, already, it appeared almost . . . excellent. Yes, I fussily decided, excellent, on him.

Heat had laid a sombre sheen along every notch and facet of his chest. He glanced down at himself, casually interested in whatever I, right now and from out here in light, could find to size up and admire. He seemed to like the spectacle he made; he looked at me, mugged an expression, gave one funny charming shrug as if to say, Not so bad, huh? – He was right, of course. That's just it.

Both thighs were black with hair; he now reached down to scratch a furry knee that plainly did not itch. Then, grinning, this punk, this small-time champ, crossed his arms and, eyes fluttering shut, let his whole head roll sideways, a smeared and languid kind of smile. It was part dare, part plea, part snarl. I thought, He surely knows what he's doing. He wants me to know he knows. Now I do. OK, but the answer is still negative. No way.

I listened to Alice's final comments, personal important ones. I wished she wouldn't hang up on me. I felt glad she was about to. I heard some yelps and, twisting right, saw one twin flip open the animal's case. A fat white Persian cat fluffed out, hurrying this way, scuddling along weeded fence, keeping low to the ground, bolting and stopping. One child chased it. The creature made towards shrubbery, where the sullen boy stood watching me. Hearing squeals, he straightened.

I leaned towards him. The creature dodged under a low limb, the child scooped up her pet, its plump tail flipping forward. Then the girl stomped away. She jerked cat's face near her own, hollered at its eyes and muzzle, 'Bad, *bad* Snowflake. You always run off. Don't you even like us any more?' Nearing the listless family, she said, 'I think Flake just *hates* vacations. To her, if it's not our yard it's way too weird to handle!' I laughed. Kids are incredible, aren't they. The things they come out with. I missed my talkative son.

Then the boy in the bushes ('The Bushes', I marvelled at the words, last heard when I was sixteen, fifteen), he wagged his head towards the woods. He signalled I should follow. Watching him, my grin died. Kids are something, all right. Watching him, I knew I would not. Do what he wanted. Could not do . . . that, he'd planned – I was someone's husband, someone's actual dad. Even if nothing if life ever *had* occurred or overwhelmed me, even if I did feel under-utilized, I couldn't sacrifice whatever'd piled up by lucky accident, right? Couldn't jeopardize all of that for one motley little roadside risk, for this one interesting wrong, right? Right. Still, I rushed last-minute conversation with my wife, said, Yes the car was fine, the food had been good but not so good as hers, as ours.

I leaned back on stainless-steel shelf. Phonebooks had been linked here till someone ripped them out. Tufts of paper binding,

one white, one yellow, spun from long and sturdy chains. I
doubted I could stand much longer. I blamed July. My voice got
cramped and wavery, my wife accepted all emotions as ones she
had inspired, Alice said, 'You'll be home in under four hours.
Your talk was a great success. There are two telegrams here. Kyle,
between his asteroids and black holes, keeps asking about you.
We'll make ice-cream with our new thing. It's in the booklet.' I
said I loved her. I hung up. I *did* love her, and very much. So much
I felt quite dizzy, so much I needed to walk over and sit down on a
table just conveniently abandoned.

I settled upon upper slats. Deck shoes rested on the bench part.
I settled faced away from highway, phones; I aimed towards trees,
towards him. I wondered how I looked – my old chinos, blue
buttondown – would I pass? Would I do, if so, why? Under the
back of my workpants, planks felt splintery and slick. Wincing in
this light, I noted a ragged crescent along woodgrain – dark oil,
wetness showing where one smooth shoulder had just pressed.
Sun dried a corner of this mark. I touched my index fingertip to
the dampest spot then tested finger against thumb. Moisture felt
like lanolin; I sniffed it. He was watching me. Let him. I was closer
to the cars than he. I could, at any moment, run for it.

Twins dashed in circles, they pretended to fly, their arms poked
out, they admired how capes looked luffing out behind. 'Am
above *build*ings,' one squealed. 'All this air is our air. We're way
way up now, look.' Parents appeared bored. Sunstroked, numb,
unworthy of their girls' imaginations. Watching, I felt something
like stagefright. I'd seen the boy ('my' boy, I almost said, 'my' boy)
slide right; he was now lost behind the wilted shrubbery. Odd, I
already missed him.

Years back, I confessed a college misdeed to Alice – how, with
my sophomore room mate, all-state lacrosse, exams over, him
with a sprained muscle in one leg, needing help with that, both of
us drunk as our excuse and amnesia . . . Alice, ready with
statistics from a famous national survey, blurted out the odds for
this occurring, said it was incredibly widespread, between boys,
the occasional lapse. After all, Alice said, when you think of it: the

world's half male, half female – occasionally, given those odds, one *had* to notice and long for a member of one's own fifty per cent. Statistically, it was bound to happen, right? 'That,' I told her gently, 'makes sense.'

Options. I sat on a picnic table, in sun, mid-summer, off highway, nowhere in particular between two minor towns upstate. I pinched the bridge of my nose; with elbows propped on knees, I pressed both hands across my face. I could feel eye sockets, goggles in the bone. I imagined him behind greenery not fifteen feet away. (I found I *could* picture him, 20/20.) He was backed against heavy-gauge steel wiring, shoulders printed with it, plaid and zigzagged, pink. He was a swarthy boy used to minimum wage, a mechanic's helper. Today, he was all itch, all smirk and certainty. He was back there, he had something back there with him, 'he had something in his pants'. Sick of my highminded life, I savoured the sleazy sound of this – 'something *good* in his pants'.

Decide. To hurry to your car, do right, speed away, lock every door and, for at least six months (till willpower bleached this memory) wonder what smut he'd had in mind for you, you two? Speeding, you could squirt detergent, purge the windshield of four states' insect life and – cleansed – appear a model citizen, pretend you'd only seen some mild rancid mirage brought on by loneliness, professional jitters, too long a drive.

Or: risk it just this once? To just risk getting nabbed by cops or hurt by him? Or catching something you might pass on to Alice? To just haul off and chance everything you've earned, to put that on the line and just stand up and follow him right now and see what might at last unlatch itself and happen finally? Which? You choose. One only.

I could not control my thoughts. I mashed butt-ends of hands against closed eyes, attempting to be rational. But, eye spheres, twitchy and slippery within skin so fine, reminded me of certain famous masculine underparts, matched sets and issued by the millions to make mischief among the world's populace, to make the world's populace. So one hand quickly shifted, pressed across my mouth, the other slammed to forehead in a fever test. Yes, heat. Yeah, leave. But it was a hundred and two degrees out here; logic was nowhere. I perspired; it probably showed. Had I been parked here for half an hour or just under seven minutes? What was the topic of a paper of someone my age and weight delivered yesterday? Applause, that I recalled. I also understood my destination, my marital condition, Mother's maiden name. But as for decency, this swarm of recollected wrongs kept interferring.

– How when I was ten, my older brother invited friends to sleep over, and how I barged into our shared attic bathroom and saw, lit by dim glow from the shower, two of brother's rangy pals (blond kids well-known at school) both studying a prized pornographic postcard (three women busy on one bony sailor in a bad hotel) and how the boy's tennis shorts were jammed around their upper legs, binding upper legs, and how – with the picture delicately suspended (a card trick) between them – they had serious hold on, of, around one another's crucials, long arms grasped to make a sinewy brown X and how – as I lunged in, then fell back against doorjamb – they gaped my way while staying bodily locked into this odd cross-referenced pose. It seems, in memory, a bond like Siamese twins' – some slab of mutual gristle, tubular and linking them – boys hooked like this for ever, sharing one rosy erection, but forked.

Their stricken faces seemed to speak: We can't help it. It grew like this. Awful, yeah, but all we've got. It is growing, still. What are we to *do* with it but what feels best? It is a fact that we can't help or stop. We check on it a lot. Here it is. We can't believe it has to look like this but . . . does. It's a monster. We're its hobby. They stared down at it – a humid brittle thing between them, pronged.

– How, in the Army, after my spinal injury on the obstacle course, a physical therapist kept rubbing my lower back with some heated implement for minute after minute; alone in the room with me, door closed, he ran this burning thing across the tops of my legs, across and all around my butt then up over my neck, burrowing it, hurtful, into scalp and how I didn't stop him,

didn't ask if this were therapy and necessary. When he said I
should turn over, I felt ashamed to. I refused. I pretended not to
hear him, I faked sleep. I was just a kid and scared to death. He
had to slap my ass, first jokingly, then not, then even less so.
Again he told me to get on to my back, 'You think you're the first
that's happened to, man? Know how many GIs I have in here
every workday? You touch guys where I've got to, just to help
them – on most guys it'll happen. It's supposed to, see? You think
you're special or something, think you interest me? Roll over,
soldier. I'm getting pretty sick of this.'

And so I did, turn over, show him. Had to, it was all right there,
right there to see. He was my age, about my build, perspiring too.
He looked down at the whole raw front of me. He diagnosed, like
a vet. It seemed I was this dog brought in to him, some dog just hit
by a car or something; he stared down with such pity, like he
thought maybe he could save me. '*Look* at you,' he said, admiring.
He gazed at me, at it, then on up to my face, comparing.

'I'm an Army therapist,' he said. 'Been trained in this. I know
everything about a guy's body.' Having explained himself, he
reached for it, he, he had it, he proved – I felt at once – he was
expert.

And, in a voice you had to believe, my fellow soldier said, 'The
backbone is one thing, real real easy to throw off. And then, of
course, there's all of this, isn't there, buddy? – There's all of this
down here that needs attention, too. Am I right?'

I didn't answer. He consulted my face again – his eyes solemn.

Gently then, he got me by the hair, he shook my whole head
back and forth, a coerced Yes to his question about need, my need.
His doing this seemed odd to me, but funny. I laughed and so did
he. It was a nice moment. I can't explain. I trusted him more. He
let my hair loose but this head, my head, kept kept kept on
nodding Yes.

'That an answer?' Again I bowed my head. Tears filled either
eye. One spilled over. I shook some.

His was a decent worthy grin. I settled back. I watched him.

And others, sure, some others. And now, in July, within hearing of a major highway at this minor patch of grass, a nameless place, some new kid was waiting for me, hidden, thinking I knew why he hid. He might be back there ready to rob me. If I disappeared here, if he took my wallet and keys, if he murdered me and buried the body deep in a hole in that birch wood past the fence, and if he stole my car and drove it to another state, nobody would know where to look for me. I would be lost for good. I would deserve to be. I followed him. I shoved off from the bench as if pushing off a pool's edge. Air had texture. I moved through it. I walked in a studied casual way. I worried that the family over there might see me step behind these bushes, I worried what the twins would think; I wanted to protect them from all knowledge of me – Since there were no bathrooms here, they would probably remember that. Yes, they'd think my motives were as innocent as that.

I stepped behind the bushes.

Somebody had clipped the fence open. Each sturdy wire was cut then peeled aside in a cylindrical coil the way you might twirl the lid off a can of smoked oysters. This made a neat narrow six-foot passage in the fence, no jagged edges, done with professional care. I was glad that some other outlaw had thought to perform this service, that he owned (or rented) the equipment, that he knew how to use it. The sign hanging over this gap still warned: 'Trespassers Will Be Prosecuted. State Land Ends.' In red spray-paint, somebody'd underlined 'Trespassers' and scrawled a ten-inch exclamation mark; the dot beneath had bled a long red droplet off the edge.

Amazed I could, this terrified, still move – I stepped through fencing. Only thought: My father would kill me. Here was a wide and downhill wood. It felt fifteen degrees cooler, it was muddy. I looked for the boy, couldn't see him. Underbrush was scuffed with paths. Other people, needing cover, also up to no good, knew this place and used it. Fastfood wrappers (red, yellow) were scattered underfoot but the birches' fine white trunks made the space look beautiful and almost planned. Then, to the left, forty feet downhill and in a grove of saplings, I saw motion. Skin was half hidden in blue shade but it was skin, his skin, his shoulder's skin, I knew that. I couldn't get a full breath. Should leave, should run out into sun and phone my wife again. Hearing her would get me past this.

Yesterday, I delivered my paper: 'The Influence of Prairie Architecture on Henry Adams' Appreciation of Mont St Michael', a work praised for its structure, vision, wit. Today I was an idiot blundering into woods, stalking nearer what I wanted (while pretending I'd come back in here to see what a typical rustic upstate glade looks like). I felt very foolish. Not enough to stop, but foolish. What I wanted wanted doing so much, it seemed mostly done already. I would just be finishing up a messy required task. Inhaling got me one quarter of the oxygen adults need.

My shoe crunched broken bottle. I wondered how he'd run so far into forest without cutting his bare feet. I worried for his feet as I'd fretted for the twins. I told myself he needs help, he is far from the road, is in some kind of trouble – I knew exactly what I wanted and yet, offering myself this lie (sad boy in need of first aid) I believed my lie at once.

Hadn't been in woods, real woods, for years. Just off highway yet it looked untamed – dense ferns, this strange lushness. I moved, was getting there, but memories – the worst ones yet – kept going off in spasm warnings. How (do you mind my telling this?) at Wiggins' Lake, when I was nine, how Father caught me with the older son of a Greek that ran the bait shop. We were in high reeds, way away from everything; I never knew how Dad found us – smell, fury? Just, suddenly, he was there, hands on hips – above us on the bank. He acted polite to the other kid. 'You may leave now,' he said, cordial. The big kid was zipping up, there was some whimpering, there was his limping off, his calling back through dense rushes, 'We didn't mean it.'

That left two of us, the right father, the wrong son. Days before, at a science fair, I'd seen the electromagnet demonstrated – a thumbtack was dropped six feet away, it skipped towards attraction and struck that magnet, humming there, immobilized and

whining with such force. I felt like that. Getting trapped quadru-
pled gravity. I considered explaining, couldn't – found I didn't
even understand. 'I wish,' Dad said, 'that I could blame him.
Spiro's boy is older but I know it was you again, wasn't it, son?' I
stood here. 'Why?' he asked. I looked at my tennis shoes – stained
grass colour: I studied reeds bent under my soles, I pitied those
reeds our weight had flattened – the wrestling, our laughing,
unbuttoning; it had seemed almost natural till getting nabbed.

Dad came over, within reach. Someone like him started hitting
me. 'This,' he said, 'And this.' Rocked side to side and yet
detached, I thought I knew why – in cartoons – they show stars
when some funny animal gets clubbed or belted in the head a lot.
It's *like* stars. Points of light, sudden, jagged, coloured, out of
nowhere, decorating what is otherwise the total dark. I heard my
father groaning, the exertion of beating me this thoroughly. I
thought: I am nine, he is thirty-four. It seemed important, a score.
I heard lapping water, distant jukebox music from the bait shop,
his grunts like ones he made while sawing wood. My T-shirt was
not the colour it'd been. Day was ending. Reeds were slick with all
I'd lost. I found myself falling, then in arms being carried down to
water.

He worried aloud (the lake cold around me) that my mother'd
faint or kill me, me coming home this cut up, this big mess. He
grumbled, blaming me for the amount I'd bled. 'I do all this for
you, Willy. Trying to get *at* whatever's in you makes you act like
this – not like your mother's family, not like me. It's just that one
part I'm after, son. Not *you*. I'd like to find that one bad spot and
. . . lance it, like I would a sty, son. Cure you.'

Bathing me, he muttered as the day gave out. Sky was slatted
with all colours bruises turn – the golden-greens, the plums, the
sulphur-yellows. 'We'll say you fell in. Yeah, tell her you fell in.
Say it like you really *did* fall. Say it, now.'

'I felw inw.' My mouth was full of misplaced liquids. Upset,
slapping water to my open face, he unbuttoned sleeves, unfastened the front and pulled his whole shirt off and all around me,
shelter, I was shivering. In late light, his neck and shoulders

looked part pink, part blue – a new colour. He saw me noticing his
chest, admiring what the late light did. I was dazed. I couldn't
judge or move my head. Whatever came into my sight I looked at.
'Haven't *learned*?' he yelled and, backhand, cuffed me. 'I hit at *it*,
not you.' He called down through all the stars he'd sired. 'I hate it
as much as I love you. That much, Will.' He pulled me close
against him so I couldn't see his front side buckling. I felt sorry for
him. I heard sounds come through his ribs; I thought, whatever's
in me that he hopes to get at – it's too far gone already – you can't
lance that far in and have the person live.

He lugged me to the car. The sky was over us, I knew that. My
features aimed towards its features. My own face was numb with
stars, inlaid, a jaw alive with green implanted ones. For nose I had
a bright-red hole, five pointed. My eyes were swollen into shiny
planets I could not see through.

'Practise. Say it.'

I hollered what we'd planned, what Dad and I had planned. I
called that up towards stars – cousins of my own. I hollered
straight up, blind. ' "Flew in"?' I hollered, blinded.

– Now, adult. Deep in the woods, I heard water running, a
brook, a ditch. Birds sang – a male called, a female answered. – I'd
only done this kind of thing maybe four or ten times since meeting
Alice. I love my wife. I remember Dad's effective lessons. This has
helped me avoid nightspots where men dance close with men, it
has helped me ignore the dark places around my hometown –
under the memorial bridge, out on certain dirt roads near the ice
plant – where men go to meet boys and other men – I've been
good, I haven't even missed it all that much.

But, sometimes, when you blunder on to something by mistake,
(you know how it is?) when Alice is two full states away, Dad
good and dead, and you find you're in an unknown place with an
even quieter more private woods to wander into (like a bonus),
and when you're coaxed back here by some kid who is no more
important than how he looks to you and how the way he looks
makes you feel while looking at him hard because he wants you
to, (can you even half imagine how it is?) and when he's some

sweet idiot kid you'll never have to see again or even speak to much . . . sometimes, in July heat this bad, no amount of fear or will or planning can quite help prevent it. And you will probably go ahead because doing it's involuntary as a heartbeat's next lurch is, helpless as the eyesight that made you notice him first, that forced you back in here, that drew you into shadow where he's waiting, where – it appears – he's fooling with himself. This isn't some deed you choose to do or not to do, this is not some minor infection you can pierce and empty out and heal, it is – scalding, simple: your eyesight, air supply, blood type, your history and aims – you, it's You.

I was shivering, had to cross my arms to hide the worst of it, to keep from jogging towards full light, back past the nice pet-owning family, back into the locked car my wife's folks had given us, back to that and out of here to safety – lack of choice. Civilization.

The kid's whole back was a show, varnish-brown, slick. I stood maybe twenty feet behind him when he scowled over one shoulder at me. He fixed me with a mean welcoming glower. Up this close, the boy looked coarser than I'd believed, he looked a little older. He looked poorer. He looked better.

I studied the calves' boxy shapes, how his legs flexed far apart. Some mud smeared across the top of one pale foot, gummed along his bristled ankle. His back was a knot-tying manual; I studied every plane and segment, how his shoulder, working in steady yanking on the front of him, widened, that arm buckling with force, dents and notches in it flattening then deepening as he – squinting at my face, my legs – pulled at something hidden, something he wanted to show me and I wanted to see.

'What do you want,' I said, and loud, to the kid's back. It sounded stupid.

He just swung his head, bull neck spreading, showing I should walk around in front of him, to look at him. I began to circle. I kept my distance, skirting the grove so far I had to steal back into it. Passing some low pines, I could see the whole front of him now. That arm was straight. I saw its big blunt fist. Across the hands' back, a cusp of black hair grew; I watched fist working on the stubby solid fact he held. He kept clamping fingers across the whole top of it. He wouldn't let me see.

I felt half-dead with this much numbing guilt, with this much excitement, same thing, same thing. On the highway, semis skimmed and blustered. Through leaves behind the kid, rectangles of silver glided North.

Step nearer. I reached into the pocket of my trousers – unable not to – I took hold of myself; my whole skull rolled back along its axis, a sigh rushed out like steam escaping. At last, I thought. Why denied so long? – If you're like me – when it starts again, when you feel how powerful, how pure, how sharp it is, (of everything, the best) you wonder: How can I have lived a day of life without this in it? From one time to the next, how can I forget how good it is?

Only then did he move his hand aside, he let me see it poking out the khaki shorts' stretched opening. It looked bouyant, worked up with a colour like dark oak. The domed tip of it was sheeny wet, split in half, all slick. He laughed at how I gawked (I guess my mouth was open). Then, amused, superior, he reached down and with an almost comic doctorly gesture – using thumb and forefinger, pulled brown skin back. The ending gap was ragged; as covering eased back, it opened like an eye. He showed me the wet thing's true shade – an almost bloody coral orange. Blunt and wide and glossy, it was the colour of a brick.

In a harsh voice, low, with what sounded like an accent, 'Come here.' Now he'd spoken, he seemed more real, more dangerous. OK, I would leave. Definitely. Under my sole, backing away, two twigs popped. Then I heard four car doors slam – first three and then a last – the family. Their car snapped across gravel, raised blue dust. When it lowered, everything went still. We were alone here. We were two young men in the woods for reasons of mischief. We were wrong to be here. Not exactly depraved, not criminal really, just mistaken. This we wanted was illegal. We were strangers but eager for the same thing. All we knew about each other was how the other looked. It seemed enough.

Who would be hurt? Who, but maybe me? I still felt afraid of him. He was like a monster in a monster movie – the one you dread seeing again, the one you paid to see – the one that eats people, the one they name the film for.

What the brown boy held out for me, there was too much of it. It belonged grafted on to someone else, some guy larger, some pro athlete, giant. His parts were like some beautiful deformity, too colourful and lurid, too ethnic – somehow too lower class, too possibly unclean, too unlike me, too swollen up with sudden black blood, too available, too . . . too nasty.

'You heard me – Said, come here.' I felt ill. Under my feet, brittle stems and paper litter crackled as I eased back two steps then paused then moved three full steps nearer. I could see his whole chest bucking now with steady breaths, expecting something. Hands hung by his sides. He glanced down at it, amused and tolerant – as at some stunt or accomplishment. On ground near his feet, the pack of Camels, a throwaway lighter, a few silver keys on a heavy brass ring.

'Look,' I said, 'don't hate me, but I'm just not sure. I saw you come back in here. I thought you were . . . in trouble or something. I didn't really know.' I hated how I sounded. Why is it so easy for some people and, for me, such perfect torture? Every victory, a relapse.

What made me ask, 'Tell me something . . . about yourself.' He cocked his head, said, 'What's to tell.' He laughed, amused by my attempt at getting personal. 'Nothing *to* tell. I got a job. Got a wife. I hate the job. Plus, lost a lot of interest in the wife – Come here. You gone this far, means you got to. You're not about to leave now, no way.' Part statement, part threat. Mostly, I thought, threat.

A sapling stood to my right; somebody'd hung a prophylactic from one branchtip; it drooped full of heavy liquid, rain and more rain. I moved past that, I moved towards him. It seemed important to, the one polite choice left me. The rasp of my own breathing alarmed me but his silence spooked me more. I thought, if I don't do something now, he'll hurt me probably. He's been too long between times. He's a garage employee; it's his one afternoon off, this is his only pleasure. He never had my advantages. I inspected the belt buckle; this near, it looked superb. I felt sorrier for him. His eyes were flirting, earnest, poisonous.

He nodded towards what waited, angled out of parted shorts. 'You didn't come way back in here just to look at it, jerk – What, have I got to spell stuff out for you, or what? First, get your own one out, let me see it.' Sleepwalking, taking orders, I did that, what he'd said.

He said he wanted I should come over there, get down on to my knees, said he had something to show me, close up, said he had plans for it and me, asked if I had a mouth, right? And if it led to a throat, right?

He smiled in a bitter tender insinuating way. The grin disgusted me. I thought, this is really a mistake. He's a crazy one. This is dangerous. I'm definitely leaving now; he read my face.

He cut between me and the road, my car. Advancing, barefoot over mud, he made no sound at all.

I felt trapped.

He stopped six feet before me.

'Look,' I tried again. 'I never do this. I'm married. Let's just say it was a lapse OK? Let's say I'm just mixed up, OK? – All right.'

He shook his head Yes, laughed, sounded decent, from a big family, forgiving. I'd risked a smile when he was on me, right hand flipped way back up near his jaw then it sped, that hand was speeding down, came flipping out and blurring past a face, my face. It weighed exactly eight pounds, the hand. It left a sound, a knock, in air, a noise upright, it was just the size of a piece of toast. It connected hard before the thought gathered, This punk is slapping you, has just cuffed you a good one, has knocked you over, down. Fool, run. My right knee hit dirt first.

A strong yellow sound whined into my right ear, that side of my face said, 'But . . .' (He couldn't even get into a junior college. Why's he allowed to do this to me? Doesn't he know who I *am*? I will have to pull rank on him now. He will cower before such credentials. He'll be sorry, he'll . . .)

My hair was being grabbed. Curly hairs that grow on your skull's backside. It burned how he was yanking those. I heard a tearing sound as his stern clutch tore some loose. This was maybe happening to someone else. He rattled my whole head so hard, top teeth hit bottoms, cut tongue; hurt. I felt a bloody nose begin, that odd ringing like a smell. 'Wait,' I called, expecting a time out. Then the metal taste as it inched and curled into my open mouth.

'OK,' I spoke towards his feet, my right eye smarting, swelling some. I knelt here – truck and birds, those sounds. At least I'm conscious. I looked up through a quarter less of everything as the blackened eye widened fast. I could see a grownman's shorts and, jammed out into air, underside foremost, the lower half of it, his. It was even stiffer now, with four fat dorsal ridges and, from down here beneath, looked very tight and weighty (a trout) made of artery and knot. It bobbed, expectant. Turned straight up, its girth was worried with forked veins wide as fingers, blue-green, some blackish. Course brown hair spilled, coiling, out the shorts' split and some of it – kind of mossy quills – grew in a stripe half up the front of it. I felt my nose's blood spill off the jaw, each droplet warming my pants' front then chilling there. Stooped, I thought, It's deep woods, who would hear my screaming; if they found us, what to *say*?

No, I must accept this, have to, he will kill me, my whole life'll be used up in this one bad mistake, my fault. Just have to find a way to live by giving him enough of what he wants so he won't hurt me even more.

He lifted me by hair. 'Please, no.' I grabbed nearest supports, legs, blunt backs of legs. I clutched the mass of either vertical, their bristles stiff but skin beneath as smooth as soapstone. Being down here, tucked underneath, his legs formed the steepled shelter that I knelt in – doghouse/temple – home.

'OK,' I said. 'I know now what I want.' I could only see one thing, his, a mess, a beauty.

My face got smeared against shorts, rough texture. Belt buckle caught between one eye, a hip, and cut into my cheek; it didn't really ache but made a sort of tremor, tickle. He still had me by scalp. He yanked me away, seeing I'd bloodied his pants. Then he pushed my upper body back so I could view all of it, thumping in place, over-ready as he yanked me, lowered, on to it, pulled my whole head overtop.

I could not see. Blind, the opening my mouth made got shoved into then past and on until my throat was open wider than a human throat can be. In my nostrils, blood rattled (a sound like frying) as I tried to breath around the total size. All I wanted was to breathe, to live through this and it.

Legs duckwalked farther apart, all his toes went curling into soft mud out beyond my own soiled knees. Straddling me, he kept shoving, stuffing, glutting my whole gullet, his full weight pitched and funnelled through hip bones as he muttered names of women, as he tore hard at my hair, as he clamped hands over my ringing ears, as he lightly slapped me till he started to hit harder. He was forcing me, kept cuffing me whenever I gagged too much in some way he didn't like. He was making me a core and hollow. I became the gap where he was throwing everything he had. I held on, was getting used – but also getting used to being used like this, I (*summa cum laude*, Bones at Yale, PhD, the thirty published articles, three books) became whatever he would choose to make of me. Released from IQ, duties, for once I knew my earthly function, perfectly: relieving him. One use. – Then I felt the boy give a low jolt, felt his pelvis lock, felt what fingers I'd worked up by accident into his back opening, the quick and jelly tucked inside, get clamped down on, bitten in spasms as he bucked, as he said, loud, 'Can't, can't, man, got . . . ah,' as he was going off whole pints, all triggered out of it and him and piped into and down me, some even rushing out edges of my mouth's gorged corners, slopping down (in shapes and pieces) flat on to my legs. It had weight, the stuff, like fibre in it, weight, a value. Then, done, he threw my head away. I went keeling back with it, half strangled, my clothes striped with his white, my red. I now shot across his legs' black hair. Everything I had spouted out of me and

I felt so good it hurt. My whole history evacuating, liquid, leaving me a fresh start where it's been packed, accumulating, surplus soured by its own long wait for light.

I was hollow, blind, his opening.

He dodged away from me, scraping wet stuff off his belly and flinging it – disgusted – on to clattering leaves, was running, deftly bending to snag up cigarettes and keys, and was gone.

I heard an engine start. It gunned. I managed to half-stand just long enough to see a rusted hulk wheel past and veer out, screeching, on to interstate. Then the stillness of just me here. I fell back, fell down again, was out at once, asleep. I slept right here. Needed blackness lasted an uncertain time. Reprieve from everything.

I woke; had Alice phoned the state police? Earth pressed – cooling – against half my face, blood there solid. I'd slept curled in on myself as children do. Spillage across clothes (stuff I'd bled, what he'd shot, all that aimed up out of me towards him) this holy slop had merged and stiffened. So now, as I tried sitting, melded liquid separated, made this awful tearing sound as if my viscera were ripping open like a pod. Despite the noise, I found it hadn't hurt a bit. I found I could have lived through the whole thing again, again. There was more of me than I'd guessed – no precious limited commodity but ore as rich as uses it was put to. I propped myself half up on arms. Where and what time, who expected me, in what house?

Evening now, and blue all over, deep in a wood. I heard something from a clearing twenty feet away. In half light, I saw one boy standing, his back to me, smeared painters' pants bunched around white ankles, his shoulders flecked with a day's work, dark-green dripped enamel. He heaved into another kid's backparts – a kid who looked too young for this, who kept whimpering, who bent face-first into a forked birch, was propped there and enduring. A striped tie curled back over his left shoulder, shirt-tail was peeled neatly from the bottom as he leaned into the sapling whose leaves shivered around him with each solid thrust, as he kept crying in a small voice, 'Shouldn't, shouldn't have, shouldn't do such, shouldn't be, we shouldn't, shouldn't, shouldn't.'

Listening to worse moans, sharper sobs, to muttered pleas, much offered thanks, then breaths breathed deeply, I heard one boy laugh at a joke, heard the other urinate, then both got wading back through ferns and, finally, the sound of some car or truck crunching into the smooth realm of headlights, traffic, legality again.

Flat on my back, staring up through tree limbs at evening sky, I thought, Stars. Only reason we can see them is: they are so busy using everything they own. Fires that end them are the only things that make them visible – a show and message – to us down here.

I wanted that. For me, my back pressed in mud (a luxury!) swollen eyes aimed up, both arms flung out as if pinned to earth for good, the face a nest of numbness and itch, I longed to stay in woods, sated, ripped, used so thoroughly I'd feel no interest in seeing sunlight ever again. I would sleep and live here, he would visit me. He would come back every evening with others. He would do more to me, they would do everything to me, in turn, in groups. I would be kept right here for ever, suspended in this creature equilibrium, ready for pleasure, anyone's, my own. I'd never need an address again. I'd be past reputation, free from any single use but this. Nobody would miss me long. Nobody would know where to look for who I'd been. They would soon give up. I'd have disappeared through perfect use.

I flattened out, a secret. Ferns helped hide me. I listened, hoping others would scuff back into this grove towards me.

Cars still moved along four lanes north, four south. I waited. I would wait. A mild breeze moved each leaf in hearing and – showing through a gap in foliage overhead, high, way high above my stunned muddy face – three white stars were out already, burning, burning – burning up.

# Notes on Authors

PAUL BAILEY was a literary fellow at the universities of Newcastle and Durham and a recipient of the E. M. Forster Award. His books have received great critical acclaim. *At the Jerusalem* won the Somerset Maugham Award and an Arts Council Award for the best first novel published between 1963 and 1967. His other books include *Trespasses* (1969), from which the selection in this anthology is excerpted, *A Distant Likeness* (1973), *Peter Smart's Confessions*, *Old Soldiers* (1980), and *Gabriel's Lament*, (1986), shortlisted for the 1986 Booker Prize.

JAMES BALDWIN, born in New York in 1924, was for a short time an evangelical preacher before leaving home at seventeen; he lived for many years as an expatriate in France, where he died in 1987. One of the major American writers of the twentieth century, he is celebrated equally for his passionate non-fiction, including *Notes of a Native Son* (1955) and *The Fire Next Time* (1963), as for his novels. *Go Tell It on the Mountain* (1953) was followed by *Giovanni's Room* (1956), which is unusual among his works in that it is set in France and that none of its principal characters is black; it was one of the few American novels of the period to deal realistically and sympathetically with questions of homosexuality. His later novels are *Another Country* (1962), *Tell Me How Long the Train's Been Gone* (1968), *If Beale Street Could Talk* (1974), and *Just Above My Head* (1979). Baldwin was also the author of a number of plays and the short-story collection *Going to Meet the Man* (1965).

NEIL BARTLETT was born in Chichester in 1958 and now lives in London. He is a theatre director, a translator, video-maker and writer. He is the author and director of the much-praised *A Vision of Love Revealed in Sleep*; his latest play is *Sarrasine*, inspired by a short story by Balzac. *Who Was That Man?* (1988), his book on Oscar Wilde, was Capital Gay Book of the Year. Most recently he has published his first novel, *Ready to Catch Him Should He Fall* (1990), from which 'Three Wedding Ceremonies' is adapted.

PAUL BOWLES, born in New York in 1910, has been an expatriate most of his life, living at various times in Europe, Mexico, Ceylon (Sri Lanka) and in Morocco, where he still resides. By turns poet, composer and translator, he is best known as a writer of stark, psychologically uncompromising fiction, including the novels *The Sheltering Sky* (1949), *Let it Come Down* (1952), *The Spider's House* (1955), and *Up Above the World* (1966). His *Collected Stories* was published in 1979. He has written an autobiography, *Without Stopping* (1972); an 'unauthorized' biography, *An Invisible Spectator* by Christopher Sawyer-Laucanno (1989), has been condemned by its subject.

WILLIAM S. BURROUGHS, born in St Louis in 1914, is associated with the Beat movement, but his often experimental or surreal works reveal broader influences and have been both widely popular and critically acclaimed, although his early novels *Junkie* (1953) and *The Naked Lunch* (1959) were condemned as degenerate and pornographic on first publication, and *Queer* was not published until many years after its composition. His primary themes, including drug addiction, secret conspiracies and homosexuality, have been treated in the novels *The Soft Machine* (1961), *Nova Express* (1964), *The Wild Boys* (1971), *Port of Saints* (1980), and *Cities of the Red Night* (1981), among others. An expatriate for many years, Burroughs now lives in Kansas, and has become widely known for his readings and performance work,.

SIMON BURT was born in Wiltshire in 1947 and educated at Downside and Trinity College, Dublin. He worked for many years as a teacher in south London. He has published a volume of short stories, *Floral Street* (1986) and a novel, *The Summer of the White Peacock* (1989). He is currently working on his second novel.

ALFRED CHESTER was born in Brooklyn in 1928. In 1955 he published in Paris the novel *Here be Dragons* and a pornographic novel *Chariot of Flesh* under the pseudonym, Malcolm Nesbit. In 1956 his novel *Jamie is My Heart's Desire* was published in England. In 1967 he wrote *The Exquisite Corpse* in Morocco. After a nervous breakdown precipitated by his abuse of alcohol and drugs, Alfred Chester died in Jerusalem in 1971 at the age of forty-two. A new volume of his collected fiction was brought out in the United States in 1990.

DENNIS COOPER is the author of two novels, *Safe* and *Closer*, three volumes of poems and prose pieces, *The Tenderness of Wolves* (1981), *The Missing Men, He Cried* (1984), and two collections of poetry, *Tiger Beat* and *Idols*. He was born in Pasadena, California, and has also lived in Amsterdam and New York City. He recently completed his third novel, *Frisk*.

JAMES M. ESTEP is a native of West Virginia. He has lived all over the continental United States and has been active for years as a gay journalist. Between 1986 and 1989 he lived in Paris, where he was a weekly columnist for *Gai Pied* and was a correspondent in France for the German gay magazine *Männer*. He now lives in New York City and is working on his third attempt at a novel.

RONALD FIRBANK, born in 1886, was the heir of a substantial railroad fortune which allowed him to travel extensively in Europe and north Africa, and to pay for the publication of most of his works. His eccentric, oblique, lapidary novels, including *Caprice* (1917), *The Flower Beneath the Foot* (1923), *Sorrow in Sunlight* (titled in the US *Prancing Nigger*, 1924), and *Concerning the Eccentricities of Cardinal Pirelli* (1926), while neither critically nor popularly successful during his lifetime, have proved to be of enduring worth, and his technical innovations have influenced, among other major writers, Virginia Woolf, Evelyn Waugh, and Ivy Compton-Burnett. Firbank died of consumption in 1926 in Rome where, although a Catholic, he was buried in the famous Protestant Cemetery. A biography by Miriam J. Benkovitz was published in 1969, and Brigid Brophy has written a critical biography, *Prancing Novelist* (1973).

E. M. FORSTER, born in England in 1879, was educated at King's College Cambridge, and travelled extensively in Europe, the Middle East, and Asia. In 1927 he delivered the Clark Lectures at Cambridge, later collected and published under the title *Aspects of the Novel*, a critical and commercial success; thereafter he was a fellow of King's College until his death in 1970. His first and most autobiographical novel (also his personal favourite), *The Longest Journey*, appeared in 1907, followed by *A Room With a View* (1908) and *Howard's End* (1910). In 1913 he composed the first draft of *Maurice*, a lyrical novel on themes of homosexuality and personal responsibility; although he circulated it privately among friends, it was not published until after his death, in 1971. His most widely known and successful novel, *A Passage to India* (1924), was also his last. A posthumous collection of short stories, *The Life to Come* (1972), includes a number of pieces written after *A Passage to India* which he did not dare publish because of their treatment of homosexuality. A two-volume biography by P. N. Furbank was published in 1977–8.

PATRICK GALE was born on the Isle of Wight in 1962. He now lives in north Cornwall with the designer Patrick Pender. His novels include *The Aerodynamics of Pork* (1987), *Ease* (1986), *Kansas in August*, *Facing the Tank*, *Little Bits of Baby* and *The Cat Sanctuary*. He is currently working on a short novel, *Caesar's Wife* and on the screenplay of *Kansas in August*.

ROBERT GLÜCK was born in 1947, and raised in the suburbs of Cleveland and Los Angeles. He has lived in San Francisco for twenty years. He is the author of a novel, *Jack the Modernist* (1985), a book of stories, *Elements of a Coffee Service* (1983), a number of books of poetry, including *Reader* and *La Fontaine* (1981), a rewriting of the *Fables* in collaboration with Bruce Boone. Glück's poetry, fiction, and critical essays have appeared in *City Lights Review*, *Semiotext(e)*, *New Directions Anthology*, *Advocate Men*, and the anthologies *Men on Men*, *Writing/Talks*, and *High Risk*. He is the Director of the Poetry Center at San Francisco State University.

ALLAN GURGANUS is the author of *Oldest Living Confederate Widow Tells All*. The novel won the Sue Kaufman Prize of the American Academy and Institute of Arts and Letters as the best first work of fiction to appear in 1989. Gurganus's new work is a collection of novellas and short stories called *White People*. A native of North Carolina, he was active during 1990 in the political campaign to unseat Senator Jesse Helms. He lives in Manhattan and Chapel Hill. His novel in progress is entitled *The Erotic History of a Southern Baptist Church*.

WILLAM HAYWOOD HENDERSON was born in 1958 and raised in Denver, Colorado. He is a graduate of the University of California at Berkeley and Brown University, and was awarded a 1989–1991 Wallace Stegner Fellowship in Creative Writing at Stanford University. His stories have appeared in the *Crescent Review* and the anthology *Men on Men 3*. The selection in this anthology is excerpted from his first novel, *Native*.

ANDREW HOLLERAN is the author of two novels, *Dancer from the Dance* (1976) and *Nights in Aruba* (1984), and a collection of essays, *Ground Zero*. His articles have been published in *New York* magazine, *Christopher Street* and other notable publications. He is currently at work on another novel.

ALAN HOLLINGHURST was born in 1954, and was educated at Magdalen College, Oxford. He has been on the staff of *The Times Literary Supplement* since 1982, and was Deputy Editor 1985–90. His first novel, *The Swimming-Pool Library*, was published in 1988. His verse translation of Racine's *Bajazet*, performed at the Almeida Theatre in 1990, will be published in September 1991.

TIMOTHY IRELAND was born in south-east England in 1959. Since graduating with a degree in English and Drama, he has struggled to combine writing with various full-time jobs. *Who Lies Inside*, his third novel, was a winner of The Other Award in 1984. Reviewing his last work, *The Novice* (1988), *Time Out* described him as 'a talent to be reckoned with'. In the nineties Timothy hopes to secure a home and a word-processor, write a screenplay, travel and have a novel earn rave reviews in the *Sunday*

*Times.* He most admires the work of the late Elizabeth Bowen. He is single. His next novel is entitled *Again.*

CHRISTOPHER ISHERWOOD, born in England in 1904, became friends with W. H. Auden at preparatory school; later, the two would collaborate on three plays and a travel book about China, *Journey to a War* (1939). Isherwood's residence in Berlin between 1929 and 1933 inspired his novels *Mr Norris Changes Trains* (1935) and *Goodbye to Berlin* (1939), published together in the US, as *The Berlin Stories* and the basis of the Broadway play *I Am a Camera* and the musical *Cabaret.* Most of his novels, including *Lions and Shadows* (1938) and *Down There on a Visit* (1962), as well as *The Berlin Stories*, are notable for a frank autobiographical basis in which the author himself is the narrator, and for their pioneering treatment of his characters' homosexuality. The short novel *A Single Man* (1964) is a sensitive and affecting portrait of bereavement. After moving to the United States at the opening of the Second World War, he settled near Hollywood and became an American citizen. His last major works were a portrait of his parents, *Kathleen and Frank* (1972), *Christopher and His Kind* (1976), which re-interprets much of the material in his autobiographical novels, and *My Guru and His Disciple* (1980), about his conversion to Vedanta. Isherwood died in 1986.

HENRY JAMES, one of the great masters of the novel in English, was born in New York in 1843, member of a family of distinguished American thinkers and writers, but settled in England in 1875, where he spent the rest of his long life, first in London, then at Lamb House in Rye, where he died in 1916. As well as his great novels, including *Daisy Miller* (1879), *Portrait of a Lady* (1881), *The Bostonians* (1886), *The Wings of the Dove* (1902) and *The Golden Bowl* (1904), in which one of his major concerns was the contrast between the American personality and the European, he also wrote many short stories, travel sketches, and essays of genius, and a number of plays, few of them staged, none successful. His most popular work may be the long ghost story *The Turn of the Screw* (1898). A four-volume biography by Leon Edel (1953–72) has recently been updated and abridged in one volume (1985).

DAVID LEAVITT was born in Pittsburgh, Pennsylvania in 1961, grew up in Northern California and graduated in 1983 from Yale University. His first collection of stories, *Family Dancing*, was published in 1984, and was a finalist for both the National Book Critics' Circle Award and the PEN/ Faulkner Prize. It was followed by two novels, *The Lost Language of Cranes* (1986) and *Equal Affections*, and a second collection, *A Place I've Never Been* (1990). He has been the recipient of grants from the National Endowment for the Arts and the Guggenheim Foundation, and was foreign writer in residence last year at the Institute of Catalan Letters in Barcelona, Spain.

He currently divides his time between Barcelona and East Hampton, New York.

DAVID MALOUF is an Australian, born in Brisbane in 1934 and now living in Sydney. He is the author of several works of fiction, including *Johnno*, *An Imaginary Life*, *Harland's Half Acre* and *Antipodes* (short stories). His most recent novel is *The Great World*.

ADAM MARS-JONES was born in London in 1954. He reviews films for the *Independent* newspaper. His publications include *Lantern Lecture* (Faber 1981, reissued 1990), *The Darker Proof* (with Edmund White, 1987) and *Venus Envy* (Chatto Counterblasts, 1990).

ARMISTEAD MAUPIN is the author of the bestselling Tales of the City novels: *Tales of the City*, *More Tales of the City*, *Further Tales of the City*, *Babycakes*, *Significant Others* and *Sure of You*. 'Suddenly Home' is one of four short stories adapted by their authors for the American musical 'Heart's Desire'. Maupin lives in San Francisco and New Zealand.

DAVID PLANTE was born in a Franco-American parish in New England in 1940. His novels include *The Family*, *The Woods*, *The Country* and *The Native*, which are set in the parish of his childhood. His novel *The Catholic* takes as its subject a homosexual's yearning for a resolution of body and soul. He has lived half his life in Europe.

JAMES PURDY was born in Ohio in 1923 and now lives in Brooklyn. His first novel, *63: Dream Palace*, and story collection, *Don't Call Me By My Right Name and Other Stories*, both published at his own expense in 1956, attracted the attention of Dame Edith Sitwell, who saw to their publication in Britain, to considerable acclaim. Since then, he has published thirteen novels as well as collections of stories, poetry, and plays, all highly praised for their remarkable and complex style and Gothic view of American society. Most recently he has published the novel *In the Hollow of His Hand* and the story collection *Candles of Your Eyes* (both 1986).

LEV RAPHAEL was born and raised in New York City. He did a Master of Fine Arts in Creative Writing at the University of Massachusetts at Amherst, where he won the Harvey Swados Fiction Prize, awarded by Martha Foley, founder and editor of *Story* magazine. His first story appeared in *Redbook*, and he has since published nearly thirty more, most recently in *Men on Men 2*, *Christopher Street*, *The James White Review*, and *Amelia*, which awarded him its Reed Smith Fiction Prize in 1988. His fiction has also appeared in *Commentary*, *Midstream*, *Hadassah*, and many other Jewish publications. He is the author of a collection of short stories, *Dancing on Tisha B'Av* (1990), and a critical study, *Edith Wharton's Prisoners of Shame*, and the co-author of a psycho-educational text, *The Dynamics of*

*Power*, and a book for middle-schoolers, *Stick Up for Yourself!* He holds a PhD in American Studies from Michigan State University, where he taught Creative Writing, Women's Studies and American-Jewish Fiction. He lives in Okemos, Michigan, where he writes full-time, and is working on a novel.

GORE VIDAL, born in 1925 at West Point, is one of the best-known literary figures in the United States, although he has lived much of his life outside the country and now divides his time between homes in Italy and California. He has written many novels, among them *Myra Breckenridge* (1968) and its sequel *Myron* (1974), a series of historical novels about American politics, *Washington, D.C.* (1967), *Burr* (1973), *1876* (1976), and *Lincoln* (1984), scripts for stage, television, and film, and several volumes of incisive essays. Following the successful *Williwaw* (1946) and *In a Yellow Wood* (1947), his third novel, *The City and the Pillar* (1948, revised 1965), although an immediate bestseller, was highly controversial because of its frank treatment of homosexuality, and cast a lasting pall on his reputation and career as a novelist. Since the 1960s, however, he has been recognized as a major contemporary writer and cultural critic.

TOM WAKEFIELD. Born of a mining family in the Midlands, Tom Wakefield now lives in London. He was awarded an Arts Council Literary Fellowship from 1980–2, based in Lancaster, and received an Oppenheim Award for Literature in 1983. His most recent books include *Mates*, *The Variety Artistes*, *Lot's Wife* and the novella *The Other Way*. 'Darts' is taken from his memoir, *Forties' Child*, published by Serpent's Tail (1990).

DENTON WELCH, born in Shanghai in 1915 but brought up in England, was a painter before being severely injured in a bicycle accident in 1935, after which he remained an invalid until his death in 1948. Although all of his published work is profoundly autobiographical, only his first book *Maiden Voyage* (1943) is identified as autobiography. His novels *In Youth is Pleasure* (1944) and the unfinished and posthumously published *A Voice Through a Cloud* (1950) are sensitive and beautifully written accounts of childhood and adolescence and of accident and illness, both of them candidly and lyrically treating the protagonists' homosexuality. A comprehensive volume of his short stories was issued in 1985, and his *Journals* were edited by Michael De-la-Noy (1984), who has also written a biography (1984).

EDMUND WHITE is the author of five novels, including *A Boy's Own Story* (1983) and *The Beautiful Room is Empty*. He is currently working on a biography of Jean Genet. He is a professor of English at Brown University, Providence, Rhode Island.

TENNESSEE WILLIAMS, one of the great American playwrights of the twentieth century, was born in 1911 in Mississippi. His first success was with the semi-autobiographical *The Glass Menagerie* (1945). Among his other major plays were *A Streetcar Named Desire* (1947), *Cat on a Hot Tin Roof* (1955), and *The Night of the Iguana* (1962). He also wrote poetry and fiction, including the novel *The Roman Spring of Mrs. Stone* (1950), and a volume of *Memoirs* (1975). He died in 1983.